GOVERNMENTAL POWERS

GOVERNMENTAL POWERS

Cases and Readings in Constitutional Law and American Democracy

COREY BRETTSCHNEIDER

Wolters Kluwer
Law & Business

Published by Wolters Kluwer Law & Business in New York.

Wolters Kluwer Law & Business serves customers worldwide with CCH, Aspen Publishers, and Kluwer Law International products. (www.wolterskluwerlb.com)

To contact Customer Service, e-mail customer.service@wolterskluwer.com, call 1-800-234-1660, fax 1-800-901-9075, or mail correspondence to:

Wolters Kluwer Law & Business
Attn: Order Department
PO Box 990
Frederick, MD 21705

Printed in the United States of America.

1 2 3 4 5 6 7 8 9 0

ISBN 978-0-7355-7984-2

Library of Congress Cataloging-in-Publication Data

Brettschneider, Corey Lang, author.
Governmental powers: cases and readings in constitutional law and American democracy / Corey Brettschneider.
pages cm
Includes bibliographical references and index.
ISBN 978-0-7355-7984-2 (alk. paper)
1. Constitutional law — United States. 2. United States — Politics and government. I. Title.
KF4550.B727 2014
342.73 — dc23

2013049262

About Wolters Kluwer Law & Business

Wolters Kluwer Law & Business is a leading global provider of intelligent information and digital solutions for legal and business professionals in key specialty areas, and respected educational resources for professors and law students. Wolters Kluwer Law & Business connects legal and business professionals as well as those in the education market with timely, specialized authoritative content and information-enabled solutions to support success through productivity, accuracy and mobility.

Serving customers worldwide, Wolters Kluwer Law & Business products include those under the Aspen Publishers, CCH, Kluwer Law International, Loislaw, ftwilliam.com and MediRegs family of products.

CCH products have been a trusted resource since 1913, and are highly regarded resources for legal, securities, antitrust and trade regulation, government contracting, banking, pension, payroll, employment and labor, and healthcare reimbursement and compliance professionals.

Aspen Publishers products provide essential information to attorneys, business professionals and law students. Written by preeminent authorities, the product line offers analytical and practical information in a range of specialty practice areas from securities law and intellectual property to mergers and acquisitions and pension/benefits. Aspen's trusted legal education resources provide professors and students with high-quality, up-to-date and effective resources for successful instruction and study in all areas of the law.

Kluwer Law International products provide the global business community with reliable international legal information in English. Legal practitioners, corporate counsel and business executives around the world rely on Kluwer Law journals, looseleafs, books, and electronic products for comprehensive information in many areas of international legal practice.

Loislaw is a comprehensive online legal research product providing legal content to law firm practitioners of various specializations. Loislaw provides attorneys with the ability to quickly and efficiently find the necessary legal information they need, when and where they need it, by facilitating access to primary law as well as state-specific law, records, forms and treatises.

ftwilliam.com offers employee benefits professionals the highest quality plan documents (retirement, welfare and non-qualified) and government forms (5500/PBGC, 1099 and IRS) software at highly competitive prices.

MediRegs products provide integrated health care compliance content and software solutions for professionals in healthcare, higher education and life sciences, including professionals in accounting, law and consulting.

Wolters Kluwer Law & Business, a division of Wolters Kluwer, is headquartered in New York. Wolters Kluwer is a market-leading global information services company focused on professionals.

For my father, Eric Brettschneider,

who brought me to my first law class at age 6

ABOUT THE AUTHOR

COREY BRETTSCHNEIDER is Professor of Political Science at Brown University, where he teaches courses in political theory and public law. He is also Professor, by courtesy, of Philosophy. Brettschneider has been a Visiting Professor of Law at Fordham Law School, a Faculty Fellow at the Princeton University Center for Human Values, a Visiting Associate Professor at Harvard Law School, and a Faculty Fellow at the Harvard Safra Center for Ethics.

Brettschneider received a Ph.D. in Politics from Princeton University and a J.D. from Stanford University. He is the author of *When the State Speaks, What Should It Say? How Democracies Can Protect Expression and Promote Equality* (Princeton University Press, 2012) and *Democratic Rights: The Substance of Self-Government* (Princeton University Press, 2007). The *Brooklyn Law Review* has published a special symposium issue on his work on free speech. His articles have appeared in top law reviews and political science journals, including *The Northwestern Law Review, The American Political Science Review,* and *Political Theory.*

SUMMARY OF CONTENTS

CONTENTS

PREFACE

Perhaps no other area of study brings together as many exciting and controversial issues as the study of constitutional law. The most hotly contested topics in our polity—from abortion rights to affirmative action to war—are found in the various areas that make up this field. But in addition to being contemporary, the topic is also by its nature historical. These contemporary topics are viewed through the lens of a document written in the eighteenth century. Thus, the study of constitutional law presents a major challenge: How can a document written so early in American history govern questions that those who wrote it could never have fathomed?

As we will see throughout this text, the question of how to interpret the Constitution, and how to apply it to today's issues, is itself contested. Rather than shying away from the controversies at the heart of constitutional law, and the related debates among citizens and academics about these issues, this book is compiled with the aim of introducing you to the terrain of these debates. Through landmark and contemporary cases as well as through other seminal readings, historical writings, and commentary by leading scholars, you will learn how to think about the most complex and important legal challenges in our nation.

In addition to presenting some of the most important cases in American history, this book emphasizes readings that place these cases in the context of wider normative and historical debates, with an emphasis on the fundamental governing institutions and structures established by the U.S. Constitution, with the hope that it can be taught both in constitutional law classes and in those that seek to combine political theory and philosophy with a study of American political development and of the Supreme Court. The approach is designed to teach you the contours of the legal debates in the area of constitutional law. But as I see it, the role of teaching constitutional law is not primarily to train future litigators—although some of you might choose that path. It is rather to give you an understanding of the Constitution itself, the primary ways in which it has been interpreted by our political institutions, and the ways you can connect your own views on these subjects with distinctly legal questions. You will thus not only come away from this book with an understanding of the positions of the Supreme Court and of major scholars on a host of issues, but you will also have become constitutional interpreters yourselves.

Corey Brettschneider
Brown University
January 2014

ACKNOWLEDGMENTS

I began this project several years ago to create a casebook that teaches constitutional doctrine by tying it to fundamental themes from constitutional theory, political theory, political science, and the study of democracy. My aim was to write a book informed by the way many scholars teach constitutional law, and one that reflects the wide research interests of those who work in the subject, and that aim has been fulfilled by the publication of *Constitutional Law and American Democracy* (2012), the parent volume to the present text as well as to my *Civil Rights and Liberties: Cases and Readings in Constitutional Law and American Democracy* (2013).

I am grateful to the many students who have taken my courses at Brown University. These books grew out of what was originally my civil liberties course, later expanded to include a discussion of governmental powers. When I first came to Brown I worked with students to create a course that had the right balance between cases and readings on larger themes related to the U.S. Constitution. As I developed drafts of the original book, I began teaching it. My students' feedback over the years has been fundamental in shaping the final product.

I am most indebted to the outstanding and inspiring team of Brown undergraduates who worked as research assistants on the project and who made its completion possible. They made working on the books a pleasure, and they were often the ones teaching me. Tobin Marcus provided invaluable support at the proposal stage. David McNamee and Manuel Possolo worked closely with me on all aspects of the original book's first draft. Together we finalized the outline, selecting the readings and cases. David and Manuel helped to find the right tone and approach in the commentaries. They also created the charts and figures in Chapter 1 of this text that illustrate the theoretical frame of the entire project. Tobin, David, and Manuel have already achieved terrific success at top law and PhD programs, working in positions of responsibility for the federal government. Brittany Harwood also provided invaluable support on the first draft.

Another impressive team of research assistants included Jasleen Salwan, Andrea Matthews, and Anthony Badami, who helped add readings, rewrite much of the commentary, and respond to excellent suggestions from reviewers. This team was essential to finishing the book, and it was a pleasure to work with them. Jasleen in particular provided a heroic and efficient effort as the manuscript reached the final stages. Her work on the accompanying products, especially the instructor's manual, shows that she is already a brilliant teacher.

I thank not only my students, but also my teachers who introduced me to the subject of constitutional law. At Princeton, Amy Gutmann, George Kateb, Stephen Macedo, and Robert George taught me early on that political theorists have an obligation to engage with constitutional issues and have a valuable contribution to make in understanding the most important document of our government. I will always be grateful to these teachers, and I deeply appreciate their continued friendship and mentorship. At Stanford Law, Lawrence Lessig was an ideal mentor who showed me how to be rigorous yet creative in thinking about doctrine. I thank him too for his continued support of my research and career. Kathleen Sullivan taught what might be the most perfect first-year constitutional law course in existence. Tom Grey supervised my independent work and provided a model of how to integrate legal theory and constitutional law.

It is also a pleasure to thank my terrific colleagues who enthusiastically supported this project from the start. James Morone, John Tomasi, Sharon Krause, David Estlund, and Charles Larmore are an extraordinarily collegial group working across the boundaries of philosophy and political science. I have been happy to build the political theory program at Brown with them. Estlund and I taught a Harvard Law course in 2009 on "Democratic Theory and the Law," related to the materials in this book. I learned an immense amount from him and from our students in the course.

I was fortunate to have two friends and colleagues who are also world-class constitutional law scholars help me to hone my presentation. Steve Calabresi has been an amazing colleague while visiting here at Brown. He provided invaluable assistance on Part III. Gordon Silverstein, who was a fellow during our year at Princeton, worked with me to improve Part II. He encouraged me to add more cases and provided assistance in creating better commentary. Together these two scholars made the parts on constitutional powers much better than they would have been.

I am indebted to the people at Aspen who made this book possible. In particular I would like to thank Carol McGeehan at Aspen for encouraging me to pursue this project, and Susan Boulanger for terrific editing work.

I thank the members of my family who talked with me about and supported this project, Allison Brettschneider, Sophie Helen Brettschneider, Susan Brettschneider,

Kim Brettschneider, Jeanne Rostaing, Robert Klopfer, Patrick Heppell, John Weisz, and Jenny Weisz. I dedicate this book to my father, Eric Brettschneider, who began talking to me about the issues here when I first learned to speak in sentences. He was attending law school at the time, and was a terrific enough father to convince me at age six that I too was a student in his class.

Finally, I am grateful to the copyright holders for permission to reprint the following materials:

Bruce Ackerman, reprinted by permission of the publisher from We the People: Volume 1, Foundations by Bruce Ackerman, pp. 8-10, 40-44, 47-52, 105, Cambridge, Mass.: The Belknap Press of Harvard University Press, Copyright © 1991 by the President and Fellows of Harvard College.

Bruce Ackerman, reprinted by permission of the publisher from We the People, Volume 2, Transformations by Bruce Ackerman, pp. 268-271, 309-311, 314, Cambridge, Mass.: The Belknap Press of Harvard University Press, Copyright © 1998 by the President and Fellows of Harvard College.

Stephen Breyer, "Judicial Review: A Practicing Judge's Perspective," Oxford Journal of Legal Studies, Vol. 19, Summer 1999, by permission of Oxford University Press.

Steven G. Calabresi & James Lindgren, "The President: Lightning Rod or King?" Yale Law Journal, Vol. 115, p. 2611, 2006. The Yale law journal by Yale Law School. Copyright 2006 Reproduced with permission of Yale Law Journal Company, Inc. in the format Textbook and Other Book via Copyright Clearance Center.

Ronald Dworkin, "The Moral Reading and the Majoritarian Premise" and "Roe in Danger" reprinted by permission of the publisher from Freedom's Law: The Moral Reading of the American Constitution by Ronald Dworkin, pp. 15-33, 44-59, Cambridge, Mass.: Harvard University Press, Copyright © 1996 by Ronald Dworkin.

John Hart Ely, War and Responsibility. Copyright © 1993 Princeton University Press. Reprinted by permission of Princeton University Press.

Richard A. Epstein, How Progressives Rewrote the Constitution. Copyright © 2006. Reproduced with permission of Cato Institute in the format Textbook and Other Book via Copyright Clearance Center.

Douglas Ginsburg, "On Constitutionalism," Cato Supreme Court Review 7, Washington, DC: Cato Institute, 2002-2003. Cato Supreme Court review 2003-2004 by Cato Institute. Center for Constitutional Studies Copyright © 2003. Reproduced with permission of Cato Institute in the format Textbook and Other Book via Copyright Clearance Center.

Andrew Koppelman, "Bad News for Mail Robbers: The Obvious Constitutionality of Health Care Reform," Yale Law Journal, Apr. 26, 2011, pp. 154-157: http://yalelawjournal.org/the-yale-law-journal-pocket-part/constitutional-law/bad-news-for-mail-robbers:-the-obvious-constitutionality-of-health-care-reform/.

Larry Kramer, "We the Court," 115 Harv. L. Rev. 4 (2001), pp. 4-169. Harvard Law Review by Harvard Law Review Association. Copyright © 2001. Reproduced with permission of Harvard Law Review Association in the format Textbook and Other Book via Copyright Clearance Center.

Lawrence Lessig & Cass Sunstein, "The President and the Administration," Columbia Law Review, Vol. 94, No. 1, Jan. 1994. Copyright © 1994. Reproduced with permission of the authors and Columbia Law Review Association, Inc. in the format Textbook and Other Book via Copyright Clearance Center.

Harvey Mansfield, "The Case for the Strong Executive: Under Some Circumstances the Rule of Law Must Yield to the Need for Energy," The Wall Street Journal, May 2, 2007. Reprinted by permission of the author.

Michael McConnell, review of Raoul Berger, "The Founders' Limits," 54 U. Chi. L. Rev. 1484. The University of Chicago law review by University of Chicago. Copyright © 1987 by University of Chicago Law School. Reproduced with permission of University of Chicago Law School in the format Textbook and Other Book via Copyright Clearance Center.

Kathleen Sullivan, "From States' Rights Blues to Blue States' Rights: Federalism After the Rehnquist Court," 75 Fordham L. Rev. 799, 2006. Reprinted by permission of the publisher.

Cass R. Sunstein & Randy E. Barnett, "Constitutive Commitments and Roosevelt's Second Bill of Rights: A Dialogue," 53 Drake L. Rev. 205, Winter, 2005. Sections I, II, VII. Reprinted by permission of Drake Law Review Copyright © 2005 in the format Textbook and Other Book via Copyright Clearance Center.

Gordon S. Wood, "The Origins of Judicial Review Revisited, or How the Marshall Court Made More Out of Less," 56 Wash. & Lee L. Rev. 787 (1999).

John Yoo, "The Continuation of Politics by Other Means: The Original Understanding of War Powers," Cal. L. Rev., Vol. 84, No. 2, Mar. 1996. Reprinted by permission of the author.

INTRODUCTION TO GOVERNMENTAL POWERS: CASES AND READINGS IN CONSTITUTIONAL LAW AND AMERICAN DEMOCRACY

In the United States, it is no longer contested that the Supreme Court has the power to strike down laws passed by Congress, the states, or municipalities that violate the Constitution. And while the Court operates under strict majoritarian rule—it takes only five of the nine justices to make these momentous decisions—the Court itself uses this power of judicial review to block and reverse the preferences of a national majority expressed through their elected representatives. This raises obvious questions: Why? Should the Supreme Court have this power? If so, how should it be exercised? These questions seem particularly puzzling in a democracy. Many Americans believe that they live in a system of self-government, in which majorities have a say in making law. Why, then, should such a small number of people be entitled to pass judgment on the preferences and will of hundreds of millions?

One answer to these questions appeals to the text of the Constitution itself. The justices, we might think, have the power to strike down legislation not in order to impose their own beliefs about policy, but rather as a means to enforce the document's requirements. The power of "judicial review," then, might be thought to stem from the Constitution's inherent supremacy over other governmental actions. Indeed, Article VI of the Constitution tells us that "this Constitution, and the Laws of the United States which shall be made in Pursuance thereof . . . shall be the supreme Law of the Land."

The claim that the Constitution is supreme, however, only raises a deeper question that will be at the heart of our inquiry into constitutional law in this book. Namely, although the Constitution is at times clear in its meaning, it is often ambiguous. In some places, it is hard to imagine much disagreement about its terms. For example, no one could argue that someone 22 years of age is eligible to be elected President of the United States. Article II, Section 1 of the Constitution explicitly states that the office excludes any "person . . . who shall not have attained to the Age of thirty five." Similarly, the Constitution is clear that "The Senate of the United States shall be composed of two Senators from each State." In contrast, consider whether the Eighth Amendment's prohibition of "cruel and unusual punishment" forbids the use of the electric chair in executions. What is "cruel"? What is "unusual"? According to whom? The Eighth Amendment does not set up a clear rule; rather, it creates a standard that must be subject to interpretation. Indeed, at points in American history, some have claimed that the death penalty constitutes "cruel and unusual" punishment. Others have disagreed, suggesting that because capital punishment is explicitly referenced in the Constitution, it cannot be prohibited by the document.

A course that merely focused on the least ambiguous provisions of the Constitution would not be very interesting. You would merely be asked obvious questions, such as the one I asked about the 22-year-old candidate for president, and would reach obvious conclusions. But fortunately, the bulk of constitutional inquiry that makes up the body of constitutional law, and that we will pursue here, is fraught with disagreement and contains some of the most interesting debates in American history. Indeed, in the United States, many of the issues discussed at our dinner tables and in our newspapers are "constitutionalized." The issues of abortion, the right to die, and the freedom of speech are among those that gain the most attention in our society. The Supreme Court, by limiting laws within these domains, has entered into the fray. Far from shying from controversy in this book, we will dive right into it.

Specifically, we will concern ourselves with two purposes. First, we will examine what the Supreme Court has said about a host of controversies. Second, rather than merely learn what the Court has said and done, we will challenge its conclusions and reasoning, taking on the task of constitutional interpretation ourselves.

Structure of the Book

We begin the book with an inquiry into the foundations of judicial review. We ask first, in Part I, why the Court should have the authority to strike down legislation passed by majoritarian institutions. Specifically, the chapters in that part ask whether the reasoning in favor of this practice is sound through an examination of case law and commentary. We also examine the origin of the Court's power of judicial review, which is never explicitly granted by the Constitution. This part revolves around a foundational problem in constitutional law—judicial authority.

In the next parts of the book, we move on to the question of which powers the particular branches of the government are afforded by the Constitution. Here, we will pivot from the question of judicial authority to questions about the powers and limits of the legislative and the executive branches. To what extent can these branches make law, and enforce it? What should be done when conflicts emerge between the branches? In addition to these questions of "separation of powers," or more precisely, "conflicts of powers," we will examine the relationship between the federal government and the states. Where does the power of the states end and the power of the federal government begin?

Throughout this book, we will be guided both by the opinions of the Supreme Court and by the most important writers thinking about these issues.

How to Read and Brief a Case

It is important for you to note that there is a specific way to read, or to decode, the cases to follow. Namely, it will be helpful, especially in the first few cases that you read, to create a "case outline" or "brief." It is essential that this be done in a particular way to ensure that you have understood the case. I will include here some essential elements that must be included in a case brief, although your instructor might point you to others. First, it is essential to understand the basic facts of the case. In some instances, this will involve one party suing another; in others, an individual who has been arrested and accused of a crime; in still others, a contract dispute between two parties. In issues about a dispute between two parties, be sure to note who the original *plaintiff* and *defendant* were at the trial level. In criminal cases, the dispute is between the *government* and the *defendant*; there is no *plaintiff* in such cases. It is important, however, not to confuse plaintiff and defendant with the *petitioner* and *respondent*, terms that refer to the party who lost at the previous level, and the party who won, respectively. Usually, though not always, the petitioner's name will be first in the name of the case.

Second, it is essential to identify what is known as the legal issue in the case. The legal issue can be summarized in one sentence. Try to see in each case if you can identify one question that summarizes the legal issue, and then see how the Court answers it. Third, we want to identify the holding of the case. The holding is sometimes as short as "yes" or "no" respecting the legal issue. For instance, when you read *District of Columbia v. Heller*, the legal issue is: Does the District of Columbia's gun ban violate the Second Amendment? The holding here answers the question in the affirmative.

Fourth, you should be able to identify the legal reasoning that explains why the holding is reached. Here, you will have to reconstruct the legal argument in order to figure out its structure. Finally, be sure to understand the outcome of the case. In whose favor did the Court rule? What are the implications of the ruling? This will not always be as obvious as you might think. In some cases, the reasoning of the Court may appear to support one side, but the judgment may nevertheless fall in favor of another side for various reasons.

Legal Citations

As you read and brief cases, you may find it useful to understand the specialized legal citation format used by judges in the writing of opinions. Each case can be cited using a relatively concise citation consisting of the name of the case, the reporter, the volume number, and page number. The year of the decision is also often included. Supreme Court opinions, which comprise the bulk of the cases in this book, are published in the official *United States Reports*, available in any law library and on the Internet. These reports are referenced with the simple abbreviation "U.S." Thus, a complete citation might look like this:

Notice that the name of the case is always italicized. On second reference, judges or commentators may refer to a case by a shorter name and will omit the full citation—here, just *Lochner*. When judges wish to cite a particular location in a case, and not merely the case itself, they may cite two page numbers. Thus, a quotation on the third page of *Lochner* would be cited as *Lochner v. New York*, 198 U.S. 45, 47 (1905).

You will also come across citations of lower courts, such as those of federal circuit courts of appeals. These decisions are typically published in the *Federal Reporter* and are cited with the abbreviations F. or F.2d (for older cases) and F.3d (for more recent ones). Select opinions from district-level courts are published in the *Federal Supplement*, abbreviated as F. Supp. or F. Supp. 2d. Cases heard in state courts have varying citation formats, which you will not need to worry about for this book. It is usually possible, however, to decipher what they refer to.

The case law you will read in this book has been edited and abridged—indeed, many of the cases you will read run to 100 pages or more in the original. If you are curious to read the original versions of any of these cases, you can find them easily in any law library or online at Web sites such as FindLaw, Westlaw, or the Cornell Law Legal Information Institute. We have also listed these cases at the Web site that accompanies this book.

INTRODUCTION TO THE CONSTITUTION AND THE SUPREME COURT

Overview of the Constitution

Before we tackle the important and controversial issues that make up the bulk of this book, it is important to clarify some basic features of the Constitution, which form the basis for most constitutional issues. You should read the entire text of the document itself, included below, starting on page xli, before reading what follows.

The first thing you should note about the document is that its first three articles establish the three branches of government. Article I creates Congress, the legislative branch; Article II the office of the President of the United States, the executive; and Article III the judiciary, including the Supreme Court. In establishing each of the branches, the Constitution grants certain powers as well as limits them. The federal government is thus known to be one of "enumerated" or "granted" powers. In contrast, the state governments have more general powers. For instance, among the powers often thought to be "reserved" to the states is the "police power" within their own jurisdictions to regulate the "welfare, health, safety, and morals" of citizens. The Tenth Amendment lays out the difference between the limited federal government and the states, declaring that "powers not delegated to the United States by the Constitution, or prohibited by it to the States, are reserved to the States respectively, or to the people."

The Three Branches of Government (Articles I, II, and III)

Article I of the Constitution creates and lays out the powers of Congress. As you look through Article I, many of the powers will seem to be straightforward. However, even several of those that seem simple at first glance turn out to be at the heart of the most difficult disputes over constitutional interpretation. Take, for instance, the Commerce Clause found in Section 8, which gives Congress the power to "regulate Commerce with foreign Nations, and among the several States." A fundamental question here is where this power of the Congress begins and where the power of states to regulate their own "intrastate" commerce ends. What kinds of activity are of an interstate nature, and what kinds belong only to the jurisdiction of one state?

As we will see in Part II, this provision also became the basis for congressional legislation in the area of civil rights, ending segregation in places of "public accommodation." The debate over whether public accommodations, such as hotels and restaurants, were involved in interstate commerce served as a battleground for achieving equality for African Americans. Indeed, from the beginning, the provisions of Article I, Section 8 have been controversial. For example, in Chapter 3 we will examine whether the so-called Necessary and Proper Clause authorized the creation of a national bank. We will soon wade into controversial territory, but for now it is worth familiarizing yourself with the various powers of the legislative branch by reading Article I. Pay particular attention to the powers to spend, to declare war, and to raise and support armies.

Article II of the Constitution establishes and delineates the powers of the executive branch. Among the powers granted to the president are the powers to make treaties, appoint judges, and choose subordinate officers. This article also states that the president shall be "Commander in Chief of the Army and Navy of the United States," a declaration that we will see used as a justification for broad executive authority in times of war. In addition, we will examine the debate over the potentially broad powers that come from the Constitution's declaration that executive power is "vested" in the presidency. Sometimes the division between the powers of Article I for Congress and those of Article II for the president is thought to outline a "separation of powers," but as will become evident in Part III, many real controversies in constitutional law concern blurred lines between presidential and congressional power. For instance, consider the tension between Congress's power to declare war and the president's status as Commander-in-Chief. As we will see, one controversy concerns when the first power limits the second. Another question we will examine concerns the president's domestic powers in times of war. Does the president's role as Commander-in-Chief enhance his or her domestic powers when the country is in the midst of a major international conflict?

Article III of the Constitution establishes the Supreme Court and grants to Congress the power to establish "inferior" courts as needed. Perhaps most notable in this article, however, is the absence of any explicit authorization of judicial review. We will examine early in Chapter 1 the controversy this has caused in regard to the Supreme Court's authority to strike down laws passed by Congress and signed by the president. Despite not being explicitly grounded in the text of the Constitution, this power was famously declared early in the Court's history in the case of *Marbury v. Madison.* Also note the distinction between the Supreme Court's "original" and "appellate" jurisdiction. The Court's "original" jurisdiction, encompassing instances in which a case can be brought directly to the Supreme Court, is quite limited. In such cases, the Court acts as a trial-level court. But in most instances, the Court does not conduct a trial, but rather acts as an appellate court. Appellate courts, in contrast to trial-level courts, only hear appeals from, or, in other words, review the decisions of, other courts. This review power, in the cases we will examine, allows the Supreme

Court to correct lower-level courts when it determines that they have committed some error in constitutional interpretation. They are about controversies of law, not about disputes over the facts of a particular case. Notice too that justices are appointed for life-long terms, "during good Behavior."

The Amendment Process (Article V)

As this book will make clear, the Constitution—in addition to setting up a government—establishes a body of law. Thus, we will study not only the structure of government, but also certain legal controversies, such as those concerning freedom of speech, freedom of religion, and equal protection of the laws. Many of these provisions, however, were not contained in the original Constitution. Rather, they had to be created through a process of amendment. Article V sets the balance between "entrenching" the Constitution as a body of law that is more permanent than statutory law passed by Congress and the recognition that the people will sometimes wish to change it. It does this by creating a "super-majority" rule for amending the Constitution.

While statutes can be passed, or repealed, by simple majorities in both houses of Congress (assuming the president does not veto them), amending the Constitution requires the approval of two-thirds supermajorities of both houses of Congress and the consent of three-fourths of the states, either through their legislatures or through state ratifying conventions. In the more than 200 years since the Constitution was ratified, only 27 amendments have been passed, with the most recent taking effect in 1992. The first ten amendments, passed just a few years after the original Constitution, are collectively known as the Bill of Rights and contain many critical elements of the modern Constitution. Another major series of revisions to the Constitution, known as the Civil War Amendments, includes the abolishment of slavery and the guarantee of equal protection of the laws. Note too that Article V permits two-thirds of state legislatures to call a constitutional convention for the purpose of proposing new amendments to the Constitution, a power that has never been used.

The Supremacy Clause (Article VI)

Article VI of the Constitution, like Article V, references the status of the document itself. Critically, it declares that the "Constitution, and the Laws of the United States which shall be made in Pursuance thereof . . . shall be the supreme Law of the Land." As we will see in Chapter 2, this provision raises questions about judicial authority. Who has the right to interpret this supreme law? Some have argued that this is the exclusive role of the Supreme Court, while others have defended a shared role among the three branches of government.

Freedom of Expression and Religion (The First Amendment)

The First Amendment to the Constitution establishes several key areas of rights. For instance, the "free speech" provision has been interpreted as protecting a variety of kinds of expression, not merely verbal "speech." The amendment also contains the right to "free exercise of religion" and the prohibition on any "establishment of religion" by the government.

Notice that the First Amendment and other elements of the Bill of Rights limit certain powers of Congress but do not explicitly say anything about the powers of the states. But with the passage of the Fourteenth Amendment after the Civil War this changed. The Fourteenth Amendment, unlike the Bill of Rights, imposes explicit limits on state governments. Today, it is commonly thought by scholars and jurists that most of the important protections of the Bill of Rights also apply to the states by virtue of the Fourteenth Amendment.

In addition, the First Amendment's reference to what Congress can or cannot do highlights that the focus here is on the actions of the government, and the text suggests a broad doctrine of constitutional law known as the "state action" doctrine. According to this doctrine, constitutional cases are only triggered when some governmental entity has acted. Thus, it is widely thought that constitutional law does not prohibit private actors from engaging in certain activities that the "state," or government, is barred from. For example, a private high school that instituted speech codes would not implicate constitutional concerns in the way that a state-run public school likely would were it to implement the same policy.

Due Process (The Fourteenth Amendment)

As you read the Fourteenth Amendment, you should notice its resemblance to the Fifth Amendment of the Bill of Rights. While the latter refers to the federal government and the former to states, both protect individuals against deprivation of "life, liberty, or property, without due process of law." This right to "due process" is certainly among the Constitution's more ambiguous provisions. As we will see, "due process," while it seems to refer only to the procedural rights of citizens, has been thought to guarantee substantive rights as well. The potential confusion in this area of law is found in the very phrase "substantive due process." Sometimes a guarantee only of "due process" is thought of as the idea that any outcome of a process that is legitimate and fair is itself legitimate. In contrast, substantive guarantees are limits on particular kinds of policy outcomes. Thus, "substantive due process" is thought by some to be a contradiction in terms. But despite this criticism, the Court has developed a doctrine of substantive due process that holds that some liberties are so fundamental that they cannot be stripped from citizens by any "process" whatsoever. Thus, among the substantive rights associated with due process are a general right to privacy and specific rights to abortion and to contraception. Most recently, this doctrine has been used to protect gay individuals from criminal prosecution for consensual sexual relations.

The doctrine of "economic substantive due process," now abandoned, was once used by a conservative court to strike down many workers' rights laws passed during the New Deal. As you read this amendment, you should ask whether this Court was right to think that economic liberties such as the right to work were so fundamental as to require "due process" protections.

Equal Protection of the Laws (The Fourteenth Amendment)

In addition to guaranteeing "due process of law," the Fourteenth Amendment also guarantees citizens "the equal protection of the laws." The provision applies particularly in cases of discrimination based on race or ethnic background. The Court affords its highest level of protection, or what it calls "strict scrutiny," to legal distinction based on these characteristics, presuming laws that use such distinctions to be invalid absent a strong justification for their enactment. At the same time, however, the Equal Protection Clause does not explicitly mention either racial or ethnic discrimination. The clause has thus been expanded to encompass questions about the legality of distinctions based on gender and sexual orientation.

Unenumerated Powers and Rights (The Ninth and Tenth Amendments)

There is great controversy over the role of the constitutional text in Supreme Court jurisprudence. In this debate, one of the more difficult and controversial provisions of the Constitution suggests an ambiguity on this issue. The Ninth Amendment to the Constitution reads: "The enumeration in the Constitution, of certain rights, shall not be construed to deny or disparage others retained by the people." The Ninth Amendment thus suggests that just because a right does not explicitly appear in the Constitution does not necessarily mean that it lacks constitutional protection. Some have gone so far as to suggest that the Ninth Amendment references a so-called unwritten Constitution, which protects basic rights not enumerated in the document itself.

In addition, some have suggested that the Tenth Amendment clarifies the overall balance between federal and state power. This amendment declares: "The powers not delegated to the United States by the Constitution, nor prohibited by it to the States, are reserved to the States respectively, or to the people." As you read this amendment, consider whether it limits the powers of the federal government, and enhances the powers of the state, beyond what is said in Articles I and II.

History of the Constitution

As you can tell from our brief tour of the Constitution, the document is not just a piece of history. Rather, it forms the textual basis for an extremely important body of contemporary law. It serves as both a way of authorizing the powers of our government and also of limiting those powers. Although our focus in this book is on the relevance of this document to the ongoing practice of constitutional law, it is important to understand some historical context about the writing of the Constitution itself.

Before the modern Constitution was written, the country was governed by the Congress of the Confederation, which adhered to the Articles of Confederation. In part due to the urging of those discontented with the Articles, famously including James Madison and Alexander Hamilton, a convention was called in Philadelphia during the summer of 1787 to consider amending this document. Among the common complaints about the Articles of Confederation was that it provided too weak a central government.

As you have seen from our examination so far, the new Constitution established both a Congress and an executive with a series of national powers. Structurally, the new Constitution retained some sovereignty for the states, but it also placed sovereignty in the hands of the federal government. The document thus dispensed with the idea that the United States was a mere alliance between fully sovereign states. As we will see in Chapter 3, this notion of "dual sovereignty" continues to pose challenges in constitutional interpretation. The convention in Philadelphia itself was not without controversy. Indeed, the final document we have today is widely regarded as the result of a series of compromises. In particular, the structure of Congress, which combines equal representation for all states in the Senate with proportional representation in the House of Representatives, is the result of a synthesis between the Virginia plan proposed by Madison, favored by large states, and the New Jersey plan, favored by small states.

Famously, too, the original document compromised on the issue of slavery. Questioning the legality of slavery was formally postponed until 1808. Notice too that Southern concerns that slaves be counted in the apportionment of representatives in the House despite not being able to vote were acknowledged by the so-called Three-Fifths Clause, which counted slaves as just that fraction of a free person for apportionment purposes. Needless to say, this document grossly ignored the interests of African Americans, who in many states were relegated to bondage and in all were denied equal status. Original defects in the Constitution would not be rectified for some time.

Because the document was to supersede the Articles of Confederation and incorporate the states into a new union of dual-sovereignty, the Philadelphia convention agreed that three-quarters of the states would have to ratify it for it to take effect. During the debates in individual states about ratification, a group of leading "Anti-Federalists" penned newspaper articles in opposition to the new Constitution and urged people to vote against it. Among their reasons, the Anti-Federalists predicted that the new Constitution would consolidate too much power in the hands of a large government, which would fail to respect either the individual sovereignty of states or the rights of citizens. The debate between Federalists and Anti-Federalists was particularly contentious in New York. In a series of periodicals, James Madison, John Jay, and Alexander Hamilton wrote articles—today known as *The Federalist Papers*—defending the Constitution and urging ratification. In this book, we have included several selections from these papers. Ultimately, the Federalists were victorious, and in mid-1788, the Constitution went into effect.

The legacy of the Anti-Federalists, however, was not entirely lost. Despite the assurances of many Federalists that the Constitution as enacted needed no explicit protections of individual rights, it was ultimately agreed to take up a Bill of Rights soon after the passage of the original document. Hamilton, for one, opposed the idea in *The Federalist No. 84*:

> I . . . affirm that bills of rights, in the sense and to the extent in which they are contended for, are not only unnecessary in the proposed Constitution, but would even be dangerous. They would contain various exceptions to powers not granted; and, on this very account, would afford a colorable pretext to claim more than were granted. For why declare that things shall not be done which there is no power to do? Why, for instance, should it be said that the liberty of the press shall not be restrained, when no power is given by which restrictions may be imposed? I will not contend that such a provision would confer a regulating power; but it is evident that it would furnish, to men disposed to usurp, a plausible pretense for claiming that power.

Despite this objection, a bill of rights was proposed by Congress in 1789 and ratified in 1791 in accordance with the Article V amendment process. Thus, of the 27 constitutional amendments that have been passed since the adoption of the original document, ten were accomplished in one fell swoop just a few years after the first version was ratified.

The Founding period is of course of significant interest to constitutional scholars. The "originalist" school of constitutional interpretation in particular places great importance on understanding the meaning of the original document in the context in which it was written. But as will soon be evident, the constitutional convention by no means resolved the controversies that would come to dominate American political life. To the contrary, these issues could only be worked out through future argument and discussion.

The Path to the Supreme Court

The Supreme Court, as the highest court in the United States, hears only a very small fraction of the total cases filed throughout the country. Needless to say, the path to the Supreme Court is fraught with obstacles, and only seldom do litigants get the chance to present their cases before this body. While it is difficult to say exactly what makes a case reviewable by the Supreme Court, it is often a necessary condition that the question of law at issue be somewhat ambiguous and require clarification. The Supreme Court does not take just any case, but rather focuses on those in which it can clarify previous rulings, overturn precedent, or correct a conflict that exists among lower court rulings. In this section, we will begin by outlining the structure of the court system and the procedures by which a case might make it to the Supreme Court. We will then go on to outline various procedural hurdles that a case must overcome for the Court to reach a decision on the merits of a particular case.

The Structure of the Courts

As we noted earlier, Article III of the Constitution grants the Supreme Court a few select areas in which it has "original jurisdiction." In such cases, the Supreme Court acts as a trial-level court, meaning that it hears evidence and makes decisions about facts. In most instances, however, such "original jurisdiction" or "trial-level" cases begin at much lower levels of either the federal or the state system. Pursuant to Article III, Congress has established a series of "inferior" federal courts. The trial-level courts are called "district courts," and are found throughout the country. There are currently 94 federal district courts. The losing party in any one of these cases can make an appeal to "circuit" courts. There are thirteen of these "courts of appeals," twelve of which hear appeals from district courts based on geographic location, while a thirteenth court of appeals in Washington, D.C., the Federal Circuit, hears appeals nationwide from district court decisions on several technical subjects like patents and trademarks.

In addition to the federal court system, a parallel judicial system exists in each state, with trial-level and top-level courts. Most, but not all, states have appellate-level courts similar to those in the federal system. Although they go by different names, each state has established its own structure for handling legal claims. Often the highest appellate court is called the "Supreme Court" of the state. This is not a reliable way of determining the level of any given court, however. New York, for example, calls the trial-level courts "Supreme Court" and the highest court the "Court of Appeals." Although the rules by which it is decided whether a claim is rightly adjudicated in state or federal court are complicated, there are a few guiding principles. For instance, parties have a right to have their case heard by federal as opposed to state courts in matters of so-called diversity jurisdiction, in which the parties are from different states. In addition, if the case implicates matters of federal law, parties can claim that there is a "federal question" at stake and seek to be heard by a federal court. Regardless, however, of whether a case originates in state or federal court, if a party claims its federal constitutional rights have been violated, it can apply for a "writ of certiorari" and seek to be heard by the Supreme Court of the United States once it has exhausted its appeals in the lower courts. Thus, the Supreme Court hears federal cases that arise both from the federal system and from the states.

Unlike at the district and circuit court level, parties do not have a right to have their case heard automatically at this level. Rather, they must petition the justices for certiorari. By custom, according to the so-called rule of four, if at least four justices vote to hear a case, the Court will schedule it for briefing and argument and issue a ruling. The process of "granting cert" is itself the subject of much speculation. Certain features of a case might make it "cert-worthy," although no one feature is sufficient to ensure that it will be accepted. Many of the justices participate in a "cert pool" in which they share the process of review. Their clerks in particular, who are typically recent law school graduates, are particularly important at this stage of decision making, reading the petitions for certiorari and helping the justices decide which cases to take. The court receives thousands of certiorari petitions each year, but will typically hear no more than about 100 cases. Thus, only the most challenging and legally pressing matters will merit the attention of the nation's top judges.

When Does the Supreme Court Hear a Case?

In contrast to courts in many other countries, the Supreme Court of the United States cannot exercise its power of judicial review at will. Although it has the power to strike down laws—federal, state, and municipal—that are in conflict with the Constitution, it must do so only in the context of a particular case brought before it. This is because Article III of the Constitution contains what is called the Case or Controversy Clause. Specifically, before the Supreme Court (or any federal court) can make a decision about the constitutionality of a law or policy, it must be presented with a relevant conflict between two parties, one of which claims a harm or potential harm from the law at issue. The Court, for example, will not hear cases in which the legal question at issue has become moot because the facts have changed. Similarly, it will not hear cases that are not "ripe" for adjudication—if, for example, it is not certain that a potential harm will be realized as an actual harm, or if critical facts remain to be resolved. Additionally, the Supreme Court does not issue "advisory opinions" on the likely outcome of hypothetical cases. Some state courts, however, do engage in this practice, as does the International Court of Justice.

Related to the "case or controversy" requirement is the issue of standing. In order to have "standing" to bring a case to federal court or an appeal before the Supreme Court, a party must be directly involved in the matter being argued. In a variety of cases, the Supreme Court has asked whether individuals can have "third-party standing," meaning that they can claim that, because of a general harm posed by a law, they can sue on behalf of citizens at large. Granting third-party standing would entail that an individual before the Court would not have been directly harmed but rather would seek to litigate on behalf of some broader interest. Repeatedly, the Supreme Court has denied such standing, thus limiting its own review power.

Deciding a Case

In addition to the readings that frame many of the issues of these chapters, a good portion of our work in this book will involve analyzing Supreme Court opinions. Unlike the legislative and executive branches, the Supreme Court issues formal written arguments revealing not only its decisions, but the reasons for those decisions. These reasoned documents are known as "opinions."

The Process of Opinion Writing

After the Court has agreed to hear a case, a number of steps will occur. First, the parties to the case will submit written briefs outlining their arguments and the legal arguments they suggest the justices rely upon. The petitioners (those who are asking the Court to reverse the lower court, or those who "petitioned" for certiorari) are then invited to have a lawyer make an oral argument before the Court and respond to questions from the bench. In practice, lawyers prepare an oral presentation but are often interrupted by the justices' questions. These questions will respond either to the oral arguments or to the written briefs. At times, justices will ask for clarification of the facts, but then will engage in legal argument with the lawyers. For instance, justices might ask the lawyers about how their suggested rules would apply in hypothetical scenarios, and what the implications of their case might be for future cases if their reasoning were adopted. After oral argument, the Court convenes a conference in which all the justices will discuss the cases in which they recently heard argument and attempt to reach a consensus. Ultimately, however, each case is subject to a vote, with the majority determining the outcome. Depending on how the vote goes, a variety of opinions can potentially be issued by the Court.

If at least five of the nine justices agree, both about the judgment and the reasoning, the senior justice in the majority will assign one of the justices to write a "majority opinion," which the other members of the majority will sign to indicate their support. Sometimes, justices will agree on the outcome of the case but not on the reasoning. In such cases, justices will often write a "concurring opinion" to distinguish their reasoning from that of the "majority opinion," although they support the ultimate judgment of the case. In cases in which fewer than five justices agree on the legal reasoning of a decision, the controlling opinion is properly called a "plurality" opinion. In some cases, the Court will issue *per curiam* ("for the court") or unsigned opinions.

Lastly, justices who disagree with the outcome of the case and with the legal reasoning will file "dissenting" opinions, outlining the legal arguments they would have adopted instead. The role of dissenting opinions in constitutional law is multi-faceted. They provide alternative kinds of reasoning that is useful in formulating possible criticisms of the majority's reasoning. In addition, however, dissenting opinions are often cited in future opinions, and indeed can become the basis for new law. For instance, Justice Oliver Wendell Holmes penned a famous dissent in *Abrams v. United States* that was later used in the founding of modern free-speech law. We include many dissents in this book, sometimes because they ultimately turned out to be controlling after a subsequent case, and sometimes because they provide interesting legal arguments.

Legal Reasoning

Now that we have discussed the process of opinion writing, we can explore some of the content of these opinions. First, it is important to learn to identify the *holding* of Supreme Court opinions. The holding explains how, in a particular case, the law applies to the facts at hand. Usually, the holding can be expressed in one sentence that ties together the legal issue discussed in the case with the decision about how this legal issue bears upon the facts. For instance, as you will see, the holding in *Lawrence v. Texas* is that state laws banning consensual sodomy violate couples' entitlement to substantive due process. Sometimes lawyers distinguish between the holding of the case and so-called *dicta.* Dicta is the area outside the specific legal adjudication, in which a particular justice will engage in reasoning that is either not strictly legal or is not necessary to decide the question before the court in the case at issue. Unlike the holding, it is not binding on future courts. The line between the holding and dicta, however, is sometimes blurry. Sometimes what is thought to be dicta becomes part of the holding, and ultimately part of the rule of law.

We will also see that much legal reasoning concerns the making and refuting of analogies to previous cases. The reason for this is that courts have an obligation to be consistent in their rulings over time, and to "treat like cases alike." In other words, the Supreme Court attempts to show respect for its prior precedent by continuing to apply similar rules to similar circumstances. The Court thus tends to follow a principle of *stare decisis,* roughly translated as "let the decision stand." Sometimes, however, the Court overturns a previous ruling. Famously, for example, the Court in *Brown v. Board of Education* overturned a previous case, *Plessy v. Ferguson,* which had enshrined the doctrine of "separate but equal." Sometimes, as in *Brown,* the Court will overrule a previous case explicitly. In other cases, such a reversal is never made explicit, though the Court may move away from or seek to marginalize a previous ruling. Thus, there is sometimes disagreement about whether a previous case has in fact been overruled.

THE CONSTITUTION OF THE UNITED STATES

We the People of the United States, in Order to form a more perfect Union, establish justice, insure domestic Tranquility, provide for the common defence, promote the general Welfare, and secure the Blessings of Liberty to ourselves and our Posterity, do ordain and establish this Constitution for the United States of America.

ARTICLE 1.

Section 1

All legislative Powers herein granted shall be vested in a Congress of the United States, which shall consist of a Senate and House of Representatives.

Section 2

The House of Representatives shall be composed of Members chosen every second Year by the People of the several States, and the Electors in each State shall have the Qualifications requisite for Electors of the most numerous Branch of the State Legislature.

No Person shall be a Representative who shall not have attained to the Age of twenty five Years, and been seven Years a Citizen of the United States, and who shall not, when elected, be an Inhabitant of that State in which he shall be chosen.

Representatives and direct Taxes shall be apportioned among the several States which may be included within this Union, according to their respective Numbers, which shall be determined by adding to the whole Number of free Persons, including those bound to Service for a Term of Years, and excluding Indians not taxed, three fifths of all other Persons.

The actual Enumeration shall be made within three Years after the first Meeting of the Congress of the United States, and within every subsequent Term of ten Years, in such Manner as they shall by Law direct. The Number of Representatives shall not exceed one for every thirty Thousand, but each State shall have at Least one Representative; and until such enumeration shall be made, the State of New

Hampshire shall be entitled to choose three, Massachusetts eight, Rhode Island and Providence Plantations one, Connecticut five, New York six, New Jersey four, Pennsylvania eight, Delaware one, Maryland six, Virginia ten, North Carolina five, South Carolina five and Georgia three.

When vacancies happen in the Representation from any State, the Executive Authority thereof shall issue Writs of Election to fill such Vacancies.

The House of Representatives shall choose their Speaker and other Officers; and shall have the sole Power of Impeachment.

Section 3

The Senate of the United States shall be composed of two Senators from each State, chosen by the Legislature thereof, for six Years; and each Senator shall have one Vote.

Immediately after they shall be assembled in Consequence of the first Election, they shall be divided as equally as may be into three Classes. The Seats of the Senators of the first Class shall be vacated at the Expiration of the second Year, of the second Class at the Expiration of the fourth Year, and of the third Class at the Expiration of the sixth Year, so that one third may be chosen every second Year; and if Vacancies happen by Resignation, or otherwise, during the Recess of the Legislature of any State, the Executive thereof may make temporary Appointments until the next Meeting of the Legislature, which shall then fill such Vacancies.

No person shall be a Senator who shall not have attained to the Age of thirty Years, and been nine Years a Citizen of the United States, and who shall not, when elected, be an Inhabitant of that State for which he shall be chosen.

The Vice President of the United States shall be President of the Senate, but shall have no Vote, unless they be equally divided.

The Senate shall choose their other Officers, and also a President pro tempore, in the absence of the Vice President, or when he shall exercise the Office of President of the United States.

The Senate shall have the sole Power to try all Impeachments. When sitting for that Purpose, they shall be on Oath or Affirmation. When the President of the United States is tried, the Chief Justice shall preside: And no Person shall be convicted without the Concurrence of two thirds of the Members present.

Judgment in Cases of Impeachment shall not extend further than to removal from Office, and disqualification to hold and enjoy any Office of honor, Trust or Profit under the United States: but the Party convicted shall nevertheless be liable and subject to Indictment, Trial, Judgment and Punishment, according to Law.

Section 4

The Times, Places and Manner of holding Elections for Senators and Representatives, shall be prescribed in each State by the Legislature thereof; but the Congress may at any time by Law make or alter such Regulations, except as to the Place of Choosing Senators.

The Congress shall assemble at least once in every Year, and such Meeting shall be on the first Monday in December, unless they shall by Law appoint a different Day.

Section 5

Each House shall be the Judge of the Elections, Returns and Qualifications of its own Members, and a Majority of each shall constitute a Quorum to do Business; but a smaller number may adjourn from day to day, and may be authorized to compel the Attendance of absent Members, in such Manner, and under such Penalties as each House may provide.

Each House may determine the Rules of its Proceedings, punish its Members for disorderly Behavior, and, with the Concurrence of two-thirds, expel a Member.

Each House shall keep a Journal of its Proceedings, and from time to time publish the same, excepting such Parts as may in their Judgment require Secrecy; and the Yeas and Nays of the Members of either House on any question shall, at the Desire of one fifth of those Present, be entered on the Journal.

Neither House, during the Session of Congress, shall, without the Consent of the other, adjourn for more than three days, nor to any other Place than that in which the two Houses shall be sitting.

Section 6

The Senators and Representatives shall receive a Compensation for their Services, to be ascertained by Law, and paid out of the Treasury of the United States. They shall in all Cases, except Treason, Felony and Breach of the Peace, be privileged from Arrest during their Attendance at the Session of their respective Houses, and in going to and returning from the same; and for any Speech or Debate in either House, they shall not be questioned in any other Place.

No Senator or Representative shall, during the Time for which he was elected, be appointed to any civil Office under the Authority of the United States which shall have been created, or the Emoluments whereof shall have been increased during such time; and no Person holding any Office under the United States, shall be a Member of either House during his Continuance in Office.

Section 7

All bills for raising Revenue shall originate in the House of Representatives; but the Senate may propose or concur with Amendments as on other Bills.

Every Bill which shall have passed the House of Representatives and the Senate, shall, before it become a Law, be presented to the President of the United States; If he approve he shall sign it, but if not he shall return it, with his Objections to that House in which it shall have originated, who shall enter the Objections at large on their Journal, and proceed to reconsider it. If after such Reconsideration two thirds of that House shall agree to pass the Bill, it shall be sent, together with the Objections, to the other House, by which it shall likewise be reconsidered, and if approved by two thirds of that House, it shall become a Law. But in all such Cases the Votes of both Houses shall be determined by Yeas and Nays, and the Names of the Persons voting for and against the Bill shall be entered on the Journal of each House respectively. If any Bill shall not be returned by the President within ten Days (Sundays excepted) after it shall have been presented to him, the Same shall be a Law, in like Manner as if he had signed it, unless the Congress by their Adjournment prevent its Return, in which Case it shall not be a Law.

Every Order, Resolution, or Vote to which the Concurrence of the Senate and House of Representatives may be necessary (except on a question of Adjournment) shall be presented to the President of the United States; and before the Same shall take Effect, shall be approved by him, or being disapproved by him, shall be repassed by two thirds of the Senate and House of Representatives, according to the Rules and Limitations prescribed in the Case of a Bill.

Section 8

The Congress shall have Power To lay and collect Taxes, Duties, Imposts and Excises, to pay the Debts and provide for the common Defence and general Welfare of the United States; but all Duties, Imposts and Excises shall be uniform throughout the United States;

To borrow money on the credit of the United States;

To regulate Commerce with foreign Nations, and among the several States, and with the Indian Tribes;

To establish an uniform Rule of Naturalization, and uniform Laws on the subject of Bankruptcies throughout the United States;

To coin Money, regulate the Value thereof, and of foreign Coin, and fix the Standard of Weights and Measures;

To provide for the Punishment of counterfeiting the Securities and current Coin of the United States;

To establish Post Offices and Post Roads;

To promote the Progress of Science and useful Arts, by securing for limited Times to Authors and Inventors the exclusive Right to their respective Writings and Discoveries;

To constitute Tribunals inferior to the supreme Court;

To define and punish Piracies and Felonies committed on the high Seas, and Offenses against the Law of Nations;

To declare War, grant Letters of Marque and Reprisal, and make Rules concerning

Captures on Land and Water;

To raise and support Armies, but no Appropriation of Money to that Use shall be for a longer Term than two Years;

To provide and maintain a Navy;

To make Rules for the Government and Regulation of the land and naval Forces;

To provide for calling forth the Militia to execute the Laws of the Union, suppress Insurrections and repel Invasions;

To provide for organizing, arming, and disciplining the Militia, and for governing such Part of them as may be employed in the Service of the United States, reserving to the States respectively, the Appointment of the Officers, and the Authority of training the Militia according to the discipline prescribed by Congress;

To exercise exclusive Legislation in all Cases whatsoever, over such District (not exceeding ten Miles square) as may, by Cession of particular States, and the acceptance of Congress, become the Seat of the Government of the United States, and to exercise like Authority over all Places purchased by the Consent of the Legislature of the State in which the Same shall be, for the Erection of Forts, Magazines, Arsenals, dock-Yards, and other needful Buildings; And

To make all Laws which shall be necessary and proper for carrying into Execution the foregoing Powers, and all other Powers vested by this Constitution in the Government of the United States, or in any Department or Officer thereof.

Section 9

The Migration or Importation of such Persons as any of the States now existing shall think proper to admit, shall not be prohibited by the Congress prior to the Year one thousand eight hundred and eight, but a tax or duty may be imposed on such Importation, not exceeding ten dollars for each Person.

The privilege of the Writ of Habeas Corpus shall not be suspended, unless when in Cases of Rebellion or Invasion the public Safety may require it.

No Bill of Attainder or ex post facto Law shall be passed.

No capitation, or other direct, Tax shall be laid, unless in Proportion to the Census or Enumeration herein before directed to be taken.

No Tax or Duty shall be laid on Articles exported from any State.

No Preference shall be given by any Regulation of Commerce or Revenue to the Ports of one State over those of another: nor shall Vessels bound to, or from, one State, be obliged to enter, clear, or pay Duties in another.

No Money shall be drawn from the Treasury, but in Consequence of Appropriations made by Law; and a regular Statement and Account of the Receipts and Expenditures of all public Money shall be published from time to time.

No Title of Nobility shall be granted by the United States: And no Person holding any Office of Profit or Trust under them, shall, without the Consent of the Congress, accept of any present, Emolument, Office, or Title, of any kind whatever, from any King, Prince or foreign State.

Section 10

No State shall enter into any Treaty, Alliance, or Confederation; grant Letters of Marque and Reprisal; coin Money; emit Bills of Credit; make any Thing but gold and silver Coin a Tender in Payment of Debts; pass any Bill of Attainder, ex post facto Law, or Law impairing the Obligation of Contracts, or grant any Title of Nobility.

No State shall, without the Consent of the Congress, lay any Imposts or Duties on Imports or Exports, except what may be absolutely necessary for executing its inspection Laws: and the net Produce of all Duties and Imposts, laid by any State on Imports or Exports, shall be for the Use of the Treasury of the United States; and all such Laws shall be subject to the Revision and Control of the Congress.

No State shall, without the Consent of Congress, lay any duty of Tonnage, keep Troops, or Ships of War in time of Peace, enter into any Agreement or Compact with another State, or with a foreign Power, or engage in War, unless actually invaded, or in such imminent Danger as will not admit of delay.

ARTICLE 2.

Section 1

The executive Power shall be vested in a President of the United States of America. He shall hold his Office during the Term of four Years, and, together with the Vice-President chosen for the same Term, be elected, as follows:

Each State shall appoint, in such Manner as the Legislature thereof may direct, a Number of Electors, equal to the whole Number of Senators and Representatives to which the State may be entitled in the Congress: but no Senator or Representative, or Person holding an Office of Trust or Profit under the United States, shall be appointed an Elector.

The Electors shall meet in their respective States, and vote by Ballot for two persons, of whom one at least shall not lie an Inhabitant of the same State with themselves. And they shall make a List of all the Persons voted for, and of the Number of Votes for each; which List they shall sign and certify, and transmit sealed to the Seat of the Government of the United States, directed to the President of the Senate. The President of the Senate shall, in the Presence of the Senate and House of Representatives, open all the Certificates, and the Votes shall then be counted. The Person having the greatest Number of Votes shall be the President, if such Number be a Majority of the whole Number of Electors appointed; and if there be more than one who have such Majority, and have an equal Number of Votes, then the House of Representatives shall immediately choose by Ballot one of them for President; and if no Person have a Majority, then from the five highest on the List the said House shall in like Manner choose the President. But in choosing the President, the Votes shall be taken by States, the Representation from each State having one Vote; a quorum for this Purpose shall consist of a Member or Members from two-thirds of the States, and a Majority of all the States shall be necessary to a Choice. In every Case, after the Choice of the President, the Person having the greatest Number of Votes of the Electors shall be the Vice President. But if there should remain two or more who have equal Votes, the Senate shall choose from them by Ballot the Vice-President.

The Congress may determine the Time of choosing the Electors, and the Day on which they shall give their Votes; which Day shall be the same throughout the United States.

No person except a natural born Citizen, or a Citizen of the United States, at the time of the Adoption of this Constitution, shall be eligible to the Office of President; neither shall any Person be eligible to that Office who shall not have attained to the Age of thirty-five Years, and been fourteen Years a Resident within the United States.

In Case of the Removal of the President from Office, or of his Death, Resignation, or Inability to discharge the Powers and Duties of the said Office, the same shall devolve on the Vice President, and the Congress may by Law provide for the Case of Removal, Death, Resignation or Inability, both of the President and Vice President, declaring what Officer shall then act as President, and such Officer shall act accordingly, until the Disability be removed, or a President shall be elected.

The President shall, at stated Times, receive for his Services, a Compensation, which shall neither be increased nor diminished during the Period for which he shall have been elected, and he shall not receive within that Period any other Emolument from the United States, or any of them.

Before he enter on the Execution of his Office, he shall take the following Oath or Affirmation:

"I do solemnly swear (or affirm) that I will faithfully execute the Office of President of the United States, and will to the best of my Ability, preserve, protect and defend the Constitution of the United States."

Section 2

The President shall be Commander in Chief of the Army and Navy of the United States, and of the Militia of the several States, when called into the actual Service of the United States; he may require the Opinion, in writing, of the principal Officer in each of the executive Departments, upon any subject relating to the Duties of their respective Offices, and he shall have Power to Grant Reprieves and Pardons for Offenses against the United States, except in Cases of Impeachment.

He shall have Power, by and with the Advice and Consent of the Senate, to make Treaties, provided two thirds of the Senators present concur; and he shall nominate, and by and with the Advice and Consent of the Senate, shall appoint Ambassadors, other public Ministers and Consuls, Judges of the supreme Court, and all other Officers of the United States, whose Appointments are not herein otherwise provided for, and which shall be established by Law: but the Congress may by Law vest the Appointment of such inferior Officers, as they think proper, in the President alone, in the Courts of Law, or in the Heads of Departments.

The President shall have Power to fill up all Vacancies that may happen during the Recess of the Senate, by granting Commissions which shall expire at the End of their next Session.

Section 3

He shall from time to time give to the Congress Information of the State of the Union, and recommend to their Consideration such Measures as he shall judge necessary and expedient; he may, on extraordinary Occasions, convene both Houses, or either of them, and in Case of Disagreement between them, with Respect to the Time of Adjournment, he may adjourn them to such Time as he shall think proper; he shall receive Ambassadors and other public Ministers; he shall take Care that the Laws be faithfully executed, and shall Commission all the Officers of the United States.

Section 4

The President, Vice President and all civil Officers of the United States, shall be removed from Office on Impeachment for, and Conviction of, Treason, Bribery, or other high Crimes and Misdemeanors.

ARTICLE 3.

Section 1

The judicial Power of the United States, shall be vested in one supreme Court, and in such inferior Courts as the Congress may from time to time ordain and establish. The Judges, both of the supreme and inferior Courts, shall hold their Offices during good Behavior, and shall, at stated Times, receive for their Services a Compensation which shall not be diminished during their Continuance in Office.

Section 2

The judicial Power shall extend to all Cases, in Law and Equity, arising under this Constitution, the Laws of the United States, and Treaties made, or which shall be made, under their Authority; to all Cases affecting Ambassadors, other public Ministers and Consuls; to all Cases of admiralty and maritime Jurisdiction; to Controversies to which the United States shall be a Party; to Controversies between two or more States; between a State and Citizens of another State; between Citizens of different States; between Citizens of the same State claiming Lands under Grants of different States, and between a State, or the Citizens thereof, and foreign States, Citizens or Subjects.

In all Cases affecting Ambassadors, other public Ministers and Consuls, and those in which a State shall be Party, the supreme Court shall have original Jurisdiction. In all the other Cases before mentioned, the supreme Court shall have appellate Jurisdiction, both as to Law and Fact, with such Exceptions, and under such Regulations as the Congress shall make.

The Trial of all Crimes, except in Cases of Impeachment, shall be by Jury; and such Trial shall be held in the State where the said Crimes shall have been committed; but when not committed within any State, the Trial shall be at such Place or Places as the Congress may by Law have directed.

Section 3

Treason against the United States, shall consist only in levying War against them, or in adhering to their Enemies, giving them Aid and Comfort. No Person shall be convicted of Treason unless on the Testimony of two Witnesses to the same overt Act, or on Confession in open Court.

The Congress shall have power to declare the Punishment of Treason, but no Attainder of Treason shall work Corruption of Blood, or Forfeiture except during the Life of the Person attainted.

ARTICLE 4.

Section 1

Full Faith and Credit shall be given in each State to the public Acts, Records, and judicial proceedings of every other State. And the Congress may by general Laws prescribe the Manner in which such Acts, Records and Proceedings shall be proved, and the Effect thereof.

Section 2

The Citizens of each State shall be entitled to all Privileges and Immunities of Citizens in the several States.

A Person charged in any State with Treason, Felony, or other Crime, who shall flee from justice, and be found in another State, shall on demand of the executive Authority of the State from which he fled, be delivered up, to be removed to the State having Jurisdiction of the Crime.

No Person held to Service or Labour in one State, under the Laws thereof, escaping into another, shall, in Consequence of any Law or Regulation therein, be discharged from such Service or Labour, But shall be delivered up on Claim of the Party to whom such Service or Labour may be due.

Section 3

New States may be admitted by the Congress into this Union; but no new States shall be formed or erected within the Jurisdiction of any other State; nor any State be formed by the Junction of two or more States, or parts of States, without the Consent of the Legislatures of the States concerned as well as of the Congress.

The Congress shall have Power to dispose of and make all needful Rules and Regulations respecting the Territory or other Property belonging to the United States; and nothing in this Constitution shall be so construed as to Prejudice any Claims of the United States, or of any particular State.

Section 4

The United States shall guarantee to every State in this Union a Republican Form of Government, and shall protect each of them against Invasion; and on Application of the Legislature, or of the Executive (when the Legislature cannot be convened) against domestic Violence.

ARTICLE 5.

The Congress, whenever two thirds of both Houses shall deem it necessary, shall propose Amendments to this Constitution, or, on the Application of the Legislatures of two thirds of the several States, shall call a Convention for proposing Amendments, which, in either Case, shall be valid to all Intents and Purposes, as part of this Constitution, when ratified by the Legislatures of three fourths of the several States, or by Conventions in three fourths thereof, as the one or the other Mode of Ratification may be proposed by the Congress; Provided that no Amendment which may be made prior to the Year One thousand eight hundred and eight shall in any Manner affect the first and fourth Clauses in the Ninth Section of the first Article; and that no State, without its Consent, shall be deprived of its equal Suffrage in the Senate.

ARTICLE 6.

All Debts contracted and Engagements entered into, before the Adoption of this Constitution, shall be as valid against the United States under this Constitution, as under the Confederation.

This Constitution, and the Laws of the United States which shall be made in Pursuance thereof; and all Treaties made, or which shall be made, under the Authority of the United States, shall be the supreme Law of the Land; and the Judges in every State shall be bound thereby, any Thing in the Constitution or Laws of any State to the Contrary notwithstanding.

The Senators and Representatives before mentioned, and the Members of the several State Legislatures, and all executive and judicial Officers, both of the United States and of the several States, shall be bound by Oath or Affirmation, to support this Constitution; but no religious Test shall ever be required as a Qualification to any Office or public Trust under the United States.

ARTICLE 7.

The Ratification of the Conventions of nine States, shall be sufficient for the Establishment of this Constitution between the States so ratifying the Same.

Done in Convention by the Unanimous Consent of the States present the Seventeenth Day of September in the Year of our Lord one thousand seven hundred and Eighty seven and of the Independence of the United States of America the Twelfth. In Witness whereof We have hereunto subscribed our Names.

Amendment 1

Congress shall make no law respecting an establishment of religion, or prohibiting the free exercise thereof; or abridging the freedom of speech, or of the press; or the right of the people peaceably to assemble, and to petition the Government for a redress of grievances.

Amendment 2

A well regulated Militia, being necessary to the security of a free State, the right of the people to keep and bear Arms, shall not be infringed.

Amendment 3

No Soldier shall, in time of peace be quartered in any house, without the consent of the Owner, nor in time of war, but in a manner to be prescribed by law.

Amendment 4

The right of the people to be secure in their persons, houses, papers, and effects, against unreasonable searches and seizures, shall not be violated, and no Warrants shall issue, but upon probable cause, supported by Oath or affirmation, and particularly describing the place to be searched, and the persons or things to be seized.

Amendment 5

No person shall be held to answer for a capital, or otherwise infamous crime, unless on a presentment or indictment of a Grand Jury, except in cases arising in the land or naval forces, or in the Militia, when in actual service in time of War or public danger; nor shall any person be subject for the same offense to be twice put in jeopardy of life or limb; nor shall be compelled in any criminal case to be a witness against himself, nor be deprived of life, liberty, or property, without due process of law; nor shall private property be taken for public use, without just compensation.

Amendment 6

In all criminal prosecutions, the accused shall enjoy the right to a speedy and public trial, by an impartial jury of the State and district wherein the crime shall have been committed, which district shall have been previously ascertained by law, and to be informed of the nature and cause of the accusation; to be confronted with the witnesses against him; to have compulsory process for obtaining witnesses in his favor, and to have the Assistance of Counsel for his defence.

Amendment 7

In Suits at common law, where the value in controversy shall exceed twenty dollars, the right of trial by jury shall be preserved, and no fact tried by a jury, shall be otherwise re-examined in any Court of the United States, than according to the rules of the common law.

Amendment 8

Excessive bail shall not be required, nor excessive fines imposed, nor cruel and unusual punishments inflicted.

Amendment 9

The enumeration in the Constitution, of certain rights, shall not be construed to deny or disparage others retained by the people.

Amendment 10

The powers not delegated to the United States by the Constitution, nor prohibited by it to the States, are reserved to the States respectively, or to the people.

Amendment 11

The Judicial power of the United States shall not be construed to extend to any suit in law or equity, commenced or prosecuted against one of the United States by Citizens of another State, or by Citizens or Subjects of any Foreign State.

Amendment 12

The Electors shall meet in their respective states, and vote by ballot for President and Vice-President, one of whom, at least, shall not be an inhabitant of the same state with themselves; they shall name in their ballots the person voted for as President, and in distinct ballots the person voted for as Vice-President, and they shall make distinct lists of all persons voted for as President, and of all persons voted for as Vice-President and of the number of votes for each, which lists they shall sign and certify, and transmit sealed to the seat of the government of the United States, directed to the President of the Senate;

The President of the Senate shall, in the presence of the Senate and House of Representatives, open all the certificates and the votes shall then be counted;

The person having the greatest Number of votes for President, shall be the President, if such number be a majority of the whole number of Electors appointed; and if no person have such majority, then from the persons having the highest numbers not exceeding three on the list of those voted for as President, the House of Representatives shall choose immediately, by ballot, the President. But in choosing the President, the votes shall be taken by states, the representation from each state having one vote; a quorum for this purpose shall consist of a member or members from two-thirds of the states, and a majority of all the states shall be necessary to a choice. And if the House of Representatives shall not choose a President whenever the right of choice shall devolve upon them, before the fourth day of March next following, then the Vice-President shall act as President, as in the case of the death or other constitutional disability of the President.

The person having the greatest number of votes as Vice-President, shall be the Vice-President, if such number be a majority of the whole number of Electors appointed, and if no person have a majority, then from the two highest numbers on the list, the Senate shall choose the Vice-President; a quorum for the purpose shall consist of two-thirds of the whole number of Senators, and a majority of the whole number shall be necessary to a choice. But no person constitutionally ineligible to the office of President shall be eligible to that of Vice-President of the United States.

Amendment 13

1. Neither slavery nor involuntary servitude, except as a punishment for crime whereof the party shall have been duly convicted, shall exist within the United States, or any place subject to their jurisdiction.

2. Congress shall have power to enforce this article by appropriate legislation.

Amendment 14

1. All persons born or naturalized in the United States, and subject to the jurisdiction thereof, are citizens of the United States and of the State wherein they reside. No State shall make or enforce any law which shall abridge the privileges or immunities of citizens of the United States; nor shall any State deprive any person of life, liberty, or property, without due process of law; nor deny to any person within its jurisdiction the equal protection of the laws.

2. Representatives shall be apportioned among the several States according to their respective numbers, counting the whole number of persons in each State, excluding Indians not taxed. But when the right to vote at any election for the choice of electors for President and Vice-President of the United States, Representatives in Congress, the Executive and Judicial officers of a State, or the members of the Legislature thereof, is denied to any of the male inhabitants of such State, being twenty-one years of age, and citizens of the United States, or in any way abridged, except for participation in rebellion, or other crime, the basis of representation therein shall be reduced in the proportion which the number of such male citizens shall bear to the whole number of male citizens twenty-one years of age in such State.

3. No person shall be a Senator or Representative in Congress, or elector of President and Vice-President, or hold any office, civil or military, under the United States, or under any State, who, having previously taken an oath, as a member of Congress, or as an officer of the United States, or as a member of any State legislature, or as an executive or judicial officer of any State, to support the Constitution of the United States, shall have engaged in insurrection or rebellion

against the same, or given aid or comfort to the enemies thereof. But Congress may by a vote of two-thirds of each House, remove such disability.

4. The validity of the public debt of the United States, authorized by law, including debts incurred for payment of pensions and bounties for services in suppressing insurrection or rebellion, shall not be questioned. But neither the United States nor any State shall assume or pay any debt or obligation incurred in aid of insurrection or rebellion against the United States, or any claim for the loss or emancipation of any slave; but all such debts, obligations and claims shall be held illegal and void.

5. The Congress shall have power to enforce, by appropriate legislation, the provisions of this article.

Amendment 15

1. The right of citizens of the United States to vote shall not be denied or abridged by the United States or by any State on account of race, color, or previous condition of servitude.

2. The Congress shall have power to enforce this article by appropriate legislation.

Amendment 16

The Congress shall have power to lay and collect taxes on incomes, from whatever source derived, without apportionment among the several States, and without regard to any census or enumeration.

Amendment 17

The Senate of the United States shall be composed of two Senators from each State, elected by the people thereof, for six years; and each Senator shall have one vote. The electors in each State shall have the qualifications requisite for electors of the most numerous branch of the State legislatures.

When vacancies happen in the representation of any State in the Senate, the executive authority of such State shall issue writs of election to fill such vacancies: Provided, That the legislature of any State may empower the executive thereof to make temporary appointments until the people fill the vacancies by election as the legislature may direct.

This amendment shall not be so construed as to affect the election or term of any Senator chosen before it becomes valid as part of the Constitution.

Amendment 18

1. After one year from the ratification of this article the manufacture, sale, or transportation of intoxicating liquors within, the importation thereof into, or

the exportation thereof from the United States and all territory subject to the jurisdiction thereof for beverage purposes is hereby prohibited.

2. The Congress and the several States shall have concurrent power to enforce this article by appropriate legislation.

3. This article shall be inoperative unless it shall have been ratified as an amendment to the Constitution by the legislatures of the several States, as provided in the Constitution, within seven years from the date of the submission hereof to the States by the Congress.

Amendment 19

The right of citizens of the United States to vote shall not be denied or abridged by the United States or by any State on account of sex.

Congress shall have power to enforce this article by appropriate legislation.

Amendment 20

1. The terms of the President and Vice President shall end at noon on the 20th day of January, and the terms of Senators and Representatives at noon on the 3d day of January, of the years in which such terms would have ended if this article had not been ratified; and the terms of their successors shall then begin.

2. The Congress shall assemble at least once in every year, and such meeting shall begin at noon on the 3d day of January, unless they shall by law appoint a different day.

3. If, at the time fixed for the beginning of the term of the President, the President elect shall have died, the Vice President elect shall become President. If a President shall not have been chosen before the time fixed for the beginning of his term, or if the President elect shall have failed to qualify, then the Vice President elect shall act as President until a President shall have qualified; and the Congress may by law provide for the case herein neither a President elect nor a Vice President elect shall have qualified, declaring who shall then act as President, or the manner in which one who is to act shall be selected, and such person shall act accordingly until a President or Vice President shall have qualified.

4. The Congress may by law provide for the case of the death of any of the persons from whom the House of Representatives may choose a President whenever the right of choice shall have devolved upon them, and for the case of the death of any of the persons from whom the Senate may choose a Vice President whenever the right of choice shall have devolved upon them.

5. Sections 1 and 2 shall take effect on the 15th day of October following the ratification of this article.

6. This article shall be inoperative unless it shall have been ratified as an amendment to the Constitution by the legislatures of three-fourths of the several States within seven years from the date of its submission.

Amendment 21

1. The eighteenth article of amendment to the Constitution of the United States is hereby repealed.

2. The transportation or importation into any State, Territory, or possession of the United States for delivery or use therein of intoxicating liquors, in violation of the laws thereof, is hereby prohibited.

3. The article shall be inoperative unless it shall have been ratified as an amendment to the Constitution by conventions in the several States, as provided in the Constitution, within seven years from the date of the submission hereof to the States by the Congress.

Amendment 22

1. No person shall be elected to the office of the President more than twice, and no person who has held the office of President, or acted as President, for more than two years of a term to which some other person was elected President shall be elected to the office of the President more than once. But this Article shall not apply to any person holding the office of President, when this Article was proposed by the Congress, and shall not prevent any person who may be holding the office of President, or acting as President, during the term within which this Article becomes operative from holding the office of President or acting as President during the remainder of such term.

2. This article shall be inoperative unless it shall have been ratified as an amendment to the Constitution by the legislatures of three-fourths of the several States within seven years from the date of its submission to the States by the Congress.

Amendment 23

1. The District constituting the seat of Government of the United States shall appoint in such manner as the Congress may direct: A number of electors of President and Vice President equal to the whole number of Senators and Representatives in Congress to which the District would be entitled if it were a State, but in no event more than the least populous State; they shall be in addition to those appointed by the States, but they shall be considered, for the purposes of the election of President and Vice President, to be electors appointed by a State; and they shall meet in the District and perform such duties as provided by the twelfth article of amendment.

2. The Congress shall have power to enforce this article by appropriate legislation.

Amendment 24

1. The right of citizens of the United States to vote in any primary or other election for President or Vice President, for electors for President or Vice President, or for Senator or Representative in Congress, shall not be denied or abridged by the United States or any State by reason of failure to pay any poll tax or other tax.

2. The Congress shall have power to enforce this article by appropriate legislation.

Amendment 25

1. In case of the removal of the President from office or of his death or resignation, the Vice President shall become President.

2. Whenever there is a vacancy in the office of the Vice President, the President shall nominate a Vice President who shall take office upon confirmation by a majority vote of both Houses of Congress.

3. Whenever the President transmits to the President pro tempore of the Senate and the Speaker of the House of Representatives his written declaration that he is unable to discharge the powers and duties of his office, and until he transmits to them a written declaration to the contrary, such powers and duties shall be discharged by the Vice President as Acting President.

4. Whenever the Vice President and a majority of either the principal officers of the executive departments or of such other body as Congress may by law provide, transmit to the President pro tempore of the Senate and the Speaker of the House of Representatives their written declaration that the President is unable to discharge the powers and duties of his office, the Vice President shall immediately assume the powers and duties of the office as Acting President.

Thereafter, when the President transmits to the President pro tempore of the Senate and the Speaker of the House of Representatives his written declaration that no inability exists, he shall resume the powers and duties of his office unless the Vice President and a majority of either the principal officers of the executive department or of such other body as Congress may by law provide, transmit within four days to the President pro tempore of the Senate and the Speaker of the House of Representatives their written declaration that the President is unable to discharge the powers and duties of his office. Thereupon Congress shall decide the issue, assembling within forty eight hours for that purpose if not in session. If the Congress, within twenty one days after receipt of the latter written declaration, or, if Congress is not in session, within twenty one days after Congress is required to assemble, determines by two thirds vote of both Houses that the President is unable to discharge the powers and duties of his office, the Vice President shall continue to discharge the same as Acting President; otherwise, the President shall resume the powers and duties of his office.

Amendment 26

1. The right of citizens of the United States, who are eighteen years of age or older, to vote shall not be denied or abridged by the United States or by any State on account of age.

2. The Congress shall have power to enforce this article by appropriate legislation.

Amendment 27

No law, varying the compensation for the services of the Senators and Representatives, shall take effect, until an election of Representatives shall have intervened.

GOVERNMENTAL POWERS

PART I

JUDICIAL AUTHORITY

Is judicial review or judicial supremacy justified? Is either constitutional? Is either democratic?

In the study of constitutional law, nothing is more problematic than the power of the Supreme Court itself. Many scholars of political science and constitutional law accept that the Court holds legitimate power to strike down both federal and state laws when those laws conflict with the U.S. Constitution. The potential problem with this power, however, lies in the fact that, at all levels of government, a large number of citizens are involved in the process of lawmaking. They do the hard work of crafting legislation, debating it in both formal and informal arenas, and participating either directly through plebiscites or indirectly through their elected representatives. In addition, at both the national and state levels of government, legislation must not only make it through the legislative branch, but must also win the approval of the executive branch, except in cases where an overwhelming supermajority in the legislature supports the legislation. Yet, in the U.S. system of government, the final decision as to whether laws are valid lies in the power of the Court to decide if legislation, despite all this effort, is consistent with the Constitution. If the Court finds that an act violates the Constitution, it has the power to strike down such legislation through the power of "judicial review." But what gives five out of nine justices of the Supreme Court the authority to make a decision about legislation that may affect millions of individuals and was approved by a majority of the people's representatives?

All that is needed to spark the Court's review power is one person who contests the constitutionality of legislation by bringing a lawsuit. Although the Court does not have the power to initiate the review of laws on its own, each person subject to the law of and present in the United States has the right to bring suit challenging the constitutionality of laws that affect him or her. Article III of the Constitution in essence gives any one person the ability to challenge the constitutionality of legislative acts.

The readings and cases in this part attempt to address the question of why the Supreme Court, prompted by suits brought by individuals or groups of individuals, should have the power of judicial review in a democracy. This problem is described perhaps most famously by Alexander Bickel. Bickel addresses what he calls the "counter-majoritarian difficulty." For him, the fundamental question of the Constitution is whether we can regard the Court's power of judicial review as democratic, given there are so few people involved in the process of judicial review, and a much larger number of people involved in the legislative process. He also challenges the idea that the Court is democratic given the fact that its members are not elected, but rather appointed by the president.

As you read through this part, it is important that you reflect on the possible answers to this challenge. The responses to this problem will help us to reflect on the question of judicial authority and the Court's review power. Indeed, the numerous questions that arise about the Constitution and its meaning throughout this book depend on our idea of judicial authority. When should the Court intercede in possible conflicts between Congress and the Constitution, or between the president and the Constitution, or even between Congress and the president? The question of intervention is no light matter, as throughout American history the courts have been involved through the power of judicial review in considering questions as fundamental as slavery, war, segregation, and abortion. Before we can discuss these specific issues, it is important to develop an understanding of when, if ever, the Court has the power and authority to intervene.

One possible line of argument that you should consider is that the rule of law itself provides an answer to the question of judicial authority. The courts, after all, are tasked with the job of interpreting the law. If the Constitution is a document of law, then it might follow that the courts should interpret the Constitution. In fact, this logic might go so far as to suggest that the Court should have the final say in various areas of law. In a contract suit, for example, the courts often are considered to have the final say. Should this finality also apply to matters of constitutional law? Something akin to this argument, as you will see, is prominent in the Court's decision in *Marbury v. Madison*, a case central to this part.

There is a long line of critics dissatisfied with grounding the Court's judicial review power in a claim about the nature of the rule of law. While courts certainly can interpret law, it does not necessarily follow that they should be the exclusive interpreter of law. Thomas Jefferson, for instance, thought that the other branches also were capable of constitutional interpretation. Some advocates of "departmentalism" have advocated for a role for the other branches, aside from the Court, in constitutional interpretation. Even further, Larry Kramer, whose article we excerpt in Chapter 2, has argued that "the people themselves" have a role in constitutional interpretation.

Another line of argumentation in defense of the Court's review power draws from its potential democratic authority. Perhaps the will of the people itself demands ceding control to the Supreme Court in particular controversies. If the people endorse the idea of representative democracy, perhaps they also endorse the idea that particular decisions about matters of constitutional law should be left to the courts. An analogous approach suggests that the courts must protect democracy itself. Perhaps the authority of the Supreme Court to enforce judicial review lies in its ability to bolster the democratic process. Similarly, those who believe rights to be fundamental to the American system might find appealing the idea that the Court's authority lies in its special ability to protect individual liberties.

What all the possible theories of the Court's authority and its review power make clear is that, to answer the counter-majoritarian difficulty, it might be necessary for you to ponder what you think democracy means. As the readings make clear, the definition of democracy is by no means obvious. Although simple majority rule is a common understanding of democratic rule, as you think about the role of the Court in a self-governing polity, also think about the meaning of democracy. Perhaps, as Ronald Dworkin believes, the protection of rights is fundamental to the meaning of democracy. Courts therefore might serve a democratic function when they protect rights, even if it means acting contrary to the will of the majority.

Some will be skeptical of both of these responses, and they will find themselves in the company of the strongest critics of judicial authority. According to some such thinkers, the Court's authority cannot be understood as anything other than antidemocratic. Some might conclude from this that there is no defense of the Court's judicial review power. But others might think that merely because it is an antidemocratic power does not mean that judicial review is not important or justified.

Indeed, even if judicial review should be a part of a system of democratic governance, as you will see, some legal scholars have debated the doctrine of "judicial supremacy." This debate concerns the question of whether the Court should be regarded as the final arbiter of the meaning of the Constitution, or if that power should instead lie with another body of government.

In sum, in order to think about whether the Court should have the power of judicial review, it is essential that you grapple with the problem of judicial authority. As you read through this part, you should seek to develop your own views about whether the Court should have *a* say, the *final* say, or *no* say in constitutional matters. This will enable you to develop informed views in other areas of constitutional controversy. If you conclude that the Supreme Court should have the power of judicial review, it will also be incumbent on you to think about how the Court should exercise this review power. Having thought about the nature of the Supreme Court and its review power will prove invaluable in this task. Indeed, your view of the reason for judicial authority will inevitably be linked to the way you think this power should be exercised. In Parts II and III of this book, you will identify and evaluate the powers held by Congress and the president. These powers are derived from the Constitution, and interpretation of the Constitution is fundamental to the question of the nature of these powers.

CHAPTER 1

THE ORIGINS OF JUDICIAL REVIEW

Although not labeled as such, the counter-majoritarian difficulty and the question of judicial authority in constitutional matters is a problem that has clearly been on the minds of scholars and jurists since the drafting of the Constitution. In *The Federalist No. 78*, Alexander Hamilton outlines two principal answers to this challenge that continue to be contested today. First, in the line of argument that would be repeated by U.S. Supreme Court Chief Justice John Marshall in the classic case of *Marbury v. Madison*, Hamilton argues that the Court's review power stems from the nature of the rule of law itself. If it is the role of courts to interpret law, and the Constitution is the law, then it follows that the courts should interpret the Constitution. This line of reasoning, often referred to as the "*Marbury* syllogism," is an often-repeated justification of the Court's authority. But this justification risks obscuring the difficult problems that underlie the counter-majoritarian difficulty not answered by this syllogism. In particular, why should the law itself command obedience? Why should courts be the exclusive interpreters of this law? The question of why the courts should have the power to interpret the law cannot be answered by reference to the law alone. Such an argument would be circular. Such questions cannot be answered without reference to a broader political theory about the justification for law. As we will see, Hamilton was aware of this problem and tried to outline a wider political theory of the power of judicial review that appealed to its importance in a democratic society. He claims in *The Federalist* that the very limits imposed by the Constitution have their source in the people themselves, as distinct from their elected representatives.

Throughout this part we examine various arguments that challenge Hamilton's understanding of the role of the Supreme Court within Article III of the Constitution. Many of these readings, however, share an assumption that the proper role of the Court should be read within the confines of Article III. These disagreements therefore are about how to interpret the Constitution. But before we examine these debates it is important to examine a fundamental challenge to Article III itself, and the very idea of a Supreme Court with review power. The excerpt included from Brutus, the pseudonym of a noted "anti-federalist" thinker, active in resisting the ratification of the Constitution by the states, suggests that the structure of Article III will lead to judicial tyranny. He suggests that the Court inevitably will need to answer questions left open by the Constitution, especially when it comes to applying broad provisions to specific facts. In such cases, the Court will have no guide. In this way, the potential arises for the Court to reach judgments that disregard the interests of the citizenry.

A more moderate critique does not seek to abolish the Supreme Court's power altogether, but would seek to limit it. The excerpt by Jefferson offers an interpretation of Article III distinct from the ones presented by both Hamilton and Brutus. Jefferson thought that a good account of democracy could not allow the Court the final word in interpreting the Constitution. In the included passage, he presents what became known later as the theory of departmentalism, or the idea that no one branch of government should have the final say in determining the meaning of the Constitution. In particular, notice his powerful metaphor about the Court's ability to mold law as though it were wax. If the Court is the final arbiter of the meaning of the Constitution, what is to prevent it from saying that the Constitution means merely what its justices wish it to say? The debate between Hamilton and Jefferson, therefore, raises a crucial issue of interpretation. Need the Constitution place its meaning in the hands of a final interpreter, or does that meaning stand apart from what any one institution claims it to mean? Does identifying the meaning of the Constitution require an institution to function as a final interpreter, or does that meaning stand on its own directly out of the document?

In his famous commentary on *Marbury v. Madison*, in which he coins the term "counter-majoritarian difficulty," Bickel poses a fundamental challenge to both Hamilton's and Jefferson's views. He is deeply skeptical of the idea that the limits on majority rule imposed by the Constitution can be called democratic. For Bickel, it is the acts of participants in democratic rule that are the source of democratic authority, and he dismisses as chimerical the maneuvers of Hamilton and Chief Justice Marshall in suggesting otherwise. Yet Bickel is also concerned with protecting the guarantees of the Constitution, and arguably he still sees a role for the Court in doing so.

Before turning to our case selection for this chapter, you will explore Gordon Wood's attempt to provide a historical context for *Marbury v. Madison*. Wood raises interesting questions about the role of the decision in the Court's current practice of judicial review. Although *Marbury v. Madison* is often considered the basis of the Court's basic review power, Wood asks whether this is a modern invention rather than an obvious historical fact. Indeed, Wood's skepticism should give deep pause to anyone who wants to find the basis of judicial review in history alone.

The case selection in this chapter begins with *Calder v. Bull*. In that case, the Court examined whether a state law violated the Constitution's ban on ex post facto laws. You will notice, too, that there is some commentary about the Court's possible power of judicial review. Although the review power is not clearly established in *Calder v. Bull*, you will see the issue examined in much greater depth when we turn next to the classic *Marbury v. Madison*, in which the Court is commonly regarded to have established the power of judicial review.

You should notice how Chief Justice Marshall's argumentation appeals to the idea of law itself in establishing the Court's authority. You should note that, although the case does not grant the petitioner his claim, Chief Justice Marshall nevertheless uses the controversy as a means by which to assert greater power for the Court. Following *Marbury v. Madison,* which was predicated on a conflict at the federal level, you will find four cases in which the Court examined whether the actions of state governments violated the federal Constitution. The clauses of the Constitution here vary from issues regarding whether the prohibition on ex post facto laws has been violated to an examination of the meaning of the Contracts Clause. In addition to addressing issues of the Court's review power, these cases also inevitably raise the issue of the federal government's relationship to the states. As you will see, the Court in these cases breaks with its earlier reluctance to review and at times overturn state laws that violate the Constitution.

Alexander Bickel

THE LEAST DANGEROUS BRANCH

Chapter 1: Establishment and General Justification of Judicial Review

New Haven, CT: Yale University Press (1986)

The least dangerous branch of the American government is the most extraordinarily powerful court of law the world has ever known. The power which distinguishes the Supreme Court of the United States is that of constitutional review of actions of the other branches of government, federal and state. Curiously enough, this power of judicial review, as it is called, does not derive from any explicit constitutional command. The authority to determine the meaning and application of a written constitution is nowhere defined or even mentioned in the document itself. This is not to say that the power of judicial review cannot be placed in the Constitution; merely that it cannot be found there.

MARBURY v. MADISON

Congress was created very nearly full blown by the Constitution itself. The vast possibilities of the presidency were relatively easy to perceive and soon, inevitably, materialized. But the institution of the judiciary needed to be summoned up out of the constitutional vapors, shaped, and maintained; and the Great Chief Justice, John Marshall — not single-handed, but first and foremost — was there to do it and did. If any social process can be said to have been "done" at a given time and by a given act, it is Marshall's achievement. The time was 1803; the act was the decision in the case of *Marbury v. Madison.*

William Marbury and some others sued Secretary Madison for delivery of their commissions as justices of the peace for the County of Washington in the District of Columbia, an office to which they had been appointed in the last moments of the administration of President John Adams. Marshall held that Marbury and the others were entitled to their commissions, but that the Supreme Court was without power to order Madison to deliver, because the section of the Judiciary Act of 1789 that purported to authorize the Court to act in such a case as this was itself unconstitutional. Thus did Marshall assume for his Court what is nowhere made explicit in the Constitution — the ultimate power to apply the Constitution, acts of Congress to the contrary notwithstanding.

"The question," Marshall's opinion begins, "whether an act repugnant to the Constitution, can become the law of the land, is a question deeply interesting to the United States; but, happily, not of an intricacy proportioned to its interest." Marshall's confidence that he could traverse the path ahead with ease is understandable, since he had already begged the question-in-chief, which was not whether an act repugnant to the Constitution could stand, but who should be empowered to decide that the act is repugnant. Marshall then posited the limited nature of the government established by the Constitution. It follows — and one may grant to Marshall that it follows as "a proposition too plain to be contested" — that the Constitution is a paramount law, and that ordinary legislative acts must conform to it. For Marshall it follows, further, that a legislative act contrary to the Constitution is not law and need not be given effect in court; else "written constitutions are absurd attempts, on the part of the people, to limit a power in its own nature illimitable." If two laws conflict, a court must obey the superior one. But Marshall knew (and, indeed, it was true in this very case) that a statute's repugnancy to the Constitution is in most instances not self-evident; it is, rather, an issue of policy that someone must decide. The problem is who: the courts, the legislature itself, the President, perhaps juries for purposes of criminal trials, or ultimately and finally the people through the electoral process?

This is the real question. Marshall addressed himself to it only partially and slightly. To leave the decision with the legislature, he said, is to allow those whose power is supposed to be limited themselves to set the limits — an absurd invitation to consistent abuse. Perhaps so, but the Constitution does not limit the power of the legislature alone. It limits that of the courts as well, and it may be equally absurd, therefore, to allow courts to set the limits. It is, indeed, more absurd, because courts are not subject to electoral control. (It may be argued that to leave the matter to the legislature is to leave it ultimately to the people at the polls. In this view the people as the principal would set the limits of the power that they have delegated to their agent.)

The case can be constructed where the conflict between a statute and the Constitution is self-evident in accordance with Marshall's general assumption. Even so, Marshall offers no real reason that the Court should have the power to nullify the statute. But Marshall did go on to some more specific textual references. His first was to Article III of the Constitution, which establishes the judiciary and reads in relevant part as follows:

> SECTION 1.The judicial Power of the United States, shall be vested in one supreme Court, and in such inferior Courts as the Congress may from time to time ordain and establish. The Judges, both of the supreme and inferior Courts, shall hold their Offices during good Behavior, and shall, at stated Times, receive for their Services a Compensation which shall not be diminished during their Continuance in Office.
>
> SECTION 2. The judicial Power shall extend to all Cases, in Law and Equity, arising under this Constitution, the Laws of the United States, and Treaties made, or which shall be made, under their Authority; — to all Cases affecting Ambassadors, or other

> public Ministers and Consuls;—to all Cases of admiralty and maritime Jurisdiction;—to Controversies to which the United States shall be a Party;—to Controversies between two or more States;—between a State and Citizens of another State;—between Citizens of different States;—between Citizens of the same State claiming Lands under Grants of different States, and between a State, or the Citizens thereof, and foreign States, Citizens or Subjects.
>
> In all Cases affecting Ambassadors, other public Ministers and Consuls, and those in which a State shall be a Party, the supreme Court shall have original Jurisdiction. In all the other Cases before mentioned, the supreme Court shall have appellate Jurisdiction, both as to Law and Fact, with such Exceptions, and under such Regulations as the Congress shall make.

Could it be, Marshall asked, that those who granted the judicial power and extended it to all cases arising under the Constitution, laws, and treaties meant that cases arising under the Constitution should be decided without examination and application of the document itself? This was for Marshall "too extravagant to be maintained." Note well, however, that what the Constitution extends to cases arising under it is "the judicial Power." Whether this power reaches as far as Marshall wanted it to go—namely, to reviewing acts of the legislature—is the question to be decided. What are the nature and extent of the function of the Court—the judicial power? Is the Court empowered, when it decides a case, to declare that a duly enacted statute violates the Constitution, and to invalidate the statute? Article III does not purport to describe the function of the Court; it subsumes whatever questions may exist as to that in the phrase "the judicial Power." It does not purport to tell the Court how to decide cases; it only specifies which kinds of cases the Court shall have jurisdiction to deal with at all. Thus, in giving jurisdiction in cases "arising under . . . the Laws" or "under . . . Treaties," the clause is not read as prescribing the process of decision to be followed. The process varies. In cases "under . . . the Laws" courts often leave determination of issues of fact and even issues that may be thought to be "of law" to administrative agencies. And under both "the Laws . . . and Treaties," much of the decision concerning meaning and applicability may be received ready-made from the Congress and the President. In some cases of all three descriptions, judicial decision may he withheld altogether—and it is for this reason that it will not do to place reliance on the word "all" in the phrase "all cases . . . arising. . . ." To the extent that the Constitution speaks to such matters, it does so in the tightly packed phrase "judicial Power."

Only in the end, and then very lightly, does Marshall come to rest on the Supremacy Clause of Article VI, which in later times has seemed to many the most persuasive textual support. The Supremacy Clause is as follows:

> This Constitution and the Laws of the United States which shall be made in Pursuance thereof; and all Treaties made, or which shall be made, under the Authority of the United States, shall be the supreme Law of the Land; and the Judges in every State shall be bound thereby, any Thing in the Constitution or Laws of any State to the Contrary notwithstanding.

"It is also not entirely unworthy of observation," Marshall wrote—and this was all he had to say on the point—that in declaring what is to be the supreme law of the land, this clause mentions the Constitution first and then not the laws of the United States generally but only those which shall be made in pursuance of the Constitution. Marshall left it at that, and what is to be concluded from this remark? First, it must be noted that nothing here is addressed to federal courts. Any command to them will have to be inferred, if there is to be one at all. Only as a forensic amusement can the phrase "Judges in every State" be taken to include federal judges, on the ground that some of them sit in the states. After all, the Supreme Court does not. The clause speaks to the constituent states of the federation and tells them that federal law will supersede any contrary state law. Further, it goes over the heads of the state governments and speaks to state judges directly, telling them that it will be their duty to enforce the supreme federal law above any contrary state law. State judges need enforce, however, only such federal law as is made in pursuance of the Constitution. Conceivably the reference here might be to more than just the mechanical provisions that describe how a federal law is to be enacted—by the concurrence of both Houses and with the signature of the President. Conceivably state judges were to be authorized to measure federal law against the federal Constitution and uphold it or strike it down in accordance with their understanding of the relevant constitutional provision. But such an arrangement, standing alone, would have been extraordinary, and it would have been self-destructive.

Judiciary acts have, from the beginning, also given the Supreme Court jurisdiction to review state court cases in which is drawn in question the validity of a treaty or statute of the United States, presumably under the federal Constitution. If that was a grant to the Supreme Court of final authority to construe the Constitution as against acts of Congress, why, then, well and good. Nothing in the text prevents such a gesture of congressional abnegation, although in that event, what Congress can give away, Congress can, at least in theory, take back. But it is question-begging so to understand this provision of the first Judiciary Act. Reading no presuppositions into it, one may as easily conclude that the Supreme Court was meant only to enforce against state courts a rule that duly enacted federal statutes are constitutional by virtue of their due enactment. There is no similar ambiguity, however, in the first Judiciary Act's grant to the Supreme Court of jurisdiction to review cases which draw in question the validity of a statute of, or an authority exercised under, any state, on the ground of its being repugnant to the Constitution, treaties, or laws of the United States. This provision would be senseless unless it was intended to authorize the Court, in these circumstances, to construe and apply the federal Constitution as well as federal statute and treaty law. Only thus could this provision serve the interest of uniformity and of the superiority of federal power—and what other purpose could it have? As we have seen, the Supremacy Clause itself does not compel, although it permits and no doubt invites, this arrangement. This being so, Congress could change it all tomorrow. And perhaps it could, if textual considerations were all that governed the matter, just as it could change the course of the Mississippi River, if all we had to indicate the location of its bed were some general description by a traveler of a body of water traversing the middle of the country from north to south.

THE COUNTER-MAJORITARIAN DIFFICULTY

The root difficulty is that judicial review is a counter-majoritarian force in our system. There are various ways of sliding over this ineluctable reality. Marshall did so when he spoke of enforcing, in behalf of "the people," the limits that they have ordained for the institutions of a limited government. But the word "people" so used is an abstraction. Not necessarily a meaningless or a pernicious one by any means; always charged with emotion, but nonrepresentational — an abstraction obscuring the reality that when the Supreme Court declares unconstitutional a legislative act or the action of an elected executive, it thwarts the will of representatives of the actual people of the here and now; it exercises control, not in behalf of the prevailing majority, but against it. That, without mystic overtones, is what actually happens. It is an altogether different kettle of fish, and it is the reason the charge can be made that judicial review is undemocratic.

Most assuredly, no democracy operates by taking continuous nose counts on the broad range of daily governmental activities. Representative democracies — that is to say, all working democracies — function by electing certain men for certain periods of time, then passing judgment periodically on their conduct of public office. . . . What we mean by democracy, therefore, is much more sophisticated and complex than the making of decisions in town meeting by a show of hands. It is true also that even decisions that have been submitted to the electoral process in some fashion are not continually resubmitted, and they are certainly not continually unmade. Once run through the process, once rendered by "the people" (using the term now in its mystic sense, because the reference is to the people in the past), myriad decisions remain to govern the present and the future despite what may well be fluctuating majorities against them at any given time. A high value is put on stability, and that is also a counter-majoritarian factor. Nevertheless, although democracy does not mean constant reconsideration of decisions once made, it does mean that a representative majority has the power to accomplish a reversal. This power is of the essence, and no less so because it is often merely held in reserve.

. . . The insights of Professor Truman and other writers into the role that groups play in our society and our politics have a bearing on judicial review. They indicate that there are other means than the electoral process, though subordinate and subsidiary ones, of making institutions of government responsive to the needs and wishes of the governed. Hence one may infer that judicial review, although not responsible, may have ways of being responsive. But nothing can finally depreciate the central function that is assigned in democratic theory and practice to the electoral process; nor can it be denied that the policy-making power of representative institutions, born of the electoral process, is the distinguishing characteristic of the system. Judicial review works counter to this characteristic.

It therefore does not follow from the complex nature of a democratic system that, because admirals and generals and the members, say, of the Federal Reserve Board or of this or that administrative agency are not electorally responsible, judges who exercise the power of judicial review need not be responsible either, and in neither case is there a serious conflict with democratic theory. For admirals and generals and the like are most often responsible to officials who are themselves elected and through whom the line runs directly to a majority. What is more significant, the policies they make are or should be interstitial or technical only and are reversible by legislative majorities.

"For myself," said the late Judge Learned Hand,

> it would be most irksome to be ruled by a bevy of Platonic Guardians, even if I knew how to choose them, which I assuredly do not. If they were in charge, I should miss the stimulus of living in a society where I have, at least theoretically, some part in the direction of public affairs. Of course I know how illusory would be the belief that my vote determined anything; but nevertheless when I go to the polls I have a satisfaction in the sense that we are all engaged in a common venture. If you retort that a sheep in the flock may feel something like it; I reply, following Saint Francis, "My brother, the Sheep."

... A further, crucial difficulty must also be faced. Besides being a counter-majoritarian check on the legislature and the executive, judicial review may, in a larger sense, have a tendency over time seriously to weaken the democratic process. Judicial review expresses, of course, a form of distrust of the legislature. "The legislatures," wrote James Bradley Thayer at the turn of the century,

> are growing accustomed to this distrust and more and more readily inclined to justify it, and to shed the considerations of constitutional restraints,—certainly as concerning the exact extent of these restrictions,—turning that subject over to the courts; and what is worse, they insensibly fall into a habit of assuming that whatever they could constitutionally do they may do,—as if honor and fair dealing and common honesty were not relevant to their inquiries. The people, all this while, become careless as to whom they send to the legislature; too often they cheerfully vote for men whom they would not trust with an important private affair, and when these unfit persons are found to pass foolish and bad laws, and the courts step in and disregard them, the people are glad that these few wiser gentlemen on the bench are so ready to protect them against their more immediate representatives .... [I]t should be remembered that the exercise of it [the power of judicial review], even when unavoidable, is always attended with a serious evil, namely, that the correction of legislative mistakes comes from the outside, and the people thus lose the political experience, and the moral education and stimulus that comes from fighting the question out in the ordinary way, and correcting their own errors. The tendency of a common and easy resort to this great function, now lamentably too common, is to dwarf the political capacity of the people, and to deaden its sense of moral responsibility. It is no light thing to do that.

To this day, in how many hundreds of occasions does Congress enact a measure that it deems expedient, having essayed consideration of its constitutionality (that is to say, of its acceptability on principle), only to abandon the attempt in the declared confidence that the Court will correct errors of principle, if any? It may well be, as has been suggested, that any lowering of the level of legislative performance is attributable to many factors other than judicial review. Yet there is no doubt that what Thayer observed remains observable.

Finally, another, though related, contention has been put forward. It is that judicial review runs so fundamentally counter to democratic theory that in a society which in all other respects rests on that theory, judicial review cannot ultimately be effective. We pay the price of a grave inner contradiction in the basic principle of our government, which is an inconvenience and a dangerous one; and in the end to no good purpose, for when the great test comes, judicial review will be unequal to it. The most arresting expression of this thought is in a famous passage from a speech of Judge Learned Hand.... Absent the institution of judicial review, Judge Hand said:

> I do not think that anyone can say what will be left of those [fundamental principles of equity and fair play which our constitutions

enshrine]; I do not know whether they will serve only as counsels; but this much I think I do know—that a society so riven that the spirit of moderation is gone, no court can save; that a society where that spirit flourishes, no court need save; that in a society which evades its responsibility by thrusting upon the courts the nurture of that spirit, that spirit in the end will perish.

THE MORAL APPROVAL OF THE LINES: PRINCIPLE

The point of departure is a truism, perhaps it even rises to the unassailability of a platitude. It is that many actions of government have two aspects: their immediate, necessarily intended, practical effects, and their perhaps unintended or unappreciated bearing on values we hold to have more general and permanent interest. It is a premise we deduce not merely from the fact of a written constitution but from the history of the race, and ultimately as a moral judgment of the good society, that government should serve not only what we conceive from time to time to be our immediate material needs but also certain enduring values. This in part is what is meant by government under law. But such values do not present themselves ready-made. They have a past always, to be sure, but they must be continually derived, enunciated, and seen in relevant application. And it remains to ask which institution of our government—if any single one in particular—should be the pronouncer and guardian of such values.

Men in all walks or public life are able occasionally to perceive this second aspect of public questions. Sometimes they are also able to base their decisions on it; that is one of the things we like to call acting on principle. Often they do not do so, however, particularly when they sit in legislative assemblies. There, when the pressure for immediate results is strong enough and emotions ride high enough, men will ordinarily prefer to act on expediency rather than take the long view. Possibly legislators—everything else being equal—are as capable as other men of following the path of principle, where the path is clear or at any rate discernible. Our system, however, like all secular systems, calls for the evolution of principle in novel circumstances, rather than only for its mechanical application. Not merely respect for the rule of established principles but the creative establishment and renewal of a coherent body of principled rules—that is what our legislatures have proven themselves ill-equipped to give us.

Initially, great reliance for principled decision was placed in the Senators and the President, who have more extended terms of office and were meant to be elected only indirectly. Yet the Senate and the President were conceived of as less closely tied to, not as divorced from, electoral responsibility and the political marketplace. And so even then the need might have been felt for an institution which stands altogether aside from the current clash of interests, and which, insofar as is humanly possible, is concerned only with principle. We cannot know whether, as Thayer believed, our legislatures are what they are because we have judicial review, or whether we have judicial review and consider it necessary because legislatures are what they are. Yet it is arguable also that the partial separation of the legislative and judicial functions—and it is not meant to be absolute—is beneficial in any event, because it makes it possible for the desires of various groups and interests concerning immediate results to be heard clearly and unrestrainedly in one place. It may be thought fitting that somewhere in government, at some stage in the process of law-making, such felt needs should find unambiguous expression. Moreover, and more importantly, courts have certain capacities for dealing with matters of principle that legislatures and executives do not possess. Judges have, or should have, the leisure, the training, and the insulation to follow the ways of the scholar in pursuing the ends of government. This is crucial in sorting out the enduring values of a society, and it is not something that institutions can do well occasionally, while operating for the most part with a different set of gears. It calls for a habit of mind, and for undeviating institutional customs. Another advantage that courts have is that questions of principle never carry the same aspect for them as they did for the legislature or the executive. Statutes, after all, deal typically with abstract or dimly foreseen problems. The courts are concerned with the flesh and blood of an actual case. This tends to modify, perhaps to lengthen, everyone's view. It also provides an extremely salutary proving ground for all abstractions; it is conducive, in a phrase of Holmes, to thinking things, not words, and thus to the evolution of principle by a process that tests as it creates.

Their insulation and the marvelous mystery of time give courts the capacity to appeal to men's better natures, to call forth their aspirations, which may have been forgotten in the moment's hue and cry. This is what Justice Stone called the opportunity for "the sober second thought." Hence it is that the courts, although they may somewhat dampen the people's and the legislatures' efforts to educate themselves, are also a great and highly effective educational institution. Judge Gibson, in the very opinion mentioned earlier, highly critical as he was, took account of this. "In the business of government," he wrote, "a recurrence to first principles answers the end of an observation at sea with a view to correct the dead reckoning; and, for this purpose, a written constitution is an instrument of inestimable value. It is of inestimable value also, in rendering its principles familiar to the mass of the people. . . ." The educational institution that both takes the observation to correct the dead reckoning and makes it known is the voice of the Constitution: the Supreme Court exercising judicial review. The Justices, in Dean Rostow's phrase, "are inevitably teachers in a vital national seminar." No other branch of the American government is nearly so well equipped to conduct one. And such a seminar can do a great deal to keep our society from becoming so riven that no court will be able to save it. Of course, we have never quite been that society in which the spirit of moderation is so richly in flower that no court need save it.

Thus, as Professor Henry M. Hart, Jr., has written, and as surely most of the profession and of informed laity believe; for if not this, what and why?—thus the Court appears "predestined in the long run, not only by the thrilling tradition of Anglo-American law but also by the hard facts of its position in the structure of American institutions, to be a voice of reason, charged with the creative function of discerning afresh and of articulating and developing impersonal and durable principles. . . ." This line of thought may perhaps blunt, if it does not meet, the force of all the arguments on the other side. No doubt full consistency with democratic theory has not been established. The heart of the democratic faith is government by the consent of the governed. The further premise is not incompatible that the good society not only will want to satisfy the immediate needs of the greatest number but also will strive to support and maintain enduring general values. I have followed the view that the elected institutions are ill fitted, or not so well-fitted as the courts, to perform the latter task. This rests on the assumption that the people themselves, by direct action at the ballot box, are surely incapable of sustaining a working system of general values specifically applied. But that much we assume throughout, being a representative, deliberative democracy. Matters of expediency are not generally submitted to direct referendum. Nor should matters of principle, which require even more intensive deliberation, be so submitted. Reference of specific policies to the people for initial decision is, with few exceptions, the fallacy of the misplaced mystics, or the way of those who would use the forms of democracy to undemocratic ends. It is not the way in which working democracies live. But democracies do live by the idea, central to the process of gaining the consent of the governed, that the majority has the ultimate power to displace the decision-makers and to reject any part of their policy. With that idea, judicial review must achieve some measure of consonance.

Gordon Wood

THE ORIGINS OF JUDICIAL REVIEW REVISITED, OR HOW THE MARSHALL COURT MADE MORE OUT OF LESS

56 Wash. & Lee L. Rev. 787 (1999)

Alexander Hamilton called the judiciary the "weakest branch" of the three branches of government, but today we know better. To us not only does the unelected, life-tenured federal judiciary seem remarkably strong, but at times it actually seems bolder and more capable than the two elective branches in setting social policy. Certainly the federal judges, and especially the Justices of the Supreme Court, precisely because they do not have periodically to face an electorate, exercise an extraordinary degree of authority over our society and culture. The Supreme Court not only sets aside laws that popularly elected legislatures pass, but also interprets and construes the law with a freedom that sometimes is virtually legislative in scope. But it is not just the Supreme Court and other federal courts that are so powerful. Even the state courts, many of which are elected periodically, are extremely influential. . . .

We have usually given the name "judicial review" to this sweeping judicial authority. But if by judicial review we mean only the power of the Supreme Court and of other courts to set aside legislative acts in violation of the Constitution, then the term is too narrow, for voiding legislation is only the most prominent part of a broader manipulative power that courts exercise over wide areas of American life.

Commentators often have given the major responsibility for creating this power of judicial review to John Marshall, the great Chief Justice of the United States who served from 1801 to 1835. Marshall, nearly everyone acknowledges, was the greatest Chief Justice in American history. During his long career as Chief Justice of the Supreme Court, which spanned the administrations of five presidents, he helped to lay the foundations for both the Supreme Court's eventual independence and the constitutional supremacy of the national government over the states. But more important, at a stroke, his decision in *Marbury v. Madison* was supposed to have created the practice of judicial review. Even a constitutional scholar as sophisticated as Alexander M. Bickel thought that Marshall had done it all. "If any social process can be said to have been 'done' at a given time and by a given act," Bickel wrote in 1962, "it is Marshall's achievement. The time was 1803; the act was the decision in the case of *Marbury v. Madison*."

Perhaps this is the way that many lawyers and jurists prefer to explain things. Perhaps they like to ransack the past in order to discover specific moments or concrete precedents, usually court decisions, which created important subsequent judicial practices and processes. The problem with this jurisprudential and unhistorical way of thinking is that it leaves its practitioners vulnerable to critics who can find other, more important precedents and moments in accounting for a practice or process. This has been the case recently with Marshall and judicial review. A number of revisionist legal scholars have argued that Marshall, in *Marbury v. Madison* or elsewhere, did not create the modern practice of judicial review.

[W]e know that judicial review of some form did develop in these early decades of the new Republic. What was it? And how did it arise? No doubt the founders were confused over judicial review: some said it was improper and dangerous, while others seem to justify it. The sources of something as significant and forbidding as judicial review never could lie in the accumulation of a few sporadic judicial precedents, or even in the decision of *Marbury v. Madison*, but had to flow from fundamental changes taking place in the Americans' ideas of government and law.

Perhaps the most crucial of these changes involved reducing the representative character of the people's agents in the legislatures and enhancing the representative character of judges. Hamilton's argument in *Federalist* No. 78 was only the most prominent of efforts to do just this. The judges, Hamilton argued, had a right to oversee the acts of the presumably sovereign legislatures and to construe statutes and even set some of them aside if they thought they conflicted with either the federal or state constitutions. And the judges could do all this because the legislators were not really sovereign; they did not fully embody the people the way Parliament embodied the people of Britain. In America real and ultimate sovereignty rested with the people themselves, not with their representatives in the legislatures. Thus the legislators were not the people, but only one kind of servant of the people with a limited delegated authority to act on their behalf. Americans, said Hamilton, had no intention of enabling "the representatives of the people to substitute their will to that of their constituents." It was in fact "far more rational to suppose, that the courts were designed to be an intermediate body between the people and the legislature, in order, among other things, to keep the latter within the limits assigned to their authority." Hamilton implied, and others drew out the implication much more fully in subsequent years, that the judges, though not elected, resembled the legislators and executives in being agents or servants of the people with a responsibility equal to that of the other two branches of government to carry out the people's will, even to the point of sharing in the making of law. Indeed, just such logic eventually would lead to the election of judges in many states. If the judges were agents of the people, not all that different from their other agents in the government, then by rights the people ought to elect them.

Redefining judges as agents of the sovereign people somehow equal in authority with the legislators and executives fundamentally altered the character of the judiciary in America and deeply affected its role in interpreting the law. But by itself it was not enough to create judicial review. Some historians and constitutional theorists have assumed that the idea of fundamental law and its embodiment in a written constitution were crucial as well.

Almost all eighteenth-century Englishmen on both sides of the Atlantic had recognized something called fundamental law as a guide to the moral rightness and constitutionality of ordinary law and politics. Nearly everyone repeatedly invoked Magna Carta and other fundamental laws of the English constitution. Theorists as different as Locke and Bolingbroke referred equally to the basic principles of the constitution as fundamental law. Even the rise of legislative sovereignty in eighteenth-century England — that is, the idea that law was the command of the legislature — did not displace this prevalent notion of fundamental law. Blackstone himself, despite his commitment to legislative sovereignty, believed that what he called an overriding natural law limited Parliament. Yet all these theoretical references to the principles of the constitution and fundamental law could not have much day-to-day practical importance. For most, this fundamental or natural law of the English constitution was seen as a kind of moral inhibition or conscience existing in the minds of legislators and others. It was so basic and primal, so imposing and political, that it really was enforceable only by the popular elective process or ultimately by the people's right of revolution. Eighteenth-century Englishmen talked about fundamental or natural law, invoked it constantly in their rhetoric, but despite the efforts of some jurists, they had difficulty calling upon this fundamental law in their everyday political and legal business.

The written constitutions of 1776 and 1777, however, gave revolutionary Americans a handle with which to grasp this otherwise insubstantial fundamental law. Suddenly the fundamental law and the first principles that Englishmen had referred to for generations had a degree of explicitness and reality that they never before quite had. The Constitution in America, said James Iredell of North Carolina in 1787, was not therefore "a mere imaginary thing, about which ten thousand different opinions may be formed, but a written document to which all may have recourse, and to which, therefore, the judges cannot willfully blind themselves."

But were the judges to have an exclusive authority to examine these fundamental laws and to determine what was constitutional and what was not? By the 1780s it seemed clear to many that legislatures in America were bound by explicitly written constitutions in ways that the English Parliament was not. But it was not yet clear that the courts by themselves were able to enforce those boundaries upon the legislatures. Said Iredell in 1786, summarizing the position of those opposed to judicial review,

> The great argument is that the Assembly have not a right to violate the constitution, yet if they in fact do so, the only remedy is, either by a humble petition that the law may be repealed, or a universal resistance of the people. But that in the mean time, their act, whatever it is, is to be obeyed as a law; for the

> judicial power is not to presume to question the power of an act of Assembly.

Both Jefferson and Madison thought that judges might act as the guardians of popular rights and might resist encroachments on these rights, but they never believed that judges had any special or unique power to interpret the Constitution. Madison admitted that "in the ordinary course of Government" the judiciary might interpret the laws and the Constitution, but surely, he said, it had no more right to determine the limits of the Constitution than did the executive or legislature. Both Jefferson and Madison remained convinced to the end of their lives that all parts of America's governments had equal authority to interpret the fundamental law of the Constitution—all departments had what Madison called "a concurrent right to expound the constitution." And when the several departments disagreed in their understanding of the fundamental law, wrote Madison in *Federalist* No. 49, only "an appeal to the people themselves, can alone declare its true meaning, and enforce its observance." Written constitutions, including the Bill of Rights, remained for Jefferson and Madison a set of great first principles that the several governmental departments, including the judiciary, could appeal to in those extraordinary occasions of violation. But because none of these departments could "pretend to an exclusive or superior right of settling the boundaries between their respective powers," the ultimate appeal in these quasi-revolutionary situations had to be to the people.

In other words, many revolutionaries or founders still thought that fundamental law, even when expressed in a written constitution, was so fundamental, so different in kind from ordinary law, that its invocation had to be essentially an exceptional and awesomely delicate political exercise. The courts might on occasion set aside legislation that violated fundamental law, but such an act could not be a part of routine judicial business. It necessarily had to be an extraordinary, even revolutionary, expression of public authority, the kind of extreme and remarkable action the people themselves would take if they could. This kind of judicial review, as Sylvia Snowiss has aptly described it, was "a substitute for revolution."

Everyone knew that setting aside legislative acts could be no ordinary matter. In *Calder v. Bull*, Justice Iredell admitted that the Supreme Court possessed the authority to declare a legislative act void, but he believed that doing so was of such "a delicate and awful nature, the Court will never resort to that authority, but in a clear and urgent case." Some congressmen actually debated establishing a regular procedure for federal judges to notify Congress officially when a court declared a law unconstitutional—so nervous were they over the gravity of such an action.

Judges realized that the burden of proving a legislative act unconstitutional beyond any doubt lay entirely with them. As Justice Samuel Chase said in *Hylton v. United States*, if the constitutionality of Congress's tax on carriages had been "doubtful," he would have been bound "to receive the construction of the legislature." As late as 1800 in *Cooper v. Telfair*, Justices Bushrod Washington and William Paterson agreed that judicial review was an exceptional act, to be exercised only infrequently. "The presumption... must always be in favour of the validity of laws, if the contrary is not clearly demonstrated," declared Washington. For the Supreme Court "to pronounce any law void," said Paterson, there "must be a clear and unequivocal breach of the constitution, not a doubtful and argumentative implication."

Thus for many Americans in the 1790s judicial review of some sort did exist. But it remained an extraordinary and solemn political action, akin perhaps to the interposition of the states that Jefferson and Madison suggested in the Kentucky and Virginia Resolutions of 1798 — something to be invoked only on the rare occasions of flagrant and unequivocal violations of the Constitution. It was not to be exercised in doubtful cases of unconstitutionality and was not yet accepted as an aspect of ordinary judicial activity.

This is where we begin to appreciate the achievement of the Marshall Court and other courts in the years following the Jeffersonian Republican revolution of 1800. The idea of fundamental law embodied in a written constitution by itself could never have accounted for the development of judicial review; indeed, emphasis on the fundamental character of the Constitution tended to inhibit the use of judicial review. Judicial review needed to be made less threatening, needed to become a normal and regular part of judicial business: This is, in fact, what the Marshall Court and other courts accomplished in the years after 1800.

In order for this to happen several things had to take place. First, America's written fundamental constitutions, its public laws, had to be transformed into laws that courts could interpret and construe as if they were routine statutes in the ordinary court system. What gives significance to our peculiar notion of a constitution is not that it is written or that it is fundamental, but rather that it runs in the ordinary court system. America's constitutions may be higher laws, special acts of the people in their sovereign capacity, but they are just like all the other lowly laws in that they are implemented through the normal practice of adversarial justice in the regular courts.

. . . American judges now treated the constitutions as commands of the sovereign people, super-statutes, if you will, that needed to be interpreted and integrated into the body of the law. In the process of reconciling constitutions and statutes, often in the name of reason and equity, courts tended to collapse the traditional distinction between fundamental and ordinary law. American judges now could construe the all-too brief words of the state and federal constitutions in relation to subject-matter, intention, context, and reasonableness as if they were the words of an ordinary statute. It was one of Marshall's great achievements, says Hobson, to apply "the familiar tools and methods of statutory construction . . . [t]o the novel task of expounding the Constitution of the United States." The result was the beginning of the creation of a special body of textual exegeses and legal expositions and precedents that we have come to call constitutional law. This accumulative body of constitutional law in America is now over two hundred years old; there is nothing quite like it anywhere else in the world.

This "legalization" of fundamental law, as Sylvia Snowiss has called it, domesticated the Constitution; it tamed what had hitherto been an object of fearful significance and wonder to the point where it could routinely run in the ordinary court system. Considering the Constitution as a kind of law that was cognizable in the regular courts permitted judges not only to expound and construe the Constitution as if it were an ordinary statute, but also to expect regular enforcement of the Constitution as if it were a simple statute. It was a momentous transformation. Because, in John Marshall's words, it was "emphatically the province and duty of the judicial department to say what the law is," treating the Constitution as mere law that judges had to expound and interpret and apply to particular cases gave special constitutional authority to American judges that judges elsewhere in the world did not share.

It was not enough, however, that constitutions run in the regular court system and be interpreted like ordinary statutes for judicial review to become acceptable. Something else was needed. If expounding constitutional law were to be simply part of the routine business of legal interpretation and not an earth-shaking political exercise, then it followed that the entire process of adjudication had to be removed from politics and from legislative tampering. Somehow or other judges had to carve out for themselves an exclusive sphere of professional legal activity.

After 1800 this is precisely what happened. Judges shed what had been a traditional political and magisterial role and adopted one that was much more exclusively legal. . . .

More and more, law grew separate from politics, all part of a larger separation between the private and public spheres that took place in these years.

This separation meant that the courts now tended to concentrate on individual cases and to avoid the most explosive and partisan political issues. Certainly the Marshall Court succeeded as well as it did because it retreated from the advanced and exposed political positions that the Federalists had tried to stake out for the national judiciary in the 1790s. . . .

The strategy behind the Marshall Court's judgments was always that less is more. The Court denied the belief of many Federalists that the common law of crimes ran in the federal court system, which was a major retreat, and it went out of its way to avoid any direct confrontation with the Republicans. In a series of conciliatory decisions, Marshall's Court recognized the authority of the Republican president and the Republican Congress over foreign affairs and matters of war. As Kent Newmyer has suggested, Marshall was so often able to get consensus out of what soon became a Republican-dominated Court because he used many of the Court's decisions to curtail governmental power — something that many Republicans eager to expand the areas of individual freedom could accept. In other words, the Marshall Court did not attempt to build up the power of the federal government, which immediately would have aroused Republican hostility everywhere. Instead, it moved to reduce governmental power, not at the federal but at the state level. By declaring a large number of state judicial interpretations and state laws invalid because they violated the national Constitution, the Court indirectly enhanced the supremacy of the nation and its own authority as well.

Even in the famous case of *Marbury v. Madison* in 1803, Marshall retreated rather than attacked. Many of the Federalists wanted Marshall to declare the Republicans' repeal of the judiciary act of 1801 unconstitutional for having abrogated the tenure of federal judges. But Marshall wisely realized that such a direct challenge to the Republicans could only harm the Court. Instead, he asserted the Court's authority to interpret the Constitution subtly and obliquely by declaring a portion of the earlier 1789 judiciary act unconstitutional for having granted the Supreme Court some original jurisdiction to which the Constitution had not entitled it.

The decision was so subtle and so oblique that most people did not see its implications. The Republicans actually liked the decision better than the

Federalists. They thought that if Marshall wanted to circumscribe the original jurisdiction of his Court, then he had every right to do so. Even Jefferson conceded the right of the Court to interpret the Constitution in matters pertaining to the judiciary, but he continued to believe that the executive and the Congress retained equal authority to interpret the Constitution. In his *Marbury* decision Marshall did not explicitly disagree with Jefferson's position. Marshall in 1803 was not embarking on a crusade for judicial supremacy. His aim was to isolate the judiciary from partisan politics as much as possible.

The *Marbury* decision was all about separating legal issues from politics. As Marshall said, some questions were political; "they respect the nation, not individual rights," and thus were "only politically examinable." But questions involving the vested rights of individuals were different; vested rights were in their "nature, judicial, and must be tried by the judicial authority." By turning all questions of individual rights into exclusively judicial issues, Marshall appropriated an enormous amount of authority for the courts. After all, even Jefferson in 1789 had conceded that judges, "kept strictly to their own department," had the authority to protect the rights of individuals. Of course, Jefferson had not anticipated Marshall's expansive notion of rights.

As far as most Federalists were concerned, the laws of the land concerning individual rights now belonged exclusively to the courts. Getting the American people to believe this was a remarkable achievement, and the Marshall Court contributed greatly to this effort. But it would not have been possible without large numbers of influential people becoming increasingly disillusioned with the kind of democratic legislative politics that was emerging in the early Republic. As St. George Tucker pointed out in 1803, since the men of greatest talents, education, and virtue were not able to compete as well as others in the new scrambling, pushy, and interest-mongering world of popular electoral politics, they could best promote the science of the law in the judiciary. Marshall himself, like all "honest men who have honorable feelings," was increasingly "disgusted with . . . the political world" he saw around him, and was "much more gloomy" about the future. Everywhere the growth of democracy encouraged the insulating of legal issues from politics; "for," as Marshall put it, "nothing is more to be deprecated than the transfer of party politics to the seat of Justice." Only separating law from popular politics could protect the rights of individuals.

Many had come to believe that a society as enterprising, unruly, and democratic as America's not only required institutions and legal processes that could adapt readily to fast-moving economic circumstances, but needed as well the moderating influence of an aristocracy. Outside of the South, however, an American aristocracy was hard to come by; but necessity invented one. As Tocqueville later pointed out, lawyers in the early nineteenth century had come to constitute whatever aristocracy America possessed, at least in the North. Through their influence on the judiciary they tempered America's turbulent majoritarian governments and protected the rights of individuals and minorities from legislative abuse. "The courts of justice," Tocqueville said, "are the visible organs by which the legal profession is enabled to control the democracy."

Alexander Hamilton

THE FEDERALIST NO. 78

The Judiciary Department

Independent Journal, Saturday, June 14, 1788

After the Constitutional Convention, the Constitution was presented to the states to ratify. Specifically, Article Seven required ratification by 9 of the 13 states before it could be enacted. Writing under the pseudonym "Publius," James Madison, John Jay, and Alexander Hamilton argued in a series of New York newspapers for ratification. The significance of the papers goes beyond this initial argument. They provided some of the most influential framing of debates about how to interpret the Constitution. In this excerpt, Hamilton addresses the role of the Supreme Court in the new Constitution and argues for its role in judicial review of legislation.

Whoever attentively considers the different departments of power must perceive, that, in a government in which they are separated from each other, the judiciary, from the nature of its functions, will always be the least dangerous to the political rights of the Constitution; because it will be least in a capacity to annoy or injure them. The Executive not only dispenses the honors, but holds the sword of the community. The legislature not only commands the purse, but prescribes the rules by which the duties and rights of every citizen are to be regulated. The judiciary, on the contrary, has no influence over either the sword or the purse; no direction either of the strength or of the wealth of the society; and can take no active resolution whatever. It may truly be said to have neither FORCE nor WILL, but merely judgment; and must ultimately depend upon the aid of the executive arm even for the efficacy of its judgments.

This simple view of the matter suggests several important consequences. It proves incontestably, that the judiciary is beyond comparison the weakest of the three departments of power; that it can never attack with success either of the other two; and that all possible care is requisite to enable it to defend itself against their attacks. It equally proves, that though individual oppression may now and then proceed from the courts of justice, the general liberty of the people can never be endangered from that quarter; I mean so long as the judiciary remains truly distinct from both the legislature and the Executive. For I agree, that "there is no liberty, if the power of judging be not separated from the legislative and executive powers." And it proves, in the last place, that as liberty can have nothing to fear from the judiciary alone, but would have everything to fear from its union with either of the other departments; that as all the effects of such a union must ensue from a dependence of the former on the latter, notwithstanding a nominal and apparent separation; that as, from the natural feebleness of the judiciary, it is in continual jeopardy of being overpowered, awed, or influenced by its co-ordinate branches; and that as nothing can contribute so much to its firmness and independence as permanency in office, this quality may therefore be justly regarded as an indispensable ingredient in its constitution, and, in a great measure, as the citadel of the public justice and the public security.

The complete independence of the courts of justice is peculiarly essential in a limited Constitution. By a limited Constitution, I understand one which contains certain specified exceptions to the legislative authority; such, for instance, as that it shall pass no bills of attainder, no ex post facto laws, and the like. Limitations of this kind can be preserved in practice no other way than through the medium of courts of justice, whose duty it must be to declare all acts contrary to the manifest tenor of the Constitution void. Without this, all the reservations of particular rights or privileges would amount to nothing.

Some perplexity respecting the rights of the courts to pronounce legislative acts void, because contrary to the Constitution, has arisen from an imagination that the doctrine would imply a superiority of the judiciary to the legislative power. It is urged that the authority which can declare the acts of another void, must necessarily be superior to the one whose acts may be declared void. As this doctrine is of great importance in all the American constitutions, a brief discussion of the ground on which it rests cannot be unacceptable.

There is no position which depends on clearer principles, than that every act of a delegated authority, contrary to the tenor of the commission under which it is exercised, is void. No legislative act, therefore, contrary to the Constitution, can be valid. To deny this, would be to affirm, that the deputy is greater than his principal; that the servant is above his master; that the representatives of the people are superior to the people themselves; that men acting by virtue of powers, may do not only what their powers do not authorize, but what they forbid.

If it be said that the legislative body are themselves the constitutional judges of their own powers, and that the construction they put upon them is conclusive upon the other departments, it may be answered, that this cannot be the natural presumption, where it is not to be collected from any particular provisions in the Constitution. It is not otherwise to be supposed, that the Constitution could intend to enable the representatives of the people to substitute their will to that of their constituents. It is far more rational to suppose, that the courts were designed to be an intermediate body between the people and the legislature, in order, among other things, to keep the latter within the limits assigned to their authority. The interpretation of the laws is the proper and peculiar province of the courts. A constitution is, in fact, and must be regarded by the judges, as a fundamental law. It therefore belongs to them to ascertain its meaning, as well as the meaning of any particular act proceeding from the legislative body. If there should happen to be an irreconcilable variance between the two, that which has the superior obligation and validity ought, of course, to be preferred; or, in other words, the Constitution ought to be preferred to the statute, the intention of the people to the intention of their agents.

Nor does this conclusion by any means suppose a superiority of the judicial to the legislative power. It only supposes that the power of the people is superior to both; and that where the will of the legislature, declared in its statutes, stands in opposition to that of the people, declared in the Constitution, the judges ought to be governed by the latter rather than the former. They ought to regulate their decisions by the fundamental laws, rather than by those which are not fundamental.

This exercise of judicial discretion, in determining between two contradictory laws, is exemplified in a familiar instance. It not uncommonly happens, that there are two statutes existing at one time, clashing in whole or in part with each other, and neither of them containing any repealing clause or expression. In such a case, it is the province of the courts to liquidate and fix their meaning and operation. So far as they can, by any fair construction, be reconciled to each other, reason and law conspire to dictate that this should be done; where this is impracticable, it becomes a matter of necessity to give effect to one, in exclusion of the other. The rule which has obtained in the courts for determining their relative validity is, that the last in order of time shall be preferred to the first. But this is a mere rule of construction, not derived from any positive law, but from the nature and reason of the thing. It is a rule not enjoined upon the courts by legislative provision, but adopted by themselves, as consonant to truth and propriety, for the direction of their conduct as interpreters of the law. They thought it reasonable, that between the interfering acts of an EQUAL authority, that which was the last indication of its will should have the preference.

But in regard to the interfering acts of a superior and subordinate authority, of an original and derivative power, the nature and reason of the thing indicate the converse of that rule as proper to be followed. They teach us that the prior act of a superior ought to be preferred to the subsequent act of an inferior and subordinate authority; and that accordingly, whenever a particular statute contravenes the Constitution, it will be the duty of the judicial tribunals to adhere to the latter and disregard the former.

It can be of no weight to say that the courts, on the pretense of a repugnancy, may substitute their own pleasure to the constitutional intentions of the legislature. This might as well happen in the case of two contradictory statutes; or it might as well happen in every adjudication upon any single statute. The courts must declare the sense of the law; and if they should be disposed to exercise WILL instead of JUDGMENT, the consequence would equally be the substitution of their pleasure to that of the legislative body. The observation, if it prove any thing, would prove that there ought to be no judges distinct from that body.

If, then, the courts of justice are to be considered as the bulwarks of a limited Constitution against legislative encroachments, this consideration will afford a strong argument for the permanent tenure of judicial offices, since nothing will contribute so much as this to that independent spirit in the judges which must be essential to the faithful performance of so arduous a duty.

This independence of the judges is equally requisite to guard the Constitution and the rights of individuals from the effects of those ill humors, which the arts of designing men, or the influence of particular conjunctures, sometimes disseminate among the people themselves, and which, though they speedily give place to better information, and more deliberate reflection, have a tendency, in the mean time, to occasion dangerous innovations in the government, and serious oppressions of the minor party in the community. Though I trust the friends of the proposed Constitution will never concur with its enemies, in questioning that fundamental principle of republican government, which admits the right of the people to alter or abolish the established Constitution, whenever they find it inconsistent with their happiness, yet it is not to be inferred from this principle, that the representatives of the people, whenever a momentary inclination happens to lay hold of a majority of their constituents, incompatible with the provisions in the existing Constitution, would, on that account, be justifiable in a violation of those provisions; or that the courts would be under a greater obligation to connive at infractions in this shape, than when they had proceeded wholly from the cabals of the representative body. Until the people have, by some solemn and authoritative act, annulled or changed the established form, it is binding upon themselves collectively, as well as individually; and no presumption, or even knowledge, of their sentiments, can warrant their representatives in a departure from it, prior to such an act. But it is easy to see, that it would require an uncommon portion of fortitude in the judges to do their duty as faithful guardians of the Constitution, where legislative invasions of it had been instigated by the major voice of the community.

But it is not with a view to infractions of the Constitution only, that the independence of the judges may be an essential safeguard against the effects of occasional ill humors in the society. These sometimes extend no farther than to the injury of the private rights of particular classes of citizens, by unjust and partial laws. Here also the firmness of the judicial magistracy is of vast importance in mitigating the severity and confining the operation of such laws. It not only serves to moderate the immediate mischiefs of those which may have been passed, but it operates as a check upon the legislative body in passing them; who, perceiving that obstacles to the success of iniquitous intention are to be expected from the scruples of the courts, are in a manner compelled, by the very motives of the injustice they meditate, to qualify their attempts. This is a circumstance calculated to have more influence upon the character of our governments, than but few may be aware of. The benefits of the integrity and moderation of the judiciary have already been felt in more States than one; and though they may have displeased those whose sinister expectations they may have disappointed, they must have commanded the esteem and applause of all the virtuous and disinterested. Considerate men, of every description, ought to prize whatever will tend to beget or fortify that temper in the courts: as no man can be sure that he may not be to-morrow the victim of a spirit of injustice, by which he may be a gainer to-day. And every man must now feel, that the inevitable tendency of such a spirit is to sap the foundations of public and private confidence, and to introduce in its stead universal distrust and distress.

That inflexible and uniform adherence to the rights of the Constitution, and of individuals, which we perceive to be indispensable in the courts of justice, can certainly not be expected from judges who hold their offices by a temporary commission. Periodical appointments, however regulated, or by whomsoever made, would, in some way or other, be fatal to their necessary independence. If the power of making them was committed either to the Executive or legislature, there would be danger of an improper complaisance to the branch which possessed it; if to both, there would be an unwillingness to hazard the displeasure of either; if to the people, or to persons chosen by them for the special purpose, there would be too great a disposition to consult popularity, to justify a reliance that nothing would be consulted but the Constitution and the laws.

Brutus

UNTITLED ESSAYS AGAINST RATIFICATION OF THE UNITED STATES CONSTITUTION

The New York Journal, 1787-1788

As the states decided whether they would or would not ratify the new Constitution, a series of essays by opponents of ratification were published in New York newspapers. These essays served as a counterbalance to The Federalist Papers, *which were meant to defend the proposed Constitution. In response to the arguments in favor of the judicial branch crafted by Article III of the Constitution, an author who called himself "Brutus" suggested why the new Supreme Court had powers that could become tyrannical and incompatible with the ideal of "free and equal government." Indeed, the name Brutus was meant to suggest a parallel between Anti-Federalists and the opponents of Julius Caesar.*

The essays, in addition to presaging future criticisms of the Court's judicial review power, help us to focus on some of the structural details of Article III. Notice in particular Brutus's worry that judicial power is left unchecked under the new Constitution. Article III requires that Supreme Court justices be appointed by the president and confirmed by the Senate. But, Brutus argues, this check does not suitably guard against the guarantee of life tenure and congressional inability to lower the salaries of the justices.

It is also worth noting as you read the argument against the review power of the Court that Brutus predicts that some justices will not stick to a literal, or what some call a "strict textual," reading of the Constitution. Instead, they will interpret the clauses broadly to claim a vast review power. Consider whether this purported judicial role follows from the way the constitutional text is written. Does it authorize a broad review power in the way Brutus suggests? If so, is this a potential problem for democratic governance? Is Brutus correct that the British system of legislative supremacy is superior to the American system? Why?

BRUTUS 1 (OCTOBER 18, 1787)

This government is to possess absolute and uncontroulable power, legislative, executive and judicial, with respect to every object to which it extends, for by the last clause of section 8th, article 1st, it is declared "that the Congress shall have power to make all laws which shall be necessary and proper for carrying into execution the foregoing powers, and all other powers vested by this constitution, in the government of the United States; or in any department or office thereof. . . ."

The judicial power of the United States is to be vested in a supreme court, and in such inferior courts as Congress may from time to time ordain and establish. The powers of these courts are very extensive; their jurisdiction comprehends all civil causes, except such as arise between citizens of the same state; and it extends to all cases in law and equity arising under the constitution. . . . These courts will be, in themselves, totally independent of the states, deriving their authority from the United States, and receiving from them fixed salaries; and in the course of human events it is to be expected, that they will swallow up all the powers of the courts in the respective states.

Brutus.

BRUTUS 11 (JANUARY 31, 1788)

The nature and extent of the judicial power of the United States, proposed to be granted by this constitution, claims our particular attention.

. . . [B]ecause those who are to be vested with it, are to be placed in a situation altogether unprecedented in a free country. They are to be rendered totally independent, both of the people and the legislature, both with respect to their offices and salaries. No errors they may commit can be corrected by any power above them, if any such power there be, nor can they be removed from office for making ever so many erroneous adjudications.

The only causes for which they can be displaced, is, conviction of treason, bribery, and high crimes and misdemeanors.

This part of the plan is so modelled, as to authorise the courts, not only to carry into execution the powers expressly given, but where these are wanting or ambiguously expressed, to supply what is wanting by their own decisions.

That we may be enabled to form a just opinion on this subject, I shall, in considering it,

1st. Examine the nature and extent of the judicial powers — and

2d. Enquire, whether the courts who are to exercise them, are so constituted as to afford reasonable ground of confidence, that they will exercise them for the general good.

In article 3d, sect. 2d, it is said, "The judicial power shall extend to all cases in law and equity arising under this constitution, the laws of the United States, and treaties made, or which shall be made, under their authority, &c."

What latitude of construction this clause should receive, it is not easy to say. At first view, one would suppose, that it meant no more than this, that the courts under the general government should exercise, not only the powers of courts of law, but also that of courts of equity, in the manner in which those powers are usually exercised in the different states. But this cannot be the meaning, because the next clause authorises the courts to take cognizance of all cases in law and equity arising under the laws of the United States; this last article, I conceive, conveys as much power to the general judicial as any of the state courts possess.

This article, therefore, vests the judicial with a power to resolve all questions that may arise on any case on the construction of the constitution, either in law or in equity.

1st. According to this mode of construction, the courts are to give such meaning to the constitution as comports best with the common, and generally received acceptation of the words in which it is expressed, regarding their ordinary and popular use, rather than their grammatical propriety. Where words are dubious, they will be explained by the context. The end of the clause will be attended to, and the words will be understood, as having a view to it; and the words will not be so understood as to bear no meaning or a very absurd one.

2d. The judicial are not only to decide questions arising upon the meaning of the constitution in law, but also in equity.

By this they are empowered, to explain the constitution according to the reasoning spirit of it, without being confined to the words or letter.

They will give the sense of every article of the constitution, that may from time to time come before them. And in their decisions they will not confine themselves to any fixed or established rules, but will determine, according to what appears to them, the reason and spirit of the constitution. The opinions of the supreme court, whatever they may be, will have the force of law; because there is no power provided in the constitution, that can correct their errors, or controul their adjudications. From this court there is no appeal. And I conceive the legislature themselves, cannot set aside a judgment of this court, because they are authorised by the constitution to decide in the last resort. The legislature must be controuled by the constitution, and not the constitution by them. They have therefore no more right to set aside any judgment pronounced upon the construction of the constitution, than they have to take from the president, the chief command of the army and navy, and commit it to some other person. The reason is plain; the judicial and executive derive their authority from the same source, that the legislature do theirs; and therefore in all cases, where the constitution does not make the one responsible to, or controulable by the other, they are altogether independent of each other.

The judicial power will operate to effect, in the most certain, but yet silent and imperceptible manner, what is evidently the tendency of the constitution: — I mean, an entire subversion of the legislative, executive and judicial powers of the individual states. Every adjudication of the supreme court, on any question that may arise upon the nature and extent of the general government, will affect the limits of the state jurisdiction. In proportion as the former enlarge the exercise of their powers, will that of the latter be restricted.

That the judicial power of the United States, will lean strongly in favour of the general government, and will give such an explanation to the constitution, as will favour an extension of its jurisdiction, is very evident from a variety of considerations.

1st. The constitution itself strongly countenances such a mode of construction. Most of the articles in this system, which convey powers of any considerable importance, are conceived in general and indefinite terms, which are either equivocal, ambiguous, or which require long definitions to unfold the extent of their meaning. The two most important powers committed to any government, those of raising money, and of raising and keeping up troops, have already been considered, and shewn to be unlimitted by any thing but the discretion of the legislature. The clause which vests the power to pass all laws which are proper and necessary, to carry the powers given into execution, it has been shewn, leaves the legislature at liberty, to do every thing, which in their judgment is best. It is said, I know, that this clause confers no power on the legislature, which they would not have had without it — though I believe this is not the fact, yet, admitting it to be, it implies that the constitution is not to receive an explanation strictly, according to its letter; but more power is implied than is expressed. And this clause, if it is to be considered, as explanatory of the extent of the powers given, rather than giving a new power, is to be understood as declaring, that in construing any of the articles conveying power, the spirit, intent and design of the clause, should be attended to, as well as the words in their common acceptation.

This constitution gives sufficient colour for adopting an equitable construction, if we consider the great end and design it professedly has in view — these appear from its preamble to be, "to form a more perfect union, establish justice, insure domestic tranquility, provide for the common defence, promote the general welfare, and secure the blessings of liberty to ourselves and posterity." The design of this system is here expressed, and it is proper to give such a meaning to the various parts, as will best promote the accomplishment of the end; this idea suggests itself naturally upon reading the preamble, and will countenance the court in giving the several articles such a sense, as will the most effectually promote the ends the constitution had in view—how this manner of explaining the constitution will operate in practice, shall be the subject of future enquiry.

2d. Not only will the constitution justify the courts in inclining to this mode of explaining it, but they will be interested in using this latitude of interpretation. Every body of men invested with office are tenacious of power; they feel interested, and hence it has become a kind of maxim, to hand down their offices, with all its rights and privileges, unimpaired to their successors; the same principle will influence them to extend their power, and increase their rights; this of itself will operate strongly upon the courts to give such a meaning to the constitution in all cases where it can possibly be done, as will enlarge the sphere of their own authority. Every extension of the power of the general legislature, as well as of the judicial powers, will increase the powers of the courts; and the dignity and importance of the judges, will be in proportion to the extent and magnitude of the powers they exercise. I add, it is highly probable the emolument of the judges will be increased, with the increase of the business they will have to transact and its importance. From these considerations the judges will be interested to extend the powers of the courts, and to construe the constitution as much as possible, in such a way as to favour it; and that they will do it, appears probable.

This power in the judicial, will enable them to mould the government, into almost any shape they please.—The manner in which this may be effected we will hereafter examine.

Brutus.

BRUTUS 15 (MARCH 20, 1788)

(Continued.)

I said in my last number, that the supreme court under this constitution would be exalted above all other power in the government, and subject to no controul. The business of this paper will be to illustrate this, and to shew the danger that will result from it. I question whether the world ever saw, in any period of it, a court of justice invested with such immense powers, and yet placed in a situation so little responsible. Certain it is, that in England, and in the several states, where we have been taught to believe, the courts of law are put upon the most prudent establishment, they are on a very different footing.

The judges in England are under the controul of the legislature, for they are bound to determine according to the laws passed by them. But the judges under this constitution will controul the legislature, for the supreme court are authorised in the last resort, to determine what is the extent of the powers of the Congress; they are to give the constitution an explanation, and there is no power above them to set aside their judgment. The framers of this constitution appear to have followed that of the British, in rendering the judges independent, by granting them their offices during good behavior, without following the constitution of England, in instituting a tribunal in which their errors may be corrected; and without adverting to this, that the judicial under this system have a power which is above the legislative, and which indeed transcends any power before given to a judicial by any free government under heaven.

Though in my opinion the judges ought to hold their offices during good behavior, yet I think it is clear, that the reasons in favour of this establishment of the judges in England, do by no means apply to this country.

The great reason assigned, why the judges in Britain ought to be commissioned during good behavior, is this, that they may be placed in a situation, not to be influenced by the crown, to give such decisions, as would tend to increase its powers and prerogatives. While the judges held their places at the will and pleasure of the king, on whom they depended not only for their offices, but also for their salaries, they were subject to every undue influence. If the crown wished to carry a favorite point, to accomplish which the aid of the courts of law was necessary, the pleasure of the king would be signified to the judges. And it required the spirit of a martyr, for the judges to determine contrary to the king's will.—They were absolutely dependent upon him both for their offices and livings. The king, holding his office during life, and transmitting it to his posterity as an inheritance, has much stronger inducements to increase the prerogatives of his office than those who hold their offices for stated periods, or even for life. Hence the English nation gained a great point, in favour of liberty. When they obtained the appointment of the judges, during good behavior, they got from the crown a concession, which deprived it of one of the most powerful engines with which it might enlarge the boundaries of the royal prerogative and encroach on the liberties of the people. But these reasons do not apply to this country, we have no hereditary monarch; those who appoint the judges do not hold their offices for life, nor do they descend to their children. The same arguments, therefore, which will conclude in favor of the tenor of the judge's offices for good behavior, lose a considerable part of their weight when applied to the state and condition of America. But much less can it be shewn, that the nature of our government requires that the courts should be placed beyond all account more independent, so much so as to be above controul.

I have said that the judges under this system will be independent in the strict sense of the word: To prove this I will shew—That there is no power above them that can controul their decisions, or correct their errors. There is no authority that can remove them from office for any errors or want of capacity, or lower their salaries, and in many cases their power is superior to that of the legislature.

1st. There is no power above them that can correct their errors or controul their decisions—The adjudications of this court are final and irreversible, for there is no court above them to which appeals can lie, either in error or on the merits.—In this respect it differs from the courts in England, for there the house of lords is the highest court, to whom appeals, in error, are carried from the highest of the courts of law.

2d. They cannot be removed from office or suffer a diminution of their salaries, for any error in judgement or want of capacity.

It is expressly declared by the constitution,—"That they shall at stated times receive a compensation for their services which shall not be diminished during their continuance in office."

The only clause in the constitution which provides for the removal of the judges from office, is that which declares, that "the president, vice-president, and all civil officers of the United States, shall be removed from office, on impeachment for, and conviction of treason, bribery, or other high crimes and misdemeanors. . . ." By this paragraph, civil officers, in which the judges are included, are removable only for crimes. Treason and bribery are named, and the rest are included under the general terms of high crimes and misdemeanors. — Errors in judgement, or want of capacity to discharge the duties of the office, can never be supposed to be included in these words, high crimes and misdemeanors. A man may mistake a case in giving judgment, or manifest that he is incompetent to the discharge of the duties of a judge, and yet give no evidence of corruption or want of integrity. To support the charge, it will be necessary to give in evidence some facts that will shew, that the judges committed the error from wicked and corrupt motives.

3d. The power of this court is in many cases superior to that of the legislature. I have shewed, in a former paper, that this court will be authorised to decide upon the meaning of the constitution, and that, not only according to the natural and ob[vious] meaning of the words, but also according to the spirit and intention of it.

In the exercise of this power they will not be subordinate to, but above the legislature. For all the departments of this government will receive their powers, so far as they are expressed in the constitution, from the people immediately, who are the source of power. The legislature can only exercise such powers as are given them by the constitution, they cannot assume any of the rights annexed to the judicial, for this plain reason, that the same authority which vested the legislature with their powers, vested the judicial with theirs — both are derived from the same source, both therefore are equally valid, and the judicial hold their powers independently of the legislature, as the legislature do of the judicial. — The supreme court then have a right, independent of the legislature, to give a construction to the constitution and every part of it, and there is no power provided in this system to correct their construction or do it away. . . . If, therefore, the legislature pass any laws, inconsistent with the sense the judges put upon the constitution, they will declare it void; and therefore in this respect their power is superior to that of the legislature.

Perhaps nothing could have been better conceived to facilitate the abolition of the state governments than the constitution of the judicial. They will be able to extend the limits of the general government gradually, and by insensible degrees, and to accommodate themselves to the temper of the people. Their decisions on the meaning of the constitution will commonly take place in cases which arise between individuals, with which the public will not be generally acquainted; one adjudication will form a precedent to the next, and this to a following one. These cases will immediately affect individuals only; so that a series of determinations will probably take place before even the people will be informed of them. In the mean time all the art and address of those who wish for the change will be employed to make converts to their opinion. The people will be told, that their state officers, and state legislatures are a burden and expense without affording any solid advantage, for that all the laws passed by them, might be equally well made by the general legislature. If to those who will be interested in the change, be added, those who will be under their influence, and such who will submit to almost any change of government, which they can be persuaded to believe will ease them of taxes, it is easy to see, the party who will favor the abolition of the state governments would be far from being inconsiderable.—In this situation, the general legislature, might pass one law after another, extending the general and abridging the state jurisdictions, and to sanction their proceedings would have a course of decisions of the judicial to whom the constitution has committed the power of explaining the constitution.—If the states remonstrated, the constitutional mode of deciding upon the validity of the law, is with the supreme court, and neither people, nor state legislatures, nor the general legislature can remove them or reverse their decrees.

Had the construction of the constitution been left with the legislature, they would have explained it at their peril; if they exceed their powers, or sought to find, in the spirit of the constitution, more than was expressed in the letter, the people from whom they derived their power could remove them, and do themselves right; and indeed I can see no other remedy that the people can have against their rulers for encroachments of this nature. A constitution is a compact of a people with their rulers; if the rulers break the compact, the people have a right and ought to remove them and do themselves justice; but in order to enable them to do this with the greater facility, those whom the people chuse at stated periods, should have the power in the last resort to determine the sense of the compact; if they determine contrary to the understanding of the people, an appeal will lie to the people at the period when the rulers are to be elected, and they will have it in their power to remedy the evil; but when this power is lodged in the hands of men independent of the people, and of their representatives, and who are not, constitutionally, accountable for their opinions, no way is left to controul them but with a high hand and an outstretched arm.

Thomas Jefferson

LETTER TO JUDGE SPENCER ROANE

September 6, 1819

In contrast to the strong view of judicial authority defended by Alexander Hamilton, this selection from Thomas Jefferson advocates a role for each branch of government in interpreting the Constitution. Does the power of judicial review transform the Constitution into "a mere thing of wax in the hands of the judiciary," as Jefferson argues? As will become apparent in Chapter 2, the Court's role in interpreting the Constitution remains highly controversial.

I had read in the Enquirer, and with great approbation, the pieces signed Hampden, and have read them again with redoubled approbation, in the copies you have been so kind as to send me. I subscribe to every title of them. They contain the true principles of the revolution of 1800, for that was as real a revolution in the principles of our government as that of 1776 was in its form; not effected indeed by the sword, as that, but by the rational and peaceable instrument of reform, the suffrage of the people. The nation declared its will by dismissing functionaries of one principle, and electing those of another, in the two branches, executive and legislative, submitted to their election. Over the judiciary department, the constitution had deprived them of their control. That, therefore, has continued the reprobated system, and although new matter has been occasionally incorporated into the old, yet the leaven of the old mass seems to assimilate to itself the new, and after twenty years' confirmation of the federal system by the voice of the nation, declared through the medium of elections, we find the judiciary on every occasion, still driving us into consolidation.

In denying the right they usurp of exclusively explaining the constitution, I go further than you do, if I understand rightly your quotation from the Federalist, of an opinion that "the judiciary is the last resort in relation to the other departments of the government, but not in relation to the rights of the parties to the compact under which the judiciary is derived." If this opinion be sound, then indeed is our constitution a complete felo de se. For intending to establish three departments, co-ordinate and independent, that they might check and balance one another, it has given, according to this opinion, to one of them alone, the right to prescribe rules for the government of the others, and to that one too, which is unelected by, and independent of the nation.... The constitution, on this hypothesis, is a mere thing of wax in the hands of the judiciary, which they may twist, and shape into any form they please. It should be remembered, as an axiom of eternal truth in politics, that whatever power in any government is independent, is absolute also; in theory only, at first, while the spirit of the people is up, but in practice, as fast as that relaxes. Independence can be trusted nowhere but with the people in mass. They are inherently independent of all but moral law. My construction of the constitution is very different from that you quote. It is that each department is truly independent of the others, and has an equal right to decide for itself what is the meaning of the constitution in the cases submitted to its action; and especially, where it is to act ultimately and without appeal....

CALDER v. BULL

3 U.S. 386 (1798)

Majority: Chase, joined by Ellsworth, Wilson, Cushing, Paterson
Concurrence: Paterson
Concurrence: Iredell
Concurrence: Cushing

The following case considers whether the actions of the Connecticut legislature, in retroactively canceling the will of a deceased citizen, violated the Constitution's prohibition of ex post facto laws. An ex post facto law is legislation that retroactively alters the legal status of past acts, in contrast to legislation regulating future acts. In reading this case, consider why the Constitution might prohibit such laws. In addition to illuminating this substantive matter, this case serves as an early example of the Court's examination of the question of whether the Supreme Court has the power of judicial review over legislative acts. How is this issue handled? Are any of Brutus's concerns about judicial tyranny present in this case? Pay particular attention as you read to the concurrence by Justice Iredell. What is his argument in favor of judicial review? Notice that the Court explicitly refuses to address the question of judicial review of acts of Congress. We examine that question in our next case selection.

CHASE, J., *opinion.*

The Legislature of Connecticut, on the 2d Thursday of May, 1795, passed a resolution or law, which for the reasons assigned, set aside a decree of the court of Probate for Hartford, on the 21st of March, 1793, which decree disapproved of the will of Normand Morrison (the grandson) made the 21st of August, 1779, and refused to record the said will; and granted a new hearing by the said Court of Probate, with liberty of appeal therefrom, in six months. A new hearing was had, in virtue of this resolution, or law, before the said Court of Probate, who, on the 27th of July, 1795, approved the said will, and ordered it to be recorded. At August, 1795, appeal was then had to the superior court at Hartford, who at February term, 1796, affirmed the decree of the Court of Probate. Appeal was had to the Supreme Court of errors of Connecticut, who in June, 1796, adjudged, that there were no errors. More than 18 months elapsed from the decree of the Court of Probate (on the 1st of March, 1793) and thereby Caleb Bull and wife were barred of all right of appeal, by a statute of Connecticut. There was no law of that State whereby a new hearing, or trial, before the said court of Probate might be obtained. Calder and wife claim the premises in question, in right of his wife, as heiress of N. Morrison, a physician; Bull and wife claim under the will of N. Morrison, the grandson.

The Counsel for the Plaintiffs in error, contend, that the said resolution or law of the Legislature of Connecticut, granting a new hearing, in the above case, is an ex post facto law, prohibited by the Constitution of the United States; that any law of the Federal government, or of the State governments, contrary to the constitution of the United States, is void; and that this court possesses the power to declare such law void.

It appears to me a self-evident proposition, that the several State Legislatures retain all the powers of legislation, delegated to them by the State Constitutions; which are not expressly taken away by the Constitution of the United States....

The effect of the resolution or law of Connecticut, above stated, is to review a decision of one of its Inferior Courts, called the Court of Probate for Hartford, and to direct a new hearing of the case by the same Court of Probate, that passed the decree against the will of Normand Morrison. By the existing law of Connecticut a right to recover certain property had vested in Calder and his wife (the appellants) in consequence, this right to recover certain property declared to be in Bull and wife, the appellees. The sole enquiry is, whether this resolution or law of Connecticut, having such operation, is an ex post facto law, within the prohibition of the Federal Constitution?

Whether the Legislature of any of the States can revise and correct by law, a decision of any of its Courts of Justice, although not prohibited by the Constitution of the State, is a question of very great importance, and not necessary now to be determined; because the resolution or law in question does not go so far. I cannot subscribe to the omnipotence of a State Legislature, or that it is absolute and without controul; although its authority should not be expressly restrained by the Constitution, or fundamental law, of the State. There are acts which the Federal, or State, Legislature cannot do, without exceeding their authority. There are certain vital principles in our free Republican governments, which will determine and over-rule an apparent and flagrant abuse of legislative power; as to authorize manifest injustice by positive law; or to take away that security for personal liberty, or private property, for the protection whereof the government was established. An act of the Legislature (for I cannot call it a law) contrary to the great first principles of the social compact, cannot be considered a rightful exercise of legislative authority.... A law that punished a citizen for an innocent action, or, in other words, for an act, which when done, was in violation of no existing law; a law that destroys, or impairs, the lawful private contracts of citizens; a law that makes a man a Judge in his own cause; or a law that takes property from A and gives it to B. It is against all reason and justice, for a people to entrust a Legislature with such powers; and, therefore, it cannot be presumed that they have done it. The genius, the nature, and the spirit, of our State Governments, amount to a prohibition of such acts of legislation; and the general principles of law and reason forbid them. The Legislature may enjoin, permit, forbid, and punish; they may declare new crimes; and establish rules of conduct for all its citizens in future cases; they may command what is right, and prohibit what is wrong; but they cannot change innocence into guilt; or punish innocence as a crime; or violate the right of an antecedent lawful private contract; or the right of private property. To maintain that our Federal, or State, Legislature possesses such powers, if they had not been expressly restrained, would, in my opinion, be a political heresy, altogether inadmissible in our free republican governments.

The prohibition, in the letter, is not to pass any law concerning and after the fact; but the plain and obvious meaning and intention of the prohibition is this; that the Legislatures of the several states shall not pass laws, after a fact done by a subject, or citizen, which shall have relation to such fact, and shall punish him for having done it. The prohibition considered in this light, is an additional bulwark in favour of the personal security of the subject, to protect his person from punishment by legislative acts, having a retrospective operation. I do not think it was inserted to secure the citizen in his private rights, of either property, or contracts. The prohibition not to make any thing but gold and silver coin a tender in payment of debts, and not to pass any law impairing the obligation of contracts, were inserted to secure private rights; but the restriction not to pass any ex post facto law, was to secure the person of the subject from injury, or punishment, in consequence of such law. If the prohibition against making ex post facto laws was intended to secure personal rights from being affected, or injured, by such laws, and the prohibition is sufficiently extensive for that object, the other restraints, I have enumerated, were unnecessary, and therefore improper; for both of them are retrospective.

... In the present case, there is no fact done by Bull and wife, Plaintiff's in Error, that is in any manner affected by the law or resolution of Connecticut: It does not concern, or relate to, any act done by them. The decree of the Court of Probate of Hartford (on the 21st, March) in consequence of which Calder and wife claim a right to the property in question, was given before the said law or resolution, and in that sense, was affected and set aside by it; and in consequence of the law allowing a hearing and the decision in favor of the will, they have lost, what they would have been entitled to, if the Law or resolution, and the decision in consequence thereof, had not been made. The decree of the Court of probate is the only fact, on which the law or resolution operates. In my judgment the case of the Plaintiffs in Error, is not within the letter of the prohibition; and, for the reasons assigned, I am clearly of opinion, that it is not within the intention of the prohibition; and if within the intention, but out of the letter, I should not, therefore, consider myself justified to continue it within the prohibition, and therefore that the whole was void.

It was argued by the counsel for the plaintiffs in error, that the Legislature of Connecticut had no constitutional power to make the resolution (or law) in question, granting a new hearing, &c.

Without giving an opinion, at this time, whether this Court has jurisdiction to decide that any law made by Congress, contrary to the Constitution of the United States, is void; I am fully satisfied that this court has no jurisdiction to determine that any law of any state Legislature, contrary to the Constitution of such state is void. Further, if this court had such jurisdiction, yet it does not appear to me, that the resolution (or law) in question, is contrary to the charter of Connecticut, or its constitution, which is said by counsel to be composed of its charter, acts of assembly, and usages, and customs. I should think, that the courts of Connecticut are the proper tribunals to decide, whether laws, contrary to the constitution thereof, are void. In the present case they have, both in the inferior and superior courts, determined that the resolution (or law) in question was not contrary to either their state, or the federal, constitution.

I admit, an act unlawful in the beginning may, in some cases, become lawful by matter of after fact.

I also agree, that the words "ex post facto" have the meaning contended for, and no other, in the cases cited, and in all similar cases; where they are used unconnected with, and without relation to, Legislative acts, or laws.

There appears to me a manifest distinction between the case where one fact relates to, and affects another fact, as where an after fact, by operation of law, makes a former fact, either lawful or unlawful; and the case where a law made after a fact done, is to operate on, and to affect, such fact. In the first case both the acts are done by private persons. In the second case the first act is done by a private person, and the second act is done by the legislature to affect the first act.

If the term ex post facto law is to be construed to include and to prohibit the enacting any law after a fact, it will greatly restrict the power of the federal and state legislatures; and the consequences of such a construction may not be foreseen.

If the prohibition to make no ex post facto law extends to all laws made after the fact, the two prohibitions, not to make anything but old and silver coin a tender in payment of debts; and not to pass any law impairing the obligation of contracts, were improper and unnecessary.

It was further urged, that if the provision does not extend to prohibit the making any law after a fact, then all choses in action; all lands by Devise, all personal property by bequest, or distribution; by Elegit; by execution; by judgments, particularly on torts; will be unprotected from the legislative power of the states; rights vested may be divested at the will and pleasure of the state legislatures; and, therefore, that the true construction and meaning of the prohibition is, that the states pass no law to deprive a citizen of any right vested in him by existing laws.

It is not to be presumed, that the federal or state legislatures will pass laws to deprive citizens of rights vested in them by existing laws; unless for the benefit of the whole community; and on making full satisfaction. The restraint against making any ex post facto laws was not considered, by the framers of the constitution, as extending to prohibit the depriving a citizen even of a vested right to property; or the provision, "that private property should not be taken for public use, without just compensation," was unnecessary.

It seems to me, that the right of property, in its origin, could only arise from compact express, or implied, and I think it the better opinion, that the right as well as the mode, or manner, of acquiring property, and of alienating or transferring, inheriting, or transmitting it, is conferred by society; it is regulated by civil institution, and is always subject to the rules prescribed by positive law. When I say that a right is vested in a citizen, I mean, that he has the power to do certain actions; or to possess certain things, according to the law of the land.

I cannot agree, that a right to property vested in Calder and wife, in consequence of the decree (of the 21st of March, 1783) disapproving of the will of Morrison, the Grandson. If the will was valid, Mrs. Calder could have no right, as heiress of Morrison, the physician; but if the will was set aside, she had an undoubted title.

The resolution (or law) alone had no manner of effect on any right whatever vested in Calder and wife. The resolution (or law) combined with the new hearing, and the decision, in virtue of it, took away their right to recover the property in question. But when combined they took away no right of property vested in Calder and wife; because the decree against the will (21st. March, 1783) did not vest in or transfer any property to them.

I am under a necessity to give a construction, or explanation of the words "ex post facto laws," because they have not any certain meaning attached to them. But I will not go farther than I feel myself bound to do; and if I ever exercise the jurisdiction I will not decide any law to be void, but in a very clear case.

I am of opinion, that the decree of the Supreme Court of Errors of Connecticut be affirmed, with costs.

IREDELL, J. [*concurring in the judgment.*]

Though I concur in the general result of the opinions, which have been delivered, I cannot entirely adopt the reasons that are assigned upon the occasion.

From the best information to be collected, relative to the Constitution of Connecticut, it appears, that the Legislature of that State has been in the uniform, uninterrupted, habit of exercising a general superintending power over its courts of law, by granting new trials. It may, indeed, appear strange to some of us, that in any form, there should exist a power to grant, with respect to suits depending or adjudged, new rights of trial, new privileges of proceeding, not previously recognized and regulated by positive institutions; but such is the established usage of Connecticut, and it is obviously consistent with the general superintending authority of her Legislature. Nor is it altogether without some sanction for a Legislature to act as a court of justice. In England, we know, that one branch of the Parliament, the house of Lords, not only exercises a judicial power in cases of impeachment, and for the trial of its own members, but as the court of dernier resort, takes cognizance of many suits at law, and in equity: And that in construction of law, the jurisdiction there exercised is by the King in full Parliament; which shews that, in its origin, the causes were probably heard before the whole Parliament. When Connecticut was settled, the right of empowering her Legislature to superintend the Courts of Justice, was, I presume, early assumed; and its expediency, as applied to the local circumstances and municipal policy of the State, is sanctioned by a long and uniform practice. The power, however, is judicial in its nature; and whenever it is exercised, as in the present instance, it is an exercise of judicial, not of legislative, authority.

But, let us, for a moment, suppose, that the resolution, granting a new trial, was a legislative act, it will by no means follow, that it is an act affected by the constitutional prohibition, that "no State shall pass any ex post facto law." I will endeavour to state the general principles, which influence me, on this point, succinctly and clearly, though I have not had an opportunity to reduce my opinion to writing.

If, then, a government, composed of Legislative, Executive and Judicial departments, were established, by a Constitution, which imposed no limits on the legislative power, the consequence would inevitably be, that whatever the legislative power chose to enact, would be lawfully enacted, and the judicial power could never interpose to pronounce it void. It is true, that some speculative jurists have held, that a legislative act against natural justice must, in itself, be void; but I cannot think that, under such a government, any Court of Justice would possess a power to declare it so. Sir William Blackstone, having put the strong case of an act of Parliament, which authorise a man to try his own cause, explicitly adds, that even in that case, "there is no court that has power to defeat the intent of the Legislature, when couched in such evident and express words, as leave no doubt whether it was the intent of the Legislature, or no." 1 Bl. Com. 91.

In order, therefore, to guard against so great an evil, it has been the policy of all the American states, which have, individually, framed their state constitutions since the revolution, and of the people of the United States, when they framed the Federal Constitution, to define with precision the objects of the legislative power, and to restrain its exercise within marked and settled boundaries. If any act of Congress, or of the Legislature of a state, violates those constitutional provisions, it is unquestionably void; though, I admit, that as the authority to declare it void is of a delicate and awful nature, the Court will never resort to that authority, but in a clear and urgent case. If, on the other hand, the Legislature of the Union, or the Legislature of any member of the Union, shall pass a law, within the general scope of their constitutional power, the Court cannot pronounce it to be void, merely because it is, in their judgment, contrary to the principles of natural justice. The ideas of natural justice are regulated by no fixed standard: the ablest and the purest men have differed upon the subject; and all that the Court could properly say, in such an event, would be, that the Legislature (possessed of an equal right of opinion) had passed an act which, in the opinion of the judges, was inconsistent with the abstract principles of natural justice. There are then but two lights, in which the subject can be viewed: 1st. If the Legislature pursue the authority delegated to them, their acts are valid. 2d. If they transgress the boundaries of that authority, their acts are invalid. In the former case, they exercise the discretion vested in them by the people, to whom alone they are responsible for the faithful discharge of their trust: but in the latter case, they violate a fundamental law, which must be our guide, whenever we are called upon as judges to determine the validity of a legislative act.

Still, however, in the present instance, the act or resolution of the Legislature of Connecticut, cannot be regarded as an ex post facto law; for, the true construction of the prohibition extends to criminal, not to civil, cases. It is only in criminal cases, indeed, in which the danger to be guarded against, is greatly to be apprehended. The history of every country in Europe will furnish flagrant instances of tyranny exercised under the pretext of penal dispensations. Rival factions, in their efforts to crush each other, have superseded all the forms, and suppressed all the sentiments, of justice; while attainders, on the principle of retaliation and proscription, have marked all the vicissitudes of party triumph. The temptation to such abuses of power is unfortunately too alluring for human virtue; and, therefore, the framers of the American Constitutions have wisely denied to the respective Legislatures, Federal as well as State, the possession of the power itself: They shall not pass any ex post facto law; or, in other words, they shall not inflict a punishment for any act, which was innocent at the time it was committed; nor increase the degree of punishment previously denounced for any specific offence.

The policy, the reason and humanity, of the prohibition, do not, I repeat, extend to civil cases, to cases that merely affect the private property of citizens. Some of the most necessary and important acts of Legislation are, on the contrary, founded upon the principle, that private rights must yield to public exigencies. Highways are run through private grounds. Fortifications, Lighthouses, and other public edifices, are necessarily sometimes built upon the soil owned by individuals. In such, and similar cases, if the owners should refuse voluntarily to accommodate the public, they must be constrained, as far as the public necessities require; and justice is done, by allowing them a reasonable equivalent. Without the possession of this power the operations of Government would often be obstructed, and society itself would be endangered. It is not sufficient to urge, that the power may be abused, for, such is the nature of all power, — such is the tendency of every human institution: and, it might as fairly be said, that the power of taxation, which is only circumscribed by the discretion of the Body, in which it is vested, ought not to be granted, because the Legislature, disregarding its true objects, might, for visionary and useless projects, impose a tax to the amount of nineteen shillings in the pound. We must be content to limit power where we can, and where we cannot, consistently with its use, we must be content to repose a salutary confidence. It is our consolation that there never existed a Government, in ancient or modern times, more free from danger in this respect, than the Governments of America.

Upon the whole, though there cannot be a case, in which an ex post facto law in criminal matters is requisite, or justifiable (for Providence never can intend to promote the prosperity of any country by bad means) yet, in the present instance the objection doesnot [sic] arise: Because, 1st. if the act of the Legislature of Connecticut was a judicial act, it is not within the words of the Constitution; and 2d. even if it was a legislative act, it is not within the meaning of the prohibition.

MARBURY v. MADISON

5 U.S. 137 (1803)

Opinion: Marshall, joined by Paterson, Chase, Washington

After the controversial election of 1800, outgoing President John Adams made a series of "midnight appointments," filling intermediate-level civil service positions with loyal Federalists before the inauguration of Democratic-Republican President-elect Thomas Jefferson. Through these appointments, the Federalist Party attempted to retain influence over the judiciary even though it no longer controlled the presidency. Adams appointed William Marbury to serve as justice of the peace in the District of Columbia, but his commission was never delivered by the new administration. In this case, Marbury sought a writ of mandamus — a mandatory court order — requiring Jefferson's Secretary of State, James Madison, to deliver this commission.

Clearly, Chief Justice John Marshall must have realized that any attempt to take sides in this dispute by the Court would be seen as a partisan intervention. If Chief Justice Marshall were to issue the writ of mandamus, he risked the perception that the Supreme Court was not independent from partisan politics. In reading the case, consider whether this political and historical context influenced either the decision of the case or the kind of arguments presented in it. Does Chief Justice Marshall succeed in making an argument that both asserts the Court's power and that keeps it from seeming like it is acting in a partisan manner?

In addition to thinking about the political context of the case, it is also essential to understand the legal issues involved. Fundamental among them is the question of whether the Supreme Court has the power of judicial review in the first place. If you reread Article III of the Constitution, you will not find any explicit mention of the Court's review power. The Court therefore needed another argument for the establishment of this power aside from a clear grant from Article III. The case addresses a number of questions, including (a) whether Marbury has a legal right to his commission, (b) whether it is constitutional for the Judiciary Act of 1789 to allow Marbury to bring his case directly before the Supreme Court rather than beginning his litigation in a lower court, and (c) whether the Supreme Court can strike down an unconstitutional law. Bearing in mind the readings from Gordon Wood and Alexander Bickel, as well as Alexander Hamilton's claim in The Federalist No. 78 *that, "The interpretation of the laws is the proper and peculiar province of the courts," it is important to consider how Chief Justice Marshall weaves these issues together. Is his case for judicial review persuasive?*

As you prepare to read this case, it would be helpful to familiarize yourself with the processes by which the Supreme Court can hear a case by looking both to Box 1-1 below and to Article III itself. As you will see, the Court often acts as an "appellate court," reviewing the decision of lower courts for mistakes about the law. In these cases an "inferior" court will have heard a case before it comes to the Supreme Court on appeal. But in some cases it acts as a Court of "original jurisdiction" in which a litigant brings his or her original suit to the Supreme Court.

MR. CHIEF JUSTICE MARSHALL *delivered the opinion of the Court.*

In the order in which the court has viewed this subject, the following questions have been considered and decided.

1st. Has the applicant a right to the commission he demands?

2dly. If he has a right, and that right has been violated, do the laws of his country afford him a remedy?

3dly. If they do afford him a remedy, is it a mandamus issuing from this court?

The first object of enquiry is,

1st. Has the applicant a right to the commission he demands?

His right originates in an act of congress passed in February, 1801, concerning the district of Columbia.

After dividing the district into two counties, the 11th section of this law, enacts, "that there shall be appointed in and for each of the said counties, such number of discreet persons to be justices of the peace as the president of the United States shall, from time to time, think expedient, to continue in office for five years."

It appears, from the affidavits, that in compliance with this law, a commission for

William Marbury as a justice of peace for the county of Washington, was signed by John Adams, then president of the United States; after which the seal of the United States was affixed to it; but the commission has never reached the person for whom it was made out.

In order to determine whether he is entitled to this commission, it becomes necessary to enquire whether he has been appointed to the office. For if he has been appointed, the law continues him in office for five years, and he is entitled to the possession of those evidences of office, which, being completed, became his property.

The 2d section of the 2d article of the constitution, declares, that "the president shall nominate, and, by and with the advice and consent of the senate, shall appoint ambassadors, other public ministers and consuls, and all other officers of the United States, whose appointments are not otherwise provided for."

The third section declares, that "he shall commission all the officers of the United States."

An act of congress directs the secretary of state to keep the seal of the United States, "to make out and record, and affix the said seal to all civil commissions to officers of the United States, to be appointed by the President, by and with the consent of the senate, or by the President alone; provided that the said seal shall not be affixed to any commission before the same shall have been signed by the President of the United States."

These are the clauses of the constitution and laws of the United States, which affect this part of the case. They seem to contemplate three distinct operations:

1st. The nomination. This is the sole act of the President, and is completely voluntary.

2d. The appointment. This is also the act of the President, and is also a voluntary act, though it can only be performed by and with the advice and consent of the senate.

3d. The commission. To grant a commission to a person appointed, might perhaps be deemed a duty enjoined by the constitution. "He shall," says that instrument, "commission all the officers of the United States."

This is an appointment by the President, by and with the advice and consent of the senate, and is evidenced by no act but the commission itself. In such a case therefore the commission and the appointment seem inseparable. . . . [T]he commission is not necessarily the appointment; though conclusive evidence of it.

It is . . . decidedly the opinion of the court, that when a commission has been signed by the President, the appointment is made; and that the commission is complete, when the seal of the United States has been affixed to it by the secretary of state.

Where an officer is removable at the will of the executive, the circumstance which completes his appointment is of no concern; because the act is at any time revocable; and the commission may be arrested, if still in the office. But when the officer is not removable at the will of the executive, the appointment is not revocable, and cannot be annulled. It has conferred legal rights which cannot be resumed.

The discretion of the executive is to be exercised until the appointment has been made. But having once made the appointment, his power over the office is terminated in all cases, where, by law, the officer is not removable by him. The right to the office is then in the person appointed, and he has the absolute, unconditional, power of accepting or rejecting it.

Mr. Marbury, . . . since his commission was signed by the President, and sealed by the secretary of state, was appointed; and as the law creating the office, gave the officer a right to hold for five years, independent of the executive, the appointment was not revocable; but vested in the officer legal rights, which are protected by the laws of his country.

To withhold his commission, therefore, is an act deemed by the court not warranted by law, but violative of a vested legal right.

This brings us to the second enquiry; which is,

2dly. If he has a right, and that right has been violated, do the laws of his country afford him a remedy?

The very essence of civil liberty certainly consists in the right of every individual to claim the protection of the laws, whenever he receives an injury. One of the first duties of government is to afford that protection. In Great Britain the king himself is sued in the respectful form of a petition, and he never fails to comply with the judgment of his court.

The government of the United States has been emphatically termed a government of laws, and not of men. It will certainly cease to deserve this high appellation, if the laws furnish no remedy for the violation of a vested legal right.

By the constitution of the United States, the President is invested with certain important political powers, in the exercise of which he is to use his own discretion, and is accountable only to his country in his political character, and to his own conscience. To aid him in the performance of these duties, he is authorized to appoint certain officers, who act by his authority and in conformity with his orders.

In such cases, their acts are his acts; and whatever opinion may be entertained of the manner in which executive discretion may be used, still there exists, and can exist, no power to control that discretion. The subjects are political. They respect the nation, not individual rights, and being entrusted to the executive, the decision of the executive is conclusive. The application of this remark will be perceived by adverting to the act of congress for establishing the department of foreign affairs. This office, as his duties were prescribed by that act, is to conform precisely to the will of the President. He is the mere organ by whom that will is communicated. The acts of such an officer, as an officer, can never be examinable by the courts.

But when the legislature proceeds to impose on that officer other duties; when he is directed peremptorily to perform certain acts; when the rights of individuals are dependent on the performance of those acts; he is so far the officer of the law; is amenable to the laws for his conduct; and cannot at his discretion sport away the vested rights of others.

The conclusion from this reasoning is, that where the heads of departments are the political or confidential agents of the executive, merely to execute the will of the President, or rather to act in cases in which the executive possesses a constitutional or legal discretion, nothing can be more perfectly clear than that their acts are only politically examinable. But where a specific duty is assigned by law, and individual rights depend upon the performance of that duty, it seems equally clear that the individual who considers himself injured, has a right to resort to the laws of his country for a remedy.

If this be the rule, let us enquire how it applies to the case under the consideration of the court.

The power of nominating to the senate, and the power of appointing the person nominated, are political powers, to be exercised by the President according to his own discretion. When he has made an appointment, he has exercised his whole power, and his discretion has been completely applied to the case. If, by law, the officer be removable at the will of the President, then a new appointment may be immediately made, and the rights of the officer are terminated. But as a fact which has existed cannot be made never to have existed, the appointment cannot be annihilated; and consequently if the officer is by law not removable at the will of the President; the rights he has acquired are protected by the law, and are not resumable by the President. They cannot be extinguished by executive authority, and he has the privilege of asserting them in like manner as if they had been derived from any other source.

The question whether a right has vested or not, is, in its nature, judicial, and must be tried by the judicial authority. If, for example, Mr. Marbury had taken the oaths of a magistrate, and proceeded to act as one; in consequence of which a suit had been instituted against him, in which his defence had depended on his being a magistrate; the validity of his appointment must have been determined by judicial authority.

So, if he conceives that, by virtue of his appointment, he has a legal right, either to the commission which has been made out for him, or to a copy of that commission, it is equally a question examinable in a court, and the decision of the court upon it must depend on the opinion entertained of his appointment.

That question has been discussed, and the opinion is, that the latest point of time which can be taken as that at which the appointment was complete, and evidenced, was when, after the signature of the president, the seal of the United States was affixed to the commission.

It is then the opinion of the court,

1st. That by signing the commission of Mr. Marbury, the president of the United States appointed him a justice of peace, for the county of Washington in the district of Columbia; and that the seal of the United States, affixed thereto by the secretary of state, is conclusive testimony of the verity of the signature, and of the completion of the appointment; and that the appointment conferred on him a legal right to the office for the space of five years.

2dly. That, having this legal title to the office, he has a consequent right to the commission; a refusal to deliver which, is a plain violation of that right, for which the laws of his country afford him a remedy.

It remains to be enquired whether,

3dly. He is entitled to the remedy for which he applies. This depends on,

1st. The nature of the writ applied for, and,

2dly. The power of this court.

1st. The nature of the writ.

Blackstone, in the 3d volume of his commentaries, page 110, defines a mandamus to be, "a command issued in the King's name from the court of King's Bench, and directed to any person, corporation, or inferior court of judicature within the King's dominions, requiring them to do some particular thing therein specified, which appertains to their office and duty, and which the court of King's Bench has previously determined, or at least supposed, to be consonant to right and justice."

The province of the court is, solely, to decide on the rights of individuals, not to enquire how the executive, or executive officers, perform duties in which they have a discretion. Questions, in their nature political, or which are, by the constitution and laws, submitted to the executive, can never be made in this court.

It is not by the office of the person to whom the writ is directed, but the nature of the thing to be done that the propriety or impropriety of issuing a mandamus, is to be determined. Where the head of a department acts in a case, in which executive discretion is to be exercised; in which he is the mere organ of executive will; it is again repeated, that any application to a court to control, in any respect, his conduct, would be rejected without hesitation.

But where he is directed by law to do a certain act affecting the absolute rights of individuals, in the performance of which he is not placed under the particular direction of the President, and the performance of which, the President cannot lawfully forbid, and therefore is never presumed to have forbidden; as for example, to record a commission, or a patent for land, which has received all the legal solemnities; or to give a copy of such record; in such cases, it is not perceived on what ground the courts of the country are further excused from the duty of giving judgment, that right be done to an injured individual, than if the same services were to be performed by a person not the head of a department.

It was at first doubted whether the action of detinue was not a specified legal remedy for the commission which has been withheld from Mr. Marbury; in which case a mandamus would be improper. But this doubt has yielded to the consideration that the judgment in detinue is for the thing itself, or its value. The value of a public office not to be sold, is incapable of being ascertained; and the applicant has a right to the office itself, or to nothing. He will obtain the office by obtaining the commission, or a copy of it from the record.

This, then, is a plain case for a mandamus, either to deliver the commission, or a copy of it from the record; and it only remains to be enquired,

Whether it can issue from this court.

The act to establish the judicial courts of the United States authorizes the supreme court "to issue writs of mandamus, in cases warranted by the principles and usages of law, to any courts appointed, or persons holding office, under the authority of the United States."

The secretary of state, being a person holding an office under the authority of the United States, is precisely within the letter of the description; and if this court is not authorized to issue a writ of mandamus to such an officer, it must be because the law is unconstitutional, and therefore absolutely incapable of conferring the authority, and assigning the duties which its words purport to confer and assign.

The constitution vests the whole judicial power of the United States in one supreme court, and such inferior courts as congress shall, from time to time, ordain and establish. This power is expressly extended to all cases arising under the laws of the United States; and consequently, in some form, may be exercised over the present case; because the right claimed is given by a law of the United States.

In the distribution of this power it is declared that "the supreme court shall have original jurisdiction in all cases affecting ambassadors, other public ministers and consuls, and those in which a state shall be a party. In all other cases, the supreme court shall have appellate jurisdiction."

It has been insisted, at the bar, that as the original grant of jurisdiction, to the supreme and inferior courts, is general, and the clause, assigning original jurisdiction to the supreme court, contains no negative or restrictive words; the power remains to the legislature, to assign original jurisdiction to that court in other cases than those specified in the article which has been recited; provided those cases belong to the judicial power of the United States.

If it had been intended to leave it to the discretion of the legislature to apportion the judicial power between the supreme and inferior courts according to the will of that body, it would certainly have been useless to have proceeded further than to have defined the judicial powers, and the tribunals in which it should be vested. The subsequent part of the section is mere surplusage, is entirely without meaning, if such is to be the construction. If congress remains at liberty to give this court appellate jurisdiction, where the constitution has declared their jurisdiction shall be original; and original jurisdiction where the constitution has declared it shall be appellate; the distribution of jurisdiction, made in the constitution, is form without substance.

Affirmative words are often, in their operation, negative of other objects than those affirmed; and in this case, a negative or exclusive sense must be given to them or they have no operation at all.

It cannot be presumed that any clause in the constitution is intended to be without effect; and therefore such a construction is inadmissible, unless the words require it.

That they should have appellate jurisdiction in all other cases, with such exceptions as congress might make, is no restriction; unless the words be deemed exclusive of original jurisdiction.

When an instrument organizing fundamentally a judicial system, divides it into one supreme, and so many inferior courts as the legislature may ordain and establish; then enumerates its powers, and proceeds so far to distribute them, as to define the jurisdiction of the supreme court by declaring the cases in which it shall take original jurisdiction, and that in others it shall take appellate jurisdiction; the plain import of the words seems to be, that in one class of cases its jurisdiction is original, and not appellate; in the other it is appellate, and not original. If any other construction would render the clause inoperative, that is an additional reason for rejecting such other construction, and for adhering to their obvious meaning.

To enable this court then to issue a mandamus, it must be shown to be an exercise of appellate jurisdiction, or to be necessary to enable them to exercise appellate jurisdiction.

It is the essential criterion of appellate jurisdiction, that it revises and corrects the proceedings in a cause already instituted, and does not create that cause. Although, therefore, a mandamus may be directed to courts, yet to issue such a writ to an officer for the delivery of a paper, is in effect the same as to sustain an original action for that paper, and therefore seems not to belong to appellate, but to original jurisdiction. Neither is it necessary in such a case as this, to enable the court to exercise its appellate jurisdiction.

The authority, therefore, given to the supreme court, by the act establishing the judicial courts of the United States, to issue writs of mandamus to public officers, appears not to be warranted by the constitution; and it becomes necessary to enquire whether a jurisdiction, so conferred, can be exercised.

The question, whether an act, repugnant to the constitution, can become the law of the land, is a question deeply interesting to the United States; but, happily, not of an intricacy proportioned to its interest. It seems only necessary to recognize certain principles, supposed to have been long and well established, to decide it.

That the people have an original right to establish, for their future government, such principles as, in their opinion, shall most conduce to their own happiness, is the basis, on which the whole American fabric has been erected. The exercise of this original right is a very great exertion; nor can it, nor ought it to be frequently repeated. The principles, therefore, so established, are deemed fundamental. And as the authority, from which they proceed, is supreme, and can seldom act, they are designed to be permanent.

This original and supreme will organizes the government, and assigns, to different departments, their respective powers. It may either stop here; or establish certain limits not to be transcended by those departments.

The government of the United States is of the latter description. The powers of the legislature are defined, and limited; and that those limits may not be mistaken, or forgotten, the constitution is written. To what purpose are powers limited, and to what purpose is that limitation committed to writing, if these limits may, at any time, be passed by those intended to be restrained? The distinction, between a government with limited and unlimited powers, is abolished, if those limits do not confine the persons on whom they are imposed, and if acts prohibited and acts allowed, are of equal obligation. It is a proposition too plain to be contested, that the constitution controls any legislative act repugnant to it; or, that the legislature may alter the constitution by an ordinary act.

Between these alternatives there is no middle ground. The constitution is either a superior, paramount law, unchangeable by ordinary means, or it is on a level with ordinary legislative acts, and like other acts, is alterable when the legislature shall please to alter it.

If the former part of the alternative be true, then a legislative act contrary to the constitution is not law: if the latter part be true, then written constitutions are absurd attempts, on the part of the people, to limit a power, in its own nature illimitable.

Certainly all those who have framed written constitutions contemplate them as forming the fundamental and paramount law of the nation, and consequently the theory of every such government must be, that an act of the legislature, repugnant to the constitution, is void.

This theory is essentially attached to a written constitution, and is consequently to be considered, by this court, as one of the fundamental principles of our society. It is not therefore to be lost sight of in the further consideration of this subject.

It is emphatically the province and duty of the judicial department to say what the law is. Those who apply the rule to particular cases, must of necessity expound and interpret that rule. If two laws conflict with each other, the courts must decide on the operation of each.

So if a law be in opposition to the constitution; if both the law and the constitution apply to a particular case, so that the court must either decide that case conformably to the law, disregarding the constitution; or conformably to the constitution, disregarding the law; the court must determine which of these conflicting rules governs the case. This is of the very essence of judicial duty.

If then the courts are to regard the constitution; and the constitution is superior to any ordinary act of the legislature; the constitution, and not such ordinary act, must govern the case to which they both apply.

Those then who controvert the principle that the constitution is to be considered, in court, as a paramount law, are reduced to the necessity of maintaining that courts must close their eyes on the constitution, and see only the law.

This doctrine would subvert the very foundation of all written constitutions. It would declare that an act, which, according to the principles and theory of our government, is entirely void; is yet, in practice, completely obligatory. It would declare, that if the legislature shall do what is expressly forbidden, such act, notwithstanding the express prohibition, is in reality effectual. It would be giving to the legislature a practical and real omnipotence, with the same breath which professes to restrict their powers within narrow limits. It is prescribing limits, and declaring that those limits may be passed at pleasure.

That it thus reduces to nothing what we have deemed the greatest improvement on political institutions a written constitution would of itself be sufficient, in America, where written constitutions have been viewed with so much reverence, for rejecting the construction. But the peculiar expressions of the constitution of the United States furnish additional arguments in favor of its rejection.

The judicial power of the United States is extended to all cases arising under the constitution.

Could it be the intention of those who gave this power, to say that, in using it, the constitution should not be looked into? That a case arising under the constitution should be decided without examining the instrument under which it arises?

This is too extravagant to be maintained.

In some cases then, the constitution must be looked into by the judges. And if they can open it at all, what part of it are they forbidden to read, or to obey?

There are many other parts of the constitution which serve to illustrate this subject.

It is declared that "no tax or duty shall be laid on articles exported from any state." Suppose a duty on the export of cotton, of tobacco, or of flour; and a suit instituted to recover it. Ought judgment to be rendered in such a case? Ought the judges to close their eyes on the constitution, and only see the law.

The constitution declares that "no bill of attainder or ex post facto law shall be passed."

If, however, such a bill should be passed and a person should be prosecuted under it; must the court condemn to death those victims whom the constitution endeavors to preserve?

"No person," says the constitution, "shall be convicted of treason unless on the testimony of two witnesses to the fame overt act, or on confession in open court."

Here the language of the constitution is addressed especially to the courts. It prescribes, directly for them, a rule of evidence not to be departed from. If the legislature should change that rule, and declare one witness, or a confession out of court, sufficient for conviction, must the constitutional principle yield to the legislative act?

From these, and many other selections which might be made, it is apparent, that the framers of the constitution contemplated that instrument, as a rule for the government of courts, as well as of the legislature.

It is also not entirely unworthy of observation, that in declaring what shall be the supreme law of the land, the constitution itself is first mentioned; and not the laws of the United States generally, but those only which shall be made in pursuance of the constitution, have that rank.

Thus, the particular phraseology of the constitution of the United States confirms and strengthens the principle, supposed to be essential to all written constitutions, that a law repugnant to the constitution is void; and that courts, as well as other departments, are bound by that instrument.

The rule must be discharged.

CASE QUESTIONS

1. **Some commentators have argued that this opinion, which found against William Marbury, was an ingenious political move that succeeded in securing the power of judicial review for the Court without seeming like a partisan power grab. In claiming that the Supreme Court had the power of judicial review and by striking down the Judiciary Act of 1787, Chief Justice John Marshall gave legal precedence to the**

arguments of Alexander Hamilton and to his own Federalist Party. He also scored a moral victory for the Federalists by claiming, even while finding in James Madison's favor, that Marbury's rights had been denied.

At the same time, Chief Justice Marshall was able to keep the Court above the partisan fray. Although he asserts the broader power of the Court to strike down unconstitutional laws, Chief Justice Marshall agrees with Thomas Jefferson's administration that the Court is powerless to enforce Marbury's particular claim. Even though Marbury has a "right" to have his appointment certified, Chief Justice Marshall rules that the procedures Marbury followed were unconstitutional. Does Chief Justice Marshall succeed in securing the power of the Court while retaining a sense of the Court's political independence? Consider here Gordon Wood's remarks about the challenges of a Supreme Court dominated by the Federalist Party retaining its power in a Democratic-Republican administration.

2. One crucial aspect of the case concerns the question of whether Congress can alter the kind of "original jurisdiction" held by the Supreme Court. While the Judiciary Act of 1789 provides that Marbury could bring his argument directly before the Supreme Court, Article III of the Constitution only allows this kind of "original jurisdiction" in a limited range of cases. Should Congress have been allowed to enhance the Supreme Court's powers of original jurisdiction? What does Chief Justice Marshall say about this issue?

3. This case is prominent because of Chief Justice Marshall's argument for the Court's judicial review power. What is his argument? Is it successful? Does it overcome concerns about the counter-majoritarian difficulty?

Box 1-1 The Pathways to the Supreme Court

In most cases (except for cases under original jurisdiction and limited instances of mandatory appeals), the Supreme Court has *discretionary* jurisdiction, which means that it can choose whether or not to hear an appeal. Often, the Court chooses to hear cases that might clear up areas of the law where lower courts have contradicted each other, or cases that bear on weighty legal issues. The Court agrees to hear an appeal by granting a petition for the writ of *certiorari*, also known as "granting cert."

Under Article III of the Constitution, the Supreme Court has the power to interpret the law in "all cases . . . arising under this Constitution, the laws of the United States, and treaties." Sometimes the Supreme Court, like lower federal courts, hears cases that concern matters of state law. Typically, these cases land in federal court under "diversity jurisdiction," when two parties in a civil matter hail from different states. The idea is that a federal courtroom provides an impartial forum to decide such cases, but federal judges are required to apply relevant state law in these instances. The Court can also review the decisions of state courts, but only when state cases touch on matters of federal law as well, such as when a state law is alleged to violate the U.S. Constitution. In certain circumstances, a case in state court can jump to a federal court lower than the Supreme Court, as when a prisoner challenges her conviction in state court as unconstitutional.

In thinking about the issues raised in *Marbury v. Madison*, the following chart might be helpful. It outlines various routes by which a case might reach the Supreme Court:

Figure 1.1. Various Paths to the Supreme Court

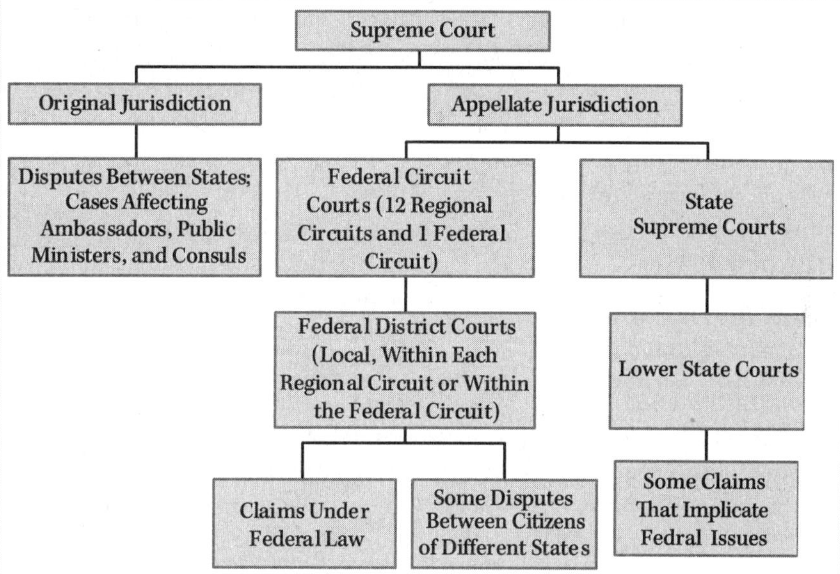

FLETCHER v. PECK

10 U.S. 87 (1810)

Opinion: Marshall, joined by Washington, Livingston, Todd
Dissent: Johnson

Under the "Yazoo Land Act," the State of Georgia sold very large tracts of land to private citizens. Believing that the Act and the process of selling the land had become deeply corrupted, a later legislature invalidated the sale. Of course, those who had bought land under this scheme were aggrieved by this result. Robert Fletcher had bought land from John Peck, one of the original purchasers of the land. When the sale was voided by the State of Georgia, Fletcher sued for damages, claiming the contract falsely represented Peck as the legal owner of the land. In order to decide whether Peck really was the legal owner, and thus entitled to sell the land to Fletcher, the Court focused on whether the law invalidating the purchases of the land was unconstitutional. Specifically, pay close attention to the discussion about whether the legislature in this decision is bound from revoking the sale by the Contracts Clause of the U.S. Constitution, located in Article I, Section 10. You will notice that the Court pits the rights of individuals under this clause against the right of the legislature to make policy. Notice, too, that this is a question of the federal constitutionality of a state law, and thus raises questions about the relative power of the U.S. Constitution and that of state legislatures. Notice also that, in addition to the discussion of the Contracts Clause, this case raises an ex post facto question similar to the one we have just examined: Can a legislature invalidate a sale of land after the sale has occurred?

MR. CHIEF JUSTICE MARSHALL *delivered the opinion of the Court.*

The suit was instituted on several covenants contained in a deed made by John Peck, the defendant in error, conveying to Robert Fletcher, the plaintiff in error, certain lands which were part of a large purchase made by James Gunn and others, in the year 1795, from the State of Georgia, the contract for which was made in the form of a bill passed by the Legislature of that State.

... The ... count ... alleges that, in consequence of these practices and of other causes, a subsequent Legislature passed an act annulling and rescinding the law under which the conveyance to the original grantees was made, declaring that conveyance void, and asserting the title of the State to the lands it contained. The count proceeds to recite at large, this rescinding act, and concludes with averring that, by reason of this act, the title of the said Peck in the premises was constitutionally and legally impaired and rendered null and void.

... The importance and the difficulty of the questions, presented by these pleadings are deeply felt by the Court. The lands in controversy vested absolutely in James Gunn and others, the original grantees, by the conveyance of the Governor, made in pursuance of an act of assembly to which the Legislature was fully competent. Being thus in full possession of the legal estate, they, for a valuable consideration, conveyed portions of the land to those who were willing to purchase. If the original transaction was infected with fraud, these purchasers did not participate in it, and had no notice of it. They were innocent. Yet the Legislature of Georgia has involved them in the fate of the first parties to the transaction, and, if the act be valid, has annihilated their rights also.

The Legislature of Georgia was a party to this transaction, and for a party to pronounce its own deed invalid, whatever cause may be assigned for its invalidity, must be considered as a mere act of power which must find its vindication in a train of reasoning not often heard in courts of justice.

But the real party, it is said, are the people, and when their agents are unfaithful, the acts of those agents cease to be obligatory.

It is, however, to be recollected that the people can act only by these agents, and that, while within the powers conferred on them, their acts must be considered as the acts of the people. If the agents be corrupt, others may be chosen, and, if their contracts be examinable, the common sentiment, as well as common usage of mankind, points out a mode by which this examination may be made, and their validity determined.

... If the Legislature felt itself absolved from those rules of property which are common to all the citizens of the United States, and from those principles of equity which are acknowledged in all our courts, its act is to be supported by its power alone, and the same power may devest any other individual of his lands if it shall be the will of the Legislature so to exert it.

The principle is this: that a legislature may, by its own act, devest the vested estate of any man whatever, for reasons which shall, by itself, be deemed sufficient.

. . . Is the power of the Legislature competent to the annihilation of such title, and to a resumption of the property thus held?

The principle asserted is that one Legislature is competent to repeal any act which a former legislature was competent to pass, and that one legislature cannot abridge the powers of a succeeding legislature.

The correctness of this principle, so far as respects general legislation, can never be controverted. But if an act be done under a law, a succeeding legislature cannot undo it.

When, then, a law is in its nature a contract, when absolute rights have vested under that contract, a repeal of the law cannot devest those rights; and the act of annulling them, if legitimate, is rendered so by a power applicable to the case of every individual in the community.

It may well be doubted whether the nature of society and of government does not prescribe some limits to the legislative power; and, if any be prescribed, where are they to be found if the property of an individual, fairly and honestly acquired, may be seized without compensation?

To the Legislature all legislative power is granted, but the question whether the act of transferring the property of an individual to the public be in the nature of the legislative power is well worthy of serious reflection.

It is the peculiar province of the legislature to prescribe general rules for the government of society; the application of those rules to individuals in society would seem to be the duty of other departments. How far the power of giving the law may involve every other power, in cases where the Constitution is silent, never has been, and perhaps never can be, definitely stated.

The validity of this rescinding act, then, might well be doubted, were Georgia a single sovereign power. But Georgia cannot be viewed as a single, unconnected, sovereign power, on whose legislature no other restrictions are imposed than may be found in its own Constitution. She is a part of a large empire; she is a member of the American Union; and that Union has a Constitution the supremacy of which all acknowledge, and which imposes limits to the legislatures of the several States which none claim a right to pass. The Constitution of the United States declares that no State shall pass any bill of attainder, ex post facto law, or law impairing the obligation of contracts.

Does the case now under consideration come within this prohibitory section of the Constitution?

In considering this very interesting question, we immediately ask ourselves what is a contract? Is a grant a contract?

A contract is a compact between two or more parties, and is either executory or executed. An executory contract is one in which a party binds himself to do, or not to do, a particular thing; such was the law under which the conveyance was made by the Governor. A contract executed is one in which the object of contract is performed, and this, says Blackstone, differs in nothing from a grant. The contract between Georgia and the purchasers was executed by the grant. A contract executed, as well as one which is executory, contains obligations binding on the parties. A grant, in its own nature, amounts to an extinguishment of the right of the grantor, and implies a contract not to reassert that right. A party is therefore always estopped by his own grant.

Since, then, in fact, a grant is a contract executed, the obligation of which still continues, and since the Constitution uses the general term "contract" without distinguishing between those which are executory and those which are executed, it must be construed to comprehend the latter as well as the former. A law annulling conveyances between individuals, and declaring that the grantors should stand seised of their former estates, notwithstanding those grants, would be as repugnant to the Constitution as a law discharging the vendors of property from the obligation of executing their contracts by conveyances. It would be strange if a contract to convey was secured by the Constitution, while an absolute conveyance remained unprotected.

If, under a fair construction the Constitution, grants are comprehended under the term "contracts," is a grant from the State excluded from the operation of the provision? Is the clause to be considered as inhibiting the State from impairing the obligation of contracts between two individuals, but as excluding from that inhibition contracts made with itself?

The words themselves contain no such distinction. They are general, and are applicable to contracts of every description. If contracts made with the State are to be exempted from their operation, the exception must arise from the character of the contracting party, not from the words which are employed.

The State legislatures can pass no ex post facto law. An ex post facto law is one which renders an act punishable in a manner in which it was not punishable when it was committed. Such a law may inflict penalties on the person, or may inflict pecuniary penalties which swell the public treasury. The legislature is then prohibited from passing a law by which a man's estate, or any part of it, shall be seized for a crime which was not declared by some previous law to render him liable to that punishment. Why, then, should violence be done to the natural meaning of words for the purpose of leaving to the legislature the power of seizing for public use the estate of an individual in the form of a law annulling the title by which he holds that estate? The Court can perceive no sufficient grounds for making this distinction. This rescinding act would have the effect of an ex post facto law.

The argument in favour of presuming an intention to except a case not excepted by the words of the Constitution is susceptible of some illustration from a principle originally ingrafted in that instrument, though no longer a part of it. The Constitution, as passed, gave the courts of the United States jurisdiction in suits brought against individual States. A State, then, which violated its own contract was suable in the courts of the United States for that violation. Would it have been a defence in such a suit to say that the State had passed a law absolving itself from the contract? It is scarcely to be conceived that such a defence could be set up. And yet, if a State is neither restrained by the general principles of our political institutions nor by the words of the Constitution from impairing the obligation of its own contracts, such a defence would be a valid one. This feature is no longer found in the Constitution, but it aids in the construction of those clauses with which it was originally associated.

It is, then, the unanimous opinion of the Court that, in this case, the estate having passed into the hands of a purchaser for a valuable consideration, without notice, the State of Georgia was restrained, either by general principles which are common to our free institutions or by the particular provisions of the Constitution of the United States, from passing a law whereby the estate of the plaintiff in the premises so purchased could be constitutionally and legally impaired and rendered null and void. Judgement affirmed with costs.

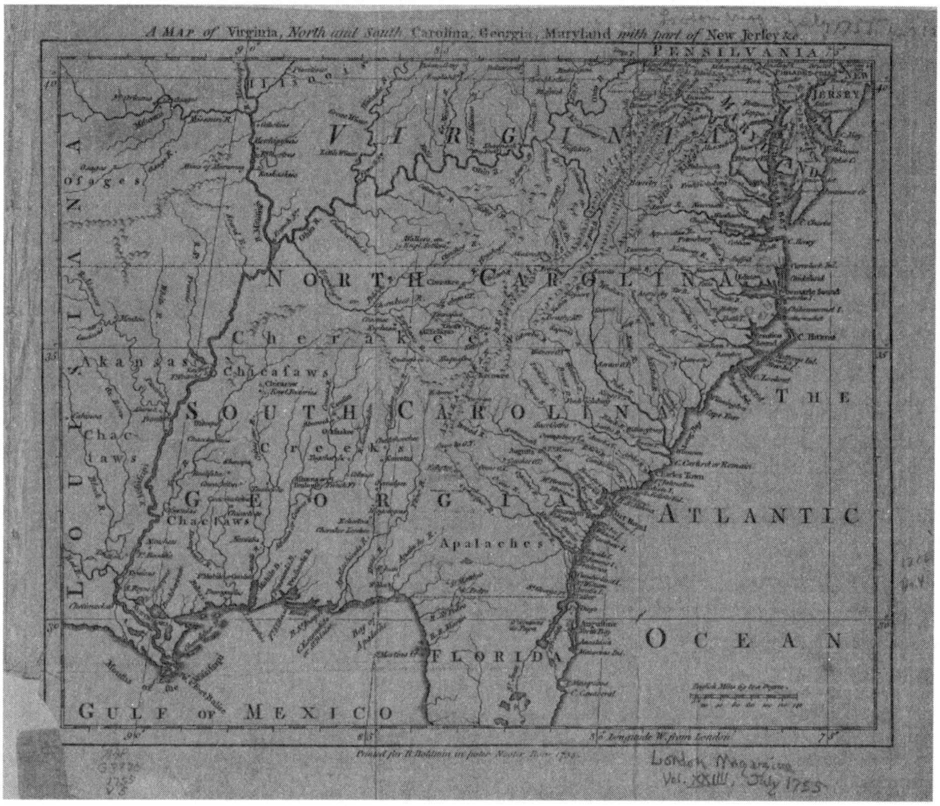

Courtesy of Hargrett Rare Book and Manuscript Library/University of Georgia Library

In Martin v. Hunter's Lessee, *the Supreme Court put an end to a dispute over land in Virginia, but also asserted the superiority of its rulings to those of state courts.*

MARTIN v. HUNTER'S LESSEE

14 U.S. 304 (1816)

Opinion: Story, joined by Duvall, Johnson, Livingston, Todd
Concurrence: Washington

Marbury v. Madison *declared the authority of the Supreme Court to review the constitutionality of federal laws. The Marshall Court extended its reasoning in* Marbury v. Madison *to establish judicial review of state laws as well in the landmark cases of* Martin v. Hunter's Lessee *and* Cohens v. Virginia.

Martin v. Hunter's Lessee *concerned a land dispute between the Commonwealth of Virginia and Denny Martin. Martin claimed the land as part of his inheritance from the British Lord Fairfax, and he argued that a treaty between Britain and the United States protected his inheritance. While the highest court of Virginia acknowledged that the U.S. treaty was superior to state law, it interpreted the treaty narrowly so that it did not prohibit the confiscation of Martin's property. On appeal, the U.S. Supreme Court held in*

Martin's favor that the confiscation was a violation of U.S. treaty obligations, and that, as the highest court in the land, its reading of the treaty trumped the Virginia court's interpretation. A central element of the Martin decision is its assertion that the Supreme Court can review state court rulings and has the final say on how to interpret federal law. In particular, at issue was the constitutionality of the 25th section of the Judiciary Act of 1789, which authorized the Supreme Court's jurisdiction in the case.

As you read, consider whether the fact that these cases involve appeals from state — not federal — courts affects the Court's willingness to assert the power of judicial review. Should the Court's judicial review power be more deferential when reviewing state courts' interpretations of federal law within their territory?

MR. JUSTICE STORY *delivered the opinion of the Court.*

... The Constitution of the United States was ordained and established not by the States in their sovereign capacities, but emphatically, as the preamble of the Constitution declares, by "the people of the United States." There can be no doubt that it was competent to the people to invest the general government with all the powers which they might deem proper and necessary, to extend or restrain these powers according to their own good pleasure, and to give them a paramount and supreme authority. As little doubt can there be that the people had a right to prohibit to the States the exercise of any powers which were, in their judgment, incompatible with the objects of the general compact, to make the powers of the State governments, in given cases, subordinate to those of the nation, or to reserve to themselves those sovereign authorities which they might not choose to delegate to either. The Constitution was not, therefore, necessarily carved out of existing State sovereignties, nor a surrender of powers already existing in State institutions, for the powers of the States depend upon their own Constitutions, and the people of every State had the right to modify and restrain them according to their own views of the policy or principle. On the other hand, it is perfectly clear that the sovereign powers vested in the State governments by their respective Constitutions remained unaltered and unimpaired except so far as they were granted to the Government of the United States.

These deductions do not rest upon general reasoning, plain and obvious as they seem to be. They have been positively recognized by one of the articles in amendment of the Constitution, which declares that "The powers not delegated to the United States by the Constitution, nor prohibited by it to the States, are reserved to the States respectively, or to the people. . . ."

It was foreseen that, in the exercise of their ordinary jurisdiction, State courts would incidentally take cognizance of cases arising under the Constitution, the laws, and treaties of the United States. Yet to all these cases the judicial power, by the very terms of the Constitution, is to extend. It cannot extend by original jurisdiction if that was already rightfully and exclusively attached in the State courts, which (as has been already shown) may occur; it must therefore extend by appellate jurisdiction, or not at all. It would seem to follow that the appellate power of the United States must, in such cases, extend to State tribunals; and if in such cases, there is no reason why it should not equally attach upon all others within the purview of the Constitution.

It has been argued that such an appellate jurisdiction over State courts is inconsistent with the genius of our Governments, and the spirit of the Constitution. That the latter was never designed to act upon State sovereignties, but only upon the people, and that, if the power exists, it will materially impair the sovereignty of the States, and the independence of their courts. We cannot yield to the force of this reasoning; it assumes principles which we cannot admit, and draws conclusions to which we do not yield our assent....

[The Constitution] is crowded with provisions which restrain or annul the sovereignty of the States in some of the highest branches of their prerogatives. The tenth section of the first article contains a long list of disabilities and prohibitions imposed upon the States. Surely, when such essential portions of State sovereignty are taken away or prohibited to be exercised, it cannot be correctly asserted that the Constitution does not act upon the States. The language of the Constitution is also imperative upon the States as to the performance of many duties. It is imperative upon the State legislatures to make laws prescribing the time, places, and manner of holding elections for senators and representatives, and for electors of President and Vice-President. And in these as well as some other cases, Congress have a right to revise, amend, or supersede the laws which may be passed by State legislatures. When therefore the States are stripped of some of the highest attributes of sovereignty, and the same are given to the United States; when the legislatures of the States are, in some respects, under the control of Congress, and in every case are, under the Constitution, bound by the paramount authority of the United States, it is certainly difficult to support the argument that the appellate power over the decisions of State courts is contrary to the genius of our institutions. The courts of the United States can, without question, revise the proceedings of the executive and legislative authorities of the States, and if they are found to be contrary to the Constitution, may declare them to be of no legal validity. Surely the exercise of the same right over judicial tribunals is not a higher or more dangerous act of sovereign power....

On the whole, the Court are of opinion that the appellate power of the United States does extend to cases pending in the State courts, and that the 25th section of the judiciary act, which authorizes the exercise of this jurisdiction in the specified cases by a writ of error, is supported by the letter and spirit of the Constitution. We find no clause in that instrument which limits this power, and we dare not interpose a limitation where the people have not been disposed to create one....

It is the opinion of the whole Court that the judgment of the Court of Appeals of Virginia, rendered on the mandate in this cause, be reversed, and the judgment of the District Court, held at Winchester, be, and the same is hereby, affirmed.

TRUSTEES OF DARTMOUTH COLLEGE v. WOODWARD

17 U.S. (4 Wheat.) 518 (1819)

Opinion: Marshall, joined by Johnson, Livingston
Concurrence: Washington, joined by Livingston
Concurrence: Story, joined by Livingston
Dissent: Duvall

Like Fletcher v. Peck, *this early act of judicial review concerned the Contracts Clause of the Constitution, which prohibits states from passing laws "impairing the obligation of contracts." When the trustees of Dartmouth College removed that college's president, the state legislature tried to make the college public in the hopes of reinstating him. The*

Court asked whether such an act violated the Contracts Clause. The case serves as an early example of the competition between judicial authority and the authority of state legislatures. As in Fletcher v. Peck, *the narrower constitutional question concerns the degree to which the Constitution protects interests in private property from the control of state legislatures. Specifically, the Court investigates the entitlements of a private corporation to be protected from the state. In reading this case, you should focus on the distinct question of whether the Supreme Court has a role in enforcing the relationship between private ownership and the authority of state legislatures. Even if the Court is correct about the meaning of the Contracts Clause, should it attempt to enforce its interpretation over the objection of a state's legislature?*

MR. CHIEF JUSTICE MARSHALL *delivered the opinion of the Court.*

This is an action of trover, brought by the Trustees of Dartmouth College against William H. Woodward, in the State court of New Hampshire, for the book of records, corporate seal, and other corporate property, to which the plaintiffs allege themselves to be entitled.

A special verdict, after setting out the rights of the parties, finds for the defendant, if certain acts of the Legislature of New Hampshire, passed on the 27th of June, and on the 18th of December 1816, be valid, and binding on the Trustees, without their assent, and not repugnant to the Constitution of the United States; otherwise, it finds for the plaintiffs.

The Superior Court of judicature of New Hampshire rendered a judgment upon this verdict for the defendant, which judgment has been brought before this court by writ of error. The single question now to be considered is do the acts to which the verdict refers violate the Constitution of the United States?

This court can be insensible neither to the magnitude nor delicacy of this question. The validity of a legislative act is to be examined; and the opinion of the highest law tribunal of a State is to be revised — an opinion which carries with it intrinsic evidence of the diligence, of the ability, and the integrity, with which it was formed. On more than one occasion, this Court has expressed the cautious circumspection with which it approaches the consideration of such questions, and has declared that in no doubtful case would it pronounce a legislative act to be contrary to the Constitution. But the American people have said in the Constitution of the United States that "no State shall pass any bill of attainder, ex post facto law, or law impairing the obligation of contracts." In the same instrument, they have also said, "that the judicial power shall extend to all cases in law and equity arising under the Constitution." On the judges of this Court, then, is imposed the high and solemn duty of protecting, from even legislative violation, those contracts which the Constitution of our country has placed beyond legislative control; and however irksome the task may be, this is a duty from which we dare not shrink.

. . . The defendant claims under three acts of the Legislature of New Hampshire, the most material of which was passed on the 27th of June, 1816, and is entitled "An act to amend the charter, and enlarge and improve the corporation of Dartmouth College." . . . The majority of the Trustees of the college have refused to accept this amended charter, and have brought this suit for the corporate property, which is in possession of a person holding by virtue of the acts which have been stated.

It can require no argument to prove that the circumstances of this case constitute a contract. . . . The points for consideration are, 1. Is this contract protected by the Constitution of the United States? 2. Is it impaired by the acts under which the defendant holds?

. . . This is plainly a contract to which the donors, the Trustees, and the Crown (to whose rights and obligations New Hampshire succeeds) were the original parties. . . . It is, then, a contract within the letter of the Constitution, and within its spirit also, unless the fact that the property is invested by the donors in Trustees for the promotion of religion and education, for the benefit of persons who are perpetually changing, though the objects remain the same, shall create a particular exception taking this case out of the prohibition contained in the Constitution.

It is more than possible that the preservation of rights of this description was not particularly in the view of the framers of the Constitution when the clause under consideration was introduced into that instrument. It is probable that interferences of more frequent occurrence, to which the temptation was stronger, and of which the mischief was more extensive, constituted the great motive for imposing this restriction on the State legislatures. But although a particular and a rare case may not, in itself, be of sufficient magnitude to induce a rule, yet it must be governed by the rule, when established, unless some plain and strong reason for excluding it can be given. It is not enough to say that this particular case was not in the mind of the convention when the article was framed, nor of the American people when it was adopted. It is necessary to go further and to say that, had this particular case been suggested, the language would have been so varied as to exclude it, or it would have been made a special exception. The case, being within the words of the rule, must be within its operation likewise, unless there be something in the literal construction so obviously absurd or mischievous or repugnant to the general spirit of the instrument as to justify those who expound the Constitution in making it an exception.

On what safe and intelligible ground can this exception stand? There is no expression in the Constitution, no sentiment delivered by its contemporaneous expounders, which would justify us in making it. In the absence of all authority of this kind, is there in the nature and reason of the case itself that which would sustain a construction of the Constitution not warranted by its words? Are contracts of this description of a character to excite so little interest that we must exclude them from the provisions of the Constitution as being unworthy of the attention of those who framed the instrument? Or does public policy so imperiously demand their remaining exposed to legislative alteration as to compel us, or rather permit us, to say that these words, which were introduced to give stability to contracts and which in their plain import comprehend this contract, must yet be so construed as to exclude it?

Almost all eleemosynary corporations, those which are created for the promotion of religion, of charity, or of education, are of the same character. The law of this case is the law of all. In every literary or charitable institution, unless the objects of the bounty be themselves incorporated, the whole legal interest is in Trustees, and can be asserted only by them. The donors, or claimants of the bounty, if they can appear in Court at all, can appear only to complain of the Trustees. In all other situations, they are identified with, and personated by, the Trustees, and their rights are to be defended and maintained by them. . . . Are they of so little estimation in the United States that contracts for their benefit must be excluded from the protection of words which in their natural import include them? Or do such contracts so necessarily require new modeling by the authority of the legislature that the ordinary rules of construction must be disregarded in order to leave them exposed to legislative alteration?

All feel that these objects are not deemed unimportant in the United States. The interest which this case has excited proves that they are not. The framers of the Constitution did not deem them unworthy of its care and protection. They have, though in a different mode, manifested their respect for science by reserving to the government of the Union the power "to promote the progress of science and useful arts by securing for limited times, to authors and inventors, the exclusive right to their respective writings and discoveries."

They have so far withdrawn science and the useful arts from the action of the State governments. Why then should they be supposed so regardless of contracts made for the advancement of literature as to intend to exclude them from provisions, made for the security of ordinary contracts between man and man? No reason for making this supposition is perceived.

The motives suggested at the bar grow out of the original appointment of the Trustees, which is supposed to have been in a spirit hostile to the genius of our government, and the presumption that, if allowed to continue themselves, they now are, and must remain forever, what they originally were. Hence is inferred the necessity of applying to this corporation, and to other similar corporations, the correcting and improving hand of the legislature.

The opinion of the Court, after mature deliberation, is that this is a contract the obligation of which cannot be impaired without violating the Constitution of the United States. This opinion appears to us to be equally supported by reason and by the former decisions of this Court.

2. We next proceed to the inquiry whether its obligation has been impaired by those acts of the Legislature of New Hampshire to which the special verdict refers.

. . . It has been already stated that the act "to amend the charter, and enlarge and improve the corporation of Dartmouth College" increases the number of Trustees to twenty-one, gives the appointment of the additional members to the executive of the State, and creates a Board of Overseers, to consist of twenty-five persons, of whom twenty-one are also appointed by the Executive of New Hampshire, who have power to inspect and control the most important acts of the Trustees.

According to the tenor of the charter, then, the Trustees might, without impropriety, appoint a President and other professors from their own body. This is a power not entirely unconnected with an interest. Even if the proposition of the counsel for the defendant were sustained, if it were admitted that those contracts only are protected by the Constitution, a beneficial interest in which is vested in the party, who appears in Court to assert that interest, yet it is by no means clear that the Trustees of Dartmouth College have no beneficial interest in themselves. But the Court has deemed it unnecessary to investigate this particular point, being of opinion on general principles that, in these private eleemosynary institutions, the body corporate, as possessing the whole legal and equitable interest and completely representing the donors for the purpose of executing the trust, has rights which are protected by the Constitution.

It results from this opinion that the acts of the Legislature of New Hampshire which are stated in the special verdict found in this cause are repugnant to the Constitution of the United States, and that the judgment on this special verdict ought to have been for the plaintiffs. The judgment of the State Court must, therefore, be reversed.

COHENS v. VIRGINIA

19 U.S. 264 (1821)

Opinion: Marshall, joined by Duvall, Johnson, Livingston, Story, Todd

In this case, two brothers violated state law by selling District of Columbia lottery tickets in Virginia. The brothers argued that, because Congress had authorized the sale of those tickets, their arrest was an unconstitutional violation of the Supremacy Clause found in Article VI, which reads, "This Constitution, and the Laws of the United States which shall be made in Pursuance thereof; and all Treaties made, or which shall be made, under the Authority of the United States, shall be the supreme Law of the Land; and the Judges in every State shall be bound thereby, any Thing in the Constitution or Laws of any State to the Contrary notwithstanding." Again, the Supreme Court articulated its power to review state court decisions. Although the Court upheld the defendants' convictions, it rejected the Virginia court's claim that it could not review the constitutionality of state criminal proceedings.

MR. CHIEF JUSTICE MARSHALL *delivered the opinion of the Court.*

The American States, as well as the American people, have believed a close and firm Union to be essential to their liberty and to their happiness. They have been taught by experience that this Union cannot exist without a government for the whole, and they have been taught by the same experience that this government would be a mere shadow, that must disappoint all their hopes, unless invested with large portions of that sovereignty which belongs to independent States. Under the influence of this opinion, and thus instructed by experience, the American people, in the conventions of their respective States, adopted the present Constitution.

If it could be doubted whether, from its nature, it were not supreme in all cases where it is empowered to act, that doubt would be removed by the declaration that "this Constitution, and the laws of the United States, which shall be made in pursuance thereof, and all treaties made, or which shall be made, under the authority of the United States, shall be the supreme law of the land; and the judges in every State shall be bound thereby; any thing in the Constitution or laws of any State to the contrary notwithstanding."

This is the authoritative language of the American people, and, if gentlemen please, of the American States. It marks, with lines too strong to be mistaken the characteristic distinction between the government of the Union and those of the States. The general government, though limited as to its objects, is supreme with respect to those objects. This principle is a part of the Constitution, and if there be any who deny its necessity, none can deny its authority.

The powers of the Union, on the great subjects of war, peace, and commerce, and on many others, are in themselves limitations of the sovereignty of the States; but, in addition to these, the sovereignty of the States is surrendered in many instances where the surrender can only operate to the benefit of the people, and where, perhaps, no other power is conferred on Congress than a conservative power to maintain the principles established in the Constitution. The maintenance of these principles in their purity is certainly among the great duties of the government. One of the instruments by which this duty may be peaceably performed is the judicial department. It is authorized to decide all cases of every description arising under the Constitution or laws of the United States.

From this general grant of jurisdiction, no exception is made of those cases in which a State may be a party. When we consider the situation of the government of the Union and of a State in relation to each other; the nature of our Constitution; the subordination of the State governments to that Constitution; the great purpose for which jurisdiction over all cases arising under the Constitution and laws of the United States is confided to the judicial department; are we at liberty to insert in this general grant an exception of those cases in which a State may be a party? Will the spirit of the Constitution justify this attempt to control its words? We think it will not. We think a case arising under the Constitution or laws of the United States is cognizable in the Courts of the Union whoever may be the parties to that case.

Box 1-2 Frequency of the Judicial Review Power

Judicial review was originally invoked primarily in an attempt to define the proper scope of governmental powers. In the twentieth century, the power was invoked much more frequently than in the nineteenth century. Does this suggest the impact of the decision in *Marbury v. Madison* was felt more strongly in the twentieth century than at the time it was decided? Figure 1.2 illustrates the number of laws struck down in the nineteenth and twentieth centuries, both state and federal, as well as the total number of laws (including local ordinances) invalidated by the Court. As shown in the graph, in the nineteenth century, judicial review was primarily directed against state governments. In the twentieth century, as the Court grew increasingly confident in striking down federal legislation, the number of invalidated state laws skyrocketed as well.

Figure 1.2. Cases Ruling Laws Unconstitutional

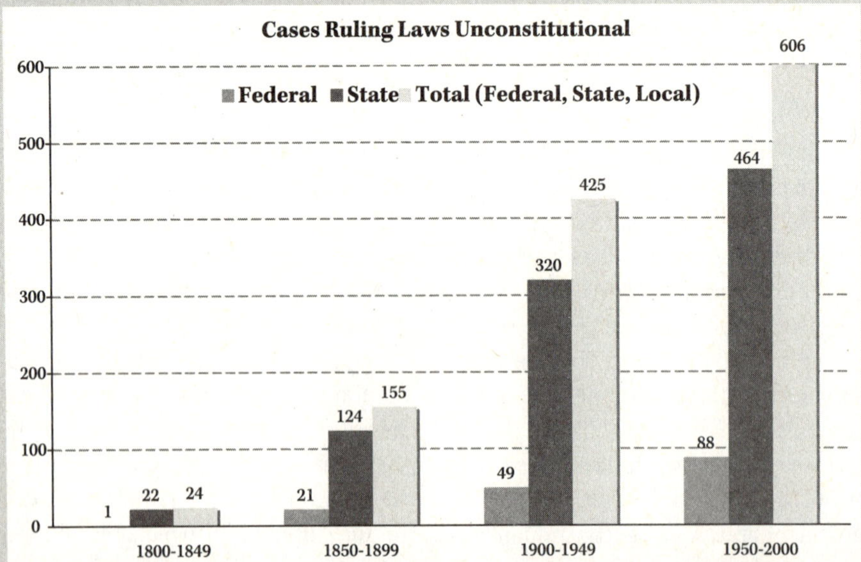

Data from *Analysis and Interpretation of the Constitution, Annotations of Cases Decided by the Supreme Court of the United States*, Senate Document No. 108-17, 2002 Edition. Available at *http://www.gpoaccess.gov/constitution/*.

Figure 1.3 paints a more fine-grained picture of the history of judicial review. Prior to the Civil War, the Supreme Court would occasionally strike down state laws, and it only invalidated two federal statutes: the Judiciary Act of 1789 in *Marbury v. Madison*, and the Missouri Compromise in the notorious case of *Dred Scott v. Sandford*. During the Reconstruction era, the Court increasingly asserted its power, reacting against legislation ushered in by the overwhelmingly Republican Congress and enforcing the rights in the new Fourteenth Amendment against the states. By the turn of the century, the Court was leaning heavily on the Fourteenth Amendment to protect economic liberty, striking down a bevy of progressive labor regulations at the state level. The Court also sought to obstruct President Franklin D. Roosevelt's first New Deal program, but eventually it backed down, ushering in a period of deference to democratically enacted law. U.S. Supreme Court Chief Justice Earl Warren's tenure during the 1960s witnessed new heights in the exercise of judicial review, expanding constitutional protections of individual rights. At the close of the twentieth century, a turn toward federalism led to a decline in the number of state statutes overturned, even as the amount of federal legislation invalidated increased.

Figure 1.3. Cases Ruling Laws Unconstitutional by 12-Year Period

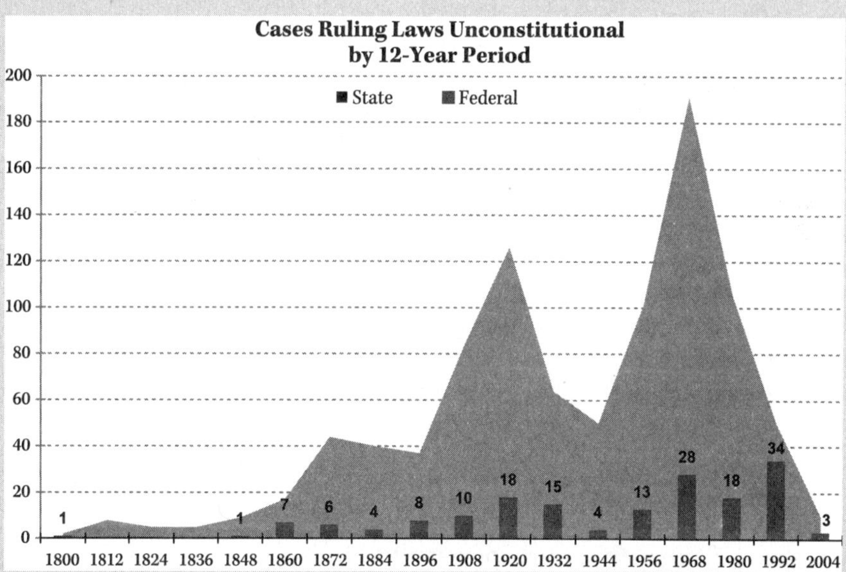

Data from *Analysis and Interpretation of the Constitution, Annotations of Cases Decided by the Supreme Court of the United States*, Senate Document No. 108-17, 2002 Edition, and 2008 Supplement. Available at *http://www.gpoaccess.gov/constitution/*.

SYNTHESIS QUESTIONS FOR FURTHER DISCUSSION: CHAPTER 1

1. The power of the Supreme Court to strike down federal laws as unconstitutional does not appear in the text of the Constitution itself. Does this fact give weight to Alexander Bickel's concern about whether the Court, an unelected body, should have the power to strike down laws passed by elected officials in a nation that considers itself democratic? Both Chief Justice John Marshall, in his opinion in *Marbury v. Madison*, and Alexander Hamilton, in *The Federalist*, attempt to answer this challenge by appealing to the idea of the rule of law itself. The Court's authority, they argue, derives from its role in interpreting law. Given that the Constitution is law, they claim, the Court should interpret it. Is this a persuasive argument for the Court's judicial review power?

In evaluating the arguments of Chief Justice Marshall and Hamilton in favor of the Court's review power, it might be helpful to consider the following questions:

a. Does the lack of constitutional text authorizing judicial review delegitimize this practice? Does the fact that *The Federalist*, including our reading from Hamilton, played a part in convincing citizens to ratify the Constitution mean that these papers themselves have a particular kind of constitutional weight?
b. Is there anything about the training of justices of the Supreme Court that gives them inherent authority over constitutional interpretation? For instance, although legal training is not required by the Constitution for appointment to the Court, does it matter that judges have been trained in law? Given that the ranks of top lawyers do not usually accurately reflect the population as a whole, is there an elitist element in the Court's decisions? Does legal training equip lawyers who are appointed to the Court with a set of skills that make the justices uniquely positioned to interpret the Constitution?
c. The Court is appointed by the president in consultation with the Senate. Do the democratic credentials of these two bodies give the Court a further claim to authority?

2. Bickel challenges the Court's power of judicial review, and others have argued further that this power inheres also in the other branches of government. Thomas Jefferson's challenge to Hamilton is commonly seen as the original view of the theory of constitutional interpretation now known as departmentalism. In his letter, Jefferson stresses that the rights enshrined in the Constitution have a meaning independent of any particular institutional actor's interpretation. Why then, Jefferson asks, should any one body, even the Supreme Court, have a monopoly on constitutional interpretation? In particular, Jefferson is concerned with the potential fallibility of the Court. If we assume that the Court is the final arbiter of the Constitution, might that inhibit citizens from recognizing its mistakes? It might be interesting to consider how Hamilton and Chief Justice Marshall would have responded to this claim. Are there any reasons to suggest that the Supreme Court might make fewer mistakes in matters of constitutional interpretation than elected bodies?

3. While the letter from Jefferson to Judge Spencer Roane emphasizes the role of other branches of the federal government in constitutional interpretation, Jefferson also held the view that states should have a role in this process. In particular, when the Federalist President John Adams and Congress crafted the Alien and Sedition Acts, which limited the free speech rights of political dissidents, Jefferson and James Madison drafted the Kentucky and Virginia resolutions declaring these acts unconstitutional. The Supreme Court was notably silent on the constitutionality of the Alien and Sedition Acts, and after its failure to speak, Jefferson and Madison turned to state legislatures in an attempt to declare them unconstitutional. Is there reason to believe, given the example of the Alien and Sedition Acts, that it is beneficial to give the states, in addition to the Court, a role in constitutional interpretation? What problems might accompany a departmentalist theory that allows for constitutional interpretation among the various branches of government? What problems might accompany a theory that provides a role for the states in interpreting the ultimate meaning of the Constitution? In answering these questions, consider the Court opinions you read in which the Supreme Court reviewed the constitutionality of state as opposed to federal law.

4. Brutus's arguments against ratification tend to emphasize that the Court will inevitably become an unchecked power that will fail to respect the interests of citizens. In contrast to Hamilton's defense of the Court and its review power, does Jefferson's notion of departmentalism offer a different retort to Brutus? What might Jefferson say about Brutus's contentions about the power of the Court under Article III, including his contention that the Court will be unchecked because justices are appointed for life?

5. In *Dartmouth College v. Woodward*, you saw the Supreme Court invalidate an act by a state legislature attempting to turn the institution from a private to a public entity. Are there any particular problems for democratic self-government that are raised when the Court strikes down state as opposed to federal law? Consider whether this case challenges the Court's democratic credentials with respect to our readings from Bickel and Brutus.

KEY TERMS

bill of attainder: Legislation that declares an individual guilty of a crime without the benefit of a trial.

Democratic-Republican Party: The party of Thomas Jefferson, the President of the United States when *Marbury v. Madison* was decided.

departmentalism: The view that the various branches of government ought to have a say in constitutional interpretation.

ex post facto law: A law retroactively imposed on parties, in contrast to laws that govern future action.

Federalist Party: The party of President John Adams, Chief Justice John Marshall, and William Marbury.

judicial review: The power to strike down legislative or executive acts on grounds that they are incompatible with a provision or provisions of the Constitution.

judicial supremacy: The view that the Court is the final and supreme interpreter of constitutional meaning.

original jurisdiction: The power of the Court to be the first court to hear a case. This is in contrast to appellate jurisdiction, where the Court reviews a lower court decision.

CHAPTER 2

FROM JUDICIAL REVIEW TO JUDICIAL SUPREMACY

In the previous chapter, we examined historical justifications for the Court's review power. At this point in American history, this power of the Supreme Court is well established and widely accepted. Yet, when it comes to the question of whether the Court *should* have this power, there is controversy among scholars. Not all contemporary polities, after all, have judicial review of legislation. In contrast to our system, some systems retain "legislative supremacy" in which the legislature, not the court, has the final word about review of legislation. In this chapter, we will see that the Supreme Court itself has now declared in *Boerne v. Flores* that it not only has the power of judicial review but that its word is the final, decisive interpretation of the Constitution. This view is widely known as "judicial supremacy." Our readings begin with a look at the Court's contemporary judicial review power and examine its legitimacy, or lack thereof.

Whereas the previous chapter grounded the question of judicial authority in debates that took place during the Founding, this chapter examines the contemporary extension of this controversy.

We begin with a reading by U.S. Supreme Court Justice Stephen Breyer, in which he tackles the problem of the Court's democratic nature. For Justice Breyer, the counter-majoritarian difficulty should be answered not by looking beyond democracy but rather by rethinking the meaning of democracy. Justice Breyer rejects the idea that democracy is brute majoritarianism. Instead, he focuses on the ways in which the Supreme Court can bring about results that enhance democracy. Whereas Alexander Bickel had seen the Court as posing a threat to democracy, Breyer argues that there is in fact a role for the Supreme Court in promoting what he refers to as the "active liberty" of self-government.

Ronald Dworkin extends Justice Breyer's argument that the Court has a fundamentally democratic purpose. He argues that when the Court serves the goals of democracy by protecting rights, self-government suffers no loss. For instance, he argues that the decision by the Court to strike down an anti-flag burning law in Texas was not undemocratic because the right of free speech was protected even though the Court was forced to strike down a decision in which many had participated through the democratic process. You might also think about Dworkin's framework when reading *Cooper v. Aaron*, a case in which there was massive resistance to the Supreme Court's desegregation order by the people of Arkansas. It is clear that both Justice Breyer and Dworkin think that there is a strong role for judicial review in a democracy. But does either or both of them defend judicial supremacy, the notion that the Court's role is final? Does either of these thinkers leave any role for constitutional interpretation by the other branches, the "departmentalism" urged by Thomas Jefferson in the previous chapter? In examining the possible contemporary relevance of departmentalism, it is also helpful to consider instances where the Court refuses to even hear a dispute that concerns the other branches. In *Nixon v. United States*, the Court employed its "political question" doctrine, according to which it does not hear some disputes on the grounds that they are better resolved by the political, elected branches of government. We will consider whether this doctrine, which is clearly an instance of judicial restraint, is a form of departmentalism.

Whereas Justice Breyer and Dworkin are among the most prominent contemporary defenders of judicial review, Larry Kramer and Jeremy Waldron are among its greatest critics. Kramer in particular modernizes Jefferson's classic worry that judicial review by the Supreme Court could turn into judicial supremacy. Kramer argues that many of the Court's decisions in recent years have been a power grab in which the democratic process has been usurped by a few powerful individuals. In its *Boerne v. Flores* decision, which we excerpt here, the Supreme Court declared itself the sole authority in determining the meaning of the Constitution and rejected Congress's own attempt to correct the Court's interpretive framework. Indeed, Kramer goes so far as to claim that the Court's intervention in the 2000 election dispute between candidates George Bush and Al Gore is emblematic of its power grab. The Court is no mere interpreter of the Constitution, according to Kramer; rather, it has usurped the power of the democratic process in a way that verges upon tyranny.

Kramer does not dispute the Court's judicial review power, long established as part of the American tradition. Rather, he questions whether the Court has an exclusive right to interpret the Constitution, as it seems to suggest in several of its decisions. On a view of judicial supremacy, perhaps best exemplified by the *Boerne v. Flores* case, the Court's interpretation of the meaning of the Constitution cannot be corrected by any of the other branches, including direct attempts by Congress to reverse Supreme Court decisions by statute as opposed to constitutional amendment. One problem with an understanding of the Court as a supreme interpreter is that it seems to suggest that even when the Court interprets the Constitution in a way that is flawed (think, for instance, of *Plessy v. Ferguson*, establishing the principle that segregation is consistent with the Equal Protection Clause of the Fourteenth Amendment), its decisions still must be respected as final and authoritative interpretations. Such a view leaves no room for constitutional interpretation by either democratically elected branches or citizens. As you read through this chapter, consider whether Kramer's criticisms of judicial supremacy are correct.

Waldron, in contrast to any of the other thinkers we examine in this part, presents a comprehensive critique of judicial review in its entirety. Going further than Kramer, Waldron is with Bickel in thinking that the power of judicial review in the hands of the Court should be understood as fundamentally undemocratic. Rejecting the theories of democracy posited by Justice Breyer and Dworkin, as well as that of Alexander Hamilton, Waldron claims that democracy is best understood as majority rule. Moreover, unlike Bickel, he believes that there is no justification for overturning the people's power to decide. Like many other scholars that we have examined in this chapter, Waldron is concerned with the protection of rights. Because citizens disagree about the content of rights, Waldron claims, the power to determine such rights is best left to the legislature.

Our case selection includes two of the most central controversies in the modern practice of judicial review, *Boerne v. Flores* and *Bush v. Gore.* The cases are notable because in both the Court asserts power over other branches of government, thus clearly raising the specter of judicial supremacy. In reading *Boerne v. Flores* you will enter into one of the clearest conflicts between Congress and the Supreme Court over the meaning of the Constitution. As you will see, in this case Congress attempted to correct what it regarded as a mistaken Supreme Court interpretation of the First Amendment's Free Exercise Clause. In studying this case, we ask whether Congress can correct the Court's interpretation of a fundamental right.

Bush v. Gore will likely be remembered as one of the Court's most controversial cases of all time. As was the case in *Marbury v. Madison, Bush v. Gore* raised potential issues of partisanship. Ultimately, the question the Court faced was whether it would, in effect, end the controversy over the 2000 election. As you will see, the legal issues in the case concern the Equal Protection Clause of the Fourteenth Amendment and the issue about the requirements of the Court's Article III powers. But as you read it, think (with *Marbury v. Madison* in mind) about whether the Court should have taken the case or issued a ruling with such a drastic consequence. Did the Court here rest its argument on an assumption of judicial supremacy?

Although this part contains many examples of what might be considered judicial supremacy as well as readings charging the Court with usurping the authority of the other branches, we also include in this chapter two cases that illustrate limits on the power of the contemporary Court. In *United States v. Nixon,* we examine the political question doctrine, which limits the power of the Court to overturn decisions that the Constitution leaves to other branches. We also examine, in *Lujan v. Defenders of Wildlife,* the "standing doctrine" and the "case or controversy" requirement as examples of procedural limits on the Court. As we will see, the Court has limitations on its ability to initiate policy that the executive and the legislative branches do not.

Justice Stephen Breyer

JUDICIAL REVIEW: A PRACTICING JUDGE'S PERSPECTIVE

19 Oxford J. Legal Stud. 153 (1999)

My description will try to help you evaluate one important criticism of "independent judicial review" by which I mean the grant of legal authority to judges to set aside statutes upon the ground that they violate provisions of a written constitution. Such a system, says the criticism, substitutes for the views of legislators the views of judges. The judges are unelected, they interpret highly abstract constitutional language, e.g. the word "liberty," and they work in an ivory tower. The results are undemocratic, subjective, and impractical.

At the outset let me remind you of several features of our Supreme Court and our Constitution, with which many of you are already familiar. I do so because of their relevance to the later discussion. First, the Court's membership reflects a diversity of backgrounds and points of view. Vacancies arise infrequently because a President must appoint, and the Senate confirm, each of its nine members (currently seven men, two women) "for life." American judges enter their judicial career typically in mid-life after experience elsewhere. Eight of the present justices have had previous judicial experience in lower courts; and, before that, six had experience as lawyers in government; four in private practice; four as law professors. Republican Presidents appointed seven of us; a Democratic President, two. Length of term and the appointment process tend to guarantee diversity of constitutional views.

Second, the Court's role in judicial decision-making is limited. Much of our work involves the resolution of lower court conflicts about the interpretation of federal law. That law—the federal Constitution, congressional statutes, federal agency action—is itself limited, because the 50 states, not the federal government, are responsible for much of American law, including family law, property law, contract law, tort law, most criminal law, and most other commercial law. Perhaps 95 per cent or more of all judicial proceedings take place in state courts. Moreover, within the area of federal law, we hear only a handful of cases. We receive about 7600 requests for hearings each year; we grant and decide fewer than 100. (Overall, there may be more than 10 million court cases brought annually in the USA.)

Third, our decisions, like those of Supreme, or Constitutional, Courts in other nations have considerable legal and practical significance. In part that is because, like the House of Lords, the cases we take, by definition, are those that present open legal issues, with strong arguments on both sides. In part it is because most of our decisions, as a practical matter, are final. In part it is because our history includes certain decisions, such as those involving desegregation or electoral reapportionment, that have changed the life of our nation. I shall return to the way in which the finality of our decisions can affect what we do. For the moment, simply keep in mind the fact that our Court is comprised of a small number of men and women of diverse views and backgrounds, appointed for life, who decide a small number of cases involving federal law, and whose decisions are usually final and frequently have considerable practical significance.

Let me also remind you of several relevant features of our Constitution. The document, adopted in 1789 and importantly amended after our 19th century Civil War, established the federal government and, in doing so, sets forth a framework for democratic government. It initially included: an explicit delegation of powers to the federal government (reserving all others to the states); an allocation of governmental powers (among three branches of federal government); protections of certain liberties (such as free speech, press, and religion, and against unreasonable searches and seizures) from federal interference; and guarantees of fair procedures for those threatened with criminal prosecution. The Civil War amendments extended the scope of these protections by guaranteeing them against infringement by state governments; and it added guarantees to individual citizens of fair, and equal, treatment by all government.

For present purposes it is important also to remember that: the document is brief—seven Articles, 27 Amendments. Often its language is open ended, e.g. "no state shall . . . deprive any person of life, liberty, or property, without due process of law; nor deny to any person . . . the equal protection of the laws." It is difficult to amend—amendment ordinarily requiring the affirmative vote of two-thirds of each house of Congress plus approval by three-quarters of the states (or a special "convention"). And it is not simply a set of aspirations, but a legal document setting forth rules with legal force.

Judicial interpretations of the Constitution have binding legal force, not subject to legislative override (except through constitutional amendment). The judicial power to set aside laws, including congressional statutes, as unconstitutional rests upon a judicial interpretation of the Constitution, which the Court made nearly 200 years ago, in *Marbury v. Madison*. The Court's authority to set aside unconstitutional laws is now accepted. The public defers to nearly all judicial interpretations of the document, even when those interpretations are unpopular, controversial, and of debatable merit.

To summarize: the framework-creating document is brief, general, permanent, and effective.

Let me now describe the "democratic anomaly," a matter central to how citizens, constitutional scholars, and judges think about constitutional decision-making, and which appears frequently as the subject of public and academic constitutional debate. The question at the heart of the anomaly is why a democracy—a political system based on representation and accountability—should entrust the final, or near final, making of such highly significant decisions to judges—unelected, independent, and insulated from the direct impact of public opinion.

I can narrow the anomaly by pointing out that all government, to achieve flexibility, must involve the exercise of delegated authority. Given delegation, enacted law will not necessarily reflect the views of a particular electorate; nor will law that takes the form of treaties, regulations, and administrative rulings necessarily reflect the views of a particular legislature. Democracies also delegate authority to judges—and properly so. Who would want to convict a person accused of murder on the basis of a popular vote? Nor could one reasonably advocate a system of civil law that instantly changed to reflect the views of a popular majority, for such law would lack the stability that any form of government under law requires.

For that matter, any actual democracy contains many non-majoritarian institutions (e.g. a Senate) and procedures (e.g. seniority).

I can narrow the anomaly further by pointing out that many non-constitutional judicial decisions are already, in a sense, immune from later legislative revision. As a practical matter, lack of legislative time or interest or the popularity of a judicial decision, means that the legislature usually will not overturn a judge's statutory decision despite its legal power to do so. . . .

I may have narrowed the anomaly, but it still exists. In fact, one could claim that the very systems just described still embody that anomaly to the extent that they offer special protection from the popular will. In any event, our own system does not permit a legislative override (except through amendment). Can we "resolve" the remaining "democratic" anomaly by admitting it and then trying to justify it? Let me remind you of several classic efforts to do so.

Some have pointed out, for example, that many, though not all, of the basic rights that our Constitution protects are themselves important preconditions of a well-functioning democratic system of government. The guarantee of free speech, for example, by helping to secure citizens' access to even the most bizarre points of view assures voters the opportunity to exercise an informed democratic choice. Many "equal protection" guarantees mean that government will not improperly weigh the voice of one citizen more heavily than that of another.

Others have argued that the American Constitution, with its allocation of powers among many different governmental units, requires a "referee" (i.e. the courts) to prevent overreaching. Still others say that "democracy" simply is, not only majority rule, but also the protection of minority rights — a method, for example, of preventing the "people drunk" from undoing the will of the "people sober." Given the 20th century's history of governments unable to withstand popular demands for mistreatment of minorities and the abandonment of democracy, one might see judicial review as a kind of institutional ballast, helping to stabilize the kind of democracy that so many nations today enjoy.

Still, there remains much to reconcile with "majoritarian" democracy, for example, certain constitutional protections such as the Eighth Amendment's prohibition of "cruel and unusual punishments," or the Fourteenth Amendment's protection of certain aspects of family life that fall within the scope of the word "liberty." Nor can one easily justify, as necessary to the preservation of that democracy, the independent determination by judges of related claims, based either upon constitutional words such as "liberty" (e.g. the claim of a constitutionally protected "right to die") or upon the words in a Court opinion interpreting those words (such as a claim about the constitutionally required implementation of a court decree forbidding certain kinds of racial discrimination). And, of course, in a sense, once one feels it necessary to justify the "anomaly," one has thereby admitted the problem.

Thus, I should like to return to narrowing: our judiciary, aware of the anomaly, tries to minimize its impact through the use of rules, standards or canons that recognize the problem. For example, the standard of constitutionality applicable to statutes focuses, not on the statute's wisdom, but on its constitutionality, which often concerns the statute's "rationality"; the rule (stare decisis) for determining when to overrule a previous case is less strict in constitutional than in statutory matters; a canon of interpretation requires courts to try to save a statute by interpreting it in a way that will avoid a serious constitutional problem. There are others. I also believe it important to note that judges, aware of the anomaly, often seek through their interpretive attitude to reflect the constitutionally vested primacy of legislative decision-making, even in cases that do not fall squarely within an interpretive canon.

But however much I may narrow, ultimately there remains an important set of cases, for example, cases involving privacy or religious freedom, that can require us, when interpreting or applying the Constitution, directly to frustrate the legislature's express objective. I turn to that set of cases — those in which there is an inevitable tension between the will of the elected legislature and the work of the unelected judge. Does judicial decision-making there mean subjective, impractical decision-making — or, to return to Lord Copper, up to what point?

You are aware that language, history, and precedent will answer many constitutional questions. Moreover, some fine constitutional judges have believed that, even in more difficult cases, a single factor, such as the Constitution's language, or its history, can itself significantly constrain subjective decision-making. For myself, however, I cannot find a touchstone in any such single factor. Instead, I believe that a realistic appraisal of subjectivity must take account of certain constraints, related to each other, which I shall describe in five parts and follow with an example.

First, judges of a constitutional court, like all judges, find constraints in the "rules," canons, principles, and institutional understandings of the judicial enterprise itself. Judge Learned Hand answered the charge of "subjectivity" by pointing to "those books." I assume he meant metaphorically to include (in common law matters) the common law tradition, and (in statutory matters) language, structure, history, precedent, purpose, and consequences — all of which permit a judge to find a "better" and a "worse" answer even to the most difficult of statutory questions, even where language (for example, antitrust law's "contract, combination or conspiracy in restraint of trade") is open-ended.

Second, as is true of any craft, experience both teaches and constrains its practitioners. And constitutional court judges do develop a kind of special experience. Our work differs in kind from most trial court work, for unlike trial courts we do not determine facts or apply previously elaborated law to those facts. It also differs in kind from some of the work of the courts of appeals, in that we do not review for error the trial court's application of previously elaborated law to the facts of a particular case. As Chief Justice Taft pointed out in 1921, "Litigants . . . have [already] had two chances." Rather we most frequently hear and decide cases that involve conflicts of interpretation among the lower courts, thereby producing uniform national law. That "law interpreting" work resembles that of the courts of appeals when it involves statutes. Our work does not resemble theirs when we interpret the Constitution. Since all federal and state courts have the power to interpret the Constitution, the difference is one of degree, not kind. But it is one of considerable degree, for open questions of constitutional law in our Court become a steady diet. And the difference in degree is important in that the experience, the steadiness, and diversity of a constitutional diet, naturally lead a judge to try to see, and to understand, the Constitution as a coherent whole.

Third, that effort, in my view, leads one to see the Constitution as a "framework"—a concept that I believe plays as central a role in our Constitutional decision-making as does the notion of "legislative purpose" in statutory interpretation, or "comparative institutional expertise" in administrative law. The concept acts as a functional limitation, for it reminds us that we almost always must determine, not whether a statute or other legal rule is wise (e.g. whether handguns should be regulated or whether doctors should be free to assist a patient's suicide), but rather who has the legal power to make such a decision: individual or government? state or federal government? executive, legislative, or judicial branch? And it reminds us (as does our small size and limited docket capacity) that a constitutional power-allocating answer must last, irrespective of today's politics, for many years to come.

The concept acts as a substantive limitation in that the Constitution's provisions (read together) create a framework for a certain kind of workable government: that government is characterized by the rule of law; democratic responsibility for decision-making; the protection of basic human liberties; fair procedures; equal treatment of citizens; and widespread dispersal of governmental powers (among different levels and branches of government) to assure that no small group of individuals becomes too powerful. . . .

Fourth, I find constraint in the need for each decision to fit within what one might call the legal "fabric," a fabric that is itself tied, through purpose and through consequence, to actual human behavior. To say this is, in a sense, to repeat my first point, for every legal decision interacts (one might say "horizontally") with other decisions, principles, standards, practices, and institutional understandings, always modifying the "web" of the law; and every decision affects (one might say "vertically") the way in which that web, in turn, affects the world. Judges must often take account of "vertical" effects both because individual laws have particular individual purposes that guide legal interpretation and because legal institutions themselves are designed to help us solve the human problems that called them into being.

I suggest, however, that, in respect to constitutional matters, estimates of "vertical" effects, i.e. the real world consequences of "horizontal" interactions, have a particularly important role to play. In order to write an opinion, one might for example, ask not only the obvious "horizontal" questions, about say language, history, and precedent, but also such "vertical" questions as: (a) How will lower courts, lawyers, government officials, and other institutions (e.g. businesses, trade unions), who must rely upon the Court's cases for authoritative guidance, implement the opinion's holding? For example, should a constitutional rule that excludes illegally seized evidence from criminal trials be applied to court officials who negligently fail to check a computer-generated suspect list, in light of the need for a uniform, easily administered basic rule, or should it except them from the rule on the ground that their inclusion is administratively unnecessary? (b) What theme or "music" does the opinion's rhetorical language generate? Consider the powerful practical effects, above and beyond an opinion's holding, that use of a word like "sovereignty," or a metaphor such as "public forum," can have in cases involving, say, Indian tribes or free speech. Think, too, of the disastrous practical impact of the phrase "separate but equal" on American life and the Court's consequent difficulties in extricating the law from the phrase's implication in the segregated society that it helped to bring about.

(c) What effect will the opinion have upon the working relations between courts and other major governmental institutions? How will it affect the way in which the Court itself works as an institution? (d) Should the opinion focus only on the facts characterized narrowly—say, to avoid commitment to a "theme," where consequences are not known, or where such commitment might mislead the public, or will so narrow a focus prevent the opinion from generating any clear and important principle?

Ultimately, what is the opinion's real-world impact (its effect, not its popularity), considered in light of basic constitutional objectives?

The answers to these practical questions constrain. Where a serious discrepancy develops between the world as described in terms of the Constitution's ultimate objectives and the world a particular decision helped to create, the constitutional rule will change. The Supreme Court realized by 1954, for example, that the Constitution's Equal Protection Clause could not tolerate the racially segregated society that the Court's earlier "separate but equal" cases had helped to establish. It properly overruled those cases, thereby indicating that constitutional interpretation itself is an ongoing, iterative, and self-correcting process.

Fifth, constraints arise out of the judge's own need for personal consistency over time. Justice O'Connor has described a judge's initial decisions as creating footprints that later decisions will follow. Moreover, the appointment process likely assures that judges have awareness, through prior experience of the nation's history and cultural heritage. Those facts, combined with diversity of membership and longevity of service, help to dampen radical swings in the Court's approach to constitutional problems.

I have tried to put the classical criticisms—"undemocratic," "subjective," "impractical"—in perspective. Since the interpretive system I describe is not mechanical but depends upon human judgment, since the constraints I mention only bind to a degree, and since the Court at certain times in its history has gone seriously awry, I cannot deny that the criticisms retain validity—"up to a point." Why then, why, one might ask, as democratic forms of government have become increasingly prevalent, in for example, Latin America and the former Eastern Bloc, have democratic societies increasingly tried to create independent judiciaries with final, or near final, authority to interpret basic legal documents that guarantee basic rights?

The obvious answer is that these nations increasingly have measured the criticisms against what they see as a need, a need for the protection of democratically structured government and of basic liberties that an independent judiciary can help to provide. That independent judiciary may protect them by helping gradually to develop among citizens and legislators liberty-protecting habits based in part upon their expectation that liberty-infringing laws will turn out not to be laws. And such protection might seem particularly necessary in a new democracy or one with a highly diverse citizenry or sizeable minority groups. That independent judiciary may also protect through the kind of force—ultimately based upon habit and expectations—that a court can bring to bear when, faced with a law that clearly violates a constitutional provision, that court says "no."

Several months ago I heard Justice Kennedy at New York University Law School welcome members of Russia's constitutional court into a profession that he said was both lonely and demanding of "courage." He was not then referring to the need to resolve difficult line-drawing problems correctly; but rather to the courage required at some times and in some places, to provide the proper answer to a clear violation.

These countervailing benefits, considered in light of the size of the USA, the diversity of its population, its history, its reliance upon law, may help to explain why, in my country, there is general public support for the institution of judicial review, whether or not that public praises or deplores the result in any particular case. You may understand both need and benefits if, of the many cases I might mention, I remind you of only one, the desegregation case *Brown v. Board of Education.*

Ronald Dworkin

FREEDOM'S LAW: THE MORAL READING OF THE AMERICAN CONSTITUTION

Introduction

Cambridge, MA: Harvard University Press (1996)

THE MAJORITARIAN PREMISE

Democracy means government by the people. But what does that mean? No explicit definition of democracy is settled among political theorists or in the dictionary. On the contrary, it is a matter of deep controversy what democracy really is. People disagree about which techniques of representation, which allocation of power among local, state, and national governments, which schedule and pattern of elections, and which other institutional arrangements provide the best available version of democracy. But beneath these familiar arguments over the structures of democracy there lies, I believe, a profound philosophical dispute about democracy's fundamental value or point, and one abstract issue is crucial to that dispute, though this is not always recognized. Should we accept or reject what I shall call the majoritarian premise?

This is a thesis about the fair outcomes of a political process: it insists that political procedures should be designed so that, at least on important matters, the decision that is reached is the decision that a majority or plurality of citizens favors, or would favor if it had adequate information and enough time for reflection. That goal sounds very reasonable, and many people, perhaps without much reflection, have taken it to provide the very essence of democracy. They believe that the complex political arrangements that constitute the democratic process should be aimed at and tested by this goal: that the laws that the complex democratic process enacts and the policies that it pursues should be those, in the end, that the majority of citizens would approve.

The majoritarian premise does not deny that individuals have important moral rights the majority should respect. It is not necessarily tied to some collectivist or utilitarian theory according to which such rights are nonsense. In some political communities, however — in Great Britain, for example — the majoritarian premise has been thought to entail that the community should defer to the majority's view about what these individual rights are, and how they are best respected and enforced. It is sometimes said that Britain has no constitution, but that is a mistake. Britain has an unwritten as well as a written constitution, and part of the former consists in understandings about what laws Parliament should not enact. It is part of the British constitution, for example, that freedom of speech is to be protected.

In the United States, however, most people who assume that the majoritarian premise states the ultimate definition of and justification for democracy nevertheless accept that on some occasions the will of the majority should not govern. They agree that the majority should not always be the final judge of when its own power should be limited to protect individual rights, and they accept that at least some of the Supreme Court's decisions that overturned popular legislation, as the *Brown* decision did, were right. The majoritarian premise does not rule out exceptions of that kind, but it does insist that in such cases, even if some derogation from majoritarian government is overall justified, something morally regrettable has happened, a moral cost has been paid. The premise supposes, in other words, that it is *always* unfair when a political majority is not allowed to have its way, so that even when there are strong enough countervailing reasons to justify this, the unfairness remains.

If we reject the majoritarian premise, we need a different, better account of the value and point of democracy. I will defend an account—which I call the constitutional conception of democracy—that does reject the majoritarian premise. It denies that it is a defining goal of democracy that collective decisions always or normally be those that a majority or plurality of citizens would favor if fully informed and rational. It takes the defining aim of democracy to be a different one that collective decisions be made by political institutions whose structure, composition, and practices treat all members of the community, as individuals, with equal concern and respect. This alternate account of the aim of democracy, it is true, demands much the same structure of government as the majoritarian premise does. It requires that day-to-day political decisions be made by officials who have been chosen in popular elections. But the constitutional conception requires these majoritarian procedures out of a concern for the equal status of citizens, and not out of any commitment to the goals of majority rule. So it offers no reason why some nonmajoritarian procedure should not be employed on special occasions when this would better protect or enhance the equal status that it declares to be the essence of democracy, and it does not accept that these exceptions are a cause of moral regret.

The constitutional conception of democracy, in short, takes the following attitude to majoritarian government. Democracy means government subject to conditions—we might call these the "democratic" conditions—of equal status for all citizens. When majoritarian institutions provide and respect the democratic conditions, then the verdicts of these institutions should be accepted by everyone for that reason. But when they do not, or when their provision or respect is defective, there can be no objection, in the name of democracy, to other procedures that protect and respect them better. The democratic conditions plainly include, for example, a requirement that public offices must in principle be open to members of all races and groups on equal terms. If some law provided that only members of one race were eligible for public office, then there would be no moral cost — no matter for moral regret at all — if a court that enjoyed the power to do so under a valid constitution struck down that law as unconstitutional. That would presumably be an occasion on which the majoritarian premise was flouted, but though this is a matter of regret according to the majoritarian conception of democracy, it is not according to the constitutional conception. Of course, it may be controversial what the democratic conditions, in detail, really are, and whether a particular law does offend them, But, according to the constitutional conception, it would be the question to object to a practice assigning those controversial questions for final decision to a court, on the ground that that practice is undemocratic, because that objection assumes that the laws in question respect the democratic conditions, and that is the very issue in controversy.

I hope it is now clear that the majoritarian premise has had a potent — if often unnoticed — grip on the imagination of American constitutional scholars and lawyers. Only that diagnosis explains the near unanimous view I described: that judicial review compromises democracy, so that the central question of constitutional theory must be whether and when that compromise is justified. That opinion is the child of a majoritarian conception of democracy, and therefore the grandchild of the majoritarian premise. It provokes the pointless search I described, for an interpretive strategy "intermediate" between the moral reading and originalism, and it tempts distinguished theorists into constructing Ptolemaic epicycles trying to reconcile constitutional practice with majoritarian principles.

So a complex issue of political morality — the validity of the majoritarian premise — is in fact at the heart of the long constitutional argument. The argument will remain confused until that issue is identified and addressed.

WE THE PEOPLE

We say that in a democracy government is by the people; we mean that the people collectively do things — elect leaders, for example — that no individual does or can do alone. There are two kinds of collective action, however — statistical and communal — and our view of the majoritarian premise may well turn on which kind of collective action we take democratic government to require.

Collective action is statistical when what the group does is only a matter of some function, rough or specific, of what the individual members of the group do on their own, that is, with no sense of doing something as a group.

Collective action is communal, however, when it cannot be reduced just to some statistical function of individual action, when it presupposes a special, distinct, collective *agency.* It is a matter of individuals acting together in a way that merges their separate actions into a further, unified, act that is together *theirs.*

I have already distinguished two conceptions of democracy: majoritarian and constitutional. The first accepts and the second rejects the majoritarian premise. The difference between statistical and communal collective action allows us to draw a second distinction, this time between two readings of the idea that democracy is government by "the people." The first reading is a statistical one: that in a democracy political decisions are made in accordance with the votes or wishes of some function — a majority or plurality — of individual citizens. The second is a communal reading: that in a democracy political decisions are taken by a distinct entity — the people as *such* — rather than by any set of individuals one by one.

DOES CONSTITUTIONALISM UNDERMINE LIBERTY?

The majoritarian premise insists that something of moral importance is lost or compromised whenever a political decision contradicts what the majority of citizens would prefer or judge right if they reflected on the basis of adequate information. We must try to identify that moral cost. What is lost or compromised? Many people think the answer is: equality. I shall consider that apparently natural answer shortly, but I begin with a different suggestion, which is that when constitutional disabling provisions, like those found in the Bill of Rights, limit what a majority can enact, the result is to compromise the community's freedom.

That suggestion plainly appeals to what Isaiah Berlin and others have called positive as distinct from negative liberty, and what Benjamin Constant described as the liberty of the ancients as distinct from that of the moderns. It is the kind of freedom that statesmen and revolutionaries and terrorists and humanitarians have in mind when they insist that freedom must include the right of "self-determination" or the right of the "people" to govern themselves. Since the suggestion that constitutional rights compromise freedom appeals to positive rather than negative liberty, it might be said to pit the two kinds of liberty against each other. Constitutionalism, on this view, protects "negative" liberties, like free speech and "privacy," at the cost of the "positive" freedoms of self-determination.

This means, however, that this argument from liberty we are considering must be based on a communal rather than a statistical reading of government by the "people." On the statistical reading, an individual's control over the collective decisions that affect his life is measured by his power, on his own, to influence the result, and in a large democracy the power of any individual over national decisions is so tiny that constitutional restraints cannot be thought to diminish it enough to count as objectionable for that reason. On the contrary, constraints on majority will might well expand any particular individual's control of his own fate. On the communal reading, however, liberty is a matter not of any relation between government and citizens one by one, but rather of the relation between government and the whole citizenry understood collectively. Positive liberty, so understood, is the state of affairs when "the people" rule their officials, at least in the final analysis, rather than vice versa, and that is the liberty said to be compromised when the majority is prevented from securing its will.

Self-determination is the most potent — and dangerous — political ideal of our time. People fervently want to be governed by a group not just to which they belong, but with which they identify in some particular way. They want to be governed by members of the same religion or race or nation or linguistic community or historical nation-state rather than by any other group, and they regard a political community that does not satisfy this demand as a tyranny, no matter how otherwise fair and satisfactory it is.

This is partly a matter of narrow self-interest. People think that decisions made by a group most of whose members share their values will be better decisions for them. The great power of the ideal lies deeper, however. It lies in half-articulate convictions about when people are free, because they govern themselves, in spite of the fact that in a statistical sense, as individuals, they are not free, because they must often bend to the will of others. For us moderns, the key to this liberty of the ancients lies in democracy. As John Kenneth Galbraith has said, "When people put their ballots in the boxes, they are, by that act, inoculated against the feeling that the government is not theirs. They then accept, in some measure, that its errors are their errors, its aberrations their aberrations, that any revolt will be against them." We think we are free when we accept a majority's will in place of our own, but not when we bow before the doom of a monarch or the ukase of any aristocracy of blood or faith or skill. It is not difficult to see the judiciary as an aristocracy claiming dominion. Learned Hand described judges who appeal to the moral reading of the Constitution as "a bevy of Platonic guardians," and said he could not bear to be ruled by such a body of elites even if he knew how to select those fit for the task.

But powerful as the idea of democratic self-governance is, it is also deeply mysterious. Why am I *free*—how could I be thought to be governing *myself*—when I must obey what other people decide even if I think it wrong or unwise or unfair to me and my family? What difference can it make how many people must think the decision right and wise and fair if it is not necessary that *I* do? What kind of freedom is that? The answer to these enormously difficult questions begins in the communal conception of collective action. If I am a genuine member of a political community, its act is in some pertinent sense my act, even when I argued and voted against it, just as the victory or defeat of a team of which I am a member is my victory or defeat even if my own individual contribution made no difference either way. On no other assumption can we intelligibly think that as members of a flourishing democracy we are governing ourselves.

What could *genuine* membership in a political community mean? And in what sense *can* a collective act of a group also be the act of each member? We must describe some connection between an individual and a group that makes it *fair* to treat him—and *sensible* that he treat himself—as responsible for what it does. Let us bring those ideas together in the concept of moral membership, by which we mean the kind of membership in a political community that engages self-government. If true democracy is government by the people, in the communal sense that provides self-government, then true democracy is based on moral membership.

In this section we are considering the argument that the moral cost incurred when the majoritarian premise is flouted is a cost in liberty. We have now clarified that argument: we must understand it to mean that the people govern themselves when the majoritarian premise is satisfied, and that any compromise of that premise compromises that self-government. But that majoritarianism does not guarantee self-government unless all the members of the community in question are moral members, and the majoritarian premise acknowledges no such qualification. I do not mean that people who deny moral membership in their political community are always right. The test, as I said, is moral not psychological. But they are not wrong just because they have an equal vote with others in some standing majoritarian structure.

When I described the constitutional conception of democracy earlier, as a rival to the majoritarian conception that reflects the majoritarian premise, I said that the constitutional conception presupposes democratic conditions. These are the conditions that must be met before majoritarian decision-making can claim any automatic moral advantage over other procedures for collective decision. We have now identified the same idea through another route. The democratic conditions are the conditions of moral membership in a political community. So we can now state a strong conclusion: not just that positive liberty is not sacrificed whenever and just because the majoritarian premise is ignored, but that positive liberty is enhanced when that premise is rejected outright in favor of the constitutional conception of democracy. If it is true that self-government is possible only within a community that meets the conditions of moral membership, because only then are we entitled to refer to government by "the people" in a powerful communal rather than a barren statistical sense, we need a conception of democracy that insists that no democracy exists unless those conditions are met.

These are *relational* conditions: they describe how an individual must be treated by a genuine political community in order that he or she be a moral member of that community. A political community cannot count anyone as a moral member unless it gives that person a *part* in any collective decision, a *stake* in it, and *independence* from it. First, each person must have an opportunity to make a difference in the collective decisions, and the force of his role — the magnitude of the difference he can make — must not be structurally fixed or limited in ways that reflect assumptions about his worth or talent or ability, or the soundness of his convictions or tastes. It is that condition that insists on universal suffrage and effective elections and representation, even though it does not demand that these be the only avenues of collective decision. It also insists on free speech and expression for all opinion, not just on formal political occasions, but in the informal life of the community as well.

Second, the political process of a genuine community must express some bona fide conception of equal concern for the interests of all members, which means that political decisions that affect the distribution of wealth, benefits, and burdens must be consistent with equal concern for all. Moral membership involves reciprocity: a person is not a member unless he is treated as a member by others, which means that they treat the consequences of any collective decision for his life as equally significant a reason for or against that decision as are comparable consequences for the life of anyone else. So the communal conception of democracy explains an intuition many of us share: that a society in which the majority shows contempt for the needs and prospects of some minority is illegitimate as well as unjust.

The third condition — of moral independence — is likely to be more controversial than these first two. I believe it essential, however, in order to capture an aspect of moral membership that the first two conditions may be interpreted to omit. The root idea we are now exploring — that individual freedom is furthered by collective self-government — assumes that the members of a political community can appropriately regard themselves as partners in a joint venture, like members or a football team or orchestra in whose work and fate all share, even when that venture is conducted in ways they do not endorse. That idea is nonsense unless it can be accepted by people with self-respect, and whether it can be depends on which kinds of decisions the collective venture is thought competent to make. An orchestra's conductor can decide, for example, how the orchestra will interpret a particular piece: there must be a decision of that issue binding on all, and the conductor is the only one placed to make it. No musician sacrifices anything essential to his control over his own life, and hence to his self-respect, in accepting that someone else has that responsibility, but it would plainly be otherwise if the conductor tried to dictate not only how a violinist should play under his direction, but what standards of taste the violinist should try to cultivate. No one who accepted responsibility to decide questions of musical judgment for himself could regard himself as a partner in a joint venture that proposed to decide them for him.

People who take personal responsibility for deciding what kind of life is valuable for them can nevertheless accept that issues of justice—about how the different and sometimes competing interests of all citizens should be accommodated—must be decided collectively, so that one decision is taken as authoritative for all. There is nothing in that proposition that challenges an individual's own responsibility to decide for himself what life to live given the resources and opportunities that such collective decisions leave to him. So he can treat himself as bound together with others in a joint effort to resolve such questions, even when his views lose. But it would be otherwise if the majority purported to decide what he should think or say about its decisions, or what values or ideals should guide how he votes or the choices he makes with the resources it assigns him. Someone who believes in his own responsibility for the central values of his life cannot yield that responsibility to a group even if he has an equal vote in its deliberations. A genuine political community must therefore be a community of independent moral agents. It must not dictate what its citizens think about matters of political or moral or ethical judgment, but must, on the contrary, provide circumstances that encourage them to arrive at beliefs on these matters through their own reflective and finally individual conviction.

EQUALITY?

Although the argument from liberty is emotionally the most powerful of the arguments that might be made for the majoritarian premise, an argument from equality is more familiar. The dimension of equality in question is presumably political equality, because there is nothing in majoritarianism that could be thought automatic to promote any other form of equality, particularly not economic equality. True, if a society's economic structure is pyramidal, with progressively more people at progressively lower economic levels, then universal suffrage and majoritarian decisions might well push toward greater economic equality. But in the United States, and in other advanced capitalist countries where the profile of distribution is now very different, people in the majority often vote to protect their own wealth against the demands of those worse off than they are.

So the argument that equality is compromised when the majoritarian premise is ignored must appeal to some concept of political equality. But which concept this is depends on which of the two readings of collective action we have in mind. If we take government by "the people" to be only a statistical matter, then the equality in question is the political equality of citizens taken one by one. Such equality was certainly denied before women were permitted to vote, and it was compromised by the electoral system in Victorian Britain, which in effect gave university graduates extra votes. But what metric do we use in making most judgments? What is political equality according to the statistical concept of collective political action?

Perhaps surprisingly, we cannot capture political equality if we define it as equality of political *power*, because we have no interpretation of "power" that would make equality of power even an attractive, let alone an attainable, ideal. Suppose we take political power to be a matter of impact, understood in the following way: my political impact, as a citizen of the United States, is a matter of how far my favoring a particular decision, just on its own, increases the antecedent likelihood of that being the collective decision, making no assumptions about what opinion any other citizen has or forms. Impact cannot be equal in a representative democracy: it must inevitably make a greater difference to the antecedent probability of a trade measure being approved that any particular senator favors it than that I do. In any case, impact does not capture any intuitively appealing concept of political power, because impact is insensitive to what is the most important source of unequal political power in modern democracies, which is the inequality of wealth that allows some people vast opportunity to influence public opinion. Ross Perot and I have only one vote each, but he can buy massive television time to persuade others to his opinion, and I cannot buy any.

This might suggest an improved account: that political power is a matter not of impact but of influence, understood as my overall power to affect political decisions, taking into account my power to affect the opinions of others. But equality of influence is plainly an unattractive — as well as unrealizable — goal. We do not want wealth to affect political decisions, but that is because wealth is unequally and unfairly distributed. We certainly do want influence to be unequal in politics for other reasons: we want those with better views, or who can argue more cogently, to have more influence. We could not eliminate differential influence from such sources without savage transformations of our whole society, and these would mean the end, not the triumph, of deliberation in our politics.

We must begin again. Political equality, on the statistical model of collective action, must be defined as a matter not of power but of the kind of *status* I discussed in connection with the conditions of democratic self-government. Male-only suffrage and university votes were inegalitarian because they presupposed that some people were worthier or better fit to participate in collective decisions than others. But mere political authority — the power attached to political office for which all are in principle eligible — carries no such presupposition. That is why the special power of political officials does not destroy true political equality, and it does not matter, for that point, whether or not the officials are directly elected. Many officials who are appointed rather than elected wield great power. An acting ambassador to Iraq can create a Gulf War and the chairman of the Federal Reserve Board can bring the economy to its knees. There is no inegalitarian premise of status — no supposition of first- and second-class citizenship — in the arrangements that produce this power. Nor is there any inegalitarian premise in the parallel arrangements that give certain American judges, appointed and approved by elected officials, authority over constitutional adjudication.

So the statistical reading of collective political action makes little sense of the idea that political equality is compromised whenever majority will is thwarted. And this idea is silly anyway, if we have the statistical reading in mind. In a large, continental democracy, any ordinary citizen's political power is minuscule, on any understanding of what political power is, and the diminution of that individual power traceable to constitutional constraints on majority will is more minuscule still. The egalitarian argument for the majoritarian premise seems initially more promising, however, if we detach it from the statistical reading of collective action and recast it from the perspective of the communal reading. From that perspective, equality is not a matter of any relation among citizens one by one, but rather a relation between the citizenry, understood collectively as "the people," and their governors. Political equality is the state of affairs in which the people rule their officials, in the final analysis, rather than vice versa. This provides a less silly argument for the proposition that judicial review or other compromises of the majoritarian premise damage political equality. It might be said that when judges apply constitutional provisions to strike down legislation that the people, through their representatives, have enacted, the people are no longer in charge.

But this argument is exactly the same as the argument considered in the last section: it appeals, once again, to the ideals of political self-determination. Positive liberty and the sense of equality that we extracted from the communal understanding of "we the people" are the very same virtues. (That is hardly surprising, since liberty and equality are, in general, aspects of the same ideal, not, as is often supposed, rivals.) The objections described in the last section, which are fatal to any attempt to ground a majoritarian premise in positive liberty, are also decisive against the same argument when it cries equality instead.

WHAT FOLLOWS?

In a decent working democracy, like the United States, the democratic conditions set out in the Constitution are sufficiently met in practice so that there is no unfairness in allowing national and local legislatures the powers they have under standing arrangements. On the contrary, democracy would be extinguished by any general constitutional change that gave an oligarchy of unelected experts power to overrule and replace any legislative decision they thought unwise or unjust. It is different, however, when the question is plausibly raised whether some rule or regulation or policy itself undercuts or weakens the democratic character of the community, and the constitutional arrangement assigns *that* question to a court. Suppose the legislature enacts a law making it a crime for someone to burn his own American flag as an act of protest. Suppose this law is challenged on the ground that it impairs democratic self-government, by wrongly constricting the liberty of speech, and a court accepts this charge and strikes down the law. If the court's decision is correct—if laws against flag-burning do in fact violate the democratic conditions set out in the Constitution as these have been interpreted and formed by American history—the decision is not antidemocratic, but, on the contrary, improves democracy. No moral cost has been paid, because no one, individually or collectively, is worse off in any of the dimensions we have now canvassed. No one's power to participate in a self-governing community has been worsened, because everyone's power in that respect has been improved. No one's equality has been compromised, because equality, in the only pertinent sense, has been strengthened. No one has been cheated of the ethical advantages of a role in principled deliberation if he or she had a chance to participate in the public discussion about whether the decision was right. If the court had not intervened—if the legislature's decision had been left standing — everyone would have been worse off, in all the dimensions of democracy, and it would be perverse to regard that as in any way or sense a democratic victory. Of course, if we assume that the court's decision was wrong, then none of this is true. Certainly it impairs democracy when an authoritative court makes the wrong decision about what the democratic conditions require — but no more than it does when a majoritarian legislature makes a wrong constitutional decision that is allowed to stand. The possibility of error is symmetrical. So the majoritarian premise is confused, and it must be abandoned.

Larry Kramer

WE THE COURT

115 Harv. L. Rev. 4 (2001)

In recent years, scholars have drawn on Thomas Jefferson's notion of departmentalism to argue against judicial supremacy. Even if the Supreme Court rightly has a power of judicial review, this should not mean, they argue, that the Supreme Court is the supreme arbiter of the Constitution. The idea that aside from the Court, the "people themselves," to use Larry Kramer's phrase, should have the power of judicial review might strike some people as problematic. After all, most people are not lawyers, so why should they be able to interpret the Constitution? But as you have seen, the question of what the Constitution means is itself deeply contested. Moreover, in the following excerpt, Kramer argues that there has historically been a tradition of the people interpreting the Constitution. The move to judicial supremacy, he suggests, is a recent one, found mostly in the doctrines of the Rehnquist Court. But this move from judicial review to judicial supremacy is a mistake, he argues. We should return at least some of the power of judicial interpretation to the people themselves.

In this selection, Kramer attempts to revive Jefferson's theory of departmentalism. Clearly, the debate over judicial authority did not die with Jefferson and Alexander Hamilton. It is very much alive today. As you read this selection, consider the ways in which Jefferson and Kramer agree. You might also ask what judicial review without judicial supremacy might look like in light of Kramer's suggestion that the two need not go together.

For all his genius, John Marshall is seldom included among American's great political or legal rhetoricians. He penned some decent enough lines, but nothing with the power routinely displayed by a Holmes or a Lincoln, or, even among his contemporaries, by a Jefferson or a Paine. There is one line, though, that every lawyer and law student knows by heart, almost by instinct: "It is, emphatically, the province and duty of the judicial department, to say what the law is." There supposedly, in one pithy sentence, is the Supreme Court's own Declaration of Independence.

But what does Marshall's statement mean — on the ground, in operation? In 1958, the Court insisted in the almost-as-famous case of *Cooper v. Aaron* that *Marbury* "declared the basic principle that the federal judiciary is supreme in the exposition of the law of the Constitution," adding that this idea "has ever since been respected by this Court and the Country as a permanent and indispensable feature of our constitutional system." Well, hardly. As we shall see below (though it is by now conventional wisdom), *Marbury* staked out a considerably more modest position, venturing only that it was proper for the Court to interpret the Constitution without in any way suggesting that its interpretations were superior to those of the other branches. And certainly, as we shall also see below (though this, too, is conventional wisdom), the idea of judicial supremacy was not cheerfully embraced in the years after *Marbury*. The Court's periodic tugs of war with the likes of Jefferson, Jackson, Lincoln, the Reconstruction Congress, and FDR, to name only a few, are familiar terrain even to non-historians.

But here is the striking thing: in the years since *Cooper v. Aaron*, the idea of judicial supremacy—the notion that judges have the last word when it comes to constitutional interpretation and that their decisions determine the meaning of the Constitution for everyone—has finally found widespread approbation. The Court's decisions are often still controversial. State legislatures sometimes enact laws they know the Justices will strike down, and compliance with the Court's most contentious rulings, like those on abortion and school prayer, is willfully slack in many places. But these incidents of non-compliance have become forms of protest more than claims of interpretive superiority. Outright defiance in the shape of denying that Supreme Court decisions define constitutional law has, quite simply, disappeared....

There is, I believe, a simple explanation both for the general acceptance of judicial supremacy and for the defensiveness of its critics. Put simply, everyone—friend or foe of supremacy—begins with a shared understanding of the Constitution as ordinary law. It is "supreme," meaning it is superior to other forms of positive law and so trumps them when conflicts arise. But in every other respect, the Constitution is just "law" in the conventional sense in which lawyers use the word. It follows, naturally and ineluctably, that judges should be the ones to interpret it. Law is, after all, the stuff of judges; it is what they do. If the law is unclear, interpreting it to clarify its meaning is among the judiciary's central missions. It follows, almost as ineluctably, that judicial interpretations should be treated as conclusive by the other branches. Insofar as questions arise about what a legal text means, courts are where we go to get answers. And once a court has spoken, or at least once the Supreme Court has done so, its interpretations are supposed to trump those of other political actors unless and until the law is formally changed. This is universally acknowledged when it comes to statutes, and insofar as the Constitution shares the same status as these of positive law, there is no reason suddenly to abandon the practice.

... If the Constitution is law, after all, it is not (supposed to be) politics. It is, of course, political, in the sense that all law is political: it has political consequences, those who interpret and apply it cannot help but bring their politics with them into the interpretive process, and so forth. But modern recognition of the inherently political nature and structure of law still accepts the fundamental premise that law can and should be separated from politics. Law is, if you will, the part of politics that is supposed to be left to courts and judges. Placing something in a "law" box thus shifts our expectations and assumptions about authority to interpret. If the Constitution is law, then it is those who would argue that courts should not be its authoritative expositor who bear the burden of justifying what amounts to an exception to our normal practice.

The Founding generation did not see the Constitution this way and, as a result, had very different views about the role of the judiciary. Their Constitution was not ordinary law, not peculiarly the stuff of courts and judges. It was, as Part II will show, a special form of popular law, law made by the people to bind their governors, and so subject to rules and considerations that made it qualitatively different from (and not just superior to) statutory or common law.

Americans of the Founding era felt the wonder of popular government in a way that we, who take so much for granted, do not. The United States was then the only country in the world with a government founded explicitly on the consent of its people, and the people who gave that consent were intensely, profoundly conscious of the fact. And proud. This pride, this awareness of the fragility and importance of their venture in popular government, informed everything the Founders did. It was, as Gordon Wood said, "the deeply felt meaning of the Revolution." Modern commentators, especially legal commentators, read the Founders' letters and speeches anachronistically, giving too much weight, or the wrong kind of weight, to complaints about "the excess of democracy." We depict the men who framed the Constitution as striving to create a self-correcting system of checks and balances whose fundamental operations would all take place from within the government itself, with minimal involvement or interference from the people. Our political grammar is saturated with this reading of the Founding, which sees the movement to write a new Constitution almost exclusively in anti-democratic terms.

. . . The Founding generation's ideas about constitutional reform remained thoroughly embedded in a political ideology that celebrated the central role of "the people" in supplying the government with its energy and direction. Preserving liberty demanded a constitution whose internal architecture was carefully arranged to check power, just as it demanded leaders of sufficient "character" and "virtue." But structural innovations and virtuous leadership were devices to channel and control popular politics, not to isolate or eliminate it. The people remained responsible for making things work.

When Tucker and his contemporaries invoked "the people," they were not conjuring an empty abstraction or describing a mythic philosophical justification for government. "The people" they knew could speak, and had done so. "The people" they knew had fought a revolution, expressed dissatisfaction with the first fruits of independence, and debated and adopted a new charter to govern itself. Certainly the Founders were concerned about the perils of popular government, some of them obsessively so. But they were also captivated by its possibilities and in awe of its importance. Their Constitution remained, fundamentally, an act of popular will: the people's charter, made by the people. And, as we shall see, it was the people themselves — working through or responding to their agents in the government — who were responsible for seeing that the Constitution was properly interpreted and implemented. The idea of turning this responsibility over to judges was unthinkable.

. . . The American people learned a great deal during the early years of their Republic[.] . . . Among the lessons they learned . . . were first, that it was difficult to keep courts out of the business of interpreting a written constitution, and second, that popular constitutionalism of the eighteenth-century variety was not well suited for American's new circumstances. That courts might play a role enforcing the Constitution had been understood by some even before Ratification; by the time *Marbury* was decided in 1803, this role had expanded to permit courts routinely to act on their own best understanding of the Constitution's meaning. That it might extend further, that judges might be assigned the final word in disputes over how to interpret the Constitution, was already being debated by the early decades of the nineteenth century. It may have taken until some time after *Cooper v. Aaron* for this proposition to achieve acceptance, but the idea of judicial supremacy had entered America's political lexicon by the 1830s.

There is, nevertheless, a world of difference between having the last word and having the only word: between judicial supremacy and judicial sovereignty. We may choose to accept judicial supremacy, because we need someone to settle certain constitutional questions and, for a variety of historical and jurisprudential reasons, the Supreme Court seems like our best option. But it does not follow either that the Court must wield its authority over every question or that, when it does, the Court can dismiss or too quickly supplant the views of other, more democratic institutions. Nothing in the doctrine of judicial supremacy, in other words, requires denying either that the Constitution has qualities that set it apart from ordinary law, or that these qualities confer legitimate interpretive authority on political actors as a means of ensuring continued popular input in shaping constitutional meaning.

The trick, of course, is to find the proper balance, a problem courts have struggled with throughout American history. The various tussles between prior Supreme Courts and prior Presidents and Congresses should be seen in this light, for they reflect both the historical persistence of popular constitutionalism and the country's efforts to reconcile it with the practice of judicial supremacy. For much of the nineteenth century, an expansive notion of "political questions" and a sharp law/politics distinction among issues of constitutional law served to reconcile these conflicting principles. This doctrinal framework broke down during the *Lochner* era, triggering a prolonged struggle that culminated in the New Deal settlement most famously reflected in *Carolene Products*' footnote four. The accommodation thus reached — roughly a division between questions of defining grants of power and questions of protecting individual rights — proved stable for more than half a century. The Warren Court was activist, for example, but it remained strictly within the terms of the New Deal accommodation.

Which brings us to the Rehnquist Court. [S]omething significant has happened on Chief Justice Rehnquist's watch: a subtle, unacknowledged shift in the Court's understanding of judicial review that has troubling consequences for constitutional doctrine and for constitutionalism generally. As opposition to judicial supremacy has receded, the seeming naturalness of the Court's power to interpret has grown, and with it the Court's own apparent sense that interpretation by non-judicial actors is somehow unnatural. The Court has reacted by abandoning the *Carolene Products* accommodation — not because it has a better or more sensible one in mind, but because this Court sees no need to accommodate the political branches at all. The Rehnquist Court no longer views itself as first among equals, but has instead staked its claim to being the only institution empowered to speak with authority when it comes to the meaning of the Constitution. The other branches get to have their say, of course, for they must interpret the Constitution when deciding whether and how to act—just as you or I must do with respect to whatever law governs us. But executive or legislative understandings of the Constitution are, in the eyes of the Rehnquist Court, hardly more authoritative than yours or mine. Only the Court's own interpretations matter; only these have the force of constitutional law. If deference is still given to the President or Congress (and this is becoming rarer by the term), it is because the Court views deferring as pragmatic or sees the Constitution as indifferent to a problem, not because it thinks these branches have equal standing to interpret the text. The last, faint traces of popular constitutionalism are fading, threatened by a Court that truly sees the Constitution as nothing more than ordinary law. Judicial supremacy is becoming judicial sovereignty.

We see this development reflected in the Court's thinking in a number of ways. It appears in the Justices' rhetoric, which increasingly ignores or affirmatively denies legitimacy to the views of other actors. It appears as well in their willingness to cast aside long-established doctrines created specifically to preserve the interpretive authority of other branches, especially that of Congress. These include rational basis scrutiny under the Commerce Clause and, more ominously, deferential review of congressional fact finding. But the effects of judicial sovereignty extend beyond the abandonment of deference, for the Court's felt need to protect its control over constitutional meaning has itself become a doctrine-shaping imperative. Where prior Courts put restrictions on judicial review to accommodate the views of other branches, this Court has revamped the doctrine to eliminate the other branches' interpretive space and protect its own exclusive custody of the Constitution. This, as we shall see, is a central thrust of the Court's recent federalism decisions, especially those limiting Congress's power under Section 5 of the Fourteenth Amendment. And, of course, this shift in the Court's attitude toward the competence of other branches to address constitutional questions goes far toward explaining its extraordinarily aggressive actions in last Term's most notorious decision, *Bush v. Gore.*

From one perspective, the historical development of judicial review stands as hugely ironic. We have moved from a world in which the interpretive authority of the political branches was clear and that of the Supreme Court questionable and uncertain, to one in which the Court's authority stands unchallenged while that of everyone else is under siege. The point is not originalist, and I will make no claim that we should reserve space for popular constitutionalism just because the Founders did. The historical experience that led to the emergence of judicial review and judicial supremacy suggests reasons for preserving bounded versions of both practices. But nothing similar justifies the drift to judicial sovereignty. . . .

. . . [D]eliberations in Congress . . . attested to the widening acceptance of the possibility and rightness of judicial review as an element of the constitutional system. A lengthy debate in the House of Representatives over the President's removal power in June 1789 generated considerable discussion of the courts' role, and while there was a great deal of ambiguity about the theory and scope of judicial review, most of the speakers accepted or assumed its existence. . . .

Courts exercising judicial review made no claim to treat fundamental law as ordinary law. They justified their refusal to enforce laws as a "political-legal" act on behalf of the people, a responsibility required by their position as the people's faithful agents. Judicial review was a substitute for popular action, a device to maintain constitutional limits without the need for civil unrest. It was, moreover, a power to be employed cautiously, only where the unconstitutionality of a law was clear beyond doubt — though in making this determination judges were not confined strictly to the text but could draw on well-established principles of the customary constitution as well.

The emergence of judicial review, even in this limited and restrained form, still needed to be fit into a theory of the Constitution. The argument for review was ultimately straightforward — to wit, that judges, no less than any other citizen or government official, were bound to take notice of the Constitution if and when it became relevant in the ordinary course of business. Yet however innocuous the proposition might sound stated abstractly, its application in practice raised an embarrassing theoretical problem. James Madison pointed to the difficulty in his 1788 observations on Jefferson's draft constitution for Virginia: "As the Courts are generally the last in making their decisions," he explained, "it results to them by refusing or not refusing to execute a law, to stamp it with its final character. This makes the Judiciary Department paramount in fact to the Legislature, which was never intended and can never be proper."

The solution to this dilemma is known today as the "departmental" or "concurrent" or "coordinate" theory of review. Madison himself was one of its earliest and strongest proponents. During the 1789 debate over the President's removal power, and notwithstanding the misgivings he had communicated to Jefferson the previous year, Madison conceded the basic argument for judicial review. "I acknowledge, in the ordinary course of government, that the exposition of the laws and constitution devolves upon the judicial," he said. It did not follow, however, that judicial decisions should therefore acquire any special stature or status.

Thomas Jefferson, who embraced this theory throughout his political life, expressed the idea succinctly: "Each of the three departments has equally the right to decide for itself what is its duty under the constitution, without any regard to what the others may have decided for themselves under a similar question."

Modern commentators find this theory puzzling, seeing in it a formula for anarchy and chaos. Some openly concede to being "confused" by the argument. Others assume that proponents of the departmental theory must have recognized that it was incomplete and continued to search for an alternative "effective method of resolving differences over constitutional interpretation." One historian pejoratively labels the theory "arbitrary review" (because, he says, it provides no "principled functional limits" for resolving constitutional conflicts) and insists that Madison, at least, meant something other than what he quite plainly said. As noted in the introduction, even modern scholars who purport to endorse departmentalism seem to find Madison's and Jefferson's version of it unintelligible. Instead, they typically propose some sort of functional division in which different branches are assigned final authority for different questions.

This generic confusion is revealing of the extent to which we have come to see our Constitution as ordinary law. For what underlies it is the assumption not just that someone must have final authority to resolve routine constitutional conflicts, but that this someone must be a governmental entity. Such an assumption belongs to the culture of ordinary law, not the culture of popular constitutionalism. In a regime of popular constitutionalism, government officials are the regulated, not the regulators, and final interpretive authority rests with the people themselves. Thus, Madison and Jefferson had no difficulty whatsoever explaining how constitutional conflicts would finally be resolved: they would be decided by the people. Ideally, of course, the disputing branches would reach an accommodation on their own, though Jefferson once observed that "we have . . . in more than one instance, seen the opinions of different departments in opposition to each other, & no ill ensue." Accommodation among the branches, after all, was what all that checking and balancing in separation of powers theory was supposed to be about. But if no compromise was forthcoming and a final resolution was needed, it was obvious who would decide. The issue would be answered, in Madison's words, by "the will of the community, to be collected in some mode to be provided by the constitution, or one dictated by the necessity of the case." Jefferson, too, urged that "when the legislative or executive functionaries act unconstitutionally, they are responsible to the people in their elective capacity."

. . . However understood, the practice of popular constitutionalism seems, at first, difficult to harmonize with the principle of judicial supremacy. After all, there can be only one last word on the meaning of the Constitution. It may rest with the people (whether speaking independently, through parties, or through elected officials) or it may rest with the Supreme Court, but how can it rest with both? Yet this is much too simplistic a view. There is, in fact, a world of difference between having the final word and having the only word. We may come to accept judicial supremacy, because we need someone trustworthy to settle certain constitutional disputes once and for all, and for a variety of historical, jurisprudential, and political reasons, the Supreme Court seems like our best option. Given this sort of pragmatic justification, it simply does not follow that the Court must wield its authority over every question of constitutional law; nor does it follow that, when the Court does exercise review, it should dismiss or too easily supplant the views of other, more democratic institutions. Nothing in the doctrine of judicial supremacy, in other words, requires divesting either the people or the political branches of legitimate interpretive authority. Some matters may call for close judicial scrutiny while others are best left for resolution in the political domain. It is all a matter of finding the most appropriate or workable accommodation. . . .

The fragility of any accommodation based on a law/politics distinction was revealed when the Justices finally struck down an important federal law in *Dred Scott v. Sandford.* The Court was savaged in the press and suffered wounds to its reputation that took nearly a generation to heal. Recoiling from Chief Justice Taney's hamfisted assertion of judicial supremacy, Abraham Lincoln declared his support for a version of the old departmental theory and invoked Andrew Jackson's defiance of the Court as precedent. Lincoln returned to the problem of *Dred Scott* in his First Inaugural Address, where he conceded that the

Court's judgment should be enforced as to the parties immediately involved. "At the same time," he continued:

> The candid citizen must confess that if the policy of the government upon vital questions, affecting the whole people, is to be irrevocably fixed by decisions of the Supreme Court, the instant they are made, in ordinary litigation between parties, in personal actions, the people will have ceased to be their own rulers, having to that extent practically resigned their government into the hands of that eminent tribunal.

. . . [T]he Rehnquist Court has simply repudiated cardinal principles of twentieth-century jurisprudence (including rational basis scrutiny of ends-means relationships and deferential review of facts), casting aside a century and a half of hard-earned experience in a spasm of "law is law" formalism. Worse, the Court's felt need to maintain its interpretive supremacy—to ensure that it alone controls the meaning of the Constitution—has itself become a doctrine-shaping imperative. The Rehnquist Court has thus devised rules that artificially limit the authority of lawmakers because it finds such rules necessary to ensure its ability to dominate constitutional interpretation. The result is a Constitution that is less and does less, and for no better reasons than the Court's low opinion of Congress and desire to protect its position as king of the hill. . . .

[A]nxiety to squelch any appearance that other branches can render authoritative interpretations of the Constitution or that their views might affect the Court's interpretations is a recurring motif in the rhetoric of the Rehnquist Court. Apprehension along these lines played an important role in its opinion in *Casey*, for example, in which the Court emphasized its aversion to showing weakness by yielding to strongly held views from outside the Court, even if the Justices believe those views might be correct. "Whatever the premises of opposition may be," Justices O'Connor, Kennedy, and Souter wrote, "to overrule under fire in the absence of the most compelling reason to reexamine a watershed decision would subvert the Court's legitimacy beyond any serious question."

Concern for securing the Court's power to interpret was still more evident in *City of Boerne v. Flores*. In 1990, the Court had overturned three decades of precedent by ruling 5-4 that laws of general applicability do not violate the Free Exercise Clause simply because they prohibit or burden religious practices. Congress responded in 1993 with the Religious Freedom Restoration Act (RFRA), in which it sought to restore the old law by protecting such practices subject to a compelling interest test. That a unanimous House of Representatives and ninety-seven of the one hundred Senators (not to mention prior Courts, four members of the current Court, and most nonjudicial commentators) thought this was the better interpretation affected the majority's thinking not at all. Quite the contrary, it provoked a lecture on how it is Congress's job to enforce the Constitution, not to say what it is:

> When the Court has interpreted the Constitution, it has acted within the province of the Judicial Branch, which embraces the duty to say what the law is. Marbury v. Madison, 1 Cranch, at 177. When the political branches of the Government act against the background of a judicial interpretation of the Constitution already issued, it must be understood that in later cases and controversies the Court will treat its precedents with the respect due them under settled principles, including stare decisis, and contrary expectations must be disappointed.

Running through these decisions, and others that could be cited, is the Rehnquist Court's skittishness about losing control over the Constitution to other branches. The Justices seemed annoyed when lawyers for Vice President Gore argued in the election litigation that a statutory scheme (not to mention the Constitution itself) required Congress to resolve the dispute. "Are you suggesting there could be any judicial review of a decision by the Congress to count one set of electoral votes?" asked a disbelieving Chief Justice, followed by Justice Kennedy's stern warning that "we must be very careful to preserve the role of the Court." In the end, the majority chose to ignore Gore's argument, and instead concluded its opinion with the jaw-droppingly disingenuous claim that it had been "forced to confront" an "unsought responsibility." . . .

Among the more striking aspects of the Court's opinion was the argument it offered to justify this heightened scrutiny; or, rather, the absence of argument, for there was none. Chief Justice Rehnquist merely laid out a "first principle" — that the Constitution "creates a Federal Government of enumerated powers" — from which he apparently thought heightened judicial scrutiny followed automatically and without question. This unreflective conflating of constitutional limits with judicial enforcement was apparent at the end of the opinion, where the Chief Justice responded to claims that the Court's newest test was vague. Uncertainty there may be, he conceded:

> But, so long as Congress' authority is limited to those powers enumerated in the Constitution, and so long as those enumerated powers are interpreted as having judicially enforceable outer limits, congressional legislation under the Commerce Clause always will engender "legal uncertainty." . . . The Constitution mandates this uncertainty by withholding from Congress a plenary police power that would authorize enactment of every type of legislation. . . . Any possible benefit from eliminating this "legal uncertainty" would be at the expense of the Constitution's system of enumerated powers.

What is astonishing about this statement . . . is the Court's unawareness that its analysis is question-begging. The issue, after all, was whether the Constitution mandated that the enumerated powers be interpreted as having "judicially enforceable" outer limits. Not outer limits, mind you, but judicially enforceable ones. Everyone, including everyone in Congress, agrees that the Constitution's delegations have limits. The question has always been deciding who should say what these limits are.

. . . One has to guess at the Rehnquist Court's reasons for launching this wide-ranging assault on Congress, since the Justices themselves have nowhere explained or justified it. Apart from political motivations, . . . what emerges is a Court driven by a formal understanding of the nature of the Constitution and of the roles of Court and Congress under it. This understanding is never clearly stated, but rather consists of implicit assumptions that must be teased out of the opinions. But what comes across is a vision of the Constitution as ordinary law, that is, as something that generates conventional legal problems of a kind that can properly be resolved only by a court. Further animating the Justices who have led this revolution is a palpable edginess about the Supreme Court's ability to resolve these problems in a way that sticks, and a sense that past Courts have already let too much of the Constitution slip into legislative hands. Rules that do not enable the Supreme Court sufficiently to control the substantive meaning of the Constitution — rules that enable Congress to enact laws that "may become substantive in operation and effect"—are rules that need to be changed. This is true whether they are rules of process (such as standards of review) or rules of substance (such as the scope of equal protection or the reach of the Commerce Clause). What matters, above all, is keeping the Constitution safely in the Court's sole custody....

Bush v. Gore, it should by now be clear, is not such an exceptional case after all. Quite the opposite, it is from a certain perspective emblematic of the Rehnquist Court and its jurisprudence. The defining characteristic of that Court is not its commitment to political conservatism nor a love of states' rights. Such labels may accurately describe the Court's politics and outcomes, but at the base of its jurisprudence, facilitating if not driving decisions, lies the Justices' conviction that they and they alone are responsible for the Constitution. Apart from the narrow political question doctrine and a theoretic possibility of amendment, any notion that what the Constitution does or permits might best be left for the people to resolve using the ordinary devices available to express their will seems beyond the Rehnquist Court's compass. Politics begins where the Constitution leaves off, and what the Constitution allows the political branches to do is in all events to be decided by the Court. This is judicial sovereignty....

It is important in this regard to understand how the Court reached the position it has, and why the Justices seem so confident that what they are doing is right. It is too easy, in my view, to ascribe the course of the Rehnquist Court to politics alone, at least to politics in the narrow sense. That the Justices do or do not like certain laws obviously plays a role, and the political conservatism of the five who have controlled the Court's major decisions in recent years is surely part of the story, maybe even a big part. But such an account is one-dimensional. It leaves out the fact that the Justices are also lawyers who have spent the better part of their lives working in and with law. Their ideology is more than an array of preferences for one or another outcome in particular cases. It includes an ideology of constitutional law itself, a set of beliefs or ideas about the nature and meaning of the Constitution that makes them think they are right to intercede in politics as aggressively as they have. That the Justices have not been fans of some of the laws in question may have had something to do with their willingness, indeed eagerness, to take this step, just as their preference for a Republican president presumably made them more open to calling a halt to the election. But their sense that the Constitution called for them to act is surely more important still. The conservative ideology of the Rehnquist Court is, above all, a conservative jurisprudence, and it consists of certain mutually reinforcing ideas about the Constitution and the Court as well as of conservative politics in the narrow sense. These ideas constitute the intellectual matrix of the Rehnquist Court's conservative majority.

The first of these ideas—now shared, I think, by many liberals as well as by conservatives—is that the Constitution is nothing more than a species of ordinary law, hence something whose content and meaning are properly resolved by judges. Politics is where you go to amend the Constitution; courts are where you go to interpret it. The idea of constitutional politics outside the amendment process is, to the Rehnquist Court, a threatening and possibly oxymoronic prospect. A second idea seems to follow from this first one, inasmuch as conceiving the Constitution in ordinary-law terms could lead one to conclude that any limitations it imposes must be of a kind enforceable by courts. Indeed, "constitutional limitations" and "judicially enforceable" have become virtual synonyms for the Rehnquist Court, inseparable if not indistinguishable. The final piece of the puzzle is not so much an idea as an understanding of constitutional history, one that reaffirms the need for court-imposed limits by demonizing popular politics and celebrating the role of the judiciary in controlling the people. The conservative majority on the Rehnquist Court do not see themselves as usurpers. They do not see themselves as activists (because it is not activism to restore the "true" Constitution). Indeed, I have little doubt but that they see themselves as heroic, as close kin of the courageous judges who stood up against segregation in the South. *Bush v. Gore* was not a travesty from their perspective. It was their finest moment, a case of taking the political heat to do the right thing.

. . . The Founding generation did not solve the problem of constitutional interpretation and enforcement by delegating it to judges. Their thinking was more complex and, frankly, more imaginative than that. They were too steeped in republicanism to think that the solution to the problem of republican politics was to chop it off at the knees. Their structural solutions were meant to operate in politics: elections, bicameralism, an executive veto, political connections between state and national governments, and, above all, the capacity of politicians with competing interests to appeal for support to the people who made the Constitution. An idea of judicial review did eventually emerge, but it was fenced in by concern for preserving the essence of this popular constitutionalism. The precise terms on which these competing principles were accommodated have varied over time, but both have been with us all along. And no matter how often the Court repeats that it has been the ultimate expositor of the Constitution since *Marbury*, it still will not have been so. Popular constitutionalism — understood as a domain in which the people are free to settle questions of constitutional law by and for themselves in politics — has been a prominent feature of American constitutional practice from the beginning. We have never had the purely legal Constitution of the Rehnquist Court, a stripped-down fundamental law whose democratic essence has been abstracted to a distant horizon. Nor has stewardship of our Constitution ever been turned over exclusively to lawyers and judges.

I said at the outset that I would not make an originalist claim, and I do not mean to do so now. The point is not that the Rehnquist Court's vision of the Constitution is wrong because the Founding generation would have rejected it or because popular constitutionalism has been a vital part of our practice all along, though both things are true. I am not interested (here) in getting into a complex debate about how much normative weight history should carry in law. My present objective is more modest: to denaturalize a set of assumptions that are taken as natural by many, including especially the conservative majority on the Rehnquist Court and its supporters off the Court. Insofar as the Justices have chosen their path in the belief that, in doing so, they are vindicating the Constitution, either as it was originally understood or as it was viewed until recently, they are mistaken. It does not automatically follow that they are wrong to enlarge the scope of their authority. But it does follow that they need an explanation and a justification they have yet to provide. Certainly more needs to be done than quoting *Marbury* out of context or offering really bad renditions of the Founding.

Perhaps the argument should be stated more strongly. History may not compel us to embrace the Founders' exact understanding of popular constitutionalism, but it does suggest that one position at least is not plausible: the one embraced by the Rehnquist Court, which denies that popular constitutionalism is even a valid concept. In fact, both our theory and our practice have always reserved substantial space for the people to have a say in interpreting their Constitution, albeit in complex ways that have changed over time. Popular constitutionalism is not some quaint curiosity from the Founders' world. It is a vital principle that has been part of our constitutional tradition all along. To deny that there are spaces outside the Court where constitutional decisions are made, decisions to which judges are subservient, is a radical and unprecedented idea. There is a place for judicial supremacy, but it has bounds. There is no place for the totalizing claims of judicial sovereignty.

We are left, then, with a normative problem: What is the proper relationship between popular constitutionalism and judicial supremacy? How should we divide the world of constitutional law between the Court and politics? These are not easy questions, and answering them properly would require another article at least this long. We would, among other things, need to agree upon a theory of constitutional interpretation and to investigate a wide range of related philosophical and empirical matters. Anything less would not do justice to this important and daunting problem. It is enough for present purposes, I hope, to uncover the problem, and in doing so to highlight the radical nature of the Rehnquist Court's recent decisions. Beyond that, I want merely to offer some preliminary observations meant to help structure thinking about the larger normative questions that remain.

. . . [T]he Constitution is not and never has been ordinary law, that while it has many features we associate with ordinary law, it retains a substantial ingredient of popular constitutionalism. Why hold to a view of the Constitution that fails so miserably to explain our actual practice? It would be one thing if popular constitutionalism were normatively undesirable or inconsistent with the basic objectives or purposes of the Constitution. But exactly the opposite is true. The central objective of the Constitution is to facilitate democratic politics, to call into being a regime of republican self-government. Popular constitutionalism is, if anything, more consistent than judicial review with the basic concept of the Constitution — which is why it provided our historical starting point and why constitutional theorists in earlier generations thought they needed to spend all their time struggling to justify judicial review at all.

I am not suggesting that we abolish judicial review, or even judicial supremacy. Surely we need not rehearse here the familiar arguments about the many ways courts exercising review can reinforce democratic politics and enhance constitutional values, arguments our historical experience offers plenty of reasons to accept. These benefits are, however, functional and instrumental, for the history makes equally clear that judicial review is not required by the structure of our Constitution, much less implicit in the very notion of a written constitution. Judicial review emerged in response to specific conditions and for specific reasons, and it has served identifiable purposes over time. Yet if anything is implicit in the Constitution, it is a general preference for democratic solutions: that, after all, was the whole point. And the more important the problem, the stronger that preference becomes. We may still conclude that we need or want courts to settle certain problems or to counter certain endemic pathologies of party politics and representative assemblies. But less is more when it comes to limiting self-government, and we should be thinking about a minimal model of judicial review that calls upon judges to intercede only where necessary. It goes without saying that such an approach is consistent with historical experience. Yet it is virtually the opposite of the approach taken by the present Supreme Court, which presumes that questions respecting the Constitution are, by virtue of that alone, questions to be resolved by them and not us.

History may not tell us what to do. But it can tell us who we were and in this way help us understand who we have become. Legend has it that, as he left the Constitutional Convention, Benjamin Franklin was approached by a woman who asked him, "What have you given us, Dr. Franklin?" "A republic," he replied, "if you can keep it." Have we? For all the disagreement about what we mean by "republic," no one has ever doubted that self-government is its essence and a constitution the purest distillate. What kind of republic removes its constitution from the process of self-governing? Certainly not the one our Founders gave us. Is it one we prefer? The choice, after all, is ours. The Supreme Court has made its grab for power. The question is: will we let them get away with it?

Jeremy Waldron

THE CORE OF THE CASE AGAINST JUDICIAL REVIEW

115 Yale L.J. 1346 (2006)

INTRODUCTION

Should judges have the authority to strike down legislation when they are convinced that it violates individual rights? In many countries they do. The best known example is the United States. In November 2003, the Supreme Judicial Court of Massachusetts ruled that the state's marriage licensing laws violated state constitutional rights to due process and equal protection by implicitly limiting marriage to a union between a man and a woman. . . . A good decision and a process in which claims of rights are steadily and seriously considered — for many people these are reasons for cherishing the institution of judicial review. . . . We can, they argue, put up with an occasional bad outcome as the price of a practice that has given us decisions like *Lawrence*, *Roe*, and *Brown*, which upheld our society's commitment to individual rights in the face of prejudiced majorities.

. . . This Essay will argue that judicial review of legislation is inappropriate as a mode of final decisionmaking in a free and democratic society.

. . . In liberal political theory, legislative supremacy is often associated with popular self-government, and democratic ideals are bound to stand in an uneasy relation to any practice that says elected legislatures are to operate only on the sufferance of unelected judges. Alexander Bickel summed up the issue in the well-known phrase, "the counter-majoritarian difficulty." . . .

In countries that do not allow legislation to be invalidated in this way, the people themselves can decide finally, by ordinary legislative procedures, whether they want to permit abortion, affirmative action, school vouchers, or gay marriage. . . .

What I want to do is identify a core argument against judicial review that is independent of both its historical manifestations and questions about its particular effects — the decisions (good and bad) that it has yielded, the heartbreaks and affirmations it has handed down. . . .

The members of the community are committed to rights, but they disagree about rights. Most issues of rights are in need of settlement. We need settlement not so much to dispose of the issue — nothing can do that — but to provide a basis for common action when action is necessary. Now, there are all sorts of issues on which we do not need society-wide settlement — transubstantiation, the meaning of *Hamlet*, the value of a purely contemplative life — and that is fortunate, because there is little prospect of agreement in these areas. Unfortunately, on issues of rights, for which we do need settlement, there is little prospect of agreement either. The need for settlement does not make the fact of disagreement evaporate; rather, it means that a common basis for action has to be forged in the heat of our disagreements.

In the real world, the need for settlement confronts us in the legislative arena. We legislate in certain areas, and the legislation we enact raises issues of rights. Those issues may not be facially prominent in the legislation. The legislation may be on marriage formalities, minimum working hours, campaign finance reform, or the historic preservation of city centers, but what happens is that somebody notices that its application happens to raise an issue of rights and it is in connection with that issue — is the legislation to be applied according to its terms or not? — that the need for settlement arises.

Let us assume, for now, that the legislature is broadly aware of the issues of rights that a given bill gives rise to and that, having deliberated on the matter, it resolves — through debate and voting — to settle those issues in a particular way. The legislature takes sides on one or more of the disagreements we imagined in assumption four. The question we face is whether that resolution of the legislature should be dispositive or whether there is reason to have it second-guessed and perhaps overruled by the judiciary.

How should we answer this question? I have heard people say that the decision-rule should be this: The legislature's decision stands, except when it violates rights. But clearly this will not do. We are assuming that the members of the society disagree about whether a given legislative proposal violates rights. We need a way of resolving that disagreement. The point is as old as Hobbes: We must set up a decision-procedure whose operation will settle, not reignite, the controversies whose existence called for a decision-procedure in the first place. This means that even though the members of the society we are imagining disagree about rights, they need to share a theory of legitimacy for the decision-procedure that is to settle their disagreements. So, in thinking about the reasons for setting up such a procedure, we should think about reasons that can be subscribed to by people on both sides of any one of these disagreements.

No decision-procedure will be perfect. Whether it is a process of legislation that cannot be reviewed or whether it is a process of judicial review, it will sometimes come to the wrong decision, betraying rights rather than upholding them. This is a fact of life in politics. Everyone must concede that there will sometimes be a dissonance between what they take to be the right choice and what they take to be the choice yielded by the decision-procedure they regard as legitimate. Richard Wollheim called this "a paradox in the theory of democracy," because it allows one and the same citizen to assert that A ought not to be enacted, where A is the policy he voted against, and A ought to be enacted, because A is the policy chosen by the majority. But Wollheim was wrong to ascribe this paradox to democracy. It is a general paradox in the theory of politics affecting any political theory that complements its account of what ought to be done with an account of how decisions ought to be made when there is disagreement about what ought to be done.

With that caution in mind, what are the reasons that need to be taken into account in designing or evaluating a decision-procedure for settling disagreements about rights? Two sorts of reasons may be considered. I shall call them "outcome-related" and "process-related" reasons, though they are both relevant to the issue of decision-procedure.

Process-related reasons are reasons for insisting that some person make, or participate in making, a given decision that stand independently of considerations about the appropriate outcome. In personal life, we sometimes say that a parent has the right to make the decision as to whether her child should be disciplined for a given infraction: It is not for a passer-by on the street or another passenger on the bus to make that decision. We may say that while reserving judgment on whether the child should be disciplined. Indeed, we may say that even though we think the passer-by is likely to make a better decision on this than the parent. In politics, the most familiar process-related reasons are those based on political equality and the democratic right to vote, the right to have one's voice counted even when others disagree with what one says.

Outcome-related reasons, by contrast, are reasons for designing the decision-procedure in a way that will ensure the appropriate outcome (i.e., a good, just, or right decision). Our subject matter is disagreements about rights. Because rights are important, it is likewise important that we get them right and so we must take outcome-related reasons very seriously indeed. Wrong answers may be tolerable in matters of policy; but on matters of principle, if the wrong answer is given, then rights will be violated. The members of the society we are imagining understand how important it is to avoid such outcomes or minimize them to the extent they can.

Of course, it may not be easy to identify outcome-related reasons that people on opposing sides of rights-disagreements can agree upon. As I said earlier, the design of a decision-procedure must be independent of the particular disagreement it is supposed to settle; it is no good if it simply reignites it. So we must avoid outcome-related reasons that aim specifically at particular controversial outcomes — e.g., favoring a decision-procedure because it is more likely to generate a pro-choice than a pro-life outcome. A decision-procedure chosen on this basis will hardly command the allegiance of the pro-life advocates. Given the disagreement, the whole point here is to set up a procedure for generating settlements in a way that can be recognized as legitimate on both sides.

So, how do we weigh these process-related and outcome-related considerations? We face the familiar problem of trying to maximize the value of two variables, like asking someone to buy the fastest car at the lowest price. There are various ways we can set up the question. We could ask: "What method is most likely to get at the truth about rights, while at the same time adequately respecting the equal claim to be heard of the voices of those affected?" Or we could ask: "What method best respects the equal claim to be heard of the voices of those affected, while at the same time being reasonably likely to get at the truth about rights?" I think I can cut through this Gordian knot. What I will argue . . . is that the outcome-related reasons are at best inconclusive. They are important, but they do not (as is commonly thought) establish anything like a clear case for judicial review. The process-related reasons, however, are quite one-sided. They operate mainly to discredit judicial review while leaving legislative decisionmaking unscathed. Thus, it seems to me the legislative side wins on either formulation of the question. And that will be the core of the case against judicial review.

It is tempting to associate outcome-related reasons with the case for judicial review (and process-related reasons with the case against it). This is a mistake. It is true that many of the more important process-related reasons are participatory and therefore favor elective or representative institutions. But it does not follow that all or most outcome-related reasons argue the other way. Outcome-related reasons, as we shall see, cut in both directions. There are things about legislatures that sometimes make them vulnerable to the sorts of pressures that rights are supposed to guard against; but there are also things about courts that make it difficult for them to grapple directly with the moral issues that rights-disagreements present.

In general, what I notice when I read outcome-related arguments in favor of judicial review is that people assume that an outcome-related case must be able to be made in favor of courts, if only because the most familiar arguments against judicial review are non-outcome-related. People strain to associate outcome-related reasons with the judiciary, and in so doing they often peddle a quite unrealistic picture of what judicial decisionmaking is like. Opponents of judicial review are often accused of adopting a naively optimistic view of legislatures. But sometimes we do this deliberately, matching one optimistic picture with another in the face of the refusal of the defenders of courts to give a realistic account of what happens there.

People sometimes argue that the wonderful thing about judicial reasoning on rights (as opposed to legislative reasoning on rights) is that issues of rights present themselves to judges in the form of flesh-and-blood individual situations. . . .

But this is mostly a myth. By the time cases reach the high appellate levels we are mostly talking about in our disputes about judicial review, almost all trace of the original flesh-and-blood right-holders has vanished, and argument such as it is revolves around the abstract issue of the right in dispute. Plaintiffs or petitioners are selected by advocacy groups precisely in order to embody the abstract characteristics that the groups want to emphasize as part of a general public policy argument. . . .

The process of legislation is open to consideration of individual cases, through lobbying, in hearings, and in debate. Indeed, there is a tendency these days to initiate legislation on the basis of notorious individual cases — Megan's Law, for example. Hard cases make bad law, it is sometimes said. To the extent that this is true, it seems to me that legislatures are much better positioned to mount an assessment of the significance of an individual case in relation to a general issue of rights that affects millions and affects them in many different ways.

We are imagining a society with a Bill of Rights, and if there is to be judicial review of legislation, it will presumably center on the Bill of Rights. The Bill of Rights, we have assumed, has been adopted in the society pursuant to members' shared commitment to the idea of individual and minority rights notwithstanding the fact that they disagree about what these rights are and what they entail. Now, when rights-disagreements erupt in regard to legislation, there is a question about the role that the established Bill of Rights should play in the decision-process in which the issue is posed. From an outcome-related point of view, is it a good idea or a bad idea that rights-disagreements be fought out in relation to the terms of a Bill of Rights?

One reason for thinking it is a good idea is that the written formulations of the Bill of Rights can help disputants focus on the abstract rights-issues at stake. But there are powerful reasons on the other side. The forms of words used in the Bill of Rights will not have been chosen with rights-disagreements in mind. Or, if they were, they will have been chosen in order to finesse the disagreements about rights that existed at the time the Bill of Rights was set up. Their platitudes may be exactly the wrong formulations to focus clear-headed, responsible, and good faith explorations of rights-disagreements.

The written formulations of a Bill of Rights also tend to encourage a certain rigid textual formalism. A legal right that finds protection in a Bill of Rights finds it under the auspices of some canonical form of words in which the provisions of the Bill are enunciated. One lesson of American constitutional experience is that the words of each provision tend to take on a life of their own, becoming the obsessive catchphrase for expressing everything one might want to say about the right in question. . . .

. . . [C]ourts will tend to be distracted in their arguments about rights by side arguments about how a text like the Bill of Rights is best approached by judges. American experience bears this out: The proportion of argument about theories of interpretation to direct argument about the moral issues is skewed in most judicial opinions in a way that no one who thinks the issues themselves are important can possibly regard as satisfactory. This is partly because the legitimacy of judicial review is itself so problematic. Because judges (like the rest of us) are concerned about the legitimacy of a process that permits them to decide these issues, they cling to their authorizing texts and debate their interpretation rather than venturing out to discuss moral reasons directly.

It is often thought that the great advantage of judicial decisionmaking on issues of individual rights is the explicit reasoning and reason-giving associated with it. Courts give reasons for their decisions, we are told, and this is a token of taking seriously what is at stake, whereas legislatures do not. In fact, this is a false contrast. Legislators give reasons for their votes just as judges do. The reasons are given in what we call debate and they are published in Hansard or the Congressional Record....

Perhaps this argument is not really about the presence or absence of reason-giving, but rather about its quality. In my view, however, the reasons that courts tend to give when they are exercising powers of judicial review of legislation are seldom the reasons that would be canvassed in a full deliberative discussion. . . . Partly this is the point mentioned earlier — that the reasons will be oriented toward the terminology of the Bill of Rights....

Courts' reason-giving also involves attempts to construct desperate analogies or disanalogies between the present decision they face and other decisions that happen to have come before them (and in which they were engaged in similar contortions). There is laborious discussion of precedent, even though it is acknowledged at the highest levels of adjudication that precedent does not settle the matter. (So there is also laborious discussion of the circumstances in which precedent should or shouldn't be overridden.) And all the time, the real issues at stake in the good faith disagreement about rights get pushed to the margins....

... Courts are concerned about the legitimacy of their decisionmaking and so they focus their "reason-giving" on facts that tend to show that they are legally authorized — by constitution, statute, or precedent — to make the decision they are proposing to make. This is an understandable thing to do. But it counts heavily against the courts in the outcome-related argument about the preferability of judicial review over legislation. Distracted by these issues of legitimacy, courts focus on what other courts have done, or what the language of the Bill of Rights is, whereas legislators — for all their vices — tend at least to go directly to the heart of the matter.

I am sure there is more to be said on the outcome-related question. It is certainly the case that just as courts address questions of rights in ways that distort what is really at stake, so too can legislative reasoning be a disgrace, as legislative majorities act out of panic, recklessly, or simply parrot popular or sectarian slogans in their pseudo-debates. The question is this: Which defects in deliberation should be regarded as normal and which as aberrations in the way that the respective institutions — courts and legislatures — are supposed to behave? Despite Dworkin's rhetoric about "forums of principle," I think courts are expected to behave in the ways that I have criticized, focusing on precedent, text, doctrine, and other legalisms. Our assumption about courts — assumption two — is about institutions that behave in that way, indeed behave well by those (legalistic) standards. In the case of legislatures, however, hasty or sectarian legislating is not part of the normal theory of what legislatures are set up to do. It is not what we should assume for the core case of legislative decisionmaking in a society most of whose members respect rights. There may be some countries — perhaps the United States — in which peculiar legislative pathologies have developed. If that is so, then Americans should confine their non-core argument for judicial review to their own exceptional circumstances....

COOPER v. AARON

358 U.S. 1 (1958)

Opinion: Warren, Black, Frankfurter, Douglas, Burton, Clark, Harlan, Brennan, Whittaker
Concurrence: Frankfurter

Following the Supreme Court's 1954 decision in Brown v. Board of Education, *which held that racial discrimination in public schools is an unconstitutional violation of the Equal Protection Clause of the Fourteenth Amendment, Little Rock, Arkansas, adopted a plan to integrate its schools beginning in 1957. Massive resistance in the form of popular discontent, mob violence, and obstructive measures by the state legislature and Governor Orval Faubus disrupted these efforts. Only the intervention of federal troops allowed the integrated schools to continue operating safely. In response to these difficulties, local officials sought to suspend implementation of the desegregation proposal. In a unanimous decision, the Supreme Court reaffirmed its holding in* Brown v. Board of Education *and maintained that state officials were bound to enforce and abide by that decision. In a separate concurrence, U.S. Supreme Court Justice Felix Frankfurter argued that the rule of law requires that the Court have the final say in the face of open resistance.*

Opinion of the Court by **THE CHIEF JUSTICE, MR. JUSTICE BLACK, MR. JUSTICE FRANKFURTER, MR. JUSTICE DOUGLAS, MR. JUSTICE BURTON, MR. JUSTICE CLARK, MR. JUSTICE HARLAN, MR. JUSTICE BRENNAN,** *and* **MR. JUSTICE WHITTAKER.**

The constitutional rights of respondents are not to be sacrificed or yielded to the violence and disorder which have followed upon the actions of the Governor and Legislature. As this Court said some 41 years ago in a unanimous opinion in a case involving another aspect of racial segregation: "It is urged that this proposed segregation will promote the public peace by preventing race conflicts. Desirable as this is, and important as is the preservation of the public peace, this aim cannot be accomplished by laws or ordinances which deny rights created or protected by the Federal Constitution." Thus law and order are not here to be preserved by depriving the Negro children of their constitutional rights. The record before us clearly establishes that the growth of the Board's difficulties to a magnitude beyond its unaided power to control is the product of state action. Those difficulties, as counsel for the Board forthrightly conceded on the oral argument in this Court, can also be brought under control by state action. The controlling legal principles are plain. The command of the Fourteenth Amendment is that no "State" shall deny to any person within its jurisdiction the equal protection of the laws. "A State acts by its legislative, its executive, or its judicial authorities. It can act in no other way. The constitutional provision, therefore, must mean that no agency of the State, or of the officers or agents by whom its powers are exerted, shall deny to any person within its jurisdiction the equal protection of the laws. Whoever, by virtue of public position under a State government, . . . denies or takes away the equal protection of the laws, violates the constitutional inhibition; and as he acts in the name and for the State, and is clothed with the State's power, his act is that of the State. This must be so, or the constitutional prohibition has no meaning." *Ex parte Virginia.* Thus the prohibitions of the Fourteenth

Amendment extend to all action of the State denying equal protection of the laws; whatever the agency of the State taking the action, or whatever the guise in which it is taken. In short, the constitutional rights of children not to be discriminated against in school admission on grounds of race or color declared by this Court in the *Brown* case can neither be nullified openly and directly by state legislators or state executive or judicial officers, nor nullified indirectly by them through evasive schemes for segregation whether attempted "ingeniously or ingenuously."

... [W]e should answer the premise of the actions of the Governor and Legislature that they are not bound by our holding in the *Brown* case. It is necessary only to recall some basic constitutional propositions which are settled doctrine.

Article VI of the Constitution makes the Constitution the "supreme Law of the Land." In 1803, Chief Justice Marshall, speaking for a unanimous Court, referring to the Constitution as "the fundamental and paramount law of the nation," declared in the notable case of *Marbury v. Madison*, that "It is emphatically the province and duty of the judicial department to say what the law is." This decision declared the basic principle that the federal judiciary is supreme in the exposition of the law of the Constitution, and that principle has ever since been respected by this Court and the Country as a permanent and indispensable feature of our constitutional system. It follows that the interpretation of the Fourteenth Amendment enunciated by this Court in the *Brown* case is the supreme law of the land, and Art. VI of the Constitution makes it of binding effect on the States "any Thing in the Constitution or Laws of any State to the Contrary notwithstanding." Every state legislator and executive and judicial officer is solemnly committed by oath taken pursuant to Art. VI, cl. 3, "to support this Constitution." Chief Justice Taney, speaking for a unanimous Court in 1859, said that this requirement reflected the framers' "anxiety to preserve it [the Constitution] in full force, in all its powers, and to guard against resistance to or evasion of its authority, on the part of a State...."

No state legislator or executive or judicial officer can war against the Constitution without violating his undertaking to support it. Chief Justice Marshall spoke for a unanimous Court in saying that: "If the legislatures of the several states may, at will, annul the judgments of the courts of the United States, and destroy the rights acquired under those judgments, the constitution itself becomes a solemn mockery. . . ." A Governor who asserts a power to nullify a federal court order is similarly restrained. If he had such power, said Chief Justice Hughes, in 1932, also for a unanimous Court, "it is manifest that the fiat of a state Governor, and not the Constitution of the United States, would be the supreme law of the land; that the restrictions of the Federal Constitution upon the exercise of state power would be but impotent phrases...."

It is, of course, quite true that the responsibility for public education is primarily the concern of the States, but it is equally true that such responsibilities, like all other state activity, must be exercised consistently with federal constitutional requirements as they apply to state action. The Constitution created a government dedicated to equal justice under law. The Fourteenth Amendment embodied and emphasized that ideal. State support of segregated schools through any arrangement, management, funds, or property cannot be squared with the Amendment's command that no State shall deny to any person within its jurisdiction the equal protection of the laws. The right of a student not to be segregated on racial grounds in schools so maintained is indeed so fundamental and pervasive that it is embraced in the concept of due process of law. *Bolling v. Sharpe*. The basic decision in *Brown* was unanimously reached by this Court only after the case had been briefed and twice argued and the issues had been given the most serious consideration. Since the first *Brown* opinion three new Justices have come to the Court. They are at one with the Justices still on the Court who participated in that basic decision as to its correctness, and that decision is now unanimously reaffirmed. The principles announced in that decision and the obedience of the States to them, according to the command of the Constitution, are indispensable for the protection of the freedoms guaranteed by our fundamental charter for all of us. Our constitutional ideal of equal justice under law is thus made a living truth.

JUSTICE FRANKFURTER, *concurring.*

By working together, by sharing in a common effort, men of different minds and tempers, even if they do not reach agreement, acquire understanding and thereby tolerance of their differences. This process was under way in Little Rock. The detailed plan formulated by the Little Rock School Board, in the light of local circumstances, had been approved by the United States District Court in Arkansas as satisfying the requirements of this Court's decree in *Brown v. Board of Education*. The Little Rock School Board had embarked on an educational effort "to obtain public acceptance" of its plan. Thus the process of the community's accommodation to new demands of law upon it, the development of habits of acceptance of the right of colored children to the equal protection of the laws guaranteed by the Constitution, had peacefully and promisingly begun. The condition in Little Rock before this process was forcibly impeded by those in control of the government of Arkansas was thus described by the District Court, and these findings of fact have not been controverted:

> "Up to this time, no crowds had gathered about Central High School and no acts of violence or threats of violence in connection with the carrying out of the plan had occurred. Nevertheless, out of an abundance of caution, the school authorities had frequently conferred with the Mayor and Chief of Police of Little Rock about taking appropriate steps by the Little Rock police to prevent any possible disturbances or acts of violence in connection with the attendance of the 9 colored students at Central High School. The Mayor considered that the Little Rock police force could adequately cope with any incidents which might arise at the opening of school. The Mayor, the Chief of Police, and the school authorities made no request to the Governor or any representative of his for State assistance in maintaining peace and order at Central High School. Neither the Governor nor any other official of the State government consulted with the Little Rock authorities about whether the Little Rock police were prepared to cope with any incidents which might arise at the school, about any need for State assistance in maintaining peace and order, or about stationing the Arkansas National Guard at Central High School."

All this was disrupted by the introduction of the state militia and by other obstructive measures taken by the State. The illegality of these interferences with the constitutional right of Negro children qualified to enter the Central High School is unaffected by whatever action or non-action the Federal Government had seen fit to take. Nor is it neutralized by the undoubted good faith of the Little Rock School Board in endeavoring to discharge its constitutional duty.

The use of force to further obedience to law is in any event a last resort and one not congenial to the spirit of our Nation. But the tragic aspect of this disruptive tactic was that the power of the State was used not to sustain law but as an instrument for thwarting law. The State of Arkansas is thus responsible for disabling one of its subordinate agencies, the Little Rock School Board, from peacefully carrying out the Board's and the State's constitutional duty. Accordingly, while Arkansas is not a formal party in these proceedings and a decree cannot go against the State, it is legally and morally before the Court.

We are now asked to hold that the illegal, forcible interference by the State of Arkansas with the continuance of what the Constitution commands, and the consequences in disorder that it entrained, should be recognized as justification for undoing what the School Board had formulated, what the District Court in 1955 had directed to be carried out, and what was in process of obedience. No explanation that may be offered in support of such a request can obscure the inescapable meaning that law should bow to force. To yield to such a claim would be to enthrone official lawlessness, and lawlessness if not checked is the precursor of anarchy. On the few tragic occasions in the history of the Nation, North and South, when law was forcibly resisted or systematically evaded, it has signaled the breakdown of constitutional processes of government on which ultimately rest the liberties of all. Violent resistance to law cannot be made a legal reason for its suspension without loosening the fabric of our society. What could this mean but to acknowledge that disorder under the aegis of a State has moral superiority over the law of the Constitution? For those in authority thus to defy the law of the land is profoundly subversive not only of our constitutional system but of the presuppositions of a democratic society. The State "must . . . yield to an authority that is paramount to the State." . . .

When defiance of law judicially pronounced was last sought to be justified before this Court, views were expressed which are now especially relevant:

> "The historic phrase 'a government of laws and not of men' epitomizes the distinguishing character of our political society. When John Adams put that phrase into the Massachusetts Declaration of Rights he was not indulging in a rhetorical flourish. He was expressing the aim of those who, with him, framed the Declaration of Independence and founded the Republic. 'A government of laws and not of men' was the rejection in positive terms of rule by fiat, whether by the fiat of governmental or private power. Every act of government may be challenged by an appeal to law, as finally pronounced by this Court. Even this Court has the last say only for a time. Being composed of fallible men, it may err. But revision of its errors must be by orderly process of law. The Court may be asked to reconsider its decisions, and this has been done successfully again and again throughout our history. Or, what this Court has deemed its duty to decide may be changed by legislation, as it often has been, and, on occasion, by constitutional amendment.
>
> "But from their own experience and their deep reading in history, the Founders knew that Law alone saves a society from being rent by internecine strife or ruled by mere brute power however disguised. 'Civilization involves subjection of force to reason, and the agency of this subjection is law.' The conception of a government by laws dominated the thoughts of those who founded this Nation and designed its Constitution, although they knew as well as the belittlers of the conception that laws have to be made, interpreted and enforced by men. To that end, they set apart a body of men, who were to be the depositories of law, who by their disciplined training and character and by withdrawal from the usual temptations of private interest may reasonably be expected to be 'as free, impartial, and independent as the lot of

> humanity will admit.' So strongly were the framers of the Constitution bent on securing a reign of law that they endowed the judicial office with extraordinary safeguards and prestige. No one, no matter how exalted his public office or how righteous his private motive, can be judge in his own case. That is what courts are for."

The duty to abstain from resistance to "the supreme Law of the Land," U.S. Const., Art. VI, para. 2, as declared by the organ of our Government for ascertaining it, does not require immediate approval of it nor does it deny the right of dissent. Criticism need not be stilled. Active obstruction or defiance is barred. Our kind of society cannot endure if the controlling authority of the Law as derived from the Constitution is not to be the tribunal specially charged with the duty of ascertaining and declaring what is "the supreme Law of the Land." Particularly is this so where the declaration of what "the supreme Law" commands on an underlying moral issue is not the dubious pronouncement of a gravely divided Court but is the unanimous conclusion of a long-matured deliberative process. The Constitution is not the formulation of the merely personal views of the members of this Court, nor can its authority be reduced to the claim that state officials are its controlling interpreters. Local customs, however hardened by time, are not decreed in heaven. Habits and feelings they engender may be counteracted and moderated. Experience attests that such local habits and feelings will yield, gradually though this be, to law and education. And educational influences are exerted not only by explicit teaching. They vigorously flow from the fruitful exercise of the responsibility of those charged with political official power and from the almost unconsciously transforming actualities of living under law.

The process of ending unconstitutional exclusion of pupils from the common school system—"common" meaning shared alike—solely because of color is no doubt not an easy, overnight task in a few States where a drastic alteration in the ways of communities is involved. Deep emotions have, no doubt, been stirred. They will not be calmed by letting violence loose—violence and defiance employed and encouraged by those upon whom the duty of law observance should have the strongest claim—nor by submitting to it under whatever guise employed. Only the constructive use of time will achieve what an advanced civilization demands and the Constitution confirms.

That the responsibility of those who exercise power in a democratic government is not to reflect inflamed public feeling but to help form its understanding, is especially true when they are confronted with a problem like a racially discriminating public school system. This is the lesson to be drawn from the heartening experience in ending enforced racial segregation in the public schools in cities with Negro populations of large proportions. Compliance with decisions of this Court, as the constitutional organ of the supreme Law of the Land, has often, throughout our history, depended on active support by state and local authorities. It presupposes such support. To withhold it, and indeed to use political power to try to paralyze the supreme Law, precludes the maintenance of our federal system as we have known and cherished it for one hundred and seventy years.

Lincoln's appeal to "the better angels of our nature" failed to avert a fratricidal war. But the compassionate wisdom of Lincoln's First and Second Inaugurals bequeathed to the Union, cemented with blood, a moral heritage which, when drawn upon in times of stress and strife, is sure to find specific ways and means to surmount difficulties that may appear to be insurmountable.

NIXON v. UNITED STATES

506 U.S. 224 (1993)

Opinion: Rehnquist, joined by O'Connor, Blackmun, Scalia, Kennedy, Thomas
Concurrence: White, joined by Blackmun
Concurrence: Stevens
Concurrence: Souter

Although, as we will see in the next case, the Supreme Court has suggested that it not only has a role in interpreting the Constitution but that its interpretive power is supreme, this has not meant that the modern Court has failed to show restraint in decisions involving the other branches of government. The following selection is an example of the Court's political question doctrine, under which it refuses to review a case because it deems it a matter under the authority of the other branches. In reading this case, consider whether the political question doctrine is compatible with the notion of judicial supremacy. Is deferring to the legislative branch of government on this issue equivalent to deferring to its interpretation of the Constitution?

The political question doctrine recognizes that the Constitution explicitly grants some powers of decision making to either the Congress or the executive branch and suggests that they might be the appropriate forum for judging the meaning of the Constitution in those arenas. The more expansive the political question doctrine, arguably, the more the Court exercises restraint in matters of constitutional interpretation. But, does the fact that the Court itself determines when the political question doctrine is appropriately invoked provide evidence that it is compatible with an idea of judicial supremacy? Consider this question as you read this case.

CHIEF JUSTICE REHNQUIST *delivered the opinion of the Court.*

Petitioner Walter L. Nixon, Jr., asks this court to decide whether Senate Rule XI, which allows a committee of Senators to hear evidence against an individual who has been impeached and to report that evidence to the full Senate, violates the Impeachment Trial Clause, Art. I, §3, cl. 6. That Clause provides that the "Senate shall have the sole Power to try all Impeachments." But before we reach the merits of such a claim, we must decide whether it is "justiciable," that is, whether it is a claim that may be resolved by the courts. We conclude that it is not.

Nixon, a former Chief Judge of the United States District Court for the Southern District of Mississippi, was convicted by a jury of two counts of making false statements before a federal grand jury and sentenced to prison. The grand jury investigation stemmed from reports that Nixon had accepted a gratuity from a Mississippi businessman in exchange for asking a local district attorney to halt the prosecution of the businessman's son. Because Nixon refused to resign from his office as a United States District Judge, he continued to collect his judicial salary while serving out his prison sentence.

On May 10, 1989, the House of Representatives adopted three articles of impeachment for high crimes and misdemeanors. The first two articles charged Nixon with giving false testimony before the grand jury and the third article charged him with bringing disrepute on the Federal Judiciary.

After the House presented the articles to the Senate, the Senate voted to invoke its own Impeachment Rule XI, under which the presiding officer appoints a committee of Senators to "receive evidence and take testimony." The Senate committee held four days of hearings, during which 10 witnesses, including Nixon, testified. Pursuant to Rule XI, the committee presented the full Senate with a complete transcript of the proceeding and a report stating the uncontested facts and summarizing the evidence on the contested facts. Nixon and the House impeachment managers submitted extensive final briefs to the full Senate and delivered arguments from the Senate floor during the three hours set aside for oral argument in front of that body. Nixon himself gave a personal appeal, and several Senators posed questions directly to both parties. The Senate voted by more than the constitutionally required two thirds majority to convict Nixon on the first two articles. The presiding officer then entered judgment removing Nixon from his office as United States District Judge.

Nixon thereafter commenced the present suit, arguing that Senate Rule XI violates the constitutional grant of authority to the Senate to "try" all impeachments because it prohibits the whole Senate from taking part in the evidentiary hearings. Nixon sought a declaratory judgment that his impeachment conviction was void and that his judicial salary and privileges should be reinstated. The District Court held that his claim was nonjusticiable, and the Court of Appeals for the District of Columbia Circuit agreed.

A controversy is nonjusticiable—*i.e.*, involves a political question—where there is "a textually demonstrable constitutional commitment of the issue to a coordinate political department; or a lack of judicially discoverable and manageable standards for resolving it. . . ." *Baker v. Carr.* But the courts must, in the first instance, interpret the text in question and determine whether and to what extent the issue is textually committed. *Powell v. McCormack.* As the discussion that follows makes clear, the concept of a textual commitment to coordinate political department is not completely separate from the concept of a lack of judicially discoverable and manageable standards for resolving it; the lack of judicially manageable standards may strengthen the conclusion that there is a textually demonstrable commitment to a coordinate branch.

In this case, we must examine Art. I, §3, cl. 6, to determine the scope of authority conferred upon the Senate by the Framers regarding impeachment. It provides:

> "The Senate shall have the sole Power to try all Impeachments. When sitting for that Purpose, they shall be on Oath or Affirmation. When the President of the United States is tried, the Chief Justice shall preside: And no Person shall be convicted without the Concurrence of two thirds of the Members present."

The language and structure of this Clause are revealing. The first sentence is a grant of authority to the Senate, and the word "sole" indicates that this authority is reposed in the Senate and nowhere else. The next two sentences specify requirements to which the Senate proceedings shall conform: the Senate shall be on oath or affirmation, a two thirds vote is required to convict, and when the President is tried the Chief Justice shall preside.

Petitioner argues that the word "try" in the first sentence imposes by implication an additional requirement on the Senate in that the proceedings must be in the nature of a judicial trial. From there petitioner goes on to argue that this limitation precludes the Senate from delegating to a select committee the task of hearing the testimony of witnesses, as was done pursuant to Senate Rule XI. "'[T]ry' means more than simply 'vote on' or 'review' or 'judge.' In 1787 and today, trying a case means hearing the evidence, not scanning a cold record." Petitioner concludes from this that courts may review whether or not the Senate "tried" him before convicting him.

There are several difficulties with this position which lead us ultimately to reject it. The word "try," both in 1787 and later, has considerably broader meanings than those to which petitioner would limit it. Older dictionaries define try as "[t]o examine" or "[t]o examine as a judge." In more modern usage the term has various meanings. For example, try can mean "to examine or investigate judicially," "to conduct the trial of," or "to put to the test by experiment, investigation, or trial." Petitioner submits that "try," as contained in T. Sheridan, *Dictionary of the English Language* (1796), means "to examine as a judge; to bring before a judicial tribunal." Based on the variety of definitions, however, we cannot say that the Framers used the word "try" as an implied limitation on the method by which the Senate might proceed in trying impeachments. "As a rule the Constitution speaks in general terms, leaving Congress to deal with subsidiary matters of detail as the public interests and changing conditions may require. . . ." *Dillon v. Gloss.*

The conclusion that the use of the word "try" in the first sentence of the Impeachment Trial Clause lacks sufficient precision to afford any judicially manageable standard of review of the Senate's actions is fortified by the existence of the three very specific requirements that the Constitution does impose on the Senate when trying impeachments: the members must be under oath, a two thirds vote is required to convict, and the Chief Justice presides when the President is tried. These limitations are quite precise, and their nature suggests that the Framers did not intend to impose additional limitations on the form of the Senate proceedings by the use of the word "try" in the first sentence.

Petitioner devotes only two pages in his brief to negating the significance of the word "sole" in the first sentence of Clause 6. As noted above, that sentence provides that "[t]he Senate shall have the sole Power to try all Impeachments." We think that the word "sole" is of considerable significance. Indeed, the word "sole" appears only one other time in the Constitution — with respect to the House of Representatives' "*sole* Power of Impeachment." The common sense meaning of the word "sole" is that the Senate alone shall have authority to determine whether an individual should be acquitted or convicted. The dictionary definition bears this out. "Sole" is defined as "having no companion," "solitary," "being the only one," and "functioning . . . independently and without assistance or interference." If the courts may review the actions of the Senate in order to determine whether that body "tried" an impeached official, it is difficult to see how the Senate would be "functioning . . . independently and without assistance or interference."

The history and contemporary understanding of the impeachment provisions support our reading of the constitutional language. The parties do not offer evidence of a single word in the history of the Constitutional Convention or in contemporary commentary that even alludes to the possibility of judicial review in the context of the impeachment powers. This silence is quite meaningful in light of the several explicit references to the availability of judicial review as a check on the Legislature's power with respect to bills of attainder, *ex post-facto* laws, and statutes.

The Framers labored over the question of where the impeachment power should lie. Significantly, in at least two considered scenarios the power was placed with the Federal Judiciary. Indeed, Madison and the Committee of Detail proposed that the Supreme Court should have the power to determine impeachments. Despite these proposals, the Convention ultimately decided that the Senate would have "the sole Power to Try all Impeachments." According to Alexander Hamilton, the Senate was the "most fit depositary of this important trust" because its members are representatives of the people. The Supreme Court was not the proper body because the Framers "doubted whether the members of that tribunal would, at all times, be endowed with so eminent a portion of fortitude as would be called for in the execution of so difficult a task" or whether the Court "would possess the degree of credit and authority" to carry out its judgment if it conflicted with the accusation brought by the Legislature — the people's representative. In addition, the Framers believed the Court was too small in number: "The awful discretion, which a court of impeachments must necessarily have, to doom to honor or to infamy the most confidential and the most distinguished characters of the community, forbids the commitment of the trust to a small number of persons."

. . . We agree with the Court of Appeals that opening the door of judicial review to the procedures used by the Senate in trying impeachments would "expose the political life of the country to months, or perhaps years, of chaos." This lack of finality would manifest itself most dramatically if the President were impeached. The legitimacy of any successor, and hence his effectiveness, would be impaired severely, not merely while the judicial process was running its course, but during any retrial that a differently constituted Senate might conduct if its first judgment of conviction were invalidated. Equally uncertain is the question of what relief a court may give other than simply setting aside the judgment of conviction. Could it order the reinstatement of a convicted federal judge, or order Congress to create an additional judgeship if the seat had been filled in the interim?

. . . In the case before us, there is no separate provision of the Constitution which could be defeated by allowing the Senate final authority to determine the meaning of the word "try" in the Impeachment Trial Clause. We agree with Nixon that courts possess power to review either legislative or executive action that transgresses identifiable textual limits. As we have made clear, "whether the action of [either the Legislative or Executive Branch] exceeds whatever authority has been committed, is itself a delicate exercise in constitutional interpretation, and is a responsibility of this Court as ultimate interpreter of the Constitution." *Baker v. Carr.* But we conclude, after exercising that delicate responsibility, that the word "try" in the Impeachment Clause does not provide an identifiable textual limit on the authority which is committed to the Senate.

For the foregoing reasons, the judgment of the Court of Appeals is

Affirmed.

LUJAN v. DEFENDERS OF WILDLIFE

504 U.S. 555 (1992)

Opinion: With respect to Parts I, II, III-A, and IV: Scalia, joined by Rehnquist, White, Kennedy, Souter, Thomas
With respect to Part III-B: Scalia, joined by Rehnquist, White, Thomas
Concurrence: Kennedy, joined by Souter
Concurrence: Stevens
Dissent: Blackmun, joined by O'Connor

Although there is a very real question about whether the Supreme Court now exercises judicial supremacy rather than just judicial review, it is important to keep in mind that there are procedural constraints on the Court's power that keep it from completely usurping the other two branches. In addition to the constraints suggested by the political question doctrine, which we examined the previous case, the Constitution's requirement that the Supreme Court only hear matters in which there is a "case or controversy" (Article III, Section 2) also poses a major limit on its power. In the following case, the Supreme Court denies standing to an individual who has not suffered a concrete enough injury that the Court can actually redress. In short, the Supreme Court, as this case makes clear, does not have the power to simply decide upon the constitutionality of a law or policy without an injured party bringing a suit. As you read this case, you might consider the degree to which the Court's decision not to grant unaffected parties "standing" limits the reach of the Court and perhaps pushes against any worries that it has become too powerful.

JUSTICE SCALIA *delivered the opinion of the Court.*

The ESA seeks to protect species of animals against threats to their continuing existence caused by man. The ESA instructs the Secretary of the Interior to promulgate by regulation a list of those species which are either endangered or threatened under enumerated criteria, and to define the critical habitat of these species. Section 7(a)(2) of the Act then provides, in pertinent part:

> "Each Federal agency shall, in consultation with and with the assistance of the Secretary [of the Interior], insure that any action authorized, funded, or carried out by such agency... is not likely to jeopardize the continued existence of any endangered species or threatened species or result in the destruction or adverse modification of habitat of such species which is determined by the Secretary, after consultation as appropriate with affected States, to be critical."

In 1978, the Fish and Wildlife Service (FWS) and the National Marine Fisheries Service (NMFS), on behalf of the Secretary of the Interior and the Secretary of Commerce respectively, promulgated a joint regulation stating that the obligations imposed by §7(a)(2) extend to actions taken in foreign nations. The next year, however, the Interior Department began to reexamine its position. A revised joint regulation, reinterpreting §7(a)(2) to require consultation only for actions taken in the United States or on the high seas, was proposed in 1983, and promulgated in 1986.

Shortly thereafter, respondents, organizations dedicated to wildlife conservation and other environmental causes, filed this action against the Secretary of the Interior, seeking a declaratory judgment that the new regulation is in error as to the geographic scope of §7(a)(2), and an injunction requiring the Secretary to promulgate a new regulation restoring the initial interpretation. The District Court granted the Secretary's motion to dismiss for lack of standing. The Court of Appeals for the Eighth Circuit reversed by a divided vote. On remand, the Secretary moved for summary judgment on the standing issue, and respondents moved for summary judgment on the merits. The District Court denied the Secretary's motion, on the ground that the Eighth Circuit had already determined the standing question in this case; it granted respondents' merits motion, and ordered the Secretary to publish a revised regulation. The Eighth Circuit affirmed. We granted certiorari.

While the Constitution of the United States divides all power conferred upon the Federal Government into "legislative Powers," "[t]he executive Power," and "[t]he judicial Power," it does not attempt to define those terms. To be sure, it limits the jurisdiction of federal courts to "Cases" and "Controversies," but an executive inquiry can bear the name "case" (the Hoffa case) and a legislative dispute can bear the name "controversy" (the Smoot Hawley controversy). Obviously, then, the Constitution's central mechanism of separation of powers depends largely upon common understanding of what activities are appropriate to legislatures, to executives, and to courts. In *The Federalist* No. 48, Madison expressed the view that "[i]t is not infrequently a question of real nicety in legislative bodies whether the operation of a particular measure will, or will not, extend beyond the legislative sphere," whereas "the executive power [is] restrained within a narrower compass and . . . more simple in its nature," and "the judiciary [is] described by landmarks still less uncertain." One of those landmarks, setting apart the "Cases" and "Controversies" that are of the justiciable sort referred to in Article III — "serv[ing] to identify those disputes which are appropriately resolved through the judicial process," *Whitmore v. Arkansas* — is the doctrine of standing. Though some of its elements express merely prudential considerations that are part of judicial self government, the core component of standing is an essential and unchanging part of the case or controversy requirement of Article III.

Over the years, our cases have established that the irreducible constitutional minimum of standing contains three elements: First, the plaintiff must have suffered an "injury in fact" — an invasion of a legally protected interest which is (a) concrete and particularized, and (b) "actual or imminent, not 'conjectural' or 'hypothetical.'" Second, there must be a causal connection between the injury and the conduct complained of — the injury has to be "fairly . . . trace[able] to the challenged action of the defendant, and not . . . th[e] result [of] the independent action of some third party not before the court." *Simon v. Eastern Kentucky Welfare Rights Org.* Third, it must be "likely," as opposed to merely "speculative," that the injury will be "redressed by a favorable decision."

The party invoking federal jurisdiction bears the burden of establishing these elements. See *FW/PBS, Inc. v. Dallas.* Since they are not mere pleading requirements but rather an indispensable part of the plaintiff's case, each element must be supported in the same way as any other matter on which the plaintiff bears the burden of proof, i.e., with the manner and degree of evidence required at the successive stages of the litigation. At the pleading stage, general factual allegations of injury resulting from the defendant's conduct may suffice, for on a motion to dismiss we "presum[e] that general allegations embrace those specific facts that are necessary to support the claim," *National Wildlife Federation.* In response to a summary judgment motion, however, the plaintiff can no longer rest on such "mere allegations," but must "set forth" by affidavit or other evidence "specific facts," which for purposes of the summary judgment motion will be taken to be true. And at the final stage, those facts (if controverted) must be "supported adequately by the evidence adduced at trial," *Gladstone.*

When the suit is one challenging the legality of government action or inaction, the nature and extent of facts that must be averred (at the summary judgment stage) or proved (at the trial stage) in order to establish standing depends considerably upon whether the plaintiff is himself an object of the action (or forgone action) at issue. If he is, there is ordinarily little question that the action or inaction has caused him injury, and that a judgment preventing or requiring the action will redress it. When, however, as in this case, a plaintiff's asserted injury arises from the government's allegedly unlawful regulation (or lack of regulation) of *someone else*, much more is needed. In that circumstance, causation and redressability ordinarily hinge on the response of the regulated third party to the government action or inaction — and perhaps on the response of others as well. The existence of one or more of the essential elements of standing "depends on the unfettered choices made by independent actors not before the courts and whose exercise of broad and legitimate discretion the courts cannot presume either to control or to predict," *ASARCO Inc. v. Kadish* (opinion of Kennedy, J.); and it becomes the burden of the plaintiff to adduce facts showing that those choices have been or will be made in such manner as to produce causation and permit redressability of injury. Thus, when the plaintiff is not himself the object of the government action or inaction he challenges, standing is not precluded, but it is ordinarily "substantially more difficult" to establish. *Allen.*

. . . Ms. Kelly stated that she traveled to Egypt in 1986 and "observed the traditional habitat of the endangered Nile crocodile there and intend[s] to do so again, and hope[s] to observe the crocodile directly," and that she "will suffer harm in fact as a result of [the] American . . . role . . . in overseeing the rehabilitation of the Aswan High Dam on the Nile . . . and [in] develop[ing] . . . Egypt's . . . Master Water Plan." Ms. Skilbred averred that she traveled to Sri Lanka in 1981 and "observed th[e] habitat" of "endangered species such as the Asian elephant and the leopard" at what is now the site of the Mahaweli Project funded by the Agency for International Development (AID), although she "was unable to see any of the endangered species"; "this development project," she continued, "will seriously reduce endangered, threatened, and endemic species habitat including areas that I visited . . . [, which] may severely shorten the future of these species"; that threat, she concluded, harmed her because she "intend[s] to return to Sri Lanka in the future and hope[s] to be more fortunate in spotting at least the endangered elephant and leopard." When Ms. Skilbred was asked at a subsequent deposition if and when she had any plans to return to Sri Lanka, she reiterated that "I intend to go back to Sri Lanka," but confessed that she had no current plans: "I don't know [when]. There is a civil war going on right now. I don't know. Not next year, I will say. In the future."

We shall assume for the sake of argument that these affidavits contain facts showing that certain agency funded projects threaten listed species — though that is questionable. They plainly contain no facts, however, showing how damage to the species will produce "imminent" injury to . . . Kelly and Skilbred. That the women "had visited" the areas of the projects before the projects commenced proves nothing. As we have said in a related context, " '[p]ast exposure to illegal conduct does not in itself show a present case or controversy regarding injunctive relief . . . if unaccompanied by any continuing, present adverse effects.' " *Lyons.* And the affiant's profession of an "inten[t]" to return to the places they had visited before — where they will presumably, this time, be deprived of the opportunity to observe animals of the endangered species — is simply not enough. Such "some day" intentions — without any description of concrete plans, or indeed even any specification of *when* the some day will be — do not support a finding of the "actual or imminent" injury that our cases require.

Besides relying upon the Kelly and Skilbred affidavits, respondents propose a series of novel standing theories. The first, inelegantly styled "ecosystem nexus," proposes that any person who uses *any part* of a "contiguous ecosystem" adversely affected by a funded activity has standing even if the activity is located a great distance away. This approach, as the Court of Appeals correctly observed, is inconsistent with our opinion in *National Wildlife Federation,* which held that a plaintiff claiming injury from environmental damage must use the area affected by the challenged activity and not an area roughly "in the vicinity" of it. It makes no difference that the general purpose section of the ESA states that the Act was intended in part "to provide a means whereby the ecosystems upon which endangered species and threatened species depend may be conserved." To say that the Act protects ecosystems is not to say that the Act creates (if it were possible) rights of action in persons who have not been injured in fact, that is, persons who use portions of an ecosystem not perceptibly affected by the unlawful action in question.

Respondents' other theories are called, alas, the "animal nexus" approach, whereby anyone who has an interest in studying or seeing the endangered animals anywhere on the globe has standing; and the "vocational nexus" approach, under which anyone with a professional interest in such animals can sue. Under these theories, anyone who goes to see Asian elephants in the Bronx Zoo, and anyone who is a keeper of Asian elephants in the Bronx Zoo, has standing to sue because the Director of AID did not consult with the Secretary regarding the AID funded project in Sri Lanka. This is beyond all reason. Standing is not "an ingenious academic exercise in the conceivable," *United States v. Students Challenging Regulatory Agency Procedures (SCRAP)*, but as we have said requires, at the summary judgment stage, a factual showing of perceptible harm. It is clear that the person who observes or works with a particular animal threatened by a federal decision is facing perceptible harm, since the very subject of his interest will no longer exist. It is even plausible — though it goes to the outermost limit of plausibility — to think that a person who observes or works with animals of a particular species in the very area of the world where that species is threatened by a federal decision is facing such harm, since some animals that might have been the subject of his interest will no longer exist, see *Japan Whaling Assn. v. American Cetacean Soc.* It goes beyond the limit, however, and into pure speculation and fantasy, to say that anyone who observes or works with an endangered species, anywhere in the world, is appreciably harmed by a single project affecting some portion of that species with which he has no more specific connection.

Besides failing to show injury, respondents failed to demonstrate redressability. Instead of attacking the separate decisions to fund particular projects allegedly causing them harm, the respondents chose to challenge a more generalized level of government action (rules regarding consultation), the invalidation of which would affect all overseas projects. This programmatic approach has obvious practical advantages, but also obvious difficulties insofar as proof of causation or redressability is concerned. As we have said in another context, "suits challenging, not specifically identifiable Government violations of law, but the particular programs agencies establish to carry out their legal obligations ... [are], even when premised on allegations of several instances of violations of law, ... rarely if ever appropriate for federal court adjudication." *Allen.*

The most obvious problem in the present case is redressability. Since the agencies funding the projects were not parties to the case, the District Court could accord relief only against the Secretary: He could be ordered to revise his regulation to require consultation for foreign projects. But this would not remedy respondents' alleged injury unless the funding agencies were bound by the Secretary's regulation, which is very much an open question. Whereas in other contexts the ESA is quite explicit as to the Secretary's controlling authority, with respect to consultation the initiative, and hence arguably the initial responsibility for determining statutory necessity, lies with the agencies. When the Secretary promulgated the regulation at issue here, he thought it was binding on the agencies. The Solicitor General, however, has repudiated that position here, and the agencies themselves apparently deny the Secretary's authority. (During the period when the Secretary took the view that §7(a)(2) did apply abroad, AID and FWS engaged in a running controversy over whether consultation was required with respect to the Mahaweli project, AID insisting that consultation applied only to domestic actions.)

. . . The Court of Appeals found that respondents had standing for an additional reason: because they had suffered a "procedural injury." The so called "citizen suit" provision of the ESA provides, in pertinent part, that "any person may commence a civil suit on his own behalf (A) to enjoin any person, including the United States and any other governmental instrumentality or agency . . . who is alleged to be in violation of any provision of this chapter." The court held that, because §7(a)(2) requires interagency consultation, the citizen suit provision creates a "procedural righ[t]" to consultation in all "persons"—so that *anyone* can file suit in federal court to challenge the Secretary's (or presumably any other official's) failure to follow the assertedly correct consultative procedure, notwithstanding their inability to allege any discrete injury flowing from that failure. To understand the remarkable nature of this holding one must be clear about what it does *not* rest upon: This is not a case where plaintiffs are seeking to enforce a procedural requirement the disregard of which could impair a separate concrete interest of theirs (*e.g.*, the procedural requirement for a hearing prior to denial of their license application, or the procedural requirement for an environmental impact statement before a federal facility is constructed next door to them). Nor is it simply a case where concrete injury has been suffered by many persons, as in mass fraud or mass tort situations. Nor, finally, is it the unusual case in which Congress has created a concrete private interest in the outcome of a suit against a private party for the government's benefit, by providing a cash bounty for the victorious plaintiff. Rather, the court held that the injury in fact requirement had been satisfied by congressional conferral upon *all* persons of an abstract, self contained, non-instrumental "right" to have the Executive observe the procedures required by law. We reject this view.

We have consistently held that a plaintiff raising only a generally available grievance about government—claiming only harm to his and every citizen's interest in proper application of the Constitution and laws, and seeking relief that no more directly and tangibly benefits him than it does the public at large—does not state an Article III case or controversy. For example, in *Fairchild v. Hughes*, we dismissed a suit challenging the propriety of the process by which the Nineteenth Amendment was ratified. Justice Brandeis wrote for the Court:

> "[This is] not a case within the meaning of . . . Article III. . . . Plaintiff has [asserted] only the right, possessed by every citizen, to require that the Government be administered according to law and that the public moneys be not wasted. Obviously this general right does not entitle a private citizen to institute in the federal courts a suit. . . ."

. . . To be sure, our generalized grievance cases have typically involved Government violation of procedures assertedly ordained by the Constitution rather than the Congress. But there is absolutely no basis for making the Article III inquiry turn on the source of the asserted right. Whether the courts were to act on their own, or at the invitation of Congress, in ignoring the concrete injury requirement described in our cases, they would be discarding a principle fundamental to the separate and distinct constitutional role of the Third Branch — one of the essential elements that identifies those "Cases" and "Controversies" that are the business of the courts rather than of the political branches. "The province of the court," as Chief Justice Marshall said in *Marbury v. Madison*, "is, solely, to decide on the rights of individuals." Vindicating the *public* interest (including the public interest in government observance of the Constitution and laws) is the function of Congress and the Chief Executive. The question presented here is whether the public interest in proper administration of the laws (specifically, in agencies' observance of a particular, statutorily prescribed procedure) can be converted into an individual right by a statute that denominates it as such, and that permits all citizens (or, for that matter, a subclass of citizens who suffer no distinctive concrete harm) to sue. If the concrete injury requirement has the separation of powers significance we have always said, the answer must be obvious: To permit Congress to convert the undifferentiated public interest in executive officers' compliance with the law into an "individual right" vindicable in the courts is to permit Congress to transfer from the President to the courts the Chief Executive's most important constitutional duty, to "take Care that the Laws be faithfully executed." It would enable the courts, with the permission of Congress, "to assume a position of authority over the governmental acts of another and co equal department," *Frothingham v. Mellon*, and to become "'virtually continuing monitors of the wisdom and soundness of Executive action.'"

JUSTICE BLACKMUN, *with whom* **JUSTICE O'CONNOR** *joins.*

... To survive petitioner's motion for summary judgment on standing, respondents need not prove that they are actually or imminently harmed. They need show only a "genuine issue" of material fact as to standing. Fed. Rule Civ. Proc. 56(c). This is not a heavy burden. A "genuine issue" exists so long as "the evidence is such that a reasonable jury could return a verdict for the nonmoving party [respondents]." *Anderson v. Liberty Lobby, Inc.* This Court's "function is not [it]self to weigh the evidence and determine the truth of the matter but to determine whether there is a genuine issue for trial." *Id.*, at 249.

The Court never mentions the "genuine issue" standard. Rather, the Court refers to the type of evidence it feels respondents failed to produce, namely, "affidavits or other evidence showing, through specific facts" the existence of injury.... The Court thereby confuses respondents' evidentiary burden (*i.e.*, affidavits asserting "specific facts") in withstanding a summary judgment motion under Rule 56(e) with the standard of proof (*i.e.*, the existence of a "genuine issue" of "material fact") under Rule 56(c).

Were the Court to apply the proper standard for summary judgment, I believe it would conclude that the sworn affidavits and deposition testimony of Joyce Kelly and Amy Skilbred advance sufficient facts to create a genuine issue for trial concerning whether one or both would be imminently harmed by the Aswan and Mahaweli projects. In the first instance, as the Court itself concedes, the affidavits contained facts making it at least "questionable" (and therefore within the province of the factfinder) that certain agency funded projects threaten listed species. . . . The only remaining issue, then, is whether Kelly and Skilbred have shown that they personally would suffer imminent harm.

I think a reasonable finder of fact could conclude from the information in the affidavits and deposition testimony that either Kelly or Skilbred will soon return to the project sites, thereby satisfying the "actual or imminent" injury standard. The Court dismisses Kelly's and Skilbred's general statements that they intended to revisit the project sites as "simply not enough." ... But those statements did not stand alone. A reasonable finder of fact could conclude, based not only upon their statements of intent to return, but upon their past visits to the project sites, as well as their professional backgrounds, that it was likely that Kelly and Skilbred would make a return trip to the project areas. Contrary to the Court's contention that Kelly's and Skilbred's past visits "proves nothing," ... the fact of their past visits could demonstrate to a reasonable factfinder that Kelly and Skilbred have the requisite resources and personal interest in the preservation of the species endangered by the Aswan and Mahaweli projects to make good on their intention to return again. Cf. *Los Angeles v. Lyons* ("Past wrongs were evidence bearing on whether there is a real and immediate threat of repeated injury") (internal quotations omitted). Similarly, Kelly's and Skilbred's professional backgrounds in wildlife preservation, see App. 100, 144, 309-310, also make it likely — at least far more likely than for the average citizen — that they would choose to visit these areas of the world where species are vanishing.

CITY OF BOERNE v. FLORES

521 U.S. 507 (1997)

Opinion: Kennedy, joined by Rehnquist, Stevens, Thomas, Ginsburg, joined by Scalia in all but Part III-A-1
Concurrence: Stevens
Concurrence: Scalia, joined by Stevens
Dissent: O'Connor joined by Breyer in all but a portion of Part I
Dissent: Souter
Dissent: Breyer

In Employment Division v. Smith, *the Supreme Court reversed an earlier line of cases and lessened the scrutiny it applied to laws allegedly infringing religious freedoms, establishing what it regarded as a more workable and sound approach to this issue. Many citizens throughout the country, however, were angered by the Court's shift to this position, believing that it had abandoned the Constitution's strong protection of religious freedom. Concerned that the Court was not doing enough to protect religious citizens, Congress enacted the Religious Freedom Restoration Act (RFRA). The RFRA required the Court to return to its previous jurisprudence in this area and to reject the standard of religious freedom that the Court sought to adopt in its* Employment Division v. Smith *decision. Although the case raises questions of religious freedom, we focus here on the case's discussion of the proper role of Congress and the Supreme Court in constitutional interpretation. Arguably, by attempting to change the kind of interpretation of religious freedom adopted by the Court in* Employment Division v. Smith, *Congress assumed that the Court's decision on this matter was not final or supreme. In this case, the Court examines the constitutionality of the RFRA. Its decision in this case is often considered the Court's definitive modern statement on the question of judicial review. As you will see, the Court considers whether Congress, in passing the RFRA, overreached its proper role by attempting to correct the Court's own understanding of religious freedom. Although the Court recognizes that Congress has some role in enforcing constitutional rights, it regards itself as the ultimate source of constitutional interpretation. But how far does the Supreme Court go in making this case? Is the Court's interpretation the right one, solely because it says so? Is constitutional interpretation best left to the judiciary alone in certain cases? What role should Congress play in discerning the meaning of the Constitution?*

As you consider these questions, keep in mind Larry Kramer's and Jeremy Waldron's critiques of judicial supremacy. You might also consider whether Ronald Dworkin, in his excerpt, provides any theoretical support for this case.

JUSTICE KENNEDY *delivered the opinion of the Court.*

Situated on a hill in the city of Boerne, Texas, some 28 miles northwest of San Antonio, is St. Peter Catholic Church. Built in 1923, the church's structure replicates the mission style of the region's earlier history. The church seats about 230 worshippers, a number too small for its growing parish. Some 40 to 60 parishioners cannot be accommodated at some Sunday masses. In order to meet the needs of the congregation the Archbishop of San Antonio gave permission to the parish to plan alterations to enlarge the building.

A few months later, the Boerne City Council passed an ordinance authorizing the city's Historic Landmark Commission to prepare a preservation plan with proposed historic landmarks and districts. Under the ordinance, the Commission must preapprove construction affecting historic landmarks or buildings in a historic district.

Soon afterwards, the Archbishop applied for a building permit so construction to enlarge the church could proceed. City authorities, relying on the ordinance and the designation of a historic district (which, they argued, included the church), denied the application. The Archbishop brought this suit challenging the permit denial in the United States District Court for the Western District of Texas.

The complaint contained various claims, but to this point the litigation has centered on RFRA and the question of its constitutionality. The Archbishop relied upon RFRA as one basis for relief from the refusal to issue the permit. The District Court concluded that by enacting RFRA Congress exceeded the scope of its enforcement power under §5 of the Fourteenth Amendment. The court certified its order for interlocutory appeal and the Fifth Circuit reversed, finding RFRA to be constitutional. We granted certiorari and now reverse.

Congress enacted RFRA in direct response to the Court's decision in *Employment Div., Dept. of Human Resources of Ore. v. Smith.* There we considered a Free Exercise Clause claim brought by members of the Native American Church who were denied unemployment benefits when they lost their jobs because they had used peyote. Their practice was to ingest peyote for sacramental purposes, and they challenged an Oregon statute of general applicability which made use of the drug criminal. In evaluating the claim, we declined to apply the balancing test set forth in *Sherbert v. Verner*, under which we would have asked whether Oregon's prohibition substantially burdened a religious practice and, if it did, whether the burden was justified by a compelling government interest. We stated:

> "Government's ability to enforce generally applicable prohibitions of socially harmful conduct . . . cannot depend on measuring the effects of a governmental action on a religious objector's spiritual development. To make an individual's obligation to obey such a law contingent upon the law's coincidence with his religious beliefs, except where the State's interest is 'compelling' . . . contradicts both constitutional tradition and common sense."

The application of the *Sherbert* test, the *Smith* decision explained, would have produced an anomaly in the law, a constitutional right to ignore neutral laws of general applicability. The anomaly would have been accentuated, the Court reasoned, by the difficulty of determining whether a particular practice was central to an individual's religion. We explained, moreover, that it "is not within the judicial ken to question the centrality of particular beliefs or practices to a faith, or the validity of particular litigants' interpretations of those creeds."

Four Members of the Court disagreed. They argued the law placed a substantial burden on the Native American Church members so that it could be upheld only if the law served a compelling state interest and was narrowly tailored to achieve that end. . . .

These points of constitutional interpretation were debated by Members of Congress in hearings and floor debates. Many criticized the Court's reasoning, and this disagreement resulted in the passage of RFRA. . . .

RFRA prohibits "government" from "substantially burdening" a person's exercise of religion even if the burden results from a rule of general applicability unless the government can demonstrate the burden "(1) is in furtherance of a compelling governmental interest; and (2) is the least restrictive means of furthering that compelling governmental interest." . . .

Under our Constitution, the Federal Government is one of enumerated powers. The judicial authority to determine the constitutionality of laws, in cases and controversies, is based on the premise that the "powers of the legislature are defined and limited; and that those limits may not be mistaken, or forgotten, the constitution is written." *Marbury v. Madison.* Congress relied on its Fourteenth Amendment enforcement power in enacting the most far reaching and substantial of RFRA's provisions, those which impose its requirements on the States. The Fourteenth Amendment provides, in relevant part:

> "SECTION 1. . . . No State shall make or enforce any law which shall abridge the privileges or immunities of citizens of the United States; nor shall any State deprive any person of life, liberty, or property, without due process of law; nor deny to any person within its jurisdiction the equal protection of the laws. . . .
>
> "SECTION 5. The Congress shall have power to enforce, by appropriate legislation, the provisions of this article."

In defense of the Act respondent contends, with support from the United States as amicus, that RFRA is permissible enforcement legislation. Congress, it is said, is only protecting by legislation one of the liberties guaranteed by the Fourteenth Amendment's Due Process Clause, the free exercise of religion, beyond what is necessary under *Smith.* It is said the congressional decision to dispense with proof of deliberate or overt discrimination and instead concentrate on a law's effects accords with the settled understanding that §5 includes the power to enact legislation designed to prevent as well as remedy constitutional violations. It is further contended that Congress' §5 power is not limited to remedial or preventive legislation.

All must acknowledge that §5 is "a positive grant of legislative power" to Congress. . . .

Legislation which deters or remedies constitutional violations can fall within the sweep of Congress' enforcement power even if in the process it prohibits conduct which is not itself unconstitutional and intrudes into "legislative spheres of autonomy previously reserved to the States." For example, the Court upheld a suspension of literacy tests and similar voting requirements under Congress' parallel power to enforce the provisions of the Fifteenth Amendment, as a measure to combat racial discrimination in voting, despite the facial constitutionality of the tests under *Lassiter v. Northampton County Bd. of Elections*. We have also concluded that other measures protecting voting rights are within Congress' power to enforce the Fourteenth and Fifteenth Amendments, despite the burdens those measures placed on the States.

It is also true, however, that "as broad as the congressional enforcement power is, it is not unlimited." *Oregon v. Mitchell*. In assessing the breadth of §5's enforcement power, we begin with its text. Congress has been given the power "to enforce" the "provisions of this article." We agree with respondent, of course, that Congress can enact legislation under §5 enforcing the constitutional right to the free exercise of religion. The "provisions of this article," to which §5 refers, include the Due Process Clause of the Fourteenth Amendment. Congress' power to enforce the Free Exercise Clause follows from our holding in *Cantwell v. Connecticut* that the "fundamental concept of liberty embodied in [the Fourteenth Amendment's Due Process Clause] embraces the liberties guaranteed by the First Amendment."

Congress' power under §5, however, extends only to "enforcing" the provisions of the Fourteenth Amendment. The Court has described this power as "remedial." The design of the Amendment and the text of §5 are inconsistent with the suggestion that Congress has the power to decree the substance of the Fourteenth Amendment's restrictions on the States. Legislation which alters the meaning of the Free Exercise Clause cannot be said to be enforcing the Clause. Congress does not enforce a constitutional right by changing what the right is. It has been given the power "to enforce," not the power to determine what constitutes a constitutional violation. Were it not so, what Congress would be enforcing would no longer be, in any meaningful sense, the "provisions of [the Fourteenth Amendment]."

While the line between measures that remedy or prevent unconstitutional actions and measures that make a substantive change in the governing law is not easy to discern, and Congress must have wide latitude in determining where it lies, the distinction exists and must be observed. There must be a congruence and proportionality between the injury to be prevented or remedied and the means adopted to that end. Lacking such a connection, legislation may become substantive in operation and effect. History and our case law support drawing the distinction, one apparent from the text of the Amendment.

The Fourteenth Amendment's history confirms the remedial, rather than substantive, nature of the Enforcement Clause. The Joint Committee on Reconstruction of the 39th Congress began drafting what would become the Fourteenth Amendment in January 1866. The objections to the Committee's first draft of the Amendment, and the rejection of the draft, have a direct bearing on the central issue of defining Congress' enforcement power. In February, Republican Representative John Bingham of Ohio reported the following draft amendment to the House of Representatives on behalf of the Joint Committee:

> "The Congress shall have power to make all laws which shall be necessary and proper to secure to the citizens of each State all privileges and immunities of citizens in the several States, and to all persons in the several States equal protection in the rights of life, liberty, and property."

The proposal encountered immediate opposition, which continued through three days of debate. Members of Congress from across the political spectrum criticized the Amendment, and the criticisms had a common theme: The proposed Amendment gave Congress too much legislative power at the expense of the existing constitutional structure....

. . . Under the revised Amendment, Congress' power was no longer plenary but remedial. Congress was granted the power to make the substantive constitutional prohibitions against the States effective. Representative Bingham said the new draft would give Congress "the power ... to protect by national law the privileges and immunities of all the citizens of the Republic ... whenever the same shall be abridged or denied by the unconstitutional acts of any State." Representative Stevens described the new draft Amendment as "allowing Congress to correct the unjust legislation of the States." ... The revised Amendment proposal did not raise the concerns expressed earlier regarding broad congressional power to prescribe uniform national laws with respect to life, liberty, and property....

The design of the Fourteenth Amendment has proved significant also in maintaining the traditional separation of powers between Congress and the Judiciary. The first eight Amendments to the Constitution set forth self-executing prohibitions on governmental action, and this Court has had primary authority to interpret those prohibitions. The Bingham draft, some thought, departed from that tradition by vesting in Congress primary power to interpret and elaborate on the meaning of the new Amendment through legislation. Under it, "Congress, and not the courts, was to judge whether or not any of the privileges or immunities were not secured to citizens in the several States." While this separation of powers aspect did not occasion the widespread resistance which was caused by the proposal's threat to the federal balance, it nonetheless attracted the attention of various Members. As enacted, the Fourteenth Amendment confers substantive rights against the States which, like the provisions of the Bill of Rights, are self-executing. The power to interpret the Constitution in a case or controversy remains in the Judiciary.

The remedial and preventive nature of Congress' enforcement power, and the limitation inherent in the power, were confirmed in our earliest cases on the Fourteenth Amendment. In the *Civil Rights Cases,* the Court invalidated sections of the Civil Rights Act of 1875 which prescribed criminal penalties for denying to any person "the full enjoyment of" public accommodations and conveyances, on the grounds that it exceeded Congress' power by seeking to regulate private conduct. The Enforcement Clause, the Court said, did not authorize Congress to pass "general legislation upon the rights of the citizen, but corrective legislation; that is, such as may be necessary and proper for counteracting such laws as the States may adopt or enforce, and which, by the amendment, they are prohibited from making or enforcing.... " The power to "legislate generally upon" life, liberty, and property, as opposed to the "power to provide modes of redress" against offensive state action, was "repugnant" to the Constitution. Although the specific holdings of these early cases might have been superseded or modified, see, e.g., *Heart of Atlanta Motel, Inc. v. United States,* their treatment of Congress' §5 power as corrective or preventive, not definitional, has not been questioned.

Recent cases have continued to revolve around the question of whether §5 legislation can be considered remedial. In *South Carolina v. Katzenbach,* we emphasized that "the constitutional propriety of [legislation adopted under the Enforcement Clause] must be judged with reference to the historical experience ... it reflects." There we upheld various provisions of the Voting Rights Act of 1965, finding them to be "remedies aimed at areas where voting discrimination has been most flagrant," and necessary to "banish the blight of racial discrimination in voting, which has infected the electoral process in parts of our country for nearly a century." We noted evidence in the record reflecting the subsisting and pervasive discriminatory—and therefore unconstitutional—use of literacy tests. The Act's new remedies, which used the administrative resources of the Federal Government, included the suspension of both literacy tests and, pending federal review, all new voting regulations in covered jurisdictions, as well as the assignment of federal examiners to list qualified applicants enabling those listed to vote. The new, unprecedented remedies were deemed necessary given the ineffectiveness of the existing voting rights laws, and the slow costly character of case-by-case litigation.

After *South Carolina v. Katzenbach*, the Court continued to acknowledge the necessity of using strong remedial and preventive measures to respond to the widespread and persisting deprivation of constitutional rights resulting from this country's history of racial discrimination....

Any suggestion that Congress has a substantive, non-remedial power under the Fourteenth Amendment is not supported by our case law. In *Oregon v. Mitchell*, a majority of the Court concluded Congress had exceeded its enforcement powers by enacting legislation lowering the minimum age of voters from 21 to 18 in state and local elections. The five Members of the Court who reached this conclusion explained that the legislation intruded into an area reserved by the Constitution to the States....

If Congress could define its own powers by altering the Fourteenth Amendment's meaning, no longer would the Constitution be "superior paramount law, unchangeable by ordinary means." It would be "on a level with ordinary legislative acts, and, like other acts, ... alterable when the legislature shall please to alter it." *Marbury v. Madison*. Under this approach, it is difficult to conceive of a principle that would limit congressional power. Shifting legislative majorities could change the Constitution and effectively circumvent the difficult and detailed amendment process contained in Article V.

We now turn to consider whether RFRA can be considered enforcement legislation under §5 of the Fourteenth Amendment.

Respondent contends that RFRA is a proper exercise of Congress' remedial or preventive power. The Act, it is said, is a reasonable means of protecting the free exercise of religion as defined by *Smith*. It prevents and remedies laws which are enacted with the unconstitutional object of targeting religious beliefs and practices. To avoid the difficulty of proving such violations, it is said, Congress can simply invalidate any law which imposes a substantial burden on a religious practice unless it is justified by a compelling interest and is the least restrictive means of accomplishing that interest. If Congress can prohibit laws with discriminatory effects in order to prevent racial discrimination in violation of the Equal Protection Clause, then it can do the same, respondent argues, to promote religious liberty.

While preventive rules are sometimes appropriate remedial measures, there must be a congruence between the means used and the ends to be achieved. The appropriateness of remedial measures must be considered in light of the evil presented. Strong measures appropriate to address one harm may be an unwarranted response to another, lesser one. Id., at 334

A comparison between RFRA and the Voting Rights Act is instructive. In contrast to the record which confronted Congress and the judiciary in the voting rights cases, RFRA's legislative record lacks examples of modern instances of generally applicable laws passed because of religious bigotry. The history of persecution in this country detailed in the hearings mentions no episodes occurring in the past 40 years. . . . It is difficult to maintain that they are examples of legislation enacted or enforced due to animus or hostility to the burdened religious practices or that they indicate some widespread pattern of religious discrimination in this country. Congress' concern was with the incidental burdens imposed, not the object or purpose of the legislation. . . .

Regardless of the state of the legislative record, RFRA cannot be considered remedial, preventive legislation, if those terms are to have any meaning. RFRA is so out of proportion to a supposed remedial or preventive object that it cannot be understood as responsive to, or designed to prevent, unconstitutional behavior. It appears, instead, to attempt a substantive change in constitutional protections. Preventive measures prohibiting certain types of laws may be appropriate when there is reason to believe that many of the laws affected by the congressional enactment have a significant likelihood of being unconstitutional. Remedial legislation under §5 "should be adapted to the mischief and wrong which the [Fourteenth] Amendment was intended to provide against."

RFRA is not so confined. Sweeping coverage ensures its intrusion at every level of government, displacing laws and prohibiting official actions of almost every description and regardless of subject matter. RFRA's restrictions apply to every agency and official of the Federal, State, and local Governments. RFRA applies to all federal and state law, statutory or otherwise, whether adopted before or after its enactment. RFRA has no termination date or termination mechanism. Any law is subject to challenge at any time by any individual who alleges a substantial burden on his or her free exercise of religion.

The stringent test RFRA demands of state laws reflects a lack of proportionality or congruence between the means adopted and the legitimate end to be achieved. If an objector can show a substantial burden on his free exercise, the State must demonstrate a compelling governmental interest and show that the law is the least restrictive means of furthering its interest. Claims that a law substantially burdens someone's exercise of religion will often be difficult to contest. Requiring a State to demonstrate a compelling interest and show that it has adopted the least restrictive means of achieving that interest is the most demanding test known to constitutional law. If " 'compelling interest' really means what it says . . . many laws will not meet the test. . . . [The test] would open the prospect of constitutionally required religious exemptions from civic obligations of almost every conceivable kind." Laws valid under *Smith* would fall under RFRA without regard to whether they had the object of stifling or punishing free exercise. We make these observations not to reargue the position of the majority in *Smith* but to illustrate the substantive alteration of its holding attempted by RFRA. Even assuming RFRA would be interpreted in effect to mandate some lesser test, say one equivalent to intermediate scrutiny, the statute nevertheless would require searching judicial scrutiny of state law with the attendant likelihood of invalidation. This is a considerable congressional intrusion into the States' traditional prerogatives and general authority to regulate for the health and welfare of their citizens.

Our national experience teaches that the Constitution is preserved best when each part of the government respects both the Constitution and the proper actions and determinations of the other branches. When the Court has interpreted the Constitution, it has acted within the province of the Judicial Branch, which embraces the duty to say what the law is. When the political branches of the Government act against the background of a judicial interpretation of the Constitution already issued, it must be understood that in later cases and controversies the Court will treat its precedents with the respect due them under settled principles, including stare decisis, and contrary expectations must be disappointed. RFRA was designed to control cases and controversies, such as the one before us; but as the provisions of the federal statute here invoked are beyond congressional authority, it is this Court's precedent, not RFRA, which must control.

It is for Congress in the first instance to "determine whether and what legislation is needed to secure the guarantees of the Fourteenth Amendment," and its conclusions are entitled to much deference. Congress' discretion is not unlimited, however, and the courts retain the power, as they have since *Marbury v. Madison*, to determine if Congress has exceeded its authority under the Constitution. Broad as the power of Congress is under the Enforcement Clause of the Fourteenth Amendment, RFRA contradicts vital principles necessary to maintain separation of powers and the federal balance. The judgment of the Court of Appeals sustaining the Act's constitutionality is reversed.

CASE QUESTIONS

1. **Why is the Supreme Court asserting that the RFRA is unconstitutional? Is it because the RFRA interprets the Constitution in an incorrect way or because Congress should not be allowed to correct the Supreme Court on any matter of constitutional interpretation? Does the opinion leave any room for the departmentalist understanding of constitutional interpretation? Could the Court have decided *Boerne v. Flores* in a way that stopped short of judicial supremacy?**

2. **Read Section 5 of the Fourteenth Amendment. Does this provision grant Congress some power in constitutional interpretation? What does the Court say about the congressional power asserted in this section of the Fourteenth Amendment?**

3. **This case clearly raises questions about the Court's role in a democracy. In *Boerne v. Flores*, the Court overturned the RFRA. The RFRA's popularity was evidenced by its overwhelming support in the Senate, where it was passed by a vote of 97 to 3. The case is significant not only because it pitted the Court against popular will, but because it raised the question of whether Congress could offer its own judgments about constitutional interpretation. The Court's negative answer makes *Boerne v. Flores* the strongest and clearest rejection of departmentalism and the Court's most ardent statement in defense of judicial supremacy. The Constitution tasks Congress with the power to enforce the provisions of the Fourteenth Amendment, including protections of individual liberty and equal protection under the law. When Congress and the Court disagree about how far those rights extend, as with the controversy over the RFRA, must Congress let the Court have the last word?**

BUSH v. GORE

531 U.S. 98 (2000)

Opinion: Per Curiam
Concurrence: Rehnquist, joined by Scalia, Thomas
Dissent: Stevens joined by Ginsburg, Breyer
Dissent: Souter, joined by Breyer and by Stevens and Ginsburg in all but Part C
Dissent: Ginsburg, joined by Stevens and by Souter and Breyer in Part I
Dissent: Breyer, joined by Stevens and Ginsburg in all but Part I-A-1 and by Souter in Part I

In the 2000 presidential election between George Bush and Albert Gore, the electoral vote was close, so close that a victory in Florida for either candidate would have ensured a victory in the presidential election. On Sunday, November 26, 2000, Florida Secretary of State Katherine Harris certified Bush as the winner of the election in the state. Subsequent litigation on behalf of Gore resulted in the Florida Supreme Court ordering a recount. The following decision focuses on two legal issues, one concerning equal protection and the second concerning Article II of the Constitution. In addition to thinking about the U.S. Supreme Court's arguments with regard to these two matters, you should think about whether the Court is the proper body to resolve this dispute in the context of the larger questions of judicial authority examined in this chapter. Is this a proper use of the Court's review power? Or is it an instance of the Court improperly adjudicating a political question?

PER CURIAM.

On December 8, 2000, the Supreme Court of Florida ordered that the Circuit Court of Leon County tabulate by hand 9,000 ballots in Miami-Dade County. It also ordered the inclusion in the certified vote totals of 215 votes identified in Palm Beach County and 168 votes identified in Miami-Dade County for Vice President Albert Gore, Jr., and Senator Joseph Lieberman, Democratic Candidates for President and Vice President. The Supreme Court noted that petitioner, Governor George W. Bush asserted that the net gain for Vice President Gore in Palm Beach County was 176 votes, and directed the Circuit Court to resolve that dispute on remand. The court further held that relief would require manual recounts in all Florida counties where so-called "undervotes" had not been subject to manual tabulation. The court ordered all manual recounts to begin at once. Governor Bush and Richard Cheney, Republican Candidates for the Presidency and Vice Presidency, filed an emergency application for a stay of this mandate. On December 9, we granted the application, treated the application as a petition for a writ of certiorari, and granted certiorari.

The petition presents the following questions: whether the Florida Supreme Court established new standards for resolving Presidential election contests, thereby violating Art. II, §1, cl. 2, of the United States Constitution and failing to comply with 3 U.S.C. §5, and whether the use of standardless manual recounts violates the Equal Protection and Due Process Clauses. With respect to the equal protection question, we find a violation of the Equal Protection Clause.

An early case in our one person, one vote jurisprudence arose when a State accorded arbitrary and disparate treatment to voters in its different counties. The Court found a constitutional violation. We relied on these principles in the context of the Presidential selection process in *Moore v. Ogilvie*, where we invalidated a county-based procedure that diluted the influence of citizens in larger counties in the nominating process. There we observed that "the idea that one group can be granted greater voting strength than another is hostile to the one man, one vote basis of our representative government."

The State Supreme Court ratified this uneven treatment. It mandated that the recount totals from two counties, Miami-Dade and Palm Beach, be included in the certified total. The court also appeared to hold sub silentio that the recount totals from Broward County, which were not completed until after the original November 14 certification by the Secretary of State, were to be considered part of the new certified vote totals even though the county certification was not contested by Vice President Gore. Yet each of the counties used varying standards to determine what was a legal vote. Broward County used a more forgiving standard than Palm Beach County, and uncovered almost three times as many new votes, a result markedly disproportionate to the difference in population between the counties.

In addition, the recounts in these three counties were not limited to so-called undervotes but extended to all of the ballots. The distinction has real consequences. A manual recount of all ballots identifies not only those ballots which show no vote but also those which contain more than one, the so-called overvotes. Neither category will be counted by the machine. This is not a trivial concern. At oral argument, respondents estimated there are as many as 110,000 overvotes statewide. As a result, the citizen whose ballot was not read by a machine because he failed to vote for a candidate in a way readable by a machine may still have his vote counted in a manual recount; on the other hand, the citizen who marks two candidates in a way discernible by the machine will not have the same opportunity to have his vote count, even if a manual examination of the ballot would reveal the requisite indicia of intent. Furthermore, the citizen who marks two candidates, only one of which is discernible by the machine, will have his vote counted even though it should have been read as an invalid ballot. The State Supreme Court's inclusion of vote counts based on these variant standards exemplifies concerns with the remedial processes that were under way.

That brings the analysis to yet a further equal protection problem. The votes certified by the court included a partial total from one county, Miami-Dade. The Florida Supreme Court's decision thus gives no assurance that the recounts included in a final certification must be complete. Indeed, it is respondent's submission that it would be consistent with the rules of the recount procedures to include whatever partial counts are done by the time of final certification, and we interpret the Florida Supreme Court's decision to permit this. This accommodation no doubt results from the truncated contest period established by the Florida Supreme Court in *Bush I*, at respondents' own urging. The press of time does not diminish the constitutional concern. A desire for speed is not a general excuse for ignoring equal protection guarantees.

In addition to these difficulties the actual process by which the votes were to be counted under the Florida Supreme Court's decision raises further concerns. That order did not specify who would recount the ballots. The county canvassing boards were forced to pull together ad hoc teams comprised of judges from various Circuits who had no previous training in handling and interpreting ballots.

Furthermore, while others were permitted to observe, they were prohibited from objecting during the recount.

The recount process, in its features here described, is inconsistent with the minimum procedures necessary to protect the fundamental right of each voter in the special instance of a statewide recount under the authority of a single state judicial officer. Our consideration is limited to the present circumstances, for the problem of equal protection in election processes generally presents many complexities.

The question before the Court is not whether local entities, in the exercise of their expertise, may develop different systems for implementing elections. Instead, we are presented with a situation where a state court with the power to assure uniformity has ordered a statewide recount with minimal procedural safeguards. When a court orders a statewide remedy, there must be at least some assurance that the rudimentary requirements of equal treatment and fundamental fairness are satisfied.

Given the Court's assessment that the recount process underway was probably being conducted in an unconstitutional manner, the Court stayed the order directing the recount so it could hear this case and render an expedited decision. The contest provision, as it was mandated by the State Supreme Court, is not well calculated to sustain the confidence that all citizens must have in the outcome of elections. The State has not shown that its procedures include the necessary safeguards. The problem, for instance, of the estimated 110,000 overvotes has not been addressed, although Chief Justice Wells called attention to the concern in his dissenting opinion.

Upon due consideration of the difficulties identified to this point, it is obvious that the recount cannot be conducted in compliance with the requirements of equal protection and due process without substantial additional work. It would require not only the adoption (after opportunity for argument) of adequate statewide standards for determining what is a legal vote, and practicable procedures to implement them, but also orderly judicial review of any disputed matters that might arise. In addition, the Secretary of State has advised that the recount of only a portion of the ballots requires that the vote tabulation equipment be used to screen out undervotes, a function for which the machines were not designed. If a recount of overvotes were also required, perhaps even a second screening would be necessary. Use of the equipment for this purpose, and any new software developed for it, would have to be evaluated for accuracy by the Secretary of State, as required by Fla. Stat. §101.015 (2000).

The Supreme Court of Florida has said that the legislature intended the State's electors to "participate fully in the federal electoral process," as provided in 3 U.S.C. §5. That statute, in turn, requires that any controversy or contest that is designed to lead to a conclusive selection of electors be completed by December 12. That date is upon us, and there is no recount procedure in place under the State Supreme Court's order that comports with minimal constitutional standards. Because it is evident that any recount seeking to meet the December 12 date will be unconstitutional for the reasons we have discussed, we reverse the judgment of the Supreme Court of Florida ordering a recount to proceed.

None are more conscious of the vital limits on judicial authority than are the members of this Court, and none stand more in admiration of the Constitution's design to leave the selection of the President to the people, through their legislatures, and to the political sphere. When contending parties invoke the process of the courts, however, it becomes our unsought responsibility to resolve the federal and constitutional issues the judicial system has been forced to confront.

The judgment of the Supreme Court of Florida is reversed, and the case is remanded for further proceedings not inconsistent with this opinion.

CHIEF JUSTICE REHNQUIST, *with whom* **JUSTICE SCALIA** *and* **JUSTICE THOMAS** *join, concurring.*

We join the per curiam opinion. We write separately because we believe there are additional grounds that require us to reverse the Florida Supreme Court's decision.

We deal here not with an ordinary election, but with an election for the President of the United States. . . .

In most cases, comity and respect for federalism compel us to defer to the decisions of state courts on issues of state law. That practice reflects our understanding that the decisions of state courts are definitive pronouncements of the will of the States as sovereigns. Of course, in ordinary cases, the distribution of powers among the branches of a State's government raises no questions of federal constitutional law, subject to the requirement that the government be republican in character. But there are a few exceptional cases in which the Constitution imposes a duty or confers a power on a particular branch of a State's government. This is one of them. Article II, §1, cl. 2, provides that "each State shall appoint, in such Manner as the *Legislature* thereof may direct," electors for President and Vice President. (Emphasis added.) Thus, the text of the election law itself, and not just its interpretation by the courts of the States, takes on independent significance.

3 U.S.C. §5 informs our application of Art. II, §1, cl. 2, to the Florida statutory scheme, which, as the Florida Supreme Court acknowledged, took that statute into account. Section 5 provides that the State's selection of electors "shall be conclusive, and shall govern in the counting of the electoral votes" if the electors are chosen under laws enacted prior to election day, and if the selection process is completed six days prior to the meeting of the electoral college. . . .

If we are to respect the legislature's Article II powers, therefore, we must ensure that post-election state-court actions do not frustrate the legislative desire to attain the "safe harbor" provided by §5.

. . . Though we generally defer to state courts on the interpretation of state law, there are of course areas in which the Constitution requires this Court to undertake an independent, if still deferential, analysis of state law.

The scope and nature of the remedy ordered by the Florida Supreme Court jeopardizes the "legislative wish" to take advantage of the safe harbor provided by 3 U.S.C. §5. December 12, 2000, is the last date for a final determination of the Florida electors that will satisfy §5. Yet in the late afternoon of December 8th—four days before this deadline—the Supreme Court of Florida ordered recounts of tens of thousands of so-called "undervotes" spread through 64 of the State's 67 counties. This was done in a search for elusive—perhaps delusive—certainty as to the exact count of 6 million votes. But no one claims that these ballots have not previously been tabulated; they were initially read by voting machines at the time of the election, and thereafter reread by virtue of Florida's automatic recount provision. No one claims there was any fraud in the election. The Supreme Court of Florida ordered this additional recount under the provision of the election code giving the circuit judge the authority to provide relief that is "appropriate under such circumstances."

Surely when the Florida Legislature empowered the courts of the State to grant "appropriate" relief, it must have meant relief that would have become final by the cut-off date of 3 U.S.C. §5. In light of the inevitable legal challenges and ensuing appeals to the Supreme Court of Florida and petitions for certiorari to this Court, the entire recounting process could not possibly be completed by that date. Whereas the majority in the Supreme Court of Florida stated its confidence that "the remaining undervotes in these counties can be [counted] within the required time frame," it made no assertion that the seemingly inevitable appeals could be disposed of in that time. Although the Florida Supreme Court has on occasion taken over a year to resolve disputes over local elections, it has heard and decided the appeals in the present case with great promptness. But the federal deadlines for the Presidential election simply do not permit even such a shortened process.

JUSTICE GINSBURG, *with whom* **JUSTICE STEVENS** *joins, and with whom* **JUSTICE SOUTER** *and* **JUSTICE BREYER** *join as to Part I, dissenting.*

Rarely has this Court rejected outright an interpretation of state law by a state high court. *Fairfax's Devisee v. Hunter's Lessee, NAACP v. Alabama ex rel. Patterson*, and *Bouie v. City of Columbia*, cited by the Chief Justice, are three such rare instances. But those cases are embedded in historical contexts hardly comparable to the situation here....

The Chief Justice's casual citation of these cases might lead one to believe they are part of a larger collection of cases in which we said that the Constitution impelled us to train a skeptical eye on a state court's portrayal of state law. But one would be hard pressed, I think, to find additional cases that fit the mold. As Justice Breyer convincingly explains, this case involves nothing close to the kind of recalcitrance by a state high court that warrants extraordinary action by this Court. The Florida Supreme Court concluded that counting every legal vote was the overriding concern of the Florida Legislature when it enacted the State's Election Code. The court surely should not be bracketed with state high courts of the Jim Crow South.

The Chief Justice says that Article II, by providing that state legislatures shall direct the manner of appointing electors, authorizes federal superintendence over the relationship between state courts and state legislatures, and licenses a departure from the usual deference we give to state court interpretations of state law. The Framers of our Constitution, however, understood that in a republican government, the judiciary would construe the legislature's enactments. In light of the constitutional guarantee to States of a "Republican Form of Government," Article II can hardly be read to invite this Court to disrupt a State's republican regime. Yet the Chief Justice today would reach out to do just that. By holding that Article II requires our revision of a state court's construction of state laws in order to protect one organ of the State from another, the Chief Justice contradicts the basic principle that a State may organize itself as it sees fit. Article II does not call for the scrutiny undertaken by this Court.

The extraordinary setting of this case has obscured the ordinary principle that dictates its proper resolution: Federal courts defer to state high courts' interpretations of their state's own law. This principle reflects the core of federalism, on which all agree. "The Framers split the atom of sovereignty. It was the genius of their idea that our citizens would have two political capacities, one state and one federal, each protected from incursion by the other."

Were the other members of this Court as mindful as they generally are of our system of dual sovereignty, they would affirm the judgment of the Florida Supreme Court.

The Court assumes that time will not permit "orderly judicial review of any disputed matters that might arise." But no one has doubted the good faith and diligence with which Florida election officials, attorneys for all sides of this controversy, and the courts of law have performed their duties. Notably, the Florida Supreme Court has produced two substantial opinions within 29 hours of oral argument. In sum, the Court's conclusion that a constitutionally adequate recount is impractical is a prophecy the Court's own judgment will not allow to be tested. Such an untested prophecy should not decide the Presidency of the United States.

I dissent.

JUSTICE BREYER, *with whom* **JUSTICE STEVENS** *and* **JUSTICE GINSBURG** *join except as to Part I-A-1, and with whom* **JUSTICE SOUTER** *joins as to Part I, dissenting.*

The Court was wrong to take this case. It was wrong to grant a stay. It should now vacate that stay and permit the Florida Supreme Court to decide whether the recount should resume.

I

The political implications of this case for the country are momentous. But the federal legal questions presented, with one exception, are insubstantial.

A

1

The majority raises three Equal Protection problems with the Florida Supreme Court's recount order: first, the failure to include overvotes in the manual recount; second, the fact that all ballots, rather than simply the undervotes, were recounted in some, but not all, counties; and third, the absence of a uniform, specific standard to guide the recounts. As far as the first issue is concerned, petitioners presented no evidence, to this Court or to any Florida court, that a manual recount of overvotes would identify additional legal votes. The same is true of the second, and, in addition, the majority's reasoning would seem to invalidate any state provision for a manual recount of individual counties in a statewide election.

The majority's third concern does implicate principles of fundamental fairness. The majority concludes that the Equal Protection Clause requires that a manual recount be governed not only by the uniform general standard of the "clear intent of the voter," but also by uniform subsidiary standards (for example, a uniform determination whether indented, but not perforated, "undervotes" should count). The opinion points out that the Florida Supreme Court ordered the inclusion of Broward County's undercounted "legal votes" even though those votes included ballots that were not perforated but simply "dimpled," while newly recounted ballots from other counties will likely include only votes determined to be "legal" on the basis of a stricter standard. In light of our previous remand, the Florida Supreme Court may have been reluctant to adopt a more specific standard than that provided for by the legislature for fear of exceeding its authority under Article II. However, since the use of different standards could favor one or the other of the candidates, since time was, and is, too short to permit the lower courts to iron out significant differences through ordinary judicial review, and since the relevant distinction was embodied in the order of the State's highest court,

I agree that, in these very special circumstances, basic principles of fairness may well have counseled the adoption of a uniform standard to address the problem. In light of the majority's disposition, I need not decide whether, or the extent to which, as a remedial matter, the Constitution would place limits upon the content of the uniform standard.

2

Nonetheless, there is no justification for the majority's remedy, which is simply to reverse the lower court and halt the recount entirely. An appropriate remedy would be, instead, to remand this case with instructions that, even at this late date, would permit the Florida Supreme Court to require recounting all undercounted votes in Florida, including those from Broward, Volusia, Palm Beach, and Miami-Dade Counties, whether or not previously recounted prior to the end of the protest period, and to do so in accordance with a single-uniform substandard.

By halting the manual recount, and thus ensuring that the uncounted legal votes will not be counted under any standard, this Court crafts a remedy out of proportion to the asserted harm. And that remedy harms the very fairness interests the Court is attempting to protect. The manual recount would itself redress a problem of unequal treatment of ballots. . . .

II

Despite the reminder that this case involves "an election for the President of the United States," no preeminent legal concern, or practical concern related to legal questions, required this Court to hear this case, let alone to issue a stay that stopped Florida's recount process in its tracks. With one exception, petitioners' claims do not ask us to vindicate a constitutional provision designed to protect a basic human right. See, e.g., *Brown v. Board of Education.* Petitioners invoke fundamental fairness, namely, the need for procedural fairness, including finality. But with the one "equal protection" exception, they rely upon law that focuses, not upon that basic need, but upon the constitutional allocation of power. Respondents invoke a competing fundamental consideration—the need to determine the voter's true intent. But they look to state law, not to federal constitutional law, to protect that interest. Neither side claims electoral fraud, dishonesty, or the like. And the more fundamental equal protection claim might have been left to the state court to resolve if and when it was discovered to have mattered. It could still be resolved through a remand conditioned upon issuance of a uniform standard; it does not require reversing the Florida Supreme Court.

Of course, the selection of the President is of fundamental national importance. But that importance is political, not legal. And this Court should resist the temptation unnecessarily to resolve tangential legal disputes, where doing so threatens to determine the outcome of the election.

The Constitution and federal statutes themselves make clear that restraint is appropriate. They set forth a road map of how to resolve disputes about electors, even after an election as close as this one. That road map foresees resolution of electoral disputes by state courts. But it nowhere provides for involvement by the United States Supreme Court.

To the contrary, the Twelfth Amendment commits to Congress the authority and responsibility to count electoral votes. A federal statute, the Electoral Count Act, enacted after the close 1876 Hayes-Tilden Presidential election, specifies that, after States have tried to resolve disputes (through "judicial" or other means), Congress is the body primarily authorized to resolve remaining disputes.

The legislative history of the Act makes clear its intent to commit the power to resolve such disputes to Congress, rather than the courts:

> "The two Houses are, by the Constitution, authorized to make the count of electoral votes. They can only count legal votes, and in doing so must determine, from the best evidence to be had, what are legal votes .... The power to determine rests with the two Houses, and there is no other constitutional tribunal."

... The decision by both the Constitution's Framers and the 1886 Congress to minimize this Court's role in resolving close federal presidential elections is as wise as it is clear. However awkward or difficult it may be for Congress to resolve difficult electoral disputes, Congress, being a political body, expresses the people's will far more accurately than does an unelected Court. And the people's will is what elections are about.

... I think it not only legally wrong, but also most unfortunate, for the Court simply to have terminated the Florida recount. Those who caution judicial restraint in resolving political disputes have described the quintessential case for that restraint as a case marked, among other things, by the "strangeness of the issue," its "intractability to principled resolution," its "sheer momentousness, . . . which tends to unbalance judicial judgment," and "the inner vulnerability, the self-doubt of an institution which is electorally irresponsible and has no earth to draw strength from." Those characteristics mark this case.

At the same time, as I have said, the Court is not acting to vindicate a fundamental constitutional principle, such as the need to protect a basic human liberty. No other strong reason to act is present. Congressional statutes tend to obviate the need. And, above all, in this highly politicized matter, the appearance of a split decision runs the risk of undermining the public's confidence in the Court itself. That confidence is a public treasure. It has been built slowly over many years, some of which were marked by a Civil War and the tragedy of segregation. It is a vitally necessary ingredient of any successful effort to protect basic liberty and, indeed, the rule of law itself. We run no risk of returning to the days when a President (responding to this Court's efforts to protect the Cherokee Indians) might have said, "John Marshall has made his decision; now let him enforce it!" But we do risk a self-inflicted wound — a wound that may harm not just the Court, but the Nation.

I fear that in order to bring this agonizingly long election process to a definitive conclusion, we have not adequately attended to that necessary "check upon our own exercise of power," "our own sense of self-restraint." Justice Brandeis once said of the Court, "The most important thing we do is not doing." What it does today, the Court should have left undone. I would repair the damage done as best we now can, by permitting the Florida recount to continue under uniform standards.

I respectfully dissent.

CASE QUESTION

This case raises fundamental questions about the role of the Supreme Court in a democracy. The Court effectively determined the outcome of the 2000 presidential election. One argument in favor of the Court's intervention, proposed by federal judge and legal theorist Richard Posner, is that the decision ended what could have been a highly divisive and

overly drawn out public battle over the election. In this sense, *Bush v. Gore* was pragmatic because it settled a critical matter that could have become destabilizing to the American polity. The included reading from Justice Stephen Breyer also lauds the importance of pragmatic decision making by the Court, but Justice Breyer opposed the Court's decision in *Bush v. Gore*. Is Justice Breyer's dissenting stance consistent with his pragmatist approach to judicial interpretation? Is there a way to give a pragmatist defense of his position?

SYNTHESIS QUESTIONS FOR FURTHER DISCUSSION: CHAPTER 2

1. The Court's claim to judicial supremacy has become closely associated with its attempt to desegregate the Southern states in the face of fierce opposition. Many Southern politicians invoked a version of departmentalism, arguing that the Court was mistaken in reading the Equal Protection Clause as forbidding segregation. It is important to note that some of these arguments also suggested that, because the Court was wrong, it could not impose its decision on Southern politicians who read the Constitution in a different way. The Court's decision in *Cooper v. Aaron*, enforcing a desegregation order in the face of a defiant governor and other local politicians, sought to deflate this debate by asserting judicial supremacy. Clearly, the arguments of Larry Kramer and Jeremy Waldron are not caught up in the racism that motivated much of the resistance to the Court in the era of desegregation, but could there have been a way to decide *Cooper v. Aaron* without invoking judicial supremacy? Are arguments for desegregation potentially consistent with departmentalism?

2. The theory of departmentalism has been revived recently by thinkers, such as Kramer, who focus on issues in which the Court's substantive decisions are at odds with the views of most contemporary Americans. Kramer's version of departmentalism is known as "popular constitutionalism." It therefore makes sense that he would focus his readers' attention on matters where the Court's decisions seem at odds with popular will. In the late nineteenth and early twentieth centuries, the Court struck down a number of statutes including wage, hour, and safety regulations for workers, as well as child labor protections. In cases such as *Lochner v. New York* and *Hammer v. Dagenhart*, the Supreme Court invalidated these laws for being incompatible with economic liberty. Since that time, workers' rights legislation has come to be seen by a vast majority as essential to the American system of government. But at times the Court has challenged legislatures and Congress on issues of personal liberties, such as gay rights and civil rights. Ronald Dworkin argues that rights protections by the Court are sometimes important despite popular opposition. How might Kramer reply to the challenge that some freedoms should be upheld even if legislatures or Congress violates them?

3. Is there any way to reconcile the Court's act of restraint in *Nixon v. United States* with Kramer's charge that the Rehnquist Court fully embraced judicial supremacy? Is judicial supremacy compatible with the political question doctrine?

KEY TERMS

departmentalism: The view that the various branches of government ought to have a say in constitutional interpretation.

judicial review: The power to strike down legislative or executive acts on grounds that they are incompatible with a provision or provisions of the Constitution.

judicial supremacy: The view that the Court is the final and supreme interpreter of constitutional meaning.

per curiam opinion: An unsigned opinion issued on behalf of the Court.

standing doctrine: The doctrine the Court uses to determine whether an individual has suffered a constitutionally cognizable harm sufficient to permit his or her claim to be heard in federal court.

PART II

CONGRESSIONAL AUTHORITY AND ITS LIMITS

In this part, we turn to the question of Congress's authority and power to make law. In contrast to the Court's judicial review power, Congress's specific powers are explicitly articulated in Article I of the Constitution. But despite this specific articulation, controversy remains about how far these powers extend and when they should be limited.

Specifically, in Chapter 4 we explore the question of how far congressional power extends relative to state governments. In Chapter 5, we go on to examine Congress's power in relation to the executive branch and the judiciary. Traditionally, questions about Congress's power relative to the states are referred to as the problems of "federalism," while the question of inter-branch authority is referred to as "separation of powers." Importantly, the question of federalism in regard to the relationship between the state governments and the federal government should not be confused with the specific positions of the "Federalist" party or of *The Federalist Papers.*

The first thing that should stand out about the question of Congress's power relative to that of state legislatures is that both are democratic branches of government. The Congress of the United States is made up of two houses, the Senate and the House of Representatives. Although the members of the Senate were originally appointed by state legislatures, this was changed by the Seventeenth Amendment, adopted in 1913. Since then, both Houses of Congress have been directly elected by the people. Just as the U.S. Congress has democratic credentials, so too do state legislatures, which are also made up of members directly elected by the people. Since both the state and the national legislatures can pass laws that govern the lives of individual citizens, we have to consider how to sort out the constitutional limits of the powers of each of these levels of government and what should happen if there is a conflict between them.

We might think about how to resolve conflicts over powers by asking what would be the most democratic relationship between the federal and state governments. Some have argued that state governments are closer to the people—both geographically and in terms of the more intimate connection between the voters and their representatives, since state legislators usually represent vastly smaller constituencies. This suggests that state government might be inherently more democratic. The national and state governments also differ in the range of their powers. Article I spells out a specific list of powers allocated to the national legislature, and while the "Necessary and Proper Clause," sometimes referred to as the "Elastic Clause," certainly expands those powers, the Tenth Amendment suggests that there are limits to the powers of the national government: Specifically, the Tenth Amendment declares that "[t]he powers not delegated to the United States by the Constitution, nor prohibited by it to the States, are reserved to the States respectively, or to the people." This suggests that while there are some specific limits on what the states are allowed to do (Article I, Section 10), the national government may do only those things assigned to it—while the states are left free to do as they choose (unless their own state constitution blocks them). Among the key powers left to the states are what are known as the "police powers," which are defined as the right to regulate the health, safety, welfare, and morals of the population. In contrast to the states, the federal government enjoys no such general police power.

The national government's powers may be limited, but they are strong powers with wide reach—just how wide, of course, is a matter of much debate. Any such debate would include a close consideration of the so-called Elastic Clause: Article I gives Congress a long list of powers, and then adds that Congress has the authority to make laws "necessary and proper for carrying into execution the foregoing Powers and all other Powers vested by this Constitution in the Government of the United States, or in any Department or Officer thereof." As our readings from Thomas Jefferson and Alexander Hamilton make clear, controversy over the meaning of this clause was evident from the Founding. In addition to this clause, the Constitution grants federal legislation supremacy over state legislation. Article VI, paragraph 2 asserts that "the laws of the United States [are the] supreme Law of the Land; and the Judges in every State shall be bound thereby, any Thing in the Constitution or Laws of any State to the Contrary notwithstanding." This "Supremacy Clause" has been invoked to make federal legislation supreme in relation to state laws that conflict with it. According to the doctrine of "preemption," states are prohibited from enacting laws that invade the realm of congressional powers. Congress has exercised power under each of the allocations provided in Article I, Section 8 — but it has made particularly extensive use of the power "to regulate Commerce with foreign Nations, and among the several States, and with the Indian Tribes." While the "Commerce Clause" would ultimately come to be interpreted in a broad way, the Court struggled for decades in an attempt to draw a clear line between commerce that was exclusively within one state and that was "among the states" — that is to say, interstate commerce.

As you read this part, you will see that there is now — and long has been — a debate over the meaning of the clauses that give Congress its various powers, as well as the scope, range, and reach of these powers, particularly as they clash with the powers thought to be reserved to the states. You will be asked to think about the proper constitutional balance between congressional and state power. As you will see, the Commerce Clause has been a frequent site of contestation between those who wish to expand federal power and those who wish to limit it. Part of our inquiry will be guided by the text of the Constitution, but we will also continue to examine approaches to constitutional interpretation that do not emphasize a strict textualism. As you saw in the previous chapters, there is a robust debate about how to interpret the Constitution in general, and the debate about how to interpret clauses related to congressional and state power is part of that discussion.

In order to understand the debate about how to interpret Congress's power, it is important for you to be familiar with some of the background debates that often framed these issues. Among the most profound struggles you will consider is one that emerged in the twentieth century. On one side of this debate were those who saw the Constitution as a document of strict limits on national government power; they argued for strict constitutional limits on governmental authority to interfere with individual property and economic rights. Notably, these supporters of limited governmental power asserted that a fundamental right to contract was enshrined in the Fourteenth Amendment. On the other side were those who saw the Constitution quite differently, asserting that the Constitution provided the government with the authority (and even the obligation) to ensure the economic welfare of all citizens, including protections against what was seen as a great inequality of power between employers and employees. Those who insisted on a strictly limited role for government might today be referred to as "libertarians"; many modern conservatives share many of these concerns and commitments. Those on the other side initially identified themselves as "progressives," and coalesced around Presidents Theodore Roosevelt and Woodrow Wilson, but they eventually galvanized under the leadership of President Franklin D. Roosevelt, seeking a vastly increased role for the federal government in regulating the economy and securing workers' rights.

The debate between progressives and libertarians came to a head in *Lochner v. New York*. In *Lochner v. New York*, the Court struck down an attempt by a state government to regulate the hours and working conditions of bread bakers. Supporters of this legislation argued that at its root, it was a legitimate exercise of governmental power designed to protect the health and safety of these workers and the public, which would consume the product of their labor. The Supreme

Court saw the legislation in a very different light, arguing that the law infringed upon the economic rights of both the workers and their employers — the right of each to agree to contracts that would define hours and working conditions. This right to contract, they insisted, was a vital and fundamental right embedded in the Constitution.

Importantly, *Lochner v. New York* concerned legislation that originated in the State of New York. If the regulation at issue in *Lochner v. New York*, however, had originated in the U.S. Congress, its opponents might have questioned its authority on the grounds that the Congress had no constitutional power to regulate the economy. Indeed, this issue defined a face-off between progressives and libertarians in the 1930s, some years after *Lochner v. New York*, over a range of national efforts to regulate the economy and the relations between employers and employees. These debates in the 1930s concerned the limits of what the national government could regulate or forbid, including particularly contentious struggles over the power to delegate broad discretionary power to the president as well as the power to create executive and even independent governmental agencies that could protect workers' rights. Specifically, the debate at this time focused on the constitutionality of the "New Deal," a staggering array of legislation passed by Congress and signed into law during President Franklin Roosevelt's first term of office between 1933 and 1936. President Roosevelt's New Deal had sought a larger role for the federal government in regulating the economy (including banks, stock exchanges, and agriculture), in promoting employment, and in protecting workers' rights. This new role for the federal government raised the important question, however, of whether Congress, in passing the New Deal, was exceeding its authority under the Constitution. Opponents of the New Deal argued that Congress had no constitutional power to enact it. As our case selection will make clear, President Roosevelt faced a Supreme Court that challenged his contention that the federal government had the constitutional power and authority to carry out the New Deal.

With these political and historical considerations in mind, we can better appreciate the debate over constitutional interpretation in regards to federal power. "Originalist" interpretations of the clauses that grant federal power have tended to stress the limited nature of congressional authority. According to these readings, we should take a narrow rather than an expansive view of the clauses that grant federal power, including the Commerce Clause, the Necessary and Proper Clause, and the Supremacy Clause. This is consistent with the general approach of originalism, which emphasizes the importance of the text as it was presumably understood by the public at the time it was drafted. But in contrast to originalist understandings, a pragmatist, emphasizing the need to look to the consequences of Supreme Court rulings for the social good, might stress the need for an increase of federal power. Indeed, many of the arguments faced by President Roosevelt and his administration in their quest to seek an expanded role for federal power in regulating the economy were born out of the Great Depression, and the belief that the Constitution must be read in a way that would allow the government to combat this great emergency. A pragmatic approach to constitutional interpretation might justify an expanded federal government's role on grounds that it would better ensure economic stability. Of course, such pragmatic arguments are also vulnerable to the worry that such a federal role might backfire. The role of the moral reading in interpreting these clauses would depend on the kind of morality one thinks is central to the Constitution. As you read through these four chapters, you should ask yourself what kind of interpretation each of these theories might support.

Now that we have examined the ideological and interpretative debate surrounding congressional authority, it is important to provide a broad overview of the history of the Supreme Court's jurisprudence about the boundaries between congressional and state powers, especially in the twentieth century. This will give you the background necessary to understand the in-depth debates raised in the readings and case law we examine in this part. It will also give you a sense of how the historical cases you will read from previous centuries continue to shape and influence the major struggles in the twentieth century and on to the present. In the nineteenth century, congressional power remained somewhat limited. Although the Court had clearly recognized that Congress had the power to regulate some interstate economic interaction in *Gibbons v. Ogden*, which we examine in Chapter 3, it also limited that right. In the late nineteenth century, the Court struck down attempts by Congress to regulate monopolies in *United States v. E.C. Knight Co.*, when it struck down portions of the Sherman Anti-Trust Act. This case did not entirely gut Congress of its ability to regulate monopolies, however. In *Swift & Co. v. United States*, the Court upheld Congress's authority to regulate products in the "stream of commerce." Despite the Court's affirmation of Congress's Commerce Clause power in *Swift*, it would nonetheless remain a limited power. In fact, the Court would soon begin to strike down major pieces of progressive legislation.

After *Swift*, a conservative Supreme Court, seeking to protect property rights and fearful of increased federal power in economic regulation, sought to establish limits on congressional authority. In 1918, well before the New Deal, the Supreme Court in *Hammer v. Dagenhart* struck down workers' rights legislation aimed at protecting children. The notion that Congress had expansive authority under the Constitution, however, would find a champion in President Roosevelt, who sought to build upon the progressives' commitment to workers' rights and to establish a federal role in regulating the economy. In the face of the nation's deepest economic crisis, and under intense political pressure from President Roosevelt, the critical swing vote on a deeply divided Supreme Court (Justice Owen Roberts) shifted his vote away from the implacable conservative bloc of four justices (Justices Willis Van Devanter, James Clark McReynolds, George Sutherland, and Pierce Butler) and upheld a key New Deal provision. This change famously became known as the "switch in time that saved nine." Realizing that they were now consigned to be a permanent minority, the four conservatives soon left the Court (three retired; Justice Butler died), and they were all replaced by justices nominated by President Roosevelt. The Court would soon develop a very different jurisprudence, shifting from a narrow vision of national power to a very broad reading in which they would give Congress wide leeway in regulating the economy. The Court's announcement in *Wickard v. Filburn*, that Congress was free to regulate just about any activity that might have even an indirect and seemingly trivial impact on the national economy, opened the possibility of nearly limitless congressional power.

During the Civil Rights movement, it would be the Commerce Clause that would serve as the constitutional foundation for congressional power to end segregation not only in government institutions but in all sorts of areas that had traditionally been thought to be private businesses, including transportation, restaurants, hotels, amusement parks, recreation facilities, and other public accommodations. You might have thought that the constitutional basis for this legislation would have been found in the Fourteenth Amendment's guarantee of equal protection. This clause was interpreted narrowly by the Court in the years immediately following its addition to the Constitution, and would only be applied where the government itself was involved — it would be triggered only where there was "state action." But when a privately owned hotel or restaurant or bar decided to exclude African Americans from their property, there appeared to be no state action involved. This led President Lyndon Johnson's administration to rest its landmark Civil Rights Act of 1964 — which banned such discrimination — on the Commerce Clause. This choice was ratified by the Supreme Court in two 1964 cases — *Heart of Atlanta Motel v. United States* and *Katzenbach v. McClung*. These cases, many would argue, marked the final and perhaps most dramatic expansion of the Commerce Clause as the critical and unassailable foundation for national power.

Or at least it seemed that way. By the late 1960s, it was widely assumed that there was virtually nothing that Congress might like to do that could not be grounded in the Commerce Clause. But that assumption was shaken in the mid-1970s as the liberal Warren Court was slowly replaced through retirement by far more conservative justices named to the Court by President Richard Nixon, including U.S. Supreme Court Chief Justice Warren Burger and then–Associate Justice William Rehnquist, who joined the Court in 1971. Echoing both Thomas Jefferson and the pre–New Deal Court, Justice Rehnquist sought to restore a textual limit to the reach of the Commerce Clause. In key cases concerning the power of the national government to regulate hand guns, domestic violence, and municipal workers' wages and hours, Justice Rehnquist led the Court in striking down legislation that the majority deemed to have exceeded congressional authority under the Commerce Clause, insisting that some commerce is truly local and thus not subject to the regulation of the national government.

The so-called New Federalism championed by Justice Rehnquist has appeared to many to be a conservative idea. Indeed, perhaps because of the Civil Rights era in which the defenders of states' rights were regarded as defenders of segregation and racism, limits on the federal government were seen to suggest an anti-progressive agenda. But as the reading by Kathleen Sullivan in Chapter 5 suggests, it is arguable whether this debate should be understood along a left-right divide. As the federal government grew increasingly conservative in the early twenty-first century, with a Republican president and Congress, some liberals began to think that limits on federalism might be consistent with a progressive agenda. In particular, the federal government's restriction of medical marijuana, its foray into regulating the kinds of abortions that medical doctors can perform, and its resistance to same-sex marriage have all led progressives to question whether there is virtue in leaving these choices to the states rather than the national government. In other words, perhaps there is nothing inherently conservative or liberal about federal power over the states. Ask yourself whether you favor a limited or expansive federal government in the various policy areas presented in the cases and readings included in this part. Keep in mind how your position about the role of Congress's power relates to your views on the policies at hand.

In many ways, the battle over health-care reform represents the most important political and constitutional controversy of the past decade. Much of the constitutional debate over health-care reform centered on whether the "New Federalism" would culminate in the Court striking down the most major piece of social welfare legislation passed by Congress since the New Deal. The controversy focused on whether the Commerce Clause power extended to Congress's entitlement to "mandate" the purchase of health insurance through government-run exchanges or other means for all citizens. Such a requirement was thought by some to exceed congressional power to regulate commerce because the provision regulated not "action," but only inaction. The case contained a surprise for observers, however. Although the Commerce Clause did not authorize the mandate, Chief Justice Roberts wrote on behalf of the Court that it *was* authorized by a separate provision: the power of Congress to tax. With one hand Roberts seemed to reduce congressional power under the Commerce Clause, while with the other he authorized the legislation. In addition to examining this issue we also will look at the question of whether Congress exceeded its spending power in seeking to expand Medicaid coverage. Chapter 6 on health-care reform thus culminates this part of the text, bringing together the various themes that have been built throughout these four chapters.

CHAPTER 3

THE IDEA OF ENUMERATED POWERS

What are the sources of congressional power? How does enumerating powers protect liberty? Does it lead to effective governance?

In this chapter we turn to the origins of the Supreme Court's rulings on congressional power. As you will see, although the Constitution sets out a number of areas in which Congress is authorized to act, from the beginning of our nation's history there has been a question as to how far these powers extend. Part of the question here is interpretive. Should we interpret these powers in a broad or narrow way? But behind this interpretive question lies a puzzle about what powers are granted to Congress by the Constitution and what kind of balance between state and federal power it requires. Fundamental to any discussion of American federalism is the case of *McCulloch v. Maryland*, which concerned the constitutionality of the Second Bank of the United States and the related question as to whether the bank could be taxed by state governments. Nowhere in the Constitution is there a mention of a power for Congress to create a bank, but do other provisions allow for its creation?

In addition to this specific question about the bank lies the more general issue of the way to strike the balance between state and federal power in the American constitutional order. Those who argue against the bank's constitutionality stress the notion of state sovereignty. Pointing out, for instance, that the Constitution was ratified by the states, they argue that the heart of American democracy lies in state government. Therefore, if federal congressional power were extended beyond the narrow provisions in Article I, it might impede the power of the states, and thus the sovereign authority of the states as realized in the people. This defense of states' rights as the basis for American democracy is most closely associated with Thomas Jefferson, whose views we examine in this chapter. It was Jefferson's political party, the Democratic-Republicans, who most prominently promoted the view in the early Republic that state governments were closer to the people than the federal government and therefore could better represent their interests.

In contrast to Jefferson's emphasis on the power of the states, Alexander Hamilton emphasizes the power of a strong national government. You will see that Hamilton makes both pragmatic and textual arguments about the constitutionality of the bank. But more importantly, he is arguing that the structure of American democracy has a large role for the federal government and Congress. Although the debate between Hamilton and Jefferson concerned the constitutionality of the First Bank of the United States, it would not be until the establishment of a second bank that the Supreme Court would rule on this important issue. As you will see in his opinion, U.S. Supreme Court Chief Justice John Marshall rejects the arguments of Jefferson and of those who claim that the people's sovereignty is only realized through state governments. But Chief Justice Marshall does not entirely reject a role for the state governments or deny that they are one location of the people's sovereignty. Instead, he announces what has come to be known as a theory of "dual-sovereignty" in both the federal government and in the states. The challenge for a theory of dual-sovereignty, however, is how to balance state and federal power given that both are sovereign entities.

The cases in this chapter will guide you as you attempt to understand what it might mean for both the states and the federal government to be sovereign under the U.S. Constitution. As you read through *McCulloch v. Maryland* and the two other cases, you will focus on three clauses that grant congressional power: (1) the Necessary and Proper Clause (in *McCulloch v. Maryland*); (2) the Interstate Commerce Clause (in *Gibbons v. Ogden*); and (3) the Spending Clause (in *South Dakota v. Dole*). Some of our inquiry, therefore, will be about the meaning of these three provisions. But, questions of textual interpretation are also controversial. Through what lens should we read each of these three clauses? Some of you will be tempted to ask what these clauses meant to the relevant legal community at the time they were written and would also interpret them based on a narrow reading, or "to the letter of the law." But one complication with this approach, as will be made clear in our first two readings, is that Hamilton and Jefferson, two prominent members of the Founding generation, disagreed about how these clauses should be understood. While Jefferson argued for an understanding that was narrow and limited, Hamilton suggested the importance of reading the Necessary and Proper Clause and the other clauses enumerating congressional authority in a broad way so as to heighten congressional power. For instance, in addition to the Necessary and Proper Clause, Congress is given the power to spend money raised through taxation. Together these clauses might be thought to suggest a more general power to intervene in national economic matters. As you will see, the controversy over how broadly or narrowly to read these clauses has not disappeared. Indeed, the Spending Clause itself has in the past 100 years become a central way that Congress has expanded its power. In *South Dakota v. Dole*, for instance, you will see that federal power to spend money on highways becomes linked to Congress's policy goal to create a national drinking age of 21. As you read the case, consider the kinds of arguments that Hamilton and Jefferson might have brought to this more recent controversy.

Another, more pragmatic approach might place less emphasis on specific clauses and more on the general question of whether increased federal power would be beneficial to the country. In particular, the question of the Second Bank of the United States could be framed as one about the need to create a national economy. Some pragmatists might argue that increased federal power was necessary if the young United States was to develop a thriving national economy. But this empirical claim might be contested by others who have suggested that federal intervention into the economy at this time depressed rather than stimulated it. Should these considerations be taken into account in deciding the extent to which congressional power is authorized?

It will become clearer in the next two chapters that beneath questions of federalism lie fundamental moral issues. In particular, in Chapter 4, the debate over the Commerce Clause moves from one solely concerned with commerce to one that is focused on race. The Civil Rights Act of 1964 outlawed segregation between the races in areas of so-called public accommodations, such as restaurants and hotels. Where did Congress get this authority? The Fourteenth Amendment was thought not to serve as a textual home for the power to enact this legislation because it had been narrowly interpreted by the Court in the *Civil Rights Cases* shortly after it was ratified and was thought to concern only discrimination that involved the government itself. By contrast, the Commerce Clause, which by 1964 had been broadly interpreted and applied, seemed a far more promising foundation for congressional authority. Opponents of this legislation argued that because many of these accommodations were not part of interstate commerce, Congress had no power to outlaw segregation as it did in this Act. Perhaps the legitimacy of the purpose of the legislation is as important as the textual meanings of the clauses. Similarly, proponents of the moral reading might defend President Franklin Roosevelt's push to use the Commerce Clause power during the New Deal on such grounds. Thus, while the moral reading might not be obviously relevant to this chapter, as we study the development of the Commerce Clause in Chapter 4, it will be central to our inquiry. In general, throughout this part, you should continue to ask how a variety of methods of interpretation might help us to analyze issues of congressional power and the problem of federalism.

Alexander Hamilton

OPINION AS TO THE CONSTITUTIONALITY OF THE BANK OF THE UNITED STATES*

1791

The creation of a national bank was one of the most heated controversies of the early Republic, both as a matter of public policy and as a question of constitutional interpretation. Congress's power to authorize a central bank is now well settled, as reflected in Federal Reserve Chairman Ben Bernanke's broad control of America's money supply during the recent financial crisis. But from the time of the Founding through President Andrew Jackson's

*Available at *http://avalon.law.yale.edu/18th_century/bank-ah.asp.*

dramatic veto of the renewal of the charter of the Second Bank of the United States in 1832, the issue was never far from the heart of public partisan debate — not unlike contemporary disagreements over abortion rights and affirmative action.

In 1791, President Washington requested written opinions on the constitutionality of the bank charter before signing it into law. Alexander Hamilton, as Secretary of the Treasury, believed that a national bank was essential to creating financial stability and establishing the nation's credit. Thomas Jefferson, writing as Secretary of State, adamantly opposed the bank, as well as the excise taxes that would finance its incorporation. Their arguments as to the constitutionality of incorporating the bank are reproduced below.

. . . [T]his general principle is inherent in the very definition of government, and essential to every step of progress to be made by that of the United States, namely: That every power vested in a government is in its nature sovereign, and includes, by force of the term, a right to employ all the means requisite and fairly applicable to the attainment of the ends of such power, and which are not precluded by restrictions and exceptions specified in the Constitution, or not immoral, or not contrary to the essential ends of political society.

This principle, in its application to government in general, would be admitted as an axiom; and it will be incumbent upon those who may incline to deny it, to prove a distinction, and to show that a rule which, in the general system of things, is essential to the preservation of the social order, is inapplicable to the United States.

The circumstance that the powers of sovereignty are in this country divided between the National and State governments, does not afford the distinction required. It does not follow from this, that each of the portion of powers delegated to the one or to the other, is not sovereign with regard to its proper objects. It will only follow from it, that each has sovereign power as to certain things, and not as to other things. To deny that the Government of the United States has sovereign power, as to its declared purposes and trusts, because its power does not extend to all cases would be equally to deny that the State governments have sovereign power in any case, because their power does not extend to every case. The tenth section of the first article of the Constitution exhibits a long list of very important things which they may not do. And thus the United States would furnish the singular spectacle of a political society without sovereignty, or of a people governed, without government.

If it would be necessary to bring proof to a proposition so clear, as that which affirms that the powers of the Federal Government, as to its objects, were sovereign, there is a clause of its Constitution which would be decisive. It is that which declares that the Constitution, and the laws of the United States made in pursuance of it, and all treaties made, or which shall be made, under their authority, shall be the supreme law of the land.

. . . [W]here the authority of the government is general, it can create corporations in all cases; where it is confined to certain branches of legislation, it can create corporations only in those cases.

. . . [A]ll government is a delegation of power. But how much is delegated in each case, is a question of fact, to be made out by fair reasoning and construction, upon the particular provisions of the Constitution, taking as guides the general principles and general ends of governments.

It is not denied that there are implied, as well as express powers, and that the former are as effectually delegated as the latter.... It will not be doubted, that if the United States should make a conquest of any of the territories of its neighbors, they would possess sovereign jurisdiction over the conquered territory. This would be rather a result, from the whole mass of the powers of the government, and from the nature of political society, than a consequence of either of the powers specially enumerated.

... [A]s a power of erecting a corporation may as well be implied as any other thing, it may as well be employed as an instrument or mean of carrying into execution any of the specified powers, as any other instrument or mean whatever. The only question must be in this, as in every other case, whether the mean to be employed or in this instance, the corporation to be erected, has a natural relation to any of the acknowledged objects or lawful ends of the government. Thus a corporation may not be erected by Congress for superintending the police of the city of Philadelphia, because they are not authorized to regulate the police of that city. But one may be erected in relation to the collection of taxes, or to the trade with foreign countries, or to the trade between the States, or with the Indian tribes; because it is the province of the Federal Government to regulate those objects, and because it is incident to a general sovereign or legislative power to regulate a thing, to employ all the means which relate to its regulation to the best and greatest advantage.

... To this mode of reasoning respecting the right of employing all the means requisite to the execution of the specified powers of the government, it is to be objected, that none but necessary and proper means are to be employed; and the Secretary of State maintains, that no means are to be considered necessary but those without which the grant of the power would be nugatory. Nay, so far does he go in his restrictive interpretation of the word, as even to make the case of necessity which shall warrant the constitutional exercise of the power to depend on casual and temporary circumstances; an idea which alone refutes the construction. The expediency of exercising a particular power, at a particular time, must, indeed, depend on circumstances; but the constitutional; right of exercising it must be uniform and invariable, the same to-day as to-morrow.

... It is certain that neither the grammatical nor popular sense of the term requires that construction. According to both, necessary often means no more than needful, requisite, incidental, useful, or conducive to. It is a common mode of expression to say, that it is necessary for a government or a person to do this or that thing, when nothing more is intended or understood, than that the interests of the government or person require, or will be promoted by, the doing of this or that thing. The imagination can be at no loss for exemplifications of the use of the word in this sense. And it is the true one in which it is to be understood as used in the Constitution. The whole turn of the clause containing it indicates, that it was the intent of the Convention, by that clause, to give a liberal latitude to the exercise of the specified powers. The expressions have peculiar comprehensiveness. They are, "to make all laws necessary and proper for carrying into execution the foregoing powers, and all other powers vested by the Constitution in the Government of the United States, or in any department or officer thereof."

To understand the word as the Secretary of State does, would be to depart from its obvious and popular sense, and to give it a restrictive operation, an idea never before entertained. It would be to give it the same force as if the word absolutely or indispensably had been prefixed to it.

Such a construction would beget endless uncertainty and embarrassment. The cases must be palpable and extreme, in which it could be pronounced, with certainty, that a measure was absolutely necessary, or one, without which the exercise of a given power would be nugatory. There are few measures of any government which would stand so severe a test....

The practice of the government is against the rule of construction advocated by the Secretary of State. Of this, the act concerning lighthouses, beacons, buoys, and public piers, is a decisive example. This, doubtless, must be referred to the powers of regulating trade, and is fairly relative to it. But it cannot be affirmed that the exercise of that power in this instance was strictly necessary or that the power itself would be nugatory, without that of regulating establishments of this nature.

This restrictive interpretation of the word necessary is also contrary to this sound maxim of construction; namely, that the powers contained in a constitution of government, especially those which concern the general administration of the affairs of a country, its finances, trade, defence, etc., ought to be construed liberally in advancement of the public good. This rule does not depend on the particular form of a government, or on the particular demarcation of the boundaries of its powers, but on the nature and objects of government itself. The means by which national exigencies are to be provided for, national inconveniences obviated, national prosperity promoted, are of such infinite variety, extent, and complexity, that there must of necessity be great latitude of discretion in the selection and application of those means. Hence, consequently, the necessity and propriety of exercising the authorities intrusted to a government on principles of liberal construction.

. . . It is no valid objection to the doctrine to say, that it is calculated to extend the power of the General Government throughout the entire sphere of State legislation. The same thing has been said, and may be said, with regard to every exercise of power by implication or construction.

. . . But the doctrine which is contended for is not chargeable with the consequences imputed to it. It does not affirm that the National Government is sovereign in all respects, but that it is sovereign to a certain extent—that is, to the extent of the objects of its specified powers.

It leaves, therefore, a criterion of what is constitutional, and of what is not so. This criterion is the end, to which the measure relates as a means. If the end be clearly comprehended within any of the specified powers, and if the measure have an obvious relation to that end, and is not forbidden by any particular provision of the Constitution, it may safely be deemed to come within the compass of the national authority. There is also this further criterion, which may materially assist the decision: Does the proposed measure abridge a pre-existing right of any State or of any individual? If it does not, there is a strong presumption in favor of its constitutionality, and slighter relations to any declared object of the Constitution may be permitted to turn the scale.

. . . The proposed bank is to consist of an association of persons, for the purpose of creating a joint capital, to be employed chiefly and essentially in loans. So far the object is not only lawful, but it is the mere exercise of a right which the law allows to every individual. The Bank of New York, which is not incorporated, is an example of such an association. The bill proposes, in addition, that the government shall become a joint proprietor in this undertaking, and that it shall permit the bills of the company, payable on demand, to be receivable in its revenues; and stipulates that it shall not grant privileges, similar to those which are to be allowed to this company, to any others. All this is incontrovertibly within the compass of the discretion of the government. The only question is, whether it has a right to incorporate this company, in order to enable it the more effectually to accomplish ends which are in themselves lawful.

To establish such a right, it remains to show the relation of such an institution to one or more of the specified powers of the government. Accordingly it is affirmed that it has a relation, more or less direct, to the power of collecting taxes, to that of borrowing money, to that of regulating trade between the States, and to those of raising and maintaining fleets and armies....

A bank relates to the collection of taxes in two ways—indirectly, by increasing the quantity of circulating medium and quickening circulation, which facilitates the means of paying directly, by creating a convenient species of medium in which they are to be paid.

To designate or appoint the money or thing in which taxes are to be paid, is not only a proper, but a necessary exercise of the power of collecting them....

And among the expedients which may be adopted, is that of bills issued under the authority of the United States.

Now the manner of issuing these bills is again matter of discretion. The government might doubtless proceed in the following manner:

It might provide that they should be issued under the direction of certain officers, payable on demand; and, in order to support their credit, and give them a ready circulation, it might, besides giving them a currency in its taxes, set apart, out of any moneys in its treasury, a given sum, and appropriate it, under the direction of those officers, as a fund for answering the bills, as presented for payment.

The constitutionality of all this would not admit of a question, and yet it would amount to the institution of a bank, with a view to the more convenient collection of taxes. . . . [I]f the place where the fund to be set apart was kept should be made a receptacle of the moneys of all other persons who should incline to deposit them there for safe-keeping; and would become still more so, if the officers charged with the direction of the fund were authorized to make discounts at the usual rate of interest, upon good security. To deny the power of the government to add these ingredients to the plan, would be to refine away all government.

. . . Suppose, when the species of bank which has been described was about to be instituted, it was to be urged that, in order to secure to it a due degree of confidence, the fund ought not only to be set apart and appropriated generally, but ought to be specifically vested in the officers who were to have the direction of it, and in their successors in office, to the end that it might acquire the character of private property. . . . [S]uch a disposition of the thing would amount to the erection of a corporation; for the true definition of a corporation seems to be this: It is a legal person, or a person created by act of law, consisting of one or more natural persons authorized to hold property....

...Suppose, also, that, by some of those adverse conjunctures which occasionally attend nations, there had been a very great drain of the specie of the country, so as not only to cause general distress for want of an adequate medium of circulation, but to produce, in consequence of that circumstance, considerable defalcations in the public revenues. Suppose, also, that there was no bank instituted in any State; in such a posture of things, would it not be most manifest, that the incorporation of a bank like that proposed by the bill would be a measure immediately relative to the effectual collection of the taxes, and completely within the province of the sovereign power of providing, by all laws necessary and proper, for that collection? . . .

A bank has a direct relation to the power of borrowing money, because it is a[n] usual, and in sudden emergencies an essential, instrument in the obtaining of loans to government.

A nation is threatened with a war; large sums are wanted on a sudden to make the necessary preparations. Taxes are laid for the purpose, but it requires time to obtain the benefit of them. Anticipation is indispensable. If there be a bank the supply can at once be had. If there be none, loans from individuals must be sought. The progress of these is often too slow for the exigency; in some situations they are not practicable at all. Frequently when they are, it is of great consequence to be able to anticipate the product of them by advance from a bank.

. . . Let it then be supposed that the necessity existed, (as but for a casualty would be the case), that proposals were made for obtaining a loan; that a number of individuals came forward and said, we are willing to accommodate the government with the money; . . . but in order to do this, it is indispensable that we should be incorporated as a bank. . . .

Can it be believed that a compliance with this proposition would be unconstitutional? . . .

The institution of a bank has also a natural relation to the regulation of trade between the States, in so far as it is conducive to the creation of a convenient medium of exchange between them, and to the keeping up a full circulation, by preventing the frequent displacement of the metals in reciprocal remittances. Money is the very hinge on which commerce turns. And this does not merely mean gold and silver; many other things have served the purpose, with different degrees of utility. Paper has been extensively employed.

The Secretary of State further argues, that if this was a regulation of commerce, it would be void, as extending as much to the internal commerce of every State as to its external. But what regulation of commerce does not extend to the internal commerce of every State? . . . [W]hat regulation of trade between the States but must affect the internal trade of each State? What can operate upon the whole, but must extend to every part?

The relation of a bank to the execution of the powers that concern the common defence has been anticipated. It has been noted, that, at this very moment, the aid of such an institution is essential to the measures to be pursued for the protection of our frontiers.

It now remains to show that the incorporation of a bank is within the operation of the provision which authorizes Congress to make all needful rules and regulations concerning the property of the United States. . . .

The support of government — the support of troops for the common defence — the payment of the public debt, are the true final causes for raising money. The disposition and regulation of it, when raised, are the steps by which it is applied to the ends for which it was raised, not the ends themselves. Hence, therefore, the money to be raised by taxes, as well as any other personal property, must be supposed to come within the meaning, as they certainly do within the letter, of authority to make all needful rules and regulations concerning the property of the United States.

A power to make all needful rules and regulations concerning territory, has been construed to mean a power to erect a government. A power to regulate trade, is a power to make all needful rules and regulations concerning trade. Why may it not, then, include that of erecting a trading company, as well as, in other cases, to erect a government?

. . . [T]he very general power of laying and collecting taxes, and appropriating their proceeds — that of borrowing money indefinitely — that of coining money, and regulating foreign coins — that of making all needful rules and regulations respecting the property of the United States. These powers combined, as well as the reason and nature of the thing, speak strongly this language: that it is the manifest design and scope of the Constitution to vest in Congress all the powers requisite to the effectual administration of the finances of the United States. As far as concerns this object, there appears to be no parsimony of power. . . .

Thomas Jefferson

OPINION ON THE CONSTITUTIONALITY OF A NATIONAL BANK*

1791

. . . I consider the foundation of the Constitution as laid on this ground: That "all powers not delegated to the United States, by the Constitution, nor prohibited by it to the States, are reserved to the States or to the people." To take a single step beyond the boundaries thus specially drawn around the powers of Congress, is to take possession of a boundless field of power, no longer susceptible of any definition.

The incorporation of a bank, and the powers assumed by this bill, have not, in my opinion, been delegated to the United States, by the Constitution.

I.

They are not among the powers specially enumerated: for these are:

1. A power to lay taxes for the purpose of paying the debts of the United States; but no debt is paid by this bill, nor any tax laid. Were it a bill to raise money, its origination in the Senate would condemn it by the Constitution.

2. "To borrow money." But this bill neither borrows money nor ensures the borrowing of it. The proprietors of the bank will be just as free as any other money holders, to lend or not to lend their money to the public. The operation proposed in the bill first, to lend them two millions, and then to borrow them back again, cannot change the nature of the latter act, which will still be a payment, and not a loan, call it by what name you please.

3. To "regulate commerce with foreign nations, and among the States, and with the Indian tribes." To erect a bank, and to regulate commerce, are very different acts. He who erects a bank, creates a

*Available at *http://avalon.law.yale.edu/18th_century/bank-tj.asp*.

subject of commerce in its bills, so does he who makes a bushel of wheat, or digs a dollar out of the mines; yet neither of these persons regulates commerce thereby. To make a thing which may be bought and sold, is not to prescribe regulations for buying and selling. Besides, if this was an exercise of the power of regulating commerce, it would be void, as extending as much to the internal commerce of every State, as to its external. For the power given to Congress by the Constitution does not extend to the internal regulation of the commerce of a State (that is to say of the commerce between citizen and citizen) which remain exclusively with its own legislature; but to its external commerce only, that is to say, its commerce with another State, or with foreign nations, or with the Indian tribes. Accordingly the bill does not propose the measure as a regulation of trade, but as "productive of considerable advantages to trade." Still less are these powers covered by any other of the special enumerations.

II.

Nor are they within either of the general phrases, which are the two following:

1. To lay taxes to provide for the general welfare of the United States, that is to say, "to lay taxes for the purpose of providing for the general welfare." For the laying of taxes is the power, and the general welfare the purpose for which the power is to be exercised. They are not to lay taxes ad libitum for any purpose they please; but only to pay the debts or provide for the welfare of the Union. In like manner, they are not to do anything they please to provide for the general welfare, but only to lay taxes for that purpose. To consider the latter phrase, not as describing the purpose of the first, but as giving a distinct and independent power to do any act they please, which might be for the good of the Union, would render all the preceding and subsequent enumerations of power completely useless.

It would reduce the whole instrument to a single phrase, that of instituting a Congress with power to do whatever would be for the good of the United States; and, as they would be the sole judges of the good or evil, it would be also a power to do whatever evil they please.

It is an established rule of construction where a phrase will bear either of two meanings, to give it that which will allow some meaning to the other parts of the instrument, and not that which would render all the others useless. Certainly no such universal power was meant to be given them. It was intended to lace them up straitly within the enumerated powers, and those without which, as means, these powers could not be carried into effect. It is known that the very power now proposed as a means was rejected as an end by the Convention which formed the Constitution. A proposition was made to them to authorize Congress to open canals, and an amendatory one to empower them to incorporate. But the whole was rejected, and one of the reasons for rejection urged in debate was, that then they would have a power to erect a bank, which would render the great cities, where there were prejudices and jealousies on the subject, adverse to the reception of the Constitution.

2. The second general phrase is, "to make all laws necessary and proper for carrying into execution the enumerated powers." But they can all be carried into execution without a bank. A bank therefore is not necessary, and consequently not authorized by this phrase.

It has been urged that a bank will give great facility or convenience in the collection of taxes. Suppose this were true: yet the Constitution allows only the means which are "necessary," not those which are merely "convenient" for effecting the enumerated powers. If such a latitude of construction be allowed to this phrase as to give any non-enumerated power, it will go to everyone, for there is not one which ingenuity may not torture into a convenience in some instance or other, to some one of so long a list of enumerated powers. It would swallow up all the delegated powers, and reduce the whole to one power, as before observed. Therefore it was that the Constitution restrained them to the necessary means, that is to say, to those means without which the grant of power would be nugatory.

But let us examine this convenience and see what it is. The report on this subject, page 3, states the only general convenience to be, the preventing the transportation and re-transportation of money between the States and the treasury (for I pass over the increase of circulating medium, ascribed to it as a want, and which, according to my ideas of paper money, is clearly a demerit). Every State will have to pay a sum of tax money into the treasury; and the treasury will have to pay, in every State, a part of the interest on the public debt, and salaries to the officers of government resident in that State. In most of the States there will still be a surplus of tax money to come up to the seat of government for the officers residing there. The payments of interest and salary in each State may be made by treasury orders on the State collector. This will take up the greater part of the money he has collected in his State, and consequently prevent the great mass of it from being drawn out of the State. If there be a balance of commerce in favor of that State against the one in which the government resides, the surplus of taxes will be remitted by the bills of exchange drawn for that commercial balance. And so it must be if there was a bank. But if there be no balance of commerce, either direct or circuitous, all the banks in the world could not bring up the surplus of taxes, but in the form of money. Treasury orders then, and bills of exchange may prevent the displacement of the main mass of the money collected, without the aid of any bank; and where these fail, it cannot be prevented even with that aid.

Perhaps, indeed, bank bills may be a more convenient vehicle than treasury orders. But a little difference in the degree of convenience cannot constitute the necessity which the Constitution makes the ground for assuming any non-enumerated power.

Besides, the existing banks will, without a doubt, enter into arrangements for lending their agency, and the more favorable, as there will be a competition among them for it; whereas the bill delivers us up bound to the national bank, who are free to refuse all arrangement, but on their own terms, and the public not free, on such refusal, to employ any other bank. That of Philadelphia I believe, now does this business, by their post-notes, which, by an arrangement with the treasury, are paid by any State collector to whom they are presented. This expedient alone suffices to prevent the existence of that necessity which may justify the assumption of a non-enumerated power as a means for carrying into effect an enumerated one. The thing may be done, and has been done, and well done, without this assumption, therefore it does not stand on that degree of necessity which can honestly justify it.

It may be said that a bank whose bills would have a currency all over the States, would be more convenient than one whose currency is limited to a single State. So it would be still more convenient that there should be a bank, whose bills should have a currency all over the world. But it does not follow from this superior convenienc, that there exists anywhere a power to establish such a bank; or that the world may not go on very well without it.

Can it be thought that the Constitution intended that for a shade or two of convenience, more or less, Congress should be authorized to break down the most ancient and fundamental laws of the several States; such as those against Mortmain, the laws of Alienage, the rules of descent, the acts of distribution, the laws of escheat and forfeiture, the laws of monopoly? Nothing but a necessity invincible by any other means, can justify such a prostitution of laws, which constitute the pillars of our whole system of jurisprudence. Will Congress be too strait-laced to carry the Constitution into honest effect, unless they may pass over the foundation-laws of the State government for the slightest convenience of theirs?

The negative of the President is the shield provided by the Constitution to protect against the invasions of the legislature: 1. The right of the Executive. 2. Of the Judiciary. 3. Of the States and State legislatures. The present is the case of a right remaining exclusively with the States, and consequently one of those intended by the Constitution to be placed under its protection.

McCULLOCH v. MARYLAND

17 U.S. 316 (1819)

Opinion: Marshall, joined by Washington, Johnson, Livingston, Todd, Duvall, Story

While the charter for the First Bank of the United States expired in 1811, Congress passed a charter for a second bank in 1816. Maryland levied a tax against all banks not chartered within the state, and the president of the Baltimore branch of the national bank, James McCulloch, refused to pay the tax. He claimed that the tax was unconstitutional because it interfered with a valid exercise of congressional power. In reading the case, pay particular attention to the kind of boundaries the holding establishes between federal and state power. According to Chief Justice Marshall, what is the source of congressional power to create the bank? In what ways does he think this power limits the various powers of the states? It is worth noting that by examining whether Congress had the power to authorize the bank, the Court was engaging in an early act of judicial review over federal legislation not long after Marbury v. Madison.

MR. CHIEF JUSTICE MARSHALL *delivered the opinion of the Court.*

In the case now to be determined, the defendant, a sovereign State, denies the obligation of a law enacted by the legislature of the Union, and the plaintiff, on his part, contests the validity of an act which has been passed by the legislature of that State. . . .

The first question made in the cause is, has Congress power to incorporate a bank?

It has been truly said, that this can scarcely be considered as an open question, entirely unprejudiced by the former proceedings of the nation respecting it. The principle now contested was introduced at a very early period of our history, has been recognised by many successive legislatures, and has been acted upon by the judicial department, in cases of peculiar delicacy, as a law of undoubted obligation.

... [A] doubtful question, one on which human reason may pause, and the human judgment be suspended, in the decision of which the great principles of liberty are not concerned, but the respective powers of those who are equally the representatives of the people, are to be adjusted; if not put at rest by the practice of the government, ought to receive a considerable impression from that practice. An exposition of the constitution, deliberately established by legislative acts, on the faith of which an immense property has been advanced, ought not to be lightly disregarded.

The power now contested was exercised by the first Congress elected under the present constitution. The bill for incorporating the bank of the United States did not steal upon an unsuspecting legislature, and pass unobserved. Its principle was completely understood, and was opposed with equal zeal and ability. After being resisted, first in the fair and open field of debate, and afterwards in the executive cabinet, with as much persevering talent as any measure has ever experienced, and being supported by arguments which convinced minds as pure and as intelligent as this country can boast, it became a law. The original act was permitted to expire; but a short experience of the embarrassments to which the refusal to revive it exposed the government, convinced those who were most prejudiced against the measure of its necessity, and induced the passage of the present law....

. . . [T]he counsel for the State of Maryland have deemed it of some importance, in the construction of the constitution, to consider that instrument not as emanating from the people, but as the act of sovereign and independent States. The powers of the general government, it has been said, are delegated by the States, who alone are truly sovereign; and must be exercised in subordination to the States, who alone possess supreme dominion.

It would be difficult to sustain this proposition.... The government proceeds directly from the people; is "ordained and established" in the name of the people; and is declared to be ordained, "in order to form a more perfect union, establish justice, ensure domestic tranquillity, and secure the blessings of liberty to themselves and to their posterity." The assent of the States, in their sovereign capacity, is implied in calling a Convention, and thus submitting that instrument to the people. But the people were at perfect liberty to accept or reject it; and their act was final. It required not the affirmance, and could not be negatived, by the State governments. The constitution, when thus adopted, was of complete obligation, and bound the State sovereignties.

It has been said, that the people had already surrendered all their powers to the State sovereignties, and had nothing more to give. But, surely, the question whether they may resume and modify the powers granted to government does not remain to be settled in this country. Much more might the legitimacy of the general government be doubted, had it been created by the States. The powers delegated to the State sovereignties were to be exercised by themselves, not by a distinct and independent sovereignty, created by themselves. To the formation of a league, such as was the confederation, the State sovereignties were certainly competent. But when, "in order to form a more perfect union," it was deemed necessary to change this alliance into an effective government, possessing great and sovereign powers, and acting directly on the people, the necessity of referring it to the people, and of deriving its powers directly from them, was felt and acknowledged by all.

If any one proposition could command the universal assent of mankind, we might expect it would be this — that the government of the Union, though limited in its powers, is supreme within its sphere of action. This would seem to result necessarily from its nature. It is the government of all; its powers are delegated by all; it represents all, and acts for all. Though any one State may be willing to control its operations, no State is willing to allow others to control them. The nation, on those subjects on which it can act, must necessarily bind its component parts. But this question is not left to mere reason: the people have, in express terms, decided it, by saying, "this constitution, and the laws of the United States, which shall be made in pursuance thereof," "shall be the supreme law of the land," and by requiring that the members of the State legislatures, and the officers of the executive and judicial departments of the States, shall take the oath of fidelity to it.

The government of the United States, then, though limited in its powers, is supreme; and its laws, when made in pursuance of the constitution, form the supreme law of the land, "any thing in the constitution or laws of any State to the contrary notwithstanding."

Among the enumerated powers, we do not find that of establishing a bank or creating a corporation. But there is no phrase in the instrument which, like the articles of confederation, excludes incidental or implied powers; and which requires that every thing granted shall be expressly and minutely described. Even the 10th amendment, which was framed for the purpose of quieting the excessive jealousies which had been excited, omits the word "expressly," and declares only that the powers "not delegated to the United States, nor prohibited to the States, are reserved to the States or to the people"; thus leaving the question, whether the particular power which may become the subject of contest has been delegated to the one government, or prohibited to the other, to depend on a fair construction of the whole instrument. The men who drew and adopted this amendment had experienced the embarrassments resulting from the insertion of this word in the articles of confederation, and probably omitted it to avoid those embarrassments. A constitution, to contain an accurate detail of all the subdivisions of which its great powers will admit, and of all the means by which they may be carried into execution, would partake of the prolixity of a legal code, and could scarcely be embraced by the human mind. It would probably never be understood by the public. Its nature, therefore, requires, that only its great outlines should be marked, its important objects designated, and the minor ingredients which compose those objects be deduced from the nature of the objects themselves. . . . [W]e must never forget that it is a constitution we are expounding.

Although, among the enumerated powers of government, we do not find the word "bank" or "incorporation," we find the great powers to lay and collect taxes; to borrow money; to regulate commerce; to declare and conduct a war; and to raise and support armies and navies. . . . [A] government, entrusted with such ample powers, on the due execution of which the happiness and prosperity of the nation so vitally depends, must also be entrusted with ample means for their execution. The power being given, it is the interest of the nation to facilitate its execution. It can never be their interest, and cannot be presumed to have been their intention, to clog and embarrass its execution by withholding the most appropriate means. . . . Can we adopt that construction (unless the words imperiously require it) which would impute to the framers of that instrument, when granting these powers for the public good, the intention of impeding their exercise by withholding a choice of means? If, indeed, such be the mandate of the constitution, we have only to obey; but that instrument does not profess to enumerate the means by which the powers it confers may be executed; nor does it prohibit the creation of a corporation, if the existence of such a being be essential to the beneficial exercise of those powers. It is, then, the subject of fair inquiry, how far such means may be employed.

The creation of a corporation, it is said, appertains to sovereignty. This is admitted. But to what portion of sovereignty does it appertain? Does it belong to one more than to another? In America, the powers of sovereignty are divided between the government of the Union, and those of the States. They are each sovereign, with respect to the objects committed to it, and neither sovereign with respect to the objects committed to the other.... The power of creating a corporation, though appertaining to sovereignty, is not, like the power of making war, or levying taxes, or of regulating commerce, a great substantive and independent power, which cannot be implied as incidental to other powers, or used as a means of executing them. It is never the end for which other powers are exercised, but a means by which other objects are accomplished.... The power of creating a corporation is never used for its own sake, but for the purpose of effecting something else. No sufficient reason is, therefore, perceived, why it may not pass as incidental to those powers which are expressly given, if it be a direct mode of executing them.

But the constitution of the United States has not left the right of Congress to employ the necessary means, for the execution of the powers conferred on the government, to general reasoning. To its enumeration of powers is added that of making "all laws which shall be necessary and proper, for carrying into execution the foregoing powers, and all other powers vested by this constitution, in the government of the United States, or in any department thereof."

The counsel for the State of Maryland have urged various arguments, to prove that this clause, though in terms a grant of power, is not so in effect; but is really restrictive of the general right, which might otherwise be implied, of selecting means for executing the enumerated powers. . . . Congress is not empowered by it to make all laws, which may have relation to the powers conferred on the government, but such only as may be "necessary and proper" for carrying them into execution. The word "necessary," is considered as controlling the whole sentence, and as limiting the right to pass laws for the execution of the granted powers, to such as are indispensable, and without which the power would be nugatory. That it excludes the choice of means, and leaves to Congress, in each case, that only which is most direct and simple.

Is it true, that this is the sense in which the word "necessary" is always used? . . . [W]e find that it frequently imports no more than that one thing is convenient, or useful, or essential to another. To employ the means necessary to an end, is generally understood as employing any means calculated to produce the end, and not as being confined to those single means, without which the end would be entirely unattainable.... The word "necessary" . . . admits of all degrees of comparison; and is often connected with other words, which increase or diminish the impression the mind receives of the urgency it imports. A thing may be necessary, very necessary, absolutely or indispensably necessary. To no mind would the same idea be conveyed, by these several phrases. This comment on the word is well illustrated, by the passage cited at the bar, from the 10th section of the 1st article of the constitution. It is, we think, impossible to compare the sentence which prohibits a State from laying "imposts, or duties on imports or exports, except what may be absolutely necessary for executing its inspection laws," with that which authorizes Congress "to make all laws which shall be necessary and proper for carrying into execution" the powers of the general government, without feeling a conviction that the convention understood itself to change materially the meaning of the word "necessary," by prefixing the word "absolutely." This word, then, like others, is used in various senses; and, in its construction, the subject, the context, the intention of the person using them, are all to be taken into view.

. . . The subject is the execution of those great powers on which the welfare of a nation essentially depends. It must have been the intention of those who gave these powers, to insure, as far as human prudence could insure, their beneficial execution. This could not be done by confiding the choice of means to such narrow limits as not to leave it in the power of Congress to adopt any which might be appropriate, and which were conducive to the end. This provision is made in a constitution intended to endure for ages to come, and, consequently, to be adapted to the various crises of human affairs. To have prescribed the means by which government should, in all future time, execute its powers, would have been to change, entirely, the character of the instrument, and give it the properties of a legal code. It would have been an unwise attempt to provide, by immutable rules, for exigencies which, if foreseen at all, must have been seen dimly, and which can be best provided for as they occur. To have declared that the best means shall not be used, but those alone without which the power given would be nugatory, would have been to deprive the legislature of the capacity to avail itself of experience, to exercise its reason, and to accommodate its legislation to circumstances. If we apply this principle of construction to any of the powers of the government, we shall find it so pernicious in its operation that we shall be compelled to discard it. . . .

So, with respect to the whole penal code of the United States: whence arises the power to punish in cases not prescribed by the constitution? All admit that the government may, legitimately, punish any violation of its laws; and yet, this is not among the enumerated powers of Congress.

Take, for example, the power "to establish post offices and post roads." This power is executed by the single act of making the establishment. But, from this has been inferred the power and duty of carrying the mail along the post road, from one post office to another. And, from this implied power, has again been inferred the right to punish those who steal letters from the post office, or rob the mail. It may be said, with some plausibility, that the right to carry the mail, and to punish those who rob it, is not indispensably necessary to the establishment of a post office and post road. This right is indeed essential to the beneficial exercise of the power, but not indispensably necessary to its existence. So, of the punishment of the crimes of stealing or falsifying a record or process of a Court of the United States, or of perjury in such Court. To punish these offences is certainly conducive to the due administration of justice. But courts may exist, and may decide the causes brought before them, though such crimes escape punishment.

. . . This clause, as construed by the State of Maryland, would abridge, and almost annihilate this useful and necessary right of the legislature to select its means. That this could not be intended, is, we should think, had it not been already controverted, too apparent for controversy. We think so for the following reasons:

1st. The clause is placed among the powers of Congress, not among the limitations on those powers.

2nd. Its terms purport to enlarge, not to diminish the powers vested in the government. It purports to be an additional power, not a restriction on those already granted. No reason has been, or can be assigned for thus concealing an intention to narrow the discretion of the national legislature under words which purport to enlarge it....

The result of the most careful and attentive consideration bestowed upon this clause is, that if it does not enlarge, it cannot be construed to restrain the powers of Congress, or to impair the right of the legislature to exercise its best judgment in the selection of measures to carry into execution the constitutional powers of the government. If no other motive for its insertion can be suggested, a sufficient one is found in the desire to remove all doubts respecting the right to legislate on that vast mass of incidental powers which must be involved in the constitution, if that instrument be not a splendid bauble.

We admit, as all must admit, that the powers of the government are limited, and that its limits are not to be transcended. But we think the sound construction of the constitution must allow to the national legislature that discretion, with respect to the means by which the powers it confers are to be carried into execution, which will enable that body to perform the high duties assigned to it, in the manner most beneficial to the people. Let the end be legitimate, let it be within the scope of the constitution, and all means which are appropriate, which are plainly adapted to that end, which are not prohibited, but consist with the letter and spirit of the constitution, are constitutional.

That a corporation must be considered as a means not less usual, not of higher dignity, not more requiring a particular specification than other means, has been sufficiently proved.... The power to "make all needful rules and regulations respecting the territory or other property belonging to the United States," is not more comprehensive, than the power "to make all laws which shall be necessary and proper for carrying into execution" the powers of the government. Yet all admit the constitutionality of a territorial government, which is a corporate body.

. . . Should Congress, in the execution of its powers, adopt measures which are prohibited by the constitution; or should Congress, under the pretext of executing its powers, pass laws for the accomplishment of objects not entrusted to the government; it would become the painful duty of this tribunal, should a case requiring such a decision come before it, to say that such an act was not the law of the land. But where the law is not prohibited, and is really calculated to effect any of the objects entrusted to the government, to undertake here to inquire into the degree of its necessity, would be to pass the line which circumscribes the judicial department, and to tread on legislative ground. This court disclaims all pretensions to such a power.

After this declaration, it can scarcely be necessary to say, that the existence of State banks can have no possible influence on the question.... [T]he choice of means implies a right to choose a national bank in preference to State banks, and Congress alone can make the election.

2. Whether the State of Maryland may, without violating the constitution, tax that branch?

That the power of taxation is one of vital importance; that it is retained by the States; that it is not abridged by the grant of a similar power to the government of the

Union; that it is to be concurrently exercised by the two governments: are truths which have never been denied. But, such is the paramount character of the constitution, that its capacity to withdraw any subject from the action of even this power, is admitted.... [I]f it may restrain a State from the exercise of its taxing power on imports and exports; the same paramount character would seem to restrain, as it certainly may restrain, a State from such other exercise of this power, as is in its nature incompatible with, and repugnant to, the constitutional laws of the Union....

On this ground the counsel for the bank place its claim to be exempted from the power of a State to tax its operations. There is no express provision for the case, but the claim has been sustained on a principle which so entirely pervades the constitution, is so intermixed with the materials which compose it, so interwoven with its web, so blended with its texture, as to be incapable of being separated from it, without rending it into shreds.

This great principle is, that the constitution and the laws made in pursuance thereof are supreme; that they control the constitution and laws of the respective States, and cannot be controlled by them. From this, which may be almost termed an axiom, other propositions are deduced as corollaries, on the truth or error of which, and on their application to this case, the cause has been supposed to depend. These are, 1st. that a power to create implies a power to preserve. 2nd. That a power to destroy, if wielded by a different hand, is hostile to, and incompatible with these powers to create and to preserve. 3d. That where this repugnancy exists, that authority which is supreme must control, not yield to that over which it is supreme.

The power of Congress to create, and of course to continue, the bank, was the subject of the preceding part of this opinion; and is no longer to be considered as questionable.

That the power of taxing it by the States may be exercised so as to destroy it, is too obvious to be denied. But taxation is said to be an absolute power, which acknowledges no other limits than those expressly prescribed in the constitution, and like sovereign power of every other description, is trusted to the discretion of those who use it. But the very terms of this argument admit that the sovereignty of the State, in the article of taxation itself, is subordinate to, and may be controlled by the constitution of the United States....

The argument on the part of the State of Maryland, is, not that the States may directly resist a law of Congress, but that they may exercise their acknowledged powers upon it, and that the constitution leaves them this right in the confidence that they will not abuse it.

[T]he power of taxing the people and their property is essential to the very existence of government, and may be legitimately exercised on the objects to which it is applicable, to the utmost extent to which the government may chuse to carry it. The only security against the abuse of this power, is found in the structure of the government itself. In imposing a tax the legislature acts upon its constituents. This is in general a sufficient security against erroneous and oppressive taxation.

The people of a State, therefore, give to their government a right of taxing themselves and their property, and as the exigencies of government cannot be limited, they prescribe no limits to the exercise of this right, resting confidently on the interest of the legislator, and on the influence of the constituents over their representative, to guard them against its abuse. But the means employed by the government of the Union have no such security, nor is the right of a State to tax them sustained by the same theory. Those means are not given by the people of a particular State, not given by the constituents of the legislature, which claim the right to tax them, but by the people of all the States. They are given by all, for the benefit of all — and upon theory, should be subjected to that government only which belongs to all.

If we apply the principle for which the State of Maryland contends, to the constitution generally, we shall find it capable of changing totally the character of that instrument. We shall find it capable of arresting all the measures of the government, and of prostrating it at the foot of the States. The American people have declared their constitution, and the laws made in pursuance thereof, to be supreme; but this principle would transfer the supremacy, in fact, to the States.

If the States may tax one instrument, employed by the government in the execution of its powers, they may tax any and every other instrument. They may tax the mail; they may tax the mint; they may tax patent rights; they may tax the papers of the custom-house; they may tax judicial process; they may tax all the means employed by the government, to an excess which would defeat all the ends of government. This was not intended by the American people. They did not design to make their government dependent on the States.

The question is, in truth, a question of supremacy; and if the right of the States to tax the means employed by the general government be conceded, the declaration that the constitution, and the laws made in pursuance thereof, shall be the supreme law of the land, is empty and unmeaning declamation.

[T]he States have no power, by taxation or otherwise, to retard, impede, burden, or in any manner control, the operations of the constitutional laws enacted by Congress to carry into execution the powers vested in the general government. This is, we think, the unavoidable consequence of that supremacy which the constitution has declared.

We are unanimously of opinion, that the law passed by the legislature of Maryland, imposing a tax on the Bank of the United States, is unconstitutional and void.

GIBBONS v. OGDEN

22 U.S. 1 (1824)

Opinion: Marshall, joined by Washington, Todd, Duvall, Story
Concurrence: Johnson

While McCulloch v. Maryland *established the framework for how we think about congressional power, perhaps the most significant source of Congress's authority is the Commerce Clause. Partly in response to economic inefficiencies and trade barriers under the Articles of Confederation, the Founders gave Congress the power "to regulate commerce . . . among the several states." But the text alone leaves many questions open, and as we will see in the next chapter, the answers have evolved over time. Does all economic activity count as "commerce"? How extensive must this activity be in order to qualify as commerce among the states? An expansive answer to these questions would significantly enlarge the scope of congressional power, giving the federal government purview over broad swaths of economic life—just as a narrow answer would significantly weaken it.*

The Supreme Court addressed these questions in Gibbons v. Ogden. *After the State of New York granted his employer the exclusive navigation rights between New York and New Jersey, Thomas Gibbons sued to enjoin Aaron Ogden from operating a competing ferry service. Ogden countered that the New York monopoly violated federal law and was void. Notice once again that this case is about both an authorization for congressional action and also the limits that authorization presents for the powers of the states. It is important to note that in addition to being about Congress's commerce power, the case is significant in that it is often thought to be the origin of limits on state power currently referred to as the "dormant commerce clause." According to this doctrine, it is implied in the grant of congressional power to regulate interstate commerce that the states cannot interfere with the regulation of interstate commerce. As you read, concentrate on the Court's perspective on whether Congress is authorized to regulate this area of economic activity and whether an individual state is prohibited from regulating it.*

MR. CHIEF JUSTICE MARSHALL *delivered the opinion of the Court, and, after stating the case, proceeded as follows:*

The appellant contends that this decree is erroneous, because the laws which purport to give the exclusive privilege it sustains, are repugnant to the constitution and laws of the United States.

The State of New-York maintains the constitutionality of these laws; and their Legislature, their Council of Revision, and their Judges, have repeatedly concurred in this opinion....

. . . [W]hen these allied sovereigns [the states] converted their league into a government, when they converted their Congress of Ambassadors, deputed to deliberate on their common concerns, and to recommend measures of general utility, into a Legislature, empowered to enact laws on the most interesting subjects, the whole character in which the States appear, underwent a change, the extent of which must be determined by a fair consideration of the instrument by which that change was effected.

This instrument contains an enumeration of powers expressly granted by the people to their government. It has been said, that these powers ought to be construed strictly. . . . What do gentlemen mean, by a strict construction? . . . If they contend for that narrow construction which, in support of some theory not to be found in the constitution, would deny to the government those powers which the words of the grant, as usually understood, import, and which are consistent with the general views and objects of the instrument; for that narrow construction, which would cripple the government, and render it unequal to the object, for which it is declared to be instituted, and to which the powers given, as fairly understood, render it competent; then we cannot perceive the propriety of this strict construction, nor adopt it as the rule by which the constitution is to be expounded.... If, from the imperfection of human language, there should be serious doubts respecting the extent of any given power, it is a well settled rule, that the objects for which it was given, especially when those objects are expressed in the instrument itself, should have great influence in the construction. We know of no reason for excluding this rule from the present case. The grant does not convey power which might be beneficial to the grantor, if retained by himself, or which can enure solely to the benefit of the grantee; but is an investment of power for the general advantage, in the hands of agents selected for that purpose; which power can never be exercised by the people themselves, but must be placed in the hands of agents, or lie dormant. We know of no rule for construing the extent of such powers, other than is given by the language of the instrument which confers them, taken in connexion with the purposes for which they were conferred.

The words are, "Congress shall have power to regulate commerce with foreign nations, and among the several States, and with the Indian tribes."

The subject to be regulated is commerce; and our constitution being, as was aptly said at the bar, one of enumeration, and not of definition, to ascertain the extent of the power, it becomes necessary to settle the meaning of the word. The counsel for the appellee would limit it to traffic, to buying and selling, or the interchange of commodities, and do not admit that it comprehends navigation. This would restrict a general term, applicable to many objects, to one of its significations. Commerce, undoubtedly, is traffic, but it is something more: it is intercourse. It describes the commercial intercourse between nations, and parts of nations, in all its branches, and is regulated by prescribing rules for carrying on that intercourse. The mind can scarcely conceive a system for regulating commerce between nations, which shall exclude all laws concerning navigation, which shall be silent on the admission of the vessels of the one nation into the ports of the other, and be confined to prescribing rules for the conduct of individuals, in the actual employment of buying and selling, or of barter.

If commerce does not include navigation, the government of the Union has no direct power over that subject, and can make no law prescribing what shall constitute American vessels, or requiring that they shall be navigated by American seamen. Yet this power has been exercised from the commencement of the government, has been exercised with the consent of all, and has been understood by all to be a commercial regulation. All America understands, and has uniformly understood, the word "commerce," to comprehend navigation....

It is a rule of construction, acknowledged by all, that the exceptions from a power mark its extent; for it would be absurd, as well as useless, to except from a granted power, that which was not granted — that which the words of the grant could not comprehend. If, then, there are in the constitution plain exceptions from the power over navigation, plain inhibitions to the exercise of that power in a particular way, it is a proof that those who made these exceptions, and prescribed these inhibitions, understood the power to which they applied as being granted.

The 9th section of the 1st article declares, that "no preference shall be given, by any regulation of commerce or revenue, to the ports of one State over those of another." This clause cannot be understood as applicable to those laws only which are passed for the purposes of revenue, because it is expressly applied to commercial regulations; and the most obvious preference which can be given to one port over another, in regulating commerce, relates to navigation. But the subsequent part of the sentence is still more explicit. It is, "nor shall vessels bound to or from one State, be obliged to enter, clear, or pay duties, in another." These words have a direct reference to navigation.

The universally acknowledged power of the government to impose embargoes, must also be considered as showing, that all America is united in that construction which comprehends navigation in the word commerce....

The word used in the constitution, then, comprehends, and has been always understood to comprehend, navigation within its meaning; and a power to regulate navigation, is as expressly granted, as if that term had been added to the word "commerce."

To what commerce does this power extend? The constitution informs us, to commerce "with foreign nations, and among the several States, and with the Indian tribes."

It has, we believe, been universally admitted, that these words comprehend every species of commercial intercourse between the United States and foreign nations. . . .

If this be the admitted meaning of the word, in its application to foreign nations, it must carry the same meaning throughout the sentence, and remain a unit, unless there be some plain intelligible cause which alters it.

The subject to which the power is next applied, is to commerce "among the several States." The word "among" means intermingled with. A thing which is among others, is intermingled with them. Commerce among the States, cannot stop at the external boundary line of each State, but may be introduced into the interior.

Comprehensive as the word "among" is, it may very properly be restricted to that commerce which concerns more States than one. The phrase is not one which would probably have been selected to indicate the completely interior traffic of a State, because it is not an apt phrase for that purpose; and the enumeration of the particular classes of commerce, to which the power was to be extended, would not have been made, had the intention been to extend the power to every description. The enumeration presupposes something not enumerated; and that something, if we regard the language or the subject of the sentence, must be the exclusively internal commerce of a State. The genius and character of the whole government seem to be, that its action is to be applied to all the external concerns of the nation, and to those internal concerns which affect the States generally; but not to those which are completely within a particular State, which do not affect other States, and with which it is not necessary to interfere, for the purpose of executing some of the general powers of the government. The completely internal commerce of a State, then, may be considered as reserved for the State itself.

Can a trading expedition between two adjoining States, commence and terminate outside of each? And if the trading intercourse be between two States remote from each other, must it not commence in one, terminate in the other, and probably pass through a third? Commerce among the States must, of necessity, be commerce with the States. In the regulation of trade with the Indian tribes, the action of the law, especially when the constitution was made, was chiefly within a State. The power of Congress, then, whatever it may be, must be exercised within the territorial jurisdiction of the several States. . . .

It is the power to regulate; that is, to prescribe the rule by which commerce is to be governed. This power, like all others vested in Congress, is complete in itself, may be exercised to its utmost extent, and acknowledges no limitations, other than are prescribed in the constitution. These are expressed in plain terms, and do not affect the questions which arise in this case, or which have been discussed at the bar. If, as has always been understood, the sovereignty of Congress, though limited to specified objects, is plenary as to those objects, the power over commerce with foreign nations, and among the several States, is vested in Congress as absolutely as it would be in a single government, having in its constitution the same restrictions on the exercise of the power as are found in the constitution of the United States. The wisdom and the discretion of Congress, their identity with the people, and the influence which their constituents possess at elections, are, in this, as in many other instances, as that, for example, of declaring war, the sole restraints on which they have relied, to secure them from its abuse. They are the restraints on which the people must often rely solely, in all representative governments.

The power of Congress, then, comprehends navigation, within the limits of every State in the Union; so far as that navigation may be, in any manner, connected with "commerce with foreign nations, or among the several States, or with the Indian tribes." It may, of consequence, pass the jurisdictional line of New-York, and act upon the very waters to which the prohibition now under consideration applies.

But it has been urged with great earnestness, that, although the power of Congress to regulate commerce with foreign nations, and among the several States, be co-extensive with the subject itself, and have no other limits than are prescribed in the constitution, yet the States may severally exercise the same power, within their respective jurisdictions. In support of this argument, it is said, that they possessed it as an inseparable attribute of sovereignty, before the formation of the constitution, and still retain it, except so far as they have surrendered it by that instrument; that this principle results from the nature of the government, and is secured by the tenth amendment; that an affirmative grant of power is not exclusive, unless in its own nature it be such that the continued exercise of it by the former possessor is inconsistent with the grant, and that this is not of that description.

It has been contended by the counsel for the appellant, that, as the word "to regulate" implies in its nature, full power over the thing to be regulated, it excludes, necessarily, the action of all others that would perform the same operation on the same thing. That regulation is designed for the entire result, applying to those parts which remain as they were, as well as to those which are altered. It produces a uniform whole, which is as much disturbed and deranged by changing what the regulating power designs to leave untouched, as that on which it has operated.

There is great force in this argument, and the Court is not satisfied that it has been refuted.

Since, however, in exercising the power of regulating their own purely internal affairs, whether of trading or police, the States may sometimes enact laws, the validity of which depends on their interfering with, and being contrary to, an act of Congress passed in pursuance of the constitution, the Court will enter upon the inquiry, whether the laws of New-York, as expounded by the highest tribunal of that State, have, in their application to this case, come into collision with an act of Congress, and deprived a citizen of a right to which that act entitles him. Should this collision exist, it will be immaterial whether those laws were passed in virtue of a concurrent power "to regulate commerce with foreign nations and among the several States," or, in virtue of a power to regulate their domestic trade and police. In one case and the other, the acts of New-York must yield to the law of Congress; and the decision sustaining the privilege they confer, against a right given by a law of the Union, must be erroneous.

The nullity of any act, inconsistent with the constitution, is produced by the declaration, that the constitution is the supreme law. The appropriate application of that part of the clause which confers the same supremacy on laws and treaties, is to such acts of the State Legislatures as do not transcend their powers, but, though enacted in the execution of acknowledged State powers, interfere with, or are contrary to the laws of Congress, made in pursuance of the constitution, or some treaty made under the authority of the United States. In every such case, the act of Congress, or the treaty, is supreme; and the law of the State, though enacted in the exercise of powers not controverted, must yield to it.

. . . Congress has passed "an act for enrolling or licensing ships or vessels to be employed in the coasting trade and fisheries, and for regulating the same." The counsel for the respondent contend, that this act does not give the right to sail from port to port, but confines itself to regulating a pre-existing right, so far only as to confer certain privileges on enrolled and licensed vessels in its exercise.

It will at once occur, that, when a Legislature attaches certain privileges and exemptions to the exercise of a right over which its control is absolute, the law must imply a power to exercise the right. The privileges are gone, if the right itself be annihilated. It would be contrary to all reason, and to the course of human affairs, to say that a State is unable to strip a vessel of the particular privileges attendant on the exercise of a right, and yet may annul the right itself; that the State of New-York cannot prevent an enrolled and licensed vessel, proceeding from Elizabethtown, in New-Jersey, to New-York, from enjoying, in her course, and on her entrance into port, all the privileges conferred by the act of Congress; but can shut her up in her own port, and prohibit altogether her entering the waters and ports of another State. To the Court it seems very clear, that the whole act on the subject of the coasting trade, according to those principles which govern the construction of statutes, implies, unequivocally, an authority to licensed vessels to carry on the coasting trade.

If the power reside in Congress, as a portion of the general grant to regulate commerce, then acts applying that power to vessels generally, must be construed as comprehending all vessels. If none appear to be excluded by the language of the act, none can be excluded by construction. Vessels have always been employed to a greater or less extent in the transportation of passengers, and have never been supposed to be, on that account, withdrawn from the control or protection of Congress. Packets which ply along the coast, as well as those which make voyages between Europe and America, consider the transportation of passengers as an important part of their business. Yet it has never been suspected that the general laws of navigation did not apply to them....

But all inquiry into this subject seems to the Court to be put completely at rest by the act already mentioned, entitled, "An act for the enrolling and licensing of steamboats."

This act authorizes a steamboat employed, or intended to be employed, only in a river or bay of the United States, owned wholly or in part by an alien, resident within the United States, to be enrolled and licensed as if the same belonged to a citizen of the United States.

This act demonstrates the opinion of Congress that steamboats may be enrolled and licensed, in common with vessels using sails. They are, of course, entitled to the same privileges, and can no more be restrained from navigating waters and entering ports which are free to such vessels than if they were wafted on their voyage by the winds, instead of being propelled by the agency of fire. The one element may be as legitimately used as the other for every commercial purpose authorized by the laws of the Union, and the act of a State inhibiting the use of either to any vessel having a license under the act of Congress comes, we think, in direct collision with that act.

As this decides the cause, it is unnecessary to enter in an examination of that part of the constitution which empowers Congress to promote the progress of science and the useful arts.

The Court is aware that, in stating the train of reasoning by which we have been conducted to this result, much time has been consumed in the attempt to demonstrate propositions which may have been thought axioms. It is felt that the tediousness inseparable from the endeavour to prove that which is already clear is imputable to a considerable part of this opinion. But it was unavoidable. The conclusion to which we have come depends on a chain of principles which it was necessary to preserve unbroken, and although some of them were thought nearly self-evident, the magnitude of the question, the weight of character belonging to those from whose judgment we dissent, and the argument at the bar demanded that we should assume nothing.

Powerful and ingenious minds, taking, as postulates, that the powers expressly granted to the government of the Union, are to be contracted by construction, into the narrowest possible compass, and that the original powers of the States are retained, if any possible construction will retain them, may, by a course of well digested, but refined and metaphysical reasoning, founded on these premises, explain away the constitution of our country, and leave it, a magnificent structure, indeed, to look at, but totally unfit for use. They may so entangle and perplex the understanding, as to obscure principles, which were before thought quite plain, and induce doubts where, if the mind were to pursue its own course, none would be perceived. In such a case, it is peculiarly necessary to recur to safe and fundamental principles to sustain those principles, and, when sustained, to make them the tests of the arguments to be examined.

MR. JUSTICE JOHNSON, *concurring.*

The judgment entered by the Court in this cause, has my entire approbation, but, having adopted my conclusions on views of the subject materially different from those of my brethren, I feel it incumbent on me to exhibit those views. . . .

The power of a sovereign state over commerce . . . amounts to nothing more than a power to limit and restrain it at pleasure. And since the power to prescribe the limits to its freedom necessarily implies the power to determine what shall remain unrestrained, it follows that the power must be exclusive; it can reside but in one potentate, and hence the grant of this power carries with it the whole subject, leaving nothing for the State to act upon. . . .

Commerce, in its simplest signification, means an exchange of goods, but in the advancement of society, labour, transportation, intelligence, care, and various mediums of exchange become commodities, and enter into commerce, the subject, the vehicle, the agent, and their various operations become the objects of commercial regulation. Shipbuilding, the carrying trade, and propagation of seamen are such vital agents of commercial prosperity that the nation which could not legislate over these subjects would not possess power to regulate commerce.

That such was the understanding of the framers of the Constitution is conspicuous from provisions contained in that instrument.

Box 3-1 Other Sources of Congressional Power

In addition to the commerce power, the Constitution also enumerates a number of congressional powers, including the power to declare war, the power to regulate patents, and the power to pass laws governing bankruptcies. You should turn to Article I, Section 8, to review this list of powers and reflect on which modern-day laws these powers correspond to. The principle in *Gibbons v. Ogden* states that each of these enumerated powers is "plenary," which means that Congress has complete control over regulating these areas. The principle in *McCulloch v. Maryland* tells us that the Necessary and Proper Clause also generates certain implied powers — such as the power to incorporate a national bank — so long as they are sufficiently related to the other powers enumerated in the list. Together, these twin constitutional principles secure a broad foundation of congressional power.

Outside of Article I, several amendments after the Civil War also expressly grant congressional powers. These amendments sought to prohibit slavery (the Thirteenth Amendment), secure due process and equal protection rights for all citizens (the Fourteenth Amendment), and prevent discrimination in the right to vote based on race or sex (the Fifteenth and Nineteenth Amendments, respectively). In addition to articulating these substantive commitments, these amendments also empower Congress to enforce their provisions through legislation. *City of Boerne v. Flores*, which we read in Chapter 2, limited these textual provisions. According to the majority in *Boerne v. Flores*, only the Court has the power to interpret what these provisions mean or require, and Congress must enforce these requirements with remedies that are congruent and proportional to the constitutional harm.

SOUTH DAKOTA v. DOLE

483 U.S. 203 (1987)

Opinion: Rehnquist, joined by White, Marshall, Blackmun, Powell, Stevens, Scalia
Dissent: Brennan
Dissent: O'Connor

There are two key questions that tie together the cases and readings in this part. First, do the enumerated provisions of the Constitution grant Congress a significant amount of power, extending even beyond what the text itself prescribes? The second question concerns whether the ultimate extent of this power is limited and where the boundaries that constrain Congress's actions lie. One such limit might be thought to lie in the set of individual rights protected by the Constitution. The other chief limit might be thought to be the principle of federalism, embodied in the Tenth Amendment and considered to protect a certain sphere of activity that only states may regulate. Some of these areas have traditionally included family law, criminal law, and education.

But even if Congress cannot directly legislate in these areas, it can influence the decisions that states make through its power to tax and spend. Take, for example, education policy. While Congress may lack the power to impose standards on state governments, the federal government contributes to a significant portion of education spending each year. Should Congress have the authority to condition this funding on the state governments' meeting certain requirements? Or would such a policy merely be a guise for imposing unconstitutional demands on the states?

The Supreme Court evaluated the constitutionality of conditioning funds in South Dakota v. Dole. *In exchange for a portion of federal highway funds, Congress demanded that all states raise the drinking age to at least 21. Chief Justice William Rehnquist's opinion discusses the line where "pressure turns into compulsion." Where does he draw that constitutional line? In Chief Justice Rehnquist's view, how closely related should the conditions be to the purpose of the funds in question?*

CHIEF JUSTICE REHNQUIST *delivered the opinion of the Court.*

Petitioner South Dakota permits persons 19 years of age or older to purchase beer containing up to 3.2% alcohol. In 1984 Congress enacted 23 U.S.C. §158, which directs the Secretary of Transportation to withhold a percentage of federal highway funds otherwise allocable from States "in which the purchase or public possession . . . of any alcoholic beverage by a person who is less than twenty-one years of age is lawful." The State sued in United States District Court seeking a declaratory judgment that §158 violates the constitutional limitations on congressional exercise of the spending power and violates the Twenty-first Amendment to the United States Constitution. . . .

Here, Congress has acted indirectly under its spending power to encourage uniformity in the States' drinking ages. As we explain below, we find this legislative effort within constitutional bounds even if Congress may not regulate drinking ages directly.

The Constitution empowers Congress to "lay and collect Taxes, Duties, Imposts, and Excises, to pay the Debts and provide for the common Defence and general Welfare of the United States." Incident to this power, Congress may attach conditions on the receipt of federal funds, and has repeatedly employed the power "to further broad policy objectives by conditioning receipt of federal moneys upon compliance by the recipient with federal statutory and administrative directives." The breadth of this power was made clear in United States v. Butler, 297 U.S. 1, 66 (1936), where the Court, resolving a longstanding debate over the scope of the Spending Clause, determined that "the power of Congress to authorize expenditure of public moneys for public purposes is not limited by the direct grants of legislative power found in the Constitution." Thus, objectives not thought to be within Article I's "enumerated legislative fields," id., at 65, may nevertheless be attained through the use of the spending power and the conditional grant of federal funds.

The spending power is of course not unlimited, but is instead subject to several general restrictions articulated in our cases. The first of these limitations is derived from the language of the Constitution itself: the exercise of the spending power must be in pursuit of "the general welfare." In considering whether a particular expenditure is intended to serve general public purposes, courts should defer substantially to the judgment of Congress. Second, we have required that if Congress desires to condition the States' receipt of federal funds, it "must do so unambiguously . . . , enabl[ing] the States to exercise their choice knowingly, cognizant of the consequences of their participation." Third, our cases have suggested (without significant elaboration) that conditions on federal grants might be illegitimate if they are unrelated "to the federal interest in particular national projects or programs." Finally, we have noted that other constitutional provisions may provide an independent bar to the conditional grant of federal funds.

South Dakota does not seriously claim that §158 is inconsistent with any of the first three restrictions mentioned above. We can readily conclude that the provision is designed to serve the general welfare, especially in light of the fact that "the concept of welfare or the opposite is shaped by Congress. . . ." Congress found that the differing drinking ages in the States created particular incentives for young persons to combine their desire to drink with their ability to drive, and that this interstate problem required a national solution. The means it chose to address this dangerous situation were reasonably calculated to advance the general welfare. The conditions upon which States receive the funds, moreover, could not be more clearly stated by Congress. And the State itself, rather than challenging the germaneness of the condition to federal purposes, admits that it "has never contended that the congressional action was . . . unrelated to a national concern in the absence of the Twenty-first Amendment." Indeed, the condition imposed by Congress is directly related to one of the main purposes for which highway funds are expended — safe interstate travel. This goal of the interstate highway system had been frustrated by varying drinking ages among the States. A Presidential commission appointed to study alcohol-related accidents and fatalities on the Nation's highways concluded that the lack of uniformity in the States' drinking ages created "an incentive to drink and drive" because "young persons commut[e] to border States where the drinking age is lower." By enacting §158, Congress conditioned the receipt of federal funds in a way reasonably calculated to address this particular impediment to a purpose for which the funds are expended.

The remaining question about the validity of §158 — and the basic point of disagreement between the parties — is whether the Twenty-first Amendment constitutes an "independent constitutional bar" to the conditional grant of federal funds. . . . But our cases show that this "independent constitutional bar" limitation on the spending power is not of the kind petitioner suggests. *United States v. Butler*, for example, established that the constitutional limitations on Congress when exercising its spending power are less exacting than those on its authority to regulate directly.

We have also held that a perceived Tenth Amendment limitation on congressional regulation of state affairs did not concomitantly limit the range of conditions legitimately placed on federal grants. In Oklahoma v. Civil Service Comm'n, 330 U.S. 127 (1947), the Court considered the validity of the Hatch Act insofar as it was applied to political activities of state officials whose employment was financed in whole or in part with federal funds. The State contended that an order under this provision to withhold certain federal funds unless a state official was removed invaded its sovereignty in violation of the Tenth Amendment. Though finding that "the United States is not concerned with, and has no power to regulate, local political activities as such of state officials," the Court nevertheless held that the Federal

Government "does have power to fix the terms upon which its money allotments to states shall be disbursed." The Court found no violation of the State's sovereignty because the State could, and did, adopt "the 'simple expedient' of not yielding to what she urges is federal coercion. The offer of benefits to a state by the United States dependent upon cooperation by the state with federal plans, assumedly for the general welfare, is not unusual."

These cases establish the "independent constitutional bar" limitation on the spending power is not, as petitioner suggests, a prohibition on the indirect achievement of objectives which Congress is not empowered to achieve directly. Instead, we think that the language in our earlier opinions stands for the unexceptionable proposition that the power may not be used to induce the States to engage in activities that would themselves be unconstitutional. Thus, for example, a grant of federal funds conditioned on invidiously discriminatory state action or the infliction of cruel and unusual punishment would be an illegitimate exercise of the Congress' broad spending power. But no such claim can be or is made here. Were South Dakota to succumb to the blandishments offered by Congress and raise its drinking age to 21, the State's action in so doing would not violate the constitutional rights of anyone.

Our decisions have recognized that in some circumstances the financial inducement offered by Congress might be so coercive as to pass the point at which "pressure turns into compulsion." Here, however, Congress has directed only that a State desiring to establish a minimum drinking age lower than 21 lose a relatively small percentage of certain federal highway funds. Petitioner contends that the coercive nature of this program is evident from the degree of success it has achieved. We cannot conclude, however, that a conditional grant of federal money of this sort is unconstitutional simply by reason of its success in achieving the congressional objective.

When we consider, for a moment, that all South Dakota would lose if she adheres to her chosen course as to a suitable minimum drinking age is 5% of the funds otherwise obtainable under specified highway grant programs, the argument as to coercion is shown to be more rhetoric than fact.

Here Congress has offered relatively mild encouragement to the States to enact higher minimum drinking ages than they would otherwise choose. But the enactment of such laws remains the prerogative of the States not merely in theory but in fact. Even if Congress might lack the power to impose a national minimum drinking age directly, we conclude that encouragement to state action found in §158 is a valid use of the spending power. Accordingly, the judgment of the Court of Appeals is Affirmed.

JUSTICE BRENNAN, *dissenting.*

I agree with Justice O'Connor that regulation of the minimum age of purchasers of liquor falls squarely within the ambit of those powers reserved to the States by the Twenty-first Amendment. . . . Since States possess this constitutional power, Congress cannot condition a federal grant in a manner that abridges this right. The Amendment, itself, strikes the proper balance between federal and state authority. I therefore dissent.

JUSTICE O'CONNOR, *dissenting.*

The Court today upholds the National Minimum Drinking Age Amendment, 23 U.S.C. §158 (1982 ed., Supp. III), as a valid exercise of the spending power conferred by Article I, §8. But §158 is not a condition on spending reasonably related to the expenditure of federal funds, and cannot be justified on that ground. Rather, it is an attempt to regulate the sale of liquor, an attempt that lies outside Congress' power to regulate commerce because it falls within the ambit of §2 of the Twenty-first Amendment.

My disagreement with the Court is relatively narrow on the spending power issue: it is a disagreement about the application of a principle, rather than a disagreement on the principle itself. I agree with the Court that Congress may attach conditions on the receipt of federal funds to further "the federal interest in particular national projects or programs...."

But the Court's application of the requirement that the condition imposed be reasonably related to the purpose for which the funds are expended is cursory and unconvincing. We have repeatedly said that Congress may condition grants under the spending power only in ways reasonably related to the purpose of the federal program.... In my view, establishment of a minimum drinking age of 21 is not sufficiently related to interstate highway construction to justify so conditioning funds appropriated for that purpose....

When Congress appropriates money to build a highway, it is entitled to insist that the highway be a safe one. But it is not entitled to insist as a condition of the use of highway funds that the State impose or change regulations in other areas of the State's social and economic life because of an attenuated or tangential relationship to highway use or safety. Indeed, if the rule were otherwise, the Congress could effectively regulate almost any area of a State's social, political, or economic life on the theory that use of the interstate transportation system is somehow enhanced. If, for example, the United States were to condition highway moneys upon moving the state capital, I suppose it might argue that interstate transportation is facilitated by locating local governments in places easily accessible to interstate highways—or, conversely, that highways might become overburdened if they had to carry traffic to and from the state capital. In my mind, such a relationship is hardly more attenuated than the one which the Court finds supports §158. *Cf.* Tr. of Oral Arg. 39 (counsel for the United States conceding that to condition a grant upon adoption of a unicameral legislature would violate the "germaneness" requirement).

There is a clear place at which the Court can draw the line between permissible and impermissible conditions on federal grants. It is the line identified in the Brief for the National Conference of State Legislatures *et al.* as *Amici Curiae:*

> "Congress has the power to *spend* for the general welfare, it has the power to *legislate* only for delegated purposes...."
>
> "The appropriate inquiry, then, is whether the spending requirement or prohibition is a condition on a grant or whether it is regulation. The difference turns on whether the requirement specifies in some way how the money should be spent, so that Congress' intent in making the grant will be effectuated. Congress has no power under the Spending Clause to impose requirements on a grant that go beyond specifying how the money should be spent. A requirement that is not such a specification is not a condition, but a regulation, which is valid only if it falls within one of Congress' delegated regulatory powers." *Id.* at 19-20....

The immense size and power of the Government of the United States ought not obscure its fundamental character. It remains a Government of enumerated powers.... Because 23 U.S.C. §158 (1982 ed., Supp. III) cannot be justified as an exercise of any power delegated to the Congress, it is not authorized by the Constitution. The Court errs in holding it to be the law of the land, and I respectfully dissent.

SYNTHESIS QUESTIONS FOR FURTHER DISCUSSION: CHAPTER 3

1. Alexander Hamilton contends that Congress possesses the "implied" power to incorporate a national bank, because this authority flows from other provisions enumerated in Article I. How persuasive is this claim? Is this argument compatible with the notion that the Constitution empowers Congress to legislate in only certain limited areas? What theories of interpretation might align with this political philosophy of implied power?

2. In *McCulloch v. Maryland*, how does Chief Justice John Marshall's opinion draw from Hamilton's and Jefferson's earlier arguments? Chief Justice Marshall proposes the following standard for determining whether the use of congressional power is constitutional: First, is the purpose of the law constitutionally legitimate? Second, are the law's means plainly adapted to that end? Does this announced legal standard more closely reflect Jefferson's or Hamilton's approach?

What does Chief Justice Marshall mean when he states that "we must never forget that it is a constitution we are expounding," in contrast to "the prolixity of a legal code"? What kind of an interpretive approach does this reminder recommend? Is his standard for evaluating the limits of constitutional power found in the Constitution, as he claims, or does it rely on an interpretive approach that would go beyond the text of the Constitution?

3. In *Gibbons v. Ogden*, Chief Justice Marshall broadly construes "Commerce . . . among the several States" to cover all navigation, and he suggests that it encompasses a number of other related activities. On this theory, when the Constitution grants Congress an enumerated power, that power is "plenary," or complete, and state laws may not interfere with it. But at the same time, Chief Justice Marshall states that the federal government cannot regulate commerce that is "completely internal" to the state itself. Are these positions consistent? How limited or expansive does this decision leave Congress's commerce power? Finally, consider how this opinion reflects the power granted to Congress in *McCulloch v. Maryland*. In general, what do *Gibbons v. Ogden* and *McCulloch v. Maryland* suggest about where congressional power ends and state power begins?

4. The debate over implied powers continues in the modern era. Consider, for instance, the spending power discussed at the end of this chapter. Does such a power include a right to condition funds on certain public policy goals? Is this power implied by a power to spend? Does the spending power require that there be a connection between the public policy goal and the kind of spending that is authorized by Congress? What powers, if any, are not implied by the spending power?

KEY TERMS

dual-sovereignty: The theory that suggests that both the states and the federal government are sovereign entities under the Constitution. On this theory, each retains certain exclusive powers. In particular, it holds that the Tenth Amendment and other provisions ensure a particular role for state power and limit federal power.

enumerated powers: Those powers specifically granted to Congress by the Constitution, in contrast to the states' more general police powers to regulate the "welfare, health, safety, and morals" of its population.

implied powers: Powers not explicitly stated in the Constitution, but thought granted by general phrases such as the Necessary and Proper Clause and the General Welfare Clause, often thought central to the decision in *McCulloch v. Maryland.*

plenary powers: Exclusive powers explicitly granted to Congress, not shared with the states.

CHAPTER 4

THE BATTLE OVER ECONOMIC REGULATION

Do federal efforts to promote the general welfare and regulate the economy usurp states' powers? Are they consistent with liberty?

So far, we have seen that congressional authority depends on powers enumerated in Article I of the U.S. Constitution. In contrast to the general powers of the states, congressional powers to enact legislation must be granted through specific clauses in Article I. The twentieth century saw two major shifts in the scope of these powers. As you read through this chapter, you will be asked to evaluate whether these two shifts were consistent with the powers granted to Congress in Article I. In particular, we examine shifting understandings of the Commerce Clause, which grants Congress the power to regulate interstate commerce and implicitly limits the states from passing laws that impede this ability.

We begin with a discussion in *Swift & Co. v. United States* about the degree to which Congress has the authority to regulate economic activity and monopolistic practices. As you will see, this discussion highlights the notion of a stream of commerce and provides some leeway for congressional legislation on matters of economic regulation. But despite the fact that *Swift & Co. v. United States* authorized congressional action, the early twentieth century is also marked by distinct limits on Congress's Commerce Clause power, especially as concerned much progressive legislation. You will note that in *Hammer v. Dagenhart* the Court limited Congress's power to regulate child labor. In many ways, *Hammer v. Dagenhart* marks the limits on congressional power, prominent in the Court's jurisprudence before the first shift we examine.

This first shift concerns President Franklin Roosevelt's decision during the New Deal era to expand the role of the federal government as a means of both regulating the national economy and stimulating economic growth. President Roosevelt believed that the Great Depression presented a major challenge to the nation's stability. On his view, the crisis of the Depression could be solved by an increased federal role in the economy, including providing jobs directly to citizens, creating new federal agencies, and seeking greater regulation of various economic sectors. As you will see in his famous "four freedoms" speech, President Roosevelt believed that government's role should not be limited to protecting private property, but should also include securing individual welfare for all. He thus rejected the "laissez-faire" approach to government, exemplified by the *Lochner v. New York* Court and libertarian thinkers such as Herbert Spencer, which suggested that financial markets and labor markets should be left free from government intervention. But President Roosevelt's attempt to expand the federal government raised a constitutional puzzle. What enumerated power granted Congress the ability to pass New Deal legislation? President Roosevelt's administration argued that the Commerce Clause provided the textual basis for much of the New Deal, as the nation had developed into one national economy in which interstate commerce was connected to a variety of aspects of life traditionally regulated by the states. President Roosevelt argued, moreover, that there was a need for a national effort to coordinate areas of economic life that the states, on their own, would be unable to do. The Supreme Court, however, struck down some New Deal legislation on grounds that it exceeded Congress's power under the Interstate Commerce Clause. For instance, in *Schechter Poultry Corp. v. United States*, the Court struck down President Roosevelt's National Industrial Recovery Act. In addition, in *Carter v. Carter Coal Company*, the Court struck down Congress's attempt at regulation of the coal industry.

President Roosevelt, however, was determined to push through his legislation over the Court's objections. He threatened to continue to add new justices to the Supreme Court, or "pack the Court," until the existing justices' votes were diluted. But President Roosevelt never had to follow through with this threat since, in 1937, U.S. Supreme Court Justice Owen Roberts changed his position from deeming the New Deal program and its economic regulations unconstitutional to upholding them. Justice Roberts's change in judicial philosophy (and his switch to join those upholding the president's position) became known as the "switch in time that saved nine." In other words, he saved the power of the nine Supreme Court justices from being diluted by a packed Court. Specifically, it was in a case about the State of Washington's minimum wage law, *West Coast Hotel v. Parrish*, that is generally considered the case in which the switch first occurred. Even though *West Coast Hotel v. Parrish* was about the constitutionality of state law and the end of the Court's use of its "substantive due process" doctrine to oppose economic regulations by the government, it signaled the end of opposition to the Court's willingness to strike down New Deal legislation at the federal level because of a perceived lack of congressional power. The Court's switch from striking down New Deal legislation to upholding it under the Commerce Clause raises a fundamental matter of constitutional interpretation. Should the Commerce Clause be understood to authorize a vast array of congressional powers to regulate and stimulate the economy? As you read the chapter, you should ask whether President Roosevelt's philosophy of the four freedoms should play a role in interpreting the Commerce Clause.

The second major shift in the scope of congressional power during the twentieth century came during the Civil Rights era. The Commerce Clause also played a critical role in this shift. In 1964, in the wake of President John F. Kennedy's assassination, Congress passed the Civil Rights Act. Among other things, the Act outlawed racial segregation in areas of so-called public accommodations, such as hotels and restaurants. Clearly, the Civil Rights movement centered on the value of equality and was not, like the New Deal, primarily focused on economic regulation. But the "Equal Protection Clause" was held to apply only to state action. Specifically, the Court's jurisprudence, starting in the nineteenth century and continuing into the twentieth, held that the Equal Protection Clause prohibited segregation in government institutions but not in public accommodations. Given this long-standing constraint, the Court instead chose to once again employ the Commerce Clause as the textual basis for congressional power to outlaw segregation in public accommodations. As you read the cases of *Heart of Atlanta Motel v. United States* and *Katzenbach v. McClung*, you should ask whether this was indeed the most compelling source of constitutional authorization for congressional power in the area of civil rights. One possible defense of the Court's action comes from the moral reading, given the inherent injustice of segregation. But is the moral reading an appropriate interpretive lens for a clause that seems to have no obvious concern for equality? Could a different lens of constitutional interpretation justify this use of the Commerce Clause?

Our readings in this chapter help to frame the controversy over the Commerce Clause during the New Deal era. For Bruce Ackerman, President Roosevelt's four freedoms are not part of the original understanding of the Constitution, but rather represent a new constitutional moment brought about by the New Deal. This moment of transformation, embodied in the Court's "switch in time," effectively amended the Constitution outside of Article V.

In Cass Sunstein's view, the four freedoms are fundamental aspects of the constitutional guarantee of welfare that should be understood alongside the more specific guarantees laid out in the Bill of Rights. The protections found in the National Labor Relations Act, the Fair Labor Standards Act, and the Social Security Act create what he refers to as "constitutive commitments" on a par with other constitutional guarantees. He therefore sees President Roosevelt not as declaring war on the meaning of the Constitution, but rather as using congressional power to pursue a fundamental mandate of the Constitution.

While Ackerman and Sunstein applaud President Roosevelt's expansion of congressional authority to bring about what they regard as economic freedom, Judge Douglas Ginsburg, a former Supreme Court nominee, and Richard Epstein argue for a different conception of economic freedom and offer an argument against President Roosevelt's expansion of congressional power. For Judge Ginsburg and Epstein, economic liberty entails protecting property rights and limiting the federal government's power to intrude upon a free market. Epstein in particular offers a defense of the pre–New Deal Court's framework for understanding Congress's authority under the Constitution on the grounds that it allowed for diverse policies among the states. Free citizens in a federal republic, he argues, should be able to choose among the several states when deciding where to live, work, or do business; these states should therefore have diverse social and economic circumstances. He thus applauds the earlier Court's restriction of congressional authority.

Although the focus of our readings is largely on the shift from a Commerce Clause that limited federal power to enact the New Deal to one that authorized it, these thinkers also offer insights that will be helpful in analyzing *Heart of Atlanta Motel v. United States* and *Katzenbach v. McClung* and the general power of Congress to enact the Civil Rights Act of 1964 under the Commerce Clause. Even if we grant that the Court shifts its understanding of the Commerce Clause in these cases, you should try to decide whether you think this shift is justified by the gravity of the Civil Rights movement and the need to eliminate segregation. Could Sunstein's suggestion that the general welfare provision of the Constitution serves as a textual basis for the New Deal also justify Congress's authority to enact civil rights legislation? Finally, do Judge Ginsburg's and Epstein's critiques of the New Deal also commit them to argue against Congress's power to enact civil rights legislation? Of course, the cases related to the New Deal and the Civil Rights Act dealt with very different subjects, but both concerned the Court's decision to expand congressional power through the Commerce Clause. Throughout this chapter, you should continue to ask whether these shifts in the Court's stance on congressional authority were or were not justified.

Bruce Ackerman

WE THE PEOPLE

Volume I: Foundations; and Volume II: Transformations

Cambridge, MA: Harvard University Press (1991)

Bruce Ackerman argues that the "switch in time"—Justice Owen Roberts's sudden shift in judicial philosophy to support New Deal policies—marked a "constitutional moment." According to Ackerman, a constitutional moment consists of a historical shift in the understanding of the Constitution that occurs outside of the normal amendment process. Although the Constitution requires an amendment to be formally changed, Ackerman believes that some shifts in judicial interpretation, backed by popular support, are so extreme that they also profoundly shift the meaning of the document. For example, in the following excerpt he contends that the Court's subsequent decisions effectively ratified the New Deal as an amendment to the Constitution outside of Article V, which creates a formal process for amending the document. This is quite a striking claim, but it does command a certain degree of explanatory power. The New Deal indeed marks a discontinuity in our constitutional development, after which the federal government assumed responsibility for regulating the national economy. The rest of this chapter traces the history of that struggle.

You should consider the feasibility of Ackerman's theory of constitutional moments and how it figures into his understanding of the ways in which the Supreme Court responds to democratic will. Does Ackerman succeed in laying out clear criteria for when a constitutional moment occurs?

Above all else, a dualist Constitution seeks to distinguish between two different decisions that may be made in a democracy. The first is a decision by the American people; the second, by their government.

Decisions by the People occur rarely, and under special constitutional conditions. Before gaining the authority to make supreme law in the name of the People, a movement's political partisans must, first, convince an extraordinary number of their fellow citizens to take their proposed initiative with a seriousness that they do not normally accord to politics; second, they must allow their opponents a fair opportunity to organize their own forces; third, they must convince a majority of their fellow Americans to support their initiative as its merits are discussed, time and again, in the deliberative fora provided for "higher lawmaking." It is only then that a political movement earns the enhanced legitimacy the dualist Constitution accords to decisions made by the People.

Decisions made by the government occur daily, and also under special conditions. Most importantly, key officials must be held accountable regularly at the ballot box. In addition, they must be given incentives to take a broad view of the public interest without the undue influence of narrow interest groups. Even when this system of "normal lawmaking" is operating well, however, the dualist Constitution prevents elected politicians from exaggerating their authority.

They are not to assert that a normal electoral victory has given them a mandate to enact an ordinary statute that overturns the considered judgments previously reached by the People. If they wish to claim this higher form of democratic legitimacy, they must take to the specially onerous obstacle course provided by a dualist Constitution for purposes of higher lawmaking. Only if they succeed in mobilizing their fellow citizens and gaining their repeated support in response to their opponents' counterattacks may they finally earn the authority to proclaim that *the People* have changed their mind and have given their government new marching orders.

. . . [A]t its root, monism is very simple: Democracy requires the grant of plenary lawmaking authority to the winners of the last general election — so long, at least, as the election was conducted under free and fair ground rules and the winners don't try to prevent the next scheduled round of electoral challenges.

This idea motivates, in turn, a critical institutional conclusion: during the period between elections, all institutional checks upon the electoral victors are presumptively antidemocratic. For sophisticated monists, this is only a presumption. Perhaps certain constitutional checks may prevent the victors from abrogating the next scheduled election; perhaps others might be justified once one considers the deeper ways normal elections fail to satisfy our ideals of electoral fairness. While these exceptions may have great practical importance, monists refuse to let them obscure the main point: when the Supreme Court, or anybody else, invalidates a statute, it suffers from a "counter-majoritarian difficulty" which must be overcome before a good democrat can profess satisfaction with this extraordinary action.

. . . The monist begs a big question when he asserts that the winner of a fair and open election is entitled to rule with the full authority of We the People. It is much better, of course, for electoral winners to take office rather than suffer an authoritarian putsch by the losers.

But it does not follow that all statutes gaining the support of a legislative majority in Washington, D.C., represent the considered judgment of a mobilized majority of American citizens. Instead, the dualist sees a profoundly democratic point to many of the distinctive practices that baffle the monist. For her, they express our Constitution's effort to require elected politicians to operate within a two-track system. If politicians hope to win normal democratic legitimacy for an initiative, they are directed down the normal lawmaking path and told to gain the assent of the House, Senate, and President in the usual ways. If they hope for higher lawmaking authority, they are directed down a specially onerous lawmaking path. . . . Only if a political movement successfully negotiates the special challenges of the higher lawmaking system can it rightfully claim that its initiative represents the constitutional judgment of We the People.

Once the two-track character of the system is recognized, the Supreme Court appears in a different light. Consider that all the time and effort required to push an initiative down the higher lawmaking track would be wasted unless the Constitution prevented future normal politicians from enacting statutes that ignored the movement's higher law achievement. If future politicians could so easily ignore established higher law, why would any mass movement take the trouble to overcome the special hurdles placed on the higher lawmaking track?

To maintain the integrity of higher lawmaking, all dualist constitutions must provide for one or more institutions to discharge a preservationist function. These institutions must effectively block efforts to repeal established constitutional principles by the simple expedient of passing a normal statute and force the reigning group of elected politicians to move onto the higher lawmaking track if they wish to question the judgments previously made by We the People. Only after negotiating this more arduous obstacle course can a political elite earn the authority to say that We the People have changed our mind.

It follows, then, that the dualist will view the Supreme Court from a very different perspective than the monist. The monist treats every act of judicial review as presumptively antidemocratic and strains to save the Supreme Court from the "counter-majoritarian difficulty" by one or another ingenious argument. In contrast, the dualist sees the discharge of the preservationist function by the courts as an essential part of a well-ordered democratic regime. Rather than threatening democracy by frustrating the statutory demands of the political elite in Washington, the courts serve democracy by protecting the hard-won principles of a mobilized citizenry against erosion by political elites who have failed to gain broad and deep popular support for their innovations. . . .

. . . When modern lawyers and judges look to the deep past, they tell themselves a story that has a distinctive structure. Though special problems may lead them to appreciate the relevance of one or another aspect of America's constitutional history, three historical periods stand out from the rest. These eras have a pervasive significance: the lessons a judge draws from them organizes her entire approach to concrete cases. The first of these jurisgenerative eras is the Founding itself — the framing of the original Constitution and the Bill of Rights, the Supreme Court's initial assertion of judicial review in *Marbury v. Madison.* A second great period occurs two generations later, with the bloody struggles that ultimately yield the Reconstruction amendments. Then there is another pause of two generations before a third great turning point. This one centers on the 1930's and the dramatic confrontation between the New Deal and the Old Court that ends in the constitutional triumph of the activist welfare state.

... While all lawyers recognize that the 1930's mark the definitive constitutional triumph of activist national government, they tell themselves a story which denies that anything deeply creative was going on. This view of the 1930's is obtained by imagining a Golden Age in which Chief Justice Marshall got things right for all time by propounding a broad construction of the national governments lawmaking authority. The period between Reconstruction and the New Deal can then be viewed as a (complex) story about the fall from grace — wherein most of the Justices strayed from the path of righteousness and imposed their laissez-faire philosophy on the nation through the pretext of constitutional interpretation. Predictably, these acts of judicial usurpation increasingly set the judges at odds with more democratic institutions, which acutely perceived the failure of laissez-faire to do justice to an increasingly interdependent world.

The confrontation between the New Deal and the Old Court climaxes this traditional morality play of decline, fall, and resurrection. Only Justice Roberts's "switch in time," and the departure of the worst judicial offenders, permitted the Court to expiate its counter-majoritarian sins without permanent institutional damage. If only the Justices had not strayed from Marshall's original path, perhaps all this unpleasantness could have been avoided!

... [I]n contrast to the first two turning points, modern lawyers do not describe either the substantive or the procedural aspects of the New Deal by telling themselves a tale of constitutional creation. The triumph of activist national government is mediated by a myth of rediscovery — as if the Founding Federalists had foreseen the works of Franklin Delano Roosevelt and would have been surprised to learn that the great struggles of the 1930's were necessary to gain the welfare state's constitutional legitimation.

... I mean to question the prevailing interpretive schema. Despite its familiarity, it is built on sand. If we return to our sources, they tell a very different story. They reveal both Reconstruction Republicans and New Deal Democrats engaging in self-conscious acts of constitutional creation that rivaled the Founding Federalists' in their scope and depth. In each case, the new spokesmen for the people refused to follow the path of constitutional revision set out by their successors; like the Federalists before them, they transformed existing systems of higher lawmaking in the process of changing the fundamental direction of political development....

THE NEW DEAL

According to the modern myth of rediscovery: the New Dealers did not even contribute new substantive principles to our higher law, let alone rework the very process of higher lawmaking. Instead, their redefinition of American government involved little more than the recollection of some forgotten bits of Founding Wisdom.

My counterthesis: Like the Reconstruction Republicans, the New Deal Democrats relied on the national separation of powers between Congress, President, and Court to create a new institutional framework through which the American People might define, debate, and finally decide their constitutional future. The key institutional difference between the two periods involves the Presidency.

Franklin Roosevelt remained at the helm of the reformist coalition throughout the Democrats' period of constitutional transformation, whereas Lincoln's assassination deprived Republican reformers of Presidential support during the critical struggle over the Fourteenth Amendment. Roosevelt's long tenure had fundamental, if unsurprising, implications for the Presidency's role in the process of higher lawmaking. While the Republicans successfully experimented with Presidential leadership in the process of legitimating the Thirteenth Amendment, they could not build on this experience once Andrew Johnson declared war on the Fourteenth Amendment. In contrast, the Democrats were in a position to develop the power of the Presidency in a far more incisive fashion.

When due allowances are made for the defection of President Johnson from the Republican coalition, however, it will be possible to identify remarkable similarities in the way in which the separation of powers tested, and finally legitimated, the constitutional revisions proposed by nineteenth-century Republicans and twentieth-century Democrats. Each higher lawmaking exercise began with the reformers in control of only part of the national government—in the case of the Republicans, it was Congress that took on the mantle of reform leadership with Johnson's defection; in the case of the Democrats, the Presidency was the leading reform branch. In both cases, the constitutional reformers' proposals were exposed to an initial period of incisive critique by conservative branches, which publicly appealed to the People to decisively reject the dangerous innovations proposed by the reformers. In the case of the Republicans, the leading conservative branch was the Presidency; for the Democrats, it was the Supreme Court.

These institutional differences were important, of course, in explaining the different dynamics of constitutional debate and decision. But it is even more important to see the deeper similarities. In both cases, the institutional deadlock in Washington forced both sides to mobilize their supporters in the country at large. These remarkable efforts at popular mobilization, in turn, gave extraordinary constitutional meaning to the next regularly scheduled election. If one or another side could win a decisive victory at the polls, it would try to use its popular support to break the institutional impasse.

This process of interbranch struggle and popular mobilization made the elections of 1866 and 1936 decisive events in constitutional history. On both occasions, the reformers returned to Washington with a clear victory at the polls. They proceeded to proclaim that the election results gave them a "mandate from the People," and that the time had come for the conservative branches to end their constitutional resistance.

This demand by the electorally victorious reformers inaugurated the period of ratification—in which the conservative branches considered whether to continue their resistance or to recognize that the People had indeed given their fixed support to the reformist movement. In both cases, this decision was not made in silent contemplation but in response to a challenge by the reformist branches to the conservatives' continued legitimacy. During Reconstruction, the reformist Congress finally threatened President Johnson with impeachment if he continued to use his office to sabotage ratification of the Fourteenth Amendment. During the New Deal, it was the reformist President's threat of packing the Court that provoked the conservative Justices to consider the wisdom of continued resistance. In both cases, however, the question was very much the same: Should the conservatives in the dissenting branches finally recognize that *the People had spoken?*

In both cases, the conservatives' answer was the same. Rather than escalating the constitutional crisis further, they decided, with evident reluctance, that further resistance would endanger too many of the very values they held fundamental. They made the "switch in time": Johnson called off his effort to prevent the formal ratification of the Fourteenth Amendment; the Supreme Court repudiated its doctrinal defense of laissez-faire capitalism and began to build new constitutional foundations for activist national government.

In turn, the victorious reformers responded in the same way. The Republicans refused to convict the President, allowing Johnson to remain in office to proclaim the validity of the Fourteenth Amendment; the Democrats called off the threat of court-packing, allowing the Old Court to proclaim that activist New Deal government was constitutionally legitimate.

As a consequence of these "switches in time," all three branches emerge from the period of democratic testing once again united, and the separation of powers remains intact for use by the next constitutional regime. But it is now in the service of the new constitutional solution that had previously been so controversial. . . .

Time and again, the New Dealers invoked Reconstruction precedents in their efforts to build a modern model of Presidential leadership in the higher lawmaking process. The challenge is to *listen* to these voices, not insist upon viewing the New Deal reformers as if they were exhausted epigones, capable only of returning to the forgotten wisdom of the Founders. Only after we define what is really new about the New Deal can we begin to confront the deep problems they left for us. Should the New Deal model of Presidential leadership once again be revised to better confront the higher lawmaking challenges of the next century?

FROM PAST TO PRESENT

. . . While the Reconstruction Republicans broke new ground in their use of the separation of powers as the principal engine of constitutional revision, they nonetheless managed to codify their reforms in legal instruments that bore the surface appearance of "constitutional amendments." These Reconstruction texts are only amendment-simulacra, since they were not generated in accordance with the principles laid down by the Federalist Constitution. Nonetheless, at least the Republicans managed to pour their new constitutional wine into old legal bottles.

In contrast, the New Dealers rejected the traditional form of an amendment; instead they relied on the New Deal Court to elaborate their new activist vision through a series of transformative opinions. It is worth emphasizing that this decision was entirely self-conscious and public. We will hear President Roosevelt and leading spokesmen of his Administration explaining why it was wrong to codify the New Deal transformation through forms sanctioned by Article Five; why we should rely instead on the appointment of new judges to give new meaning to the Constitution. After 1937, moreover, Roosevelt and Congress used this technique of transformative judicial appointment with unprecedented success. By the early 1940's, a reconstituted Court had not contented itself with rejecting a few offending decisions of a bygone era. It revolutionized reigning constitutional doctrine in a thoroughgoing way—to the point where the Court was now unanimously rejecting fundamental doctrines that shaped the entire body of constitutional law only a decade before. . . .

RETHINKING THE NEW DEAL

New Deal Democracy marked another great leap along the arc of nationalistic self-definition initiated by the American Revolution. Although the Founders broke with the state-centered Articles of Confederation, they did not clearly establish the priority of national over state citizenship; although the Reconstructers resolved this fundamental question in favor of the Union, they did not frontally challenge the Founding notion that the national government had limited powers over economic and social development; with the New Deal, this Founding principle was decisively repudiated. Henceforth, the federal government would operate as a truly national government, speaking for the People on all matters that sufficiently attracted the interest of lawmakers in Washington, D.C.

Not that the states were deprived of their general lawmaking jurisdiction. They too could legislate on any subject they found in the public interest — subject to preemption by national lawmakers and judicial scrutiny for prejudicial impact upon out-of-staters. A commitment to federalism, however, was no longer thought to require a constitutional strategy that restrained the national government to a limited number of enumerated powers over economic and social life.

. . . When the New Deal generation won positions of authority in the courts and the law schools, they took full advantage of their opportunity to warn their successors against repeating the Old Court's mistakes. These doctrinal teachings were greatly enhanced by the penetration of New Deal premises into American government. The millions of Social Security checks mailed each month attest to the government's ongoing concern with fair income distribution. The thousands of pages published annually in the *Federal Register* (founded in 1936) contain countless reminders by a host of alphabet agencies — SEC, NLRB, EPA, OSHA . . . — that unregulated capitalism endangers a series of fundamental values, ranging from environmental purity to worker dignity. Each day's headlines report on the ongoing effort by the national government to sustain general prosperity through the flexible tools of macroeconomic policy made possible by the New Deal's repudiation of the Gold Standard. Until the Reagan Presidency, no victorious political movement had questioned the propriety of this complex governmental effort to improve upon the invisible hand. To one or another extent, each Administration had built upon the efforts of its predecessors in the three basic areas of activist concern marked out in the Roosevelt years: the pursuit of distributive justice, the correction of market failure, and the assurance of general prosperity.

Little wonder that modern lawyers have little trouble recalling the broad outlines of the great constitutional crisis of the 1930's. It is only their recollection of the Supreme Court's retreat before the New Deal that provides the vast statutory superstructure of the activist state with a firm constitutional foundation. It was different before 1932. Each new activist initiative then provoked anxious foreboding: How to evade the entrenched constitutional principles that cast intervention into the "free market" under a dark cloud? The answer, in particular cases, depended upon the complexities of constitutional doctrine and the vagaries of judicial personnel. But there was no mistaking the constitutionally problematic character of the activist enterprise. So far as the judges were concerned, We the People had *not* authorized state regulation of the marketplace whenever political majorities concluded that this would serve the nation's general welfare; the Constitution emerging after the Civil War contained fundamental limitations on such dubious enterprises.

These boundaries disintegrated during the New Deal revolution. A complex web of doctrine, woven by two generations of judges in the long period between 1873 and 1932, was swept away in the space of a decade. If the partisans of laissez-faire lost their battle in the legislature, they could no longer hope that the courts might reverse their opponents' victory. After the New Deal revolution, it became clear to judges that We the People had stripped free market solutions to social problems of their previously privileged position.

Lochner v. New York serves as the paradigm. In 1905, the Court struck down the effort by New York to limit the work week to sixty hours as a violation of freedom of contract. By the end of the Roosevelt era, *Lochner* became the symbol of a repudiated era of laissez-faire jurisprudence. Henceforward, courts would uphold the authority of American government to act against all forms of social or economic exploitation that were condemned by a democratically elected majority.

This turnaround was all the more wrenching in connection with the national government. The Supreme Court had never denied the states a broad (though not unlimited) power to police the economy, but it had taken a different view of Congressional authority. *Hammer v. Dagenhart* can serve as paradigm. In 1916, Congress had acted against child labor by excluding its products from interstate commerce. But the Court struck down this effort: "[t]he Commerce Clause was not intended to give to Congress a general authority to equalize . . . conditions." If Congress could not take steps to express the nation's condemnation of a shocking abuse like child labor, its powers were limited indeed. If the New Deal was to prevail, this vision of limited government could not survive.

And it did not. By the early 1940's, the New Deal Court was ringing the death knell in unanimous decisions that would have astounded lawyers a decade before. But the bar proved very adaptable. Under the Court's emphatic tutelage, lawyers learned to look upon the case law of the preceding Republican regime with the peculiar mix of ignorance and contempt reserved for abandoned precedent. Whatever their personal political convictions, they quickly mastered the New Deal language for courtroom use. A half-century later, the New Deal Constitution — far less respectful of the rights of property and contract, far more respectful of national power — had been woven into the very fabric of the modern polity, shaping the expectations of ordinary citizens as well as the daily interactions of the President, Congress, and the Supreme Court. . . .

THE VIEW FROM ARTICLE FIVE

We can now begin to triangulate our problem by considering the New Deal's relationship to the Founding. Speaking broadly, the higher lawmaking efforts of the 1930's broke with the premises of Article Five in two ways.

The first involved a break from the Founding system of authorizing institutions. Article Five rests upon a federalist premise: in order to speak in the name of the People, a movement must gain the assent of *both* national and state institutions. The New Dealers took a more nation-centered course — using a series of national electoral victories as mandates that ultimately induced all three branches of the national government to recognize that the People had endorsed activist national government. So long, then, as modern lawyers suppose that all successful popular movements must take a federalist path to higher lawmaking authority, they will never surmount this first hurdle to a mature recognition of the New Deal's constitutional creativity.

But it shouldn't be too hard to jump over this hurdle. As we have seen, it was the Reconstruction Republicans, not the New Deal Democrats, who first established that We the People could speak through national institutions and demand that the states accept the primacy of American citizenship. If Reconstruction Republicans could use national institutions to legitimate their claims, why not New Deal Democrats, especially when they had gained the sustained consent of majorities in *all* regions of the country, while the Republicans had a lot more support in the North than in the South?

Which brings us to a second aspect of the New Deal break with Article Five. While the Reconstruction Republicans repudiated the federalist premises of the Founding, they memorialized their revolutionary reforms by placing them in legal packages that resemble Article Five amendments — bearing the numbers XIII and XIV and placing themselves in sober sequence with other amendments of less uncertain pedigree. In contrast, when modern lawyers seek to recall the New Deal's contribution, they do not turn to writings that pose as Article Five amendments but to *transformative judicial opinions* written in the aftermath of the Court-packing crisis. These great cases mark the decisive institutional moment at which the Supreme Court joined the other branches in rejecting the Republican vision of limited government, symbolized by *Hammer v. Dagenhart* and *Lochner v. New York*. Indeed, modern judges are more disturbed by the charge of *Lochnering* than the charge of ignoring the intentions of the Federalists and Republicans who wrote the formal text. To mark this point, I shall say that the transformative opinions handed down by the New Deal Court function as *amendment-analogues* that anchor constitutional meanings in the same symbolically potent way achieved by Article Five amendments.

Undoubtedly, this New Deal use of amendment-analogues requires thoughtful reappraisal of some pious platitudes — including the sense in which Americans live under a *written* constitution. Two centuries after the Founding, this platitude remains valid only on an expanded understanding of the constitutional canon. The corpus of authoritative texts includes not only those formal amendments generated by the procedures of Article Five but also: (a) the *amendment-simulacra* generated by the Republicans under the nationalistic procedures developed during Reconstruction and (b) the transformative opinions that serve as *amendment-analogues* under the nationalistic procedures developed by the Democrats during the Great Depression. So long as lawyers continue to accept the text-simulacra generated by the Reconstruction Republicans, they should not lightly reject the amendment-analogues generated by the New Deal Democrats.

Especially when this use of transformative opinions is hardly unprecedented in American constitutional history. As we already saw, the Republican Court's opinions in the *Legal Tender* and *Slaughterhouse Cases* discharged analogous constitutional functions toward the end of

Reconstruction; and even before the Civil War, the opinions of the Taney Court had served to codify the constitutional meaning of Jacksonian Democracy.

Looking beyond the confines of constitutional law, there are countless other cases in which judicial opinions substitute for formal legislative texts. Consider the problem that arises when judges are obliged to coordinate statutory commands and the common law tradition.

In this familiar situation, common law courts regularly appeal to common law cases whenever they find a hole in a statutory scheme. Indeed, this use of judicial precedents in the absence of statutes is the single most important feature distinguishing Anglo-American legal systems from those dominant in Europe. From this vantage, the New Deal innovation is best seen as another case in which American lawyers, at moments of great crisis, creatively adapt traditional ideas (here, the common law use of cases in the absence of statutes) for new constitutional purposes (here, the use of cases in the absence of formal amendments). While this unconventional adaptation does challenge constitutional theory, this is the kind of challenge that has allowed the American people to sustain a continuous constitutional identity for the past two centuries. . . .

. . . The New Deal's substitution of transformative opinions for formal amendments was not the result of some inexplicable failure to attend to the terms of Article Five. It was a creative elaboration of higher lawmaking changes initiated much earlier in American history. The struggle over Reconstruction, not the Great Depression, first led Americans to break with the federalist premises of Article Five. The struggle over Reconstruction, not the Great Depression, first led the President, Congress, and Court to develop new higher lawmaking procedures more in keeping with the constitutive will of We the People of the *United* States. The basic New Deal innovation followed from the Democrats' greater success in sustaining their control over the Presidency throughout the period of constitutional creativity. . . .

. . . It is no small thing for a political system to focus on fundamentals in this incisive way. Most of the credit goes to the American people — who rejected the demagogues around them eager to drag them toward the moral abyss.

But the Constitution also deserves its share — for the way it structured the evolving struggle so as to allow the antagonists to join issue, rather than talk past one another. Despite Roosevelt's assertion to the contrary, the election of 1932 had little relationship to "the people's mandate" as he was now defining it. At that time, Americans had simply repudiated Hoover's style of progressive Republicanism as utterly inadequate; Roosevelt's mandate, as he well understood, was to experiment with more activist approaches — without any certainty that Americans would approve. Only with the 1934 elections could the President begin to claim genuine popular support for his more affirmative program. Even then his vision was very different from the one he was presenting to the Philadelphia convention. The NIRA was no assault on "economic royalism." If anything, it consolidated the hold of the business elite on their industrial fiefdoms — suspending the antitrust laws and giving dominant firms a central role in the emerging industrial order. This was, of course, why men like Brandeis enthusiastically joined in striking it down.

Only in response to the Supreme Court did Roosevelt and his New Dealers rethink their course — leading to the statutory initiatives of the Second New Deal and the Philadelphia effort to frame the meaning of their initiatives in self-consciously constitutional terms. Roosevelt's watchword was now the rebirth of freedom, not the imperative of central planning. But it was a new freedom, defined in the light of modern realities that would otherwise defeat the claims of equal opportunity. It was a freedom that could not be achieved in opposition to the state, but only through democratic control of the marketplace: "If the average citizen is guaranteed equal opportunity in the polling place, he must have equal opportunity in the market place."

This is the point where the Republicans jumped off the train. While [1936 Republican presidential nominee Governor Alfred] Landon was willing to endorse a more activist version of progressive Republicanism, he was unwilling to revise the old constitutional definition of freedom — tightly linked to principles of limited national government, freedom of contract, and private property. At most, he could endorse a constitutional amendment that authorized state (not federal) regulation of hours and wages. But he was entirely unwilling to accept the New Deal claim that modern freedom could only be achieved through the state and not against it; or endorse Roosevelt's assertion that the old constitutional regime had degenerated into a legalistic smokescreen for a world in which "life was no longer free; liberty no longer real; men could no longer follow the pursuit of happiness." To the contrary, the New Deal promise of freedom raised alarming prospects: "[Will] he attempt to get around the Constitution by tampering with the Supreme Court?"

With such questions ringing in their ears, Americans went to the polls — and gave Roosevelt and the New Deal Congress the greatest victory in American history. Landon gained the electoral votes of only Maine and New Hampshire; he managed to win only 36.5 percent of the popular vote, his share rising as high as 45 percent in no more than four states. The Republicans were left with eighty-nine seats in the House; sixteen in the Senate. No less important, the election of 1936 cemented the hold of the Democratic Party on American life for the next generation. Indeed, we have yet to see another example of such a massive and enduring political realignment.

The same is true if we look backwards. Despite breakthroughs in the theory of popular sovereignty, the majoritarian achievements of the Federalists and the Republicans were actually quite modest. On both occasions, the revolutionary reformers won the consent of paper-thin majorities for their unconventional movements toward a "more perfect Union." In contrast, New Deal Democracy achieved in practice what Federalists and Republicans had sought in theory — the escalating support of a decisive majority of Americans throughout the nation in the face of an eloquent effort by conservatives to draw the line short of revolutionary reform.

Of course, all Americans had not been magically transformed into enthusiastic New Dealers. Alf Landon did attract 17 million voters into the Republican column in 1936, and the Supreme Court's resistance played an especially important role in reconciling these dissenters to the larger transformation. However bitterly the remaining Republicans might condemn "that man in the White House," there was something that none of them could reasonably deny. In gaining reelection, Roosevelt had been obliged to seek popular support in the face of a withering constitutional critique led by the Court. But when Landon energetically called the People to rise up in defense of their traditional Constitution, Americans were more impressed with the urgent need for revolutionary reform. While Republicans might conscientiously believe that their fellow citizens had made a tragic mistake, they could hardly deny that the People had given decisive support to the Democrats with their eyes open. By raising the question of constitutional principle so eloquently during Roosevelt's first term of experimentation, the Supreme Court had played a key role in establishing, *even to New Deal opponents*, that the People were indeed supporting a change in their governing philosophy....

... Roosevelt made the first big move with his plan for judicial reorganization—which would have allowed him to make six new appointments to the Supreme Court. This provoked a remarkably sophisticated constitutional debate. The President's leading opponents did not present themselves as staunch defenders of the traditional jurisprudence. No less than Roosevelt, they recognized that the People were demanding a fundamental change in constitutional direction.

They denied, however, that the President had hit upon the right way to implement the shift. On their view, there was only one way the President and his party could credibly speak for the People in a higher lawmaking voice—and that was by using the forms provided by Article Five of the original Constitution. To establish their good faith, opponents came forward with constitutional amendments and pleaded with the Administration to put its weight behind one or another proposal. In response, the President was obliged to explain why Article Five was inadequate, presenting an increasingly self-conscious defense of Presidential leadership in higher lawmaking.

The President's initiative, in short, catapulted the country into a great debate of central importance to my main thesis: Was the President right in claiming that the Democrats' electoral victories had given the New Dealers a mandate from the People to take unconventional action to constitutionalize their revolutionary reforms? Or were his opponents right in insisting on a monopolistic interpretation of Article Five?

Just then, the Court chose to make its switch in time. While particular decisions became landmarks, the Justices' new-found consistency was even more important. Never again would the Court find a New Deal reform beyond the power of government. As a consequence, the political protagonists relaxed their own creative efforts to work out the terms of a new constitutional solution and allowed the Court to codify the terms of the New Deal revolution....

President Franklin Roosevelt

ADDRESS TO CONGRESS—"FOUR FREEDOMS"*

January 6, 1941

The following two speeches by President Franklin Roosevelt during 1941 and 1944 seek to anchor his New Deal programs in the context of World War II, painting the same joint purpose for them both: to secure and fulfill the great American promise of freedom. But President Roosevelt's vision is a significant break from the traditional idea that freedom requires only protections

*Available at *http://www.americanrhetoric.com/speeches/fdrthefourfreedoms.htm.*

against interference by the state. In contrast, President Roosevelt's conception of freedom includes an active role for government to help citizens navigate the dynamic economy and weather the storms of economic insecurity. How does this political theory help to justify expansive federal programs, such as wage and hour regulations, social security, and government works projects? Is this understanding of federal power consistent with Alexander Hamilton's or Thomas Jefferson's arguments, or does it go beyond either of them?

I address you, the members of this new Congress, at a moment unprecedented in the history of the union. I use the word "unprecedented" because at no previous time has American security been as seriously threatened from without as it is today.

I suppose that every realist knows that the democratic way of life is at this moment being directly assailed in every part of the world—assailed either by arms or by secret spreading of poisonous propaganda by those who seek to destroy unity and promote discord in nations that are still at peace. During 16 long months this assault has blotted out the whole pattern of democratic life in an appalling number of independent nations, great and small. And the assailants are still on the march, threatening other nations, great and small.

Therefore, as your President, performing my constitutional duty to "give to the Congress information of the state of the union," I find it unhappily necessary to report that the future and the safety of our country and of our democracy are overwhelmingly involved in events far beyond our borders.

As men do not live by bread alone, they do not fight by armaments alone. Those who man our defenses and those behind them who build our defenses must have the stamina and the courage which come from unshakable belief in the manner of life which they are defending. The mighty action that we are calling for cannot be based on a disregard of all the things worth fighting for.

The nation takes great satisfaction and much strength from the things which have been done to make its people conscious of their individual stake in the preservation of democratic life in America. Those things have toughened the fiber of our people, have renewed their faith and strengthened their devotion to the institutions we make ready to protect.

Certainly this is no time for any of us to stop thinking about the social and economic problems which are the root cause of the social revolution which is today a supreme factor in the world. For there is nothing mysterious about the foundations of a healthy and strong democracy.

The basic things expected by our people of their political and economic systems are simple. They are:

Equality of opportunity for youth and for others.

Jobs for those who can work.

Security for those who need it.

The ending of special privilege for the few.

The preservation of civil liberties for all.

The enjoyment—The enjoyment of the fruits of scientific progress in a wider and constantly rising standard of living.

These are the simple, the basic things that must never be lost sight of in the turmoil and unbelievable complexity of our modern world. The inner and abiding strength of our economic and political systems is dependent upon the degree to which they fulfill these expectations.

Many subjects connected with our social economy call for immediate improvement. As examples:

We should bring more citizens under the coverage of old-age pensions and unemployment insurance.

We should widen the opportunities for adequate medical care.

We should plan a better system by which persons deserving or needing gainful employment may obtain it.

I have called for personal sacrifice, and I am assured of the willingness of almost all Americans to respond to that call. A part of the sacrifice means the payment of more money in taxes. In my budget message I will recommend that a greater portion of this great defense program be paid for from taxation than we are paying for today. No person should try, or be allowed to get rich out of the program, and the principle of tax payments in accordance with ability to pay should be constantly before our eyes to guide our legislation.

If the Congress maintains these principles the voters, putting patriotism ahead pocketbooks, will give you their applause.

In the future days, which we seek to make secure, we look forward to a world founded upon four essential human freedoms.

The first is freedom of speech and expression — everywhere in the world.

The second is freedom of every person to worship God in his own way — everywhere in the world.

The third is freedom from want, which, translated into world terms, means economic understandings which will secure to every nation a healthy peacetime life for its inhabitants — everywhere in the world.

The fourth is freedom from fear, which, translated into world terms, means a world-wide reduction of armaments to such a point and in such a thorough fashion that no nation will be in a position to commit an act of physical aggression against any neighbor — anywhere in the world.

That is no vision of a distant millennium. It is a definite basis for a kind of world attainable in our own time and generation. That kind of world is the very antithesis of the so-called "new order" of tyranny which the dictators seek to create with the crash of a bomb.

To that new order we oppose the greater conception — the moral order. A good society is able to face schemes of world domination and foreign revolutions alike without fear.

Since the beginning of our American history we have been engaged in change, in a perpetual, peaceful revolution, a revolution which goes on steadily, quietly, adjusting itself to changing conditions without the concentration camp or the quicklime in the ditch. The world order which we seek is the cooperation of free countries, working together in a friendly, civilized society.

This nation has placed its destiny in the hands and heads and hearts of its millions of free men and women, and its faith in freedom under the guidance of God. Freedom means the supremacy of human rights everywhere. Our support goes to those who struggle to gain those rights and keep them. Our strength is our unity of purpose.

To that high concept there can be no end save victory.

President Franklin Roosevelt

STATE OF THE UNION MESSAGE TO CONGRESS — "SECOND BILL OF RIGHTS"*

January 11, 1944

To the Congress:

This Nation in the past two years has become an active partner in the world's greatest war against human slavery.

The one supreme objective for the future, which we discussed for each Nation individually, and for all the United Nations, can be summed up in one word: Security.

And that means not only physical security which provides safety from attacks by aggressors. It means also economic security, social security, moral security — in a family of Nations.

The best interests of each Nation, large and small, demand that all freedom-loving Nations shall join together in a just and durable system of peace. In the present world situation, evidenced by the actions of Germany, Italy, and Japan, unquestioned military control over disturbers of the peace is as necessary among Nations as it is among citizens in a community. And an equally basic essential to peace is a decent standard of living for all individual men and women and children in all Nations. Freedom from fear is eternally linked with freedom from want.

It is our duty now to begin to lay the plans and determine the strategy for the winning of a lasting peace and the establishment of an American standard of living higher than ever before known. We cannot be content, no matter how high that general standard of living may be, if some fraction of our people — whether it be one-third or one-fifth or one-tenth — is ill-fed, ill-clothed, ill-housed, and insecure.

This Republic had its beginning, and grew to its present strength, under the protection of certain inalienable political rights — among them the right of free speech, free press, free worship, trial by jury, freedom from unreasonable searches and seizures. They were our rights to life and liberty.

As our Nation has grown in size and stature, however — as our industrial economy expanded — these political rights proved inadequate to assure us equality in the pursuit of happiness.

We have come to a clear realization of the fact that true individual freedom cannot exist without economic security and independence. "Necessitous men are not free men." People who are hungry and out of a job are the stuff of which dictatorships are made.

In our day these economic truths have become accepted as self-evident. We have accepted, so to speak, a second Bill of Rights under which a new basis of security and prosperity can be established for all — regardless of station, race, or creed.

Among these are:

The right to a useful and remunerative job in the industries or shops or farms or mines of the Nation;

The right to earn enough to provide adequate food and clothing and recreation;

The right of every farmer to raise and sell his products at a return which will give him and his family a decent living;

* Available at *http://www.fdrlibrary.marist.edu/archives/address_text.html.*

The right of every businessman, large and small, to trade in an atmosphere of freedom from unfair competition and domination by monopolies at home or abroad;

The right of every family to a decent home;

The right to adequate medical care and the opportunity to achieve and enjoy good health;

The right to adequate protection from the economic fears of old age, sickness, accident, and unemployment;

The right to a good education.

All of these rights spell security. And after this war is won we must be prepared to move forward, in the implementation of these rights, to new goals of human happiness and well-being.

America's own rightful place in the world depends in large part upon how fully these and similar rights have been carried into practice for our citizens. For unless there is security here at home there cannot be lasting peace in the world.

One of the great American industrialists of our day—a man who has rendered yeoman service to his country in this crisis—recently emphasized the grave dangers of "rightist reaction" in this Nation. All clear-thinking businessmen share his concern. Indeed, if such reaction should develop—if history were to repeat itself and we were to return to the so-called "normalcy" of the 1920's—then it is certain that even though we shall have conquered our enemies on the battlefields abroad, we shall have yielded to the spirit of Fascism here at home.

I ask the Congress to explore the means for implementing this economic bill of rights—for it is definitely the responsibility of the Congress so to do. Many of these problems are already before committees of the Congress in the form of proposed legislation. I shall from time to time communicate with the Congress with respect to these and further proposals. In the event that no adequate program of progress is evolved, I am certain that the Nation will be conscious of the fact.

Our fighting men abroad—and their families at home—expect such a program and have the right to insist upon it. It is to their demands that this Government should pay heed rather than to the whining demands of selfish pressure groups who seek to feather their nests while young Americans are dying.

The foreign policy that we have been following—the policy that guided us at Moscow, Cairo, and Teheran—is based on the common sense principle which was best expressed by Benjamin Franklin on July 4, 1776: "We must all hang together, or assuredly we shall all hang separately."

I have often said that there are no two fronts for America in this war. There is only one front. There is one line of unity which extends from the hearts of the people at home to the men of our attacking forces in our farthest outposts. When we speak of our total effort, we speak of the factory and the field, and the mine as well as of the battleground—we speak of the soldier and the civilian, the citizen and his Government.

Each and every one of us has a solemn obligation under God to serve this Nation in its most critical hour—to keep this Nation great—to make this Nation greater in a better world.

Cass R. Sunstein & Randy E. Barnett

CONSTITUTIVE COMMITMENTS AND ROOSEVELT'S SECOND BILL OF RIGHTS: A DIALOGUE

53 Drake L. Rev. 205 (Winter 2005)

We include here Cass Sunstein's defense of President Franklin Roosevelt's vision of freedom as well as a response to that defense by Randy Barnett. Notice that Barnett challenges Sunstein's constitutional argument and also President Roosevelt's conception of freedom. Does Sunstein succeed in providing a constitutional basis for President Roosevelt's vision?

I. ROOSEVELT'S SECOND BILL OF RIGHTS

Cass R. Sunstein

On January 11, 1944, the United States was involved in its longest conflict since the Civil War. The war effort was going well. In a remarkably short period, the tide had turned sharply in favor of the Allies. Ultimate victory was no longer in serious doubt. The real question was the nature of the peace.

At noon, America's optimistic, aging, self-assured, wheelchair-bound president, Franklin Delano Roosevelt, delivered his State of the Union Address to Congress. His speech was not elegant. It was messy, sprawling, unruly, a bit of a pastiche, and not at all literary. It was the opposite of Lincoln's tight, poetic Gettysburg Address. But because of what it said, this forgotten address, proposing a "Second Bill of Rights," has a strong claim to being the greatest speech of the twentieth century.

What made the Second Bill of Rights possible? Part of the answer lies in a simple idea, one pervasive in the American legal culture during Roosevelt's time: No one really opposes government intervention. Markets and wealth depend on government. Without government creating and protecting property rights, property itself cannot exist. Even the people who most loudly denounce government interference depend on it every day. Their own rights do not come from minimizing government but are a product of government.... Think, for example, of the owner of a radio station, a house in the suburbs, an expensive automobile, or a large bank account. Every such owner depends, every day of every year, on the protection given by a coercive and well-funded state, equipped with a police force, judges, prosecutors, and an extensive body of criminal and civil law.

From the beginning, Roosevelt's White House understood all this quite well. In accepting the Democratic nomination in 1932, Roosevelt insisted that "we must lay hold of the fact that economic laws are not made by nature. They are made by human beings." ...

In this light it was implausible to contend that government should simply "stay out of the way" or "let people fend for themselves." Against the backdrop of the Great Depression, and the threat from fascism, Roosevelt was entirely prepared to insist that government should "protect individualism" not only by protecting property rights but also by ensuring decent opportunities and minimal security for all. The ultimate result was his proposal for the Second Bill of Rights.

By virtue of its effect on the Universal Declaration, the Second Bill has influenced dozens of constitutions throughout the world. In one form or another, it can be found in countless political and legal documents. . . .

In fact the United States itself continues to live, at least some of the time, under Roosevelt's constitutional vision. A consensus underlies several of the rights he listed, including the right to education, the right to social security, and the right to be free from monopoly. In the 1950s and 1960s, the Supreme Court started to go much further, embarking on a process of giving constitutional recognition to some of the rights that Roosevelt listed.

In a short period from 1957 through 1969, the Court explored several of these issues, and it reacted sympathetically to people's complaints. In some of them, the Court went so far as to hold that the government must subsidize poor people in certain domains. In several, the Court ruled that indigent criminal defendants have a right to a lawyer at taxpayer expense. Building on "the right to protect your rights," the Court struck down poll taxes. In other cases, the Court went further still. In *Shapiro v. Thompson*, the Court seemed to come close to saying that the Constitution conferred a right to welfare benefits. . . .

In *Goldberg*, the Court abandoned the right-privilege distinction and ruled that welfare was indeed a form of constitutional "property." Under the Due Process Clause, the government must provide a hearing before it removes people from the rolls. In *Goldberg*, the Court emphasized the "brutal need" of those who depended on welfare benefits. In its most extraordinary passage, it noted that "from its founding the Nation's basic commitment has been to foster the dignity and well-being of all persons within its borders. We have come to recognize that forces not within the control of the poor contribute to their poverty." Here is a clear reminder of a central lesson of the Great Depression . . . .

. . . By the late 1960s, respected constitutional thinkers could conclude that the Court was on the verge of recognizing a right to be free from desperate conditions — a right that captures many of the rights that Roosevelt attempted to catalogue. But all this was undone as a result of the election of President Richard Nixon in 1968. President Nixon promptly appointed four justices — Warren Burger, William Rehnquist, Lewis Powell, and Harry Blackmun — who showed no interest in the Second Bill. In a series of decisions, the new justices, joined by one or two others, rejected the claim that the existing Constitution protects the rights that Roosevelt catalogued.

Roosevelt himself did not argue for constitutional change (and on this I believe that he was right). He wanted the Second Bill to be part of the nation's deepest commitments, to be recognized and vindicated by the public, not by federal judges. He thought that the Second Bill should be seen in the same way as the Declaration of Independence — as a statement of the fundamental aspirations of the United States, which we might see as the nation's constitutive commitments. . . .

II. CONSTITUTIVE COMMITMENTS

Cass R. Sunstein

It is standard to distinguish between constitutional requirements and mere policies. An appropriation for Head Start is a policy, which can be changed however Congress wishes; by contrast, the principle of free speech overrides whatever Congress seeks to do. But there is something important, rarely unnoticed, and in between — much firmer than mere policies, but falling short of constitutional requirements. These are constitutive commitments. . . .

Constitutive commitments have a special place in the sense that they are widely accepted and cannot be eliminated without a fundamental change in national understandings. These rights are "constitutive" in the sense that they help to create, or to constitute, a society's basic values. They are also commitments, in the sense that they have a degree of stability over time. A violation would amount to a kind of breach — a violation of a trust.

Current examples include the right to some kind of social security program; the right not to be fired by a private employer because of your skin color or your sex; the right to protection through some kind of antitrust law. As with constitutional provisions, we disagree about what, specifically, these rights entail; but there is not much national disagreement about the rights themselves. (At least not at the moment.)

We could learn a lot about a nation's history if we explored what falls in the category of constitutional rights, constitutive commitments, and mere policies — and even more if we identified migrations over time. Maybe some of the commitments just mentioned will turn into mere policies. Sometimes policies are rapidly converted into constitutive commitments (consider the 1964 Civil Rights Act). Sometimes constitutive commitments end up getting constitutional status (the right to sexual privacy is, to some extent, an example, with the line of cases from *Griswold v. Connecticut* to *Lawrence v. Texas*).

Back to FDR's Second Bill of Rights: He was not proposing a formal constitutional change; he did not want to alter a word of the founding document. He was proposing to identify a set of constitutive commitments. One possible advantage of that strategy is that it avoids a role for federal judges; another possible advantage is that it allows a lot of democratic debate, over time, about what the constitutive commitments specifically entail.

VII. CONSTITUTIVE COMMITMENTS DO NOT MATTER, BUT IF THEY DO . . .

Randy E. Barnett

Suppose I deny that there is a natural right to a decent home, by which I mean that one person has no enforceable moral claim on another person, or group of persons, to provide him with a house. Classical natural rights thinkers distinguished between "perfect rights" which ought to be enforceable and "imperfect rights" which entail unenforceable moral duties. By denying that there is a perfect right to a house, I would not be denying that some persons could decide to give a portion of their property to others so that they may afford a house. Likewise, a government program could be created to provide housing by means of tax dollars (unless taxation itself is theft, in which case such a program would be unjust for that reason). The denial of the alleged "right" to a home would be denying only that, in the absence of government, one person can demand that another person be compelled to labor for him to build him a house. What policies government chooses to adopt, even in the absence of an enforceable moral claim, is another matter.

Supposing that it is possible to identify the constitutive commitments of an entire society of 280 million diverse persons and that it matters what these commitments may be, the particular constitutive commitments emphasized by Cass are highly contestable. First, the exact content of the alleged commitment is contestable — for example, is a commitment to an enforceable or "perfect right" of the poor to the assistance of others, or a commitment to voluntarily honor an unenforceable duty or "imperfect right" to provide assistance to those in need by means of a voluntary public program? As a purely descriptive matter, it seems that it is the latter, not the former, that has "real foundations in our history," but who can be sure? And how could this interpretive dispute about unwritten constitutive commitments ever be settled? That is the point of my doubts about the uncertain conditions of what makes a commitment constitutive and how we would know one if it existed.

Second, assuming there are such things as constitutive commitments, it is not at all clear that ours today are the same as those in Roosevelt's day. In the 1940s, the idea of a national welfare state had great appeal among intellectuals. It promised a more effective means to achieve the liberal ends of individual well-being. Then it was tried. Remember "The Great Society" with its "War on Poverty" and "Urban Renewal," which was initiated during the Johnson Administration and greatly expanded by Richard Nixon (who also added the "War on Drugs" to the program)? Did poverty end? Were cities restored to their previous greatness? Was illicit drug use eradicated? Well, no. The underclass expanded as more people came to rely on government benefits as "entitlements." The inner cities grew more impoverished and dangerous. Government housing projects were erected and fell into the control of gangs and thugs, and are now being demolished. Government schools declined precipitously. Stagflation hit the national economy. The War on Drugs has fueled inner city street gangs and international terrorist organizations, and undermined democracy in Third World countries.

All these pernicious effects of implementing something like Roosevelt's Second Bill of Rights are the reasons why "welfare state" is now an epithet rather than a noble goal. Why courts in the 1980s backed away from imposing these policies as constitutional rights. Why Ronald Reagan was elected in 1980. Why Republicans took control of the House of Representatives in 1994, ending 50 years of Democratic dominance. Why all three branches of government are now controlled by Republicans. Why European social welfare states, all built on Rooseveltian foundations, are in grave economic crisis, with intractably high unemployment and obligations to pay for social programs outstripping the ability to tax those who work.

In short, our real world experience since the 1940s undermined any "constitutive commitment" that may have existed to a Second Bill of Rights in a manner that no academic argument ever could. But academic arguments explaining theoretically why Roosevelt's approach leads to disastrous consequences have also boomed since his speech, beginning with the explosive popularity of F.A. Hayek's *The Road to Serfdom* in 1949. If forced to choose whether the vision of Roosevelt or of Hayek is ascendant, I think clearly it is the latter. . . .

Nor were classical liberals somehow confused, as Cass seems to think, about the need for government to "positively" enforce properly defined natural rights of property and contract, when they opposed governmental interference with these rights. Indeed, the purpose for making claims of perfect rights is as much to justify government protection of these rights as it is to deny government the power to interfere with their proper exercise. That the first duty of government is the equal protection of properly defined rights was always at the heart of the Lockean justification of government itself. That government is thought to be needed to enforce properly defined rights, therefore, provides no support whatsoever for extending governmental enforcement to rights claims that themselves interfere with properly defined rights.

So what then are our "constitutive commitments" today? Today more than any time since the nineteenth century, American culture is committed to rights of private property and freedom of contract. It is against this intellectual tide that Cass Sunstein makes his plea, asserting Rooseveltian constitutive commitments as a sort of rear guard action. But this American commitment to property and contract is tempered by the age-old classical liberal concern with the welfare of those who slip between the cracks — the group that used to be called the "deserving poor."

True, today most still accept the Progressive proposition that government rather than private institutions should assist these people. Nevertheless, most also complain that the nondeserving poor are assisted as well as those who deserve aid, a complaint that led to historic welfare reforms in the 1990s. I believe both the deserving poor and the greater society would be better served if more of this well-motivated assistance were channeled through private competitive institutions, as it once was. Time will tell whether we will move farther in this direction or be frozen in place.

But the proof of the pudding is in the eating. To the extent it matters, Roosevelt's Second Bill of Rights was abandoned as a constitutive commitment — if it was ever truly adopted — by the bitter taste of the Great Society. If increased reliance on the voluntary duty of beneficence is allowed by the political establishment to be tried and it proves to work better in practice than government welfare programs, as theory says that it should, then such an approach is likely to expand. The principal obstacle to discovering who is correct as a practical matter is the effective obstruction of these reforms by reactionaries in academia, the media and public sector unions who call themselves, ironically, "Progressives." In the end, individual liberty is the one continuous constitutive commitment of the American polity. Only time will tell whether the best means to that end is Roosevelt's or Hayek's. I know on whom my bet would be placed.

Judge Douglas Ginsburg

ON CONSTITUTIONALISM*

Kenneth Simon Lecture in Constitutional Thought

September 17, 2002

Bruce Ackerman and Cass Sunstein contend that, at least in some sense, the New Deal effectively amended the Constitution outside of the formal Article V process. But does this kind of claim concede that President Franklin Roosevelt's efforts to regulate the national economy were in fact unconstitutional at the time they were proposed? Judge Douglas Ginsburg and libertarian scholar Richard Epstein express skepticism about whether the New Deal's

* Available at *www.cato.org/pubs/scr/2003/constitutional.pdf.*

expansion of the commerce power was constitutional—or even desirable.

Does fidelity to the written nature of constitutional text require that its meaning remain fixed, insulated from changing conditions? Are political and policy judgments about the New Deal really separable from judgments about its constitutionality? If the critics are right and the New Deal was unconstitutional, what difference does 70 years of reliance on these mistaken precedents make? Would constitutional fidelity require uprooting these precedents, or simply "cutting our losses" and refusing to allow federal power to continue its growth?

I begin with an observation so fundamental, so straightforward and obvious, that it could be controversial only in the most elite law schools. That observation, to which I will devote considerable attention, is that ours is a written Constitution. When I say ours is a written constitution, I refer, of course, to the actual Constitution, the Constitution of the United States, the document reprinted in this little pamphlet in my hand. I do not refer to the legion of Supreme Court decisions interpreting the Constitution, applying it to particular factual situations, and in many cases providing us with an extended exegesis on its meaning. Those decisions are not the Constitution; as a practical matter, they are reasonably reliable guides to its application in future cases, but they are not the Constitution itself. To maintain otherwise is to ascribe to the Supreme Court a doctrine of infallibility it has never claimed for itself....

To be faithful to our written Constitution, a jurist must recognize and respect the limiting nature of its terms. Granted, what a term such as "due process" requires in a particular circumstance is not always clear. Nevertheless, there should be no question at all about whether a 34-year-old or a naturalized citizen may become President of the United States. That the terms giving rise to most questions of constitutional meaning lie somewhere between inherent ambiguity and mathematical certainty is no excuse from the duty of fidelity to the text. Rather, to be faithful to the written Constitution a jurist must make it his goal to illuminate the meaning of the text as the Framers understood it. To be sure, there will be disagreements even among principled jurists whose only goal is fidelity to the text, but with the aid of historical sources such disagreements will be confined to the ordinarily narrow and determinate zone within which competing constructions of a word or phrase are reasonable.

Despite sporadic departures like *Dred Scott*, respect for the text of the Constitution was the norm from *Marbury* through the first third of the twentieth century. But the Great Depression and the determination of the Roosevelt Administration placed the Supreme Court's commitment to the Constitution as written under severe stress in the 1930s, and it was then that the wheels began to come off.

Among the powers granted to the Congress in the Constitution is the power "[t]o regulate commerce . . . among the several states." From early in the history of the Republic, this authority was recognized to extend to articles in commerce among the states, while jurisdiction over health, safety, or other exercises of the police power was reserved exclusively to the states. The Clause was deemed broad enough, therefore, to allow regulation not only of ferries and railroads that transported goods in interstate commerce, but also of ancillary facilities, such as stockyards, described as "a throat through which the current [of commerce] flows." The power did not encompass regulation of child labor, however, because "the use of interstate transportation was [not] necessary to the accomplishment of harmful results." Desirable though a prohibition upon child labor may have been, therefore, the Congress was without power to enact it. A contrary result would have allowed the Congress to regulate almost anything pursuant to its power over interstate commerce, regardless whether the subject regulated was within the police power of the states.

During the 1930s, President Roosevelt proposed and the Congress enacted New Deal legislation in the teeth of the Court's prior decisions explicating the limits of the written Constitution. In effect, the President and the Congress dared the Court to strike down laws with strong popular support. Then President Roosevelt announced, after his landslide victory in 1936, his plan to "pack" the Supreme Court—that is, in the name of efficiency, to add another seat to the Court for each active justice over the age of 70, which would have given him six additional appointments. The Court-packing plan was voted down overwhelmingly by the Senate, but until then the threat of some change in the composition of the Court must have added to the strain placed upon the Justices' adherence to their announced understanding of the Constitution. After all, the power of the sword of Damocles is not that it falls, but that it hangs.

It was under the threat of the Court-packing plan that the Justices decided *NLRB v. Jones & Laughlin Steel Corp.*, upholding the power of the Congress to require employers to recognize and bargain with unions representing their employees. The Court's loose reasoning appears entirely too familiar from our contemporary perspective: strikes and other labor strife burden interstate commerce; therefore, employer-employee relations are subject to the power of the Congress to regulate interstate commerce.

In context, however, it is clear that the decision was a stark break from the Court's precedent. Whereas the Court had previously determined that the national government could not intrude upon the police power of the states by proscribing child labor, it now threw open the door to national regulation of employment relations—and much more. Not only interstate commerce but anything that affects interstate commerce came within the reach of the Congress. Indeed, not until *United States v. Lopez* in 1995 did the Court find another federally regulated subject beyond the reach of the Commerce Clause, and that was the possession near a school of a gun that was not shown to have moved in interstate commerce.

I have singled out the Court's interpretation of the Commerce Clause not because it is extreme but because it is illustrative. To take another example, the Constitution carefully separates legislative and executive powers. "All legislative powers herein granted shall be vested in a Congress of the United States," whereas "[t]he Executive Power shall be vested in a President of the United States of America." From that clear demarcation the Court had once inferred there must be a limit upon the ability of the Congress to delegate lawmaking functions to the executive branch. By delegating its legislative function the Congress avoids political accountability—therein lies the appeal of delegation—and frustrates the Framers' purpose in separating governmental powers. Accordingly, in the years before *Jones & Laughlin* the Supreme Court invalidated delegations of legislative power that contained no "intelligible principle to which the person or body authorized to take action is directed to conform." After the watershed New Deal cases expanding the reach of the Congress through the commerce power, however, the Court never again found an Act of Congress, however open-ended, to violate the Non-Delegation Doctrine.

If renewed fidelity to the Constitution as written is possible — and I think it is — then it will come only through a change in the legal culture. The ranks of scholars and judges advocating greater fidelity to constitutional text is still small but it is growing. Scholars are attending more to the original meaning of at least some of the clauses of the Constitution instead of focusing exclusively upon the Court's prior decisions. I daresay there has been more study of the Commerce Power and the Non-Delegation Doctrine in the last 10 years than in the prior half-century. Like archaeologists, legal and historical researchers have been rediscovering neglected clauses, dusting them off, and in some instances even imagining how they might be returned to active service. As the new legal scholarship gains acceptance, and students are exposed to the competing vision it represents, they will as lawyers begin to present more textual arguments, some of which may eventually win acceptance in the courts.

Richard Epstein

HOW PROGRESSIVES REWROTE THE CONSTITUTION

Washington, D.C.: Cato Institute (2006)

. . . The traditional classical liberal ideas of constitutional government — private property and freedom of contract, coupled with limited government and low levels of taxation and regulation, and, in the American context, federalism — may be traced to ancient times. They had a profound influence during the fertile founding period of our own Constitution. As historical landmarks, they stand as a constant reminder that it is possible to think of constitutional law without embracing the ideals of the modern social welfare state.

These debates swirl around many modern controversies, but they often come to a head whenever a new Supreme Court nomination is in the wings. However great my affection for the classical ideals that animated some, but not all, of the pre–New Deal jurisprudence, the opposition to that position is every bit as intense. Proponents of the modern position often make their lives far easier than they ought to be by their own extravagant misdescriptions of key doctrines of the now-reviled "Old Court." They are quite happy to place anyone opposed to their ideals in an imaginary "Constitution-in-Exile" movement, as though employing that term (Judge Douglas Ginsburg coined it) makes their opponents as legitimate as, say, deposed Bourbon royalists yearning for a return to some bygone age.

Overblown rhetoric to one side, just what might such a supposed movement support? We are often told that defenders of the pre–New Deal world order believe in an "unregulated America," when what they typically support is a legal order that does not regulate the prices, terms, and conditions on which goods and services are sold in a competitive market. It is often said that defenders of the pre–New Deal world believe that all property rights are inviolable. In fact, the classical liberal tradition in which I write accepts proportionate taxation. It also insists that government at all levels can use the power of eminent domain but only for public uses and upon payment of just compensation. That position also accepts the use of a police power that allows for regulation without compensation, which historically embraced law that addressed the public health, safety, morals, and general welfare, to use the formulation followed in the controversial case of *Lochner v. New York.* In some cases, that theory (like much of the modern law of privacy and sexual association) rejects some pre–New Deal legislation, such as that which is intended to promote the "morals" of the public at large. The classical liberal position is not "frozen" in the past; nor does it line up with modern left/right or Red/Blue divisions. The constant theme that drives the analysis is that of small government, which offers as little comfort to the new generation of religious and social conservatives as it does to the traditional American left.

Of course, I endorse some propositions that many other critics of modern American constitutional law most emphatically do not accept. Years ago, in my 1985 book *Takings*, I took the position that the standard interferences with employment contracts, such as minimum wage laws, antidiscrimination laws (in competitive markets only), collective bargaining laws, and Social Security requirements, were unconstitutional, all on the ground that the state has no better knowledge of what individuals need than individuals themselves do. I stand unapologetically by those positions today and think that the invalidation of those programs rests not on some narrowly egoistical view of private property but on the correct *social* ground that this view does us more good in the long run than the endless creation of various "unfair" practices, such as those under modern labor law, that introduce various forms of state monopolies, each of which further saps the productive juices from American society. At the same time, I fully recognize that the mistakes of the past, such as the creation of Social Security, cannot be undone today in light of the extensive reliance interests that have been created. Many institutions that are not defensible as a matter of first principle become so embedded in our social life that they cannot be undone without grievous harm. But that acceptance of change should never be confused with the mistaken belief that long usage of accepted doctrine renders it necessarily immune from rational criticism and constitutional change; for if that were the case, then the doctrine of "separate-but-equal," announced in 1896 in *Plessy v. Ferguson,* would have been affirmed, not overturned *58* years later in *Brown v. Board of Education.* There is no easy metric to solve the "second-best" of what, if anything, should be done to correct past constitutional errors. . . .

. . . [T]he same intellectuals who attacked the members of the Old Court because of their narrow and prescientific point of view were guilty of a massive disregard of the basic established principles of economics that were well known to Adam Smith and David Ricardo. Those principles were trampled by the mercantilist impulses of the day. No judgment about social welfare can be made simply by celebrating the gains to one preferred group. A complete social analysis must look at all the effects, negative and positive. Any program that works like a cartel makes sure that one group gets a larger share of a smaller pie from which it may profit in the long run (although long-term profitability could easily be impaired as others seek to evade legal restrictions). But the situation is always a double disaster for those individuals whom regulation leaves with a smaller share of a smaller pie.

The decisive criticism of the Progressive program, then, does not depend on any exaggerated sense of individualism — of the 18th century or of more modern vintage. It depends on an overall programmatic critique that examines the effect that policy initiatives have on the full range of relevant parties. The only programs that should survive are those that produce some *net* social improvement. Accordingly, there is no good sense in saying that one bad program justifies a second, any more than there is in insisting on making a second hole in the bottom of a boat instead of patching the first. Yet that is what happened under the Progressive regime where one bad turn justified a second. The workers whom the Progressives reflexively supported on matters of employment suffered under the agricultural regimes imposed to benefit dairy and wheat farmers, just as those farmers suffered from the legal regime that the Progressives adopted for labor unions. Neither error cancels out the other. Rather, the two errors compound each other. The intellectuals who scoffed at Adam Smith and his archaic conceptions of liberty fell into the timeless traps about which he so eloquently warned.

The Court's Commerce Clause jurisprudence thus represents a dubious textual reading for an antisocial political end. The language of the clause is contorted so "commerce" now includes the home consumption that everyone took to be its verbal opposite. Politically, this tour-de-force of constitutional interpretation was justified by an ostensible social need to inject the federal government into problems too big to be left to the states. But so long as market liberalization is the path toward a rational agricultural and labor policy, the Progressive vision of American constitutionalism continues to prop up the most dubious of federal institutions. . . .

. . . [T]he Progressive tradition was . . . bankrupt on Commerce Clause and economic issues . . . in two distinct but related senses.

The first of these is that it failed as a matter of constitutional interpretation. Although inconsistent on several points, the Framers of the original Constitution, the Bill of Rights, and the Civil War Amendments did start with some strong preference in favor of protecting liberty, property, and the social institutions they foster — competition and free trade in all areas of human endeavor. A good theory of constitutional interpretation is not one that starts and stops with some rote meaning of text, but this charge could not be lodged against the Old Court whose understanding of the need to introduce the nontextual element of the police power shows a sensitivity to structure and function as well as text. Nor can it be said that the interpretation that the justices of the Old Court gave to liberty or property is at variance with ordinary usage or with the larger mission of strong individual protections under a regime of limited government. They made mistakes along the way, and they were forced to make peace with a doctrine that had more protectionist elements than is ideal. But it is hard to charge them with any wholesale betrayal of the original design.

The same cannot be said of the Progressives. They saw in constitutional interpretation the opportunity to rewrite a Constitution that showed at every turn the influence of John Locke and James Madison into a different Constitution, which reflected the wisdom of the leading intellectual reformers of their own time. That effort to switch the terms of discourse fails because it violates the first tenet of interpretation. If you disagree with the original text, then you cannot mend your disagreements by adding to its basic rule some exceptions that change the tenor and purpose of the document. That standard is not meant to privilege the Old Court against modern rivals. The same principle applies to modern constitutions that often are overendowed with positive rights: a right to decent housing does not become a right to purchase decent housing if you can afford it. A grant of positive rights, whether wise or foolish, should not disappear in a blaze of interpretation. The same applies to modern statutes. The National Labor Relations Act should not become the charter of free markets in labor, and the civil rights acts should not be interpreted to allow racial discrimination against any person in the name of ending discrimination. The point here is that anyone on any side of the political spectrum can play fast and loose with authoritative text, and those evasions are no more palatable when done by one side than by the other. The Progressives were wrong on matters of constitutional interpretation because they consciously used their intellectual powers to rewrite, not understand, key provisions of the constitutional text.

Worse perhaps, the Progressives were wrong as a matter of political theory. Assume that they could write their own constitution on a blank slate. What principles of political economy would so captivate their imaginations that they would want to preserve cartels and monopolies in all areas of social life? There are, of course, special cases — patents, telecommunications — where some guarded use of monopoly power may be needed to spur invention or to assemble network industries. But the Progressives were not interested in working through those special cases. Rather, they were determined that their vision of the managed economy should take precedence in all areas of life. Although they purported to have great sophistication on economic and social matters, their understanding of those matters was primitive, and their disdain for the evident signs of social improvement colored their vision of the success of the older order. In the end, they cannot hide behind any notion of judicial restraint or high-minded social virtue. The Progressives and their modern defenders have to live with the stark truth that the noblest innovations of the Progressive Era were its greatest failures.

SWIFT AND COMPANY v. UNITED STATES

196 U.S. 375 (1905)

Opinion: Holmes, joined by Harlan, Brewer, Brown, White, Peckham, McKenna, Day

Toward the end of the nineteenth century, members of the Progressive movement sought to apply the federal government's power to address social and economic problems such as labor conditions, food safety, and monopolies. In response to this movement, the Court insisted on a narrow reading of Gibbons v. Ogden, *distinguishing interstate commerce from purely local economic activity like production and consumption. Although the Court interpreted these latter spheres of activity to be within the purview of state governments alone, the justices struck down Progressive regulations at the state level— albeit on different grounds.*

In United States v. E.C. Knight Co., *the Supreme Court severely weakened the Sherman Anti-Trust Act. Because of its narrow reading of the commerce power, the Court construed the Act not to cover monopoly activity that occurred strictly within a state, such as in manufacturing. Although the justices did not invalidate this landmark legislation, their limited understanding of the commerce power rendered it difficult to enforce.*

However, despite denying Progressives the Commerce Clause power as a means of enacting legislation to regulate working conditions and wages within the states, the Court did allow the use of the commerce power to regulate what it labeled the "stream" of commerce. In Swift & Co. v. United States, *the Court upheld the federal government's attempts to regulate cattle and prevent local monopolistic practices under the Sherman Anti-Trust Act. Even if each individual transaction involved in the cattle trade did not involve the crossing of state lines, the industry as a whole was involved, U.S. Supreme Court Justice Oliver Wendell Holmes argued, in a "stream of commerce." To some degree* Swift & Co. v. United States *might have marked a more lenient Commerce Clause jurisprudence. But as you will see in the following case, the Court was very concerned not to allow too much federal power to be authorized under this clause. As you read this case, you should pay attention to how broadly the Court reads the Commerce Clause.*

MR. JUSTICE HOLMES *delivered the opinion of the Court.*

Although the combination alleged embraces restraint and monopoly of trade within a single state, its effect upon commerce among the states is not accidental, secondary, remote, or merely probable. On the allegations of the bill the latter commerce no less, perhaps even more, than commerce within a single state, is an object of attack. Moreover, it is a direct object; it is that for the sake of which the several specific acts and courses of conduct are done and adopted. Therefore the case is not like *United States v. E.C. Knight Co.*, where the subject-matter of the combination was manufacture, and the direct object monopoly of manufacture within a state. However likely monopoly of commerce among the states in the article manufactured was to follow from the agreement, it was not a necessary consequence nor a primary end. Here the subject-matter is sales, and the very point of the combination is to restrain and monopolize commerce among the states in respect to such sales. The two cases are near to each other, as sooner or later always must happen where lines are to be drawn, but the line between them is distinct.

So, again, the line is distinct between this case and *Hopkins v. United States.* All that was decided there was that the local business of commission merchants was not commerce among the states, even if what the brokers were employed to sell was an object of such commerce. The brokers were not like the defendants before us, themselves the buyers and sellers. They only furnished certain facilities for the sales. Therefore, there again the effects of the combination of brokers upon the commerce was only indirect, and not within the act.

For the foregoing reasons we are of opinion that the carrying out of the scheme alleged, by the means set forth, properly may be enjoined, and that the bill cannot be dismissed.

So far it has not been necessary to consider whether the facts charges in any single paragraph constitute commerce among the states or show an interference with it. There can be no doubt, we apprehend, as to the collective effect of all the facts, if true, and if the defendants entertain the intent alleged. We pass now to the particulars, and will consider the corresponding parts of the injunction at the same time. The first question arises on the 6th section. That charges a combination of independent dealers to restrict the competition of their agents when purchasing stock for them in the stock yards. The purchasers and their slaughtering establishments are largely in different States from those of the stock-yards, and the sellers of the cattle, perhaps it is not too much to assume, largely in different States from either. The intent of the combination is not merely to restrict competition among the parties, but, as we have said, by force of the general allegation at the end of the bill, to aid in an attempt to monopolize commerce among the States.

It is said that this charge is too vague, and that it does not set forth a case of commerce among the States. Taking up the latter objection first, commerce among the States is not a technical legal conception, but a practical one, drawn from the course of business. When cattle are sent for sale from a place in one State, with the expectation that they will end their transit, after purchase, in another, and when, in effect, they do so, with only the interruption necessary to find a purchaser at the stock-yards, and when this is a typical, constantly recurring course, the current thus existing is a current of commerce among the States, and the purchase of the cattle is a part and incident of such commerce. What we say is true at least of such a purchase by residents in another State from that of the seller and of the cattle. And we need not trouble ourselves at this time as to whether the statute could be escaped by any arrangement as to the place where the sale, in point of law, is consummated. *See Norfolk & Western Ry. v. Sims.* But the sixth section of the bill charges an interference with such sales, a restraint of the parties by mutual contract and a combination not to compete in order to monopolize. It is immaterial if the section also embraces domestic transactions.

It should be added that the cattle in the stockyard are not at rest even to the extent that was held sufficient to warrant taxation in *American Steel & Wire Co. v. Speed.* But it may be that the question of taxation does not depend upon whether the article taxed may or may not be said to be in the course of commerce between the States, but depends upon whether the tax so far affects that commerce as to amount to a regulation of it. The injunction against taking part in a combination, the effect of which will be a restraint of trade among the States by directing the defendants' agents to refrain from bidding against one another at the sales of livestock, is justified so far as the subject matter is concerned.

The injunction, however, refers not to trade among the States in cattle, concerning which there can be no question of original packages, but to trade in fresh meats, as the trade forbidden to be restrained, and it is objected that the trade in fresh meats described in the second and third sections of the bill is not commerce among the States, because the meat is sold at the slaughtering places, or, when sold elsewhere, may be sold in less than the original packages. But the allegations of the second section, even if they import a technical passing of title at the slaughtering places, also import that the sales are to persons in other States, and that the shipments to other States are part of the transaction — "pursuant to such sales" — and the third section imports that the same things which are sent to agents are sold by them, and sufficiently indicates that some, at least, of the sales are of the original packages. Moreover, the sales are by persons in one State to persons in another. But we do not mean to imply that the rule which marks the point at which state taxation or regulation becomes permissible necessarily is beyond the scope of interference by Congress in cases where such interference is deemed necessary for the protection of commerce among the States. Nor do we mean to intimate that the statute under consideration is limited to that point. Beyond what we have said above, we leave those questions as we find them. They were touched upon in the *Northern Securities Company*'s case.

We are of opinion, further, that the charge in the sixth section is not too vague. The charge is not of a single agreement, but of a course of conduct intended to be continued. Under the act, it is the duty of the court, when applied to, to stop the conduct. The thing done and intended to be done is perfectly definite: with the purpose mentioned, directing the defendants' agents and inducing each other to refrain from competition in bids. The defendants cannot be ordered to compete, but they properly can be forbidden to give directions or to make agreements not to compete. *See Addyston Pipe & Steel Co. v. United States.* The injunction follows the charge. No objection was made on the ground that it is not confined to the places specified in the bill. It seems to us, however, that it ought to set forth more exactly the transactions in which such directions and agreements are forbidden. The trade in fresh meat referred to should be defined somewhat as it is in the bill, and the sales of stock should be confined to sales of stock at the stockyards named, which stock is sent from other States to the stockyards for sale or is bought at those yards for transport to another State.

HAMMER v. DAGENHART

247 U.S. 251 (1918)

Opinion: Day, joined by White, Pitney, Van Devanter, McReynolds
Dissent: Holmes, joined by McKenna, Brandeis, Clarke

Perhaps the most striking example of the Court's limits on the commerce power is Hammer v. Dagenhart. *The Child Labor Act of 1916 sought to ban the exchange of goods produced by child labor across state lines. This measure might seem to fit under even the narrowest understanding of "commerce . . . among the several states," because it did not directly ban child labor but instead concentrated on the products that were produced by that labor. But the Court argued that there was nothing dangerous or illicit about these products and thus this legislation was a poorly disguised effort to regulate wages and working conditions within the states themselves—which, they insisted, was beyond the reach of the Commerce Clause.*

As you read Hammer v. Dagenhart, *pay attention to the reasons why the legislation at issue is deemed not to be part of the stream of commerce. Why does the Court take this stance? Do you agree that this law is not authorized by the Commerce Clause? Pay particular attention to the dissent by Justice Oliver Wendell Holmes, the author of the majority decision in* Swift & Co. v. United States. *What arguments does he make against the Court's holding that this law is not authorized under the Commerce Clause?*

MR. JUSTICE DAY *delivered the opinion of the Court.*

A bill was filed in the United States District Court for the Western District of North Carolina by a father in his own behalf and as next friend of his two minor sons, one under the age of fourteen years and the other between the ages of fourteen and sixteen years, employees in a cotton mill at Charlotte, North Carolina, to enjoin the enforcement of the act of Congress intended to prevent interstate commerce in the products of child labor. Act of Sept. 1, 1916, c. 432, 39 Stat. 675:

> That no producer, manufacturer, or dealer shall ship or deliver for shipment in Interstate or foreign commerce any article or commodity the product of any mine or quarry, situated in the United States, in which within thirty days prior to the time of the removal of such product therefrom children under the age of sixteen years have been employed or permitted to work, or any article or commodity the product of any mill, cannery, workshop, factory, or manufacturing establishment, situated in the United States, in which within thirty days prior to the removal of such product there from children under the age of fourteen years have been employed or permitted to work, or children between the ages of fourteen years and sixteen years have been employed or permitted to work more than eight hours in any day, or more than six days in any week, or after the hour of seven o'clock postmeridian, or before the hour of six o'clock antemeridian.

Other sections of the act contain provisions for its enforcement and prescribe penalties for its violation.

The attack upon the act rests upon three propositions: First: It is not a regulation of interstate and foreign commerce; Second: It contravenes the Tenth Amendment to the Constitution; Third: It conflicts with the Fifth Amendment to the Constitution.

The controlling question for decision is: Is it within the authority of Congress in regulating commerce among the States to prohibit the transportation in interstate commerce of manufactured goods, the product of a factory in which, within thirty days prior to their removal there from, children under the age of fourteen have been employed or permitted to work, or children between the ages of fourteen and sixteen years have been employed or permitted to work more than eight hours in any day, or more than six days in any week, or after the hour of seven o'clock P.M. or before the hour of 6 o'clock A.M.?

The power essential to the passage of this act, the Government contends, is found in the Commerce Clause of the Constitution which authorizes Congress to regulate commerce with foreign nations and among the States.

. . . [T]he power is one to control the means by which commerce is carried on, which is directly the contrary of the assumed right to forbid commerce from moving and thus destroy it as to particular commodities. But it is insisted that adjudged cases in this court establish the doctrine that the power to regulate given to Congress incidentally includes the authority to prohibit the movement of ordinary commodities and therefore that the subject is not open for discussion. The cases demonstrate the contrary. They rest upon the character of the particular subjects dealt with and the fact that the scope of governmental authority, state or national, possessed over them is such that the authority to prohibit is as to them but the exertion of the power to regulate.

In each of these instances the use of interstate transportation was necessary to the accomplishment of harmful results. In other words, although the power over interstate transportation was to regulate, that could only be accomplished by prohibiting the use of the facilities of interstate commerce to effect the evil intended.

This element is wanting in the present case. The thing intended to be accomplished by this statute is the denial of the facilities of interstate commerce to those manufacturers in the States who employ children within the prohibited ages. The act in its effect does not regulate transportation among the States, but aims to standardize the ages at which children may be employed in mining and manufacturing within the States. The goods shipped are of themselves harmless. The act permits them to be freely shipped after thirty days from the time of their removal from the factory. When offered for shipment, and before transportation begins, the labor of their production is over, and the mere fact that they were intended for interstate commerce transportation does not make their production subject to federal control under the commerce power.

Commerce "consists of intercourse and traffic . . . and includes the transportation of persons and property, as well as the purchase, sale and exchange of commodities." The making of goods and the mining of coal are not commerce, nor does the fact that these things are to be afterwards shipped or used in interstate commerce, make their production a part thereof.

Over interstate transportation, or its incidents, the regulatory power of Congress is ample, but the production of articles, intended for interstate commerce, is a matter of local regulation.

When the commerce begins is determined, not by the character of the commodity, nor by the intention of the owner to transfer it to another state for sale, nor by his preparation of it for transportation, but by its actual delivery to a common carrier for transportation, or the actual commencement of its transfer to another state. . . . If it were otherwise, all manufacture intended for interstate shipment would be brought under federal control to the practical exclusion of the authority of the States, a result certainly not contemplated by the framers of the Constitution when they vested in Congress the authority to regulate commerce among the States.

It is further contended that the authority of Congress may be exerted to control interstate commerce in the shipment of child-made goods because of the effect of the circulation of such goods in other States where the evil of this class of labor has been recognized by local legislation, and the right to thus employ child labor has been more rigorously restrained than in the State of production. In other words, that the unfair competition, thus engendered, may be controlled by closing the channels of interstate commerce to manufacturers in those States where the local laws do not meet what Congress deems to be the more just standard of other States.

There is no power vested in Congress to require the States to exercise their police power so as to prevent possible unfair competition. Many causes may cooperate to give one State, by reason of local laws or conditions, an economic advantage over others. The Commerce Clause was not intended to give to Congress a general authority to equalize such conditions. In some of the States laws have been passed fixing minimum wages for women, in others the local law regulates the hours of labor of women in various employments. Business done in such States may be at an economic disadvantage when compared with States which have no such regulations; surely, this fact does not give Congress the power to deny transportation in interstate commerce to those who carry on business where the hours of labor and the rate of compensation for women have not been fixed by a standard in use in other States and approved by Congress.

The grant of power to Congress over the subject of interstate commerce was to enable it to regulate such commerce, and not to give it authority to control the States in their exercise of the police power over local trade and manufacture.

The grant of authority over a purely federal matter was not intended to destroy the local power always existing and carefully reserved to the States in the Tenth Amendment to the Constitution.

That there should be limitations upon the right to employ children in mines and factories in the interest of their own and the public welfare, all will admit. That such employment is generally deemed to require regulation is shown by the fact that the brief of counsel states that every State in the Union has a law upon the subject, limiting the right to thus employ children. In North Carolina, the State wherein is located the factory in which the employment was had in the present case, no child under twelve years of age is permitted to work.

It may be desirable that such laws be uniform, but our Federal Government is one of enumerated powers; "this principle," declared Chief Justice Marshall in *McCulloch v. Maryland,* 4 Wheat. 316, "is universally admitted."

The maintenance of the authority of the States over matters purely local is as essential to the preservation of our institutions as is the conservation of the supremacy of the federal power in all matters entrusted to the Nation by the Federal Constitution.

Thus the act in a twofold sense is repugnant to the Constitution. It not only transcends the authority delegated to Congress over commerce but also exerts a power as to a purely local matter to which the federal authority does not extend. The far reaching result of upholding the act cannot be more plainly indicated than by pointing out that if Congress can thus regulate matters entrusted to local authority by prohibition of the movement of commodities in interstate commerce, all freedom of commerce will be at an end, and the power of the States over local matters may be eliminated, and thus our system of government be practically destroyed.

MR. JUSTICE HOLMES, *dissenting.*

[I]f an act is within the powers specifically conferred upon Congress, it seems to me that it is not made any less constitutional because of the indirect effects that it may have, however obvious it may be that it will have those effects, and that we are not at liberty upon such grounds to hold it void.

The first step in my argument is to make plain what no one is likely to dispute — that the statute in question is within the power expressly given to Congress if considered only as to its immediate effects and that if invalid it is so only upon some collateral ground. The statute confines itself to prohibiting the carriage of certain goods in interstate or foreign commerce. Congress is given power to regulate such commerce in unqualified terms. It would not be argued today that the power to regulate does not include the power to prohibit. Regulation means the prohibition of something, and when interstate commerce is the matter to be regulated I cannot doubt that the regulation may prohibit any part of such commerce that Congress sees fit to forbid.

The question then is narrowed to whether the exercise of its otherwise constitutional power by Congress can be pronounced unconstitutional because of its possible reaction upon the conduct of the States in a matter upon which I have admitted that they are free from direct control. I should have thought that that matter had been disposed of so fully as to leave no room for doubt. I should have thought that most conspicuous decisions of this Court had made it clear that the power to regulate commerce and other constitutional powers could not be cut down or qualified by the fact that it might interfere with the carrying out of the domestic policy of any State.

The manufacture of oleomargarine is as much a matter of state regulation as the manufacture of cotton cloth. Congress levied a tax upon the compound when colored so as to resemble butter that was so great as obviously to prohibit the manufacture and sale. . . . Fifty years ago a tax on state banks, the obvious purpose and actual effect of which was to drive them, or at least their circulation, out of existence, was sustained, although the result was one that Congress had no constitutional power to require. . . . [T]he Sherman Act has been made an instrument for the breaking up on combinations in restraint of trade and monopolies, using the power to regulate commerce as a foothold, but not proceeding because that commerce was the end actually in mind. The objection that the control of the States over production was interfered with was urged again and again but always in vain.

The Pure Food and Drug Act which was sustained in *Hipolite Egg Co. v. United States*, with the intimation that "no trade can be carried on between the States to which it [the power of Congress to regulate commerce] does not extend," applies not merely to articles that the changing opinions of the time condemn as intrinsically harmful but to others innocent in themselves, simply on the ground that the order for them was induced by a preliminary fraud. It does not matter whether the supposed evil precedes or follows the transportation. It is enough that in the opinion of Congress the transportation encourages the evil.

The notion that prohibition is any less prohibition when applied to things now thought evil I do not understand. But if there is any matter upon which civilized countries have agreed—far more unanimously than they have with regard to intoxicants and some other matters over which this country is now emotionally aroused—it is the evil of premature and excessive child labor. I should have thought that if we were to introduce our own moral conceptions where in my opinion they do not belong, this was preeminently a case for upholding the exercise of all its powers by the United States.

But I had thought that the propriety of the exercise of a power admitted to exist in some cases was for the consideration of Congress alone and that this Court always had disavowed the right to intrude its judgment upon questions of policy or morals. It is not for this Court to pronounce when prohibition is necessary to regulation if it ever may be necessary—to say that it is permissible as against strong drink but not as against the product of ruined lives.

The act does not meddle with anything belonging to the States. They may regulate their internal affairs and their domestic commerce as they like. But when they seek to send their products across the state line they are no longer within their rights. If there were no Constitution and no Congress their power to cross the line would depend upon their neighbors. Under the Constitution such commerce belongs not to the States but to Congress to regulate. It may carry out its views of public policy whatever indirect effect they may have upon the activities of the States. Instead of being encountered by a prohibitive tariff at her boundaries the State encounters the public policy of the United States which it is for Congress to express.

The public policy of the United States is shaped with a view to the benefit of the nation as a whole. . . . The national welfare as understood by Congress may require a different attitude within its sphere from that of some self-seeking State. It seems to me entirely constitutional for Congress to enforce its understanding by all the means at its command.

A.L.A. SCHECHTER POULTRY CORP. v. UNITED STATES

295 U.S. 495 (1935)

Opinion: Hughes, joined by Van Devanter, McReynolds, Brandeis, Sutherland, Butler, Roberts
Concurrence: Cardozo, joined by Stone

During the initial attempts of President Franklin Roosevelt to implement his New Deal, the Court repeatedly struck down congressional legislation as lacking any federal power in the Constitution. Although Congress had tried to assert its Commerce Clause power in passing much of this legislation, the Court often held that Congress had exceeded its authority. For example, in Schechter Poultry Co. v. United States, *the Court struck down national labor and safety regulations as they applied to a New York slaughterhouse and poultry market. "Commerce . . . among the several states" did not extend to local production—and that meant that many of President Roosevelt's New Deal policies were unconstitutional. The following year, in* Carter v. Carter Coal Company, *the Court struck down an attempt by the federal government to regulate the coal industry on the grounds that it lacked the Commerce Clause power to do so.*

MR. CHIEF JUSTICE HUGHES *delivered the opinion of the Court.*

The question of the application of the provisions of the Live Poultry Code to intrastate transactions. Although the validity of the codes (apart from the question of delegation) rests upon the commerce clause of the Constitution, §3(a) is not, in terms, limited to interstate and foreign commerce. From the generality of its terms, and from the argument of the Government at the bar, it would appear that §3(a) was designed to authorize codes without that limitation. But, under §3(f), penalties are confined to violations of a code provision "in any transaction in or affecting interstate or foreign commerce." This aspect of the case presents the question whether the particular provisions of the Live Poultry Code, which the defendants were convicted for violating and for having conspired to violate, were within the regulating power of Congress.

These provisions relate to the hours and wages of those employed by defendants in their slaughterhouses in Brooklyn, and to the sales there made to retail dealers and butchers.

(1) Were these transactions "*in*" interstate commerce? Much is made of the fact that almost all the poultry coming to New York is sent there from other States. But the code provisions, as here applied, do not concern the transportation of the poultry from other States to New York, or the transactions of the commission men or others to whom it is consigned, or the sales made by such consignees to defendants. When defendants had made their purchases, whether at the West Washington Market in New York City or at the railroad terminals serving the City, or elsewhere, the poultry was trucked to their slaughterhouses in Brooklyn for local disposition. The interstate transactions in relation to that poultry then ended. Defendants held the poultry at their slaughterhouse markets for slaughter and local sale to retail dealers and butchers who, in turn, sold directly to consumers. Neither the slaughtering nor the sales by defendants were transactions in interstate commerce. *Brown v. Houston*; *Public Utilities Comm'n v. Landon*; *Industrial Association v. States*; *Atlantic Coast Line v. Standard Oil Co.*

The undisputed facts thus afford no warrant for the argument that the poultry handled by defendants at their slaughterhouse markets was in a "*current*" or "*flow*" of interstate commerce, and was thus subject to congressional regulation. The mere fact that there may be a constant flow of commodities into a State does not mean that the flow continues after the property has arrived, and has become commingled with the mass of property within the State, and is there held solely for local disposition and use. So far as the poultry here in question is concerned, the flow in interstate commerce had ceased. The poultry had come to a permanent rest within the State. It was not held, used, or sold by defendants in relation to any further transactions in interstate commerce, and was not destined for transportation to other States. Hence, decisions which deal with a stream of interstate commerce — where goods come to rest within a State temporarily and are later to go forward in interstate commerce — and with the regulations of transactions involved in that practical continuity of movement, are not applicable here. *See Swift & Co. v. United States*; *Lemke v. Farmers Grain Co.*; *Stafford v. Wallace*; *Chicago Board of Trade v. Olsen*; *Tagg Bros. & Moorhead v. United States.*

(2) Did the defendants' transactions directly "*affect*" interstate commerce, so as to be subject to federal regulation? The power of Congress extends not only to the regulation of transactions which are part of interstate commerce, but to the protection of that commerce from injury. It matters not that the injury may be due to the conduct of those engaged in intrastate operations. Thus, Congress may protect the safety of those employed in interstate transportation "no matter what may be the source of the dangers which threaten it." *Southern Ry. Co. v. United States*. We said in *Second Employers' Liability Cases*, that it is the "effect upon interstate commerce," not "the source of the injury," which is "the criterion of congressional power." We have held that, in dealing with common carriers engaged in both interstate and intrastate commerce, the dominant authority of Congress necessarily embraces the right to control their intrastate operations in all matters having such a close and substantial relation to interstate traffic that the control is essential or appropriate to secure the freedom of that traffic from interference or unjust discrimination and to promote the efficiency of the interstate service. *The Shreveport Case*; *Wisconsin Railroad Comm'n v. Chicago, B. & Q. R. Co.* And combinations and conspiracies to restrain interstate commerce, or to monopolize any part of it, are nonetheless within the reach of the Anti-Trust Act because the conspirators seek to attain their end by means of intrastate activities. *Coronado Coal Co. v. United Mine Workers*; *Bedford Cut Stone Co. v. Stone Cutters Assn.*

We recently had occasion, in *Local 677 v. United States*, to apply this principle in connection with the live poultry industry. That was a suit to enjoin a conspiracy to restrain and monopolize interstate commerce in violation of the Anti-Trust Act. It was shown that marketmen, teamsters and slaughterers (*shochtim*) had conspired to burden the free movement of live poultry into the metropolitan area in and about New York City. Marketmen had organized an association, had allocated retailers among themselves, and had agreed to increase prices. To accomplish their objects, large amounts of money were raised by levies upon poultry sold, men were hired to obstruct the business dealers who resisted, wholesalers and retailers were spied upon, and, by violence and other forms of intimidation, were prevented from freely purchasing live poultry. Teamsters refused to handle poultry for recalcitrant marketmen, and members of the *shochtim* union refused to slaughter. In view of the proof of that conspiracy, we said that it was unnecessary to decide when interstate commerce ended and when intrastate commerce began. We found that the proved interference by the conspirators "with the unloading, the transportation, the sales by marketmen to retailers, the prices charged, and the amount of profits exacted" operated "substantially and directly to restrain and burden the untrammeled shipment and movement of the poultry" while unquestionably it was in interstate commerce. The intrastate acts of the conspirators were included in the injunction because that was found to be necessary for the protection of interstate commerce against the attempted and illegal restraint. *Id.* pp. 297, 299, 300.

The instant case is not of that sort. This is not a prosecution for a conspiracy to restrain or monopolize interstate commerce in violation of the Anti-Trust Act. Defendants have been convicted not upon direct charges of injury to interstate commerce or of interference with persons engaged in that commerce, but of violations of certain provisions of the Live Poultry Code and of conspiracy to commit these violations. Interstate commerce is brought in only upon the charge that violations of these provisions — as to hours and wages of employees and local sales — "*affected*" interstate commerce.

In determining how far the federal government may go in controlling intrastate transactions upon the ground that they "affect" interstate commerce, there is a necessary and well established distinction between direct and indirect effects. The precise line can be drawn only as individual cases arise, but the distinction is clear in principle. Direct effects are illustrated by the railroad cases we have cited, as, *e.g.*, the effect of failure to use prescribed safety appliances on railroads which are the highways of both interstate and intrastate commerce, injury to an employee engaged in interstate transportation by the negligence of an employee engaged in an intrastate movement, the fixing of rates for intrastate transportation which unjustly discriminate against interstate commerce. But where the effect of intrastate transactions upon interstate commerce is merely indirect, such transactions remain within the domain of state power. If the commerce clause were construed to reach all enterprise and transactions which could be said to have an indirect effect upon interstate commerce, the federal authority would embrace practically all the activities of the people, and the authority of the State over its domestic concerns would exist only by sufferance of the federal government. Indeed, on such a theory, even the development of the State's commercial facilities would be subject to federal control.

The distinction between direct and indirect effects has been clearly recognized in the application of the Anti-Trust Act. Where a combination or conspiracy is formed, with the intent to restrain interstate commerce or to monopolize any part of it, the violation of the statute is clear. *Coronado Coal Co. v. United Mine Workers.* But where that intent is absent, and the objectives are limited to intrastate activities, the fact that there may be an indirect effect upon interstate commerce does not subject the parties to the federal statute, notwithstanding its broad provisions. This principle has frequently been applied in litigation growing out of labor disputes.

While these decisions related to the application of the federal statute, and not to its constitutional validity, the distinction between direct and indirect effects of intrastate transactions upon interstate commerce must be recognized as a fundamental one, essential to the maintenance of our constitutional system. Otherwise, as we have said, there would be virtually no limit to the federal power, and, for all practical purposes, we should have a completely centralized government. We must consider the provisions here in question in the light of this distinction.

The question of chief importance relates to the provisions of the Code as to the hours and wages of those employed in defendants' slaughterhouse markets. It is plain that these requirements are imposed in order to govern the details of defendants' management of their local business. The persons employed in slaughtering and selling in local trade are not employed in interstate commerce. Their hours and wages have no direct relation to interstate commerce. The question of how many hours these employees should work and what they should be paid differs in no essential respect from similar questions in other local businesses which handle commodities brought into a State and there dealt in as a part of its internal commerce. This appears from an examination of the considerations urged by the Government with respect to conditions in the poultry trade. Thus, the Government argues that hours and wages affect prices; that slaughterhouse men sell at a small margin above operating costs; that labor represents 50 to 60 percent of these costs; that a slaughterhouse operator paying lower wages or reducing his cost by exacting long hours of work translates his saving into lower prices; that this results in demands for a cheaper grade of goods, and that the cutting of prices brings about a demoralization of the price structure. Similar conditions may be adduced in relation to other businesses. The argument of the Government proves too much. If the federal government may determine the wages and hours of employees in the internal commerce of a State, because of their relation to cost and prices and their indirect effect upon interstate commerce, it would seem that a similar control might be exerted over other elements of cost also affecting prices, such as the number of employees, rents, advertising, methods of doing business, etc. All the processes of production and distribution that enter into cost could likewise be controlled. If the cost of doing an intrastate business is, in itself, the permitted object of federal control, the extent of the regulation of cost would be a question of discretion, and not of power.

The Government also makes the point that efforts to enact state legislation establishing high labor standards have been impeded by the belief that, unless similar action is taken generally, commerce will be diverted from the States adopting such standards, and that this fear of diversion has led to demands for federal legislation on the subject of wages and hours. The apparent implication is that the federal authority under the commerce clause should be deemed to extend to the establishment of rules to govern wages and hours in intrastate trade and industry generally throughout the country, thus overriding the authority of the States to deal with domestic problems arising from labor conditions in their internal commerce.

It is not the province of the Court to consider the economic advantages or disadvantage of such a centralized system.

It is sufficient to say that the Federal Constitution does not provide for it. Our growth and development have called for wide use of the commerce power of the federal government in its control over the expanded activities of interstate commerce, and in protecting that commerce from burdens, interferences, and conspiracies to restrain and monopolize it. But the authority of the federal government may not be pushed to such an extreme as to destroy the distinction, which the commerce clause itself establishes, between commerce "among the several States" and the internal concerns of a State. The same answer must be made to the contention that is based upon the serious economic situation which led to the passage of the Recovery Act—the fall in prices, the decline in wages and employment, and the curtailment of the market for commodities. Stress is laid upon the great importance of maintaining wage distributions which would provide the necessary stimulus in starting "the cumulative forces making for expanding commercial activity." Without in any way disparaging this motive, it is enough to say that the recuperative efforts of the federal government must be made in a manner consistent with the authority granted by the Constitution.

We are of the opinion that the attempt, through the provisions of the Code, to fix the hours and wages of employees of defendants in their intrastate business was not a valid exercise of federal power.

CARTER v. CARTER COAL COMPANY

298 U.S. 238 (1936)

Opinion: Sutherland, joined by Van Devanter, McReynolds, Butler, Roberts
Concurrence: Hughes
Dissent: Cardozo, joined by Brandeis, Stone

MR. JUSTICE SUTHERLAND *delivered the opinion of the Court.*

Another group of cases, of which *Swift & Co. v. United States,* is an example, rest upon the circumstance that the acts in question constituted direct interferences with the "flow" of commerce among the states. In the *Swift* case, livestock was consigned and delivered to stockyards—not as a place of final destination, but, as the court said in *Stafford v. Wallace,* "a throat through which the current flows." The sales which ensued merely changed the private interest in the subject of the current, without interfering with its continuity. *Industrial Assn. v. United States.* It was nowhere suggested in these cases that the interstate commerce power extended to the growth or production of the things which, after production, entered the flow. If the court had held that the raising of the cattle, which were involved in the *Swift* case, including the wages paid to and working conditions of the herders and others employed in the business, could be regulated by Congress, that decision and decisions holding similarly would be in point, for it is that situation, and not the one with which the court actually dealt, which here concerns us.

The distinction suggested is illustrated by the decision in *Arkadelphia Milling Co. v. St. Lois S.W. Ry. Co.* That case dealt with orders of a state commission fixing railroad rates. One of the questions considered was whether certain shipments of rough material from the forest to mills in the same state for manufacture, followed by the forwarding of the finished product to points outside the state, was a continuous movement in interstate commerce. It appeared that, when the rough material reached the mills, it was manufactured into various articles which were stacked or placed in kilns to dry, the processes occupying several months. Markets for the manufactured articles were almost entirely in other states or in foreign countries. About 95% of the finished articles was made for outbound shipment. When the rough material was shipped to the mills, it was expected by the mills that this percentage of the finished articles would be so sold and shipped outside the state. And all of them knew and intended that this 95% of the finished product would be so sold and shipped. This court held that the state order did not interfere with interstate commerce, and that the *Swift* case was not in point, as it is not in point here.

The restricted field covered by the *Swift* and kindred cases is illustrated by the *Schechter* case, *supra*, p. 543. There, the commodity in question, although shipped from another state, had come to rest in the state of its destination, and, as the court pointed out, was no longer in a current or flow of interstate commerce. The *Swift* doctrine was rejected as inapposite. In the *Schechter* case, the flow had ceased. Here it had not begun. The difference is not one of substance. The applicable principle is the same.

But §1 (the preamble) of the act now under review declares that all production and distribution of bituminous coal "bear upon and directly affect its interstate commerce," and that regulation thereof is imperative for the protection of such commerce. The contention of the government is that the labor provisions of the act may be sustained in that view.

That the production of every commodity intended for interstate sale and transportation has some effect upon interstate commerce may be, if it has not already been, freely granted, and we are brought to the final and decisive inquiry, whether here that effect is direct, as the "preamble" recites, or indirect. The distinction is not formal, but substantial in the highest degree, as we pointed out in the *Schechter* case, *supra*, p. 546, *et seq.* "If the commerce clause were construed," we there said,

> to reach all enterprises and transactions which could be said to have an indirect effect upon interstate commerce, the federal authority would embrace practically all the activities of the people, and the authority of the State over its domestic concerns would exist only by sufferance of the federal government. Indeed, on such a theory, even the development of the State's commercial facilities would be subject to federal control.

It was also pointed out, p. 548, that

> the distinction between direct and indirect effects of intrastate transactions upon interstate commerce must be recognized as a fundamental one, essential to the maintenance of our constitutional system.

Whether the effect of a given activity or condition is direct or indirect is not always easy to determine. The word "direct" implies that the activity or condition invoked or blamed shall operate proximately—not mediately, remotely, or collaterally—to produce the effect. It connotes the absence of an efficient intervening agency or condition. And the extent of the effect bears no logical relation to its character. The distinction between a direct and an indirect effect turns not upon the magnitude of either the cause or the effect, but entirely upon the manner in which the effect has been brought about. If the production by one man of a single ton of coal intended for interstate sale and shipment, and actually so sold and shipped, affects interstate commerce indirectly, the effect does not become direct by multiplying the tonnage, or increasing the number of men employed, or adding to the expense or complexities of the business, or by all combined. It is quite true that rules of law are sometimes qualified by considerations of degree, as the government argues. But the matter of degree has no bearing upon the question here, since that question is not what is the extent of the local activity or condition, or the extent of the effect produced upon interstate commerce, but what is the relation between the activity or condition and the effect?

Much stress is put upon the evils which come from the struggle between employers and employees over the matter of wages, working conditions, the right of collective bargaining, etc., and the resulting strikes, curtailment and irregularity of production and effect on prices, and it is insisted that interstate commerce is greatly affected thereby. But, in addition to what has just been said, the conclusive answer is that the evils are all local evils over which the federal government has no legislative control. The relation of employer and employee is a local relation. At common law, it is one of the domestic relations. The wages are paid for the doing of local work. Working conditions are obviously local conditions. The employees are not engaged in or about commerce, but exclusively in producing a commodity. And the controversies and evils which it is the object of the act to regulate and minimize are local controversies and evils affecting local work undertaken to accomplish that local result. Such effect as they may have upon commerce, however extensive it may be, is secondary and indirect. An increase in the greatness of the effect adds to its importance. It does not alter its character.

NATIONAL LABOR RELATIONS BOARD v. JONES & LAUGHLIN STEEL CORP.

301 U.S. 1 (1937)

Opinion: Hughes, joined by Brandeis, Stone, Roberts, Cardozo
Dissent: McReynolds, joined by Van Devanter, Sutherland, Butler

Although the Supreme Court obstructed federal efforts to regulate the national economy for decades, culminating in the rejection of Congress's power to enact the early New Deal, the year 1937 saw the Court reverse course. In the following case, the Court began to embrace a far broader view of the commerce power, and with it, much of President Franklin Roosevelt's New Deal. This case was decided soon after West Coast Hotel v. Parrish, *often thought to be the case in which the Court's "switch in time" occurred. As some see it,* West Coast Hotel v. Parrish, *which concerns substantive due process, marked a change from the Court striking down New Deal legislation, as it did in* A.L.A. Schechter Poultry Corp. v. United States *and* Carter v. Carter Coal Co., *to upholding it. Some attribute the Court's change to President Roosevelt's threat to pack the Court with new justices. Regardless of the reasons, however, the change from the limits on Congress's Commerce Clause power before 1937, and the more expansive view of this power after 1937, is stark.*

The following three cases consider the National Labor Relations Act, the Fair Labor Standards Act, and the Agricultural Adjustment Act—each a cornerstone of President Roosevelt's economic recovery plan. It is important to read these cases as a group with the following questions in mind: How broadly do these cases define the stream of commerce? Does it only include production and other economic activity that cross state lines?

MR. CHIEF JUSTICE HUGHES *delivered the opinion of the Court.*

In a proceeding under the National Labor Relations Act of 1935, the National Labor Relations Board found that the respondent, Jones & Laughlin Steel Corporation, had violated the Act by engaging in unfair labor practices affecting commerce. . . . The unfair labor practices charged were that the corporation was discriminating against members of the union with regard to hire and tenure of employment, and was coercing and intimidating its employees in order to interfere with their self-organization. The discriminatory and coercive action alleged was the discharge of certain employees.

The National Labor Relations Board, sustaining the charge, ordered the corporation to cease and desist from such discrimination and coercion, to offer reinstatement to ten of the employees named, to make good their losses in pay, and to post for thirty days notices that the corporation would not discharge or discriminate against members, or those desiring to become members, of the labor union. As the corporation failed to comply, the Board petitioned the Circuit Court of Appeals to enforce the order. The court denied the petition, holding that the order lay beyond the range of federal power. We granted certiorari.

Contesting the ruling of the Board, the respondent argues (1) that the Act is in reality a regulation of labor relations and not of interstate commerce; (2) that the Act can have no application to the respondent's relations with its production employees because they are not subject to regulation by the federal government; and (3) that the provisions of the Act violate §2 of Article III and the Fifth and Seventh Amendments of the Constitution of the United States.

First. The scope of the Act.—The Act is challenged in its entirety as an attempt to regulate all industry, thus invading the reserved powers of the States over their local concerns. It is asserted that the references in the Act to interstate and foreign commerce are colorable at best; that the Act is not a true regulation of such commerce or of matters which directly affect it but on the contrary has the fundamental object of placing under the compulsory supervision of the federal government all industrial labor relations within the nation. . . .

If this conception of terms, intent and consequent inseparability were sound, the Act would necessarily fall by reason of the limitation upon the federal power which inheres in the constitutional grain, as well as because of the explicit reservation of the Tenth Amendment. But we are not at liberty to deny effect to specific provisions, which Congress has constitutional power to enact, by superimposing upon them inferences from general legislative declarations of an ambiguous character.

We think it clear that the National Labor Relations Act may be construed so as to operate within the sphere of constitutional authority. The jurisdiction conferred upon the Board, and invoked in this instance, is found in §10 (a), which provides:

> "SEC. 10 (a). The Board is empowered, as hereinafter provided, to prevent any person from engaging in any unfair labor practice (listed in section 8) affecting commerce."

The critical words of this provision, prescribing the limits of the Board's authority in dealing with the labor practices, are "affecting commerce." The Act specifically defines the "commerce" to which it refers (§2(6)):

> "The term 'commerce' means trade, traffic, commerce, transportation, or communication among the several States . . . or between points in the same State but through any other State or any Territory or the District of Columbia or any foreign country."

The Act also defines the term "affecting commerce" (§2 (7)):

> "The term 'affecting commerce' means in commerce, or burdening or obstructing commerce or the free flow of commerce, or having led or tending to lead to a labor dispute burdening or obstructing commerce or the free flow of commerce."

This definition is one of exclusion as well as inclusion. The grant of authority to the Board does not purport to extend to the relationship between all industrial employees and employers. Its terms do not impose collective bargaining upon all industry regardless of effects upon interstate or foreign commerce. It purports to reach only what may be deemed to burden or obstruct that commerce and, thus qualified, it must be construed as contemplating the exercise of control within constitutional bounds. It is a familiar principle that acts which directly burden or obstruct interstate or foreign commerce, or its free flow, are within the reach of the congressional power. Acts having that effect are not rendered immune because they grow out of labor disputes. It is the effect upon commerce, not the source of the injury, which is the criterion. Whether or not particular action does affect commerce in such a close and intimate fashion as to be subject to federal control, and hence to lie within the authority conferred upon the Board, is left by the statute to be determined as individual cases arise. We are thus to inquire whether in the instant case the constitutional boundary has been passed.

Second. The unfair labor practices in question.—The unfair labor practices found by the Board are those defined in §8, subdivisions (1) and (3). These provide:

> Sec. 8. It shall be an unfair labor practice for an employer—
>
> "(1) To interfere with, restrain, or coerce employees in the exercise of the rights guaranteed in section 7."
>
> "(3) By discrimination in regard to hire or tenure of employment or any term or condition of employment to encourage or discourage membership in any labor organization: . . ."

Section 8, subdivision (1), refers to §7, which is as follows:

> "Sec. 7. Employees shall have the right to self-organization, to form, join, or assist labor organizations, to bargain collectively through representatives of their own choosing, and to engage in concerted activities, for the purpose of collective bargaining or other mutual aid or protection."

Thus, in its present application, the statute goes no further than to safeguard the right of employees to self-organization and to select representatives of their own choosing for collective bargaining or other mutual protection without restraint or coercion by their employer.

That is a fundamental right. Employees have as clear a right to organize and select their representatives for lawful purposes as the respondent has to organize its business and select its own officers and agents. Discrimination and coercion to prevent the free exercise of the right of employees to self-organization and representation is a proper subject for condemnation by competent legislative authority. Long ago we stated the reason for labor organizations. We said that they were organized out of the necessities of the situation; that a single employee was helpless in dealing with an employer; that he was dependent ordinarily on his daily wage for the maintenance of himself and family; that if the employer refused to pay him the wages that he thought fair, he was nevertheless unable to leave the employ and resist arbitrary and unfair treatment; that union was essential to give laborers opportunity to deal on an equality with their employer. . . .

Third. The application of the Act to employees engaged in production.—The principle involved. — Respondent says that whatever may be said of employees engaged in interstate commerce, the industrial relations and activities in the manufacturing department of respondent's enterprise are not subject to federal regulation. The argument rests upon the proposition that manufacturing in itself is not commerce.

The various parts of respondent's enterprise are described as interdependent and as thus involving "a great movement of iron ore, coal and limestone along well-defined paths to the steel mills, thence through them, and thence in the form of steel products into the consuming centers of the country — a definite and well-understood course of business." It is urged that these activities constitute a "stream" or "flow" of commerce, of which the Aliquippa manufacturing plant is the focal point, and that industrial strife at that point would cripple the entire movement.

. . . [But] we do not find it necessary to determine whether these features of defendant's business dispose of the asserted analogy to the "stream of commerce" cases. The instances in which that metaphor has been used are but particular, and not exclusive, illustrations of the protective power which the Government invokes in support of the present Act. The congressional authority to protect interstate commerce from burdens and obstructions is not limited to transactions which can be deemed to be an essential part of a "flow" of interstate or foreign commerce. Burdens and obstructions may be due to injurious action springing from other sources. The fundamental principle is that the power to regulate commerce is the power to enact "all appropriate legislation" for "its protection and advancement"; to adopt measures "to promote its growth and insure its safety"; "to foster, protect, control and restrain." That power is plenary and may be exerted to protect interstate commerce "no matter what the source of the dangers which threaten it." Although activities may be intrastate in character when separately considered, if they have such a close and substantial relation to interstate commerce that their control is essential or appropriate to protect that commerce from burdens and obstructions, Congress cannot be denied the power to exercise that control. Undoubtedly the scope of this power must be considered in the light of our dual system of government and may not be extended so as to embrace effects upon interstate commerce so indirect and remote that to embrace them, in view of our complex society, would effectually obliterate the distinction between what is national and what is local and create a completely centralized government. The question is necessarily one of degree. . . .

The close and intimate effect which brings the subject within the reach of federal power may be due to activities in relation to productive industry although the industry when separately viewed is local. This has been abundantly illustrated in the application of the federal Anti-Trust Act. . . .

Upon the same principle, the Anti-Trust Act has been applied to the conduct of employees engaged in production. . . . The Court ruled that while the mere reduction in the supply of an article to be shipped in interstate commerce by the illegal or tortious prevention of its manufacture or production is ordinarily an indirect and remote obstruction to that commerce, nevertheless when the "intent of those unlawfully preventing the manufacture or production is shown to be to restrain or control the supply entering and moving in interstate commerce, or the price of it in interstate markets, their action is a direct violation of the Anti-Trust Act." And the existence of that intent may be a necessary inference from proof of the direct and substantial effect produced by the employees' conduct.

It is thus apparent that the fact that the employees here concerned were engaged in production is not determinative. The question remains as to the effect upon interstate commerce of the labor practice involved.

Fourth. Effects of the unfair labor practice in respondent's enterprise. — Giving full weight to respondent's contention with respect to a break in the complete continuity of the "stream of commerce" by reason of respondent's manufacturing operations, the fact remains that the stoppage of those operations by industrial strife would have a most serious effect upon interstate commerce. In view of respondent's far-flung activities, it is idle to say that the effect would be indirect or remote. It is obvious that it would be immediate and might be catastrophic. We are asked to shut our eyes to the plainest facts of our national life and to deal with the question of direct and indirect effects in an intellectual vacuum. . . . When industries organize themselves on a national scale, making their relation to interstate commerce the dominant factor in their activities, how can it be maintained that their industrial labor relations constitute a forbidden field into which Congress may not enter when it is necessary to protect interstate commerce from the paralyzing consequences of industrial war? We have often said that interstate commerce itself is a practical conception. It is equally true that interferences with that commerce must be appraised by a judgment that does not ignore actual experience.

Experience has abundantly demonstrated that the recognition of the right of employees to self-organization and to have representatives of their own choosing for the purpose of collective bargaining is often an essential condition of industrial peace. Refusal to confer and negotiate has been one of the most prolific causes of strife.

The steel industry is one of the great basic industries of the United States, with ramifying activities affecting interstate commerce at every point. The Government aptly refers to the steel strike of 1919–1920 with its far-reaching consequences. The fact that there appears to have been no major disturbance in that industry in the more recent period did not dispose of the possibilities of future and like dangers to interstate commerce which Congress was entitled to foresee and to exercise its protective power to forestall. It is not necessary again to detail the facts as to respondent's enterprise. Instead of being beyond the pale, we think that it presents in a most striking way the close and intimate relation which a manufacturing industry may have to interstate commerce and we have no doubt that Congress had constitutional authority to safeguard the right of respondent's employees to self-organization and freedom in the choice of representatives for collective bargaining.

UNITED STATES v. DARBY

312 U.S. 100 (1940)

Opinion: Stone, joined by Hughes, Roberts, Black, Reed, Frankfurter, Douglas, Murphy

MR. JUSTICE STONE *delivered the opinion of the Court.*

The two principal questions raised by the record in this case are, first, whether Congress has constitutional power to prohibit the shipment in interstate commerce of lumber manufactured by employees whose wages are less than a prescribed minimum or whose weekly hours of labor at that wage are greater than a prescribed maximum, and, second, whether it has power to prohibit the employment of workmen in the production of goods "for interstate commerce" at other than prescribed wages and hours....

The Fair Labor Standards Act set up a comprehensive legislative scheme for preventing the shipment in interstate commerce of certain products and commodities produced in the United States under labor conditions as respects wages and hours which fail to conform to standards set up by the Act.

Section 15 of the statute prohibits certain specified acts and §16 (a) punishes willful violation of it by a fine of not more than $10,000 and punishes each conviction after the first by imprisonment of not more than six months or by the specified fine or both. Section 15 (1) makes unlawful the shipment in interstate commerce of any goods "in the production of which any employee was employed in violation of section 6 or section 7," which provide, among other things, that during the first year of operation of the Act a minimum wage of 25 cents per hour shall be paid to employees "engaged in [interstate] commerce or the production of goods for [interstate] commerce," and that the maximum hours of employment for employees "engaged in commerce or the production of goods for commerce" without increased compensation for overtime, shall be forty-four hours a week.

There are numerous counts charging appellee with the shipment in interstate commerce from Georgia to points outside the state of lumber in the production of which, for interstate commerce, appellee has employed workmen at less than the prescribed minimum wage or more than the prescribed maximum hours without payment to them of any wage for overtime....

The demurrer, so far as now relevant to the appeal, challenged the validity of the Fair Labor Standards Act under the Commerce Clause and the Fifth and Tenth Amendments. The district court quashed the indictment in its entirety upon the broad grounds that the Act, which it interpreted as a regulation of manufacture within the states, is unconstitutional. It declared that manufacture is not interstate commerce and that the regulation by the Fair Labor Standards Act of wages and hours of employment of those engaged in the manufacture of goods which it is intended at the time of production "may or will be" after production "sold in interstate commerce in part or in whole" is not within the congressional power to regulate interstate commerce.

While manufacture is not of itself interstate commerce, the shipment of manufactured goods interstate is such commerce and the prohibition of such shipment by Congress is indubitably a regulation of the commerce. The power to regulate commerce is the power "to prescribe the rule by which commerce is governed." It extends not only to those regulations which aid, foster and protect the commerce, but embraces those which prohibit it. It is conceded that the power of Congress to prohibit transportation in interstate commerce includes noxious articles, stolen articles, kidnapped persons, and articles such as intoxicating liquor or convict made goods, traffic in which is forbidden or restricted by the laws of the state of destination.

But it is said that the present prohibition falls within the scope of none of these categories; that . . . under the guise of a regulation of interstate commerce, it undertakes to regulate wages and hours within the state contrary to the policy of the state which has elected to leave them unregulated.

The power of Congress over interstate commerce "is complete in itself, may be exercised to its utmost extent, and acknowledges no limitations other than are prescribed in the Constitution." That power can neither be enlarged nor diminished by the exercise or non-exercise of state power. Congress, following its own conception of public policy concerning the restrictions which may appropriately be imposed on interstate commerce, is free to exclude from the commerce articles whose use in the states for which they are destined it may conceive to be injurious to the public health, morals or welfare, even though the state has not sought to regulate their use.

Such regulation is not a forbidden invasion of state power merely because either its motive or its consequence is to restrict the use of articles of commerce within the states of destination; and is not prohibited unless by other Constitutional provisions. It is no objection to the assertion of the power to regulate interstate commerce that its exercise is attended by the same incidents which attend the exercise of the police power of the states.

In the more than a century which has elapsed since the decision of *Gibbons v. Ogden*, these principles of constitutional interpretation have been so long and repeatedly recognized by this Court as applicable to the Commerce Clause, that there would be little occasion for repeating them now were it not for the decision of this Court twenty-two years ago in *Hammer v. Dagenhart*. In that case it was held by a bare majority of the Court over the powerful and now classic dissent of Mr. Justice Holmes setting forth the fundamental issues involved, that Congress was without power to exclude the products of child labor from interstate commerce. The reasoning and conclusion of the Court's opinion there cannot be reconciled with the conclusion which we have reached, that the power of Congress under the Commerce Clause is plenary to exclude any article from interstate commerce subject only to the specific prohibitions of the Constitution.

Hammer v. Dagenhart has not been followed. The distinction on which the decision was rested that Congressional power to prohibit interstate commerce is limited to articles which in themselves have some harmful or deleterious property — a distinction which was novel when made and unsupported by any provision of the Constitution — has long since been abandoned. . . . The conclusion is inescapable that *Hammer v. Dagenhart* was a departure from the principles which have prevailed in the interpretation of the Commerce Clause both before and since the decision and that such vitality, as a precedent, as it then had has long since been exhausted. It should be and now is overruled.

The power of Congress over interstate commerce is not confined to the regulation of commerce among the states. It extends to those activities intrastate which so affect interstate commerce or the exercise of the power of Congress over it as to make regulation of them appropriate means to the attainment of a legitimate end, the exercise of the granted power of Congress to regulate interstate commerce.

In the absence of Congressional legislation on the subject state laws which are not regulations of the commerce itself or its instrumentalities are not forbidden even though they affect interstate commerce.

But it does not follow that Congress may not by appropriate legislation regulate intrastate activities where they have a substantial effect on interstate commerce. A recent example is the National Labor Relations Act for the regulation of employer and employee relations in industries in which strikes, induced by unfair labor practices named in the Act, tend to disturb or obstruct interstate commerce. But long before the adoption of the National Labor

Relations Act this Court had many times held that the power of Congress to regulate interstate commerce extends to the regulation through legislative action of activities intrastate which have a substantial effect on the commerce or the exercise of the Congressional power over it.

Congress, having by the present Act adopted the policy of excluding from interstate commerce all goods produced for the commerce which do not conform to the specified labor standards, it may choose the means reasonably adapted to the attainment of the permitted end, even though they involve control of intrastate activities. Such legislation has often been sustained with respect to powers, other than the commerce power granted to the national government, when the means chosen, although not themselves within the granted power, were nevertheless deemed appropriate aids to the accomplishment of some purpose within an admitted power of the national government. A familiar like exercise of power is the regulation of intrastate transactions which are so commingled with or related to interstate commerce that all must be regulated if the interstate commerce is to be effectively controlled. Similarly Congress may require inspection and preventive treatment of all cattle in a disease infected area in order to prevent shipment in interstate commerce of some of the cattle without the treatment. It may prohibit the removal, at destination, of labels required by the Pure Food & Drugs Act to be affixed to articles transported in interstate commerce. And we have recently held that Congress in the exercise of its power to require inspection and grading of tobacco shipped in interstate commerce may compel such inspection and grading of all tobacco sold at local auction rooms from which a substantial part but not all of the tobacco sold is shipped in interstate commerce.

The Sherman Act and the National Labor Relations Act are familiar examples of the exertion of the commerce power to prohibit or control activities wholly intrastate because of their effect on interstate commerce.

The means adopted by §15(a)(2) for the protection of interstate commerce by the suppression of the production of the condemned goods for interstate commerce is so related to the commerce and so affects it as to be within the reach of the commerce power. Congress, to attain its objective in the suppression of nationwide competition in interstate commerce by goods produced under substandard labor conditions, has made no distinction as to the volume or amount of shipments in the commerce or of production for commerce by any particular shipper or producer. It recognized that in present day industry, competition by a small part may affect the whole and that the total effect of the competition of many small producers may be great....

Our conclusion is unaffected by the Tenth Amendment which provides "The powers not delegated to the United States by the Constitution, nor prohibited by it to the States, are reserved to the States respectively, or to the people." The amendment states but a truism that all is retained which has not been surrendered. There is nothing in the history of its adoption to suggest that it was more than declaratory of the relationship between the national and state governments as it had been established by the Constitution before the amendment or that its purpose was other than to allay fears that the new national government might seek to exercise powers not granted, and that the states might not be able to exercise fully their reserved powers.

From the beginning and for many years the amendment has been construed as not depriving the national government of authority to resort to all means for the exercise of a granted power which are appropriate and plainly adapted to the permitted end. Whatever doubts may have arisen of the soundness of that conclusion, they have been put at rest by the decisions under the Sherman Act and the National Labor Relations Act which we have cited.

WICKARD v. FILBURN

317 U.S. 111 (1942)

Opinion: Jackson, joined by Stone, Roberts, Black, Reed, Frankfurter, Douglas, Murphy

As you will see, Wickard v. Filburn *explains that Congress may regulate any economic activity that, in the aggregate, would "substantially affect" interstate commerce. If this proposition stretches so far as to cover a farmer who grows wheat for his own use, then is there any real limit on the commerce power?*

One puzzle that arises from the expanded commerce power concerns the meaning and relevance of the Tenth Amendment to the Constitution. That amendment claims that the "powers not delegated to the United States by the Constitution, nor prohibited by it to the States, are reserved to the States respectively, or to the people." But are there any powers left to the states if the Commerce Clause grants such expansive powers to Congress? What should we make of U.S. Supreme Court Chief Justice Harlan F. Stone's claim in United States v. Darby *that the Tenth Amendment "states but a truism"? Even if the Court is right to overturn* Hammer v. Dagenhart, *does the Constitution nonetheless articulate some positive principle of state sovereignty?*

MR. JUSTICE JACKSON *delivered the opinion of the Court.*

The appellee for many years past has owned and operated a small farm in Montgomery County, Ohio, maintaining a herd of dairy cattle, selling milk, raising poultry, and selling poultry and eggs. It has been his practice to raise a small acreage of winter wheat, sown in the Fall and harvested in the following July; to sell a portion of the crop; to feed part to poultry and livestock on the farm, some of which is sold; to use some in making flour for home consumption; and to keep the rest for the following seeding. The intended disposition of the crop here involved has not been expressly stated.

In July of 1940, pursuant to the Agricultural Adjustment Act of 1938, as then amended, there were established for the appellee's 1941 crop a wheat acreage allotment of 11.1 acres and a normal yield of 20.1 bushels of wheat an acre. He was given notice of such allotment in July of 1940, before the Fall planting of his 1941 crop of wheat, and again in July of 1941, before it was harvested. He sowed, however, 23 acres, and harvested from his 11.9 acres of excess acreage 239 bushels, which under the terms of the Act as amended on May 26, 1941, constituted farm marketing excess, subject to a penalty of 49 cents a bushel, or $117.11 in all. . . .

The general scheme of the Agricultural Adjustment Act of 1938 as related to wheat is to control the volume moving in interstate and foreign commerce in order to avoid surpluses and shortages and the consequent abnormally low or high wheat prices and obstructions to commerce.

Within prescribed limits and by prescribed standards the Secretary of Agriculture is directed to ascertain and proclaim each year a national acreage allotment for the next crop of wheat, which is then apportioned to the states and their counties, and is eventually broken up into allotments for individual farms. Loans and payments to wheat farmers are authorized in stated circumstances.

It is urged that under the Commerce Clause of the Constitution, Article I, §8, clause 3, Congress does not possess the power it has in this instance sought to exercise. The question would merit little consideration since our decision in *United States v. Darby*, sustaining the federal power to regulate production of goods for commerce, except for the fact that this Act extends federal regulation to production not intended in any part for commerce but wholly for consumption on the farm. The Act includes a definition of "market" and its derivatives, so that as related to wheat, in addition to its conventional meaning, it also means to dispose of "by feeding (in any form) to poultry or livestock which, or the products of which, are sold, bartered, or exchanged, or to be so disposed of." Hence, marketing quotas not only embrace all that may be sold without penalty but also what may be consumed on the premises. Wheat produced on excess acreage is designated as "available for marketing" as so defined, and the penalty is imposed thereon. Penalties do not depend upon whether any part of the wheat, either within or without the quota, is sold or intended to be sold. The sum of this is that the Federal Government fixes a quota including all that the farmer may harvest for sale or for his own farm needs, and declares that wheat produced on excess acreage may neither be disposed of nor used except upon payment of the penalty, or except it is stored as required by the Act or delivered to the Secretary of Agriculture.

Appellee says that this is a regulation of production and consumption of wheat. Such activities are, he urges, beyond the reach of Congressional power under the Commerce Clause, since they are local in character, and their effects upon interstate commerce are at most "indirect." In answer the Government argues that the statute regulates neither production nor consumption, but only marketing; and, in the alternative, that if the Act does go beyond the regulation of marketing it is sustainable as a "necessary and proper" implementation of the power of Congress over interstate commerce.

The Government's concern lest the Act be held to be a regulation of production or consumption, rather than of marketing, is attributable to a few dicta and decisions of this Court which might be understood to lay it down that activities such as "production," "manufacturing," and "mining" are strictly "local" and, except in special circumstances which are not present here, cannot be regulated under the commerce power because their effects upon interstate commerce are, as matter of law, only "indirect." Even today, when this power has been held to have great latitude, there is no decision of this Court that such activities may be regulated where no part of the product is intended for interstate commerce or intermingled with the subjects thereof. We believe that a review of the course of decision under the Commerce Clause will make plain, however, that questions of the power of Congress are not to be decided by reference to any formula which would give controlling force to nomenclature such as "production" and "indirect" and foreclose consideration of the actual effects of the activity in question upon interstate commerce.

The Court's recognition of the relevance of the economic effects in the application of the Commerce Clause . . . has made the mechanical application of legal formulas no longer feasible. Once an economic measure of the reach of the power granted to Congress in the Commerce Clause is accepted, questions of federal power cannot be decided simply by finding the activity in question to be "production," nor can consideration of its economic effects be foreclosed by calling them "indirect." The present Chief Justice has said in summary of the present state of the law: "The commerce power is not confined in its exercise to the regulation of commerce among the states. It extends to those activities intrastate which so affect interstate commerce, or the exertion of the power of Congress over it, as to make regulation of them appropriate means to the attainment of a legitimate end, the effective execution of the granted power to regulate interstate commerce. . . . The power of Congress over interstate commerce is plenary and complete in itself, may be exercised to its utmost extent, and acknowledges no limitations other than are prescribed in the Constitution. . . . It follows that no form of state activity can constitutionally thwart the regulatory power granted by the Commerce Clause to Congress. Hence the reach of that power extends to those intrastate activities which in a substantial way interfere with or obstruct the exercise of the granted power."

Whether the subject of the regulation in question was "production," "consumption," or "marketing" is, therefore, not material for purposes of deciding the question of federal power before us.... [E]ven if appellee's activity be local and though it may not be regarded as commerce, it may still, whatever its nature, be reached by Congress if it exerts a substantial economic effect on interstate commerce, and this irrespective of whether such effect is what might at some earlier time have been defined as "direct" or "indirect."

The wheat industry has been a problem industry for some years. Largely as a result of increased foreign production and import restrictions, annual exports of wheat and flour from the United States during the ten-year period ending in 1940 averaged less than 10 per cent of total production, while during the 1920's they averaged more than 25 per cent. The decline in the export trade has left a large surplus in production which, in connection with an abnormally large supply of wheat and other grains in recent years, caused congestion in a number of markets; tied up railroad cars; and caused elevators in some instances to turn away grains, and railroads to institute embargoes to prevent further congestion.

In the absence of regulation, the price of wheat in the United States would be much affected by world conditions. During 1941, producers who cooperated with the Agricultural Adjustment program received an average price on the farm of about $1.16 a bushel, as compared with the world market price of 40 cents a bushel.

Differences in farming conditions, however, make these benefits mean different things to different wheat growers. . . . Except in regions of large-scale production, wheat is usually grown in rotation with other crops; for a nurse crop for grass seeding; and as a cover crop to prevent soil erosion and leaching. Some is sold, some kept for seed, and a percentage of the total production much larger than in areas of specialization is consumed on the farm and grown for such purpose. Such farmers, while growing some wheat, may even find the balance of their interest on the consumer's side.

The effect of consumption of homegrown wheat on interstate commerce is due to the fact that it constitutes the most variable factor in the disappearance of the wheat crop. Consumption on the farm where grown appears to vary in an amount

Special Collections and Archives, Georgia State University Library

The Heart of Atlanta Motel, whose practice of turning away African-American customers was held to violate the Civil Rights Act of 1964. The Supreme Court ruled that the Commerce Clause of the Constitution permitted the 1964 law.

greater than 20 per cent of average production. The total amount of wheat consumed as food varies but relatively little, and use as seed is relatively constant.

The maintenance by government regulation of a price for wheat undoubtedly can be accomplished as effectively by sustaining or increasing the demand as by limiting the supply. The effect of the statute before us is to restrict the amount which may be produced for market and the extent as well to which one may forestall resort to the market by producing to meet his own needs. That appellee's own contribution to the demand for wheat may be trivial by itself is not enough to remove him from the scope of federal regulation where, as here, his contribution, taken together with that of many others similarly situated, is far from trivial.

It is well established by decisions of this Court that the power to regulate commerce includes the power to regulate the prices at which commodities in that commerce are dealt in and practices affecting such prices. One of the primary purposes of the Act in question was to increase the market price of wheat, and to that end to limit the volume thereof that could affect the market. It can hardly be denied that a factor of such volume and variability as home-consumed wheat would have a substantial influence on price and market conditions. This may arise because being in marketable condition such wheat overhangs the market and, if induced by rising prices, tends to flow into the market and check price increases. But if we assume that it is never marketed, it supplies a need of the man who grew it which would otherwise be reflected by purchases in the open market. Home-grown wheat in this sense competes with wheat in commerce. The stimulation of commerce is a use of the regulatory function quite as definitely as prohibitions or restrictions thereon. This record leaves us in no doubt that Congress may properly have considered that wheat consumed on the farm where grown, if wholly outside the scheme of regulation, would have a substantial effect in defeating and obstructing its purpose to stimulate trade therein at increased prices.

HEART OF ATLANTA MOTEL, INC. v. UNITED STATES

379 U.S. 241 (1964)

Opinion: Clark, joined by Warren, Douglas, Harlan, Brennan, Stewart, White, Goldberg
Concurrence: Black
Concurrence: Douglas
Concurrence: Goldberg

The Civil Rights movement of the 1950s and 1960s culminated in one of the nation's most important legislative legacies, the Civil Rights Act of 1964. This law far surpassed earlier legislation in its efforts to root out discrimination by federally funded entities, its allocation of meaningful enforcement power to the Justice Department, and its nationwide prohibition against segregating public accommodations such as restaurants, hotels, and movie theaters.

After reviewing the various sources of congressional power laid out in the previous section, you might guess that this legislation finds its roots in the power to enforce the equal protection provision of the Fourteenth Amendment. But in the Civil Rights Cases *(1883), the Court ruled that the guarantee of equal protection applies only to state action, not to private conduct by business owners. Not wanting to disturb this 80-year-old precedent, the Court instead upheld the 1964 law on Commerce Clause grounds. In* Heart of Atlanta Motel v. United States *and* Katzenbach v. McClung, *the Supreme Court ruled that racial segregation imposes "a substantial and harmful effect" on interstate commerce, and thus Congress has the power to prohibit it. Does this ruling go farther than* United States v. Darby *and* Wickard v. Filburn? *Does it leave any activity to be regulated by the states? Are Commerce Clause grounds the best way to decide the case, or should the Court have instead overturned the* Civil Rights Cases *and found a textual home for this legislation in the Equal Protection Clause?*

MR. JUSTICE CLARK *delivered the opinion of the Court.*

The case comes here on admissions and stipulated facts. Appellant owns and operates the Heart of Atlanta Motel which has 216 rooms available to transient guests. The motel is . . . readily accessible to interstate highways 75 and 85 and state highways 23 and 41. Appellant solicits patronage from outside the State of Georgia through various national advertising media, including magazines of national circulation; it maintains over 50 billboards and highway signs within the State, soliciting patronage for the motel; it accepts convention trade from outside Georgia and approximately 75% of its registered guests are from out of State. Prior to passage of the [Civil Rights Act of 1964,] the motel had followed a practice of refusing to rent rooms to Negroes, and it alleged that it intended to continue to do so. In an effort to perpetuate that policy this suit was filed.

Title II of the Act . . . provides that:

> "All persons shall be entitled to the full and equal enjoyment of the goods, services, facilities, privileges, advantages, and accommodations of any place of public accommodation, as defined in this section, without discrimination or segregation on the ground of race, color, religion, or national origin."

There are listed in §201(b) four classes of business establishments, each of which "serves the public" and "is a place of public accommodation" within the meaning of §201(a) "if its operations affect commerce, or if discrimination or segregation by it is supported by State action." The covered establishments are:

> "(1) any inn, hotel, motel, or other establishment which provides lodging to transient guests, other than an establishment located within a building which contains not more than five rooms for rent or hire and which is actually occupied by the proprietor of such establishment as his residence;
>
> "(2) any restaurant, cafeteria . . . [not here involved];
>
> "(3) any motion picture house . . . [not here involved];
>
> "(4) any establishment . . . which is physically located within the premises of any establishment otherwise covered by this subsection, or . . . within the premises of which is physically located any such covered establishment . . . [not here involved]."

Section 201(c) defines the phrase "affect commerce" as applied to the above establishments. It first declares that "any inn, hotel, motel, or other establishment which provides lodging to transient guests" affects commerce per se. Restaurants, cafeterias, etc., in class two affect commerce only if they serve or offer to serve interstate travelers or if a substantial portion of the food which they serve or products which they sell have "moved in commerce." Motion picture houses and other places listed in class three affect commerce if they customarily present films, performances, etc., "which move in commerce." And the establishments listed in class four affect commerce if they are within, or include within their own premises, an establishment "the operations of which affect commerce." Private clubs are excepted under certain conditions. See §201(e).

Section 201(d) declares that "discrimination or segregation" is supported by state action when carried on under color of any law, statute, ordinance, regulation or any custom or usage required or enforced by officials of the State or any of its subdivisions.

In addition, §202 affirmatively declares that all persons "shall be entitled to be free, at any establishment or place, from discrimination or segregation of any kind on the ground of race, color, religion, or national origin, if such discrimination or segregation is or purports to be required by any law, statute, ordinance, regulation, rule, or order of a State or any agency or political subdivision thereof."

Finally, §203 prohibits the withholding or denial, etc., of any right or privilege secured by §201 and §202 or the intimidation, threatening or coercion of any person with the purpose of interfering with any such right or the punishing, etc., of any person for exercising or attempting to exercise any such right.

The remaining sections of the Title are remedial ones for violations of any of the previous sections. . . .

It is admitted that the operation of the motel brings it within the provisions of §201 (a) of the Act and that appellant refused to provide lodging for transient Negroes because of their race or color and that it intends to continue that policy unless restrained.

The sole question posed is, therefore, the constitutionality of the Civil Rights Act of 1964 as applied to these facts. The legislative history of the Act indicates that Congress based the Act on §5 and the Equal Protection Clause of the Fourteenth Amendment as well as its power to regulate interstate commerce under Art. I, §8, cl. 3, of the Constitution.

The Senate Commerce Committee made it quite clear that the fundamental object of Title II was to vindicate "the deprivation of personal dignity that surely accompanies denials of equal access to public establishments." At the same time, however, it noted that such an objective has been and could be readily achieved "by congressional action based on the commerce power of the Constitution." Our study of the legislative record, made in the light of prior cases, has brought us to the conclusion that Congress possessed ample power in this regard, and we have therefore not considered the other grounds relied upon. This is not to say that the remaining authority upon which it acted was not adequate, a question upon which we do not pass, but merely that since the commerce power is sufficient for our decision here we have considered it alone. Nor is §201(d) or §202, having to do with state action, involved here and we do not pass upon either of those sections.

In light of our ground for decision, it might be well at the outset to discuss the *Civil Rights Cases*, supra, which declared provisions of the Civil Rights Act of 1875 unconstitutional. We think that decision inapposite, and without precedential value in determining the constitutionality of the present Act. Unlike Title II of the present legislation, the 1875 Act broadly proscribed discrimination in "inns, public conveyances on land or water, theaters, and other places of public amusement," without limiting the categories of affected businesses to those impinging upon interstate commerce. In contrast, the applicability of Title II is carefully limited to enterprises having a direct and substantial relation to the interstate flow of goods and people, except where state action is involved. Further, the fact that certain kinds of businesses may not in 1875 have been sufficiently involved in interstate commerce to warrant bringing them within the ambit of the commerce power is not necessarily dispositive of the same question today. Our populace had not reached its present mobility, nor were facilities, goods and services circulating as readily in interstate commerce as they are today. . . . Finally, there is language in the *Civil Rights Cases* which indicates that the Court did not fully consider whether the 1875 Act could be sustained as an exercise of the commerce power.

While the Act as adopted carried no congressional findings the record of its passage through each house is replete with evidence of the burdens that discrimination by race or color places upon interstate commerce. This testimony included the fact that our people have become increasingly mobile with millions of people of all races traveling from State to State; that Negroes in particular have been the subject of discrimination in transient accommodations, having to travel great distances to secure the same; that often they have been unable to obtain accommodations and have had to call upon friends to put them up overnight, and that these conditions had become so acute as to require the listing of available lodging for Negroes in a special guidebook which was itself "dramatic testimony to the difficulties" Negroes encounter in travel.... This testimony indicated a qualitative as well as quantitative effect on interstate travel by Negroes. The former was the obvious impairment of the Negro traveler's pleasure and convenience that resulted when he continually was uncertain of finding lodging. As for the latter, there was evidence that this uncertainty stemming from racial discrimination had the effect of discouraging travel on the part of a substantial portion of the Negro community. . . . We shall not burden this opinion with further details since the voluminous testimony presents overwhelming evidence that discrimination by hotels and motels impedes interstate travel.

The power of Congress to deal with these obstructions depends on the meaning of the Commerce Clause. . . . [T]he determinative test of the exercise of power by the Congress under the Commerce Clause is simply whether the activity sought to be regulated is "commerce which concerns more States than one" and has a real and substantial relation to the national interest. Let us now turn to this facet of the problem.

[I]n 1917 in *Caminetti v. United States*, Mr. Justice Day held for the Court:

> "The transportation of passengers in interstate commerce, it has long been settled, is within the regulatory power of Congress, under the Commerce Clause of the Constitution, and the authority of Congress to keep the channels of interstate commerce free from immoral and injurious uses has been frequently sustained, and is no longer open to question."

The same interest in protecting interstate commerce which led Congress to deal with segregation in interstate carriers and the white-slave traffic has prompted it to extend the exercise of its power to gambling, to criminal enterprises, to deceptive practices in the sale of products, to fraudulent security transactions, to misbranding of drugs, to wages and hours, *United States v. Darby*, to members of labor unions, to crop control, to discrimination against shippers, to the protection of small business from injurious price cutting, to resale price maintenance, to professional football, and to racial discrimination by owners and managers of terminal restaurants.

That Congress was legislating against moral wrongs in many of these areas rendered its enactments no less valid. In framing Title II of this Act Congress was also dealing with what it considered a moral problem. But that fact does not detract from the overwhelming evidence of the disruptive effect that racial discrimination has had on commercial intercourse. It was this burden which empowered Congress to enact appropriate legislation, and, given this basis for the exercise of its power, Congress was not restricted by the fact that the particular obstruction to interstate commerce with which it was dealing was also deemed a moral and social wrong.

It is said that the operation of the motel here is of a purely local character. But, assuming this to be true, "if it is interstate commerce that feels the pinch, it does not matter how local the operation which applies the squeeze." As Chief Justice Stone put it in *United States v. Darby*:

> "The power of Congress over interstate commerce is not confined to the regulation of commerce among the states. It extends to those activities intrastate which so affect interstate commerce or the exercise of the power of Congress over it as to make regulation of them appropriate means to the attainment of a legitimate end, the exercise of the granted power of Congress to regulate interstate commerce."

Thus the power of Congress to promote interstate commerce also includes the power to regulate the local incidents thereof, including local activities in both the States of origin and destination, which might have a substantial and harmful effect upon that commerce. One need only examine the evidence which we have discussed above to see Congress may — as it has — prohibit racial discrimination by motels serving travelers, however "local" their operations may appear.

We, therefore, conclude that the action of the Congress in the adoption of the Act as applied here to a motel which concededly serves interstate travelers is within the power granted it by the Commerce Clause of the Constitution, as interpreted by this Court for 140 years. It may be argued that Congress could have pursued other methods to eliminate the obstructions it found in interstate commerce caused by racial discrimination. But this is a matter of policy that rests entirely with the Congress not with the courts. How obstructions in commerce may be removed — what means are to be employed — is within the sound and exclusive discretion of the Congress. It is subject only to one caveat — that the means chosen by it must be reasonably adapted to the end permitted by the Constitution. We cannot say that its choice here was not so adapted. The Constitution requires no more.

APPENDIX TO OPINION OF THE COURT

Title II — Injunctive Relief Against Discrimination in Places of Public Accommodation

"SEC. 201. (a) All persons shall be entitled to the full and equal enjoyment of the goods, services, facilities, privileges, advantages, and accommodations of any place of public accommodation, as defined in this section, without discrimination or segregation on the ground of race, color, religion, or national origin.

"(b) Each of the following establishments which serves the public is a place of public accommodation within the meaning of this title if its operations affect commerce, or if discrimination or segregation by it is supported by State action:

"(1) any inn, hotel, motel, or other establishment which provides lodging to transient guests, other than an establishment located within a building which contains not more than five rooms for rent or hire and which is actually occupied by the proprietor of such establishment as his residence;

"(2) any restaurant, cafeteria, lunchroom, lunch counter, soda fountain, or other facility principally engaged in selling food for consumption on the premises, including, but not limited to, any such facility located on the premises of any retail establishment; or any gasoline station;

"(3) any motion picture house, theater, concert hall, sports arena, stadium or other place of exhibition or entertainment; and

"(4) any establishment (A)(i) which is physically located within the premises of any establishment otherwise covered by this subsection, or (ii) within the premises of which is physically located any such covered establishment, and (B) which holds itself out as serving patrons of such covered establishment.

"(c) The operations of an establishment affect commerce within the meaning of this title if (1) it is one of the establishments described in paragraph (1) of subsection (b); (2) in the case of an establishment described in paragraph (2) of subsection (b), it serves or offers to serve interstate travelers or a substantial portion of the food which it serves, or gasoline or other products which it sells, has moved in commerce; (3) in the case of an establishment described in paragraph (3) of subsection (b), it customarily presents films, performances, athletic teams, exhibitions, or other sources of entertainment which move in commerce; and (4) in the case of an establishment described in paragraph (4) of subsection (b), it is physically located within the premises of, or there is physically located within its premises, an establishment the operations of which affect commerce within the meaning of this subsection. For purposes of this section, 'commerce' means travel, trade, traffic, commerce, transportation, or communication among the several States, or between the District of Columbia and any State, or between any foreign country or any territory or possession and any State or the District of Columbia, or between points in the same State but through any other State or the District of Columbia or a foreign country.

"(d) Discrimination or segregation by an establishment is supported by State action within the meaning of this title if such discrimination or segregation (1) is carried on under color of any law, statute, ordinance, or regulation; or (2) is carried on under color of any custom or usage required or enforced by officials of the State or political subdivision thereof; or (3) is required by action of the State or political subdivision thereof.

"(e) The provisions of this title shall not apply to a private club or other establishment not in fact open to the public, except to the extent that the facilities of such establishment are made available to the customers or patrons of an establishment within the scope of subsection (b).

"SEC. 202. All persons shall be entitled to be free, at any establishment or place, from discrimination or segregation of any kind on the ground of race, color, religion, or national origin, if such discrimination or segregation is or purports to be required by any law, statute, ordinance, regulation, rule, or order of a State or any agency or political subdivision thereof.

"SEC. 203. No person shall (a) withhold, deny, or attempt to withhold or deny, or deprive or attempt to deprive, any person of any right or privilege secured by section 201 or 202, or (b) intimidate, threaten, or coerce, or attempt to intimidate, threaten, or coerce any person with the purpose of interfering with any right or privilege secured by section 201 or 202, or (c) punish or attempt to punish any person for exercising or attempting to exercise any right or privilege secured by section 201 or 202.

"SEC. 204. (a) Whenever any person has engaged or there are reasonable grounds to believe that any person is about to engage in any act or practice prohibited by section 203, a civil action for preventive relief, including an application for a permanent or temporary injunction, restraining order, or other order, may be instituted by the person aggrieved and, upon timely application, the court may, in its discretion, permit the Attorney General to intervene in such civil action if he certifies that the case is of general public importance. Upon application by the complainant and in such circumstances as the court may deem just, the court may appoint an attorney for such complainant and may authorize the commencement of the civil action without the payment of fees, costs, or security.

"(b) In any action commenced pursuant to this title, the court, in its discretion, may allow the prevailing party, other than the United States, a reasonable attorney's fee as part of the costs, and the United States shall be liable for costs the same as a private person.

"(c) In the case of an alleged act or practice prohibited by this title which occurs in a State, or political subdivision of a State, which has a State or local law prohibiting such act or practice and establishing or authorizing a State or local authority to grant or seek relief from such practice or to institute criminal proceedings with respect thereto upon receiving notice thereof, no civil action may be brought under subsection (a) before the expiration of thirty days after written notice of such alleged act or practice has been given to the appropriate State or local authority by registered mail or in person, provided that the court may stay proceedings in such civil action pending the termination of State or local enforcement proceedings.

"(d) In the case of an alleged act or practice prohibited by this title which occurs in a State, or political subdivision of a State, which has no State or local law prohibiting such act or practice, a civil action may be brought under subsection (a): Provided, That the court may refer the matter to the Community Relations Service established by title X of this Act for as long as the court believes there is a reasonable possibility of obtaining voluntary compliance, but for not more than sixty days: Provided further, That upon expiration of such sixty-day period, the court may extend such period for an additional period, not to exceed a cumulative total of one hundred and twenty days, if it believes there then exists a reasonable possibility of securing voluntary compliance.

"SEC. 205. The Service is authorized to make a full investigation of any complaint referred to it by the court under section 204(d) and may hold such hearings with respect thereto as may be necessary. The Service shall conduct any hearings with respect to any such complaint in executive session, and shall not release any testimony given therein except by agreement of all parties involved in the complaint with the permission of the court, and the Service shall endeavor to bring about a voluntary settlement between the parties.

"SEC. 206. (a) Whenever the Attorney General has reasonable cause to believe that any person or group of persons is engaged in a pattern or practice of resistance to the full enjoyment of any of the rights secured by this title, and that the pattern or practice is of such a nature and is intended to deny the full exercise of the rights herein described, the Attorney General may bring a civil action in the appropriate district court of the United States by filing with it a complaint (1) signed by him (or in his absence the Acting Attorney General), (2) setting forth facts pertaining to such pattern or practice, and (3) requesting such preventive relief, including an application for a permanent or temporary injunction, restraining order or other order against the person or persons responsible for such pattern or practice, as he deems necessary to insure the full enjoyment of the rights herein described.

"(b) In any such proceeding the Attorney General may file with the clerk of such court a request that a court of three judges be convened to hear and determine the case. Such request by the Attorney General shall be accompanied by a certificate that, in his opinion, the case is of general public importance. A copy of the certificate and request for a three-judge court shall be immediately furnished by such clerk to the chief judge of the circuit (or in his absence, the presiding circuit judge of the circuit) in which the case is pending. Upon receipt of the copy of such request it shall be the duty of the chief judge of the circuit or the presiding circuit judge, as the case may be, to designate immediately three judges in such circuit, of whom at least one shall be a circuit judge and another of whom shall be a district judge of the court in which the proceeding was instituted, to hear and determine such case, and it shall be the duty of the judges so designated to assign the case for hearing at the earliest practicable date, to participate in the hearing and determination thereof, and to cause the case to be in every way expedited. An appeal from the final judgment of such court will lie to the Supreme Court.

"In the event the Attorney General fails to file such a request in any such proceeding, it shall be the duty of the chief judge of the district (or in his absence, the acting chief judge) in which the case is pending immediately to designate a judge in such district to hear and determine the case. In the event that no judge in the district is available to hear and determine the case, the chief judge of the district, or the acting chief judge, as the case may be, shall certify this fact to the chief judge of the circuit (or in his absence, the acting chief judge) who shall then designate a district or circuit judge of the circuit to hear and determine the case.

"It shall be the duty of the judge designated pursuant to this section to assign the case for hearing at the earliest practicable date and to cause the case to be in every way expedited.

"SEC. 207. (a) The district courts of the United States shall have jurisdiction of proceedings instituted pursuant to this title and shall exercise the same without regard to whether the aggrieved party shall have exhausted any administrative or other remedies that may be provided by law.

"(b) The remedies provided in this title shall be the exclusive means of enforcing the rights based on this title, but nothing in this title shall preclude any individual or any State or local agency from asserting any right based on any other Federal or State law not inconsistent with this title, including any statute or ordinance requiring nondiscrimination in public establishments or accommodations, or from pursuing any remedy, civil or criminal, which may be available for the vindication or enforcement of such right."

MR. JUSTICE DOUGLAS, *concurring.*

Though I join the Court's opinions, I am somewhat reluctant here ... to rest solely on the Commerce Clause. My reluctance is not due to any conviction that Congress lacks power to regulate commerce in the interests of human rights. It is rather my belief that the right of people to be free of state action that discriminates against them because of race, like the "right of persons to move freely from State to State" (*Edwards v. California*) "occupies a more protected position in our constitutional system than does the movement of cattle, fruit, steel and coal across state lines." Moreover ... the result reached by the Court is for me much more obvious as a protective measure under the Fourteenth Amendment than under the Commerce Clause. For the former deals with the constitutional status of the individual not with the impact on commerce of local activities or vice versa.

Hence I would prefer to rest on the assertion of legislative power contained in §5 of the Fourteenth Amendment which states: "The Congress shall have power to enforce, by appropriate legislation, the provisions of this article"—a power which the Court concedes was exercised at least in part in this Act.

A decision based on the Fourteenth Amendment would have a more settling effect, making unnecessary litigation over whether a particular restaurant or inn is within the commerce definitions of the Act or whether a particular customer is an interstate traveler. Under my construction, the Act would apply to all customers in all the enumerated places of public accommodation. And that construction would put an end to all obstructionist strategies and finally close one door on a bitter chapter in American history.

I think the Court is correct in concluding that the Act is not founded on the Commerce Clause to the exclusion of the Enforcement Clause of the Fourteenth Amendment.

In determining the reach of an exertion of legislative power, it is customary to read various granted powers together. As stated in *McCulloch v. Maryland*:

> "We admit, as all must admit, that the powers of the government are limited, and that its limits are not to be transcended. But we think the sound construction of the constitution must allow to the national legislature that discretion, with respect to the means by which the powers it confers are to be carried into execution, which will enable that body to perform the high duties assigned to it, in the manner most beneficial to the people. Let the end be legitimate, let it be within the scope of the constitution, and all means which are appropriate, which are plainly adapted to that end, which are not prohibited, but consist with the letter and spirit of the constitution, are constitutional."

The "means" used in the present Act are in my view "appropriate" and "plainly adapted" to the end of enforcing Fourteenth Amendment rights as well as protecting interstate commerce.

Section 201(a) declares in Fourteenth Amendment language the right of equal access:

> "All persons shall be entitled to the full and equal enjoyment of the goods, services, facilities, privileges, advantages, and accommodations of any place of public accommodation, as defined in this section, without discrimination or segregation on the ground of race, color, religion, or national origin."

The rights protected are clearly within the purview of our decisions under the Equal Protection Clause of the Fourteenth Amendment.

"State action"—the key to Fourteenth Amendment guarantees—is defined by §201(d) as follows:

> "Discrimination or segregation by an establishment is supported by State action within the meaning of this title if such discrimination or segregation (1) is carried on under color of any law, statute, ordinance, or regulation; or (2) is carried on under color of any custom or usage required or enforced by officials of the State or political subdivision thereof; or (3) is required by action of the State or political subdivision thereof."

That definition is within our decision of *Shelley v. Kraemer*, for the "discrimination" in the present cases is "enforced by officials of the State," i.e., by the state judiciary under the trespass laws.

Section 202 declares the right of all persons to be free from certain kinds of state action at any public establishment—not just at the previously enumerated places of public accommodation:

> "All persons shall be entitled to be free, at any establishment or place, from discrimination or segregation of any kind on the ground of race, color, religion, or national origin, if such discrimination or segregation is or purports to be required by any law, statute, ordinance,

> regulation, rule, or order of a State or any agency or political subdivision thereof."

Thus the essence of many of the guarantees embodied in the Act are those contained in the Fourteenth Amendment.

The Commerce Clause, to be sure, enters into some of the definitions of "place of public accommodation" in §§201(b) and (c). Thus a "restaurant" is included, §201(b)(2), "if . . . it serves or offers to serve interstate travelers or a substantial portion of the food which it serves . . . has moved in commerce." §201(c)(2). But any "motel" is included "which provides lodging to transient guests, other than an establishment located within a building which contains not more than five rooms for rent or hire and which is actually occupied by the proprietor of such establishment as his residence." §§201(b)(1) and (c)(1). Providing lodging "to transient guests" is not strictly Commerce Clause talk, for the phrase aptly describes any guest — local or interstate.

Thus some of the definitions of "place of public accommodation" in §201(b) are in Commerce Clause language and some are not. Indeed §201(b) is explicitly bifurcated. An establishment "which serves the public is a place of public accommodation," says §201(b), under either of two conditions: first, "if its operations affect commerce," or second, "if discrimination or segregation by it is supported by State action."

The House Report emphasizes these dual bases on which the Act rests — a situation which a minority recognized was being attempted and which it opposed.

Thus while I agree with the Court that Congress in fashioning the present Act used the Commerce Clause to regulate racial segregation, it also used (and properly so) some of its power under §5 of the Fourteenth Amendment.

I repeat what I said earlier, that our decision should be based on the Fourteenth Amendment, thereby putting an end to all obstructionist strategies and allowing every person — whatever his race, creed, or color — to patronize all places of public accommodation without discrimination whether he travels interstate or intrastate.

KATZENBACH v. McCLUNG

379 U.S. 294 (1964)

Opinion: Clark, joined by Warren, Harlan, Brennan, Stewart, White
Concurrence: Douglas
Concurrence: Goldberg
Concurrence: Black

MR. JUSTICE CLARK *delivered the opinion of the Court.*

This case was argued with No. 515, *Heart of Atlanta Motel v. United States*, decided this date, . . . in which we upheld the constitutional validity of Title II of the Civil Rights Act of 1964 against an attack by hotels, motels, and like establishments.

Ollie's Barbecue is a family-owned restaurant in Birmingham, Alabama, specializing in barbecued meats and homemade pies, with a seating capacity of 220 customers. It is located on a state highway 11 blocks from an interstate one and a somewhat greater distance from railroad and bus stations. The restaurant caters to a family and white-collar trade with a take-out service for Negroes. It employs 36 persons, two-thirds of whom are Negroes.

In the 12 months preceding the passage of the Act, the restaurant purchased locally approximately $150,000 worth of food, $69,683 or 46% of which was meat that it bought from a local supplier who had procured it from outside the State. The District Court expressly found that a substantial portion of the food served in the restaurant had moved in interstate commerce. The restaurant has refused to serve Negroes in its dining accommodations since its original opening in 1927, and since July 2, 1964, it has been operating in violation of the Act. . . .

The basic holding in *Heart of Atlanta Motel*, answers many of the contentions made by the appellees. There we outlined the overall purpose and operational plan of Title II and found it a valid exercise of the power to regulate interstate commerce insofar as it requires hotels and motels to serve transients without regard to their race or color. In this case we consider its application to restaurants which serve food a substantial portion of which has moved in commerce.

Section 201(a) of Title II commands that all persons shall be entitled to the full and equal enjoyment of the goods and services of any place of public accommodation without discrimination or segregation on the ground of race, color, religion, or national origin; and §201(b) defines establishments as places of public accommodation if their operations affect commerce or segregation by them is supported by state action. Sections 201(b)(2) and (c) place any "restaurant . . . principally engaged in selling food for consumption on the premises" under the Act "if . . . it serves or offers to serve interstate travelers or a substantial portion of the food which it serves . . . has moved in commerce."

Ollie's Barbecue admits that it is covered by these provisions of the Act. The Government makes no contention that the discrimination at the restaurant was supported by the State of Alabama. There is no claim that interstate travelers frequented the restaurant. The sole question, therefore, narrows down to whether Title II, as applied to a restaurant annually receiving about $70,000 worth of food which has moved in commerce, is a valid exercise of the power of Congress. The Government has contended that Congress had ample basis upon which to find that racial discrimination at restaurants which receive from out of state a substantial portion of the food served does, in fact, impose commercial burdens of national magnitude upon interstate commerce.

As we noted in *Heart of Atlanta Motel* both Houses of Congress conducted prolonged hearings on the Act. And, as we said there, while no formal findings were made, which of course are not necessary, it is well that we make mention of the testimony at these hearings. . . . The record is replete with testimony of the burdens placed on interstate commerce by racial discrimination in restaurants. A comparison of per capita spending by Negroes in restaurants, theaters, and like establishments indicated less spending, after discounting income differences, in areas where discrimination is widely practiced. . . . This diminutive spending springing from a refusal to serve Negroes and their total loss as customers has, regardless of the absence of direct evidence, a close connection to interstate commerce. The fewer customers a restaurant enjoys the less food it sells and consequently the less it buys. In addition, the Attorney General testified that this type of discrimination imposed "an artificial restriction on the market" and interfered with the flow of merchandise. In addition, there were many references to discriminatory situations causing wide unrest and having a depressant effect on general business conditions in the respective communities.

Moreover there was an impressive array of testimony that discrimination in restaurants had a direct and highly restrictive effect upon interstate travel by Negroes. This resulted, it was said, because discriminatory practices prevent Negroes from buying prepared food served on the premises while on a trip, except in isolated and unkempt restaurants and under most unsatisfactory and often unpleasant conditions. This obviously discourages travel and obstructs interstate commerce for one can hardly travel without eating. Likewise, it was said, that discrimination deterred professional, as well as skilled, people from moving into areas where such practices occurred and thereby caused industry to be reluctant to establish there.

We believe that this testimony afforded ample basis for the conclusion that established restaurants in such areas sold less interstate goods because of the discrimination, that interstate travel was obstructed directly by it, that business in general suffered and that many new businesses refrained from establishing there as a result of it.

It goes without saying that, viewed in isolation, the volume of food purchased by Ollie's Barbecue from sources supplied from out of state was insignificant when compared with the total foodstuffs moving in commerce. But, as our late Brother Jackson said for the Court in *Wickard v. Filburn*:

> "That appellee's own contribution to the demand for wheat may be trivial by itself is not enough to remove him from the scope of federal regulation where, as here, his contribution, taken together with that of many others similarly situated, is far from trivial."

Article I, §8, cl. 3, confers upon Congress the power "to regulate Commerce . . . among the several States" and Clause 18 of the same Article grants it the power "to make all Laws which shall be necessary and proper for carrying into Execution the foregoing Powers. . . ." This grant, as we have pointed out in *Heart of Atlanta Motel* "extends to those activities intrastate which so affect interstate commerce, or the exertion of the power of Congress over it, as to make regulation of them appropriate means to the attainment of a legitimate end, the effective execution of the granted power to regulate interstate commerce." Much is said about a restaurant business being local but "even if appellee's activity be local and though it may not be regarded as commerce, it may still, whatever its nature, be reached by Congress if it exerts a substantial economic effect on interstate commerce. . . ."

This Court has held time and again that this power extends to activities of retail establishments, including restaurants, which directly or indirectly burden or obstruct interstate commerce. We have detailed the cases in *Heart of Atlanta Motel*, and will not repeat them here.

Congress has determined for itself that refusals of service to Negroes have imposed burdens both upon the interstate flow of food and upon the movement of products generally. Of course, the mere fact that Congress has said when particular activity shall be deemed to affect commerce does not preclude further examination by this Court. But where we find that the legislators, in light of the facts and testimony before them, have a rational basis for finding a chosen regulatory scheme necessary to the protection of commerce, our investigation is at an end. The only remaining question — one answered in the affirmative by the court below — is whether the particular restaurant either serves or offers to serve interstate travelers or serves food a substantial portion of which has moved in interstate commerce.

Confronted as we are with the facts laid before Congress, we must conclude that it had a rational basis for finding that racial discrimination in restaurants had a direct and adverse effect on the free flow of interstate commerce. Insofar as the sections of the Act here relevant are concerned, §§201(b)(2) and (c), Congress prohibited discrimination only in those establishments having a close tie to interstate commerce, i.e., those, like the McClungs', serving food that has come from out of the State. We think in so doing that Congress acted well within its power to protect and foster commerce in extending the coverage of Title II only to those restaurants offering to serve interstate travelers or serving food, a substantial portion of which has moved in interstate commerce.

The absence of direct evidence connecting discriminatory restaurant service with the flow of interstate food, a factor on which the appellees place much reliance, is not, given the evidence as to the effect of such practices on other aspects of commerce, a crucial matter.

The power of Congress in this field is broad and sweeping; where it keeps within its sphere and violates no express constitutional limitation it has been the rule of this Court, going back almost to the founding days of the Republic, not to interfere. The Civil Rights Act of 1964, as here applied, we find to be plainly appropriate in the resolution of what the Congress found to be a national commercial problem of the first magnitude. We find it in no violation of any express limitations of the Constitution and we therefore declare it valid.

SYNTHESIS QUESTIONS FOR FURTHER DISCUSSION: CHAPTER 4

1. When President Franklin Roosevelt calls for a "Second Bill of Rights," does he actually advocate amending the text of the Constitution? What branch of government would be best suited to enforce these positive, socio-economic rights? Cass Sunstein believes that the New Deal successfully entrenched many of President Roosevelt's proposed rights as "constitutive commitments." Like Bruce Ackerman, Sunstein argues that these commitments, including landmark legislation such as the Social Security Act, register the same constitutional status as the text itself. Do you agree that these entitlements have similar constitutional status as some of the rights established by the Constitution? Does it matter that many of the rights are "negative" restrictions on state power as opposed to "positive" entitlements that grant citizens rights to receive certain benefits?

2. Issues regarding congressional power are sometimes couched in solely procedural terms, apart from any of the substantive or moral issues involved in these cases. Does it matter that child labor was a particularly controversial issue at the time? For instance, do you think Justice Oliver Wendell Holmes is justified in appealing to the "evil of premature and excessive child labor" in his dissent in *Hammer v. Dagenhart*, or is the morality of the legislation at issue in the "powers" cases in this chapter irrelevant to constitutional analysis?

3. In learning that the debate about civil rights legislation passed in the 1960s hinged on questions regarding the commerce power, many students express surprise. The debate about civil rights, we often assume, is about equality, a value more closely enshrined in the Fourteenth Amendment's guarantee of "equal protection." Another route in discussing the constitutionality of this legislation would have been through the power granted to Congress under the fifth section of the Fourteenth Amendment, to enforce laws related to equal protection. Should this have been the constitutional hook for Congress's civil rights legislation, instead of the Commerce Clause?

KEY TERMS

enumerated powers: Those powers specifically granted to Congress by the Constitution, in contrast to the states' more general police powers to regulate the "welfare, health, safety, and morals" of its population.

plenary powers: Exclusive powers explicitly granted to Congress, not shared with the states.

Progressive movement: A movement of the early twentieth century that sought increased roles for government in guaranteeing basic welfare for all and increased federal regulation of the economy and in stimulating economic growth.

CHAPTER 5

THE NEW FEDERALISM

Do states have a role in protecting liberty? How far does economic activity extend?

If some claim the New Deal illustrates an important lesson about the need for Congress to regulate the national economy, others believe it raises questions about whether this broad reach is compatible with a Constitution of limited federal powers. Under the sweeping reach of the Court's post–1937 decisions, Congress could regulate virtually any activity, so long as it produced some kind of "substantial effect" on interstate commerce. Furthermore, courts have largely deferred to the legislature in economic judgments, such as how substantial an effect on commerce might be. The only constitutional requirement that an economic regulation would have to meet is that it possesses some rational basis.

But if "commerce . . . among the several states" can cover virtually any activity, then is Congress still limited to the specific powers enumerated in the Constitution? Or did the New Deal give rise to a single, unitary government? In determining whether questions of federalism — which for a time were forgotten as the public came to accept broader congressional powers without question — are important contemporary constitutional controversies, we examine a question of doctrine and a question of theory. First, where can we draw a clear line beyond which federal power cannot extend? Second, why do the principles of federalism matter in the first place?

In relation to the first question, the issue of balance between state authority and congressional authority might have been a moot point had it not been for a relatively recent development in constitutional law. As you saw in *Wickard v. Filburn* and in *Heart of Atlanta v. United States*, the Supreme Court after the "switch in time" adopted a broad understanding of interstate commerce. In *Wickard v. Filburn*, for instance, it upheld the regulation on the cultivation of wheat for private use on grounds that while the grower might use this wheat strictly for personal consumption, that would mean he was not buying that same wheat in the open market — thus depressing demand and therefore the price of wheat other farmers could command. While this one farmer might not be significant, if every wheat farmer in America did the same thing, the aggregation of these small effects would be substantial and significantly affect the larger national market in wheat. After *Wickard v. Filburn*, it might appear that the question of congressional authority was largely settled and accepted as not only expansive but potentially limitless.

However, as you will see, decades later, in *National League of Cities v. Usery*, then–U.S. Supreme Court Associate Justice William Rehnquist, writing for the Court, revived the issue of federalism. Although Justice Rehnquist would face some setbacks, he played a crucial role in asserting the power of the states in relation to the federal government in contemporary constitutional jurisprudence. Indeed, some have suggested that his role in constitutional debates about federalism was central to what some have called the "Rehnquist Revolution" in the Supreme Court's recent history. Specifically, *National League of Cities v. Usery* concerned the federal government's regulation of state employees. Justice Rehnquist argued that the Tenth Amendment, which states that "powers not delegated to the United States by the Constitution . . . are reserved to the States," still presented significant limits on federal power, including limits on its power to regulate interstate commerce. In striking down the regulation, Justice Rehnquist hoped to signal the reemergence of boundaries on congressional authority and to reassert the power of the states. However, his plan faced a setback in *Garcia v. San Antonio Metropolitan Transit Authority* (1985), where the Court reversed *National League of Cities v. Usery*. It might appear that *Garcia v. San Antonio* would once and for all establish virtually unlimited congressional power in relation to the states. However, although the ruling in *Garcia v. San Antonio* seemed to signal continued expansive federal power, it contained a dissent from Justice Rehnquist, excerpted here, which presaged a pushback against the Court's expansive jurisprudence in regard to the Commerce Clause. Indeed, ten years later, in *United States v. Lopez*, the Supreme Court would strike down legislation establishing gun-free school zones on grounds that it exceeded Congress's power under the Commerce Clause. In *Printz v. United States*, Justice Scalia argued that the Tenth Amendment prohibited the "commandeering" of state officials by the federal government. Again in *United States v. Morrison*, the Court would strike down the Violence Against Women Act on grounds that Congress lacked the authority to enact this legislation, which it deemed not a matter of interstate commerce. In both of these cases, the Court rejects the idea that commerce should be interpreted broadly to include matters that are not clearly economic. These cases, therefore, once again raise a puzzle about the meaning of this clause and the importance of federalism altogether.

The Court's revival of limits on Congress's commerce power came on the heels of another development in American politics. The development of constitutional interpretation is not merely an abstract exercise — it turns alongside the gears of history, evolving in step with the influence of political movements. Just as President Franklin Roosevelt eventually replaced the entire body of the Supreme Court, conservative presidents like Richard Nixon and Ronald Reagan have also left their mark on the Court. Specifically, during his terms in office,

President Reagan announced a "New Federalism" that would restore power to the states. The idea of New Federalism was meant to serve as a direct rejection of President Roosevelt's New Deal. After President Reagan left office, the Court's decisions in *United States v. Lopez* and *United States v. Morrison* seemed to echo this call, ushering in a New Federalism jurisprudence under the leadership of appointees of Presidents Nixon and Reagan, including Justice Rehnquist, who was elevated to Chief Justice by President Reagan in 1986, after serving on the Court since 1972. The cases in this chapter detail this development in constitutional law.

Although arguments for the New Federalism have traditionally been associated with the more conservative end of the political spectrum, in recent years progressives have begun to argue for the importance of constraints on congressional power. In the reading from Kathleen Sullivan we see the suggestion that during periods of conservative dominance in Congress, federalist arguments in favor of states' rights might be an important tool for liberals to use in pushing back against encroachments on liberty. Although federalism is often associated with conservative resistance to the New Deal and civil rights in the name of states' rights, Sullivan's piece raises a question about whether those who defend more leftist understandings of economics and civil liberties might also appeal to this doctrine. In particular, defenders of a freedom to use medical marijuana might be tempted to agree with U.S. Supreme Court Justice Clarence Thomas's dissent in *Gonzales v. Raich*, which argued that the federal government does not have the power to outlaw and regulate medical marijuana. Is there room for those on the left of the political spectrum to embrace federalism? Should state governments have the leeway, free from congressional intervention, to pursue progressive ideas for promoting individual freedom and equality, including stem cell research, same-sex marriage, medical marijuana, and physician-assisted suicide?

We also read in this chapter a piece by Michael McConnell, who attempts to defend federalism by appealing to the history and political theory of the Constitution itself. These selections demonstrate that federalism is no longer a mere abstract question of philosophy, but rather fundamental to the Supreme Court's decisions and its jurisprudence. McConnell raises the relationship between federalism and democracy, and thus ties the topic of this chapter to a theme that has been prominent in this book. Specifically, notice McConnell's contention that state governments are closer to the people and more democratic, as opposed to the cumbersome, monopoly-like qualities of a centralized form of national government. Do you agree with McConnell that federalism is an inherently democratic idea and that it would be a mistake to move toward centralized control? Or, on the contrary, are you sympathetic to President Roosevelt's use of federal power and the Supreme Court's decision to grant that power under the Commerce Clause?

Michael W. McConnell

FEDERALISM: EVALUATING THE FOUNDERS' DESIGN

54 U. Chi. L. Rev. 1484 (1987)

During the debates over the drafting and ratification of the Constitution, supporters and opponents alike came to articulate complex and sophisticated theories of federalism (which, it should be stressed, was a uniquely American blend of national systems — like the French — and confederate systems — like the ancient Greek and early modern Dutch). The "natural attachment" of the people in 1787 to their states was augmented by practical arguments about how the new system of dual sovereignty would promote three complementary objectives: (1) "[t]o secure the public good," (2) to protect "private rights," and (3) "to preserve the spirit and form of popular government." Achievement of these ends, according to Madison, was the "great object" of the Constitution. To understand the "founders' design" we must look again at those arguments. As the people of 1987, we must look at them in light of modern experience and knowledge about political decision making. The arguments of 1787 stand up remarkably well.

A. TO "SECURE THE PUBLIC GOOD"

Rejecting both pure confederation and consolidation, the "Federal Farmer" (the ablest and most influential of the antifederalist pamphleteers) argued that a "partial consolidation" is the only system "that can secure the freedom and happiness of this people." He reasoned that "one government and general legislation alone, never can extend equal benefits to all parts of the United States: Different laws, customs, and opinions exist in the different states, which by a uniform system of laws would be unreasonably invaded." The framers sought, the Federal Farmer concluded, to preserve decentralized decision making because smaller units of government are better able to further the interests and general welfare of the people.

Three important advantages of decentralized decision making emerge from an examination of the founders' arguments and the modern literature. First, decentralized decision making is better able to reflect the diversity of interests and preferences of individuals in different parts of the nation. Second, allocation of decision making authority to a level of government no larger than necessary will prevent mutually disadvantageous attempts by communities to take advantage of their neighbors. And third, decentralization allows for innovation and competition in government.

1. Responsiveness to diverse interests and preferences. The first, and most axiomatic, advantage of decentralized government is that local laws can be adapted to local conditions and local tastes, while a national government must take a uniform — and hence less desirable — approach. So long as preferences for government policies are unevenly distributed among the various localities, more people can be satisfied by decentralized decision making than by a single national authority. . . .

For example, assume that there are only two states, with equal populations of 100 each. Assume further that 70 percent of State A, and only 40 percent of State B, wish to outlaw smoking in public buildings. The others are opposed. If the decision is made on a national basis by a majority rule, 110 people will be pleased, and 90 displeased. If a separate decision is made by majorities in each state, 130 will be pleased, and only 70 displeased. The level of satisfaction will be still greater if some smokers in State A decide to move to State B, and some anti-smokers in State B decide to move to State A. In the absence of economies of scale in government services, significant externalities, or compelling arguments from justice, this is a powerful reason to prefer decentralized government. States are preferably governing units to the federal government, and local government to states. Modern public choice theory provides strong support for the framers' insight on this point.

2. Destructive competition for the benefits of government. A second consideration in designing a federal structure is more equivocal. The unit of decision making must be large enough so that decisions reflect the full costs and benefits, but small enough that destructive competition for the benefits of central government action is minimized. In economic language, this is the problem of "externalities."

Externalities present the principal countervailing consideration in favor of centralized government: if the costs of government action are borne by the citizens of State C, but the benefits are shared by the citizens of States D, E, and F, State C will be unwilling to expend the level of resources commensurate with the full social benefit of the action. This was the argument in Federalist 25 for national control of defense. Since an MX missile in Pennsylvania will deter a Soviet attack on Connecticut and North Carolina as well as Pennsylvania, optimal levels of investment in MX's require national decisions and national taxes. Or, similarly, since expenditures on water pollution reduction in Kentucky will benefit riparians all the way to New Orleans, it makes sense to nationalize decisions about water pollution regulation and treatment. Thus, as James Wilson explained to the Pennsylvania ratifying convention, "[w]hatever the object of government extends, in its operation, beyond the bounds of a particular state, should be considered as belonging to the government of the United States" (quoted at pp. 169-70).

That significant external effects of this sort provide justification for national decisions is well understood — hence federal funding of defense, interstate highways, national parks, and medical research, and federal regulation of interstate commerce, pollution, and national labor markets. It is less well understood that nationalizing decisions where the impact is predominantly local has an equal and opposite effect. The framers' awareness that ill consequences flow as much from excessive as from insufficient centralization is fundamental to their insistence on enumerating and thus limiting the powers of the federal government. Hence the other half of Wilson's explanation: "Whatever object of government is confined in its operation and effect, within the bounds of a particular State, should be considered as belonging to the government of that State" (p. 169). This stands in marked contrast to the modern tendency to resolve all doubts in favor of federal control.

The point is quite general. It applies to lawmaking and regulation no less than to taxing and spending. A major effect of regulation is to shift burdens from one region or locality to another. Familiar examples are environmental laws that protect eastern "dirty" coal from competition from western "clean" coal and railroad regulation that enables low density areas to maintain service at the expense of other traffic. But the effect is especially obvious in the case of federal spending. If the national treasury is seen as a common pool resource for financing schemes of predominantly local benefit, it will be oversubscribed. Current budgetary woes are largely attributable to this fiscal "tragedy of the commons."

3. Innovation and competition in government. A final reason why federalism has been thought to advance the public good is that state and local governmental units will have greater opportunity and incentive to pioneer useful changes. A consolidated national government has all the drawbacks of a monopoly: it stifles choice and lacks the goad of competition.

Lower levels of government are more likely to depart from established consensus simply because they are smaller and more numerous. Elementary statistical theory holds that a greater number of independent observations will produce more instances of deviation from the mean. If innovation is desirable, it follows that decentralization is desirable. This statistical proposition is strengthened, moreover, by the political reality that a smaller unit of government is more likely to have a population with preferences that depart from the majority's. It is, therefore, more likely to try an approach that could not command a national majority.

Perhaps more important is that smaller units of government have an incentive, beyond the mere political process, to adopt popular policies. If a community can attract additional taxpayers, each citizen's share of the overhead costs of government is proportionately reduced. Since people are better able to move among states or communities than to emigrate from the United States, competition among governments for taxpayers will be far stronger at the state and local than at the federal level. Since most people are taxpayers, this means that there is a powerful incentive for decentralized governments to make things better for most people. In particular, the desire to attract taxpayers and jobs will promote policies of economic growth and expansion.

It is well known, for example, that families often choose a community on the basis of the school system; a better school system encourages development and raises property values. Competition among communities is therefore likely to result in superior education (as well as more cost-effective ways of providing it). This is especially likely given the strong business support for education. Because of the need for a well-educated work force, businesses often choose to locate in communities with a superior educational system and push for improved education in communities where they already have facilities. The chairman of Xerox Corporation has been quoted as saying, "Education is a bigger factor in productivity growth [rates] than increased capital, economies of scale or better allocation of resources."

To be sure, the results of competition among states and localities will not always be salutary. State-by-state determination of the laws of incorporation likely results in the most efficient forms of corporate organization, but state-by-state determination of the law of products liability seems to have created a liability monster. This is because each state can benefit in-state plaintiffs by more generous liability rules, the costs being exported to largely out-of-state defendants; while no state can do much to protect its in-state manufacturers from suits by plaintiffs in the other states. Thus, competition among the states in this arena leads to one-sidedly pro-plaintiff rules of law.

The most important example of this phenomenon is the effect of state-by-state competition on welfare and other redistributive policies. In most cases, immigration of investment and of middle- to upper-income persons is perceived as desirable, while immigration of persons dependent on public assistance is viewed as a drain on a community's finances. Yet generous welfare benefits paid by higher taxes will lead the rich to leave and the poor to come. This creates an incentive, other things being equal, against redistributive policies. Indeed, it can be shown that the level of redistribution in a decentralized system is likely to be lower even if there is virtually unanimous agreement among the citizens that higher levels would be desirable. Where redistribution is the objective, therefore, advocates should and do press for federal programs, or at least for minimum federal standards.

Thus, the competition among states has an uncertain effect: often salutary but sometimes destructive. There are races to the bottom as well as races to the top. Often one's view of the allocation of authority for specific issues will depend on a prediction as to substantive outcomes rather than a general theory of federalism.

B. TO PROTECT "PRIVATE RIGHTS"

The most important reason offered by the defenders of state sovereignty was that state and local governments are better protectors of liberty. Patrick Henry went to the heart of the matter when he told the Virginia ratifying convention:

> You are not to inquire how your trade may be increased, nor how you are to become a great and powerful people, but how your liberties can be secured; for liberty ought to be the direct end of your Government.

The most eloquent of the opponents of the Constitution, Henry stated flatly that in the "alarming transition, from a Confederacy to a consolidated Government," the "rights and privileges" of Americans were "endangered." He was far from alone in this fear.

At a distance of 200 years, it is this aspect of the Founders' thought that is most difficult for us to understand. After *Brown v. Board of Education* and the various civil rights acts, after the revolution in criminal procedure fostered by federal law and federal courts, after the imposition of uniform federal standards for basic liberties under the Bill of Rights, and after the proliferation of novel statutory "rights" arising from the interventions of the welfare-regulatory state, it is the federal government, not the states, that appears to be our system's primary protector of individual liberties. This seems to be the premise of the Fourteenth Amendment and of much of New Deal legislation. The view at the founding, however, was much more divided and ambivalent.

Madison's most important contribution to the debate over ratification is his challenging argument that individual liberties, such as property rights and freedom of religion, are better protected at the national than the state level. Madison's argument, greatly simplified, is that the most serious threat to individual liberty is the tyranny of a majority faction. Since any given faction is more likely to be concentrated in a particular locality, and to be no more than a small minority in the nation as a whole, it follows that factional tyranny is more likely in the state legislatures than in the Congress of the United States. This argument is supplemented by others, based on the "proper structure of the Union" — deliberative representation, separation of powers, and checks and balances — that also suggest that the federal government is a superior protector of rights. Here I shall concentrate on the argument from the "extent . . . of the Union." Madison's argument blunted the anti-federalists' appeal to state sovereignty as the guarantor of liberty. It was, however, only partially successful. Why?

Modern public choice theory has cast some doubt on elements of Madison's theory. In particular, Madison's assumption that the possibility of minority tyranny is neutralized by majority vote requirements and that minority factions are inherently vulnerable to majority tyranny is undermined by studies showing that a small, cohesive faction intensely interested in a particular outcome can exercise disproportionate influence in the political arena. Madison underestimated both the dangers of minority rule and the defensive resources of minority groups. Moreover, some observers have suggested that the conditions of modern federal politics — especially the balkanized, issue-oriented conjunction of bureaucratic agencies and committee staffs — is especially susceptible to factional politics. Professor Richard Stewart has dubbed the result "Madison's Nightmare." Proponents of greater state sovereignty in 1787-89 may have been rightly skeptical of Madison's claims that there would be less danger of factional oppression at the federal level.

But even taking Madison's fundamental insight as correct — and surely it has much to commend it — the argument on its own terms cautions against total centralization of authority in Washington. It points instead to a hybrid system in which states retain a major role in the protection of individual liberties. There are three basic reasons.

1. Liberty through mobility. Madison's argument demonstrates that factional oppression is more likely to occur in the smaller, more homogenous jurisdictions of individual states. But it does not deny that oppression at the federal level, when it occurs, is more dangerous. The lesser likelihood must be balanced against the greater magnitude of the danger. The main reason oppression at the federal level is more dangerous is that it is more difficult to escape. If a single state chose, for example, to prohibit divorce, couples seeking a divorce could move (or perhaps merely travel) to other states where their desires can be fulfilled. Oppressive measures at the state level are easier to avoid. Important recent examples of this phenomenon are the migration of homosexuals to cities like San Francisco, where they received official toleration, and the migration of individuals from Massachusetts to New Hampshire to escape high rates of taxation. A more contentious example is the regulation of abortion. If the power to regulate abortion is returned to the states, there is little likelihood of effective enforcement of anti-abortion laws, since permissive jurisdictions would attract business from more restrictive states. On the other hand, a nationwide rule — either voted by Congress or adopted by the courts as a construction of the due process clause — would have far more dramatic consequences.

2. Self-interested government. Madison held that there are two different and distinct dangers inherent in republican government: the "oppression of [the] . . . rulers" and the "injustice" of "one part of the society against . . . the other part." The first concern is that government officials will rule in their own interest instead of the interest of the people. The second is that some persons, organized in factions, will use the governmental powers to oppress

others. Significantly, while Madison argued that the danger of faction is best met at the federal level (for the reasons summarized above), he conceded that the danger of self-interested representation is best tackled at the state level. "As in too small a sphere oppressive combinations may be too easily formed ag[ainst] the weaker party; so in too extensive a one, a defensive concert may be rendered too difficult against the oppression of those entrusted with the administration." Consequently, while powers most likely to be abused for factional advantage ought to be vested in the federal government, powers that are most likely to be abused by self-aggrandizing officials should be left in the states, where direct popular control is stronger.

3. Diffusion of power. Madison himself did not view his argument as establishing the superiority of a consolidated national government; rather, he presented his famous argument about the tyranny of factions in favor of the intermediate, federalist solution of dual sovereignty. In Federalist 51, he underscored that "the rights of the people" are best protected in a system in which "two distinct governments," federal and state, "will control each other." The diffusion of power, in and of itself, is protective of liberty. In Tocqueville's evocative words, "Municipal bodies and county administrations are like so many hidden reefs retarding or dividing the flood of the popular will."

. . . [T]he framers of the Constitution and Bill of Rights believed that state governments were, in some vital respects, safer repositories of power over individual liberties than the federal government. It is thus no accident that the "police power" — the protection of public health, safety, and morals — was left to the states, with the federal government entrusted with less sensitive powers like those over interstate and foreign commerce. As Berger comments, "Moral issues . . . are best left to the States, precisely as the Founders intended" (p.146). Given the diversity of views about issues of morality, and the potential for oppression, it is natural that lovers of liberty would be inclined toward decentralized decision making.

At this point, an important qualification is in order. The arguments from the "public good" and from "private rights" make sense only if one presupposes that the decision in question is appropriate to democratic decision making at some level, be it state or federal. Some issues are so fundamental to basic justice that they must be taken out of majoritarian control altogether. This is why both state and federal governments are prohibited, for example, from passing ex post facto laws and bills of attainder. These issues are thus subject to a single national rule; the reason, however, has nothing to do with federalism. Federalism is a system for allocation of democratic decision making power. For those few but important matters on which democracy itself cannot be trusted, neither the "public good" nor the "private rights" argument for state autonomy can hold sway.

C. TO PRESERVE "THE SPIRIT AND FORM OF POPULAR GOVERNMENT"

It was an article of faith among advocates of state autonomy that republicanism could survive only in a small jurisdiction. As stated by the prominent anti-federalist essayist, "Brutus," "a free republic cannot succeed over a country of such immense extent, containing such a number of inhabitants, and these increasing in such rapid progression as that of the whole United States." They believed consolidated national government would lead to aristocratic or despotic rule. Their reasons may be reduced to three major themes: (1) enforcement of laws, (2) nature of representation, and (3) cultivation of public spiritedness.

1. Enforcement of laws. Obedience to the law can arise from two different sources: fear of punishment and voluntary compliance. A republican government, which has a minimal coercive apparatus, must rely predominantly upon the latter. As Brutus explained, in a free republic "the government must rest for its support upon the confidence and respect which the people have for their government and laws." To the advocates of decentralized government, this necessarily implied that the units of government must be small and close to the people. . . .

2. Nature of representation. One of the principal arguments for substantial state autonomy was that representatives in a smaller unit of government will be closer to the people. Patrick Henry, for example, warned in the Virginia ratifying convention that "throwing the country into large districts . . . will destroy that connection that ought to subsist between the electors and the elected." Assuming representative bodies of roughly the same number, any given representative will have fewer constituents and a smaller district at the state or local level. Each citizen's influence on his representative, therefore, will be proportionately greater, and geographically concentrated minorities are more likely to achieve representation.

Because federal electoral districts must of necessity be larger and more populous, representation is likely to be skewed in favor of the well-known few—what were known at the time as the "aristocratic" element. The Federal Farmer argued that increasing the number of representatives would make the nation "more democratical and secure, strengthen the confidence of the people in it, and thereby render it more nervous and energetic." However, the sheer size of the United States makes it impossible to increase the number of representatives sufficiently, without turning the Congress into what Madison called "the confusion of a multitude." . . .

3. Public spiritedness. Critics of governmental centralization warned that public spiritedness—then called "public virtue"—could be cultivated only in a republic of small dimensions. Republicanism, it was thought, depended to an extraordinary degree on the willingness of each citizen to submerge his own passions and interests for the common good. The only substitute for public virtue was an unacceptable degree of coercion, compatible only with nonrepublican forms of government.

There were two reasons to believe that a centralized government would undermine republican virtue. First, public spiritedness is a product of participation in deliberation over the public good. If the citizens are actively engaged in the public debate they will have more of a stake in the community. The federal government is too distant and its compass too vast to permit extensive participation by ordinary citizens in its policy formulations. By necessity, decision making will be delegated to agents. But as they are cut off from active participation in the commonwealth, the citizens will become less attached to it and more inclined to attend to their private affairs.

Second, the natural sentiment of benevolence, which lies at the heart of public spiritedness, is weaker as the distance grows between the individual and the objects of benevolence. An individual is most likely to sacrifice his private interests for the good of his family, and then for his neighbors and, by extension, his community. He is unlikely to place great weight upon the well-being of strangers hundreds of miles away. It is unlikely, therefore, that citizens of a nation as large as the United States will assume an attitude of republican virtue toward national affairs....

Kathleen M. Sullivan

FROM STATES' RIGHTS BLUES TO BLUE STATES' RIGHTS: FEDERALISM AFTER THE REHNQUIST COURT

75 Fordham L. Rev. 799 (2006)

The Rehnquist Court dramatically revived the structural principles of federalism as grounds for judicial invalidation of statutes. For most of the twentieth century, the federal and state governments had been left to bargain or fight over their relationship in the realm of politics. The Rehnquist Court, by contrast, increasingly held that this relationship was a matter to be refereed in the courts. The Court grounded this approach in the history of the Founding: "Dual sovereignty is a defining feature of our Nation's constitutional blueprint. States, upon ratification of the Constitution, did not consent to become mere appendages of the Federal Government. Rather, they entered the Union with their sovereignty intact." In addition, the Court suggested that this relationship required judicial protection, not mere political self-help: "Federalism was our Nation's own discovery. The Framers split the atom of sovereignty. It was the genius of their idea that our citizens would have two political capacities, one state and one federal, each protected from incursion by the other."

For the most part, the Rehnquist Court's federalist revival restrained the federal government from incursion upon the states. In some lines of decision, the Court held that Congress had exceeded the scope of its powers. In others, it held that a federal law had wrongly intruded upon the sovereign autonomy of the states. Whether enforcing such internal or external limits on federal power, the Rehnquist Court took significant steps to rebalance power between the state and federal governments. The Court revived normative arguments for self-rule at more local levels of government and found textual and structural bases for vindicating such arguments against assertions of federal power that had gone unchallenged for decades.

Did these decisions establish a new constitutional order for federalism? . . . Any such extreme picture . . . is overstated. The Rehnquist Court surely revived the structural principles of federalism. But it maintained certain striking limits that kept these principles from bringing about a greater sea change in constitutional law. The Court did more to change the constitutional jurisprudence of federalism than it did to realign actual constitutional power. The question for the future is how much generative power this jurisprudence will have, for blue states and red states alike.

Even if the Rehnquist Court's federalism decisions did not shift power from the federal government to the states as dramatically as some have suggested, those decisions articulated a powerful set of constitutional ideals and principles supporting checks on federal incursions into state self-rule. . . . [T]his new jurisprudence . . . has the capacity to transcend traditional political alignments. States' rights have been associated historically with conservative causes, while federal power has been associated with increasing egalitarianism and protection of minorities from Reconstruction through the New Deal and the Civil Rights Acts of the 1960s. But now that federal power in all three branches has been consolidated in Republican hands to the greatest extent since 1954, champions of liberal causes might need to rethink any reflexive recoil from federalism. Gay weddings in San Francisco and Massachusetts, like popular initiatives authorizing physician-assisted suicide in Oregon and medicinal use of marijuana in California, exemplify recent progressive experimentation at the local level through policies that could not command a national majority. Under such political circumstances, liberals should hesitate before rejecting the Rehnquist Court's New Federalism. It might well contain seeds of a constitutional concept of social fluidity that can help to realize progressive as well as conservative ideals.

The first line of cases reintroduced, for the first time since the New Deal, judicial enforcement of the limits of power granted to Congress by the Commerce Clause. In *United States v. Lopez*, the Court invalidated a federal criminal prohibition on gun possession within the vicinity of a school, reasoning that gun possession, standing alone, does not have a substantial effect on interstate commerce. In *United States v. Morrison*, the Court invalidated the civil damages provisions of the federal Violence Against Women Act, reasoning that acts such as date rape or domestic battery are not economic activities with a substantial effect on interstate commerce. Both decisions declined to defer to congressional conclusions — in *Morrison*, conclusions based on quite extensive congressional factual findings — that a regulated activity has a substantial effect on interstate commerce.

These decisions signaled the end to an anything-goes approach to congressional commerce power, reviving the theory that enumeration of powers in Article I is a structural principle warranting judicial intervention to constrain federal overreaching. These striking new constraints on the federal commerce power, however, reached their outer limit in *Gonzalez v. Raich*, which upheld the application of federal controlled substance laws to the consumption of home-grown marijuana, despite California's efforts by popular initiative to allow such consumption for medicinal purposes. The majority reasoned that the principles of federalism did not compel an exemption from federal law, even for wholly intrastate activities expressly sanctioned by a state's government, so long as a product grown and consumed locally is fungible with products sold on interstate markets and the overall congressional scheme aims at activity that might be thought to have a substantial effect on interstate commerce. Only three Justices from the *Lopez* and *Morrison* majorities stuck to their federalist guns, arguing in dissent that the Court's capacious conception of federal power over economic activities might well swallow up such wholly local activities as quilting bees.

. . . [Another] line of Rehnquist Court cases advanced federalism by limiting the federal government's ability to commandeer state officers and legislatures to serve federal ends. In *Printz v. United States*, the Court extended this holding to limit federal intrusion into state enforcement as well as enactment of law, invalidating portions of the Brady Handgun Violence Prevention Act that had required sheriffs and other local law enforcement officials to carry out federally mandated background checks on handgun purchasers.

But the Rehnquist Court's federalist revival was not as sweeping as it might appear. As described above, the Court set forth limiting principles to each of these lines. Even more important, the Court declined to go down four roads that would have pushed its New Federalism much further — despite having the apparent capacity to round up five votes to do so.

First, the Rehnquist Court never brought back the short-lived principle, set forth in 1976 in *National League of Cities v. Usery*, that there are some areas of reserved state autonomy over traditional and integral governmental functions that are absolutely immunized from federal control. *National League* was explicitly overruled a decade later by *Garcia v. San Antonio Metropolitan Transit Authority*. The bitter dissents in *Garcia* suggested that time and actuarial tables were on the side of the federalists. But Chief Justice William Rehnquist never cobbled a majority to bring back the federalist jurisprudence of *National League*, even though Presidents Ronald Reagan and George W. Bush added five new Justices to the Court, replacing most of the *Garcia* majority.

The failure to revive *National League* arguably renders the *Lopez* line of cases somewhat trivial. The majority opinion in *Lopez* spoke of criminal law, education, and family law as areas traditionally regulated by the states, suggesting a faint echo of *National League*'s notion of state islands in the stream of commerce. But if a traditional state activity does not enjoy affirmative immunity from congressional regulation, then the Rehnquist Court's internal limits on Congress's commerce power will provide thin constraint; it is a relatively small trick for Congress to make adequate findings that such an activity has a substantial effect on interstate commerce. If there is any doubt, Congress may simply employ an express jurisdictional nexus.

Second, the Rehnquist Court did not overrule *South Dakota v. Dole*, which held that Congress could condition federal highway funding for the states on their raising their minimum drinking age to twenty-one. The *Dole* decision takes a broad view of Congress's ability to use its spending power as leverage to obtain state commitments to regulation that Congress could not impose directly. The Court assumed that the Twenty-First Amendment, which preserves some measure of state autonomy over alcohol traffic, precluded Congress from directly imposing such a federal regulation in this area. It also assumed that if the drinking-age requirement were not germane to the purpose of highway funding, the federal law would impose an unconstitutional condition. But the Court found teenage alcohol sales germane enough to highway funding to surmount the unconstitutional conditions problem, finding a sufficient nexus because, after all, teenage alcohol sales can cause drunk driving and drunk driving can cause damage to and require emergency services on the roads. Thus, spending conditions need only meet the most lenient test of rationality.

The failure to overrule *Dole* arguably renders trivial the . . . line of [commandeering] cases. Given the massive scale of federal spending and the large percentage of state budgets that depend upon federal subsidies, Congress has considerable leverage over the states through spending conditions. If, with little judicial oversight, Congress may bribe the states into enacting the very regulatory programs that Congress may not commandeer the states into enacting or enforcing, then the anti-commandeering cases can do little as a practical matter to shift power from the federal government to the states.

The Rehnquist Court's federalism revival was theoretically deep even if practically limited. The Rehnquist Court's federalism decisions suggested two principal theoretical bases for devolving greater power to local levels of government, one deontological and the other utilitarian. The first, deontological justification for federalism emphasizes self-rule: the notion of giving government to oneself. On this view, it is immoral to cede self-government to a distant bureaucrat in a remote capital rather than engaging in self-government alongside nearby neighbors. This position implies a default rule in favor of local power and requires very strong justifications for federal intervention.

The second justification, based on utilitarianism, takes the view that different levels of government have different expertise and competence in serving the general welfare. States are better at solving some and the nation better at solving other local and national problems. For example, the federal government can correct market failures that defy state control, such as regulating externalities like pollution that cross over state borders, providing public goods like national defense that would have free-rider problems if provided by the states, preventing races to the bottom that would occur if the states were left to compete among themselves on labor or welfare legislation, or providing a larger insurance pool for disasters such as earthquakes and hurricanes that would swamp local resources. On this view, state governments will be better at just about everything else because they are more efficient, more flexible given their smaller scale, and more responsive to problems that differ across localities. This justification applies a view of federalism that entrusts neutral technocratic expertise to make utilitarian judgments about which level of government has greater comparative advantage at solving different problems.

There is a third theoretical justification for federalism that is not well developed in the Rehnquist Court cases, but that might well be desirable to elaborate going forward, especially by those favoring liberal causes. This theory sees federalism as one among many guarantees in the Constitution facilitating social fluidity, and preventing the entrenchment of individual identity. On this theory, liberals should stop singing the states' rights blues and begin embracing blue states' rights.

This is so because the traditional federalism paradigm has been inverted by the entrenchment of Republican dominance of all three branches of government over the last six years. Under the traditional structural paradigm, liberals favor federal government while conservatives favor government by the states. On this view, liberals view the federal government as an efficient means to correct market failures (as in the New Deal) and a just means to correct local tyranny (as in the Civil Rights Acts). At the same time, liberals traditionally view the states as backwaters of tyranny and discrimination epitomized by Jim Crow laws and continued resistance to desegregation in the South. On this traditional view, liberals endorse expansive views of federal governmental power and close checks on local options for the states. Conversely, under the traditional paradigm, conservatives view "big government" as the enemy, and the federal government as presumptively inefficient and unjust, stifling libertarian initiative and small business under a massive code of environmental, consumer protection, labor, and safety regulations. State governments, by contrast, traditionally appear to conservatives both more efficient and more responsive to the people, justifying, for example, the switch to block grants rather than formula grants to states during the Nixon and Reagan Administrations.

But once the Republican Party obtained simultaneous control of the White House, House, and Senate for the first time since 1954, local and state initiatives began to do more than federal programs to advance progressive social ends. Gay weddings took place through the executive action of Mayor Gavin Newsom of San Francisco and the state constitutional interpretation of Chief Justice Margaret Marshall writing for the Massachusetts Supreme Judicial Court. Oregon pioneered physician-assisted suicide while California experimented with allowing severely ill patients to use marijuana medicinally. Suddenly states' rights were no longer just for segregationist southerners. Conversely, conservatives have sought to transform entrenched control of the federal government into nationwide social restrictions — from regulating late-term abortion to limiting stem-cell research — that were once unthinkable at the federal level.

Against this backdrop, it is promising to articulate a third possible normative premise for federalism — one rooted in a larger constitutional norm of social fluidity. Social fluidity assumes that each individual has the freedom to shape and change identity without entrenchment into any fixed class, caste, nationality, religion, race, or locality. Our nation's lack of such entrenched national, tribal, or sectarian identity separates us from such balkanized societies as Belfast, Belgrade, and Beirut, in which national or religious identity determines all of one's social, economic, familial, and residential relationships.

The original Constitution contains a number of provisions that support this notion of social fluidity and that resist entrenchment of identity into fixed silos that go all the way down, constraining citizens within one group. The Establishment Clause forbids any national union of church and state. The Titles of Nobility Clause forbids the establishment of any aristocratic caste. In addition, the modern First Amendment has been held to imply a freedom of association that helps formalize Alexis de Tocqueville's observation that early nineteenth-century America had substituted ever-changing voluntary associations for fixed medieval hierarchies of guild and caste. If the Boy Scouts exclude someone for reason of sexual orientation, then there remains the option to start an alternative Boy Scouts instead. Another aspect of social fluidity is physical mobility. The right to migrate among the states, which itself migrated around the Constitution before the Court found a home for it in the Citizenship Clause, guarantees free movement across state boundaries without penalty for relocation or recency of state citizenship.

Federalism, by providing exit options from local repression, provides similar support to this crosscutting constitutional commitment to social fluidity. On this view, the answer to local prejudice is exit; a gay person inhibited by pre-*Lawrence v. Texas* Wyoming laws and social norms in a rural locale has the freedom to move to more welcoming urban environments. Federalism provides an opportunity for socially fluid self-definition according to each locality's different legislative and cultural environment. Such local norms provide an opportunity for self-definition and redefinition until a national consensus forms to extend any one local norm more universally.

This view of federalism as worthy of judicial protection to facilitate social fluidity is subject to several criticisms. First, it requires a presumption of strong judicial enforcement to maintain state and local autonomy from federal prohibitions on such activities as gay marriage and stem-cell research that fall outside the main purview of regulating the national market. This cannot please those who favor leaving issues of structure to the political safeguards of federalism. Second, by allowing economic decisions to be made at the national level while social decisions are made at the state level, such a view of federalism might seem to thwart decentralized economic policies that might allow for progressive local environmental, labor, antitakeover, and other laws. While such concepts of local economic rule might well be intuitively appealing, they also seem quixotic given the interconnectedness of a globalized economy. Third, some people will have more mobility than others to migrate across the lines that divide red and blue states—consider the gay cowboy who cannot leave Wyoming because ranching is the only job he knows and he has child support obligations, or the teenager in Montana for whom there is no in-state abortion provider. Where such constraints are present, federalism might appear to maroon some unlucky individuals in distinctly un-fluid backwaters. The only correction in such situations can be the national protection of individual rights through federal judicial decision or congressional exercise of Fourteenth Amendment enforcement powers. But there is reason to believe that federalist experimentation at the local level will help promote the ultimate spread of such norms. Massachusetts, for example, having launched an experiment in allowing gay marriage, declined the first legislative opportunity to roll back that experiment, apparently finding the effects of the experiment more salutary than pernicious.

The Rehnquist Court's revival of the structural principles of federalism has been unfairly maligned as an opportunistic vehicle for freeing gun-toters, wife-beaters, and other bigots from desirable federal laws. Under entrenched conservative dominance of all three branches of the federal government, however, federalism is better seen as protecting blue states and red states alike—that is, as a potential device for protecting progressive state and local experiments that advance the ends of liberty and equality. The Rehnquist Court did less than is often supposed to redistribute political power from the federal government to the states; its federalism decisions were qualified on their own terms and never reached as far as they might have. The Rehnquist Court did more than is often supposed, however, to redevelop the political theory of federalism, and to remind us of our more overarching constitutional commitments to social fluidity.

NATIONAL LEAGUE OF CITIES v. USERY

426 U.S. 833 (1976)

Opinion: Rehnquist, joined by Burger, Stewart, Powell
Concurrence: Blackmun
Dissent: Brennan, joined by White, Marshall
Dissent: Stevens

One clear lesson from the above readings is that the principle of federalism is an important structural feature of American constitutional government. The key question we must ask is whether this principle is compatible with Congress's power to regulate the national economy. Is there an upper boundary to the commerce power? If so, where might we draw the line? One possibility is to say that the federal government lacks the power to regulate how sovereign states conduct their internal and administrative affairs in their capacity as employers. If the Tenth Amendment secures some kind of special autonomy for states, perhaps they are immune from the same kinds of regulations that bind ordinary employers in the national economy.

In National League of Cities v. Usery, *the Court considered whether state employees were not subject to regulation because of the constitutional relationship between states and the national government. In particular, you should ask whether the Tenth Amendment requires the national government to defer to the states in matters concerning their own employees. Moreover, you should ask whether this decision begins to limit some of the federal power that we saw expanded during and after the New Deal in Chapter 4. In particular, how does this decision relate to the Court's decision in* United States v. Darby *that the Fair Labor Standards Act (FLSA) was constitutional? In then–Associate Justice William Rehnquist's opinion for the Court he wrote, "FLSA . . . would interfere with traditional aspects of state sovereignty." Do you agree?*

MR. JUSTICE REHNQUIST *delivered the opinion of the Court.*

Appellee Secretary argues that the cases in which this Court has upheld sweeping exercises of authority by Congress, even though those exercises preempted state regulation of the private sector, have already curtailed the sovereignty of the States quite as much as the 1974 amendments to the Fair Labor Standards Act. We do not agree. It is one thing to recognize the authority of Congress to enact laws regulating individual businesses necessarily subject to the dual sovereignty of the government of the Nation and of the State in which they reside. It is quite another to uphold a similar exercise of congressional authority directed not to private citizens, but to the States as States. We have repeatedly recognized that there are attributes of sovereignty attaching to every state government which may not be impaired by Congress, not because Congress may lack an affirmative grant of legislative authority to reach the matter, but because the Constitution prohibits it from exercising the authority in that manner. In *Coyle v. Oklahoma*, the Court gave this example of such an attribute:

> The power to locate its own seat of government and to determine when and how it shall be changed from one place to another, and to appropriate its own public funds for that purpose, are essentially and peculiarly state powers. That one of the original thirteen States could now be shorn of such powers by an act of Congress would not be for a moment entertained.

Id. at 565.

One undoubted attribute of state sovereignty is the States' power to determine the wages which shall be paid to those whom they employ in order to carry out their governmental functions, what hours those persons will work, and what compensation will be provided where these employees may be called upon to work overtime. The question we must resolve here, then, is whether these determinations are "functions essential to separate and independent existence," *id.* at 580, quoting from *Lane County v. Oregon, supra,* at 76, so that Congress may not abrogate the States' otherwise plenary authority to make them.

In their complaint, appellants advanced estimates of substantial costs which will be imposed upon them by the 1974 amendments. Since the District Court dismissed their complaint, we take its well pleaded allegations as true, although it appears from appellee's submissions in the District Court and in this Court that resolution of the factual disputes as to the effect of the amendments is not critical to our disposition of the case.

Judged solely in terms of increased costs in dollars, these allegation show a significant impact on the functioning of the governmental bodies involved. The Metropolitan Government of Nashville and Davidson County, Tenn., for cxample, asserted that the Act will increase its costs of providing essential police and fire protection, without any increase in service or in current salary levels, by $938,000 per year. Cape Girardeau, Mo., estimated that its annual budget for fire protection may have to be increased by anywhere from $250,000 to $400,000 over the current figure of $350,000. The State of Arizona alleged that the annual additional expenditures which will be required if it is to continue to provide essential state services may total $2.5 million. The State of California, which must devote significant portions of its budget to fire suppression endeavors, estimated that application of the Act to its employment practices will necessitate an increase in its budget of between $8 million and $16 million.

Increased costs are not, of course, the only adverse effects which compliance with the Act will visit upon state and local governments, and, in turn, upon the citizens who depend upon those governments. In its complaint in intervention, for example, California asserted that it could not comply with the overtime costs (approximately $750,000 per year) which the Act required to be paid to California Highway Patrol cadets during their academy training program. California reported that it had thus been forced to reduce its academy training program from 2,080 hours to only 960 hours, a compromise undoubtedly of substantial importance to those whose safety and welfare may depend upon the preparedness of the California Highway Patrol.

This type of forced relinquishment of important governmental activities is further reflected in the complaint's allegation that the city of Inglewood, Cal., has been forced to curtail its affirmative action program for providing employment opportunities for men and women interested in a career in law enforcement. The Inglewood police department has abolished a program for police trainees who split their week between on-the-job training and the classroom. The city could not abrogate its contractual obligations to these trainees, and it concluded that compliance with the Act in these circumstances was too financially burdensome to permit continuance of the classroom program. The city of Clovis, Cal., has been put to a similar choice regarding an internship program it was running in cooperation with a California State university. According to the complaint, because the interns' compensation brings them within the purview of the Act, the city must decide whether to eliminate the program entirely or to substantially reduce its beneficial aspects by doing away with any pay for the interns.

Quite apart from the substantial costs imposed upon the States and their political subdivisions, the Act displaces state policies regarding the manner in which they will structure delivery of those governmental services which their citizens require. The Act, speaking directly to the States *qua* States, requires that they shall pay all but an extremely limited minority of their employee the minimum wage rate currently chosen by Congress. It may well be that, as a matter of economic policy, it would be desirable that States, just as private employers, comply with these minimum wage requirement. But it cannot be gainsaid that the federal requirement directly supplant the considered policy choice of the States' elected officials and administrator as to how they wish to structure pay scale in state employment. The State might wish to employ persons with little or no training, or those who wish to work on a casual basis, or those who, for some other reason, do not possess minimum employment requirements, and pay them less than the federally prescribed minimum wage. It may wish to offer part-time or summer employment to teenagers at a figure less than the minimum wage, and, if unable to do so, may decline to offer such employment at all. But the Act would forbid such choice by the States. The only "discretion" left to them under the Act is either to attempt to increase their revenue to meet the additional financial burden imposed upon them by paying congressionally prescribed wages to their existing complement of employees or to reduce that complement to a number which can be paid the federal minimum wage without increasing revenue.

This dilemma presented by the minimum wage restriction may seem not immediately different from that faced by private employers, who have long been covered by the Act and who must find ways to increase their gross income if they are to pay higher wages while maintaining current earnings. The difference, however, is that a State is not merely a factor in the "shifting economic arrangements" of the private sector of the economy, *Kovacs v. Cooper* (Frankfurter, J., concurring), but is itself a coordinate element in the system established by the Framers for governing our Federal Union.

The degree to which the FLSA amendments would interfere with traditional aspects of state sovereignty can be seen even more clearly upon examining the overtime requirements of the Act. The general effect of these provisions is to require the States to pay their employees at premium rates whenever their work exceeds a specified number of hours in a given period. The asserted reason for these provisions is to provide a financial disincentive upon using employees beyond the work period deemed appropriate by Congress. According to appellee:

> This premium rate can be avoided if the [State] uses other employees to do the overtime work. This, in effect, tends to discourage overtime work and to spread employment, which is the result Congress intended.

Brief for Appellee 43. We do not doubt that this may be a salutary result, and that it has a sufficiently rational relationship to commerce to validate the application of the overtime provisions to private employers. But, like the minimum wage provisions, the vice of the Act as sought to be applied here is that it directly penalizes the States for choosing to hire governmental employees on terms different from those which Congress has sought to impose.

This congressionally imposed displacement of state decisions may substantially restructure traditional ways in which the local governments have arranged their affairs. Although, at this point, many of the actual effects under the proposed amendments remain a matter of some dispute among the parties, enough can be satisfactorily anticipated for an outline discussion of their general import. The requirement imposing premium rates upon any employment in excess of what Congress has decided is appropriate for a governmental employee's workweek, for example, appears likely to have the effect of coercing the States to structure work periods in some employment areas, such as police and fire protection, in a manner substantially different from practices which have long been commonly accepted among local governments of this Nation. In addition, appellee represents that the Act will require that the premium compensation for overtime worked must be paid in cash, rather than with compensatory time off, unless such compensatory time is taken in the same pay period. Supplemental Brief for Appellee 9-10; *see Dunlop v. New Jersey, cert. pending sub nom. New Jersey v. Usery,* No. 75-532. This, too, appears likely to be highly disruptive of accepted employment practices in many governmental areas where the demand for a number of employees to perform important jobs for extended periods on short notice can be both unpredictable and critical. Another example of congressional choices displacing those of the States in the area of what are, without doubt, essential governmental decisions may be found in the practice of using volunteer firemen, a source of manpower crucial to many of our smaller towns' existence. Under the regulations proposed by appellee, whether individuals are indeed "volunteers" rather than "employees" subject to the minimum wage provisions of the Act are questions to be decided in the courts. *See* Brief for Appellee 49, and n.41. It goes without saying that provisions such as these contemplate a significant reduction of traditional volunteer assistance which has been, in the past, drawn on to complement the operation of many local governmental functions.

Our examination of the effect of the 1974 amendments, as sought to be extended to the States and their political subdivisions, satisfies us that both the minimum wage and the maximum hour provisions will impermissibly interfere with the integral governmental functions of these bodies. We earlier noted some disagreement between the parties regarding the precise effect the amendments will have in application. We do not believe particularized assessments of actual impact are crucial to resolution of the issue presented, however. For even if we accept appellee's assessments concerning the impact of the amendments, their application will nonetheless significantly alter or displace the States' abilities to structure employer employee relationships in such areas as fire prevention, police protection, sanitation, public health, and parks and recreation. These activities are typical of those performed by state and local governments in discharging their dual functions of administering the public law and furnishing public services. Indeed, it is functions such as these which governments are created to provide, services such as these which the States have traditionally afforded their citizens. If Congress may withdraw from the States the authority to make those fundamental employment decisions upon which their systems for performance of these functions must rest, we think there would be little left of the States' "separate and independent existence." *Coyle.* Thus, even if appellants may have overestimated the effect which the Act will have upon their current levels and patterns of governmental activity, the dispositive factor is that Congress has attempted to exercise its Commerce Clause authority to prescribe minimum wages and maximum hours to be paid by the States in their capacities as sovereign governments. In so doing, Congress has sought to wield its power in a fashion that would impair the States' "ability to function effectively in a federal system." *Fry*. This exercise of congressional authority does not comport with the federal system of government embodied in the Constitution. We hold that, insofar as the challenged amendments operate to directly displace the States' freedom to structure integral operations in areas of traditional governmental functions, they are not within the authority granted Congress by Art. I, §8, cl. 3.

GARCIA v. SAN ANTONIO METROPOLITAN TRANSIT AUTHORITY

469 U.S. 528 (1985)

Opinion: Blackmun, joined by Brennan, White, Marshall, Stevens
Dissent: Powell, joined by Burger, Rehnquist, O'Connor
Dissent: Rehnquist
Dissent: O'Connor, joined by Rehnquist, Powell

Nine years after National League of Cities v. Usery, *U.S. Supreme Court Justice Harry Blackmun changed his vote to overturn that precedent in* Garcia v. San Antonio Metropolitan Transit Authority. *Is Justice Blackmun right that it is unworkable to distinguish between ordinary economic activity by states' governments and whatever activity reflects their special status as sovereigns?*

JUSTICE BLACKMUN *delivered the opinion of the Court.*

We revisit in these cases an issue raised in *National League of Cities v. Usery*. In that litigation, this Court, by a sharply divided vote, ruled that the Commerce Clause does not empower Congress to enforce the minimum-wage and overtime provisions of the Fair Labor Standards Act (FLSA) against the States "in areas of traditional governmental functions." Id., at 852. Although *National League of Cities* supplied some examples of "traditional governmental functions," it did not offer a general explanation of how a "traditional" function is to be distinguished from a "nontraditional" one. Since then, federal and state courts have struggled with the task, thus imposed, of identifying a traditional function for purposes of state immunity under the Commerce Clause.

In the present cases, a Federal District Court concluded that municipal ownership and operation of a mass-transit system is a traditional governmental function and thus, under *National League of Cities*, is exempt from the obligations imposed by the FLSA. Faced with the identical question, three Federal Courts of Appeals and one state appellate court have reached the opposite conclusion.

Our examination of this "function" standard applied in these and other cases over the last eight years now persuades us that the attempt to draw the boundaries of state regulatory immunity in terms of "traditional governmental function" is not only unworkable but is also inconsistent with established principles of federalism and, indeed, with those very federalism principles on which *National League of Cities* purported to rest. That case, accordingly, is overruled.

Appellees have not argued that SAMTA is immune from regulation under the FLSA on the ground that it is a local transit system engaged in intrastate commercial activity. In a practical sense, SAMTA's operations might well be characterized as "local." Nonetheless, it long has been settled that Congress' authority under the Commerce Clause extends to intrastate economic activities that affect interstate commerce. Were SAMTA a privately owned and operated enterprise, it could not credibly argue that Congress exceeded the bounds of its Commerce Clause powers in prescribing minimum wages and overtime rates for SAMTA's employees. Any constitutional exemption from the requirements of the FLSA therefore must rest on SAMTA's status as a governmental entity rather than on the "local" nature of its operations.

The prerequisites for governmental immunity under *National League of Cities* were summarized by this Court in *Hodel*. Under that summary, four conditions must be satisfied before a state activity may be deemed immune from a particular federal regulation under the Commerce Clause. First, it is said that the federal statute at issue must regulate "the 'States as States.'" Second, the statute must "address matters that are indisputably '[attributes] of state sovereignty.'" Third, state compliance with the federal obligation must "directly impair [the States'] ability 'to structure integral operations in areas of traditional governmental functions.'" Finally, the relation of state and federal interests must not be such that "the nature of the federal interest... justifies state submission."

Thus far, this Court itself has made little headway in defining the scope of the governmental functions deemed protected under *National League of Cities*. In that case the Court set forth examples of protected and unprotected functions, but provided no explanation of how those examples were identified....

Many constitutional standards involve "[undoubted] . . . gray areas," and, despite the difficulties that this Court and other courts have encountered so far, it normally might be fair to venture the assumption that case-by-case development would lead to a workable standard for determining whether a particular governmental function should be immune from federal regulation under the Commerce Clause. A further cautionary note is sounded, however, by the Court's experience in the related field of state immunity from federal taxation.... If these tax-immunity cases had any common thread, it was in the attempt to distinguish between "governmental" and "proprietary" functions....

The distinction the Court discarded as unworkable in the field of tax immunity has proved no more fruitful in the field of regulatory immunity under the Commerce Clause. Neither do any of the alternative standards that might be employed to distinguish between protected and unprotected governmental functions appear manageable. We rejected the possibility of making immunity turn on a purely historical standard of "tradition" in Long Island, and properly so. The most obvious defect of a historical approach to state immunity is that it prevents a court from accommodating changes in the historical functions of States, changes that have resulted in a number of once-private functions like education being assumed by the States and their subdivisions. At the same time, the only apparent virtue of a rigorous historical standard, namely, its promise of a reasonably objective measure for state immunity, is illusory. Reliance on history as an organizing principle results in line-drawing of the most arbitrary sort; the genesis of state governmental functions stretches over a historical continuum from before the Revolution to the present, and courts would have to decide by fiat precisely how longstanding a pattern of state involvement had to be for federal regulatory authority to be defeated.

A nonhistorical standard for selecting immune governmental functions is likely to be just as unworkable as is a historical standard. The goal of identifying "uniquely" governmental functions, for example, has been rejected by the Court in the field of government tort liability in part because the notion of a "uniquely" governmental function is unmanageable. Another possibility would be to confine immunity to "necessary" governmental services, that is, services that would be provided inadequately or not at all unless the government provided them. The set of services that fits into this category, however, may well be negligible. The fact that an unregulated market produces less of some service than a State deems desirable does not mean that the State itself must provide the service; in most if not all cases, the State can "contract out" by hiring private firms to provide the service or simply by providing subsidies to existing suppliers. It also is open to question how well equipped courts are to make this kind of determination about the workings of economic markets.

We believe, however, that there is a more fundamental problem at work here, a problem that explains why the Court was never able to provide a basis for the governmental/proprietary distinction in the intergovernmental tax-immunity cases and why an attempt to draw similar distinctions with respect to federal regulatory authority under *National League of Cities* is unlikely to succeed regardless of how the distinctions are phrased. The problem is that neither the governmental/proprietary distinction nor any other that purports to separate out important governmental functions can be faithful to the role of federalism in a democratic society. The essence of our federal system is that within the realm of authority left open to them under the Constitution, the States must be equally free to engage in any activity that their citizens choose for the common weal, no matter how unorthodox or unnecessary anyone else — including the judiciary — deems state involvement to be. Any rule of state immunity that looks to the "traditional," "integral," or "necessary" nature of governmental functions inevitably invites an unelected federal judiciary to make decisions about which state policies it favors and which ones it dislikes. "The science of government . . . is the science of experiment," and the States cannot serve as laboratories for social and economic experiment if they must pay an added price when they meet the changing needs of their citizenry by taking up functions that an earlier day and a different society left in private hands. In the words of Justice Black:

> "There is not, and there cannot be, any unchanging line of demarcation between essential and non-essential governmental functions. Many governmental functions of today have at some time in the past been non-governmental. The genius of our government provides that, within the sphere of constitutional action, the people — acting not through the courts but through their elected legislative representatives — have the power to determine as conditions demand, what services and functions the public welfare requires."

We therefore now reject, as unsound in principle and unworkable in practice, a rule of state immunity from federal regulation that turns on a judicial appraisal of whether a particular governmental function is "integral" or "traditional." Any such rule leads to inconsistent results at the same time that it disserves principles of democratic self-governance, and it breeds inconsistency precisely because it is divorced from those principles. If there are to be limits on the Federal Government's power to interfere with state functions — as undoubtedly there are — we must look elsewhere to find them. We accordingly return to the underlying issue that confronted this Court in *National League of Cities* — the manner in which the Constitution insulates States from the reach of Congress' power under the Commerce Clause.

The central theme of *National League of Cities* was that the States occupy a special position in our constitutional system and that the scope of Congress' authority under the Commerce Clause must reflect that position. Of course, the Commerce Clause by its specific language does not provide any special limitation on Congress' actions with respect to the States. . . .

What has proved problematic is not the perception that the Constitution's federal structure imposes limitations on the Commerce Clause, but rather the nature and content of those limitations. One approach to defining the limits on Congress' authority to regulate the States under the Commerce Clause is to identify certain underlying elements of political sovereignty that are deemed essential to the States' "separate and independent existence." [T]he Court concluded that decisions by a State concerning the wages and hours of its employees are an "undoubted attribute of state sovereignty." . . .

We doubt that courts ultimately can identify principled constitutional limitations on the scope of Congress' Commerce Clause powers over the States merely by relying on a priori definitions of state sovereignty. In part, this is because of the elusiveness of objective criteria for "fundamental" elements of state sovereignty, a problem we have witnessed in the search for "traditional governmental functions." There is, however, a more fundamental reason: the sovereignty of the States is limited by the Constitution itself. A variety of sovereign powers, for example, are withdrawn from the States by Article I, §10. Section 8 of the same Article works an equally sharp contraction of state sovereignty by authorizing Congress to exercise a wide range of legislative powers and (in conjunction with the Supremacy Clause of Article VI) to displace contrary state legislation. By providing for final review of questions of federal law in this Court, Article III curtails the sovereign power of the States' judiciaries to make authoritative determinations of law. Finally, the developed application, through the Fourteenth Amendment, of the greater part of the Bill of Rights to the States limits the sovereign authority that States otherwise would possess to legislate with respect to their citizens and to conduct their own affairs.

The States unquestionably do "[retain] a significant measure of sovereign authority." They do so, however, only to the extent that the Constitution has not divested them of their original powers and transferred those powers to the Federal Government. . . .

[T]he fact that the States remain sovereign as to all powers not vested in Congress or denied them by the Constitution offers no guidance about where the frontier between state and federal power lies. In short, we have no license to employ freestanding conceptions of state sovereignty when measuring congressional authority under the Commerce Clause.

Apart from the limitation on federal authority inherent in the delegated nature of Congress' Article I powers, the principal means chosen by the Framers to ensure the role of the States in the federal system lies in the structure of the Federal Government itself. It is no novelty to observe that the composition of the Federal Government was designed in large part to protect the States from overreaching by Congress. The Framers thus gave the States a role in the selection both of the Executive and the Legislative Branches of the Federal Government. The States were vested with indirect influence over the House of Representatives and the Presidency by their control of electoral qualifications and their role in Presidential elections. They were given more direct influence in the Senate, where each State received equal representation and each Senator was to be selected by the legislature of his State. The significance attached to the States' equal representation in the Senate is underscored by the prohibition of any constitutional amendment divesting a State of equal representation without the State's consent.

[T]he Framers chose to rely on a federal system in which special restraints on federal power over the States inhered principally in the workings of the National Government itself, rather than in discrete limitations on the objects of federal authority. State sovereign interests, then, are more properly protected by procedural safeguards inherent in the structure of the federal system than by judicially created limitations on federal power.

We realize that changes in the structure of the Federal Government have taken place since 1789, not the least of which has been the substitution of popular election of Senators by the adoption of the Seventeenth Amendment in 1913, and that these changes may work to alter the influence of the States in the federal political process. Nonetheless, against this background, we are convinced that the fundamental limitation that the constitutional scheme imposes on the Commerce Clause to protect the "States as States" is one of process rather than one of result. Any substantive restraint on the exercise of Commerce Clause powers must find its justification in the procedural nature of this basic limitation, and it must be tailored to compensate for possible failings in the national political process rather than to dictate a "sacred province of state autonomy."

Insofar as the present cases are concerned, then, we need go no further than to state that we perceive nothing in the overtime and minimum-wage requirements of the FLSA, as applied to SAMTA, that is destructive of state sovereignty or violative of any constitutional provision. SAMTA faces nothing more than the same minimum-wage and overtime obligations that hundreds of thousands of other employers, public as well as private, have to meet.

JUSTICE POWELL, *with whom* **THE CHIEF JUSTICE, JUSTICE REHNQUIST,** *and* **JUSTICE O'CONNOR** *join, dissenting.*

The Court today, in its 5–4 decision, overrules *National League of Cities v. Usery*, a case in which we held that Congress lacked authority to impose the requirements of the Fair Labor Standards Act on state and local governments. Because I believe this decision substantially alters the federal system embodied in the Constitution, I dissent.

There are, of course, numerous examples over the history of this Court in which prior decisions have been reconsidered and overruled. There have been few cases, however, in which the principle of stare decisis and the rationale of recent decisions were ignored as abruptly as we now witness. The reasoning of the Court in *National League of Cities*, and the principle applied there, have been reiterated consistently over the past eight years. . . .

Whatever effect the Court's decision may have in weakening the application of stare decisis, it is likely to be less important than what the Court has done to the Constitution itself. A unique feature of the United States is the federal system of government guaranteed by the Constitution and implicit in the very name of our country. Despite some genuflecting in the Court's opinion to the concept of federalism, today's decision effectively reduces the Tenth Amendment to meaningless rhetoric when Congress acts pursuant to the Commerce Clause. The Court holds that the Fair Labor Standards Act (FLSA) "contravened no affirmative limit on Congress' power under the Commerce Clause" to determine the wage rates and hours of employment of all state and local employees. . . .

To leave no doubt about its intention, the Court renounces its decision in *National League of Cities* because it "inevitably invites an unelected federal judiciary to make decisions about which state policies its favors and which ones it dislikes." In other words, the extent to which the States may exercise their authority, when Congress purports to act under the Commerce Clause, henceforth is to be determined from time to time by political decisions made by members of the Federal Government, decisions the Court says will not be subject to judicial review. I note that it does not seem to have occurred to the Court that it—an unelected majority of five Justices—today rejects almost 200 years of the understanding of the constitutional status of federalism. In doing so, there is only a single passing reference to the Tenth Amendment. Nor is so much as a dictum of any court cited in support of the view that the role of the States in the federal system may depend upon the grace of elected federal officials, rather than on the Constitution as interpreted by this Court.

The Court finds that the test of state immunity approved in *National League of Cities* and its progeny is unworkable and unsound in principle. In finding the test to be unworkable, the Court begins by mischaracterizing *National League of Cities* and subsequent cases. In concluding that efforts to define state immunity are unsound in principle, the Court radically departs from long-settled constitutional values and ignores the role of judicial review in our system of government.

Today's opinion does not explain how the States' role in the electoral process guarantees that particular exercises of the Commerce Clause power will not infringe on residual state sovereignty. Members of Congress are elected from the various States, but once in office they are Members of the Federal Government. Although the States participate in the Electoral College, this is hardly a reason to view the President as a representative of the States' interest against federal encroachment. We noted recently "[the] hydraulic pressure inherent within each of the separate Branches to exceed the outer limits of its power. . . ." *INS v. Chadha*. The Court offers no reason to think that this pressure will not operate when Congress seeks to invoke its powers under the Commerce Clause, notwithstanding the electoral role of the States.

The fact that Congress generally does not transgress constitutional limits on its power to reach state activities does not make judicial review any less necessary to rectify the cases in which it does do so. The States' role in our system of government is a matter of constitutional law, not of legislative grace. "The powers not delegated to the United States by the Constitution, nor prohibited by it to the States, are reserved to the States, respectively, or to the people."

More troubling than the logical infirmities in the Court's reasoning is the result of its holding, i.e., that federal political officials, invoking the Commerce Clause, are the sole judges of the limits of their own power. This result is inconsistent with the fundamental principles of our constitutional system. At least since *Marbury v. Madison* it has been the settled province of the federal judiciary "to say what the law is" with respect to the constitutionality of Acts of Congress. In rejecting the role of the judiciary in protecting the States from federal overreaching, the Court's opinion offers no explanation for ignoring the teaching of the most famous case in our history.

In our federal system, the States have a major role that cannot be pre-empted by the National Government. As contemporaneous writings and the debates at the ratifying conventions make clear, the States' ratification of the Constitution was predicated on this understanding of federalism. Indeed, the Tenth Amendment was adopted specifically to ensure that the important role promised the States by the proponents of the Constitution was realized.

Much of the initial opposition to the Constitution was rooted in the fear that the National Government would be too powerful and eventually would eliminate the States as viable political entities. This concern was voiced repeatedly until proponents of the Constitution made assurances that a Bill of Rights, including a provision explicitly reserving powers in the States, would be among the first business of the new Congress. . . . Antifederalists raised these concerns in almost every state ratifying convention. As a result, eight States voted for the Constitution only after proposing amendments to be adopted after ratification. All eight of these included among their recommendations some version of what later became the Tenth Amendment. So strong was the concern that the proposed Constitution was seriously defective without a specific bill of rights, including a provision reserving powers to the States, that in order to secure the votes for ratification, the Federalists eventually conceded that such provisions were necessary.

. . . Far from being "unsound in principle," . . . judicial enforcement of the Tenth Amendment is essential to maintaining the federal system so carefully designed by the Framers and adopted in the Constitution.

The Framers believed that the separate sphere of sovereignty reserved to the States would ensure that the States would serve as an effective "counterpoise" to the power of the Federal Government. The States would serve this essential role because they would attract and retain the loyalty of their citizens. The roots of such loyalty, the Founders thought, were found in the objects peculiar to state government. . . . [B]y usurping functions traditionally performed by the States, federal overreaching under the Commerce Clause undermines the constitutionally mandated balance of power between the States and the Federal Government, a balance designed to protect our fundamental liberties.

. . . [T]he Court today propounds a view of federalism that pays only lip service to the role of the States. [I]t fails to recognize the broad, yet specific areas of sovereignty that the Framers intended the States to retain. Indeed, the Court barely acknowledges that the Tenth Amendment exists. That Amendment states explicitly that "[the] powers not delegated to the United States . . . are reserved to the States." The Court recasts this language to say that the States retain their sovereign powers "only to the extent that the Constitution has not divested them of their original powers and transferred those powers to the Federal Government." This rephrasing is not a distinction without a difference; rather, it reflects the Court's unprecedented view that Congress is free under the Commerce Clause to assume a State's traditional sovereign power, and to do so without judicial review of its action. Indeed, the Court's view of federalism appears to relegate the States to precisely the trivial role that opponents of the Constitution feared they would occupy.

JUSTICE REHNQUIST, *dissenting.*

I join both Justice Powell's and Justice O'Connor's thoughtful dissents. Justice

Powell's reference to the "balancing test" approved in National League of Cities is not identical with the language in that case, which recognized that Congress could not act under its commerce power to infringe on certain fundamental aspects of state sovereignty that are essential to "the States' separate and independent existence." Nor is either test, or Justice O'Connor's suggested approach, precisely congruent with Justice Blackmun's views in 1976, when he spoke of a balancing approach which did not outlaw federal power in areas "where the federal interest is demonstrably greater." But under any one of these approaches, the judgment in these cases should be affirmed, and I do not think it incumbent on those of us in dissent to spell out further the fine points of a principle that will, I am confident, in time again command the support of a majority of this Court.

JUSTICE O'CONNOR, *dissenting.*

The Court today surveys the battle scene of federalism and sounds a retreat. Like Justice Powell, I would prefer to hold the field and, at the very least, render a little aid to the wounded. I join Justice Powell's opinion. I also write separately to note my fundamental disagreement with the majority's views of federalism and the duty of this Court.

The Court overrules *National League of Cities v. Usery*, on the grounds that it is not "faithful to the role of federalism in a democratic society." . . . "The essence of our federal system," the Court concludes, "is that, within the realm of authority left open to them under the Constitution, the States must be equally free to engage in any activity that their citizens choose for the common weal. . . ." *Ibid. National League of Cities* is held to be inconsistent with this narrow view of federalism because it attempts to protect only those fundamental aspects of state sovereignty that are essential to the States' separate and independent existence, rather than protecting all state activities "equally."

In my view, federalism cannot be reduced to the weak "essence" distilled by the majority today. There is more to federalism than the nature of the constraints that can be imposed on the States in "the realm of authority left open to them by the Constitution." The central issue of federalism, of course, is whether any realm is left open to the States by the Constitution — whether any area remains in which a State may act free of federal interference. "The issue . . . is whether the federal system has any *legal* substance, any core of constitutional right that courts will enforce." C. Black, *Perspectives in Constitutional Law* 30 (1963). The true "essence" of federalism is that the States, as States, have legitimate interests which the National Government is bound to respect even though its laws are supreme. If federalism so conceived and so carefully cultivated by the Framers of our Constitution is to remain meaningful, this Court cannot abdicate its constitutional responsibility to oversee the Federal Government's compliance with its duty to respect the legitimate interests of the States.

Due to the emergence of an integrated and industrialized national economy, this Court has been required to examine and review a breathtaking expansion of the powers of Congress. In doing so, the Court correctly perceived that the Framers of our Constitution intended Congress to have sufficient power to address national problems. But the Framers were not single-minded. The Constitution is animated by an array of intentions. *EEOC v. Wyoming* (Powell, J., dissenting). Just as surely as the Framers envisioned a National Government capable of solving national problems, they also envisioned a republic whose vitality was assured by the diffusion of power not only among the branches of the Federal Government, but also between the Federal Government and the States. *FERC v. Mississippi*, (O'Connor, J., dissenting). In the 18th century, these intentions did not conflict, because technology had not yet converted every local problem into a national one. A conflict has now emerged, and the Court today retreats rather than reconcile the Constitution's dual concerns for federalism and an effective commerce power.

We would do well to recall the constitutional basis for federalism and the development of the commerce power which has come to displace it. The text of the Constitution does not define the precise scope of state authority other than to specify, in the Tenth Amendment, that the powers not delegated to the United States by the Constitution are reserved to the States. In the view of the Framers, however, this did not leave state authority weak or defenseless; the powers delegated to the United States, after all, were "few and defined." *The Federalist* No. 45. The Framers' comments indicate that the sphere of state activity was to be a significant one, as Justice Powell's opinion clearly demonstrates. The States were to retain authority over those local concerns of greatest relevance and importance to the people. *The Federalist* No. 17. This division of authority, according to Madison, would produce efficient government and protect the rights of the people:

> "In a single republic, all the power surrendered by the people is submitted to the administration of a single government, and usurpations are guarded against by a division of the government into distinct and separate departments. In the compound republic of America, the power surrendered by the people is first divided between two distinct governments, and then the portion allotted to each subdivided among distinct and separate departments. Hence, a double security arises to the rights of the people. The different governments will controul each other at the same time that each will be controuled by itself." *The Federalist* No. 51.

Of course, one of the "few and defined" powers delegated to the National Congress was the power "To regulate Commerce with foreign Nations, and among the several States, and with the Indian Tribes." U.S. Const., Art. I, §8, cl. 3. The Framers perceived the interstate commerce power to be important but limited, and expected that it would be used primarily, if not exclusively, to remove interstate tariffs and to regulate maritime affairs and large-scale mercantile enterprise. This perception of a narrow commerce power is important not because it suggests that the commerce power should be as narrowly construed today. Rather, it explains why the Framers could believe the Constitution assured significant state authority even as it bestowed a range of powers, including the commerce power, on the Congress. In an era when interstate commerce represented a tiny fraction of economic activity and most goods and services were produced and consumed close to home, the interstate commerce power left a broad range of activities beyond the reach of Congress.

In the decades since ratification of the Constitution, interstate economic activity has steadily expanded. Industrialization, coupled with advances in transportation and communications, has created a national economy in which virtually every activity occurring within the borders of a State plays a part. The expansion and integration of the national economy brought with it a coordinate expansion in the scope of national problems. This Court has been increasingly generous in its interpretation of the commerce power of Congress, primarily to assure that the National Government would be able to deal with national economic problems. Most significantly, the Court in *NLRB v. Jones & Laughlin Steel*

Corp. and *United States v. Darby* rejected its previous interpretations of the commerce power which had stymied New Deal legislation. *Jones & Laughlin* and *Darby* embraced the notion that Congress can regulate intrastate activities that affect interstate commerce as surely as it can regulate interstate commerce directly. Subsequent decisions indicate that Congress, in order to regulate an activity, needs only a rational basis for a finding that the activity affects interstate commerce. *See Heart of Atlanta Motel, Inc. v. United States.* Even if a particular individual's activity has no perceptible interstate effect, it can be reached by Congress through regulation of that class of activity in general as long as that class, considered as a whole, affects interstate commerce. *Fry v. United States*; *Perez v. United States.*

Incidental to this expansion of the commerce power, Congress has been given an ability it lacked prior to the emergence of an integrated national economy. Because virtually every state activity, like virtually every activity of a private individual, arguably "affects" interstate commerce, Congress can now supplant the States from the significant sphere of activities envisioned for them by the Framers. It is in this context that recent changes in the workings of Congress, such as the direct election of Senators and the expanded influence of national interest groups . . . become relevant. These changes may well have lessened the weight Congress gives to the legitimate interests of States as States. As a result, there is now a real risk that Congress will gradually erase the diffusion of power between State and Nation on which the Framers based their faith in the efficiency and vitality of our Republic.

It would be erroneous, however, to conclude that the Supreme Court was blind to the threat to federalism when it expanded the commerce power. The Court based the expansion on the authority of Congress, through the Necessary and Proper Clause, "to resort to all means for the exercise of a granted power which are appropriate and plainly adapted to the permitted end." *United States v. Darby, supra,* at 124. It is through this reasoning that an intrastate activity "affecting" interstate commerce can be reached through the commerce power. Thus, in *United States v. Wrightwood Dairy Co.*, the Court stated:

> "The commerce power is not confined in its exercise to the regulation of commerce among the states. It extends to those activities intrastate which so affect interstate commerce, or the exertion of the power of Congress over it, as to make regulation of them appropriate means to the attainment of a legitimate end, the effective execution of the granted power to regulate interstate commerce . . . ."

United States v. Wrightwood Dairy Co. was heavily relied upon by *Wickard v. Filburn,* and the reasoning of these cases underlies every recent decision concerning the reach of Congress to activities affecting interstate commerce. *See, e.g., Fry v. United States, supra,* at 547; *Perez v. United States, supra,* at 151-152; *Heart of Atlanta Motel, Inc. v. United States, supra,* at 258-259.

It is worth recalling the cited passage in *McCulloch v. Maryland* that lies at the source of the recent expansion of the commerce power. "Let the end be legitimate, let it be within the scope of the constitution," Chief Justice Marshall said, "and all means which are appropriate, which are plainly adapted to that end, which are not prohibited, but consist with the letter and spirit of the constitution, are constitutional." The spirit of the Tenth Amendment, of course, is that the States will retain their integrity in a system in which the laws of the United States are nevertheless supreme. *Fry v. United States, supra,* at 547, n.7.

It is not enough that the "end be legitimate"; the means to that end chosen by

Congress must not contravene the spirit of the Constitution. Thus, many of this Court's decisions acknowledge that the means by which national power is exercised must take into account concerns for state autonomy. ("Undoubtedly, the scope of this [commerce] power must be considered in the light of our dual system of government, and may not be extended so as to embrace effects upon interstate commerce so indirect and remote that to embrace them, in view of our complex society, would effectually obliterate the distinction between what is national and what is local and create a completely centralized government"); for example, Congress might rationally conclude that the location a State chooses for its capital may affect interstate commerce, but the Court has suggested that Congress would nevertheless be barred from dictating that location because such an exercise of a delegated power would undermine the state sovereignty inherent in the Tenth Amendment. Similarly, Congress, in the exercise of its taxing and spending powers, can protect federal savings and loan associations, but if it chooses to do so by the means of converting quasi-public state savings and loan associations into federal associations, the Court has held that it contravenes the reserved powers of the States because the conversion is not a reasonably necessary exercise of power to reach the desired end. The operative language of these cases varies, but the underlying principle is consistent: state autonomy is a relevant factor in assessing the means by which Congress exercises its powers.

UNITED STATES v. LOPEZ

514 U.S. 549 (1995)

Opinion: Rehnquist, joined by O'Connor, Scalia, Kennedy, Thomas
Concurrence: Kennedy, joined by O'Connor
Concurrence: Thomas
Dissent: Breyer, joined by Stevens, Souter, Ginsburg
Dissent: Stevens
Dissent: Souter

Although it looked like National League of Cities v. Usery *might spark a resurgence of the concern for the powers of the state as opposed to the federal government, Justice Harry Blackmun's opinion in* Garcia v. San Antonio Metropolitan Transit Authority *reversed that potential trajectory. Thus, in some ways,* National League of Cities v. Usery *was a false start for asserting the sovereignty of states. Importantly, however, Justice William Rehnquist's dissent in* Garcia v. San Antonio Metropolitan Transit Authority *emphatically asserts the importance of state sovereignty. It took ten years for Justice Rehnquist's prediction that the Court would rediscover the principles of federalism to be realized. By the time the "New Federalism" finally emerged, Justice Rehnquist had been promoted to Chief Justice and liberal Justice Thurgood Marshall had been replaced by conservative Justice Clarence Thomas.*

In United States v. Lopez, *the Court struck down a provision of the Gun-Free School Zones Act prohibiting individuals from carrying a firearm within a certain distance of a school. In his opinion, Chief Justice Rehnquist argues that the possession of a handgun does not constitute "economic activity," nor does it substantially affect interstate commerce, and that therefore the law extends beyond Congress's limited powers. Is the distinction between economic activity and noneconomic activity tenable? Is it consistent with all of the landmark New Deal precedents? Recall that the* McCulloch v. Maryland *framework for congressional power is to ask whether the law in question is an appropriate means to a legitimate end. Is U.S. Supreme Court Justice Stephen Breyer correct to say that the decision grants Congress considerably less deference than precedent requires?*

CHIEF JUSTICE REHNQUIST *delivered the opinion of the Court.*

In the Gun-Free School Zones Act of 1990, Congress made it a federal offense "for any individual knowingly to possess a firearm at a place that the individual knows, or has reasonable cause to believe, is a school zone." 18 U.S.C. §922(q)(1)(A). The Act neither regulates a commercial activity nor contains a requirement that the possession be connected in any way to interstate commerce. We hold that the Act exceeds the authority of Congress "to regulate Commerce . . . among the several States. . . ."

On March 10, 1992, respondent, who was then a 12th-grade student, arrived at Edison High School in San Antonio, Texas, carrying a concealed .38 caliber handgun and five bullets. Acting upon an anonymous tip, school authorities confronted respondent, who admitted that he was carrying the weapon. He was arrested and charged under Texas law with firearm possession on school premises. The next day, the state charges were dismissed after federal agents charged respondent by complaint with violating the Gun-Free School Zones Act of 1990.

We start with first principles. The Constitution creates a Federal Government of enumerated powers. As James Madison wrote, "the powers delegated by the proposed Constitution to the federal government are few and defined. Those which are to remain in the State governments are numerous and indefinite." This constitutionally mandated division of authority "was adopted by the Framers to ensure protection of our fundamental liberties . . . a healthy balance of power between the States and the Federal Government will reduce the risk of tyranny and abuse from either front."

The Court, through Chief Justice Marshall, first defined the nature of Congress' commerce power in *Gibbons v. Ogden*:

> "Commerce, undoubtedly, is traffic, but it is something more: it is intercourse. It describes the commercial intercourse between nations, and parts of nations, in all its branches, and is regulated by prescribing rules for carrying on that intercourse."

The commerce power "is the power to regulate; that is, to prescribe the rule by which commerce is to be governed. This power, like all others vested in congress, is complete in itself, may be exercised to its utmost extent, and acknowledges no limitations, other than are prescribed in the constitution." The *Gibbons* Court, however, acknowledged that limitations on the commerce power are inherent in the very language of the Commerce Clause.

. . . *Jones & Laughlin Steel, Darby*, and *Wickard* ushered in an era of Commerce Clause jurisprudence that greatly expanded the previously defined authority of Congress under that Clause. In part, this was a recognition of the great changes that had occurred in the way business was carried on in this country. Enterprises that had once been local or at most regional in nature had become national in scope. But the doctrinal change also reflected a view that earlier Commerce Clause cases artificially had constrained the authority of Congress to regulate interstate commerce.

But even these modern-era precedents which have expanded congressional power under the Commerce Clause confirm that this power is subject to outer limits. In *Jones & Laughlin Steel*, the Court warned that the scope of the interstate commerce power "must be considered in the light of our dual system of government and may not be extended so as to embrace effects upon interstate commerce so indirect and remote that to embrace them, in view of our complex society, would effectually obliterate the distinction between what is national and what is local and create a completely centralized government." Since that time, the Court has heeded that warning and undertaken to decide whether a rational basis existed for concluding that a regulated activity sufficiently affected interstate commerce.

. . . [W]e have identified three broad categories of activity that Congress may regulate under its commerce power. First, Congress may regulate the use of the channels of interstate commerce. Second, Congress is empowered to regulate and protect the instrumentalities of interstate commerce, or persons or things in interstate commerce, even though the threat may come only from intrastate activities. Finally, Congress' commerce authority includes the power to regulate those activities having a substantial relation to interstate commerce, i.e., those activities that substantially affect interstate commerce.

We now turn to consider the power of Congress, in the light of this framework, to enact §922(q). The first two categories of authority may be quickly disposed of: §922(q) is not a regulation of the use of the channels of interstate commerce, nor is it an attempt to prohibit the interstate transportation of a commodity through the channels of commerce; nor can §922(q) be justified as a regulation by which Congress has sought to protect an instrumentality of interstate commerce or a thing in interstate commerce. Thus, if §922(q) is to be sustained, it must be under the third category as a regulation of an activity that substantially affects interstate commerce.

First, we have upheld a wide variety of congressional Acts regulating intrastate economic activity where we have concluded that the activity substantially affected interstate commerce. Examples include the regulation of intrastate coal mining; intrastate extortionate credit transactions, restaurants utilizing substantial interstate supplies, inns and hotels catering to interstate guests, and production and consumption of homegrown wheat. These examples are by no means exhaustive, but the pattern is clear. Where economic activity substantially affects interstate commerce, legislation regulating that activity will be sustained.

Even *Wickard*, which is perhaps the most far reaching example of Commerce Clause authority over intrastate activity, involved economic activity in a way that the possession of a gun in a school zone does not.

. . . Section 922(q) is a criminal statute that by its terms has nothing to do with "commerce" or any sort of economic enterprise, however broadly one might define those terms. Section 922(q) is not an essential part of a larger regulation of economic activity, in which the regulatory scheme could be undercut unless the intrastate activity were regulated. It cannot, therefore, be sustained under our cases upholding regulations of activities that arise out of or are connected with a commercial transaction, which viewed in the aggregate, substantially affects interstate commerce.

Second, §922(q) contains no jurisdictional element which would ensure, through case-by-case inquiry, that the firearm possession in question affects interstate commerce. . . .

Although as part of our independent evaluation of constitutionality under the Commerce Clause we of course consider legislative findings, and indeed even congressional committee findings, regarding effect on interstate commerce, the Government concedes that "neither the statute nor its legislative history contain[s] express congressional findings regarding the effects upon interstate commerce of gun possession in a school zone." We agree with the Government that Congress normally is not required to make formal findings as to the substantial burdens that an activity has on interstate commerce. But to the extent that congressional findings would enable us to evaluate the legislative judgment that the activity in question substantially affected interstate commerce, even though no such substantial effect was visible to the naked eye, they are lacking here.

The Government's essential contention, in fine, is that we may determine here that §922(q) is valid because possession of a firearm in a local school zone does indeed substantially affect interstate commerce. The Government argues that possession of a firearm in a school zone may result in violent crime and that violent crime can be expected to affect the functioning of the national economy in two ways. First, the costs of violent crime are substantial, and, through the mechanism of insurance, those costs are spread throughout the population. Second, violent crime reduces the willingness of individuals to travel to areas within the country that are perceived to be unsafe. The Government also argues that the presence of guns in schools poses a substantial threat to the educational process by threatening the learning environment.

A handicapped educational process, in turn, will result in a less productive citizenry. That, in turn, would have an adverse effect on the Nation's economic well-being. As a result, the Government argues that Congress could rationally have concluded that §922(q) substantially affects interstate commerce.

We pause to consider the implications of the Government's arguments. The Government admits, under its "costs of crime" reasoning, that Congress could regulate not only all violent crime, but all activities that might lead to violent crime, regardless of how tenuously they relate to interstate commerce. Similarly, under the Government's "national productivity" reasoning, Congress could regulate any activity that it found was related to the economic productivity of individual citizens: family law (including marriage, divorce, and child custody), for example. Under the theories that the Government presents in support of §922(q), it is difficult to perceive any limitation on federal power, even in areas such as criminal law enforcement or education where States historically have been sovereign. Thus, if we were to accept the Government's arguments, we are hard pressed to posit any activity by an individual that Congress is without power to regulate.

Justice Breyer rejects our reading of precedent and argues that "Congress . . . could rationally conclude that schools fall on the commercial side of the line." Justice Breyer's rationale lacks any real limits because, depending on the level of generality, any activity can be looked upon as commercial. Under the dissent's rationale, Congress could just as easily look at child rearing as "falling on the commercial side of the line" because it provides a "valuable service — namely, to equip [children] with the skills they need to survive in life and, more specifically, in the workplace." We do not doubt that Congress has authority under the Commerce Clause to regulate numerous commercial activities that substantially affect interstate commerce and also affect the educational process. That authority, though broad, does not include the authority to regulate each and every aspect of local schools.

The possession of a gun in a local school zone is in no sense an economic activity that might, through repetition elsewhere, substantially affect any sort of interstate commerce. Respondent was a local student at a local school; there is no indication that he had recently moved in interstate commerce, and there is no requirement that his possession of the firearm have any concrete tie to interstate commerce.

To uphold the Government's contentions here, we would have to pile inference upon inference in a manner that would bid fair to convert congressional authority under the Commerce Clause to a general police power of the sort retained by the States. Admittedly, some of our prior cases have taken long steps down that road, giving great deference to congressional action. The broad language in these opinions has suggested the possibility of additional expansion, but we decline here to proceed any further. To do so would require us to conclude that the Constitution's enumeration of powers does not presuppose something not enumerated, and that there never will be a distinction between what is truly national and what is truly local. This we are unwilling to do.

JUSTICE BREYER, *with whom* **JUSTICE STEVENS, JUSTICE SOUTER,** *and* **JUSTICE GINSBURG** *join, dissenting.*

The issue in this case is whether the Commerce Clause authorizes Congress to enact a statute that makes it a crime to possess a gun in, or near, a school. In my view, the statute falls well within the scope of the commerce power as this Court has understood that power over the last half century.

In reaching this conclusion, I apply three basic principles of Commerce Clause interpretation. First, the power to "regulate Commerce . . . among the several States," encompasses the power to regulate local activities insofar as they significantly affect interstate commerce. As the majority points out, the Court, in describing how much of an effect the Clause requires, sometimes has used the word "substantial" and sometimes has not. . . . I use the word "significant" because the word "substantial" implies a somewhat narrower power than recent precedent suggests. . . .

Second, in determining whether a local activity will likely have a significant effect upon interstate commerce, a court must consider, not the effect of an individual act (a single instance of gun possession), but rather the cumulative effect of all similar instances (i.e., the effect of all guns possessed in or near schools).

Third, the Constitution requires us to judge the connection between a regulated activity and interstate commerce, not directly, but at one remove. Courts must give Congress a degree of leeway in determining the existence of a significant factual connection between the regulated activity and interstate commerce—both because the Constitution delegates the commerce power directly to Congress and because the determination requires an empirical judgment of a kind that a legislature is more likely than a court to make with accuracy. The traditional words "rational basis" capture this leeway. Thus, the specific question before us, as the Court recognizes, is not whether the "regulated activity sufficiently affected interstate commerce," but, rather, whether Congress could have had "a rational basis" for so concluding.

I recognize that we must judge this matter independently. . . . And, I also recognize that Congress did not write specific "interstate commerce" findings into the law under which Lopez was convicted. Nonetheless, as I have already noted, the matter that we review independently (i.e., whether there is a "rational basis") already has considerable leeway built into it. And, the absence of findings, at most, deprives a statute of the benefit of some extra leeway. This extra deference, in principle, might change the result in a close case, though, in practice, it has not made a critical legal difference. It would seem particularly unfortunate to make the validity of the statute at hand turn on the presence or absence of findings. . . . [T]here is no special need here for a clear indication of Congress' rationale. The statute does not interfere with the exercise of state or local authority. . . .

Applying these principles to the case at hand, we must ask whether Congress could have had a rational basis for finding a significant (or substantial) connection between gun-related school violence and interstate commerce. Or, to put the question in the language of the explicit finding that Congress made when it amended this law in 1994: Could Congress rationally have found that "violent crime in school zones," through its effect on the "quality of education," significantly (or substantially) affects "interstate" or "foreign commerce"? As long as one views the commerce connection, not as a "technical legal conception," but as "a practical one," the answer to this question must be yes. Numerous reports and studies — generated both inside and outside government — make clear that Congress could reasonably have found the empirical connection that its law, implicitly or explicitly, asserts.

For one thing, reports, hearings, and other readily available literature make clear that the problem of guns in and around schools is widespread and extremely serious. These materials report, for example, that four percent of American high school students (and six percent of inner-city high school students) carry a gun to school at least occasionally, that 12 percent of urban high school students have had guns fired at them, that 20 percent of those students have been threatened with guns, and that, in any 6-month period, several hundred thousand schoolchildren are victims of violent crimes in or near their schools. And, they report that this widespread violence in schools throughout the Nation significantly interferes with the quality of education in those schools. Based on reports such as these, Congress obviously could have thought that guns and learning are mutually exclusive. Congress could therefore have found a substantial educational problem — teachers unable to teach, students unable to learn — and concluded that guns near schools contribute substantially to the size and scope of that problem.

Having found that guns in schools significantly undermine the quality of education in our Nation's classrooms, Congress could also have found, given the effect of education upon interstate and foreign commerce, that gun-related violence in and around schools is a commercial, as well as a human, problem. Education, although far more than a matter of economics, has long been inextricably intertwined with the Nation's economy. Scholars estimate that nearly a quarter of America's economic growth in the early years of this century is traceable directly to increased schooling, that investment in "human capital" (through spending on education) exceeded investment in "physical capital" by a ratio of almost two to one, and that the economic returns to this investment in education exceeded the returns to conventional capital investment.

In recent years the link between secondary education and business has strengthened, becoming both more direct and more important. Scholars on the subject report that technological changes and innovations in management techniques have altered the nature of the workplace so that more jobs now demand greater educational skills. . . .

Increasing global competition also has made primary and secondary education economically more important. The portion of the American economy attributable to international trade nearly tripled between 1950 and 1980, and more than 70 percent of American-made goods now compete with imports. Yet, lagging worker productivity has contributed to negative trade balances and to real hourly compensation that has fallen below wages in 10 other industrialized nations. At least some significant part of this serious productivity problem is attributable to students who emerge from classrooms without the reading or mathematical skills necessary to compete with their European or Asian counterparts, and, presumably, to high school dropout rates of 20 to 25 percent (up to 50 percent in inner cities)....

Finally, there is evidence that, today more than ever, many firms base their location decisions upon the presence, or absence, of a work force with a basic education.... In light of this increased importance of education to individual firms, it is no surprise that half of the Nation's manufacturers have become involved with setting standards and shaping curricula for local schools, that 88 percent think this kind of involvement is important, that more than 20 States have recently passed educational reforms to attract new business, and that business magazines have begun to rank cities according to the quality of their schools.

The economic links I have just sketched seem fairly obvious. Why then is it not equally obvious, in light of those links, that a widespread, serious, and substantial physical threat to teaching and learning also substantially threatens the commerce to which that teaching and learning is inextricably tied? That is to say, guns in the hands of six percent of inner-city high school students and gun-related violence throughout a city's schools must threaten the trade and commerce that those schools support. The only question, then, is whether the latter threat is (to use the majority's terminology) "substantial." The evidence of (1) the extent of the gun-related violence problem, see supra, at 619, (2) the extent of the resulting negative effect on classroom learning, see ibid., and (3) the extent of the consequent negative commercial effects, see supra, at 620-622, when taken together, indicate a threat to trade and commerce that is "substantial." At the very least, Congress could rationally have concluded that the links are "substantial."

Specifically, Congress could have found that gun-related violence near the classroom poses a serious economic threat (1) to consequently inadequately educated workers who must endure low paying jobs, and (2) to communities and businesses that might (in today's "information society") otherwise gain, from a well-educated work force, an important commercial advantage, of a kind that location near a railhead or harbor provided in the past. Congress might also have found these threats to be no different in kind from other threats that this Court has found within the commerce power, such as the threat that loan sharking poses to the "funds" of "numerous localities," and that unfair labor practices pose to instrumentalities of commerce. As I have pointed out, Congress has written that "the occurrence of violent crime in school zones" has brought about a "decline in the quality of education" that "has an adverse impact on interstate commerce and the foreign commerce of the United States." The violence-related facts, the educational facts, and the economic facts, taken together, make this conclusion rational. And, because under our case law, the sufficiency of the constitutionally necessary Commerce Clause link between a crime of violence and interstate commerce turns simply upon size or degree, those same facts make the statute constitutional.

To hold this statute constitutional is not to "obliterate" the "distinction between what is national and what is local," nor is it to hold that the Commerce Clause permits the Federal Government to "regulate any activity that it found was related to the economic productivity of individual citizens," to regulate "marriage, divorce, and child custody," or to regulate any and all aspects of education. First, this statute is aimed at curbing a particularly acute threat to the educational process — the possession (and use) of life-threatening firearms in, or near, the classroom. The empirical evidence that I have discussed above unmistakably documents the special way in which guns and education are incompatible. This Court has previously recognized the singularly disruptive potential on interstate commerce that acts of violence may have. Second, the immediacy of the connection between education and the national economic well-being is documented by scholars and accepted by society at large in a way and to a degree that may not hold true for other social institutions. It must surely be the rare case, then, that a statute strikes at conduct that (when considered in the abstract) seems so removed from commerce, but which (practically speaking) has so significant an impact upon commerce.

The majority's holding — that §922 falls outside the scope of the Commerce Clause — creates three serious legal problems. First, the majority's holding runs contrary to modern Supreme Court cases that have upheld congressional actions despite connections to interstate or foreign commerce that are less significant than the effect of school violence. . . .

The second legal problem the Court creates comes from its apparent belief that it can reconcile its holding with earlier cases by making a critical distinction between "commercial" and noncommercial "transaction[s]." That is to say, the Court believes the Constitution would distinguish between two local activities, each of which has an identical effect upon interstate commerce, if one, but not the other, is "commercial" in nature. As a general matter, this approach fails to heed this Court's earlier warning not to turn "questions of the power of Congress" upon "formula[s]" that would give "controlling force to nomenclature such as 'production' and 'indirect' and foreclose consideration of the actual effects of the activity in question upon interstate commerce." . . . Although the majority today attempts to categorize *Perez, McClung*, and *Wickard* as involving intrastate "economic activity," the Courts that decided each of those cases did not focus upon the economic nature of the activity regulated. Rather, they focused upon whether that activity affected interstate or foreign commerce.

. . . [I]f there is a principled distinction that could work both here and in future cases, Congress (even in the absence of vocational classes, industry involvement, and private management) could rationally conclude that schools fall on the commercial side of the line. In 1990, the year Congress enacted the statute before us, primary and secondary schools spent $230 billion — that is, nearly a quarter of a trillion dollars — which accounts for a significant portion of our $5.5 trillion gross domestic product for that year. . . . Why could Congress, for Commerce Clause purposes, not consider schools as roughly analogous to commercial investments from which the Nation derives the benefit of an educated work force?

The third legal problem created by the Court's holding is that it threatens legal uncertainty in an area of law that, until this case, seemed reasonably well settled. Congress has enacted many statutes (more than 100 sections of the United States

Code), including criminal statutes (at least 25 sections), that use the words "affecting commerce" to define their scope. More importantly, in the absence of a jurisdictional element, are the courts nevertheless to take *Wickard* as inapplicable, and to judge the effect of a single noncommercial activity on interstate commerce without considering similar instances of the forbidden conduct? However these questions are eventually resolved, the legal uncertainty now created will restrict Congress' ability to enact criminal laws aimed at criminal behavior that, considered problem by problem rather than instance by instance, seriously threatens the economic, as well as social, well-being of Americans.

CASE QUESTION

After the decision, Congress responded by adding a jurisdictional requirement, requiring prosecutors to prove in each case that the gun in question moved in or otherwise affected interstate commerce. With this minor change, the Gun-Free School Zones Act of 1995 never again received a serious constitutional challenge. Given this fact, should we understand the *Lopez* decision to undermine the precedents found in the previous section, or instead as a warning requiring Congress to legislate with greater care?

PRINTZ v. UNITED STATES

521 U.S. 898 (1997)

Opinion: Scalia, joined by Rehnquist, O'Connor, Kennedy, Thomas
Dissent: Stevens, joined by Souter, Ginsburg, Breyer

In Lopez *we examined limits on the Commerce Clause power that defined the New Federalism. We now turn to another aspect of the New Federalism: limits on federal "commandeering" of state governments. We began this chapter by examining a "false start" in the Court's Tenth Amendment jurisprudence. Although* National League of Cities *seemed to announce a broadening of the Tenth Amendment limits on federal power,* Garcia *seemed to put an end to that expansion. But here we revisit the limits of the Tenth Amendment on the power of the federal government to command, or "commandeer," state officials to implement policy. As you read* Printz v. United States *consider how, if at all, it might be distinguished from* Garcia. *You might also consider how Justice Scalia's originalism, that is, his use of the interpretive principle that seeks to decide current cases in the light of the Constitution's originally intended meaning, affects his argument for balancing state and federal power.*

MR. JUSTICE SCALIA *delivered the opinion of the Court.*

The question presented in these cases is whether certain interim provisions of the Brady Handgun Violence Prevention Act, Pub. L. 103-159, 107 Stat. 1536, commanding state and local law enforcement officers to conduct background checks on prospective handgun purchasers and to perform certain related tasks, violate the Constitution.

The Gun Control Act of 1968 (GCA), 18 U.S.C. §921 *et seq.*, establishes a detailed federal scheme governing the distribution of firearms. It prohibits firearms dealers from transferring handguns to any person under 21, not resident in the dealer's State, or prohibited by state or local law from purchasing or possessing firearms, §922(b). It also forbids possession of a firearm by, and transfer of a firearm to, convicted felons, fugitives from justice, unlawful users of controlled substances, persons adjudicated as mentally defective or committed to mental institutions, aliens unlawfully present in the United States, persons dishonorably discharged from the Armed Forces, persons who have renounced their citizenship, and persons who have been subjected to certain restraining orders or been convicted of a misdemeanor offense involving domestic violence. §§922(d) and (g).

In 1993, Congress amended the GCA by enacting the Brady Act. The Act requires the Attorney General to establish a national instant background check system by November 30, 1998, Pub. L. 103-159, as amended, Pub. L. 103-322, 103 Stat. 2074, note following 18 U.S.C. §922 and immediately puts in place certain interim provisions until that system becomes operative. Under the interim provisions, a firearms dealer who proposes to transfer a handgun must first: (1) receive from the transferee a statement (the Brady Form), §922(s)(1)(A)(i)(I), containing the name, address and date of birth of the proposed transferee along with a sworn statement that the transferee is not among any of the classes of prohibited purchasers, §922(s)(3); (2) verify the identity of the transferee by examining an identification document, §922(s)(1)(A)(i)(II); and (3) provide the "chief law enforcement officer" (CLEO) of the transferee's residence with notice of the contents (and a copy) of the Brady Form, §§922(s)(1)(A)(i)(III) and (IV). With some exceptions, the dealer must then wait five business days before consummating the sale, unless the CLEO earlier notifies the dealer that he has no reason to believe the transfer would be illegal. §922(s)(1)(A)(ii).

The Brady Act creates two significant alternatives to the foregoing scheme. A dealer may sell a handgun immediately if the purchaser possesses a state handgun permit issued after a background check, §922(s)(1)(C), or if state law provides for an instant background check, §922(s)(1)(D). In States that have not rendered one of these alternatives applicable to all gun purchasers, CLEOs are required to perform certain duties. When a CLEO receives the required notice of a proposed transfer from the firearms dealer, the CLEO must "make a reasonable effort to ascertain within 5 business days whether receipt or possession would be in violation of the law, including research in whatever State and local recordkeeping systems are available and in a national system designated by the Attorney General." §922(s)(2). The Act does not require the CLEO to take any particular action if he determines that a pending transaction would be unlawful; he may notify the firearms dealer to that effect, but is not required to do so. If, however, the CLEO notifies a gun dealer that a prospective purchaser is ineligible to receive a handgun, he must, upon request, provide the would be purchaser with a written statement of the reasons for that determination. §922(s)(6)(C). Moreover, if the CLEO does not discover any basis for objecting to the sale, he must destroy any records in his possession relating to the transfer, including his copy of the Brady Form. §922(s)(6)(B)(i). Under a separate provision of the GCA, any person who "knowingly violates [the section of the GCA amended by the Brady Act] shall be fined under this title, imprisoned for no more than 1 year, or both." §924(a)(5).

Petitioners Jay Printz and Richard Mack, the CLEOs for Ravalli County, Montana, and Graham County, Arizona, respectively, filed separate actions challenging the constitutionality of the Brady Act's interim provisions. In each case, the District Court held that the provision requiring CLEOs to perform background checks was unconstitutional, but concluded that that provision was severable from the remainder of the Act, effectively leaving a voluntary background check system in place. 856 F. Supp. 1372 (Ariz. 1994); 854 F. Supp. 1503 (Mont. 1994). A divided panel of the Court of Appeals for the Ninth Circuit reversed, finding none of the Brady Act's interim provisions to be unconstitutional. 66 F.3d 1025 (1995). We granted certiorari. 518 U.S.___ (1996).

From the description set forth above, it is apparent that the Brady Act purports to direct state law enforcement officers to participate, albeit only temporarily, in the administration of a federally enacted regulatory scheme. Regulated firearms dealers are required to forward Brady Forms not to a federal officer or employee, but to the CLEOs, whose obligation to accept those forms is implicit in the duty imposed upon them to make "reasonable efforts" within five days to determine whether the sales reflected in the forms are lawful. While the CLEOs are subjected to no federal requirement that they prevent the sales determined to be unlawful (it is perhaps assumed that their state law duties will require prevention or apprehension), they are empowered to grant, in effect, waivers of the federally prescribed 5 day waiting period for handgun purchases by notifying the gun dealers that they have no reason to believe the transactions would be illegal....

[T]he Constitution was originally understood to permit imposition of an obligation on state *judges* to enforce federal prescriptions, insofar as those prescriptions related to matters appropriate for the judicial power. That assumption was perhaps implicit in one of the provisions of the Constitution, and was explicit in another. In accord with the so called Madisonian Compromise, Article III, §1, established only a Supreme Court, and made the creation of lower federal courts optional with the Congress—even though it was obvious that the Supreme Court alone could not hear all federal cases throughout the United States. See C. Warren, The Making of the Constitution 325-327 (1928). And the Supremacy Clause, Art. VI, cl. 2, announced that "the Laws of the United States . . . shall be the supreme Law of the Land; and the Judges in every State shall be bound thereby." It is understandable why courts should have been viewed distinctively in this regard; unlike legislatures and executives, they applied the law of other sovereigns all the time. The principle underlying so called "transitory" causes of action was that laws which operated elsewhere created obligations in justice that courts of the forum state would enforce.

See, e.g., *McKenna v. Fisk*, 1 How. 241, 247-249 (1843).

The Constitution itself, in the Full Faith and Credit Clause, Art. IV, §1, generally required such enforcement with respect to obligations arising in other States. See *Hughes v. Fetter*, 341 U.S. 609 (1951).

For these reasons, we do not think the early statutes imposing obligations on state courts imply a power of Congress to impress the state executive into its service. Indeed, it can be argued that the numerousness of these statutes, contrasted with the utter lack of statutes imposing obligations on the States' executive (notwithstanding the attractiveness of that course to Congress), suggests an assumed *absence* of such power. The only early federal law the Government has brought to our attention that imposed duties on state executive officers is the Extradition Act of 1793, which required the "executive authority" of a State to cause the arrest and delivery of a fugitive from justice upon the request of the executive authority of the State from which the fugitive had fled. See Act of Feb. 12, 1793, ch. 7, §1, 1 Stat. 302. That was in direct implementation, however, of the Extradition Clause of the Constitution itself, see Art. IV, §2.

Not only do the enactments of the early Congresses, as far as we are aware, contain no evidence of an assumption that the Federal Government may command the States' executive power in the absence of a particularized constitutional authorization, they contain some indication of precisely the opposite assumption. On September 23, 1789—the day before its proposal of the Bill of Rights, see 1 Annals of Congress 912-913—the First Congress enacted a law aimed at obtaining state assistance of the most rudimentary and necessary sort for the enforcement of the new Government's laws: the holding of federal prisoners in state jails at federal expense. Significantly, the law issued not a command to the States' executive, but a recommendation to their legislatures. Congress "recommended to the legislatures of the several States to pass laws, making it expressly the duty of the keepers of their gaols, to receive and safe keep therein all prisoners committed under the authority of the United States," and offered to pay 50 cents per month for each prisoner. Act of Sept. 23, 1789, 1 Stat. 96. Moreover, when Georgia refused to comply with the request, see L. White, The Federalists 402 (1948), Congress's only reaction was a law authorizing the marshal in any State that failed to comply with the Recommendation of September 23, 1789, to rent a temporary jail until provision for a permanent one could be made, see Resolution of Mar. 3, 1791, 1 Stat. 225.

. . .

It is most implausible that the person who labored for that example of state executive officers' assisting the Federal Government believed, but neglected to mention, that they had a responsibility to execute federal laws. If it was indeed Hamilton's view that the Federal Government could direct the officers of the States, that view has no clear support in Madison's writings, or as far as we are aware, in text, history, or early commentary elsewhere.

To complete the historical record, we must note that there is not only an absence of executive commandeering statutes in the early Congresses, but there is an absence of them in our later history as well, at least until very recent years. The Government points to the Act of August 3, 1882, ch. 376, §§2, 4, 22 Stat. 214, which enlisted state officials "to take charge of the local affairs of immigration in the ports within such State, and to provide for the support and relief of such immigrants therein landing as may fall into distress or need of public aid"; to inspect arriving immigrants and exclude any person found to be a "convict, lunatic, idiot," or indigent; and to send convicts back to their country of origin "without compensation." The statute did not, however, *mandate* those duties, but merely empowered the Secretary of the Treasury "to *enter into contracts* with such State . . . officers as *may be designated* for that purpose *by the governor* of any State." (Emphasis added.)

. . .

It is incontestible that the Constitution established a system of "dual sovereignty." *Gregory v. Ashcroft,* 501 U.S. 452, 457 (1991); *Tafflin v. Levitt,* 493 U.S. 455, 458 (1990). Although the States surrendered many of their powers to the new Federal Government, they retained "a residuary and inviolable sovereignty," The Federalist No. 39, at 245 (J. Madison). This is reflected throughout the Constitution's text, *Lane County* v. *Oregon,* 7 Wall. 71, 76 (1869); *Texas v. White,* 7 Wall. 700, 725 (1869), including (to mention only a few examples) the prohibition on any involuntary reduction or combination of a State's territory, Art. IV, §3; the Judicial Power Clause, Art. III, §2, and the Privileges and Immunities Clause, Art. IV, §2, which speak of the "Citizens" of the States; the amendment provision, Article V, which requires the votes of three fourths of the States to amend the Constitution; and the Guarantee Clause, Art. IV, §4, which "presupposes the continued existence of the states and . . . those means and instrumentalities which are the creation of their sovereign and reserved rights," *Helvering v. Gerhardt,* 30 4 U.S. 405, 414-415 (1938). Residual state sovereignty was also implicit, of course, in the Constitution's conferral upon Congress of not all governmental powers, but only discrete, enumerated ones, Art. I, §8, which implication was rendered express by the Tenth Amendment's assertion that "[t]he powers not delegated to the United States by the Constitution, nor prohibited by it to the States, are reserved to the States respectively, or to the people."

The Framers' experience under the Articles of Confederation had persuaded them that using the States as the instruments of federal governance was both ineffectual and provocative of federal state conflict. See The Federalist No. 15. Preservation of the States as independent political entities being the price of union, and "[t]he practicality of making laws, with coercive sanctions, for the States as political bodies" having been, in Madison's words, "exploded on all hands," 2 Records of the Federal Convention of 1787, p. 9 (M. Farrand ed. 1911), the Framers rejected the concept of a central government that would act upon and through the States, and instead designed a system in which the state and federal governments would exercise concurrent authority over the people — who were, in Hamilton's words, "the only proper objects of government," The Federalist No. 15, at 109. We have set forth the historical record in more detail elsewhere, see *New York v. United States,* 505 U.S., at 161-166, and need not repeat it here. It suffices to repeat the conclusion: "The Framers explicitly chose a Constitution that confers upon Congress the power to regulate individuals, not States." *Id.,* at 166. The great innovation of this design was that "our citizens would have two political capacities, one state and one federal, each protected from incursion by the other" — "a legal system unprecedented in form and design, establishing two orders of government, each with its own direct relationship, its own privity, its own set of mutual rights and obligations to the people who sustain it and are governed by it." *U.S. Term Limits, Inc. v. Thornton,* 514 U.S. 779, 838 (1995) (Kennedy, J., concurring). The Constitution thus contemplates that a State's government will represent and remain accountable to its own citizens. *See New York, supra,* at 168-169; *United States v. Lopez,* 514 U.S. 549, 576-577 (1995) (Kennedy, J., concurring). Cf. *Edgar v. MITE Corp.,* 457 U.S. 624, 644 (1982) ("the State has no legitimate interest in protecting nonresident[s]"). As Madison expressed it: "[T]he local or municipal authorities form distinct and independent portions of the supremacy, no more subject, within their respective spheres, to the general authority than the general authority is subject to them, within its own sphere." The Federalist No. 39, at 245.

This separation of the two spheres is one of the Constitution's structural protections of liberty. "Just as the separation and independence of the coordinate branches of the Federal Government serve to prevent the accumulation of excessive power in any one branch, a healthy balance of power between the States and the Federal Government will reduce the risk of tyranny and abuse from either front." . . .

. . .

When we were at last confronted squarely with a federal statute that unambiguously required the States to enact or administer a federal regulatory program, our decision should have come as no surprise. At issue in *New York v. United States,* 505 U.S. 144 (1992), were the so called "take title" provisions of the Low Level Radioactive Waste Policy Amendments Act of 1985, which required States either to enact legislation providing for the disposal of radioactive waste generated within their borders, or to take title to, and possession of the waste — effectively requiring the States either to legislate pursuant to Congress's directions, or to implement an administrative solution. *Id.,* at 175-176. We concluded that Congress could constitutionally require the States to do neither. *Id.,* at 176. "The Federal Government," we held, "may not compel the States to enact or administer a federal regulatory program." *Id.,* at 188.

The Government contends that *New York* is distinguishable on the following ground: unlike the "take title" provisions invalidated there, the background check provision of the Brady Act does not require state legislative or executive officials to make policy, but instead issues a final directive to state CLEOs. It is permissible, the Government asserts, for Congress to command state or local officials to assist in the implementation of federal law so long as "Congress itself devises a clear legislative solution that regulates private conduct" and requires state or local officers to provide only "limited, non policymaking help in enforcing that law." "[T]he constitutional line is crossed only when Congress compels the States to make law in their sovereign capacities." Brief for United States 16.

. . .

Even assuming, moreover, that the Brady Act leaves no "policymaking" discretion with the States, we fail to see how that improves rather than worsens the intrusion upon state sovereignty. Preservation of the States as independent and autonomous political entities is arguably less undermined by requiring them to make policy in certain fields than (as Judge Sneed aptly described it over two decades ago) by "reduc[ing] [them] to puppets of a ventriloquist Congress," *Brown v. EPA,* 521 F.2d, at 839. It is an essential attribute of the States' retained sovereignty that they remain independent and autonomous within their proper sphere of authority. See *Texas v. White,* 7 Wall, at 725. It is no more compatible with this independence and autonomy that their officers be "dragooned" (as Judge Fernandez put it in his dissent below, 66 F.3d, at 1035) into administering federal law, than it would be compatible with the independence and autonomy of the United States that its officers be impressed into service for the execution of state laws.

. . .

We adhere to that principle today, and conclude categorically, as we concluded categorically in *New York:* "The Federal Government may not compel the States to enact or administer a federal regulatory program." *Id.,* at 188. The mandatory obligation imposed on CLEOs to perform background checks on prospective handgun purchasers plainly runs afoul of that rule.

What we have said makes it clear enough that the central obligation imposed upon CLEOs by the interim provisions of the Brady Act — the obligation to "make a reasonable effort to ascertain within 5 business days whether receipt or possession [of a handgun] would be in violation of the law, including research in whatever State and local recordkeeping systems are available and in a national system designated by the Attorney General," 18 U.S.C. §922(s)(2) — is unconstitutional. Extinguished with it, of course, is the duty implicit in the background check requirement that the CLEO accept notice of the contents of, and a copy of, the completed Brady Form, which the firearms dealer is required to provide to him, §§922(s)(1)(A)(i)(III) and (IV).

Petitioners also challenge, however, two other provisions of the Act: (1) the requirement that any CLEO "to whom a [Brady

Form] is transmitted" destroy the form and any record containing information derived from it, §922(s)(6)(B)(i), and (2) the requirement that any CLEO who "determines that an individual is ineligible to receive a handgun" provide the would be purchaser, upon request, a written statement of the reasons for that determination, §922(s)(6)(C). With the background check and implicit receipt of forms requirements invalidated, however, these provisions require no action whatsoever on the part of the CLEO. Quite obviously, the obligation to destroy all Brady Forms that he has received when he has received none, and the obligation to give reasons for a determination of ineligibility when he never makes a determination of ineligibility, are no obligations at all. These two provisions have conceivable application to a CLEO, in other words, only if he has chosen, voluntarily, to participate in administration of the federal scheme. The present petitioners are not in that position. As to them, these last two challenged provisions are not unconstitutional, but simply inoperative.

There is involved in this Brady Act conundrum a severability question, which the parties have briefed and argued: whether firearms dealers in the jurisdictions at issue here, and in other jurisdictions, remain obliged to forward to the CLEO (even if he will not accept it) the requisite notice of the contents (and a copy) of the Brady Form, §§922(s)(1)(A)(i)(III) and (IV); and to wait five business days before consummating the sale, §922(s)(1)(A)(ii). These are important questions, but we have no business answering them in these cases. These provisions burden only firearms dealers and purchasers, and no plaintiff in either of those categories is before us here. We decline to speculate regarding the rights and obligations of parties not before the Court. Cf., e.g., *New York*, *supra*, at 186-187 (addressing severability where remaining provisions at issue affected the plaintiffs).

* * *

We held in *New York* that Congress cannot compel the States to enact or enforce a federal regulatory program. Today we hold that Congress cannot circumvent that prohibition by conscripting the State's officers directly. The Federal Government may neither issue directives requiring the States to address particular problems, nor command the States' officers, or those of their political subdivisions, to administer or enforce a federal regulatory program. It matters not whether policymaking is involved, and no case by case weighing of the burdens or benefits is necessary; such commands are fundamentally incompatible with our constitutional system of dual sovereignty. Accordingly, the judgment of the Court of Appeals for the Ninth Circuit is reversed.

It is so ordered.

UNITED STATES v. MORRISON

529 U.S. 598 (2000)

Opinion: Rehnquist, joined by O'Connor, Scalia, Kennedy, Thomas
Concurrence: Thomas
Dissent: Souter, joined by Stevens, Ginsburg, Breyer
Dissent: Breyer, joined by Stevens, and by Souter and Ginsburg in Part I-A

United States v. Morrison *extends the ruling in* United States v. Lopez, *which cites education, criminal law, and family law as core examples of "noneconomic activity" beyond the purview of the Commerce Clause.* United States v. Morrison *strikes down parts of the Violence Against Women Act, limiting the use of the Commerce Clause to protect the rights of women through the use of criminal law. Does the logic of* United States v. Lopez *lead necessarily to this result? Is U.S. Supreme Court Justice David Souter correct to say that the holding here is incompatible with the Court's earlier rulings in* Heart of Atlanta Motel v. United States *and* Katzenbach v. McClung? *Does the holding in this case suggest that it is unwise to defend legislation protecting liberty and equality on Commerce Clause grounds?*

CHIEF JUSTICE REHNQUIST *delivered the opinion of the Court.*

Petitioner Christy Brzonkala enrolled at Virginia Polytechnic Institute (Virginia Tech) in the fall of 1994. In September of that year, Brzonkala met respondents Antonio Morrison and James Crawford, who were both students at Virginia Tech and members of its varsity football team. Brzonkala alleges that, within 30 minutes of meeting Morrison and Crawford, they assaulted and repeatedly raped her. After the attack, Morrison allegedly told Brzonkala, "You better not have any . . . diseases." In the months following the rape, Morrison also allegedly announced in the dormitory's dining room that he "like[d] to get girls drunk and. . . ." The omitted portions, quoted verbatim in the briefs on file with this Court, consist of boasting, debased remarks about what Morrison would do to women, vulgar remarks that cannot fail to shock and offend.

Brzonkala alleges that this attack caused her to become severely emotionally disturbed and depressed. She sought assistance from a university psychiatrist, who prescribed antidepressant medication. Shortly after the rape Brzonkala stopped attending classes and withdrew from the university.

In early 1995, Brzonkala filed a complaint against respondents under Virginia Tech's Sexual Assault Policy. During the school-conducted hearing on her complaint, Morrison admitted having sexual contact with her despite the fact that she had twice told him "no." After the hearing, Virginia Tech's Judicial Committee found insufficient evidence to punish Crawford, but found Morrison guilty of sexual assault and sentenced him to immediate suspension for two semesters.

Morrison appealed his second conviction through the university's administrative system. On August 21, 1995, Virginia Tech's senior vice president and provost set aside Morrison's punishment. She concluded that it was "excessive when compared with other cases where there has been a finding of violation of the Abusive Conduct Policy," 132 F.3d 949, 955 (CA4 1997). Virginia Tech did not inform Brzonkala of this decision. After learning from a newspaper that Morrison would be returning to Virginia Tech for the fall 1995 semester, she dropped out of the university.

In December 1995, Brzonkala sued Morrison, Crawford, and Virginia Tech in the United States District Court for the Western District of Virginia. Her complaint alleged that Morrison's and Crawford's attack violated . . . the Violence Against Women Act of 1994. It states that "persons within the United States shall have the right to be free from crimes of violence motivated by gender." To enforce that right, subsection (c) declares:

> "A person (including a person who acts under color of any statute, ordinance, regulation, custom, or usage of any State) who commits a crime of violence motivated by gender and thus deprives another of the right declared in subsection (b) of this section shall be liable to the party injured, in an action for the recovery of compensatory and punitive damages, injunctive and declaratory relief, and such other relief as a court may deem appropriate."

Section 13981 defines a "crime" of violence motivated by "gender" as "a crime of violence committed because of gender or on the basis of gender, and due, at least in part, to an animus based on the victim's gender." . . .

Further clarifying the broad scope of §13981's civil remedy, subsection (e)(2) states that "nothing" in this section requires a prior criminal complaint, prosecution, or conviction to establish the elements of a cause of action under subsection (c) of this section." And subsection (e)(3) provides a §13981 litigant with a choice of forums: Federal and state courts "shall have concurrent jurisdiction" over complaints brought under the section.

Every law enacted by Congress must be based on one or more of its powers enumerated in the Constitution. "The powers of the legislature are defined and limited; and that those limits may not be mistaken or forgotten, the constitution is written." *Marbury v. Madison.* Congress explicitly identified the sources of federal authority on which it relied in enacting §13981. It said that a "federal civil rights cause of action" is established "pursuant" to the affirmative power of Congress . . . under section 5 of the Fourteenth Amendment to the Constitution, as well as under section 8 of Article I of the Constitution." 42 U.S.C. §13981(a). We address Congress' authority to enact this remedy under each of these constitutional provisions in turn.

Due respect for the decisions of a coordinate branch of Government demands that we invalidate a congressional enactment only upon a plain showing that Congress has exceeded its constitutional bounds. With this presumption of constitutionality in mind, we turn to the question whether §13981 falls within Congress' power under Article I, §8, of the Constitution. Brzonkala and the United States rely upon the third clause of the Article, which gives Congress power "to regulate Commerce with foreign Nations, and among the several States, and with the Indian Tribes." As we discussed at length in *Lopez,* our interpretation of the Commerce Clause has changed as our Nation has developed. We need not repeat that detailed review of the Commerce Clause's history here; it suffices to say that, in the years since *NLRB v. Jones & Laughlin Steel Corp.*, Congress has had considerably greater latitude in regulating conduct and transactions under the Commerce Clause than our previous case law permitted.

Lopez emphasized, however, that even under our modern, expansive interpretation of the Commerce Clause, Congress' regulatory authority is not without effective bounds.

> "[E]ven [our] modern-era precedents which have expanded congressional power under the Commerce Clause confirm that this power is subject to outer limits. In *Jones & Laughlin Steel,* the Court warned that the scope of the interstate commerce power 'must be considered in the light of our dual system of government and may not be extended so as to embrace effects upon interstate commerce so indirect and remote that to embrace them, in view of our complex society, would effectually obliterate the distinction between what is national and what is local and create a completely centralized government.'" Id., at 556-557 (quoting *Jones & Laughlin Steel,* supra, at 37)

As we observed in *Lopez,* modern Commerce Clause jurisprudence has "identified three broad categories of activity that Congress may regulate under its commerce power. First, Congress may regulate the use of the channels of interstate commerce. Second, Congress is empowered to regulate and protect the instrumentalities of interstate commerce, or persons or things in interstate commerce, even though the threat may come only from intrastate activities. Finally, Congress' commerce authority includes the power to regulate those activities having a substantial relation to interstate commerce, . . . i.e., those activities that substantially affect interstate commerce."

Petitioners do not contend that these cases fall within either of the first two of these categories of Commerce Clause regulation. They seek to sustain §13981 as a regulation of activity that substantially affects interstate commerce. Given §13981's focus on gender-motivated violence wherever it occurs (rather than violence directed at the instrumentalities of interstate commerce, interstate markets, or things or persons in interstate commerce), we agree that this is the proper inquiry. . . . In *Lopez,* we held that the Gun-Free School Zones Act of 1990, which made it a federal crime to knowingly possess a firearm in a school zone, exceeded Congress' authority under the Commerce Clause. . . . *Lopez*'s review of Commerce Clause case law demonstrates that in those cases where we have sustained federal regulation of intrastate activity based upon the activity's substantial effects on interstate commerce, the activity in question has been some sort of economic endeavor.

The second consideration that we found important in analyzing §922(q) was that the statute contained "no express jurisdictional element which might limit its reach to a discrete set of firearm possessions that additionally have an explicit connection with or effect on interstate commerce." Such a jurisdictional element may establish that the enactment is in pursuance of Congress' regulation of interstate commerce. Third, we noted that neither §922(q) "nor its legislative history contains express congressional findings regarding the effects upon interstate commerce of gun possession in a school zone." While "Congress normally is not required to make formal findings as to the substantial burdens that an activity has on interstate commerce," the existence of such findings may "enable us to evaluate the legislative judgment that the activity in question substantially affects interstate commerce, even though no such substantial effect [is] visible to the naked eye." Finally, our decision in *Lopez* rested in part on the fact that the link between gun possession and a substantial effect on interstate commerce was attenuated.

With these principles underlying our Commerce Clause jurisprudence as reference points, the proper resolution of the present cases is clear. Gender-motivated crimes of violence are not, in any sense of the phrase, economic activity. While we need not adopt a categorical rule against aggregating the effects of any noneconomic activity in order to decide these cases, thus far in our Nation's history our cases have upheld Commerce Clause regulation of intrastate activity only where that activity is economic in nature. Like the Gun-Free School Zones Act at issue in *Lopez,* §13981 contains no jurisdictional element establishing that the federal cause of action is in pursuance of Congress' power to regulate interstate commerce. Although *Lopez* makes clear that such a jurisdictional element would lend support to the argument that §13981 is sufficiently tied to interstate commerce, Congress elected to cast §13981's remedy over a wider, and more purely intrastate, body of violent crime.

In contrast with the lack of congressional findings that we faced in *Lopez,* §13981 is supported by numerous findings regarding the serious impact that gender-motivated violence has on victims and their families. But the existence of congressional findings is not sufficient, by itself, to sustain the constitutionality of Commerce Clause legislation. As we stated in *Lopez,* "[S]imply because Congress may conclude that a particular activity substantially affects interstate commerce does not necessarily make it so." Rather, "[w]hether particular operations affect interstate commerce sufficiently to come under the constitutional power of Congress to regulate them is ultimately a judicial rather than a legislative question, and can be settled finally only by this Court."

In these cases, Congress' findings are substantially weakened by the fact that they rely so heavily on a method of reasoning that we have already rejected as unworkable if we are to maintain the Constitution's enumeration of powers. Congress found that gender-motivated violence affects interstate commerce

> "by deterring potential victims from traveling interstate, from engaging in employment in interstate business, and from transacting with business, and in places involved in interstate commerce; . . . by diminishing national productivity, increasing medical and other costs, and decreasing the supply of and the demand for interstate products."

Given these findings and petitioners' arguments, the concern that we expressed in *Lopez* that Congress might use the Commerce Clause to completely obliterate the Constitution's distinction between national and local authority seems well founded. The reasoning that petitioners advance seeks to follow the but-for causal chain from the initial occurrence of violent crime (the suppression of which has always been the prime object of the States' police power) to every attenuated effect upon interstate commerce. If accepted, petitioners' reasoning would allow Congress to regulate any crime as long as the nationwide, aggregated impact of that crime has substantial effects on employment, production, transit, or consumption. Indeed, if Congress may regulate gender-motivated violence, it would be able to regulate murder or any other type of violence since gender-motivated violence, as a subset of all violent crime, is certain to have lesser economic impacts than the larger class of which it is a part.

Petitioners' reasoning, moreover, will not limit Congress to regulating violence but may, as we suggested in *Lopez*, be applied equally as well to family law and other areas of traditional state regulation since the aggregate effect of marriage, divorce, and child rearing on the national economy is undoubtedly significant. Congress may have recognized this specter when it expressly precluded §13981 from being used in the family law context. Under our written Constitution, however, the limitation of congressional authority is not solely a matter of legislative grace.

We accordingly reject the argument that Congress may regulate noneconomic, violent criminal conduct based solely on that conduct's aggregate effect on interstate commerce. The Constitution requires a distinction between what is truly national and what is truly local. In recognizing this fact we preserve one of the few principles that has been consistent since the Clause was adopted. The regulation and punishment of intrastate violence that is not directed at the instrumentalities, channels, or goods involved in interstate commerce has always been the province of the States. Indeed, we can think of no better example of the police power, which the Founders denied the National Government and reposed in the States, than the suppression of violent crime and vindication of its victims. . . .

Because we conclude that the Commerce Clause does not provide Congress with authority to enact §13981, we address petitioners' alternative argument that the section's civil remedy should be upheld as an exercise of Congress' remedial power under §5 of the Fourteenth Amendment. As noted above, Congress expressly invoked the Fourteenth Amendment as a source of authority to enact §13981.

The principles governing an analysis of congressional legislation under §5 are well settled. Section 5 states that Congress may "'enforce,' by 'appropriate legislation' the constitutional guarantee that no State shall deprive any person of 'life, liberty or property, without due process of law,' nor deny any person 'equal protection of the laws.'" *City of Boerne v. Flores*. Section 5 is "a positive grant of legislative power" that includes authority to "prohibit conduct which is not itself unconstitutional and [to] intrude into 'legislative spheres of autonomy previously reserved to the States.'" However, "[a]s broad as the congressional enforcement power is, it is not unlimited." In fact, as we discuss in detail below, several limitations inherent in §5's text and constitutional context have been recognized since the Fourteenth Amendment was adopted.

Petitioners' §5 argument is founded on an assertion that there is pervasive bias in various state justice systems against victims of gender-motivated violence. This assertion is supported by a voluminous congressional record. Specifically, Congress received evidence that many participants in state justice systems are perpetuating an array of erroneous stereotypes and assumptions. Congress concluded that these discriminatory stereotypes often result in insufficient investigation and prosecution of gender-motivated crime, inappropriate focus on the behavior and credibility of the victims of that crime, and unacceptably lenient punishments for those who are actually convicted of gender-motivated violence. Petitioners contend that this bias denies victims of gender-motivated violence the equal protection of the laws and that Congress therefore acted appropriately in enacting a private civil remedy against the perpetrators of gender-motivated violence to both remedy the States' bias and deter future instances of discrimination in the state courts.

As our cases have established, state-sponsored gender discrimination violates equal protection unless it "serves 'important governmental objectives and ... the discriminatory means employed' are 'substantially related to the achievement of those objectives.'" However, the language and purpose of the Fourteenth Amendment place certain limitations on the manner in which Congress may attack discriminatory conduct. These limitations are necessary to prevent the Fourteenth Amendment from obliterating the Framers' carefully crafted balance of power between the States and the National Government. Foremost among these limitations is the time-honored principle that the Fourteenth Amendment, by its very terms, prohibits only state action. "The principle has become firmly embedded in our constitutional law that the action inhibited by the first section of the Fourteenth Amendment is only such action as may fairly be said to be that of the States. That Amendment erects no shield against merely private conduct, however discriminatory or wrongful."

Shortly after the Fourteenth Amendment was adopted, we decided ... the *Civil Rights Cases*. In those consolidated cases, we held that the public accommodation provisions of the Civil Rights Act of 1875, which applied to purely private conduct, were beyond the scope of the §5 enforcement power.

The force of the doctrine of stare decisis behind these decisions stems not only from the length of time they have been on the books, but also from the insight attributable to the Members of the Court at that time. Every Member had been appointed by President Lincoln, Grant, Hayes, Garfield, or Arthur—and each of their judicial appointees obviously had intimate knowledge and familiarity with the events surrounding the adoption of the Fourteenth Amendment....

Petitioners alternatively argue that, unlike the situation in the *Civil Rights Cases*, here there has been gender-based disparate treatment by state authorities, whereas in those cases there was no indication of such state action. There is abundant evidence, however, to show that the Congresses that enacted the Civil Rights Acts of 1871 and 1875 had a purpose similar to that of Congress in enacting §13981: There were state laws on the books bespeaking equality of treatment, but in the administration of these laws there was discrimination against newly freed slaves. . . . Section 13981 is not aimed at proscribing discrimination by officials which the Fourteenth Amendment might not itself proscribe; it is directed not at any State or state actor, but at individuals who have committed criminal acts motivated by gender bias. . . .

Petitioner Brzonkala's complaint alleges that she was the victim of a brutal assault. But Congress' effort in §13981 to provide a federal civil remedy can be sustained neither under the Commerce Clause nor under §5 of the Fourteenth Amendment. If the allegations here are true, no civilized system of justice could fail to provide her a remedy for the conduct of respondent Morrison. But under our federal system that remedy must be provided by the Commonwealth of Virginia, and not by the United States. The judgment of the Court of Appeals is Affirmed.

JUSTICE THOMAS, *concurring.*

The majority opinion correctly applies our decision in *United States v. Lopez*, and I join it in full. I write separately only to express my view that the very notion of a "substantial effects" test under the Commerce Clause is inconsistent with the original understanding of Congress' powers and with this Court's early Commerce Clause cases. By continuing to apply this rootless and malleable standard, however circumscribed, the Court has encouraged the Federal Government to persist in its view that the Commerce Clause has virtually no limits. Until this Court replaces its existing Commerce Clause jurisprudence with a standard more consistent with the original understanding, we will continue to see Congress appropriating state police powers under the guise of regulating commerce.

JUSTICE SOUTER, *with whom* **JUSTICE STEVENS, JUSTICE GINSBURG,** *and* **JUSTICE BREYER** *join, dissenting.*

The Court says both that it leaves Commerce Clause precedent undisturbed and that the Civil Rights Remedy of the Violence Against Women Act of 1994 exceeds Congress's power under that Clause. I find the claims irreconcilable and respectfully dissent.

Our cases, which remain at least nominally undisturbed, stand for the following propositions. Congress has the power to legislate with regard to activity that, in the aggregate, has a substantial effect on interstate commerce. The fact of such a substantial effect is not an issue for the courts in the first instance, ibid., but for the Congress, whose institutional capacity for gathering evidence and taking testimony far exceeds ours. By passing legislation, Congress indicates its conclusion, whether explicitly or not, that facts support its exercise of the commerce power. The business of the courts is to review the congressional assessment, not for soundness but simply for the rationality of concluding that a jurisdictional basis exists in fact. Any explicit findings that Congress chooses to make, though not dispositive of the question of rationality, may advance judicial review by identifying factual authority on which Congress relied. Applying those propositions in these cases can lead to only one conclusion.

One obvious difference from *United States v. Lopez*, is the mountain of data assembled by Congress, here showing the effects of violence against women on interstate commerce. Passage of the Act in 1994 was preceded by four years of hearings, which included testimony from physicians and law professors; from survivors of rape and domestic violence; and from representatives of state law enforcement and private business. The record includes reports on gender bias from task forces in 21 States, and we have the benefit of specific factual findings in the eight separate Reports issued by Congress and its committees over the long course leading to enactment.

Based on the data . . . Congress found that

> "crimes of violence motivated by gender have a substantial adverse effect on interstate commerce, by deterring potential victims from traveling interstate, from engaging in employment in interstate business, and from transacting with business, and in places involved, in interstate commerce . . . [,] by diminishing national productivity, increasing medical and other costs, and decreasing the supply of and the demand for interstate products. . . ."

Congress thereby explicitly stated the predicate for the exercise of its Commerce Clause power. Is its conclusion irrational in view of the data amassed? True, the methodology of particular studies may be challenged, and some of the figures arrived at may be disputed. But the sufficiency of the evidence before Congress to provide a rational basis for the finding cannot seriously be questioned.

Indeed, the legislative record here is far more voluminous than the record compiled by Congress and found sufficient in two prior cases upholding Title II of the Civil Rights Act of 1964 against Commerce Clause challenges. In *Heart of Atlanta Motel, Inc. v. United States*, and *Katzenbach v. McClung*, the Court referred to evidence showing the consequences of racial discrimination by motels and restaurants on interstate commerce. Congress had relied on compelling anecdotal reports that individual instances of segregation cost thousands to millions of dollars.

While Congress did not, to my knowledge, calculate aggregate dollar values for the nationwide effects of racial discrimination in 1964, in 1994 it did rely on evidence of the harms caused by domestic violence and sexual assault, citing annual costs of $3 billion in 1990 and $5 to $10 billion in 1993. Equally important, though, gender-based violence in the 1990's was shown to operate in a manner similar to racial discrimination in the 1960's in reducing the mobility of employees and their production and consumption of goods shipped in interstate commerce. Like racial discrimination, gender-based violence bars its most likely targets — women — from full participation in the national economy.

If the analogy to the Civil Rights Act of 1964 is not plain enough, one can always look back a bit further. In *Wickard*, we upheld the application of the Agricultural Adjustment Act to the planting and consumption of homegrown wheat. The effect on interstate commerce in that case followed from the possibility that wheat grown at home for personal consumption could either be drawn into the market by rising prices, or relieve its grower of any need to purchase wheat in the market. The Commerce Clause predicate was simply the effect of the production of wheat for home consumption on supply and demand in interstate commerce. Supply and demand for goods in interstate commerce will also be affected by the deaths of 2,000 to 4,000 women annually at the hands of domestic abusers, and by the reduction in the work force by the 100,000 or more rape victims who lose their jobs each year or are forced to quit. Violence against women may be found to affect interstate commerce and affect it substantially.

. . . [T]he elusive heart of the majority's analysis in these cases is its statement that Congress's findings of fact are "weakened" by the presence of a disfavored "method of reasoning." This seems to suggest that the "substantial effects" analysis is not a factual enquiry, for Congress in the first instance with subsequent judicial review looking only to the rationality of the congressional conclusion, but one of a rather different sort, dependent upon a uniquely judicial competence.

The premise that the enumeration of powers implies that other powers are withheld is sound; the conclusion that some particular categories of subject matter are therefore presumptively beyond the reach of the commerce power is, however, a non sequitur. From the fact that Art. I, §8, cl. 3 grants an authority limited to regulating commerce, it follows only that Congress may claim no authority under that section to address any subject that does not affect commerce. It does not at all follow that an activity affecting commerce nonetheless falls outside the commerce power, depending on the specific character of the activity, or the authority of a State to regulate it along with Congress. My disagreement with the majority is not, however, confined to logic, for history has shown that categorical exclusions have proven as unworkable in practice as they are unsupportable in theory.

Why is the majority tempted to reject the lesson so painfully learned in 1937? An answer emerges from contrasting *Wickard* with one of the predecessor cases it superseded. It was obvious in *Wickard* that growing wheat for consumption right on the farm was not "commerce" in the common vocabulary, but that did not matter constitutionally so long as the aggregated activity of domestic wheat growing affected commerce substantially. Just a few years before *Wickard*, however, it had certainly been no less obvious that "mining" practices could substantially affect commerce, even though *Carter Coal Co.*, supra, had held mining regulation beyond the national commerce power. When we try to fathom the difference between the two cases, it is clear that they did not go in different directions because the *Carter Coal* Court could not understand a causal connection that the *Wickard* Court could grasp; the difference, rather, turned on the fact that the Court in *Carter Coal* had a reason for trying to maintain its categorical, formalistic distinction, while that reason had been abandoned by the time *Wickard* was decided. The reason was laissez-faire economics, the point of which was to keep government interference to a minimum. The Court in *Carter Coal* was still trying to create a laissez-faire world out of the 20th-century economy, and formalistic commercial distinctions were thought to be useful instruments in achieving that object. The Court in *Wickard* knew it could not do any such thing and in the aftermath of the New Deal had long since stopped attempting the impossible.

If we now ask why the formalistic economic/noneconomic distinction might matter today, after its rejection in *Wickard*, the answer is not that the majority fails to see causal connections in an integrated economic world. The answer is that in the minds of the majority there is a new animating theory that makes categorical formalism seem useful again. Just as the old formalism had value in the service of an economic conception, the new one is useful in serving a conception of federalism. It is the instrument by which assertions of national power are to be limited in favor of preserving a supposedly discernible, proper sphere of state autonomy to legislate or refrain from legislating as the individual

States see fit. The legitimacy of the Court's current emphasis on the noncommercial nature of regulated activity, then, does not turn on any logic serving the text of the Commerce Clause or on the realism of the majority's view of the national economy. The essential issue is rather the strength of the majority's claim to have a constitutional warrant for its current conception of a federal relationship enforceable by this Court through limits on otherwise plenary commerce power. This conception is the subject of the majority's second categorical discount applied today to the facts bearing on the substantial effects test.

All of this convinces me that today's ebb of the commerce power rests on error, and at the same time leads me to doubt that the majority's view will prove to be enduring law. There is yet one more reason for doubt. Although we sense the presence of *Carter Coal*, *Schechter*, and *Usery* once again, the majority embraces them only at arm's-length. Where such decisions once stood for rules, today's opinion points to considerations by which substantial effects are discounted. . . . As our predecessors learned then, the practice of such ad hoc review cannot preserve the distinction between the judicial and the legislative, and this Court, in any event, lacks the institutional capacity to maintain such a regime for very long. This one will end when the majority realizes that the conception of the commerce power for which it entertains hopes would inevitably fail the test expressed in Justice Holmes's statement that "the first call of a theory of law is that it should fit the facts." The facts that cannot be ignored today are the facts of integrated national commerce and a political relationship between States and Nation much affected by their respective treasuries and constitutional modifications adopted by the people. The federalism of some earlier time is no more adequate to account for those facts today than the theory of laissez-faire was able to govern the national economy 70 years ago.

GONZALES v. RAICH

545 U.S. 1 (2005)

Opinion: Stevens, joined by Kennedy, Souter, Ginsburg, Breyer
Concurrence: Scalia
Dissent: O'Connor, joined by Rehnquist and Thomas in all but Part III
Dissent: Thomas

Although California state law expressly allows certain individuals to grow their own marijuana as a treatment for various medical conditions, the federal Controlled Substances Act classifies marijuana as an illegal drug and bans its possession. Does Congress have the power to regulate marijuana even though California legalizes growing it and using it for some purposes? In Gonzales v. Raich, *the Court upheld Congress's power to authorize Drug Enforcement Administration officials to seize and destroy Angel Raich's supply of medical marijuana. Although Ms. Raich did not intend to sell or distribute her crop, the Court relied on* Wickard v. Filburn *to uphold her conviction. Do you agree with the Court that the Commerce Clause authorizes federal action in this case? Consider also U.S. Supreme Court Justice Antonin Scalia's concurrence. Do you think it is consistent with the majority positions in* United States v. Lopez *and* United States v. Morrison, *which he joined?*

JUSTICE STEVENS *delivered the opinion of the Court.*

The question presented in this case is whether the power vested in Congress by Article I, §8, of the Constitution "[t]o make all Laws which shall be necessary and proper for carrying into Execution" its authority to "regulate Commerce with foreign Nations, and among the several States" includes the power to prohibit the local cultivation and use of marijuana in compliance with California law.

Respondents Angel Raich and Diane Monson are California residents who suffer from a variety of serious medical conditions and have sought to avail themselves of medical marijuana pursuant to the terms of the Compassionate Use Act. They are being treated by licensed, board-certified family practitioners, who have concluded, after prescribing a host of conventional medicines to treat respondents' conditions and to alleviate their associated symptoms, that marijuana is the only drug available that provides effective treatment. Both women have been using marijuana as a medication for several years pursuant to their doctors' recommendation, and both rely heavily on cannabis to function on a daily basis. Indeed, Raich's physician believes that forgoing cannabis treatments would certainly cause Raich excruciating pain and could very well prove fatal.

On August 15, 2002, county deputy sheriffs and agents from the federal Drug Enforcement Administration (DEA) came to Monson's home. After a thorough investigation, the county officials concluded that her use of marijuana was entirely lawful as a matter of California law. Nevertheless, after a 3-hour standoff, the federal agents seized and destroyed all six of her cannabis plants.

Respondents thereafter brought this action against the Attorney General of the United States and the head of the DEA seeking injunctive and declaratory relief prohibiting the enforcement of the federal Controlled Substances Act to the extent it prevents them from possessing, obtaining, or manufacturing cannabis for their personal medical use. In their complaint and supporting affidavits, Raich and Monson described the severity of their afflictions, their repeatedly futile attempts to obtain relief with conventional medications, and the opinions of their doctors concerning their need to use marijuana. . . .

The question before us, however, is not whether it is wise to enforce the statute in these circumstances; rather, it is whether Congress' power to regulate interstate markets for medicinal substances encompasses the portions of those markets that are supplied with drugs produced and consumed locally. Well-settled law controls our answer. The CSA is a valid exercise of federal power, even as applied to the troubling facts of this case.

Title II of that Act, the CSA, repealed most of the earlier antidrug laws in favor of a comprehensive regime to combat the international and interstate traffic in illicit drugs. The main objectives of the CSA were to conquer drug abuse and to control the legitimate and illegitimate traffic in controlled substances. Congress was particularly concerned with the need to prevent the diversion of drugs from legitimate to illicit channels.

To effectuate these goals, Congress devised a closed regulatory system making it unlawful to manufacture, distribute, dispense, or possess any controlled substance except in a manner authorized by the CSA. . . . In enacting the CSA, Congress classified marijuana as a Schedule I drug . . . because of [its] high potential for abuse, lack of any accepted medical use, and absence of any accepted safety for use in medically supervised treatment.

Respondents in this case do not dispute that passage of the CSA, as part of the Comprehensive Drug Abuse Prevention and Control Act, was well within Congress' commerce power. Nor do they contend that any provision or section of the CSA amounts to an unconstitutional exercise of congressional authority. Rather, respondents' challenge is actually quite limited; they argue that the CSA's categorical prohibition of the manufacture and possession of marijuana as applied to the intrastate manufacture and possession of marijuana for medical purposes pursuant to California law exceeds Congress' authority under the Commerce Clause.

Our case law firmly establishes Congress' power to regulate purely local activities that are part of an economic "class of activities" that have a substantial effect on interstate commerce. As we stated in *Wickard*, "even if appellee's activity be local and though it may not be regarded as commerce, it may still, whatever its nature, be reached by Congress if it exerts a substantial economic effect on interstate commerce." . . . When Congress decides that the "total incidence" of a practice poses a threat to a national market, it may regulate the entire class.

Our decision in *Wickard* is of particular relevance. In *Wickard*, we upheld the application of regulations promulgated under the Agricultural Adjustment Act of 1938, which were designed to control the volume of wheat moving in interstate and foreign commerce in order to avoid surpluses and consequent abnormally low prices. The regulations established an allotment of 11.1 acres for Filburn's 1941 wheat crop, but he sowed 23 acres, intending to use the excess by consuming it on his own farm. Filburn argued that even though we had sustained Congress' power to regulate the production of goods for commerce, that power did not authorize "federal regulation [of] production not intended in any part for commerce but wholly for consumption on the farm." Justice Jackson's opinion for a unanimous Court rejected this submission. He wrote:

> "The effect of the statute before us is to restrict the amount which may be produced for market and the extent as well to which one may forestall resort to the market by producing to meet his own needs. That appellee's own contribution to the demand for wheat may be trivial by itself is not enough to remove him from the scope of federal regulation where, as here, his contribution, taken together with that of many others similarly situated, is far from trivial."

Wickard thus establishes that Congress can regulate purely intrastate activity that is not itself "commercial," in that it is not produced for sale, if it concludes that failure to regulate that class of activity would undercut the regulation of the interstate market in that commodity.

The similarities between this case and *Wickard* are striking. Like the farmer in *Wickard*, respondents are cultivating, for home consumption, a fungible commodity for which there is an established, albeit illegal, interstate market. Just as the Agricultural Adjustment Act was designed "to control the volume [of wheat] moving in interstate and foreign commerce in order to avoid surpluses . . ." and consequently control the market price, a primary purpose of the CSA is to control the supply and demand of controlled substances in both lawful and unlawful drug markets. In *Wickard*, we had no difficulty concluding that Congress had a rational basis for believing that, when viewed in the aggregate, leaving home-consumed wheat outside the regulatory scheme would have a substantial influence on price and market conditions. Here too, Congress had a rational basis for concluding that leaving home-consumed marijuana outside federal control would similarly affect price and market conditions.

More concretely, one concern prompting inclusion of wheat grown for home consumption in the 1938 Act was that rising market prices could draw such wheat into the interstate market, resulting in lower market prices. The parallel concern making it appropriate to include marijuana grown for home consumption in the CSA is the likelihood that the high demand in the interstate market will draw such marijuana into that market. While the diversion of homegrown wheat tended to frustrate the federal interest in stabilizing prices by regulating the volume of commercial transactions in the interstate market, the diversion of homegrown marijuana tends to frustrate the federal interest in eliminating commercial transactions in the interstate market in their entirety. In both cases, the regulation is squarely within Congress' commerce power because production of the commodity meant for home consumption, be it wheat or marijuana, has a substantial effect on supply and demand in the national market for that commodity.

Nonetheless, respondents suggest that *Wickard* differs from this case in three respects: (1) the Agricultural Adjustment Act, unlike the CSA, exempted small farming operations; (2) *Wickard* involved a "quintessential economic activity" — a commercial farm — whereas respondents do not sell marijuana; and (3) the *Wickard* record made it clear that the aggregate production of wheat for use on farms had a significant impact on market prices. Those differences, though factually accurate, do not diminish the precedential force of this Court's reasoning.

The fact that Wickard's own impact on the market was "trivial by itself" was not a sufficient reason for removing him from the scope of federal regulation. That the Secretary of Agriculture elected to exempt even smaller farms from regulation does not speak to his power to regulate all those whose aggregated production was significant, nor did that fact play any role in the Court's analysis. Moreover, even though Wickard was indeed a commercial farmer, the activity he was engaged in — the cultivation of wheat for home consumption — was not treated by the Court as part of his commercial farming operation. And while it is true that the record in the *Wickard* case itself established the causal connection between the production for local use and the national market, we have before us findings by Congress to the same effect.

. . . Respondents nonetheless insist that the CSA cannot be constitutionally applied to their activities because Congress did not make a specific finding that the intrastate cultivation and possession of marijuana for medical purposes based on the recommendation of a physician would substantially affect the larger interstate marijuana market. Be that as it may, we have never required Congress to make particularized findings in order to legislate, absent a special concern such as the protection of free speech. While congressional findings are certainly helpful in reviewing the substance of a congressional statutory scheme, particularly when the connection to commerce is not self-evident, and while we will consider congressional findings in our analysis when they are available, the absence of particularized findings does not call into question Congress' authority to legislate.

In assessing the scope of Congress' authority under the Commerce Clause, we stress that the task before us is a modest one. We need not determine whether respondents' activities, taken in the aggregate, substantially affect interstate commerce in fact, but only whether a "rational basis" exists for so concluding. Given the enforcement difficulties that attend distinguishing between marijuana cultivated locally and marijuana grown elsewhere and concerns about diversion into illicit channels, we have no difficulty concluding that Congress had a rational basis for believing that failure to regulate the intrastate manufacture and possession of marijuana would leave a gaping hole in the CSA. Thus, as in *Wickard*, when it enacted comprehensive legislation to regulate the interstate market in a fungible commodity, Congress was acting well within its authority to "make all Laws which shall be necessary and proper" to "regulate Commerce . . . among the several States."

To support their contrary submission, respondents rely heavily on two of our more recent Commerce Clause cases. In their myopic focus, they overlook the larger context of modern-era Commerce Clause jurisprudence preserved by those cases. Moreover, even in the narrow prism of respondents' creation, they read those cases far too broadly.

Those two cases, of course, are *Lopez*, and *Morrison*. As an initial matter, the statutory challenges at issue in those cases were markedly different from the challenge respondents pursue in the case at hand. Here, respondents ask us to excise individual applications of a concededly valid statutory scheme. In contrast, in both *Lopez* and *Morrison*, the parties asserted that a particular statute or provision fell outside Congress' commerce power in its entirety. This distinction is pivotal for we have often reiterated that "[w]here the class of activities is regulated and that class is within the reach of federal power, the courts have no power 'to excise, as trivial, individual instances' of the class."

Unlike those at issue in *Lopez* and *Morrison*, the activities regulated by the CSA are quintessentially economic. "Economics" refers to "the production, distribution, and consumption of commodities." The CSA is a statute that regulates the production, distribution, and consumption of commodities for which there is an established, and lucrative, interstate market. Prohibiting the intrastate possession or manufacture of an article of commerce is a rational (and commonly utilized) means of regulating commerce in that product. Such prohibitions include specific decisions requiring that a drug be withdrawn from the market as a result of the failure to comply with regulatory requirements as well as decisions excluding Schedule I drugs entirely from the market. Because the CSA is a statute that directly regulates economic, commercial activity, our opinion in *Morrison* casts no doubt on its constitutionality.

. . . [T]he mere fact that marijuana — like virtually every other controlled substance regulated by the CSA — is used for medicinal purposes cannot possibly serve to distinguish it from the core activities regulated by the CSA.

Nor can it serve as an "objective marke[r]" or "objective facto[r]" to arbitrarily narrow the relevant class as the dissenters suggest. More fundamentally, if, as the principal dissent contends, the personal cultivation, possession, and use of marijuana for medicinal purposes is beyond the "'outer limits' of Congress' Commerce Clause authority," it must also be true that such personal use of marijuana (or any other homegrown drug) for recreational purposes is also beyond those "outer limits," whether or not a State elects to authorize or even regulate such use. Justice Thomas' separate dissent suffers from the same sweeping implications. That is, the dissenters' rationale logically extends to place any federal regulation (including quality, prescription, or quantity controls) of any locally cultivated and possessed controlled substance for any purpose beyond the "outer limits" of Congress' Commerce Clause authority. One need not have a degree in economics to understand why a nationwide exemption for the vast quantity of marijuana (or other drugs) locally cultivated for personal use (which presumably would include use by friends, neighbors, and family members) may have a substantial impact on the interstate market for this extraordinarily popular substance. The congressional judgment that an exemption for such a significant segment of the total market would undermine the orderly enforcement of the entire regulatory scheme is entitled to a strong presumption of validity....

Second, limiting the activity to marijuana possession and cultivation "in accordance with state law" cannot serve to place respondents' activities beyond congressional reach. The Supremacy Clause unambiguously provides that if there is any conflict between federal and state law, federal law shall prevail....

Respondents . . . contend that their activities were not "an essential part of a larger regulatory scheme" because they had been "isolated by the State of California, and [are] policed by the State of California," and thus remain "entirely separated from the market." The dissenters fall prey to similar reasoning. The notion that California law has surgically excised a discrete activity that is hermetically sealed off from the larger interstate marijuana market is a dubious proposition, and, more importantly, one that Congress could have rationally rejected.

... Respondents also raise a substantive due process claim and seek to avail themselves of the medical necessity defense. These theories of relief were set forth in their complaint but were not reached by the Court of Appeals. We therefore do not address the question whether judicial relief is available to respondents on these alternative bases. We do note, however, the presence of another avenue of relief. As the Solicitor General confirmed during oral argument, the statute authorizes procedures for the reclassification of Schedule I drugs. But perhaps even more important than these legal avenues is the democratic process, in which the voices of voters allied with these respondents may one day be heard in the halls of Congress. Under the present state of the law, however, the judgment of the Court of Appeals must be vacated. The case is remanded for further proceedings consistent with this opinion.

JUSTICE SCALIA, *concurring in the judgment.*

I agree with the Court's holding that the Controlled Substances Act (CSA) may validly be applied to respondents' cultivation, distribution, and possession of marijuana for personal, medicinal use. I write separately because my understanding of the doctrinal foundation on which that holding rests is, if not inconsistent with that of the Court, at least more nuanced.

Since *Perez v. United States*, our cases have mechanically recited that the Commerce Clause permits congressional regulation of three categories: (1) the channels of interstate commerce; (2) the instrumentalities of interstate commerce, and persons or things in interstate commerce; and (3) activities that "substantially affect" interstate commerce. The first two categories are self-evident, since they are the ingredients of interstate commerce itself. The third category, however, is different in kind, and its recitation without explanation is misleading and incomplete.

It is misleading because, unlike the channels, instrumentalities, and agents of interstate commerce, activities that substantially affect interstate commerce are not themselves part of interstate commerce, and thus the power to regulate them cannot come from the Commerce Clause alone. Rather . . . Congress's regulatory authority over intrastate activities that are not themselves part of interstate commerce (including activities that have a substantial effect on interstate commerce) derives from the Necessary and Proper Clause. And the category of "activities that substantially affect interstate commerce," is incomplete because the authority to enact laws necessary and proper for the regulation of interstate commerce is not limited to laws governing intrastate activities that substantially affect interstate commerce. Where necessary to make a regulation of interstate commerce effective, Congress may regulate even those intrastate activities that do not themselves substantially affect interstate commerce.

Our cases show that the regulation of intrastate activities may be necessary to and proper for the regulation of interstate commerce in two general circumstances. Most directly, the commerce power permits Congress not only to devise rules for the governance of commerce between States but also to facilitate interstate commerce by eliminating potential obstructions, and to restrict it by eliminating potential stimulants. That is why the Court has repeatedly sustained congressional legislation on the ground that the regulated activities had a substantial effect on interstate commerce....

This principle is not without limitation. In *Lopez* and *Morrison*, the Court—conscious of the potential of the "substantially affects" test to "obliterate the distinction between what is national and what is local"—rejected the argument that Congress may regulate noneconomic activity based solely on the effect that it may have on interstate commerce through a remote chain of inferences....

As we implicitly acknowledged in *Lopez*, however, Congress's authority to enact laws necessary and proper for the regulation of interstate commerce is not limited to laws directed against economic activities that have a substantial effect on interstate commerce.... As the Court put it in *Wrightwood Dairy*, where Congress has the authority to enact a regulation of interstate commerce, "it possesses every power needed to make that regulation effective."

Although this power "to make ... regulation effective" commonly overlaps with the authority to regulate economic activities that substantially affect interstate commerce, and may in some cases have been confused with that authority, the two are distinct. The regulation of an intrastate activity may be essential to a comprehensive regulation of interstate commerce even though the intrastate activity does not itself "substantially affect" interstate commerce. Moreover . . . Congress may regulate even noneconomic local activity if that regulation is a necessary part of a more general regulation of interstate commerce....

Today's principal dissent objects that, by permitting Congress to regulate activities necessary to effective interstate regulation, the Court reduces *Lopez* and *Morrison* to "little more than a drafting guide." (opinion of O'Connor, J.). I think that criticism unjustified. Unlike the power to regulate activities that have a substantial effect on interstate commerce, the power to enact laws enabling effective regulation of interstate commerce can only be exercised in conjunction with congressional regulation of an interstate market, and it extends only to those measures necessary to make the interstate regulation effective. As *Lopez* itself states, and the Court affirms today, Congress may regulate noneconomic intrastate activities only where the failure to do so "could ... undercut" its regulation of interstate commerce.

Lopez and *Morrison* affirm that Congress may not regulate certain "purely local" activity within the States based solely on the attenuated effect that such activity may have in the interstate market. But those decisions do not declare noneconomic intrastate activities to be categorically beyond the reach of the Federal Government. . . . To dismiss this distinction as "superficial and formalistic" is to misunderstand the nature of the Necessary and Proper Clause, which empowers Congress to enact laws in effectuation of its enumerated powers that are not within its authority to enact in isolation. See *McCulloch v. Maryland.*

The application of these principles to the case before us is straightforward. In the CSA, Congress has undertaken to extinguish the interstate market in Schedule I controlled substances, including marijuana. The Commerce Clause unquestionably permits this. The power to regulate interstate commerce "extends not only to those regulations which aid, foster and protect the commerce, but embraces those which prohibit it." To effectuate its objective, Congress has prohibited almost all intrastate activities related to Schedule I substances — both economic activities (manufacture, distribution, possession with the intent to distribute) and noneconomic activities (simple possession).... Congress's authority to enact all of these prohibitions of intrastate controlled-substance activities depends only upon whether they are appropriate means of achieving the legitimate end of eradicating Schedule I substances from interstate commerce.

By this measure, I think the regulation must be sustained. Not only is it impossible to distinguish "controlled substances manufactured and distributed intrastate" from "controlled substances manufactured and distributed interstate," but it hardly makes sense to speak in such terms. Drugs like marijuana are fungible commodities. As the Court explains, marijuana that is grown at home and possessed for personal use is never more than an instant from the interstate market — and this is so whether or not the possession is for medicinal use or lawful use under the laws of a particular State....

JUSTICE THOMAS, *dissenting.*

Respondents Diane Monson and Angel Raich use marijuana that has never been bought or sold, that has never crossed state lines, and that has had no demonstrable effect on the national market for marijuana. If Congress can regulate this under the Commerce Clause, then it can regulate virtually anything — and the Federal Government is no longer one of limited and enumerated powers.

I

Respondents' local cultivation and consumption of marijuana is not "Commerce ... among the several States." By holding that Congress may regulate activity that is neither interstate nor commerce under the Interstate Commerce Clause, the Court abandons any attempt to enforce the Constitution's limits on federal power. The majority supports this conclusion by invoking, without explanation, the Necessary and Proper Clause. Regulating respondents' conduct, however, is not "necessary and proper for carrying into Execution" Congress' restrictions on the interstate drug trade. Thus, neither the Commerce Clause nor the Necessary and Proper Clause grants Congress the power to regulate respondents' conduct.

. . . [A]t the time of the founding, the term " 'commerce' consisted of selling, buying, and bartering, as well as transporting for these purposes." Commerce, or trade, stood in contrast to productive activities like manufacturing and agriculture. Throughout founding-era dictionaries, Madison's notes from the Constitutional Convention, *The Federalist Papers*, and the ratification debates, the term "commerce" is consistently used to mean trade or exchange — not all economic or gainful activity that has some attenuated connection to trade or exchange.... Certainly no evidence from the founding suggests that "commerce" included the mere possession of a good or some purely personal activity that did not involve trade or exchange for value. In the early days of the Republic, it would have been unthinkable that Congress could prohibit the local cultivation, possession, and consumption of marijuana.

On this traditional understanding of "commerce," the Controlled Substances Act regulates a great deal of marijuana trafficking that is interstate and commercial in character. The CSA does not, however, criminalize only the interstate buying and selling of marijuana. Instead, it bans the entire market—intrastate or interstate, noncommercial or commercial—for marijuana. Respondents are correct that the CSA exceeds Congress' commerce power as applied to their conduct, which is purely intrastate and noncommercial.

More difficult, however, is whether the CSA is a valid exercise of Congress' power to enact laws that are "necessary and proper for carrying into Execution" its power to regulate interstate commerce. The Necessary and Proper Clause is not a warrant to Congress to enact any law that bears some conceivable connection to the exercise of an enumerated power. Nor is it, however, a command to Congress to enact only laws that are absolutely indispensable to the exercise of an enumerated power.

To act under the Necessary and Proper Clause . . . Congress must select a means that is "appropriate" and "plainly adapted" to executing an enumerated power; the means cannot be otherwise "prohibited" by the Constitution; and the means cannot be inconsistent with "the letter and spirit of the [C]onstitution".... However, in order to be "necessary," the intrastate ban must be more than "a reasonable means [of] effectuat[ing] the regulation of interstate commerce." It must be "plainly adapted" to regulating interstate marijuana trafficking—in other words, there must be an "obvious, simple, and direct relation" between the intrastate ban and the regulation of interstate commerce....

California's Compassionate Use Act sets respondents' conduct apart from other intrastate producers and users of marijuana. The Act channels marijuana use to "seriously ill Californians," and prohibits "the diversion of marijuana for nonmedical purposes." California strictly controls the cultivation and possession of marijuana for medical purposes. To be eligible for its program, California requires that a patient have an illness that cannabis can relieve, such as cancer, AIDS, or arthritis, and that he obtain a physician's recommendation or approval. Qualified patients must provide personal and medical information to obtain medical identification cards, and there is a statewide registry of cardholders. . . . This class of intrastate users is therefore distinguishable from others....

But even assuming that States' controls allow some seepage of medical marijuana into the illicit drug market, there is a multibillion-dollar interstate market for marijuana. It is difficult to see how this vast market could be affected by diverted medical cannabis, let alone in a way that makes regulating intrastate medical marijuana obviously essential to controlling the interstate drug market.

In sum, neither in enacting the CSA nor in defending its application to respondents has the Government offered any obvious reason why banning medical marijuana use is necessary to stem the tide of interstate drug trafficking. Congress' goal of curtailing the interstate drug trade would not plainly be thwarted if it could not apply the CSA to patients like Monson and Raich.

Even assuming the CSA's ban on locally cultivated and consumed marijuana is "necessary," that does not mean it is also "proper." The means selected by Congress to regulate interstate commerce cannot be "prohibited" by, or inconsistent with the "letter and spirit" of, the Constitution.

Here, Congress has encroached on States' traditional police powers to define the criminal law and to protect the health, safety, and welfare of their citizens. Further, the Government's rationale — that it may regulate the production or possession of any commodity for which there is an interstate market — threatens to remove the remaining vestiges of States' traditional police powers. This would convert the Necessary and Proper Clause into precisely what Chief Justice Marshall did not envision, a "pretext . . . for the accomplishment of objects not intrusted to the government."

The majority holds that Congress may regulate intrastate cultivation and possession of medical marijuana under the Commerce Clause, because such conduct arguably has a substantial effect on interstate commerce. The majority's decision is further proof that the "substantial effects" test is a "rootless and malleable standard" at odds with the constitutional design.

The majority's treatment of the substantial effects test is rootless, because it is not tethered to either the Commerce Clause or the Necessary and Proper Clause. Under the Commerce Clause, Congress may regulate interstate commerce, not activities that substantially affect interstate commerce — any more than Congress may regulate activities that do not fall within, but that affect, the subjects of its other Article I powers. Whatever additional latitude the Necessary and Proper Clause affords, the question is whether Congress' legislation is essential to the regulation of interstate commerce itself — not whether the legislation extends only to economic activities that substantially affect interstate commerce.

The majority's treatment of the substantial effects test is malleable, because the majority expands the relevant conduct. By defining the class at a high level of generality (as the intrastate manufacture and possession of marijuana), the majority overlooks that individuals authorized by state law to manufacture and possess medical marijuana exert no demonstrable effect on the interstate drug market.

This Court has never held that Congress can regulate noneconomic activity that substantially affects interstate commerce. To evade even that modest restriction on federal power, the majority defines economic activity in the broadest possible terms as "the production, distribution, and consumption of commodities." This carves out a vast swath of activities that are subject to federal regulation. If the majority is to be taken seriously, the Federal Government may now regulate quilting bees, clothes drives, and potluck suppers throughout the 50 States. This makes a mockery of Madison's assurance to the people of New York that the "powers delegated" to the Federal Government are "few and defined," while those of the States are "numerous and indefinite."

If the majority is correct that *Lopez* and *Morrison* are distinct because they were facial challenges to "particular statute[s] or provision[s]," then congressional power turns on the manner in which Congress packages legislation. Under the majority's reasoning, Congress could not enact — either as a single-subject statute or as a separate provision in the CSA — a prohibition on the intrastate possession or cultivation of marijuana. Nor could it enact an intrastate ban simply to supplement existing drug regulations. However, that same prohibition is perfectly constitutional when integrated into a piece of legislation that reaches other regulable conduct.

Our federalist system, properly understood, allows California and a growing number of other States to decide for themselves how to safeguard the health and welfare of their citizens. I would affirm the judgment of the Court of Appeals. I respectfully dissent.

SYNTHESIS QUESTIONS FOR FURTHER DISCUSSION: CHAPTER 5

1. A significant argument in Justice Harry Blackmun's *Garcia v. San Antonio Metropolitan Transit Authority* opinion is that America's robust system of federalism does not require enforcement by the courts. Instead, the very structure of the federal government protects states' interests, with multiple veto points for policy changes, the Electoral College for presidential elections, and equal representation in the Senate. This was a popular argument among scholars who defended the New Deal, made most prominently by Herbert Wechsler. See Herbert Wechsler, "The Political Safeguards of Federalism: The Role of the States in the Composition and Selection of the National Government," *Columbia Law Review*, 54, no. 4 (Apr. 1954), pp. 543-560. Is Justice Blackmun's argument persuasive? Political safeguards also exist to protect individual rights, but many defenders of judicial review believe that courts should not simply defer to majority rule on these matters of constitutional principle. Is it possible to distinguish these two types of cases?

2. Is U.S. Supreme Court Justice John Paul Stevens's result in *Gonzales v. Raich* required by *Wickard v. Filburn*? What theory might support national economic regulation but still find that Ms. Raich has the right—under the protection of state law—to grow medical marijuana? What role do *United States v. Lopez* and *United States v. Morrison* play in the reasoning in the decision? Consider Justice Antonin Scalia's concurrence, which draws from the broad *McCulloch* framework for congressional power. Are his arguments here consistent with his votes in *United States v. Lopez* and *United States v. Morrison*? How does this case differ from the way we might expect the "liberal" and "conservative" justices to vote?

3. Previously we noted that Justice Oliver Wendell Holmes could not resist moral evaluation in regard to a case about child labor even though the constitutional arguments revolved around issues of congressional and state powers. In *Gonzales v. Raich,* one of the attorneys before the Supreme Court, Randy Barnett, argued that in addition to the powers question, medical marijuana also raised issues of basic liberty. Specifically, Barnett argued that limits on medical marijuana violated constitutional rights under the doctrine of substantive due process. Should the issue of personal liberty help to frame the powers debate, or is it irrelevant to the kind of considerations we have explored in this chapter?

KEY TERMS

enumerated powers: Those powers specifically granted to Congress by the Constitution, in contrast to the states' more general police powers to regulate the "welfare, health, safety, and morals" of its population.

New Federalism: The philosophy usually associated with the Reagan revolution, which sought to retrench the role of the federal government in the economic sphere; this also might refer to the Court's jurisprudence in pulling back congressional power under the Commerce Clause.

plenary powers: Exclusive powers explicitly granted to Congress, not shared with the states.

CHAPTER 6

RECALIBRATING THE POWERS OF CONGRESS: TAXATION, COMMERCE, AND THE DEBATE OVER HEALTH CARE

What are the constitutional grounds for federal mandates? Were the Commerce Clause and taxation authority of Congress meant to compel individuals to fulfill goals of national import?

We turn now to the most momentous issue before the Court in recent memory, the constitutionality of the Patient Protection and Affordable Care Act (often referred to as the Affordable Care Act, or ACA). Passed by Congress and signed into law by President Obama in 2010, the Act overhauled the nation's health-care system and was the subject of much debate. Indeed, although there had been attempts to pass health-care reform in the past, with the aim of achieving universal health insurance coverage for all Americans, notably during the administration of Bill Clinton, this was the first time a major overhaul of the system was successful since the 1960s. To say that the battle over this legislation was fierce would be an understatement. Politicians in all regions and at all levels of government weighed in about the legislation, and it was the subject of much controversy.

But for our purposes the constitutional controversy over what is commonly referred to as "Obamacare" began after the ACA was passed. As we have seen, congressional authority must be based on a specific enumerated power. What was the basis for this legislation? Those who sought to challenge the law argued that it could not be based in the Commerce Clause because that provision only regulated activity, whereas the requirement in the legislation of the "mandate" that all citizens purchase health insurance in some form is a regulation of "inactivity." Does the Commerce Clause potentially regulate such "inactivity"?

As you know from reading the chapters in this part, even if one power does not provide a basis for a piece of legislation, another provision might. Could the requirement that all Americans purchase health insurance be authorized under Congress's taxation power? In a 2009 interview, President Obama, while advocating for passage of the Affordable Care Act, responded to an interviewer's claim that the mandate was a tax by arguing that it was not.

> No. That's not true, George. The — for us to say that you've got to take a responsibility to get health insurance is absolutely not a tax increase. What it's saying is, is that we're not going to have other people carrying your burdens for you anymore than the fact that right now everybody in America, just about, has to get auto insurance. Nobody considers that a tax increase. People say to themselves, that is a fair way to make sure that if you hit my car, that I'm not covering all the costs.*

Is Obama right? Is the mandate not a tax? If so, what does that suggest about its constitutionality absent a commerce power to enact the legislation? We begin this chapter with the debate over whether the individual mandate is authorized by the Commerce Clause. We then turn to the issue of taxation, first by examining earlier, often ignored cases on the subject followed by the holding of the Roberts Court that the Constitution's tax provision authorizes the mandate.

Andrew Koppelman

BAD NEWS FOR MAIL ROBBERS: THE OBVIOUS CONSTITUTIONALITY OF HEALTH CARE REFORM

121 Yale L.J. Online 1 (2011)

The Patient Protection and Affordable Care Act includes a so-called "individual mandate." This mandate is the focus of challenges to the law. Without the mandate, the law's protection of people with preexisting conditions would mean that healthy people could wait until they get sick to buy insurance. Because insurance pools rely on cross-subsidization of sick people by healthy participants, this would bankrupt the entire health insurance system. The individual mandate charges those people for at least some of the costs they impose on their fellow citizens. Massachusetts, acting a few years before the federal law, combined its guarantee of coverage with a mandate, but seven other states tried to protect people with preexisting conditions without mandating coverage for everyone. The results in those states ranged from huge premium increases to the complete collapse of the market. The correct legal analysis is simple. Congress has the authority to solve problems that the states cannot separately solve. It can choose any reasonable means to do that.

The principal complaint about the mandate is that Congress should only be able to regulate economic activity, and the mandate is not a regulation of any activity. David Rivkin and Lee Casey object that

* See http://abcnews.go.com/blogs/politics/2009/09/obama-mandate-is-not-a-tax/.

it will "apply to every American simply because they exist." The Virginia judge, Henry Hudson, declared that in order to be subject to regulation by Congress, an individual had to engage in "some type of self-initiated action." The Florida judge, Roger Vinson, similarly argued that failure to purchase health insurance is "inactivity" and that Congress cannot regulate inactivity.

Opponents of the mandate claim that, even if Congress can regulate health care, it cannot demand that you purchase private insurance. "Congress has never before mandated that a citizen enter into an economic transaction with a private company," writes Professor Randy Barnett, "so there can be no judicial precedent for such a law." But when Congress chartered the Bank of the United States, it had never done that before either. The underlying principle behind the individual mandate is not novel at all. The Court declared it in *McCulloch*: a government that has the right to do an act — here, to regulate health care — "must, according to the dictates of reason, be allowed to select the means."

There is, however, reason to doubt the soundness of the economic/noneconomic line. While it makes sense to say that Congress can regulate any economic transaction, the Court's language suggests that this might be the test, not only for what is included in the commerce power, but also for what is *excluded.* If that were the rule, then Congress would be deprived of authority over such nontrivial matters as the spoliation of the environment or the spread of contagious diseases across state lines. The Court has already suggested on this basis that Congress may not have the power to regulate wetlands that are wholly within a single state.

A better rule would implement the line that the Framers of the Constitution drew — a line that has nothing to do with the activity/inactivity distinction, although it supports congressional regulation of the economy. This line supports the mandate.

At Philadelphia in 1787, the Convention resolved that Congress could "legislate in all cases . . . to which the States are separately incompetent, or in which the harmony of the United States may be interrupted by the exercise of individual legislation." This was then translated by the Committee of Detail into the present enumeration of powers in Article I, Section 8, which was accepted as a functional equivalent by the Convention without much discussion. Article I, Section 8 includes the commerce and "necessary and proper" provisions.

Did the Committee of Detail botch its job, limiting congressional power more than the Convention intended and creating a regime in which Congress could not legislate in cases the separate states were incompetent to address? Did the Convention not notice the massive change? No. "[T]he purpose of enumeration," Jack Balkin observes, "was not to *displace* the principle but to *enact* it." This language was accepted without objection for good reasons. Balkin shows that the word "commerce" at the time of the framing referred to all interaction between people, and so "the commerce power authorizes Congress to regulate problems or activities that produce spillover effects between states or generate collective action problems that concern more than one state." If health care markets involve such effects or problems, then the mandate presents, once more, an easy case. The Framers' most important decision was to replace the weak Articles of Confederation with a central government strong enough to address common problems. This is not a recipe for unlimited power: grandstanding statutes that horn in on matters that are purely local, such as the federal ban on the possession of handguns near schools that the Supreme Court struck down in *Lopez*, exceed the commerce power. But the national health care insurance market is not a purely local matter.

This approach justifies congressional authority over the economy, even in its local incidents, because the United States in fact has a single unified economy. You may, however, wonder whether health care reform happens to be another unnecessary centralization of an area that states were handling perfectly well. If it is, this might raise doubts about the Court's decision—which, I emphasize, is settled law—to concede to Congress's broad economic authority, and perhaps would even justify a reshaping of settled law to put a stop to this centralization. I now address this concern.

One thing that the Framers did not anticipate was the spectacular advances of the past two hundred years in our capacity to treat disease, prolong life, and ameliorate congenital illness. Many of these innovations are expensive. So with modern medicine comes a new kind of moral horror: the patient with a treatable disease who cannot afford to pay for the treatment.

The spillover effects are clear. Individuals with preexisting conditions are deterred from pursuing new opportunities in states where insurers are allowed to deny them coverage. Those with preexisting conditions whose jobs provide insurance are locked into those jobs: they are afraid to move to a different employer or to start their own businesses. Both of these effects burden the American economy as a whole.

Health insurance regulation also presents a collective action problem. The reform of the American health care system to ensure that no one would be uninsurable or bankrupted by illness was too big a task for the states to address individually. It requires more regulatory skill than most states can muster.

How can we know that collective action problems are the reasons why states have not undertaken massive health care reform? Could it not rather be evidence that local preferences are different in different places and that federalism has enabled variation of a benign sort? It is difficult to know for certain why legislation does not get enacted. But there are several pieces of information that can be the basis of reasonable inferences. One of these is that, according to a February 2011 Kaiser poll, an overwhelming majority of Americans—72 percent—supported guaranteed insurance for people with preexisting conditions. Yet only Massachusetts managed to implement it. If states are not delivering guaranteed insurance, it is not because the electorate likes that state of affairs. Contrast the law at issue in *Lopez*: it was obvious that nothing prevented states from banning handguns near schools, because more than forty of them already had such laws.

There is also the problem of adverse selection. Any state that mandates insurance for preexisting conditions risks attracting sick people and driving away healthy ones. The magnitude of this effect is uncertain, but its effect on states' incentives is plain. There is not much evidence for the notion that high levels of public support are "welfare magnets" that attract the poor across state lines, but fear of creating such magnets has made it hard to ameliorate poverty. A similar dynamic is likely at work here. How great is the danger, really? It is hard to say. People make residence decisions based on a wide range of factors, including the availability of benefits. In the health insurance case, the answer probably varies from one place to another, depending on the costs of moving. For example, the heavy burdens borne by Tennessee's health care system may be related to the fact that its most populous city, Memphis, is bordered by Mississippi and Arkansas, which offer much lower benefits. TennCare insurers are also concerned that patients from other states may be establishing residency in Tennessee in order to obtain coverage for organ transplants. There is no data available on this question, but it is hard to believe that no one responds to incentives when failure to do so is literally suicidal. Whatever the facts are, the political obstacle is a powerful one. States are reluctant to legislate because they worry that they will lose the race to the bottom. These collective action problems mean that most states cannot reform health insurance even if they all would prefer to. It is a matter in which the states are separately incompetent. Congress has the power to regulate insurance, the Court noted in 1944, because it has power "to govern affairs which the individual states, with their limited territorial jurisdictions, are not fully capable of governing."

Compare the case of child labor. When Congress acted in 1916 to ban the interstate shipment of the products of child labor, the government warned that, absent such a law, "[t]he shipment of child-made goods outside of one State directly induces similar employment of children in competing States." The collective action problem weighed heavily on state policymakers. The Supreme Court's invalidation of the law astounded even those who had most strenuously opposed enactment and provoked a wave of national revulsion and the rapid enactment of a second law—a tax on products of child labor—which the Court also invalidated. Jonathan Adler, a prominent defender of Judge Hudson's decision, does not believe the race-to-the-bottom argument in this context either, noting that at the time every state already had a law restricting child labor. This, however, ignores the enormous variation in child labor policy: some laws were weak; others were ineffectively enforced. Interstate competition kept them weak.

The precise uncertainty that drives the objection—that it is hard to know when a race to the bottom is happening—is part of the collective action problem. States do not know whether they will be disadvantaged in interstate competition by having welfare-promoting legislation. This deters them from enacting it. Congress does not have this problem.

As noted earlier, because there is a unified national economy, courts do not and should not demand proof of collective action problems before sustaining economic regulations such as the mandate. With respect to noneconomic regulations, such as environmental laws, all that it makes sense for courts to ask for is (1) a plausible description of a collective action problem and (2) evidence of the failure of states to solve it. Neither (1) nor (2) was available in *Lopez*. Both are present in the health care context.

In the context of federalism, slippery slope arguments have an unpleasant history. When it struck down the first child labor law in 1918, the Supreme Court declared—in tones reminiscent of the Broccoli Objection—that if it upheld the law, "all freedom of commerce will be at an end, and the power of the States over local matters may be eliminated, and, thus, our system of government be practically destroyed." The decision was overruled in 1941. Our system of government was not destroyed. The real lesson of this episode is that the desire to rein in government power can create a slippery slope of its own, to a state of affairs in which collective action problems go unsolved. What the Court actually accomplished in 1918 was to thwart democracy and consign large numbers of children to the textile mills for two decades. Health care is another context in which the Court is at serious risk of ravaging the lives of large numbers of actual people. In both the child labor and health care contexts, opponents of reform flee from illusory dangers into the jaws of real ones.

If the Constitution were as defective as the bill's opponents claim it is, a regime in which national problems must remain permanently unsolved, why would it deserve our allegiance? The sensible thing to do would be to try to get free of it, to try—by amendment or judicial construction—to nullify its limits so that we can live in a humanly habitable world. To continue to live with such a perverse Constitution would be mindless ancestor worship.

But the opponents of reform have been unfair to the Framers. Chief Justice Marshall was right when he said that the Constitution does not "attempt to provide, by immutable rules, for exigencies which, if foreseen at all, must have been seen dimly, and which can be best provided for as they occur." Instead, it provides a structure for us to govern ourselves. That is what Congress did when, at long last, it took on the spectacularly broken American system of health care delivery.

Randy E. Barnett

TESTIMONY BEFORE THE SENATE JUDICIARY COMMITTEE*

February 2, 2011

In 2010 something happened in this country that has never happened before: Congress required that every person enter into a contractual relationship with a private company. Now, it is not as though the federal government never requires you to do anything. You must register for the military and serve if called, you must submit a tax form, fill out a census form, and serve on a jury. And you must join a posse organized by a U.S. Marshall. But the existence and nature of these very few duties illuminates the truly extraordinary and objectionable nature of the individual insurance mandate. Each of these duties is necessary for the operation of government itself; and each has traditionally been widely recognized as inherent in being a citizen of the United States.

Consider why, in 1918, the Supreme Court rejected the claim that the military draft violated the Thirteenth Amendment, which bars "involuntary servitude." At first glance, conscription surely looks like a form of involuntary servitude. But the Court said that it could not see how "the exaction by government from the citizen of the performance of his supreme and noble duty of contributing to the defense of the rights and honor of the nation . . . can be said to be the imposition of involuntary servitude. . . ."

Keep that phrase, "supreme and noble duty" of citizenship, in mind. For this, and nothing less than this, is what is at stake in

*Available at *http://www.judiciary.senate.gov/pdf/11-02-02%20 Barnett%20Testimony.pdf.*

the fight over the constitutionality of the individual insurance mandate. Is it part of the "supreme and noble duty" of citizenship to do whatever the Congress deems in its own discretion to be convenient to its regulation of interstate commerce? If this proposition is upheld, I submit, the relationship of the people to the federal government would fundamentally change: no longer would they fairly be called "citizens"; instead they would more accurately be described as "subjects."

In fact, in Article III, the Constitution distinguishes between citizens of the United States and "subjects" of foreign states. What is the difference? In the United States, sovereignty rests with the citizenry. The government, including the Congress, is not sovereign over the people, but is the servant of the people. In the 1886 case of *Yick Wo v. Hopkins*, the Supreme Court reaffirmed that "in our system, while sovereign powers are delegated to the agencies of government, sovereignty itself remains with the people, by whom and for whom all government exists and acts." But if Congress can mandate you do anything that is "convenient" to its regulation of the national economy, then that relationship is now reversed, and Congress has the prerogative powers of King George III.

In essence, the defenders of this bill are making the following claim: because Congress has the power to draft you into the military—a power tantamount to enslaving you to fight and die—it has the power to make you do anything less than this, including mandating that you to send your money to a private company and do business with it for the rest of your life. This simply does not follow. The greater power does not include the lesser.

One way to justify so exceptional a power would be to find it in the Constitution itself. Does the Constitution expressly give Congress a power to compel citizens to enter into contractual relations with private companies—or can it be fairly implied? Quite obviously, the answer is no.

True, the Constitution does give Congress the power to impose taxes on the people to compel them to give their money to the government for its support. And it has long been assumed that Congress can then appropriate funds to provide for the common defense and general welfare by making disbursements to private companies and individuals. Social Security and Medicare are examples of the exercise of such tax and spending powers.

Because the Supreme Court is highly deferential to Congress's use of its tax power, the primary constraint on the exercise of this power is political. That is, like the power to declare war or impose a military draft, legislators will be held politically accountable for their exercise of the great and dangerous power to tax. But for this constraint to operate, at a minimum Congress must expressly invoke this power so it can be held politically accountable for exercising its power to tax.

This is why it is of utmost significance that, when it enacted the Affordable Care Act, Congress did not refer to the penalty imposed on those who fail to buy insurance as a tax. Instead it called it a "penalty" to enforce the insurance mandate. Although the penalty was inserted into the Internal Revenue Code, Congress then expressly severed the penalty from the normal enforcement mechanisms of the tax code. The failure to pay the penalty "shall not be subject to any criminal prosecution or penalty with respect to such failure." Nor shall the IRS "file notice of lien with respect to any property of a taxpayer by reason of any failure to pay the penalty imposed by this section," or impose a "levy on any such property with respect to such failure." All of these restrictions undermine the claim that, because the penalty is inserted into the Internal Revenue Code, it is a garden-variety tax.

Nor is this merely a matter of form. As Justice Souter explained in a 1996 case, "if the concept of penalty means anything, it means punishment for an unlawful act or omission. . . ." By contrast, he described a tax as "a pecuniary burden laid upon individuals or property for the purpose of supporting the Government." But when Congress identified all the revenue raising provisions of the Affordable Care Act for the vital purpose of scoring its costs, it failed to include any revenues to be collected under the penalty.

Rather than tax everyone to provide a direct subsidy to private insurance companies to compensate them for the cost of the new regulations being imposed upon them, Congress decided to compel the people to pay insurance companies directly. And it expressly justified the mandate as an exercise of its regulatory powers under the Commerce Clause. But if the mandate to buy insurance is unconstitutional because it exceeds the commerce power, then there is nothing for the penalty to enforce, regardless of whether it is deemed to be a tax.

So the unprecedented assertion of a power to impose economic mandates on the citizenry must rise and fall on whether the mandate is within the power of Congress under the Commerce Clause "to regulate . . . commerce among the several states," or whether, under the Necessary and Proper Clause, the mandate is both "necessary and proper for carrying into Execution" its commerce power.

No one claims that the individual mandate is justified by the original meaning of either the Commerce Clause or Necessary and Proper Clause. Instead, the government and those law professors who support the mandate have rested their arguments exclusively on the decisions of the Supreme Court. So what does existing Supreme Court doctrine say about the scope of the Commerce and Necessary and Proper clauses?

Of course, given that economic mandates have never before been imposed on the American people by Congress, there cannot possibly be any Supreme Court case expressly upholding such a power. But during the New Deal, the Supreme Court used the Necessary and Proper Clause to allow Congress to go beyond the regulation of interstate commerce itself to reach wholly intrastate activities that substantially affect interstate commerce. Then in 1995, in the case of *United States v. Lopez*, it limited the reach of this power to the regulation of economic, rather than noneconomic activity.

Barring Congress from regulating noneconomic intrastate activity keeps it from reaching activity that has only a remote connection to interstate commerce, without requiring courts to assess what Alexander Hamilton referred to as the "more or less necessity or utility" of a measure. Existing Commerce Clause and Necessary and Proper Clause doctrine, therefore, allows Congress to go this far, and no farther.

But the individual mandate is not regulating any economic activity. It is quite literally regulating inactivity. Rather than regulating or prohibiting economic activity in which a citizen voluntarily chooses to engage — such as growing wheat, operating a hotel or restaurant, or growing marijuana — it is commanding that a citizen must engage in economic activity. It is as though the federal government had mandated Roscoe Filburn (of *Wickard v. Filburn*) to grow wheat, or mandated

Angel Raich (of *Gonzales v. Raich*) to grow marijuana.

The distinction between acting and not acting is pervasive in all areas of law. We are liable for our actions but, absent some preexisting duty, we cannot be penalized for inaction. So in defending the mandate, the government has been forced to offer a number of shifting arguments for why, despite the appearances, insurance mandates are actually regulations of activity.

The statute itself speaks of regulating "decisions" as though a decision is an action. But expanding the meaning of "activity" to include "decisions" not to act erases the distinction between acting and not acting. It would convert all of your "decisions" not to sell your houses or cars into economic activity that could be "regulated" or mandated if Congress deems it convenient to its regulation of interstate commerce.

The government also claims that it is regulating the activity of obtaining health care, which it says everyone eventually will seek. While the government could try to condition the activity of delivering health care on patients having previously purchased insurance, in the Affordable Care Act it did not do this. The fact that most Americans will seek health care at some point or another does not convert their failure to obtain insurance from inactivity to activity and so does not convert the mandate to buy insurance into a regulation of activity.

Just as commandeering state governments is an unconstitutional infringement of state sovereignty, commandeering the people violates the even more fundamental principle of popular sovereignty. After all, the Tenth Amendment reads: "The powers not delegated to the United States by the Constitution, nor prohibited by it to the states, are reserved to the states respectively, or *to the people*."

Should the Supreme Court decide that Congress may not commandeer the people in this way, such a doctrine would only affect one law: the Affordable Care Act of 2010. Because Congress has never done anything like this before, the Court need strike down no previous mandate. This makes a challenge to the insurance mandate more likely to succeed. But if it strikes down the individual insurance mandate, the Court may also have to strike down the mandates imposed on insurance companies. For the Affordable Care Act does not include the normal severability clause that would let the remainder stand if any part is invalidated. And the very reasons why the government argues that the individual mandate is "essential" to implement the insurance regulations, are why it is not severable.

Although the bulk of my remarks today concerned decisions of the Supreme Court, many of the Court's doctrines concerning the regulatory and taxing powers are not actually opinions about what the Constitution requires, but when the Court will defer to Congress's judgment of the scope of its own powers and when it will intervene. Each Senator and Representative takes his or her own oath to uphold the Constitution, and each must reach his or her own judgment about the scope of Congressional powers.

After the Supreme Court upheld the constitutionality of the second national bank in *McCulloch v. Maryland* by invoking the Necessary and Proper Clause, President Andrew Jackson vetoed its renewal. Jackson interpreted *McCulloch* as deferring to the judgment of the legislature as to the bank's necessity and propriety. Because he viewed the veto power as legislative in nature, and because he viewed the bank as both unnecessary and improper, he concluded that the bank was unconstitutional. "If our power over means is so absolute that the Supreme Court will not call in question the constitutionality of an act of Congress the subject of which "is not prohibited, and is really calculated to effect any of the objects intrusted to the Government," ... it becomes us to proceed in our legislation with the utmost caution."

In short, just because *the Supreme Court* defers to you, does not mean *the Constitution* lets you do anything you like. Regardless of how the Supreme Court may eventually rule, each of you must decide for yourself whether the mandate is truly necessary to provide, for example, for portability of insurance if one changes jobs or moves to another state. If not, then restricting the liberties of the American people in this way is unnecessary. Each of you must also decide if allowing Congress to regulate inactivity by mandating that Americans enter into contractual relations with a private company for the rest of their lives would be to treat them as subjects, rather than citizens. If so, then commandeering the people in this manner is improper.

If you conclude that the mandate is either unnecessary or improper then, like President Jackson, you are obligated to conclude that it is unconstitutional, and to support its repeal.

NATIONAL FEDERATION OF INDEPENDENT BUSINESS v. SEBELIUS

567 U.S. __ (2012), 132 S. Ct. 2566, 183 L. Ed. 2d 450

Opinion on mandate under the Commerce Clause: Roberts, joined by Scalia, Thomas, Alito, Kennedy
Dissent: Ginsburg, joined by Sotomayor, Breyer, Kagan

In NFIB, *the Supreme Court ruled that the individual mandate was beyond Congress's power to regulate interstate commerce. Notice the holding mainly rests on the distinction between economic activity and inactivity. This distinction is also addressed in prior Commerce Clause cases such as* Heart of Atlanta Motel *and* Wickard. *In* Heart of Atlanta Motel, *the Court held that the government can force the owners of motels to engage in economic activity by making them accept African-American guests. Refusing to accept African Americans is an economic inactivity that Congress prohibited by the Civil Rights Act of 1964.*

In Wickard, *the only interstate economic effect was the farmers' refusal to buy wheat from the market, which is a form of economic inactivity. Yet, the Court found considerable federal interest in the farmers' inactivity in a market to uphold the challenged statute.*

Does NFIB *seem consistent with* Heart of Atlanta Motel *and* Wickard?

One approach to the Commerce Clause suggests that the federal government can regulate when there exists a collective action problem that states, acting alone, cannot solve. Professor Koppelman explained that prior to the passage of the ACA, only Massachusetts managed to pass a universal health-care bill. From this, he concluded that since other states seem incapable of passing such bills themselves, then the federal government can take the initiative. What do you think about this argument?

As noted above, in this portion of U.S. Supreme Court Chief Justice John Roberts's decision, he articulates why Congress has no authority to enact the mandate in the ACA based on the Commerce Clause power. On this particular issue he joins Justices Scalia,

Thomas, Alito, and Kennedy to make a majority, although those justices, as you will see below, dissent on the holding, which upholds the mandate to purchase insurance. Although Chief Justice Roberts joins these dissenting justices on the Commerce issue, as you will see in a subsequent section of the decision, he forms a majority with Justices Kagan, Breyer, Sotomayor, and Ginsburg to uphold the mandate under Congress's taxation authority.

CHIEF JUSTICE ROBERTS *announced the judgment of the Court.*

We resolve constitutional challenges to two provisions of the Patient Protection and Affordable Care Act of 2010: the individual mandate, which requires individuals to purchase a health insurance policy providing a minimum level of coverage; and the Medicaid expansion, which gives funds to the States on the condition that they provide specified health care to all citizens whose income falls below a certain threshold.

The Government's first argument is that the individual mandate is a valid exercise of Congress's power under the Commerce Clause and the Necessary and Proper Clause.

In the Affordable Care Act, Congress addressed the problem of those who cannot obtain insurance coverage because of preexisting conditions or other health issues. It did so through the Act's "guaranteed-issue" and "community-rating" provisions. These provisions together prohibit insurance companies from denying coverage to those with such conditions or charging unhealthy individuals higher premiums than healthy individuals.

The guaranteed-issue and community-rating reforms do not, however, address the issue of healthy individuals who choose not to purchase insurance to cover potential health care needs. In fact, the reforms sharply exacerbate that problem, by providing an incentive for individuals to delay purchasing health insurance until they become sick, relying on the promise of guaranteed and affordable coverage. The reforms also threaten to impose massive new costs on insurers, who are required to accept unhealthy individuals but prohibited from charging them rates necessary to pay for their coverage. This will lead insurers to significantly increase premiums on everyone. See Brief for America's Health Insurance Plans et al. as Amici Curiae in No. 11-393 etc. 8-9.

The individual mandate was Congress's solution to these problems. By requiring that individuals purchase health insurance, the mandate prevents cost-shifting by those who would otherwise go without it. In addition, the mandate forces into the insurance risk pool more healthy individuals, whose premiums on average will be higher than their health care expenses. This allows insurers to subsidize the costs of covering the unhealthy individuals the reforms require them to accept. The Government claims that Congress has power under the Commerce and Necessary and Proper Clauses to enact this solution.

The Government contends that the individual mandate is within Congress's power because the failure to purchase insurance "has a substantial and deleterious effect on interstate commerce" by creating the cost-shifting problem. Brief for United States 34. The path of our Commerce Clause decisions has not always run smooth, see United States v. Lopez, 514 U.S. 549-559 (1995), but it is now well established that Congress has broad authority under the Clause. We have recognized, for example, that "[t]he power of Congress over interstate commerce is not confined to the regulation of commerce among the states," but extends to activities that "have a substantial effect on interstate commerce." United States v. Darby, 312 U.S. 100-119 (1941). Congress's power, moreover, is not limited to regulation of an activity that by itself substantially affects interstate commerce, but also extends to activities that do so only when aggregated with similar activities of others. See *Wickard*, 317 U.S., at 127-128.

Given its expansive scope, it is no surprise that Congress has employed the commerce power in a wide variety of ways to address the pressing needs of the time. But Congress has never attempted to rely on that power to compel individuals not engaged in commerce to purchase an unwanted product. Legislative novelty is not necessarily fatal; there is a first time for everything. But sometimes "the most telling indication of [a] severe constitutional problem . . . is the lack of historical precedent" for Congress's action. Free Enterprise Fund v. Public Company Accounting Oversight Bd., 561 U.S. ___, ___ (2010) (slip op., at 25) (internal quotation marks omitted). At the very least, we should "pause to consider the implications of the Government's arguments" when confronted with such new conceptions of federal power. *Lopez*, supra, at 564.

The Constitution grants Congress the power to "regulate Commerce." Art. I, §8, cl. 3 (emphasis added). The power to regulate commerce presupposes the existence of commercial activity to be regulated. If the power to "regulate" something included the power to create it, many of the provisions in the Constitution would be superfluous. For example, the Constitution gives Congress the power to "coin Money," in addition to the power to "regulate the Value thereof." Id., cl. 5. And it gives Congress the power to "raise and support Armies" and to "provide and maintain a Navy," in addition to the power to "make Rules for the Government and Regulation of the land and naval Forces." Id., cls. 12-14. If the power to regulate the armed forces or the value of money included the power to bring the subject of the regulation into existence, the specific grant of such powers would have been unnecessary. The language of the Constitution reflects the natural understanding that the power to regulate assumes there is already something to be regulated. See *Gibbons*, 9 Wheat., at 188 ("[T]he enlightened patriots who framed our constitution, and the people who adopted it, must be understood to have employed words in their natural sense, and to have intended what they have said").

Our precedent also reflects this understanding. As expansive as our cases construing the scope of the commerce power have been, they all have one thing in common: They uniformly describe the power as reaching "activity." It is nearly impossible to avoid the word when quoting them. . . .

The individual mandate, however, does not regulate existing commercial activity. It instead compels individuals to become active in commerce by purchasing a product, on the ground that their failure to do so affects interstate commerce. Construing the Commerce Clause to permit Congress to regulate individuals precisely because they are doing nothing would open a new and potentially vast domain to congressional authority. Every day individuals do not do an infinite number of things. In some cases they decide not to do something; in others they simply fail to do it. Allowing Congress to justify federal regulation by pointing to the effect of inaction on commerce would bring countless decisions an individual could potentially make within the scope of federal regulation, and — under the Government's theory — empower Congress to make those decisions for him.

To an economist, perhaps, there is no difference between activity and inactivity; both have measurable economic effects on commerce. But the distinction between doing something and doing nothing would not have been lost on the Framers, who were "practical statesmen," not metaphysical philosophers. Industrial Union Dept., AFL-CIO v. American Petroleum Institute, 448 U.S. 607, 673 (1980) (Rehnquist, J., concurring in judgment). As we have explained, "the framers of the Constitution were not mere visionaries, toying with speculations or theories, but practical men, dealing with the facts of political life as they understood them, putting into form the government they were creating, and prescribing in language clear and intelligible the powers that government was to take." South Carolina v. United States, 199 U.S. 437, 449 (1905). The Framers gave Congress the power to regulate commerce, not to compel it, and for over 200 years both our decisions and Congress's actions have reflected this understanding. There is no reason to depart from that understanding now.

Everyone will likely participate in the markets for food, clothing, transportation, shelter, or energy; that does not authorize Congress to direct them to purchase particular products in those or other markets today. The Commerce Clause is not a general license to regulate an individual from cradle to grave, simply because he will predictably engage in particular transactions. Any police power to regulate individuals as such, as opposed to their activities, remains vested in the States.

The Government argues that the individual mandate can be sustained as a sort of exception to this rule, because health insurance is a unique product. According to the Government, upholding the individual mandate would not justify mandatory purchases of items such as cars or broccoli because, as the Government puts it, "[h]ealth insurance is not purchased for its own sake like a car or broccoli; it is a means of financing health-care consumption and covering universal risks." Reply Brief for United States 19. But cars and broccoli are no more purchased for their "own sake" than health insurance. They are purchased to cover the need for transportation and food.

The Government says that health insurance and health care financing are "inherently integrated." Brief for United States 41. But that does not mean the compelled purchase of the first is properly regarded as a regulation of the second. No matter how "inherently integrated" health insurance and health care consumption may be, they are not the same thing: They involve different transactions, entered into at different times, with different providers. And for most of those targeted by the mandate, significant health care needs will be years, or even decades, away. The proximity and degree of connection between the mandate and the subsequent commercial activity is too lacking to justify an exception of the sort urged by the Government. The individual mandate forces individuals into commerce precisely because they elected to refrain from commercial activity. Such a law cannot be sustained under a clause authorizing Congress to "regulate Commerce."

The Government next contends that Congress has the power under the Necessary and Proper Clause to enact the individual mandate because the mandate is an "integral part of a comprehensive scheme of economic regulation"—the guaranteed-issue and community-rating insurance reforms. Brief for United States 24. Under this argument, it is not necessary to consider the effect that an individual's inactivity may have on interstate commerce; it is enough that Congress regulate commercial activity in a way that requires regulation of inactivity to be effective.

The power to "make all Laws which shall be necessary and proper for carrying into Execution" the powers enumerated in the Constitution, Art. I, §8, cl. 18, vests Congress with authority to enact provisions "incidental to the [enumerated] power, and conducive to its beneficial exercise," *McCulloch*,

4 Wheat., at 418. Although the Clause gives Congress authority to "legislate on that vast mass of incidental powers which must be involved in the constitution," it does not license the exercise of any "great substantive and independent power[s]" beyond those specifically enumerated. Id., at 411, 421. Instead, the Clause is "'merely a declaration, for the removal of all uncertainty, that the means of carrying into execution those [powers] otherwise granted are included in the grant.'" Kinsella v. United States ex rel. Singleton, 361 U.S. 234, 247 (1960) (quoting VI Writings of James Madison 383 (G. Hunt ed. 1906)).

As our jurisprudence under the Necessary and Proper Clause has developed, we have been very deferential to Congress's determination that a regulation is "necessary." We have thus upheld laws that are "'convenient, or useful' or 'conducive' to the authority's 'beneficial exercise.'" *Comstock*, 560 U.S., at ___ (slip op., at 5) (quoting *McCulloch*, supra, at 413, 418). But we have also carried out our responsibility to declare unconstitutional those laws that undermine the structure of government established by the Constitution. Such laws, which are not "consist[ent] with the letter and spirit of the constitution," McCulloch, supra, at 421, are not "proper [means] for carrying into Execution" Congress's enumerated powers. Rather, they are, "in the words of The Federalist, 'merely acts of usurpation' which 'deserve to be treated as such.'"

Applying these principles, the individual mandate cannot be sustained under the Necessary and Proper Clause as an essential component of the insurance reforms. Each of our prior cases upholding laws under that Clause involved exercises of authority derivative of, and in service to, a granted power.... The individual mandate, by contrast, vests Congress with the extraordinary ability to create the necessary predicate to the exercise of an enumerated power.

This is in no way an authority that is "narrow in scope," Comstock, supra, at ___ (slip op., at 20), or "incidental" to the exercise of the commerce power, McCulloch, supra, at 418. Rather, such a conception of the Necessary and Proper Clause would work a substantial expansion of federal authority. No longer would Congress be limited to regulating under the Commerce Clause those who by some preexisting activity bring themselves within the sphere of federal regulation. Instead, Congress could reach beyond the natural limit of its authority and draw within its regulatory scope those who otherwise would be outside of it. Even if the individual mandate is "necessary" to the Act's insurance reforms, such an expansion of federal power is not a "proper" means for making those reforms effective.

Just as the individual mandate cannot be sustained as a law regulating the substantial effects of the failure to purchase health insurance, neither can it be upheld as a "necessary and proper" component of the insurance reforms. The commerce power thus does not authorize the mandate.

JUSTICE GINSBURG, *with whom* **JUSTICES SOTOMAYOR, BREYER,** *and* **KAGAN** *join, dissenting.*

Unlike The Chief Justice, I would hold that the Commerce Clause authorizes Congress to enact the minimum coverage provision.

The Commerce Clause, it is widely acknowledged, "was the Framers' response to the central problem that gave rise to the Constitution itself." EEOC v. Wyoming, 460 U.S. 226, n.1 (1983) (Stevens, J., concurring) (citing sources). Under the Articles of Confederation, the Constitution's precursor, the regulation of commerce was left to the States. This scheme proved unworkable, because the individual States, understandably focused on their own economic interests, often failed to take actions critical to the success of the Nation as a whole. See Vices of the Political System of the United States, in James Madison: Writings 69, 71, ¶5 (J. Rakove ed. 1999) (As a result of the "want of concert in matters where common interest requires it," the "national dignity, interest, and revenue [have] suffered.").

What was needed was a "national Government . . . armed with a positive & compleat authority in all cases where uniform measures are necessary." See Letter from James Madison to Edmund Randolph (Apr. 8, 1787), in 9 Papers of James Madison 368, 370 (R. Rutland ed. 1975). See also Letter from George Washington to James Madison (Nov. 30, 1785), in 8 id., at 428, 429 ("We are either a United people, or we are not. If the former, let us, in all matters of general concern act as a nation, which ha[s] national objects to promote, and a national character to support."). The Framers' solution was the Commerce Clause, which, as they perceived it, granted Congress the authority to enact economic legislation "in all Cases for the general Interests of the Union, and also in those Cases to which the States are separately incompetent." 2 Records of the Federal Convention of 1787, pp. 131-132, ¶8 (M. Farrand rev. 1966). See also North American Co. v. SEC, 327 U.S. 686, 705 (1946) ("[The commerce power] is an affirmative power commensurate with the national needs.").

Rather than evaluating the constitutionality of the minimum coverage provision in the manner established by our precedents, The Chief Justice relies on a newly minted constitutional doctrine. The commerce power does not, The Chief Justice announces, permit Congress to "compe[l] individuals to become active in commerce by purchasing a product." Ante, at 20 (emphasis deleted).

The Chief Justice's limitation of the commerce power to the regulation of those actively engaged in commerce finds no home in the text of the Constitution or our decisions. Article I, §8, of the Constitution grants Congress the power "[t]o regulate Commerce . . . among the several States." Nothing in this language implies that Congress' commerce power is limited to regulating those actively engaged in commercial transactions. Indeed, as the D.C. Circuit observed, "[a]t the time the Constitution was [framed], to 'regulate' meant," among other things, "to require action." See Seven-Sky v. Holder, 661 F.3d 1, 16 (2011).

It is not hard to show the difficulty courts (and Congress) would encounter in distinguishing statutes that regulate "activity" from those that regulate "inactivity." As Judge Easterbrook noted, "it is possible to restate most actions as corresponding inactions with the same effect." Archie v. Racine, 847 F.2d 1211, 1213 (CA7 1988) (en banc). Take this case as an example. An individual who opts not to purchase insurance from a private insurer can be seen as actively selecting another form of insurance: self-insurance. See *Thomas More Law Center*, 651 F.3d, at 561 (Sutton, J., concurring in part) ("No one is inactive when deciding how to pay for health care, as self-insurance and private insurance are two forms of action for addressing the same risk."). The minimum coverage provision could therefore be described as regulating activists in the self-insurance market. *Wickard* is another example. Did the statute there at issue target activity (the growing of too much wheat) or inactivity (the farmer's failure to purchase wheat in the marketplace)? If anything, the Court's analysis suggested the latter. See 317 U.S., at 127-129.

Underlying The Chief Justice's view that the Commerce Clause must be confined to the regulation of active participants in a commercial market is a fear that the commerce power would otherwise know no limits. The joint dissenters express a similar apprehension. This concern is unfounded. The Chief Justice could certainly uphold the individual mandate without giving Congress carte blanche to enact any and all purchase mandates. As several times noted, the unique attributes of the health-care market render everyone active in that market and give rise to a significant free-riding problem that does not occur in other markets.

To bolster his argument that the minimum coverage provision is not valid Commerce Clause legislation, The Chief Justice emphasizes the provision's novelty. See ante, at 18 (asserting that "sometimes the most telling indication of [a] severe constitutional problem . . . is the lack of historical precedent for Congress's action" (internal quotation marks omitted)). While an insurance-purchase mandate may be novel, The Chief Justice's argument certainly is not. "[I]n almost every instance of the exercise of the [commerce] power differences are asserted from previous exercises of it and made a ground of attack." Hoke v. United States, 227 U.S. 308, 320 (1913). See, e.g., Brief for Petitioner in Perez v. United States, O.T. 1970, No. 600, p. 5 ("unprecedented exercise of power"); Supplemental Brief for Appellees in Katzenbach v. McClung, O.T. 1964, No. 543, p. 40 ("novel assertion of federal power"); Brief for Appellee in Wickard v. Filburn, O. T. 1941, No. 59, p. 6 ("complete departure"). For decades, the Court has declined to override legislation because of its novelty, and for good reason. As our national economy grows and changes, we have recognized, Congress must adapt to the changing "economic and financial realities." See supra, at 14-15. Hindering Congress' ability to do so is shortsighted; if history is any guide, today's constriction of the Commerce Clause will not endure. See supra, at 25-26.

For the reasons explained above, the minimum coverage provision is valid Commerce Clause legislation. When viewed as a component of the entire ACA, the provision's constitutionality becomes even plainer. Recall that one of Congress' goals in enacting the Affordable Care Act was to eliminate the insurance industry's practice of charging higher prices or denying coverage to individuals with preexisting medical conditions. See supra, at 9-10. The commerce power allows Congress to ban this practice, a point no one disputes. See United States v. South-Eastern Underwriters Assn., 322 U.S. 533-553 (1944) (Congress may regulate "the methods by which interstate insurance companies do business.").

Congress knew, however, that simply barring insurance companies from relying on an applicant's medical history would not work in practice. Without the individual mandate, Congress learned, guaranteed-issue and community-rating requirements would trigger an adverse-selection death-spiral in the health-insurance market: Insurance premiums would skyrocket, the number of uninsured would increase, and insurance companies would exit the market. See supra, at 10-11. When complemented by an insurance mandate, on the other hand, guaranteed issue and community rating would work as intended, increasing access to insurance and reducing uncompensated care. See supra, at 11-12. The minimum coverage provision is thus an "essential par[t] of a larger regulation of economic activity"; without the provision, "the regulatory scheme [w]ould be undercut." *Raich*, 545 U.S., at 24-25 (internal quotation marks omitted). Put differently, the minimum coverage provision, together with the guaranteed-issue and community-rating requirements, is "'reasonably adapted' to the attainment of a legitimate end under the commerce power": the elimination of pricing and sales practices that take an applicant's medical history into account. See id., at 37 (Scalia, J., concurring in judgment).

Asserting that the Necessary and Proper Clause does not authorize the minimum coverage provision, The Chief Justice focuses on the word "proper." A mandate to purchase health insurance is not "proper" legislation, The Chief Justice urges, because the command "undermine[s] the structure of government established by the Constitution." Ante, at 28. If long on rhetoric, The Chief Justice's argument is short on substance.

Lacking case law support for his holding, The Chief Justice nevertheless declares the minimum coverage provision not "proper" because it is less "narrow in scope" than other laws this Court has upheld under the Necessary and Proper Clause. Ante, at 29 (citing United States v. Comstock, 560 U.S. ___ (2010); Sabri v. United States, 541 U.S. 600 (2004); Jinks v. Richland County, 538 U.S. 456 (2003)). The Chief Justice's reliance on cases in which this Court has affirmed Congress' "broad authority to enact federal legislation" under the Necessary and Proper Clause, *Comstock*, 560 U.S., at ___ (slip op., at 5), is underwhelming.

Nor does The Chief Justice pause to explain why the power to direct either the purchase of health insurance or, alternatively, the payment of a penalty collectible as a tax is more far-reaching than other implied powers this Court has found meet under the Necessary and Proper Clause. These powers include the power to enact criminal laws, see, e.g., United States v. Fox, 95 U.S. 670, 672 (1878); the power to imprison, including civil imprisonment, see, e.g., *Comstock*, 560 U.S., at ___ (slip op., at 1); and the power to create a national bank, see *McCulloch*, 4 Wheat., at 425. See also *Jinks*, 538 U.S., at 463 (affirming Congress' power to alter the way a state law is applied in state court, where the alteration "promotes fair and efficient operation of the federal courts").

In failing to explain why the individual mandate threatens our constitutional order, The Chief Justice disserves future courts. How is a judge to decide, when ruling on the constitutionality of a federal statute, whether Congress employed an "independent power," ante, at 28, or merely a "derivative" one, ante, at 29. Whether the power used is "substantive," ante, at 30, or just "incidental," ante, at 29? The instruction The Chief Justice, in effect, provides lower courts: You will know it when you see it.

It is more than exaggeration to suggest that the minimum coverage provision improperly intrudes on "essential attributes of state sovereignty." Ibid. (internal quotation marks omitted). First, the Affordable Care Act does not operate "in [an] are[a] such as criminal law enforcement or education where States historically have been sovereign." *Lopez*, 514 U.S., at 564. As evidenced by Medicare, Medicaid, the Employee Retirement Income Security Act of 1974 (ERISA), and the Health Insurance Portability and Accountability Act of 1996 (HIPAA), the Federal Government plays a lead role in the health-care sector, both as a direct payer and as a regulator.

Second, and perhaps most important, the minimum coverage provision, along with other provisions of the ACA, addresses the very sort of interstate problem that made the commerce power essential in our federal system. See supra, at 12-14. The crisis created by the large number of U.S. residents who lack health insurance is one of national dimension that States are "separately incompetent" to handle. See supra, at 7-8, 13. See also Maryland Brief 15-26 (describing "the impediments to effective state policymaking that flow from the interconnectedness of each state's healthcare economy" and emphasizing that "state-level reforms cannot fully address the problems associated with uncompensated care"). Far from trampling on States' sovereignty, the ACA attempts a federal solution for the very reason that the States, acting separately, cannot meet the need. Notably, the ACA serves the general welfare of the people of the United States while retaining a prominent role for the States. See id., at 31-36 (explaining and illustrating how the ACA affords States wide latitude in implementing key elements of the Act's reforms).

In the early 20th century, this Court regularly struck down economic regulation enacted by the peoples' representatives in both the States and the Federal Government. See, e.g., *Carter Coal Co.*, 298 U.S., at 303-304, 309-310; *Dagenhart*, 247 U.S., at 276-277; Lochner v. New York, 198 U.S. 45, 64 (1905). The Chief Justice's Commerce Clause opinion, and even more so the joint dissenters' reasoning, see post, at 4-16, bear a disquieting resemblance to those long-overruled decisions.

JUSTICES SCALIA, KENNEDY, THOMAS, *and* **ALITO,** *dissenting.*

The Act before us here exceeds federal power in mandating the purchase of health insurance. We do not doubt that the buying and selling of health insurance contracts is commerce generally subject to federal regulation. But when Congress provides that (nearly) all citizens must buy an insurance contract, it goes beyond "adjust[ing] by rule or method," Johnson, supra, or "direct[ing] according to rule," Ash, supra; it directs the creation of commerce. In response, the Government offers two theories as to why the Individual Mandate is nevertheless constitutional. Neither theory suffices to sustain its validity.

First, the Government submits that §5000A is "integral to the Affordable Care Act's insurance reforms" and "necessary to make effective the Act's core reforms." Brief for Petitioners in No. 11-398 (Minimum Coverage Provision) 24 (hereinafter Petitioners' Minimum Coverage Brief). Congress included a "finding" to similar effect in the Act itself. See 42 U.S.C. §18091(2)(H).

The Government presents the Individual Mandate as a unique feature of a complicated regulatory scheme governing many parties with countervailing incentives that must be carefully balanced. Congress has imposed an extensive set of regulations on the health insurance industry, and compliance with those regulations will likely cost the industry a great deal. If the industry does not respond by increasing premiums, it is not likely to survive. And if the industry does increase premiums, then there is a serious risk that its products — insurance plans — will become economically undesirable for many and prohibitively expensive for the rest.

This is not a dilemma unique to regulation of the health-insurance industry. Government regulation typically imposes costs on the regulated industry — especially regulation that prohibits economic behavior in which most market participants are already engaging, such as "piecing out" the market by selling the product to different classes of people at different prices (in the present context, providing much lower insurance rates to young and healthy buyers). And many industries so regulated face the reality that, without an artificial increase in demand, they cannot continue on. When Congress is regulating these industries directly, it enjoys the broad power to enact " 'all appropriate legislation' " to " 'protec[t]' " and " 'advanc[e]' " commerce, NLRB v. Jones & Laughlin Steel Corp., 301 U.S. 1-37 (1937) (quoting *The Daniel Ball*, 10 Wall. 557, 564 (1871)). Thus, Congress might protect the imperiled industry by prohibiting low-cost competition, or by according it preferential tax treatment, or even by granting it a direct subsidy.

Here, however, Congress has impressed into service third parties, healthy individuals who could be but are not customers of the relevant industry, to offset the undesirable consequences of the regulation. Congress' desire to force these individuals to purchase insurance is motivated by the fact that they are further removed from the market than unhealthy individuals with pre-existing conditions, because they are less likely to need extensive care in the near future. If Congress can reach out and command even those furthest removed from an interstate market to participate in the market, then the Commerce Clause becomes a font of unlimited power, or in Hamilton's words, "the hideous monster whose devouring jaws . . . spare neither sex nor age, nor high nor low, nor sacred nor profane." The Federalist No. 33, p. 202 (C. Rossiter ed. 1961).

The Government was invited, at oral argument, to suggest what federal controls over private conduct (other than those explicitly prohibited by the Bill of Rights or other constitutional controls) could not be justified as necessary and proper for the carrying out of a general regulatory scheme. See Tr. of Oral Arg. 27-30, 43-45 (Mar. 27, 2012). It was unable to name any. As we said at the outset, whereas the precise scope of the Commerce Clause and the Necessary and Proper Clause is uncertain, the proposition that the Federal Government cannot do everything is a fundamental precept. See *Lopez*, 514 U.S., at 564 ("[I]f we were to accept the Government's arguments, we are hard pressed to posit any activity by an individual that Congress is without power to regulate"). Section 5000A is defeated by that proposition.

The Government's second theory in support of the Individual Mandate is that §5000A is valid because it is actually a "regulat[ion of] activities having a substantial relation to interstate commerce, . . . i.e., . . . activities that substantially affect interstate commerce." Id., at 558-559. See also *Shreveport Rate Cases*, supra. This argument takes a few different forms, but the basic idea is that §5000A regulates "the way in which individuals finance their participation in the health-care market." Petitioners' Minimum Coverage Brief 33 (emphasis added). That is, the provision directs the manner in which individuals purchase health care services and related goods (directing that they be purchased through insurance) and is therefore a straightforward exercise of the commerce power.

The primary problem with this argument is that §5000A does not apply only to persons who purchase all, or most, or even any, of the health care services or goods that the mandated insurance covers. Indeed, the main objection many have to the Mandate is that they have no intention of purchasing most or even any of such goods or services and thus no need to buy insurance for those purchases. The Government responds that the health-care market involves "essentially universal participation," id., at 35. The principal difficulty with this response is that it is, in the only relevant sense, not true. It is true enough that everyone consumes "health care," if the term is taken to include the purchase of a bottle of aspirin. But the health care "market" that is the object of the Individual Mandate not only includes but principally consists of goods and services that the young people primarily affected by the Mandate do not purchase. They are quite simply not participants in that market, and cannot be made so (and thereby subjected to regulation) by the simple device of defining participants to include all those who will, later in their lifetime, probably purchase the goods or services covered by the mandated insurance. Such a definition of market participants is unprecedented, and were it to be a premise for the exercise of national power, it would have no principled limits.

In a variation on this attempted exercise of federal power, the Government points out that Congress in this Act has purported to regulate "economic and financial decision[s] to forego [sic] health insurance coverage and [to] attempt to self-insure," 42 U.S.C. §18091(2)(A), since those decisions have "a substantial and deleterious effect on interstate commerce," Petitioners' Minimum Coverage Brief 34. But as the discussion above makes clear, the decision to forgo participation in an interstate market is not itself commercial activity (or indeed any activity at all) within Congress' power to regulate. It is true that, at the end of the day, it is inevitable that each American will affect commerce and become a part of it, even if not by choice. But if every person comes within the Commerce Clause power of Congress to regulate by the simple reason that he will one day engage in commerce, the idea of a limited Government power is at an end.

A few respectful responses to Justice Ginsburg's dissent on the issue of the Mandate are in order. That dissent duly recites the test of Commerce Clause power that our opinions have applied, but disregards the premise the test contains. It is true enough that Congress needs only a "'rational basis' for concluding that the regulated activity substantially affects interstate commerce," ante, at 15 (emphasis added). But it must be activity affecting commerce that is regulated, and not merely the failure to engage in commerce. And one is not now purchasing the health care covered by the insurance mandate simply because one is likely to be purchasing it in the future. Our test's premise of regulated activity is not invented out of whole cloth, but rests upon the Constitution's requirement that it be commerce which is regulated. If all inactivity affecting commerce is commerce, commerce is everything. Ultimately the dissent is driven to saying that there is really no difference between action and inaction, ante, at 26, a proposition that has never recommended itself, neither to the law nor to common sense. To say, for example, that the inaction here consists of activity in "the self-insurance market," ibid., seems to us wordplay. By parity of reasoning the failure to buy a car can be called participation in the non-private-car-transportation market. Commerce becomes everything.

The dissent claims that we "fai[l] to explain why the individual mandate threatens our constitutional order." Ante, at 35. But we have done so. It threatens that order because it gives such an expansive meaning to the Commerce Clause that all private conduct (including failure to act) becomes subject to federal control, effectively destroying the Constitution's division of governmental powers.

We respectfully dissent.

BAILEY v. DREXEL FURNITURE CO.

259 U.S. 20 (1922)

Opinion: Taft, joined by Brandeis, Day, Van Devanter, Holmes, McKenna, McReynolds, Pitney
Dissent: Clarke

You have just seen that the Court ruled that the Commerce Clause does not authorize the individual mandate core to the Affordable Care Act. But does another provision authorize it? As you will see, although the Court rejected the Commerce Clause argument for a power to enact the mandate, it did agree that its taxation power authorized it. Before we turn back to examine the constitutionality of the mandate, however, it is important to examine the history of that clause.

In Hammer v. Dagenhart, *the Supreme Court held that the federal regulation of the employment of children is beyond Congress's power to regulate commerce. After the Court struck down the child labor laws in* Dagenhart, *Congress passed the Child Labor Tax Law, which imposed higher taxes on businesses that employed children. In* Bailey, *those laws were challenged as exceeding Congress's power to tax. The Taxing Clause reads: "The Congress shall have Power To lay and collect Taxes, Duties, Imposts and Excises, to pay the Debts and provide for the common Defence, and general Welfare of the United States." The question before the Court, in this case, is whether Congress can use its taxing power to regulate in an area, which here is child labor. Can Congress call a "penalty" a "tax" in a statute and have it upheld as a valid exercise of its taxing power? What distinguishes a "tax" from a "penalty"?*

MR. CHIEF JUSTICE TAFT *delivered the opinion of the Court.*

This case presents the question of the constitutional validity of the Child Labor Tax Law. The plaintiff below, the Drexel Furniture Company, is engaged in the manufacture of furniture in the Western District of North Carolina. On September 20, 1921, it received a notice from Bailey, United States Collector of Internal Revenue for the District, that it had been assessed $6,312.79 for having during the taxable year 1919 employed and permitted to work in its factory a boy under fourteen years of age, thus incurring the tax of ten percent on its net profits for that year. The Company paid the tax under protest, and after rejection of its claim for a refund, brought this suit. On demurrer to an amended complaint, judgment was entered for the Company against the Collector for the full amount with interest. The writ of error is prosecuted by the Collector direct from the District Court under §238 of the Judicial Code.

The Child Labor Tax Law is Title XII of an act entitled "An Act To provide revenue, and for other purposes," approved February 24, 1919, c. 18, 40 Stat. 1057, 1138. The heading of the title is "Tax on Employment of Child Labor." Section 1200 is as follows: "[E]very person (other than a bona fide boys' or girls' canning club recognized by the Agricultural Department of a State and of the United States) operating (a) any mine or quarry situated in the United States in which children under the age of sixteen years have been employed or permitted to work during any portion of the taxable year; or (b) any mill, cannery, workshop, factory, or manufacturing establishment situated in the United States in which children under the age of fourteen years have been employed or permitted to work, or children between the ages of fourteen and sixteen have been employed or permitted to work more than eight hours in any day or more than six days in any week, or after the hour of seven o'clock post meridian, or before the hour of six o'clock ante meridian, during any portion of the taxable year, shall pay for each taxable year, in addition to all other taxes imposed by law, an excise tax equivalent to 10 percentum of the entire net profits received or accrued for such year from the sale or disposition of the product of such mine, quarry, mill, cannery, workshop, factory, or manufacturing establishment."

Section 1206 gives authority to the Commissioner of Internal Revenue, or any other person authorized by him, "to enter and inspect at any time any mine, quarry, mill, cannery, workshop, factory, or manufacturing establishment." The Secretary of Labor, or any person whom he authorizes, is given like authority in order to comply with a request of the Commissioner to make such inspection and report the same. Any person who refuses entry or obstructs inspection is made subject to fine or imprisonment or both.

The law is attacked on the ground that it is a regulation of the employment of child labor in the States — an exclusively state function under the Federal Constitution and within the reservations of the Tenth Amendment. It is defended on the ground that it is a mere excise tax levied by the Congress of the United States under its broad power of taxation conferred by §8, Article I, of the Federal Constitution. We must construe the law and interpret the intent and meaning of Congress from the language of the act. The words are to be given their ordinary meaning unless the context shows that they are differently used. Does this law impose a tax with only that incidental restraint and regulation which a tax must inevitably involve? Or does it regulate by the use of the so-called tax as a penalty? If a tax, it is clearly an excise. If it were an excise on a commodity or other thing of value, we might not be permitted under previous decisions of this court to infer solely from its heavy burden that the act intends a prohibition, instead of a tax. But this act is more. It provides a heavy exaction for a departure from a detailed and specified course of conduct in business. That course of business is that employers shall employ in mines and quarries children of an age greater than sixteen years; in mills and factories, children of an age greater than fourteen years, and shall prevent children of less than sixteen years in mills and factories from working more than eight hours a day or six days in the week. If an employer departs from this prescribed course of business, he is to pay to the Government one-tenth of his entire net income in the business for a full year. The amount is not to be proportioned in any degree to the extent or frequency of the departures, but is to be paid by the employer in full measure whether he employs five hundred children for a year, or employs only one for a day. Moreover, if he does not know the child is within the named age limit, he is not to pay; that is to say, it is only where he knowingly departs from the prescribed course that payment is to be exacted. *Scienter* is associated with penalties, not with taxes. The employer's factory is to be subject to inspection at any time not only by the taxing officers of the Treasury, the Department normally charged with the collection of taxes, but also by the Secretary of Labor and his subordinates, whose normal function is the advancement and protection of the welfare of the workers. In the light of these features of the act, a court must be blind not to see that the so-called tax is imposed to stop the employment of children within the age limits prescribed. Its prohibitory and regulatory effect and purpose are palpable. All others can see and understand this. How can we properly shut our minds to it?

Out of a proper respect for the acts of a coordinate branch of the Government, this court has gone far to sustain taxing acts as such, even though there has been ground for suspecting from the weight of the tax it was intended to destroy its subject. But, in the act before us, the presumption of validity cannot prevail, because the proof of the contrary is found on the very face of its provisions. Grant the validity of this law, and all that Congress would need to do, hereafter, in seeking to take over to its control anyone of the great number of subjects of public interest, jurisdiction of which the States have never parted with, and which are reserved to them by the Tenth Amendment, would be to enact a detailed measure of complete regulation of the subject and enforce it by a so-called tax upon departures from it. To give such magic to the word "tax" would be to break down all constitutional limitation of the powers of Congress and completely wipe out the sovereignty of the States.

The difference between a tax and a penalty is sometimes difficult to define, and yet the consequences of the distinction in the required method of their collection often are important. Where the sovereign enacting the law has power to impose both tax and penalty, the difference between revenue production and mere regulation may be immaterial, but not so when one sovereign can impose a tax only, and the power of regulation rests in another. Taxes are occasionally imposed in the discretion of the legislature on proper subjects with the primary motive of obtaining revenue from them and with the incidental motive of discouraging them by making their continuance onerous. They do not lose their character as taxes because of the incidental motive. But there comes a time in the extension of the penalizing features of the so-called tax when it loses its character as such and becomes a mere penalty with the characteristics of regulation and punishment. Such is the case in the law before us. Although Congress does not invalidate the contract of employment or expressly declare that the employment within the mentioned ages is illegal, it does exhibit its intent practically to achieve the latter result by adopting the criteria of wrongdoing and imposing its principal consequence on those who transgress its standard.

The case before us cannot be distinguished from that of *Hammer v. Dagenhart*, 247 U.S. 251. Congress there enacted a law to prohibit transportation in interstate commerce of goods made at a factory in which there was employment of children within the same ages and for the same number of hours a day and days in a week as are penalized by the act in this case. This court held the law in that case to be void. It said:

> In our view, the necessary effect of this act is, by means of a prohibition against the movement in interstate commerce of ordinary commercial commodities, to regulate the hours of labor of children in factories and mines within the States, a purely state authority.

In the case at the bar, Congress in the name of a tax which, on the face of the act, is a penalty seeks to do the same thing, and the effort must be equally futile.

The analogy of the *Dagenhart* Case is clear. The congressional power over interstate commerce is, within its proper scope, just as complete and unlimited as the congressional power to tax, and the legislative motive in its exercise is just as free from judicial suspicion and inquiry. Yet when Congress threatened to stop interstate commerce in ordinary and necessary commodities, unobjectionable as subjects of transportation, and to deny the same to the people of a State in order to coerce them into compliance with Congress' regulation of state concerns, the Court said this was not, in fact, regulation of interstate commerce, but rather that of State concerns, and was invalid. So here, the so-called tax is a penalty to coerce people of a State to act as Congress wishes them to act in respect of a matter completely the business of the state government under the Federal Constitution.

It is pressed upon us that this court has gone so far in sustaining taxing measures the effect or tendency of which was to accomplish purposes not directly within congressional power that we are bound by authority to maintain this law.

The first of these is *Veazie Bank v. Fenno*, 8 Wheat. 533. In that case, the validity of a law which increased a tax on the circulating notes of persons and state banks from one percentum to ten percentum was in question. The main question was whether this was a direct tax to be apportioned among the several States "according to their respective numbers." This was answered in the negative. The second objection was stated by the Court: "It is insisted, however, that the tax in the case before us is excessive, and so excessive as to indicate a purpose on the part of Congress to destroy the franchise of the bank, and is, therefore, beyond the constitutional power of Congress."

It will be observed that the sole objection to the tax there was its excessive character. Nothing else appeared on the face of the act. It was an increase of a tax admittedly legal to a higher rate, and that was all. There were no elaborate specifications on the face of the act, as here, indicating the purpose to regulate matters of state concern and jurisdiction through an exaction so applied as to give it the qualities of a penalty for violation of law, rather than a tax.

It should be noted, too, that the Court, speaking of the extent of the taxing power, used these cautionary words: "There are, indeed, certain virtual limitations, arising from the principles of the Constitution itself. It would undoubtedly be an abuse of the power if so exercised as to impair the separate existence and independent self-government of the States, or if exercised for ends inconsistent with the limited grants of power in the Constitution."

But, more than this, what was charged to be the object of the excessive tax was within the congressional authority, as appears from the second answer which the Court gave to the objection. After having pointed out the legitimate means taken by Congress to secure a national medium or currency, the Court said:

"Having thus, in the exercise of undisputed constitutional powers, undertaken to provide a currency for the whole country, it cannot be questioned that Congress may, constitutionally, secure the benefit of it to the people by appropriate legislation. To this end, Congress has denied the quality of legal tender to foreign coins, and has provided by law against the imposition of counterfeit and base coin on the community. To the same end, Congress may restrain, by suitable enactments, the circulation as money of any notes not issued under its own authority. Without this power, indeed, its attempts to secure a sound and uniform currency for the country must be futile."

The next case is that of *McCray v. United States*, 195 U.S. 27. That, like the *Veazie Bank* case, was the increase of an excise tax upon a subject properly taxable in which the taxpayers claimed that the tax had become invalid because the increase was excessive. It was a tax on oleomargarine, a substitute for butter. The tax on the white oleomargarine was one-quarter of a cent a pound, and on the yellow oleomargarine was first two cents and was then by the act in question increased to ten cents per pound. This court held that the discretion of Congress in the exercise of its constitutional powers to levy excise taxes could not be controlled or limited by the Courts because the latter might deem the incidence of the tax oppressive, or even destructive. It was the same principle as that applied in the *Veazie Bank* case. This was that Congress, in selecting its subjects for taxation, might impose the burden where and as it would, and that a motive disclosed in its selection to discourage sale or manufacture of an article by a higher tax than on some other did not invalidate the tax. In neither of these cases did the law objected to show on its face, as does the law before us, the detailed specifications of a regulation of a state concern and business with a heavy exaction to promote the efficacy of such regulation.

The third case is that of *Flint v. Stone Tracy Co.*, 220 U.S. 107. It involved the validity of an excise tax levied on the doing of business by all corporations, joint stock companies, associations organized for profit having a capital stock represented by shares, and insurance companies, and measured the excise by the net income of the corporations. There was not in that case the slightest doubt that the tax was a tax, and a tax for revenue, but it was attacked on the ground that such a tax could be made excessive, and thus used by Congress to destroy the existence of state corporations. To this, this court gave the same answer as in the *Veazie Bank* and *McCray* cases. It is not so strong an authority for the Government's contention as they are.

The fourth case is *United States v. Doremus*, 249 U.S. 86. That involved the validity of the Narcotic Drug Act, 38 Stat. 785, which imposed a special tax on the manufacture, importation and sale or gift of opium or coca leaves or their compounds or derivatives. It required every person subject to the special tax to register with the Collector of Internal Revenue his name and place of business, and forbade him to sell except upon the written order of the person to whom the sale was made on a form prescribed by the Commissioner of Internal Revenue. The vendor was required to keep the order for two years, and the purchaser to keep a duplicate for the same time, and both were to be subject to official inspection. Similar requirements were made as to sales upon prescriptions of a physician and as to the dispensing of such drugs directly to a patient by a physician. The validity of a special tax in the nature of an excise tax on the manufacture, importation and sale of such drugs was, of course, unquestioned. The provisions for subjecting the sale and distribution of the drugs to official supervision and inspection were held to have a reasonable relation to the enforcement of the tax, and were therefore held valid.

The court said that the act could not be declared invalid just because another motive than taxation, not shown on the face of the act, might have contributed to its passage. This case does not militate against the conclusion we have reached in respect of the law now before us. The court there made manifest its view that the provisions of the so-called taxing act must be naturally and reasonably adapted to the collection of the tax, and not solely to the achievement of some other purpose plainly within state power.

For the reason given, we must hold the Child Labor Tax Law invalid, and the judgment of the District Court is *affirmed.*

NATIONAL FEDERATION OF INDEPENDENT BUSINESS v. SEBELIUS

567 U.S. __ (2012), 132 S. Ct. 2566, 183 L. Ed. 2d 450

Opinion on mandate under taxation power: Roberts, joined by Breyer, Kagan
Concurrence: Ginsburg, joined by Sotomayor
Dissent: Kennedy, Alito, Scalia, Thomas

In Bailey, *the Court found that what was called a "tax" was a "penalty," and therefore not a valid exercise of the Congress's power under the Taxing Clause. The opinion of the Court in* NFIB, *written by Chief Justice Roberts, does the opposite by finding what is called a "penalty" a "tax." How does this holding relate to* Bailey's *explanation of the meaning of a "tax" and a "penalty"?*

Another issue of congressional power concerns the Spending Clause of Article I, examined in Chapter 3. The Supreme Court struck down the Medicaid expansion provision of the ACA with an 8–2 majority. But on U.S. Supreme Court Justice Ruth Bader Ginsburg's view, the Medicaid expansion was within the Congress's spending power because there is no constitutional requirement for the states to receive funds for their Medicaid programs from the federal government. On her view, Congress could have first stopped the already existing Medicaid funding, and then put a new Medicaid funding system in place that is in accord with the objectives of the ACA. Given that Justice Ginsburg views the provision to be accomplishable in two steps, she finds no reason for the Court to strike it down simply because it was done in one step instead. What do you think about this argument?

How does the Medicaid expansion provision in NFIB *differ from the statute in* South Dakota v. Dole, *which made a state's receiving of federal highway funds conditioned on having a 21-year old drinking age. Is the decision in this case consistent with the holding in* Dole?

The Constitution contains no Spending Clause. The power to spend, it has been argued, is derived from the power to tax read in light of the Necessary and Proper Clause. In other words, the power to spend is "necessary and proper" for "carrying into execution" the payment of debts and providing for the "common Defence and general Welfare of the United States."

Can the government attach strings for giving funds to the states? What if these strings are considered by Congress to provide for the "general Welfare" of the United States, as was the case in Dole *and* NFIB*? Can the Supreme Court argue that the Medicaid expansion provision does not further the "general Welfare" of the United States, or is that a political question that should be resolved by deferral to Congress? Is there any inconsistency in the majority's application of the presumption of constitutionality to the individual mandate as compared to the Medicaid expansion program?*

Again, above we read Chief Justice Roberts's opinion on why there is no Commerce Clause power to enact the ACA. On that issue he formed a majority with Justices Kennedy, Scalia, Thomas, and Alito. But here he departs from those justices and forms a majority with Justices Breyer, Ginsburg, Sotomayor, and Kagan, based on the taxation power, to uphold the mandate and the law.

CHIEF JUSTICE ROBERTS *announced the judgment of the Court and delivered the opinion of the Court with respect to Part III-C, and an opinion with respect to Part IV, with whom* **JUSTICE BREYER and JUSTICE KAGAN** *join.*

III-C

The exaction the Affordable Care Act imposes on those without health insurance looks like a tax in many respects. The "[s]hared responsibility payment," as the statute entitles it, is paid into the Treasury by "taxpayer[s]" when they file their tax returns. It does not apply to individuals who do not pay federal income taxes because their household income is less than the filing threshold in the Internal Revenue Code. For taxpayers who do owe the payment, its amount is determined by such familiar factors as taxable income, number of dependents, and joint filing status. The requirement to pay is found in the Internal Revenue Code and enforced by the IRS, which — as we previously explained — must assess and collect it "in the same manner as taxes." This process yields the essential feature of any tax: it produces at least some revenue for the Government. United States v. Kahriger, 345 U.S. 22, n. 4 (1953). Indeed, the payment is expected to raise about $4 billion per year by 2017. Congressional Budget Office, Payments of Penalties for Being Uninsured Under the Patient Protection and Affordable Care Act (Apr. 30, 2010), in Selected CBO Publications Related to Health Care Legislation, 2009-2010, p. 71 (rev. 2010).

It is of course true that the Act describes the payment as a "penalty," not a "tax." That choice [of label] does not, however, control whether an exaction is within Congress's constitutional power to tax. Our precedent reflects this: In 1922, we decided two challenges to the "Child Labor Tax" on the same day. In the first, we held that a suit to enjoin collection of the so-called tax was barred by the Anti-Injunction Act. *George*, 259 U.S., at 20. Congress knew that suits to obstruct taxes had to await payment under the Anti-Injunction Act; Congress called the child labor tax a tax; Congress therefore intended the Anti-Injunction Act to apply. In the second case, however, we held that the same exaction, although labeled a tax, was not in fact authorized by Congress's taxing power. *Drexel Furniture*, 259 U.S., at 38. That constitutional question was not controlled by Congress's choice of label.

We have similarly held that exactions not labeled taxes nonetheless were authorized by Congress's power to tax. In the *License Tax Cases*, for example, we held that federal licenses to sell liquor and lottery tickets — for which the licensee had to pay a fee — could be sustained as exercises of the taxing power. 5 Wall., at 471. And in *New York v. United States* we upheld as a tax a "surcharge" on out-of-state nuclear waste shipments, a portion of which was paid to the Federal Treasury. 505 U.S., at 171. We thus ask whether the shared responsibility payment falls within Congress's taxing power, "[d]isregarding the designation of the exaction, and viewing its substance and application." United States v. Constantine, 296 U.S. 287, 294 (1935); cf. Quill Corp. v. North Dakota, 504 U.S. 298, 310 (1992) ("[M]agic words or labels" should not "disable an otherwise constitutional levy" (internal quotation marks omitted)); Nelson v. Sears, Roebuck & Co., 312 U.S. 359, 363 (1941) ("In passing on the constitutionality of a tax law, we are concerned only with its practical operation, not its definition or the precise form of descriptive words which may be applied to it" (internal quotation marks omitted)); United States v. Sotelo, 436 U.S. 268, 275 (1978) ("That the funds due are referred to as a 'penalty' . . . does not alter their essential character as taxes").

Our cases confirm this functional approach. For example, in *Drexel Furniture*, we focused on three practical characteristics of the so-called tax on employing child laborers that convinced us the "tax" was actually a penalty. First, the tax imposed an exceedingly heavy burden — 10 percent of a company's net income — on those who employed children, no matter how small their infraction. Second, it imposed that exaction only on those who knowingly employed underage laborers. Such scienter requirements are typical of punitive statutes, because Congress often wishes to punish only those who intentionally break the law. Third, this "tax" was enforced in part by the Department of Labor, an agency responsible for punishing violations of labor laws, not collecting revenue. 259 U.S., at 36-37; see also, e.g., *Kurth Ranch*, 511 U.S., at 780-782 (considering, inter alia, the amount of the exaction, and the fact that it was imposed for violation of a separate criminal law); *Constantine*, supra, at 295 (same).

The same analysis here suggests that the shared responsibility payment may for constitutional purposes be considered a tax, not a penalty: First, for most Americans the amount due will be far less than the price of insurance, and, by statute, it can never be more. It may often be a reasonable financial decision to make the payment rather than purchase insurance, unlike the "prohibitory" financial punishment in *Drexel Furniture.* 259 U.S., at 37. Second, the individual mandate contains no scienter requirement. Third, the payment is collected solely by the IRS through the normal means of taxation—except that the Service is not allowed to use those means most suggestive of a punitive sanction, such as criminal prosecution. See §5000A(g)(2). The reasons the Court in *Drexel Furniture* held that what was called a "tax" there was a penalty support the conclusion that what is called a "penalty" here may be viewed as a tax.

Our precedent demonstrates that Congress had the power to impose the exaction in §5000A under the taxing power, and that §5000A need not be read to do more than impose a tax. That is sufficient to sustain it. The "question of the constitutionality of action taken by Congress does not depend on recitals of the power which it undertakes to exercise." Woods v. Cloyd W. Miller Co., 333 U.S. 138, 144 (1948).

IV

The States also contend that the Medicaid expansion exceeds Congress's authority under the Spending Clause. They claim that Congress is coercing the States to adopt the changes it wants by threatening to withhold all of a State's Medicaid grants, unless the State accepts the new expanded funding and complies with the conditions that come with it. This, they argue, violates the basic principle that the "Federal Government may not compel the States to enact or administer a federal regulatory program." *New York,* 505 U.S., at 188.

Our cases have recognized limits on Congress's power under the Spending Clause to secure state compliance with federal objectives. "We have repeatedly characterized . . . Spending Clause legislation as 'much in the nature of a contract.'" Barnes v. Gorman, 536 U.S. 181, 186 (2002) (quoting Pennhurst State School and Hospital v. Halderman, 451 U.S. 1, 17 (1981)). The legitimacy of Congress's exercise of the spending power "thus rests on whether the State voluntarily and knowingly accepts the terms of the 'contract.'" *Pennhurst,* supra, at 17. Respecting this limitation is critical to ensuring that Spending Clause legislation does not undermine the status of the States as independent sovereigns in our federal system. That system "rests on what might at first seem a counterintuitive insight, that 'freedom is enhanced by the creation of two governments, not one.'" *Bond,* 564 U.S., at ___ (slip op., at 8) (quoting Alden v. Maine, 527 U.S. 706, 758 (1999)). For this reason, "the Constitution has never been understood to confer upon Congress the ability to require the States to govern according to Congress' instructions." *New York,* supra, at 162. Otherwise the two-government system established by the Framers would give way to a system that vests power in one central government, and individual liberty would suffer.

Permitting the Federal Government to force the States to implement a federal program would threaten the political accountability key to our federal system. "[W]here the Federal Government directs the States to regulate, it may be state officials who will bear the brunt of public disapproval, while the federal officials who devised the regulatory program may remain insulated from the electoral ramifications of their decision." Id., at 169. Spending Clause programs do not pose this danger when a State has a legitimate choice whether to accept the federal conditions in exchange for federal funds. In such a situation, state officials can fairly be held politically accountable for choosing to accept or refuse the federal offer. But when the State has no choice, the Federal Government can achieve its objectives without accountability, just as in *New York* and *Printz*. Indeed, this danger is heightened when Congress acts under the Spending Clause, because Congress can use that power to implement federal policy it could not impose directly under its enumerated powers.

As our decision in *Steward Machine* confirms, Congress may attach appropriate conditions to federal taxing and spending programs to preserve its control over the use of federal funds. In the typical case we look to the States to defend their prerogatives by adopting "the simple expedient of not yielding" to federal blandishments when they do not want to embrace the federal policies as their own. Massachusetts v. Mellon, 262 U.S. 447, 482 (1923). The States are separate and independent sovereigns. Sometimes they have to act like it.

The States, however, argue that the Medicaid expansion is far from the typical case. They object that Congress has "crossed the line distinguishing encouragement from coercion," *New York*, supra, at 175, in the way it has structured the funding: Instead of simply refusing to grant the new funds to States that will not accept the new conditions, Congress has also threatened to withhold those States' existing Medicaid funds. The States claim that this threat serves no purpose other than to force unwilling States to sign up for the dramatic expansion in health care coverage effected by the Act.

Given the nature of the threat and the programs at issue here, we must agree. We have upheld Congress's authority to condition the receipt of funds on the States' complying with restrictions on the use of those funds, because that is the means by which Congress ensures that the funds are spent according to its view of the "general Welfare." Conditions that do not here govern the use of the funds, however, cannot be justified on that basis. When, for example, such conditions take the form of threats to terminate other significant independent grants, the conditions are properly viewed as a means of pressuring the States to accept policy changes.

In this case, the financial "inducement" Congress has chosen is much more than "relatively mild encouragement"—it is a gun to the head. Medicaid spending accounts for over 20 percent of the average State's total budget, with federal funds covering 50 to 83 percent of those costs. See Nat. Assn. of State Budget Officers, Fiscal Year 2010 State Expenditure Report, p. 11, Table 5 (2011); 42 U.S.C. §1396d(b). The Federal Government estimates that it will pay out approximately $3.3 trillion between 2010 and 2019 in order to cover the costs of pre-expansion Medicaid. Brief for United States 10, n. 6. . . . It is easy to see how the Dole Court could conclude that the threatened loss of less than half of one percent of South Dakota's budget left that State with a "prerogative" to reject Congress's desired policy, "not merely in theory but in fact." 483 U.S., at 211-212. The threatened loss of over 10 percent of a State's overall budget, in contrast, is economic dragooning that leaves the States with no real option but to acquiesce in the Medicaid expansion.

The Medicaid expansion, however, accomplishes a shift in kind, not merely degree. The original program was designed to cover medical services for four particular categories of the needy: the disabled, the blind, the elderly, and needy families with dependent children. See 42 U.S.C. §1396a(a)(10).

Previous amendments to Medicaid eligibility merely altered and expanded the boundaries of these categories. Under the Affordable Care Act, Medicaid is transformed into a program to meet the health care needs of the entire nonelderly population with income below 133 percent of the poverty level. It is no longer a program to care for the neediest among us, but rather an element of a comprehensive national plan to provide universal health insurance coverage.

Nothing in our opinion precludes Congress from offering funds under the Affordable Care Act to expand the availability of health care, and requiring that States accepting such funds comply with the conditions on their use. What Congress is not free to do is to penalize States that choose not to participate in that new program by taking away their existing Medicaid funding.

* * *

In this case it is reasonable to construe what Congress has done as increasing taxes on those who have a certain amount of income, but choose to go without health insurance. Such legislation is within Congress's power to tax.

As for the Medicaid expansion, that portion of the Affordable Care Act violates the Constitution by threatening existing Medicaid funding. Congress has no authority to order the States to regulate according to its instructions. Congress may offer the States grants and require the States to comply with accompanying conditions, but the States must have a genuine choice whether to accept the offer. The States are given no such choice in this case: They must either accept a basic change in the nature of Medicaid, or risk losing all Medicaid funding. The remedy for that constitutional violation is to preclude the Federal Government from imposing such a sanction. That remedy does not require striking down other portions of the Affordable Care Act.

The judgment of the Court of Appeals for the Eleventh Circuit is affirmed in part and reversed in part.

It is so ordered.

JUSTICE GINSBURG, *with whom* **JUSTICE SOTOMAYOR** *joins.*

Through Medicaid, Congress has offered the States an opportunity to furnish health care to the poor with the aid of federal financing. The ACA enlarges the population of needy people States must cover to include adults under age 65 with incomes up to 133% of the federal poverty level. The spending power conferred by the Constitution, the Court has never doubted, permits Congress to define the contours of programs financed with federal funds. See, e.g., Pennhurst State School and Hospital v. Halderman, 451 U.S. 1, 17 (1981). And to expand coverage, Congress could have recalled the existing legislation, and replaced it with a new law making Medicaid as embracive of the poor as Congress chose.

The question posed by the 2010 Medicaid expansion, then, is essentially this: To cover a notably larger population, must Congress take the repeal/reenact route, or may it achieve the same result by amending existing law? The answer should be that Congress may expand by amendment the classes of needy persons entitled to Medicaid benefits. A ritualistic requirement that Congress repeal and reenact spending legislation in order to enlarge the population served by a federally funded program would advance no constitutional principle and would scarcely serve the interests of federalism. To the contrary, such a requirement would rigidify Congress' efforts to empower States by partnering with them in the implementation of federal programs.

The Chief Justice acknowledges that Congress may "condition the receipt of [federal] funds on the States' complying with restrictions on the use of those funds," ante, at 50, but nevertheless concludes that the 2010 expansion is unduly coercive. His conclusion rests on three premises, each of them essential to his theory. First, the Medicaid expansion is, in The Chief Justice's view, a new grant program, not an addition to the Medicaid program existing before the ACA's enactment. Congress, The Chief Justice maintains, has threatened States with the loss of funds from an old program in an effort to get them to adopt a new one. Second, the expansion was unforeseeable by the States when they first signed on to Medicaid. Third, the threatened loss of funding is so large that the States have no real choice but to participate in the Medicaid expansion. The Chief Justice therefore — for the first time ever — finds an exercise of Congress' spending power unconstitutionally coercive.

Medicaid, as amended by the ACA, however, is not two spending programs; it is a single program with a constant aim — to enable poor persons to receive basic health care when they need it. Given past expansions, plus express statutory warning that Congress may change the requirements participating States must meet, there can be no tenable claim that the ACA fails for lack of notice. Moreover, States have no entitlement to receive any Medicaid funds; they enjoy only the opportunity to accept funds on Congress' terms. Future Congresses are not bound by their predecessors' dispositions; they have authority to spend federal revenue as they see fit. The Federal Government, therefore, is not, as The Chief Justice charges, threatening States with the loss of "existing" funds from one spending program in order to induce them to opt into another program. Congress is simply requiring States to do what States have long been required to do to receive Medicaid funding: comply with the conditions Congress prescribes for participation.

Yes, there are federalism-based limits on the use of Congress' conditional spending power. In the leading decision in this area, South Dakota v. Dole, 483 U.S. 203 (1987), the Court identified four criteria. The conditions placed on federal grants to States must (a) promote the "general welfare," (b) "unambiguously" inform States what is demanded of them, (c) be germane "to the federal interest in particular national projects or programs," and (d) not "induce the States to engage in activities that would themselves be unconstitutional." Id., at 207-208, 210 (internal quotation marks omitted).

The Court in Dole mentioned, but did not adopt, a further limitation, one hypothetically raised a half-century earlier: In "some circumstances," Congress might be prohibited from offering a "financial inducement . . . so coercive as to pass the point at which 'pressure turns into compulsion.'" Id., at 211 (quoting Steward Machine Co. v. Davis, 301 U.S. 548, 590 (1937)). Prior to today's decision, however, the Court has never ruled that the terms of any grant crossed the indistinct line between temptation and coercion.

This case does not present the concerns that led the Court in *Dole* even to consider the prospect of coercion. In *Dole*, the condition — set 21 as the minimum drinking age — did not tell the States how to use funds Congress provided for highway construction. Further, in view of the Twenty-First Amendment, it was an open question whether Congress could directly impose a national minimum drinking age.

The ACA, in contrast, relates solely to the federally funded Medicaid program; if States choose not to comply, Congress has not threatened to withhold funds earmarked for any other program. Nor does the ACA use Medicaid funding to induce States to take action Congress itself could not undertake. The Federal Government undoubtedly could operate its own health-care program for poor persons, just as it operates Medicare for seniors' health care.

That is what makes this such a simple case, and the Court's decision so unsettling. Congress, aiming to assist the needy, has appropriated federal money to subsidize state health-insurance programs that meet federal standards. The principal standard the ACA sets is that the state program cover adults earning no more than 133% of the federal poverty line. Enforcing that prescription ensures that federal funds will be spent on health care for the poor in furtherance of Congress' present perception of the general welfare.

Endeavoring to show that Congress created a new program, The Chief Justice cites three aspects of the expansion. First, he asserts that, in covering those earning no more than 133% of the federal poverty line, the Medicaid expansion, unlike pre-ACA Medicaid, does not "care for the neediest among us." Ante, at 53. What makes that so? Single adults earning no more than \$14,856 per year — 133% of the current federal poverty level — surely rank among the Nation's poor.

Consider also that Congress could have repealed Medicaid. See supra, at 38-39 (citing 42 U.S.C. §1304); Brief for Petitioners in No. 11-400, p. 41. Thereafter, Congress could have enacted Medicaid II, a new program combining the pre-2010 coverage with the expanded coverage required by the ACA. By what right does a court stop Congress from building up without first tearing down?

The Chief Justice finds the Medicaid expansion vulnerable because it took participating States by surprise. Ante, at 54. "A State could hardly anticipate that Congres[s]" would endeavor to "transform [the Medicaid program] so dramatically," he states. Ante, at 54-55. For the notion that States must be able to foresee, when they sign up, alterations Congress might make later on, The Chief Justice cites only one case: Pennhurst State School and Hospital v. Halderman, 451 U.S. 1.

The Chief Justice appears to find in Pennhurst a requirement that, when spending legislation is first passed, or when States first enlist in the federal program, Congress must provide clear notice of conditions it might later impose. If I understand his point correctly, it was incumbent on Congress, in 1965, to warn the States clearly of the size and shape potential changes to Medicaid might take. And absent such notice, sizable changes could not be made mandatory. Our decisions do not support such a requirement.

In any event, from the start, the Medicaid Act put States on notice that the program could be changed: "The right to alter, amend, or repeal any provision of [Medicaid]," the statute has read since 1965, "is hereby reserved to the Congress." 42 U.S.C. §1304. The "effect of these few simple words" has long been settled. See National Railroad Passenger Corporation v. Atchison, T. & S. F. R. Co., 470 U.S. 451-468, n. 22 (1985) (citing Sinking Fund Cases, 99 U.S. 700, 720 (1879)). By reserving the right to "alter, amend, [or] repeal" a spending program, Congress "has given special notice of its intention to retain . . . full and complete power to make such alterations and amendments . . . as come within the just scope of legislative power." Id., at 720.

The Chief Justice nevertheless would rewrite §1304 to countenance only the "right to alter somewhat," or "amend, but not too much." Congress, however, did not so qualify §1304. Indeed, Congress retained discretion to "repeal" Medicaid, wiping it out entirely. Cf. Delta Air Lines, Inc. v. August, 450 U. S. 346, 368 (1981) (Rehnquist,

J., dissenting) (invoking "the commonsense maxim that the greater includes the lesser"). As Bowen indicates, no State could reasonably have read §1304 as reserving to Congress authority to make adjustments only if modestly sized.

At bottom, my colleagues' position is that the States' reliance on federal funds limits Congress' authority to alter its spending programs. This gets things backwards: Congress, not the States, is tasked with spending federal money in service of the general welfare. And each successive Congress is empowered to appropriate funds as it sees fit. When the 110th Congress reached a conclusion about Medicaid funds that differed from its predecessors' view, it abridged no State's right to "existing," or "pre-existing," funds. But see ante, at 51-52; post, at 47-48 (joint opinion of Scalia, Kennedy, Thomas, and Alito, JJ.). For, in fact, there are no such funds. There is only money States anticipate receiving from future Congresses.

I would uphold the Eleventh Circuit's decision that the Medicaid expansion is within Congress' spending power.

JUSTICE SCALIA, JUSTICE KENNEDY, JUSTICE THOMAS, *and* JUSTICE ALITO, *dissenting.*

The Government contends that "the minimum coverage provision is independently authorized by congress's taxing power." Petitioners' Minimum Coverage Brief 52. The phrase "independently authorized" suggests the existence of a creature never hitherto seen in the United States Reports: A penalty for constitutional purposes that is also a tax for constitutional purposes. In all our cases the two are mutually exclusive. The provision challenged under the Constitution is either a penalty or else a tax. Of course in many cases what was a regulatory mandate enforced by a penalty could have been imposed as a tax upon permissible action; or what was imposed as a tax upon permissible action could have been a regulatory mandate enforced by a penalty. But we know of no case, and the Government cites none, in which the imposition was, for constitutional purposes, both. The two are mutually exclusive. Thus, what the Government's caption should have read was "alternatively, the minimum coverage provision is not a mandate-with-penalty but a tax." It is important to bear this in mind in evaluating the tax argument of the Government and of those who support it: The issue is not whether Congress had the power to frame the minimum-coverage provision as a tax, but whether it did so.

In answering that question we must, if "fairly possible," Crowell v. Benson, 285 U.S. 22, 62 (1932), construe the provision to be a tax rather than a mandate-with-penalty, since that would render it constitutional rather than unconstitutional (ut res magis valeat quam pereat). But we cannot rewrite the statute to be what it is not. "'"[A]lthough this Court will often strain to construe legislation so as to save it against constitutional attack, it must not and will not carry this to the point of perverting the purpose of a statute . . ." or judicially rewriting it.'" Commodity Futures Trading Comm'n v. Schor, 478 U.S. 833, 841 (1986) (quoting Aptheker v. Secretary of State, 378 U.S. 500, 515 (1964), in turn quoting Scales v. United States, 367 U.S. 203, 211 (1961)). In this case, there is simply no way, "without doing violence to the fair meaning of the words used," Grenada County Supervisors v. Brogden, 112 U.S. 261, 269 (1884), to escape what Congress enacted: a mandate that individuals maintain minimum essential coverage, enforced by a penalty.

For all these reasons, to say that the Individual Mandate merely imposes a tax is not to interpret the statute but to rewrite it. Judicial tax-writing is particularly troubling. Taxes have never been popular, see, e.g., Stamp Act of 1765, and in part for that reason, the Constitution requires tax increases to originate in the House of Representatives. See Art. I, §7, cl. 1. That is to say, they must originate in the legislative body most accountable to the people, where legislators must weigh the need for the tax against the terrible price they might pay at their next election, which is never more than two years off. The Federalist No. 58 "defend[ed] the decision to give the origination power to the House on the ground that the Chamber that is more accountable to the people should have the primary role in raising revenue." United States v. Munoz-Flores, 495 U. S. 385, 395 (1990). We have no doubt that Congress knew precisely what it was doing when it rejected an earlier version of this legislation that imposed a tax instead of a requirement-with-penalty. See Affordable Health Care for America Act, H.R. 3962, 111th Cong., 1st Sess., §501 (2009); America's Healthy Future Act of 2009, S. 1796, 111th Cong., 1st Sess., §1301. Imposing a tax through judicial legislation inverts the constitutional scheme, and places the power to tax in the branch of government least accountable to the citizenry.

***

We now consider respondents' second challenge to the constitutionality of the ACA, namely, that the Act's dramatic expansion of the Medicaid program exceeds Congress' power to attach conditions to federal grants to the States.

The States challenging the constitutionality of the ACA's Medicaid Expansion contend that, for these practical reasons, the Act really does not give them any choice at all. As proof of this, they point to the goal and the structure of the ACA. The goal of the Act is to provide near-universal medical coverage, 42 U.S.C. §18091(2)(D), and without 100% State participation in the Medicaid program, attainment of this goal would be thwarted. Even if States could elect to remain in the old Medicaid program, while declining to participate in the Expansion, there would be a gaping hole in coverage. And if a substantial number of States were entirely expelled from the program, the number of persons without coverage would be even higher.

In light of the ACA's goal of near-universal coverage, petitioners argue, if Congress had thought that anything less than 100% state participation was a realistic possibility, Congress would have provided a backup scheme. But no such scheme is to be found anywhere in the more than 900 pages of the Act. This shows, they maintain, that Congress was certain that the ACA's Medicaid offer was one that no State could refuse.

In response to this argument, the Government contends that any congressional assumption about uniform state participation was based on the simple fact that the offer of federal funds associated with the expanded coverage is such a generous gift that no State would want to turn it down.

To evaluate these arguments, we consider the extent of the Federal Government's power to spend money and to attach conditions to money granted to the States.

When federal legislation gives the States a real choice whether to accept or decline a federal aid package, the federal-state relationship is in the nature of a contractual relationship. See Barnes v. Gorman, 536 U.S. 181, 186 (2002); *Pennhurst*, 451 U.S., at 17. And just as a contract is voidable if coerced, "[t]he legitimacy of Congress' power to legislate under the spending power . . . rests on whether the State voluntarily and knowingly accepts the terms of the 'contract.'" Ibid. (emphasis added). If a federal spending program coerces participation the States have not "exercise[d] their choice"—let alone made an "informed choice." Id., at 17, 25.

Coercing States to accept conditions risks the destruction of the "unique role of the States in our system." *Davis*, supra, at 685 (Kennedy, J., dissenting). "[T]he Constitution has never been understood to confer upon Congress the ability to require the States to govern according to Congress' instructions." *New York*, 505 U.S., at 162. Congress may not "simply commandeer the legislative processes of the States by directly compelling them to enact and enforce a federal regulatory program." Id., at 161 (internal quotation marks and brackets omitted). Congress effectively engages in this impermissible compulsion when state participation in a federal spending program is coerced, so that the States' choice whether to enact or administer a federal regulatory program is rendered illusory.

Amici who support the Government argue that forcing state employees to implement a federal program is more respectful of federalism than using federal workers to implement that program. See, e.g., Brief for Service Employees International Union et al. as Amici Curiae in No. 11-398, pp. 25-26. They note that Congress, instead of expanding Medicaid, could have established an entirely federal program to provide coverage for the same group of people. By choosing to structure Medicaid as a cooperative federal-state program, they contend, Congress allows for more state control. Ibid.

This argument reflects a view of federalism that our cases have rejected—and with good reason. When Congress compels the States to do its bidding, it blurs the lines of political accountability. If the Federal Government makes a controversial decision while acting on its own, "it is the Federal Government that makes the decision in full view of the public, and it will be federal officials that suffer the consequences if the decision turns out to be detrimental or unpopular." *New York*, 505 U.S., at 168. But when the Federal Government compels the States to take unpopular actions, "it may be state officials who will bear the brunt of public disapproval, while the federal officials who devised the regulatory program may remain insulated from the electoral ramifications of their decision." Id., at 169; see *Printz*, supra, at 930. For this reason, federal officeholders may view this "departur[e] from the federal structure to be in their personal interests . . . as a means of shifting responsibility for the eventual decision." *New York*, 505 U.S., at 182-183. And even state officials may favor such a "departure from the constitutional plan," since uncertainty concerning responsibility may also permit them to escape accountability. Id., at 182. If a program is popular, state officials may claim credit; if it is unpopular, they may protest that they were merely responding to a federal directive.

Once it is recognized that spending-power legislation cannot coerce state participation, two questions remain: (1) What is the meaning of coercion in this context? (2) Is the ACA's expanded Medicaid coverage coercive? We now turn to those questions.

1. The answer to the first of these questions—the meaning of coercion in the present context—is straightforward. As we have explained, the legitimacy of attaching conditions to federal grants to the States depends on the voluntariness of the States' choice to accept or decline the offered package. Therefore, if States really have no choice other than to accept the package, the offer is coercive, and the conditions cannot be sustained under the spending power. And as our decision in *South Dakota v. Dole* makes clear, theoretical voluntariness is not enough.

2. The Federal Government's argument in this case at best pays lip service to the anticoercion principle. The Federal Government suggests that it is sufficient if States are "free, as a matter of law, to turn down" federal funds. Brief for Respondents in No. 11-400, p. 17 (emphasis added); see also id., at 25. According to the Federal Government, neither the amount of the offered federal funds nor the amount of the federal taxes extracted from the taxpayers of a State to pay for the program in question is relevant in determining whether there is impermissible coercion. Id., at 41-46.

This argument ignores reality. When a heavy federal tax is levied to support a federal program that offers large grants to the States, States may, as a practical matter, be unable to refuse to participate in the federal program and to substitute a state alternative. Even if a State believes that the federal program is ineffective and inefficient, withdrawal would likely force the State to impose a huge tax increase on its residents, and this new state tax would come on top of the federal taxes already paid by residents to support subsidies to participating States.

Acceptance of the Federal Government's interpretation of the anticoercion rule would permit Congress to dictate policy in areas traditionally governed primarily at the state or local level. Suppose, for example, that Congress enacted legislation offering each State a grant equal to the State's entire annual expenditures for primary and secondary education. Suppose also that this funding came with conditions governing such things as school curriculum, the hiring and tenure of teachers, the drawing of school districts, the length and hours of the school day, the school calendar, a dress code for students, and rules for student discipline. As a matter of law, a State could turn down that offer, but if it did so, its residents would not only be required to pay the federal taxes needed to support this expensive new program, but they would also be forced to pay an equivalent amount in state taxes. And if the State gave in to the federal law, the State and its subdivisions would surrender their traditional authority in the field of education. Asked at oral argument whether such a law would be allowed under the spending power, the Solicitor General responded that it would. Tr. of Oral Arg. 44-45 (Mar. 28, 2012).

* * *

The Court today decides to save a statute Congress did not write. It rules that what the statute declares to be a requirement with a penalty is instead an option subject to a tax. And it changes the intentionally coercive sanction of a total cut-off of Medicaid funds to a supposedly noncoercive cut-off of only the incremental funds that the Act makes available.

For the reasons here stated, we would find the Act invalid in its entirety. We respectfully dissent.

SYNTHESIS QUESTIONS FOR FURTHER DISCUSSION: CHAPTER 6

1. Is the opinion in *NFIB* a vindication of the jurisprudence of the New Federalism examined in the previous chapter or a repudiation of it? To what extent does the case suggest a weakening of federal power under the Commerce Clause? Are the circumstances unique enough to suggest no

consequence or do they push back against core precedents such as *Heart of Atlanta* and *Wickard*? Similarly, is the ruling on the taxation power and expansion of congressional power consistent with past precedents?

2. Some suggest that the power of Congress to act should not depend on isolated interpretations of clauses. Rather, the clauses should be interpreted to expand or contract together such that it is not possible to claim expansive power under one clause, such as Taxation, and restrictive power under another, such as Commerce. Do you agree?

KEY TERMS

enumerated powers: Those powers specifically granted to Congress by the Constitution, in contrast to the states' more general police powers to regulate the "welfare, health, safety, and morals" of its population.

implied powers: Powers not explicitly stated in the Constitution, but thought granted by general phrases such as the Necessary and Proper Clause and the General Welfare Clause, often thought central to the decision in *McCulloch v. Maryland*.

New Federalism: The philosophy usually associated with the Reagan revolution, which sought to retrench the role of the federal government in the economic sphere; this also might refer to the Court's jurisprudence in pulling back congressional power under the Commerce Clause.

PART III

PRESIDENTIAL AUTHORITY AND ITS LIMITS

In this part, we examine the power of the executive branch of government. Some of the Framers of the Constitution feared that the power endowed in this branch had significant potential for exploitation, and they sought to ensure that the presidency was not vulnerable to the same abuses they thought defined monarchy. The danger of the presidency arguably inheres in the very idea of the execution of law. While lawmaking and adjudication are obviously important functions, it is in the act of carrying out the law that coercive power is most present. *The Federalist No. 78* suggests, for instance, that the president "holds the sword of the community." In absolute monarchies and dictatorships, the power to execute the law is combined with the power to make law and to judge when it has been violated. But drawing on Montesquieu, an eighteenth-century French political theorist widely read by the drafters of the American Constitution, the Founders worried that such a consolidation of the powers of government would invariably lead to infringements upon individual liberty.

Montesquieu proposed the idea of the separation of powers as a way to avoid the dangers present in regimes, such as absolute monarchies, where powers to execute the laws were consolidated with the power to actually write the laws and interpret them. According to Montesquieu, liberty could best be protected by creating different institutions to carry out the three primary functions of government. Montesquieu suggests in one of our readings that "when the legislative and executive powers are united in the same person, or in the same body of magistrates, there can be no liberty." This same concern for liberty motivates the theories of federalism laid out in Chapter 2. In that chapter, you saw that the

Founders created a structure of vertical separation of powers, dividing power between the national and the state governments; in this chapter, you will see how they also established a horizontal scheme at the federal level that sets the executive, legislative, and judicial powers against each other, creating a system of checks and balances. Dividing power among rival branches, they believed, would best preserve liberty and prevent tyranny.

The philosophy of the separation of powers is embodied not only in the writings of Montesquieu and the Founders, but also in the Constitution itself. Articles I, II, and III of the Constitution specify distinct functions for lawmaking, the execution of laws, and adjudication. Within each of these articles, specific powers are enumerated to delineate varying functions. It is tempting to see these specific enumerations as separating out the powers of the branches of government into distinct institutional entities. But as you will see in the cases and readings in this part, the manner in which such separation should occur is not obvious or uncontested. The greatest challenges for constitutional governance have occurred at the intersection of the functions outlined by Montesquieu. In particular, we examine various conflicts between the branches. Indeed, while the topic of this part is often referred to as "separation of powers," it might be more accurate to think of it as "conflicts of powers."

The source of conflicts between the branches is found partly in the fact that the powers of the executive, as outlined in Article II, are somewhat general and vague. It is important to note the contrast here with Article I. Whereas Article I grants to Congress only the powers that are "herein granted," such as the power to regulate commerce, Article II states simply that "the executive power shall be vested in the President." Note, though, that the Constitution never defines the meaning of the word "executive." Although Article II does enumerate specific powers for the president, such as the power to appoint cabinet officers, to veto legislation passed by Congress, and to serve as Commander-in-Chief of the military, there may also be functions inherent in "the executive power" besides these explicit grants of power. Additionally, Article II states that the president "shall take care that the laws be faithfully executed," an obligation that some scholars have argued implies a significant amount of latitude and discretion for executive authority.

Perhaps because the language vesting the executive power in the president is vague, questions remain as to what precisely executive power means. Most importantly, we are left with the question of whether the president has exclusive power in all matters of executive concern, or whether his power must be shared with the legislature. For example, does the power of the president to appoint executive officers also imply that he has the exclusive power to remove such officers, or is he required to obtain the advice and consent of the Senate? What power does the president have to act without congressional authorization? Moreover, can power be delegated between the executive and legislative branches? For instance, if executive power lies with the president, can Congress establish laws that allow this power to be shared either with independent agencies or with Congress itself?

As you will see in the cases throughout this part that deal with the above questions, although the powers of Congress and the executive branch at times appear to be clearly demarcated, in many other instances they come into conflict. This is particularly the case where powers are shared. Most obviously, while the president is the Commander-in-Chief, the Congress retains the power to declare war, the power to raise and support an army and a navy, and the power to pass the regulations that will govern those armed forces. We must ask in such instances where the Constitution draws the boundaries between these two branches.

The conflicts we examine here between the president and Congress open up larger issues about our constitutional democracy, which we first introduced in Chapter 1. In that chapter, we questioned why the Supreme Court, an unelected body, should have the power to strike down laws passed by democratic representatives. But what does democracy demand in instances of conflict between two representative branches? Although many have raised concerns about the Electoral College in the wake of *Bush v. Gore*, which we read in Chapter 2, the fact remains that the president and vice president are the only government officials elected by all of the nation's citizens. Some, such as Steven Calabresi, believe that this gives the presidency a particularly high level of democratic legitimacy, because he or she is accountable to the people as a whole. Others worry, however, that an executive unchecked by Congress could become too powerful and thwart the will of the people. Indeed, a democratic election is no guarantee that principles such as the rule of law and respect for the interests of all citizens will be respected. We need only be reminded that dictators have often come to power through elections to see this point.

As you will see in *Youngstown Sheet & Tube Co. v. Sawyer*, which involved President Harry Truman's decision to seize private steel mills in a time of war, executive power is constitutionally limited by congressional authority. The executive power cannot encroach on areas in which Congress retains authority. Indeed, an effective way to ensure that the president has limited power is to grant another elected branch authority over some matters. The debate over war powers that we examine in Chapter 8, for instance, also highlights how the potential danger of presidential control over the military is mitigated by Congress's authority.

In the final chapter, we examine the relationship between the presidency and the rule of law. In addition to being tempered by Congress, presidential power is also limited by the Constitution itself. What role do the courts have in limiting executive power through enforcing the law? Famously, Richard Nixon declared in his post-Watergate interview with David Frost that "when the president does it, that means that it is not illegal." But, as you will see, our constitutional tradition has come to a different conclusion.

The most obvious difficulty with executive power is the worry that the president will become too powerful, and either ignore the will of Congress or the rule of law altogether. But, as you will see, another modern issue in this part concerns the democratic accountability of administrative agencies. Part of President Franklin Roosevelt's New Deal included a vast expansion of what has become known as the "administrative state." Independent agencies such as the Federal Communications Commission, the Federal Election Commission, and the

Federal Aviation Authority are appointed by the president but are not regarded as a part of the executive branch in the same way that cabinet departments are. The rationale is that some regulation should be carried out by parties that are insulated from political considerations. However, some have questioned the constitutionality of granting enormous power to these agencies of our government. The Constitution creates three branches of government, but it is unclear under which branch these agencies fall. In particular, *Humphrey's Executor v. United States* reveals that when it comes to the removal of the heads of these agencies, it is not straightforward which branch of government controls them. Indeed, according to some thinkers, the existence of these agencies may very well violate the Constitution. Others have articulated a more limited critique, demanding that the lines of accountability be clear. Do these administrative agencies have too much independence from both the executive and congressional branches? Are there examples in which the president's power over executive agencies needs to be stronger in order to ensure democratic accountability?

In considering issues related to both the rule of the law, as well as those concerning the independence of administrative agencies, both the theoretical and legal debates center on the meaning of the "unitary executive." At the Founding, there was a lively debate about whether we should have more than one person serve as the chief executive. The Framers agreed, however, that there should be one president—in other words, a unitary executive. In contemporary politics, some have proposed that we rethink this decision. For instance, instead of having the president as the only nationally elected official who has power over the attorney general, some have proposed independent elections for some cabinet members. But in the realm of constitutional interpretation, the existence of only one executive is settled. The debate, rather, is about the meaning of this structure of government, in particular in its relation to the other branches regarding the separation of powers and foreign policy. Advocates of the unitary executive generally argue that the power of the president should not be shared with any other branch. Such thinkers conceptualize separation of powers as a commitment to complete and total separation between the various branches of government. In their article, law professors Lawrence Lessig and Cass Sunstein suggest that, although the Founders did not envision a unitary executive, it has become increasingly desirable over the course of history. However, some legal scholars oppose the idea of a unitary executive. They claim that, in fact, there should be some sharing or overlap in power between Congress and the president when it comes to the execution of the laws. As you read the cases included here, you should consider not only whether the Constitution endorses a unitary executive, but also whether such a scheme of power is in fact desirable in the context of the modern administrative state.

In discerning what exactly separation of powers entails, the readings of this part look to history and the text of the Constitution. But another way to think about this problem is to theorize about the executive function itself. According to many, the very idea of the executive includes a range of "inherent" powers that are necessary for the execution of the laws. Arguably, one such inherent power is control over foreign affairs. It might be thought that a nation needs to engage in foreign relations with one clear voice. But the notion that foreign relations are the exclusive power of the president is in conflict with Article I, Section 8, which grants Congress the power to declare war, regulate foreign trade, coin money, raise taxes, and raise and support an army and navy, as well as Article II, Section 2's requirement that treaties be made with the "advice and consent" of the Senate. In Chapter 8, we consider the ways in which the debate over the unitary executive influences arguments about the president's powers when it comes to foreign affairs. Authors such as John Yoo argue that the president's power over foreign affairs is almost entirely exclusive and that the power to declare war is a narrow one. In contrast, John Hart Ely suggests that while the executive is responsible for carrying out the execution of war, the clear constitutional responsibility for its declaration, or commencement, mandates a large role for congressional deliberation in the formation of a national consensus.

Chapters 7 and 8 examine the scope of presidential power in executing legislation in matters of domestic and foreign policy. Chapter 9 asks whether and how the rule of law limits the president when executive authority oversteps its bounds. The readings and cases of that chapter broaden our area of concern and force us to question the degree to which the president is subjected to the law. A number of cases probe the question of whether the president enjoys immunity from suit or evidentiary privileges. Together, these topics point to a larger controversy over presidential prerogative. Is the president ever above the law?

CHAPTER 7

THE EXECUTIVE AND THE SEPARATION OF POWERS

What sources determine the power of the president, and how does the executive branch fit within the idea of the separation of powers? Are executive powers inherent, enumerated, or subject to congressional authorization?

This chapter begins with a selection from Montesquieu, whose writings directly influenced the thinking of the Founders. Although Montesquieu's writings about separation of powers are philosophical, they clearly provided a guide for those who were tasked with creating actual institutions of governance at the Constitutional Convention in 1787. His view is cited explicitly in *The Federalist Papers*. Despite the Founders' concern to show how the executive would be checked by both Congress and the judiciary, the Anti-Federalists worried that the executive power as it appeared in the Constitution would be tantamount to monarchy. We include from the Anti-Federalists a writing by "An Old Whig" that criticizes the presidency as the implementation of tyranny.

The modern debate about executive power revolves in large part around disputes over the interpretation of both Montesquieu and the Federalists. Defenders of a strong executive, what they label the unitary executive, argue that power should be held exclusively by the president and not shared with other branches or agencies. The unitary executive theory, defended by Lawrence Lessig and Cass Sunstein, resists such developments in American history as the independent prosecutor law and the development of shared responsibility for administrative agencies, such as the Federal Trade Commission, by the president and Congress.

Despite their many agreements, it also important to note the differences in the arguments about the unitary executive presented by Lessig and Sunstein, on the one hand, and Steven Calabresi and James Lindgren, on the other. For instance, Lessig and Sunstein pay close attention to the text of the Constitution and attempt to give an interpretation of executive power that is consistent with what they view as the original meaning of the document. With that said, their approach highlights the importance of adapting the original meaning of the Constitution to modern conditions and constraints that the Founders might not have foreseen. Calabresi's contribution here is noteworthy for its straightforward empirical arguments grounding his defense of an independent executive in arguments about democratic accountability. Calabresi addresses the worry that the presidency might be too strong, and in doing so makes way for arguments for a strong unitary executive. As you read through the case selection, keep in mind how each case raises questions about the original meaning of the Constitution, the text itself, and the more general question of the democratic accountability of the president, Congress, and the administrative agencies. To what extent do originalist arguments support limiting or expanding the power of the presidency? To what extent do concerns about democratic accountability shape the debate over the strength of the president's power?

Included in our case selection is *Youngstown Sheet & Tube Co. v. Sawyer*, the most influential modern legal formulation of how to understand conflicts between the branches. It is also notable because the opinion that has had the greatest influence was a concurrence, by U.S. Supreme Court Justice Robert H. Jackson, rather than the majority opinion. Justice Jackson's concurrence sets up a three-part structure for thinking about executive power. At one extreme are those cases where the president acts with the explicit approval of Congress. Here he acts with the maximum latitude. At the other extreme are those instances where the president acts despite congressional disapproval. Here he can do only those things explicitly assigned to the executive branch. In between is what Justice Jackson calls "the zone of twilight"—cases where Congress is silent and where the president lacks clear, explicit constitutional authority.

We also examine the question of the president's power to remove administrative appointees from office. The Constitution, you will recall, states that most administrative appointments must be made with the advice and consent of Congress, but says nothing about how these officials can be removed. This question was initially resolved in *Myers v. United States*, where the Court affirmed President Herbert Hoover's power to remove the postmaster general. But in *Humphrey's Executor v. United States*, the Court took a different view, ruling that the president's authority to remove officials could be constrained in those instances where Congress had established an explicit term of office for appointees in independent agencies. Those concerned with democratic accountability, including proponents of the unitary executive theory, worry that this undermines the ability of the public to hold these agencies accountable. This concern reached something of a zenith in a case challenging the constitutionality of the appointment of an independent prosecutor in *Morrison v. Olson*. This was a particularly fraught case, since leaving control over prosecutions of cases involving political corruption seemed to require independence from those who might actually be accused of these crimes—and the law being challenged here had been passed specifically in response to concerns about the abuse of prosecutorial discretion in the Watergate scandal.

Two cases in this chapter, *INS v. Chadha* and *Clinton v. New York*, address instances in which Congress attempted to alter the fundamental relationship between the legislative and executive branches by either increasing or weakening its own power in relation to the executive. In *INS v. Chadha*, the Court rejected an attempt by Congress to gain greater control over individual immigration cases through the so-called legislative veto. In *Clinton v. New York*, in contrast, the Court rejected an attempt by Congress to give away some of its constitutional power to write laws by granting the executive a line item veto, or the power to veto parts of congressional spending bills rather than to veto or accept in its entirety a bill passed by Congress.

As you examine both the readings and the cases in this chapter, you should formulate your own ideas about the proper balance of power between Congress and the executive. Do you think that independent agencies of the type discussed in *Myers v. United States* and *Humphrey's Executor v. United States* should be under the complete control of the executive, or should there be shared power between Congress and the executive in the appointment and approval of the officers of these agencies? Moreover, you should pay particular attention to the framework outlined by Justice Jackson in the *Youngstown Sheet & Tube Co. v. Sawyer* case. Does this three-part framework accommodate the concerns about democracy that we struggled with in Chapter 1, as well as those raised in this chapter?

In many ways, the cases and readings in this chapter serve as a framework for the rest of this part. In particular, you should keep in mind how arguments about the unitary executive relate to more specific debates about the foreign policy powers of the presidency, and whether the president should be immune to lawsuits.

Montesquieu

THE SPIRIT OF THE LAWS

Book XI, Section 6

New York, NY: Hafner Publishing Company (1949)

Political liberty is to be found only in moderate governments; and even in these it is not always found. It is there only when there is no abuse of power. But constant experience shows us that every man invested with power is apt to abuse it, and to carry his authority as far as it will go. Is it not strange, though true, to say that virtue itself has need of limits? To prevent this abuse, it is necessary from the very nature of things that power should be a check to power.

In every government there are three sorts of power: the legislative; the executive in respect to things dependent on the law of nations; and the executive in regard to matters that depend on the civil law.

By virtue of the first, the prince or magistrate enacts temporary or perpetual laws, and amends or abrogates those that have been already enacted. By the second, he makes peace or war, sends or receives embassies, establishes the public security, and provides against invasions. By the third, he punishes criminals, or determines the disputes that arise between individuals. The latter we shall call the judiciary power, and the other simply the executive power of the state.

The political liberty of the subject is a tranquillity of mind arising from the opinion each person has of his safety. In order to have this liberty, it is requisite the

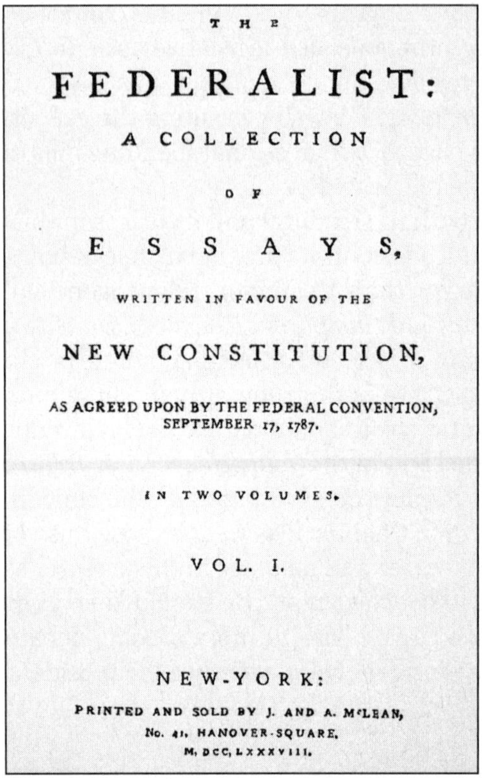
THE

FEDERALIST:

A COLLECTION

OF

ESSAYS,

WRITTEN IN FAVOUR OF THE

NEW CONSTITUTION,

AS AGREED UPON BY THE FEDERAL CONVENTION,
SEPTEMBER 17, 1787.

IN TWO VOLUMES.

VOL. I.

NEW-YORK:

PRINTED AND SOLD BY J. AND A. M'LEAN,
No. 41, HANOVER-SQUARE,
M, DCC, LXXXVIII.

Title page of the first volume of The Federalist.

government be so constituted as one man need not be afraid of another.

When the legislative and executive powers are united in the same person, or in the same body of magistrates, there can be no liberty; because apprehensions may arise, lest the same monarch or senate should enact tyrannical laws, to execute them in a tyrannical manner.

Again, there is no liberty, if the judiciary power be not separated from the legislative and executive. Were it joined with the legislative, the life and liberty of the subject would be exposed to arbitrary control; for the judge would be then the legislator. Were it joined to the executive power, the judge might behave with violence and oppression.

There would be an end of everything, were the same man or the same body, whether of the nobles or of the people, to exercise those three powers, that of enacting laws, that of executing the public resolutions, and of trying the causes of individuals.

The judiciary power ought not to be given to a standing senate; it should be exercised by persons taken from the body of the people at certain times of the year, and consistently with a form and manner prescribed by law, in order to erect a tribunal that should last only so long as necessity requires.

By this method the judicial power, so terrible to mankind, not being annexed to any particular state or profession, becomes, as it were, invisible. People have not then the judges continually present to their view; they fear the office, but not the magistrate.

The other two powers may be given rather to magistrates or permanent bodies, because they are not exercised on any private subject; one being no more than the general will of the state, and the other the execution of that general will.

As in a country of liberty, every man who is supposed a free agent ought to be his own governor; the legislative power should reside in the whole body of the people. But since this is impossible in large states, and in small ones is subject to many inconveniences, it is fit the people should transact by their representatives what they cannot transact by themselves.

The executive power ought to be in the hands of a monarch, because this branch of government, having need of despatch, is better administered by one than by many: on the other hand, whatever depends on the legislative power is oftentimes better regulated by many than by a single person.

But if there were no monarch, and the executive power should be committed to a certain number of persons selected from the legislative body, there would be an end then of liberty; by reason the two powers would be united, as the same persons would sometimes possess, and would be always able to possess, a share in both.

James Madison

THE FEDERALIST NO. 51

The Structure of the Government Must Furnish the Proper Checks and Balances Between the Different Departments

Independent Journal, Wednesday, February 6, 1788

To the People of the State of New York:

To what expedient, then, shall we finally resort, for maintaining in practice the necessary partition of power among the several departments, as laid down in the Constitution? The only answer that can be given is, that as all these exterior provisions are found to be inadequate, the defect must be supplied, by so contriving the interior structure of the government as that its several constituent parts may, by their mutual relations, be the means of keeping each other in their proper places. Without presuming to undertake a full development of this important idea, I will hazard a few general observations, which may perhaps place it in a clearer light, and enable us to form a more correct judgment of the principles and structure of the government planned by the convention.

In order to lay a due foundation for that separate and distinct exercise of the different powers of government, which to a certain extent is admitted on all hands to be essential to the preservation of liberty, it is evident that each department should have a will of its own; and consequently should be so constituted that the members of each should have as little agency as possible in the appointment of the members of the others. Were this principle rigorously adhered to, it would require that all the appointments for the supreme executive, legislative, and judiciary magistracies should be drawn from the same fountain of authority, the people, through channels having no communication whatever with one another. Perhaps such a plan of constructing the several departments would be less difficult in practice than it may in contemplation appear. Some difficulties, however, and some additional expense would attend the execution of it. Some deviations, therefore, from the principle must be admitted. In the constitution of the judiciary department in particular, it might be inexpedient to insist rigorously on the principle: first, because peculiar qualifications being essential in the members, the primary consideration ought to be to select that mode of choice which best secures these qualifications; secondly, because the permanent tenure by which the appointments are held in that department, must soon destroy all sense of dependence on the authority conferring them.

It is equally evident, that the members of each department should be as little dependent as possible on those of the others, for the emoluments annexed to their offices. Were the executive magistrate, or the judges, not independent of the legislature in this particular, their independence in every other would be merely nominal.

But the great security against a gradual concentration of the several powers in the same department, consists in giving to those who administer each department the necessary constitutional means and personal motives to resist encroachments of the others. The provision for defense must in this, as in all other cases, be made commensurate to the danger of attack. Ambition must be made to counteract ambition. The interest of the man must be connected with the constitutional rights of the place. It may be a reflection on human nature, that such devices should be necessary to control the abuses of government. But what is government itself, but the greatest of all reflections on human nature? If men were angels, no government would be necessary. If angels were to govern men, neither external nor internal controls on government would be necessary. In framing a government which is to be administered by men over men, the great difficulty lies in this: you must first enable the government to control the governed; and in the next place oblige it to control itself. A dependence on the people is, no doubt, the primary control on the government; but experience has taught mankind the necessity of auxiliary precautions.

This policy of supplying, by opposite and rival interests, the defect of better motives, might be traced through the whole system of human affairs, private as well as public. We see it particularly displayed in all the subordinate distributions of power, where the constant aim is to divide and arrange the several offices in such a manner as that each may be a check on the other—that the private interest of every individual may be a sentinel over the public rights. These inventions of prudence cannot be less requisite in the distribution of the supreme powers of the State.

AN OLD WHIG V

Philadelphia Independent Gazetteer, November 1, 1787

. . . [T]he office of President of the United States appears to me to be clothed with such powers as are dangerous. To be the fountain of all honors in the United States, commander in chief of the army, navy and militia, with the power of making treaties and of granting pardons, and to be vested with an authority to put a negative upon all laws, unless two thirds of both houses shall persist in enacting it, and put their names down upon calling the yeas and nays for that purpose, is in reality to be a KING as much *a King as the King of Great Britain*, and a King too of the worst kind; — an elective King. — If such powers as these are to be trusted in the hands of any man, they ought for the sake of preserving the peace of the community at once to be made hereditary. — Much as I abhor kingly government, yet I venture to pronounce where kings are admitted to rule they should most certainly be vested with hereditary power. The election of a King whether it be in America or Poland, will be a scene of horror and confusion; and I am perfectly serious when I declare that, as a friend to my country, I shall despair of any happiness in the United States until this office is either reduced to a lower pitch of power or made perpetual and hereditary. — When I say that our future President will be as much a king as the king of Great-Britain, I only ask of my readers to look into the constitution of that country, and then tell me what important prerogative the King of Great-Britain is entitled to, which does not also belong to the President during his continuance in office. — The King of Great-Britain it is true can create nobility which our President cannot; but our President will have the power of making all the *great men*, which comes to the same thing. — All the difference is that we shall be embroiled in contention about the choice of the man, whilst they are at peace under the security of an hereditary succession. — To be tumbled headlong from the pinnacle of greatness and be reduced to a shadow of departed royalty is a shock almost too great for human nature to endure. It will cost a man many struggles to resign such eminent powers, and ere long, we shall find, some one who will be very unwilling to part with them. — Let us suppose this man to be a favorite with his army, and that they are unwilling to part with their beloved commander in chief; or to make the thing familiar, let us suppose, a future President and commander in chief adored by his army and the militia to as great a degree as our late illustrious commander in chief; and we have only to suppose one thing more, that this man is without the virtue, the moderation and love of liberty which possessed the mind of our late general, and this country will be involved at once in war and tyranny. So far is it from its being improbable that the man who shall hereafter be in a situation to make the attempt to perpetuate his own power, should want the virtues of General Washington; that it is perhaps a chance of one hundred millions to one that the next age will not furnish an example of so disinterested a use of great power. We may also suppose, without trespassing upon the bounds of probability, that this man may not have the means of supporting in private life the dignity of his former station; that like Caesar, he may be at once ambitious and poor, and deeply involved in debt. — Such a man would die a thousand deaths rather than sink from the heights of splendor and power into obscurity and wretchedness. We are certainly about giving our president too much or too little; and in the course of less than twenty years we shall find that we have given him enough to enable him to take all. It would be infinitely more prudent to give him at once as much as would content him, so that we might be able to retain the rest in peace; for if once power is seized by violence not the least fragment of liberty will survive the shock. I would therefore advise my country-men seriously to ask themselves this question; — Whether they are prepared TO RECEIVE A KING? If they are to say at once, and make the kingly office hereditary; to frame a constitution that should set bounds to his power, and, as far as possible secure the liberty of the subject. If we are not prepared to *receive a king*, let us call another convention to revise the proposed constitution, and form it anew on the principles of a confederacy of free republics; but by no means, under pretence of a republic, to lay the foundation for a military government, which is the worst of all tyrannies.

Alexander Hamilton

THE FEDERALIST NO. 70

The Executive Department Further Considered

Independent Journal, Saturday, March 15, 1788

To the People of the State of New York:

Energy in the Executive is a leading character in the definition of good government. It is essential to the protection of the community against foreign attacks; it is not less essential to the steady administration of the laws; to the protection of property against those irregular and high-handed combinations which sometimes interrupt the ordinary course of justice; to the security of liberty against the enterprises and assaults of ambition, of faction, and of anarchy. Every man the least conversant in Roman history, knows how often that republic was obliged to take refuge in the absolute power of a single man, under the formidable title of Dictator, as well against the intrigues of ambitious individuals who aspired to the tyranny, and the seditions of whole classes of the community whose conduct threatened the existence of all government, as against the invasions of external enemies who menaced the conquest and destruction of Rome.

There can be no need, however, to multiply arguments or examples on this head. A feeble Executive implies a feeble execution of the government. A feeble execution is but another phrase for a bad execution; and a government ill executed, whatever it may be in theory, must be, in practice, a bad government.

Taking it for granted, therefore, that all men of sense will agree in the necessity of an energetic Executive, it will only remain to inquire, what are the ingredients which constitute this energy? How far can they be combined with those other ingredients which constitute safety in the republican sense? And how far does this combination characterize the plan which has been reported by the convention?

The ingredients which constitute energy in the Executive are, first, unity; secondly, duration; thirdly, an adequate provision for its support; fourthly, competent powers.

The ingredients which constitute safety in the republican sense are, first, a due dependence on the people, secondly, a due responsibility.

Those politicians and statesmen who have been the most celebrated for the soundness of their principles and for the justice of their views, have declared in favor of a single Executive and a numerous legislature. They have with great propriety, considered energy as the most necessary qualification of the former, and have regarded this as most applicable to power in a single hand, while they have, with equal propriety, considered the latter as best adapted to deliberation and wisdom, and best calculated to conciliate the confidence of the people and to secure their privileges and interests.

That unity is conducive to energy will not be disputed. Decision, activity, secrecy, and despatch will generally characterize the proceedings of one man in a much more eminent degree than the proceedings of any greater number; and in proportion as the number is increased, these qualities will be diminished.

This unity may be destroyed in two ways: either by vesting the power in two or more magistrates of equal dignity and authority; or by vesting it ostensibly in one man, subject, in whole or in part, to the control and co-operation of others, in the capacity of counsellors to him. Of the first, the two Consuls of Rome may serve as an example; of the last, we shall find examples in the constitutions of several of the States. New York and New Jersey, if I recollect right, are the only States which have intrusted the executive authority wholly to single men. Both these methods of destroying the unity of the Executive have their partisans; but the votaries of an executive council are the most numerous. They are both liable, if not to equal, to similar objections, and may in most lights be examined in conjunction.

The experience of other nations will afford little instruction on this head. As far, however, as it teaches any thing, it teaches us not to be enamoured of plurality in the Executive. We have seen that the Achaeans, on an experiment of two Praetors, were induced to abolish one. The Roman history records many instances of mischiefs to the republic from the dissensions between the Consuls, and between the military Tribunes, who were at times substituted for the Consuls. But it gives us no specimens of any peculiar advantages derived to the state from the circumstance of the plurality of those magistrates. That the dissensions between them were not more frequent or more fatal, is a matter of astonishment, until we advert to the singular position in which the republic was almost continually placed, and to the prudent policy pointed out by the circumstances of the state, and pursued by the Consuls, of making a division of the government between them. The patricians engaged in a perpetual struggle with the plebeians for the preservation of their ancient authorities and dignities; the Consuls, who were generally chosen out of the former body, were commonly united by the personal interest they had in the defense of the privileges of their order. In addition to this motive of union, after the arms of the republic had considerably expanded the bounds of its empire, it became an established custom with the Consuls to divide the administration between themselves by lot — one of them remaining at Rome to govern the city and its environs, the other taking the command in the more distant provinces. This expedient must, no doubt, have had great influence in preventing those collisions and rivalships which might otherwise have embroiled the peace of the republic.

But quitting the dim light of historical research, attaching ourselves purely to the dictates of reason and good sense, we shall discover much greater cause to reject than to approve the idea of plurality in the Executive, under any modification whatever.

Wherever two or more persons are engaged in any common enterprise or pursuit, there is always danger of difference of opinion. If it be a public trust or office, in which they are clothed with equal dignity and authority, there is peculiar danger of personal emulation and even animosity. From either, and especially from all these causes, the most bitter dissensions are apt to spring. Whenever these happen, they lessen the respectability, weaken the authority, and distract the plans and operation of those whom they divide. If they should unfortunately assail the supreme executive magistracy of a country, consisting of a plurality of persons, they might impede or frustrate the most important measures of the government, in the most critical emergencies of the state. And what is still worse, they might split the community into the most violent and irreconcilable factions, adhering differently to the different individuals who composed the magistracy.

Men often oppose a thing, merely because they have had no agency in planning it, or because it may have been planned by those whom they dislike. But if they have been consulted, and have happened to disapprove, opposition then becomes, in their estimation, an indispensable duty of self-love. They seem to think themselves bound in honor, and by all the motives of personal infallibility, to defeat the success of what has been resolved upon contrary to their sentiments. Men of upright, benevolent tempers have too many opportunities of remarking, with horror, to what desperate lengths this disposition is sometimes carried, and how often the great interests of society are sacrificed to the vanity, to the conceit, and to the obstinacy of individuals, who have credit enough to make their passions and their caprices interesting to mankind. Perhaps the question now before the public may, in its consequences, afford melancholy proofs of the effects of this despicable frailty, or rather detestable vice, in the human character.

Upon the principles of a free government, inconveniences from the source just mentioned must necessarily be submitted to in the formation of the legislature; but it is unnecessary, and therefore unwise, to introduce them into the constitution of the Executive. It is here too that they may be most pernicious. In the legislature, promptitude of decision is oftener an evil than a benefit. The differences of opinion, and the jarrings of parties in that department of the government, though they may sometimes obstruct salutary plans, yet often promote deliberation and circumspection, and serve to check excesses in the majority. When a resolution too is once taken, the opposition must be at an end. That resolution is a law, and resistance to it punishable. But no favorable circumstances palliate or atone for the disadvantages of dissension in the executive department. Here, they are pure and unmixed. There is no point at which they cease to operate. They serve to embarrass and weaken the execution of the plan or measure to which they relate, from the first step to the final conclusion of it. They constantly counteract those qualities in the Executive which are the most necessary ingredients in its composition — vigor and expedition, and this without any counterbalancing good. In the conduct of war, in which the energy of the Executive is the bulwark of the national security, every thing would be to be apprehended from its plurality.

But one of the weightiest objections to a plurality in the Executive, and which lies as much against the last as the first plan, is, that it tends to conceal faults and destroy responsibility.

Responsibility is of two kinds — to censure and to punishment. The first is the more important of the two, especially in an elective office. Man, in public trust, will much oftener act in such a manner as to render him unworthy of being any longer trusted, than in such a manner as to make him obnoxious to legal punishment. But the multiplication of the Executive adds to the difficulty of detection in either case. It often becomes impossible, amidst mutual accusations, to determine on whom the blame or the punishment of a pernicious measure, or series of pernicious measures, ought really to fall. It is shifted from one to another with so much dexterity, and under such plausible appearances, that the public opinion is left in suspense about the real author. The circumstances which may have led to any national miscarriage or misfortune are sometimes so complicated that, where there are a number of actors who may have had different degrees and kinds of agency, though we may clearly see upon the whole that there has been mismanagement, yet it may be impracticable to pronounce to whose account the evil which may have been incurred is truly chargeable.

It is evident from these considerations, that the plurality of the Executive tends to deprive the people of the two greatest securities they can have for the faithful exercise of any delegated power, *first*, the restraints of public opinion, which lose their efficacy, as well on account of the division of the censure attendant on bad measures among a number, as on account of the uncertainty on whom it ought to fall; and, *second*, the opportunity of discovering with facility and clearness the misconduct of the persons they trust, in order either to their removal from office or to their actual punishment in cases which admit of it.

The idea of a council to the Executive, which has so generally obtained in the State constitutions, has been derived from that maxim of republican jealousy which considers power as safer in the hands of a number of men than of a single man. If the maxim should be admitted to be applicable to the case, I should contend that the advantage on that side would not counterbalance the numerous disadvantages on the opposite side. But I do not think the rule at all applicable to the executive power. I clearly concur in opinion, in this particular, with a writer whom the celebrated Junius pronounces to be "deep, solid, and ingenious," that "the executive power is more easily confined when it is ONE"; that it is far more safe there should be a single object for the jealousy and watchfulness of the people; and, in a word, that all multiplication of the Executive is rather dangerous than friendly to liberty.

Lawrence Lessig & Cass R. Sunstein

THE PRESIDENT AND THE ADMINISTRATION

94 Colum L. Rev. 1 (Jan. 1994)

INTRODUCTION

Many think that under our constitutional system, the President must have the authority to control all government officials who implement the laws. The text, structure, and history of the Constitution, we are told, plainly require this result. Under this view, it is therefore something of an embarrassment that the Supreme Court has permitted conspicuous exceptions to this constitutional imperative. We now have independent special counsels, independent agencies, and other such exceptions, commonly thought to be inconsistent with the basic founding commitment to a unitary executive.

Some believe that this conception of unitariness derives from something that the framers decided—that the framers constitutionalized a strongly unitary executive, and that anyone following the original design must follow this structural pattern.

We think that the view that the framers constitutionalized anything like this vision of the executive is just plain myth. It is a creation of the twentieth century, not the eighteenth. It derives from twentieth century categories applied unreflectively to an eighteenth-century document. It ignores strong evidence that the framers imagined not a clear executive hierarchy with the President at the summit, but a large degree of congressional power to structure the administration as it thought proper.

We reach this conclusion with reluctance. A strongly unitary executive can promote important values of accountability, coordination, and uniformity in the execution of the laws, and to whatever extent these were the framers' values, they are certainly now ours. If these values are not advanced by the original design, we seemingly face an unpleasant dilemma—either we adhere to that design and sacrifice important institutional values, or we advance these institutional values and sacrifice fidelity to the original design. History apparently leads us to choose between the original design and a design many now view as indispensable.

At least this is so unless there is a compelling nonhistorical argument supporting a strong unitary design. We believe that there is indeed a plausible structural argument on behalf of the hierarchical conception of the unitary executive. This is an argument that emphasizes changed circumstances since the eighteenth century, and that accommodates the framers' design within this changed constitutional context—an argument, that is, that translates the framers' original design from the language and context of the eighteenth century into the world today. . . .

NEW CIRCUMSTANCES, OLD COMMITMENTS

We are concerned with the task of preserving initial constitutional commitments in light of changes in the constitutional context. In what follows, we first outline some relevant initial commitments, and then sketch two types of contextual change that make new applications necessary if these old commitments are to be maintained.

From our focus on what the framers said and did, we can identify a number of values that bear on whether we categorize a particular institution as executive (and hence requiring plenary presidential control) and that affect whether a particular limit on presidential control is proper. Unitariness was unquestionably one such value. As we have seen, the framers rejected a plural executive, and the Decision of 1789 shows that for some decisions, presidential control was indeed required. The framers believed that unitariness advanced the interests of coordination, accountability, and efficiency in the execution of the laws. All of these policies argued against a fragmented executive. In certain cases, it was critical that the executive be able to act with dispatch and without dissent. To account for those cases, the framers decided that the executive structure should be unitary.

The Vesting Clause of Article II—by placing the executive in one rather than many presidents—embodied this judgment. It is therefore clear that the constitutional text and structure reflect commitments to the unitary virtues of coordination, accountability, and efficiency in government. These commitments account for the unitariness of the presidency and of the executive power across a certain domain.

But it is equally certain that in some cases other values were relevant, and these values may at times constitutionally trump unitariness. On the founding view, efficiency not only justifies unitariness but also occasional legislative departures from that notion; it explains something of the relative independence of the district attorneys. So too does fear of executive and judicial aggrandizement. We have already noted the complexities in the Decision of 1789, but one lesson of that story was that sometimes the values of independence from the President could rightfully trump the interests of unitariness. The independence of adjudicative officers is one such interest. Maintaining congressional control over spending, to take another example, led the framers to reduce executive control over the Treasury, unitarian considerations notwithstanding.

From these distinct values we can draw together two that are for our purposes central. First is a value in accountability—where no special reason existed to separate responsibility from the President, the pattern of original executive structures strongly supports the conclusion that the President remains accountable for the actions of government officers. Of course, the general idea of accountability is embodied not only in the allocation of executive power, but also in the grant of legislative power to Congress, accompanied by a ban on open-ended delegations of legislative power. Second is a value of avoiding faction. This goal is, of course, at the center of the constitutional structure, and it helps explain the system of checks and balances in general.

Accountability and avoidance of factionalism, then, are two central values of the framers' original executive. Let us focus now on two sorts of changes in the current constitutional context that may require accommodation to continue to preserve these two original values.

The first, and least controversial, type of change is in the functions of what we are calling administrative agencies. What agencies do—the nature of their power and the way that power is exercised—is very different now from what it was at the framing period. Lawmaking and law-interpreting authority is now concentrated in an extraordinary array of regulatory agencies. This development has ensured that domestic policymaking is often done, not at the state level or even through Congress, but through large national bureaucracies.

This massive transformation in the institutional framework of American public law was entirely unanticipated by the framers, and it fundamentally altered the original constitutional design. We do not contend that administration was itself unanticipated, or that at the founding period it was trivial. On the contrary, the original period contained a precursor of the modern administrative state. But what we do now is not what was done then. General managerial functions were not within the domain of the national government, much less the President. Much of the organization of the national economy was left to state courts. By contrast, the national government restricted itself largely to national improvements, subsidies, tariffs, patents, tonnage, and the disposal of public lands. Whether or not Articles I and II were designed for congressional dominance, it seems clear that the early presidency involved little policymaking role in domestic affairs.

Things are of course different today. To take just one example, the Federal Communications Commission (FCC) sets national policy with respect to broadcasting. The FCC is not fully analogous to the administrative institutions at the founding, which never (or almost never) had such broad policymaking discretion. The problem is intensified when we recall that the FCC is merely one of a bewildering array of national administrative entities armed with similar power. Perhaps the immunization of such entities from presidential authority would now compromise constitutional commitments, indeed the very commitments that underlay the decision to create a (kind of) unitary presidency. Consider the original interest in coordination and the extent to which that interest would be compromised by allowing Congress to prevent the President from overseeing environmental or energy policy. For this reason, some institutions currently denominated administrative could arguably fall under presidential control as a matter of constitutional compulsion. This is because what administrative institutions do now is, in nature and scope, quite different from what administrative institutions did then—indeed, what such institutions do now is in terms of sheer importance more analogous to what unquestionably executive agencies did at the founding period. We will lay principal stress on this difference, suggesting that the framers' acquiescence in allowing some institutions to be independent of the President does not entail the conclusion that current, very different institutions can be similarly independent.

Second, and more controversially, some values may have become more or less important because we now have a better pragmatic understanding about how institutions actually function and a better understanding of the nature of the values at issue. This is the lesson from experience. Here the change consists not of new institutions raising unforeseen issues, but instead of new understandings of what certain governmental activities entail. At one time, for example, it may have been thought that an independent agency would best advance the policy interests of program X, but experience reveals that with independence, an independent agency is highly likely to fall victim to factional capture. Or it may have been thought that some sufficiently protected agencies could engage in apolitical, scientific, technocratic implementation of the laws; but now many believe that the notion of purely apolitical implementation is impossible, at least when discretionary judgments are involved. Of course assessments of this kind should be made principally by nonjudicial officials. But they may bear on constitutional interpretation as well. If either change occurred, then entities that Congress legitimately made independent when either view reigned must, perhaps, now be placed under the wing of the President as a matter of constitutional compulsion.

We begin, then, with the values of accountability and avoidance of faction, and we are confronted with changes in the types of function performed by modern regulatory agencies and in the lessons provided by experience with regulation. Consider how these two changes might work together to suggest that the modern executive must be strongly unitary, even if the framers' executive was not.

In the original understanding, officials who exercise the President's enumerated powers must operate under his control. But Congress was originally entitled to immunize some officials from presidential control when it thought proper—in particular, if those officials operated like judges, or if their duties were ministerial, or even if (as in the case of the Comptroller) their actions were discretionary but properly separated from the President's. All this of course operated in the context of a presidency that had an exceptionally narrow range of discretionary policymaking authorities in the domestic arena, at least compared to what we now find routine. Most of the functions performed by what we call the federal executive branch were originally the province of state legislatures and state courts, which had principal authority over regulation of the economy.

Now consider the character of the modern presidency. In the aftermath of the New Deal, administrative agencies carry out a wide range of highly discretionary policymaking tasks in the domestic arena. Because of delegations of discretionary authority to administrative agencies, the functions of those who execute the law have dramatically altered. Because of this discretionary authority, these agencies are now principal national policymakers — in practice, crucial lawmakers, both through regulation and interpretation. For example, control of the environment is in large measure a policy decision of the administrator of the Environmental Protection Agency. Parallel observations might be made for decisions relating to occupational safety and health, consumer products, and energy, including nuclear power. The same is true of implementation decisions. Rather than being ministerial, they involve highly discretionary choices about the content of domestic policy.

To say this is not to say that administrators at the founding had no policymaking power; of course they did. But it is hard to dispute the view that there has been a fundamental change in the legal context, involving the scope and nature of policymaking discretion that members of administrative agencies now possess. As the scope of the discretion of administrators has increased, their function has dramatically changed. At the founding, ministerial functions were freed from presidential control, and a wide range of administrative tasks plausibly could have been considered ministerial. Similarly, entities that performed judicial functions, or that engaged in tasks related to the purse, were also free of executive control. But now many administrators exercise what seem uncontroversially to be political functions, in the sense that their actions involve a great deal of discretion about policy and principle in implementing federal law. It remains true that many administrators also adjudicate; but the very process of adjudication frequently involves the creation of national policy under vague standards, as in, for example, the work of the National Labor Relations Board, the Federal Communications Commission, the Securities and Exchange Commission, and the Federal Trade Commission.

In short, in a period in which administrators exercise a wide range of discretionary authority, the very meaning of immunizing them from presidential control changes dramatically. When fundamental policy decisions are made by administrators, immunizing them from presidential control would have two significant consequences: first, it would segment fundamental policy decisions from direct political accountability and thus the capacity for coordination and democratic control; and second, it would subject these institutions to the perverse incentives of factions, by removing the insulating arm of the President, and increasing the opportunity for influence by powerful private groups. Neither of these consequences was favored by the framers. Indeed, both problems were specifically what the framers sought to avoid. For both these reasons — retaining accountability and avoiding factions — an interpreter could reasonably conclude either that it makes sense to understand the term executive to include more of the administrative power than the framers would have (specifically) included, or alternatively, that a legislative effort to insulate what is misleadingly labeled administration from the President is an improper exercise of legislative authority under the Necessary and Proper Clause.

All this describes how the function of administration has changed, and in ways that raise doubts about whether independence can be given to administrators, consistent with original constitutional commitments. Now consider a second change, one equally important.

In the last two centuries, there have been large-scale shifts in the nature of our understanding of what the administrators' power is. What was striking about the nineteenth-century view was the faith in the ability of administrative bodies to stand impartial in some scientific search for the true (rather than best) policy judgment. This was the progressive faith in administrative expertise. As Grundstein, a turn of the century theorist, wrote:

> Administration . . . was the realm of the professional, the scientist and the neutral technician, in the affairs of government, . . . set . . . apart from Politics in the sense that while the latter had to do with policies or expressions of the state will administration had to do with their execution.

But the post–New Deal view questions the very presupposition of this nineteenth-century model — the presupposition that the political can be so sharply separated from the administrative. To be sure, many insist on technocratic rationality — on the importance of expertise in helping people to make informed judgments about the relations between means and ends. This is an enduring theme in administrative law. We do not mean to disparage the importance of expertise in providing the foundation for sound public judgments. On the contrary, the absence of expertise, or the distortion of expert judgment through anecdote and interest-group power, is an important obstacle to a well-functioning system of regulatory law. But there has been an unmistakable and we believe fully warranted diminution in the progressive era's faith in the ability of expertise to solve regulatory problems on its own. This diminution has brought about a significant shift. As noted by (it is reported) Judge Scalia in the per curiam decision of a three-judge district court striking a portion of the Gramm-Rudman-Hollings Act,

> "These cases reflect considerable shifts over the course of time, not only in the Supreme Court's resolutions of particular issues relating to the removal power, but more importantly in the constitutional premises underlying those resolutions." It is not clear, moreover, that these shifts are at an end. Justice Sutherland's decision in *Humphrey's Executor* (1935) . . . is stamped with some of the political science preconceptions characteristic of its era and not of the present day. . . . It is not as obvious today as it seemed in the 1930s that there can be such things as genuinely "independent" regulatory agencies, bodies of impartial experts whose independence from the President does not entail correspondingly greater dependence upon the committees of Congress to which they are then immediately accountable; or indeed, that the decisions of such agencies so clearly involve scientific judgment rather than political choice that it is even theoretically desirable to insulate them from the democratic process.

In a world where administration is conceived as apolitical, granting administrators relatively independent authority could be thought to raise few constitutional issues. If the administrators are simply executing a technical skill, there is little reason to make their judgment subject to the review of the President. In such a world, the grant of authority to independent commissions could build directly on two precedents provided in the framing period — ministerial duties, which by definition do not involve discretion, and the quasi-adjudicative Comptroller. The Supreme Court accepted this highly technocratic conception of administration in *Humphrey's Executor v. United States*, the heyday of the progressive model within the judiciary. On progressive assumptions, *Humphrey's Executor* builds quite directly on framing premises and precedents insofar as the Court emphasized quasi-legislative and quasi-adjudicative functions — an irony in view of the widespread view that the case was a bizarre and unfounded exercise in constitutional innovation.

But once this view of administration changes — once one sees the nature of administration as fundamentally political — new questions are raised about the extent to which courts may permit this power to be independent of the President. The presupposition behind independent administration — what made it capable of drawing on analogies like the Comptroller General and the Postmaster in the founding period — is no longer sustainable. The question for interpretation is how to accommodate this fundamental change in understanding.

If all this is true, an argument for the strongly unitary executive under modern conditions takes the following form. From the actual administrative entities that the framers established, we can infer that the framers did not intend to allow administrative officials exercising broad policymaking authority to operate independently of the President. With respect to such officials, they made no explicit judgment, for their existence was not foreseen. The framers anticipated a much smaller national government, in which states would have the fundamental role and in which Congress would engage in basic policymaking, and they believed that the President would exercise a good deal of discretionary authority only in international relations. The execution of federal domestic law would often be mechanical, and crucially, nonpolitical. For this reason, the founding commitment to a unitary executive could coexist with a range of federal officials not directly subject to presidential control.

To the framers, centralization of executive power in the President was indeed designed to promote accountability, expedition, and coordination in federal law, and nothing we have said questions their commitment to a unitary executive at this level of generality. Indeed, these were fundamental constitutional principles. Our point is only that the framers did not believe that those principles would be compromised by insulating particular administrators from presidential control.

It was in the nineteenth century that one of the features distinguishing the framers' world from ours changed. Here was the rise of a massive federal bureaucracy; but unlike the legal culture today, the culture of the nineteenth-century theorists was firm in its faith in the scientific model of administration, so that the theorists did not see constitutional problems with relatively independent agencies. The nineteenth-century culture could accommodate the growth in bureaucracy by approving relatively independent agencies while staying within the bounds of fidelity.

But for us, the central fact of the eighteenth-century executive (limited national government and limited delegations to federal administrators) has changed, and the central assumption of the nineteenth-century solution (neutral, scientific administration) has failed. For now, we not only have a large administrative bureaucracy, but we also have profound skepticism about whether it is possible and desirable for that bureaucracy to operate free from political judgment. Echoing Justice Brandeis (quoting Justice Holmes) in *Erie R.R. Co. v. Tompkins*, we could say that administration in the sense in which courts speak of it today can no longer be understood to be neutral, or scientific. Politics is at its core, in the sense that value judgments are pervasive and democratic controls on policymaking are indispensable. This raises a central problem for a modern bureaucratic state. The question the interpreter must answer is how best to accommodate this current skepticism—what structure makes most sense of the framers' design, given the change in the extent of the bureaucracy and the change in our understanding of what bureaucracy is.

The answer to this question is not simple. No doubt our understandings are complex and multiple, and no doubt the principal place for registering changes in understanding is the legislature, not the judiciary. Congress' diminished enthusiasm for the independent agency form attests to the possibility that new views about expertise and factionalism can influence legislative judgments, informed by constitutional considerations, about appropriate structures. It would be possible to say that courts should not take account of changed understandings in the process of constitutional interpretation. But it is also possible to think that changes of this kind are relevant to interpretation as well as to lawmaking.

A structural argument for a unitary executive, then, comes down to this: Where the framers allocated a power that they thought of as political, that power was allocated to people who were themselves politically accountable. This was part of the fundamental commitments to accountability and avoidance of factionalism. At the founding period, the existence of a degree of independence in administration could not realistically have been thought to compromise these commitments. Today, by contrast, a strong presumption of unitariness is necessary in order to promote the original constitutional commitments. The legislative creation of domestic officials operating independently of the President but exercising important discretionary policymaking power now stands inconsistent with founding commitments.

It follows that in order to be faithful to the founding vision in changed circumstances, courts must now bar Congress, at least as a presumption, from immunizing from presidential control the activities of officials who exercise discretionary policymaking authority—at least if those officials are not adjudicators. In order to be faithful to the original design, that is, the interpreter must see as part of the constitutional structure a constraint not explicitly stated in that design, requiring that certain kinds of policymaking remain within the control of the executive.

A contrary view, set out forcefully by Abner Greene, could also be suggested by this same history—one that argues against a strongly unitary executive. Perhaps the original design reflected a carefully calibrated set of judgments about institutional authority, with a division between lawmaking and law implementation; perhaps the most important changed circumstance was the disturbance of this calibration through the delegation of policymaking authority to the President. On this view, the key founding commitments call for diffusion of power and for checks and balances between the legislature and the executive. The principal threat of the post–New Deal period lies in the concentration of lawmaking and law-executing power within the presidency. To restore the original balance, courts must now allow a high degree of independence from presidential power, so as to prevent what the framers dreaded most: the concentration of governmental power in a single institution — here, the executive.

This argument also stresses the need to maintain fidelity with the original constitutional design. It too is an argument of translation. But it takes the post–New Deal developments as a reason for more rather than less caution about unitariness in administration. The new circumstances mean that unitariness is a far greater threat than it once was — not that unitariness is a constitutionally compelled solution.

More particularly, this view fears that the new delegations have threatened to confer excessive power on the executive branch — to create an imperial presidency. The changed circumstances argue in favor of a narrow reading of executive power and for broad congressional authority under the Necessary and Proper Clause, precisely in the interest of maintaining the original commitment to a system of checks and balances. On this view, congressional power to insulate administration from presidential control is a necessary quid pro quo for the exercise of discretionary lawmaking power by people other than legislators. The rise of lawmaking by nonlegislative bodies — most especially, the downfall of the nondelegation doctrine — makes it especially necessary to insist on congressional prerogatives under the Necessary and Proper Clause, in order to prevent an aggregation of powers in the presidency. In short, Greene urges, the post–New Deal developments mean that modern interpreters should place less value on unitariness than did the framers, because of the need to maintain fidelity with the commitment to the diffusion of power.

This argument is hardly without force. It shows that there is no algorithm for deciding how to maintain fidelity with past instructions in the face of changed circumstances. But we do not believe that the argument is ultimately persuasive. The first and most fundamental problem is that the argument treats diffusion of power as an end in itself, rather than as an instrument for serving various purposes connected with the preservation of liberty. The second problem is that even if broad delegations of authority are the problem, independent agencies are not the solution.

Perhaps Congress can point to the need to limit presidential authority in order to support some isolated efforts to prevent concentration of power in the President. But it seems clear that the changed circumstances do not justify the immunization of all or most bureaucratic power from the President. This is because it is hard to identify how independent administration is a realistic solution to the constitutional problems caused by changed circumstances. Indeed, independent administration would sacrifice many values the founders saw as essential.

We conclude that if the framers thought that the realm of executive power was roughly coextensive with the realm of political choice, it makes sense to say that most of modern administration must fall under the power of the executive; and this is so even if the framers had a relatively capacious, but not specifically constitutionalized, conception of what counted as the administrative. Their conception of administrative (or permissibly nonexecutive) power certainly did not extend to the broad-scale selection of domestic policies for the country as a whole. If we are to translate their structural choices into current conditions, we may conclude that a largely hierarchical executive branch is the best way of keeping faith with the original plan. At least this is so if we are asking whether the President has a degree of removal and supervisory power over people who are authorized to make high-level discretionary decisions about the content of national policy.

Steven G. Calabresi & James Lindgren

THE PRESIDENT: LIGHTNING ROD OR KING?

115 Yale L.J. 2611 (2006)

I. THE POWERS OF A KING?

There is an idea current in the land today that presidential power has grown to the point where it is a threat to democracy. The *New York Times* editorial page writers and leading Democrats regularly accuse President George W. Bush of acting like a king or seeking kingly powers. In the academic community, Professor Bruce Ackerman has written powerfully about what he sees as the danger that presidential power poses to democracy itself. In this symposium issue, Professors Bill Marshall and Jennifer Martinez argue that the presidency has become too powerful. Marshall goes so far as to argue for reducing presidential power by separately electing the Attorney General.

In this Commentary, we suggest that when political power is examined more broadly, presidents and their parties generally have less power in the United States than commentators usually recognize. We believe the president today is less of a king than a lightning rod. Indeed, the constitutional and practical weakness of the presidency is, if not a threat to American democracy, at least a worrisome limitation on it. . . .

II. A WEAK OFFICE UNDER THE CONSTITUTION

Every four years Americans focus intently for ten months on the nation's presidential race. That race formally begins in late January with the Iowa caucuses and the New Hampshire primary, and it continues non-stop until November with a torrent of primaries, nominating conventions, presidential and vice presidential debates, and opinion polls. The unmistakable message sent to the voters is that this is it: the selection of a new president will determine which direction we go in as a society for the next four years. Electing the president is the democratic decision that really counts.

The problem with this idea is that it is not true. The president's formal powers under the Constitution are far too narrow to justify the hoopla that surrounds presidential elections. Under the Constitution, for example, presidents have very limited power over domestic policy. Anyone who doubts this should consider the fate of President Bush's proposals to reform social security and the tax code or President Clinton's attempt to introduce national health care.

The main levers that the Constitution gives the president over domestic policy are the veto power and the power to appoint principal officers in the executive and judicial branches subject to senatorial advice and consent. But the allegedly imperial George Bush has not yet vetoed even one piece of Congressional legislation. And it is easy to make too much of even the president's significant power over appointments. It is hard to induce most federal agencies to change directions (the NLRB is a notable exception), as is suggested by the successful thwarting of George Bush's recent attempts to reform the culture at the CIA. One must remember that federal departments and agencies are called *bureaucracies* for a reason. Even the significant effects of Bush's judicial appointments will be felt mainly in the period after he leaves office.

Ah, but a skeptic might say that the president has the dominant voice in foreign policy. Perhaps it is this formidable presidential power that justifies our quadrennial year-long presidential selection spectacle? Consider, however, just how little power a president really has even in this realm. Presidents can start military actions, but those military actions can be waged successfully only to the extent that Congress is willing to pay for them. Presidents can offer foreign aid, but again only to the extent Congress is willing to pay the bill. Presidents can propose free trade zones, but only if Congress is willing by a vote of both houses to go along. Presidents can negotiate treaties, but they become law only if two-thirds of the Senate approves. In short, while the president is the dominant player in foreign policy, there is almost nothing vital that the president can do even in this realm without some help from Congress. On its face, the power that voters grant to a president every four years is less than is generally supposed.

III. OF COATTAILS, MIDTERM BACKLASHES, AND LIGHTNING RODS

A. Losses in Midterm Congressional Elections

In a broader political sense, elections convey even less power to presidents and their parties than we have just described. First, as the substantial political science literature on midterm elections documents, it is an iron law of politics that the president's party almost always loses seats in Congress during the biennial midterm elections and especially during the second midterm election of an eight-year presidency. The data are consistent with the anecdotal evidence that the party holding the presidency six years into an eight-year tenure becomes a lightning rod for voter discontent.

Recently it is not just the second midterm election that has been a disaster for most presidents: often it is the first midterm election as well. Midterm losses in a president's first term can lead to his party losing control of both houses of Congress, as happened to Bill Clinton in 1994, or simply to losing enough seats that the president can no longer push his agenda, as happened to Ronald Reagan in 1982. . . .

B. Losses in State Elections

Strikingly, this midterm backlash is not confined just to federal elections. As James Campbell has nicely documented, there is a backlash against the president's party in the midterm elections for seats in state legislatures. Campbell shows that in state legislative races in presidential election years, the winning president's party benefits from his coattails, but in midterm elections the president's party suffers losses in state legislative races that approximately cancel out the gains from his coattails. Further, in an article published 35 years ago, Stephen Turrett analyzed incumbent governors' races in 1900–1969, noticing that incumbent governors were more likely to be re-elected in midterm elections if the president was of the opposing party. Turrett limited his analysis of this midterm effect to incumbent governors running for re-election and interpreted it as merely offsetting the coattail effect in presidential election years.

When one adds all gubernatorial races to the analysis, as we do in Charts 1 and 2, the backlash against the president's party in state races during a president's term is actually *stronger* overall than the coattail effect in the presidential election year. To be more specific, we find that four years after a party wins a presidential election it holds on average three *fewer* statehouses than it had *before it won* the presidential election! Perversely, winning the presidency seems to lead very shortly to losing power in the states. Since 1932 there have been eight changes of party control of the White House (1933, 1953, 1961, 1969, 1977, 1981, 1993, and 2001). In every instance but one, the party that seized the White House held more governorships in the year before they took office than in the year they lost the election leading to their leaving the White House. The only exception is that in 1980 Republicans held four fewer governorships than they held in 1992, immediately before the Republicans were voted out of the White House. Similarly, of the eleven presidents since 1933, every one except two (Kennedy and Reagan) left office with fewer governorships than his party had before he took office. Chart 1 shows this pattern.

The four-year pattern of a federal election cycle is shown in Chart 2. If one looks at the pattern since 1968, in his first year in office a president's party controls only 1.1 more governorships than the party had in the election year. Once in office, there is a backlash against the sitting president's

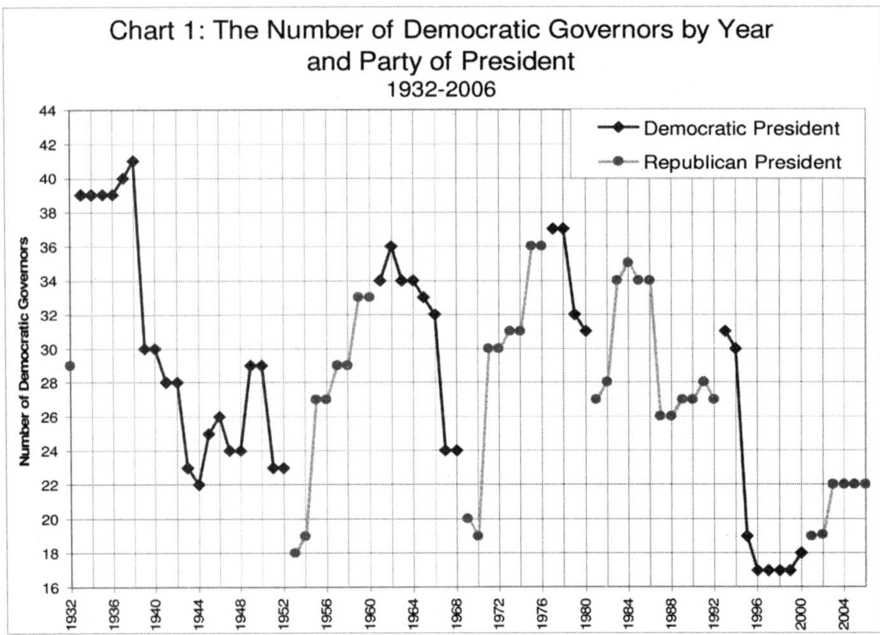

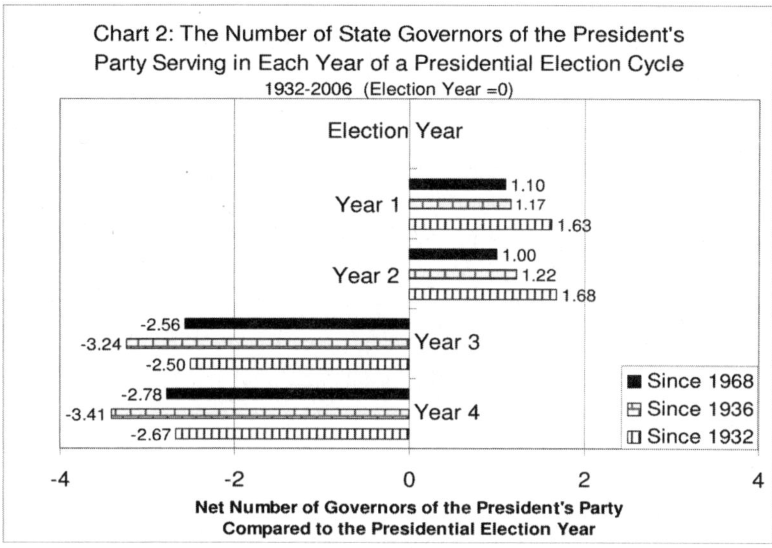

party. On average since 1968, by the third and fourth years of a four-year presidential administration he has lost nearly four seats (3.7-3.9) from his first year, thus losing not only that one "coattail effect" seat, but nearly three more governorships as well. One sees a similar, but slightly stronger pattern since 1936. If one looks at just two-term administrations since the 1950s, by the seventh year of the administration, the party winning the White House has 6 fewer governorships on average than it had before it won the White House.

C. Why We See a Lightning Rod Effect

What is driving the backlash we are documenting here? First, and most obviously, presidents become lightning rods for everything that goes wrong. Most presidents leave office less popular than when

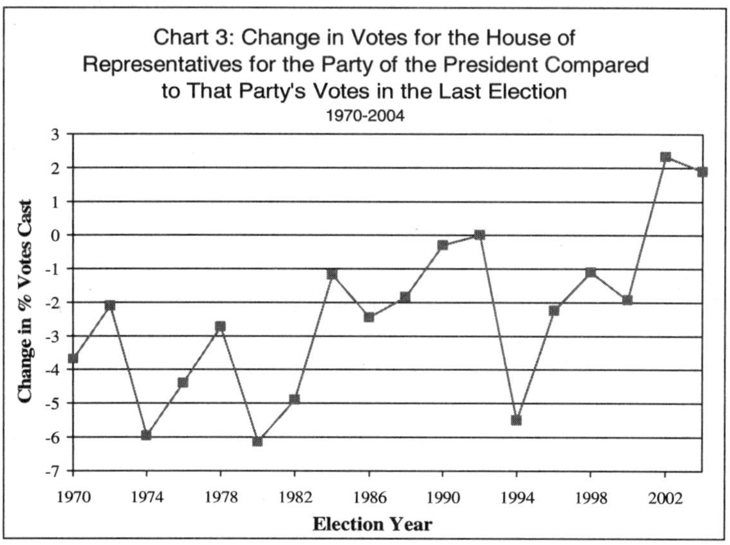

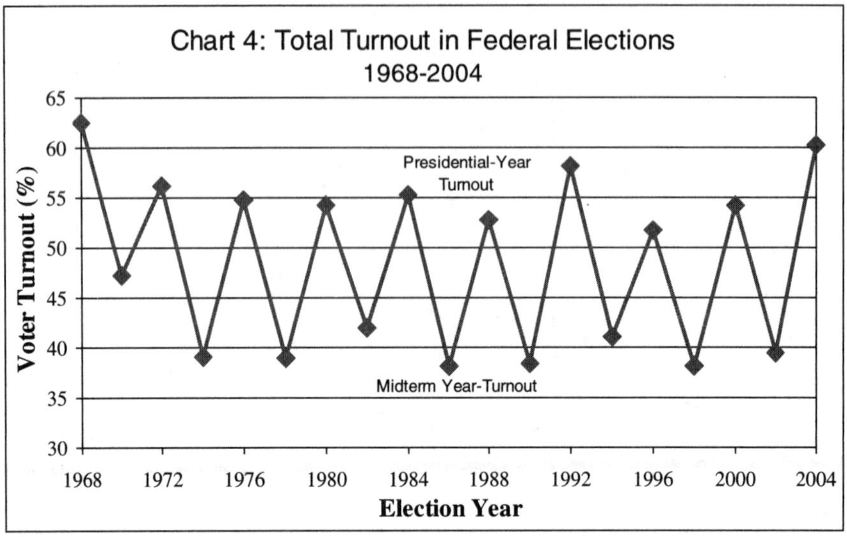

they entered, with Ronald Reagan and Bill Clinton being the only exceptions since at least Dwight Eisenhower. Even the exceptions (Reagan and Clinton) suffered major Congressional losses in their first midterm elections, at times when their job approval ratings were down substantially. Thus, the response of voters is to blame the president for whatever goes wrong, and probably as a result, to punish that president's party in midterm elections.

In Chart 3, we show that in the eighteen federal elections since 1970, in all but three of them (1992, 2002, and 2004), the party controlling the White House at the time of the election lost some of its proportion of the electorate for the House, compared with its proportion of the House vote two years before.

Second, as Chart 4 shows, not everyone votes in the midterm elections. Voter turnout is, in fact, significantly lower in midterm elections than it is during presidential years, and, as is well known, even American voter turnout in presidential years is low compared with the turnout in other Western democracies. Typically, turnout in a presidential year is about 55% of registered voters and turnout in midterm elections hovers around 40% of registered voters (Chart 4). The reasons for this are not hard to find. Americans are taught to think that the choice of a president is the key choice that gets made in their democracy, so that is the election everyone focuses on and votes in. The midterm election is of interest only to political junkies and to those voters who are mad about the direction in which the nation is going when the midterm election is held. Those angry voters in 1982 were disproportionately Democrats who were hostile to Ronald Reagan's dismantling of the safety net set up during the New Deal and Great Society years. Conversely, in 1994 the angry voters were disproportionately Republicans who were mad about everything from national health care, to gun control, to gay rights.

The effect therefore of successfully mobilizing to win the 1980 election for Ronald Reagan or the 1992 election for Bill Clinton was almost to guarantee the triumph of one's political opponents two years hence in an election where the turnout was around 40% of all registered voters, so that a mere 21% of registered voters constituted a majority. This midterm election allocated nearly as much federal power as did the presidential election and more power in the states. Yet this midterm election was one in which one's political opponents were much more likely to turn out and vote than one's allies — a very strange form of democracy indeed. Moreover, the losses suffered in the 1982 or 1994 midterm elections were of such a nature that they were unlikely to be undone until the other party again held the lightning rod office of the presidency.

The third reason for the strength of the perverse lightning rod effect is that in the mid-twentieth century, some states moved their governors' races to off-years in part to minimize the president's coattail effect and thus the effects of the presidential election cycle on state politics. Now only eleven states elect their governors on the same day as they vote for the president, while 36 states elect their governors during the year of a presidential midterm. Five other states, Kentucky, Mississippi, Louisiana, New Jersey, and Virginia, pick their governors during an odd numbered, non-presidential election year. All of the most populous (and thus politically powerful) states pick their governors during the midterm year, including California, Georgia, Florida, Illinois, Massachusetts, Michigan, New York, Pennsylvania, Ohio, and Texas. In a presidential year, the presidency, one third of the Senate, the entire House of Representatives, and eleven governorships are up for election. In the midterm year, one third of the Senate, the entire House of Representatives, and 36 governorships, including all the most important ones, are up for election with another five governorships up in odd numbered years. The huge number of governorships that are open in midterm and odd numbered years make the midterm elections of central importance to government in the United States.

In Reagan's second year, 1982, Republicans went from holding twenty-four governorships to holding sixteen — a reduction of 33%. In Clinton's second year, 1994, Republicans went from holding twenty governorships to holding thirty — an increase of 50%. The same pattern occurred in the 1960's and 1970's. In 1968, at the end of the Kennedy-Johnson years, Republicans held thirty-one governorships. In 1976, at the end of the Nixon-Ford years, Republicans held only twelve governorships.

IV. CONCLUSION

The American political landscape changes, not just every four years, but every two years as well. What has not been adequately recognized in the scholarly literature is that the changes in control in the states in the gubernatorial off-year elections are indeed larger than any coattail effect in the presidential election year, largely because only eleven small states elect their governors at the same time as they vote for president. The net effect is that by the time a president is up for re-election, his party controls fewer governorships than even before he won the election. Winning the presidency seems to lead very shortly to losing power, not only in Congress, but in state governorships as well. When one adds this perverse effect to the constitutional weakness of the presidency, the extraordinary emphasis on the presidential election every four years seems misplaced.

No American president has ever seriously threatened our democratic system of government, but democracy may be undermined when people regularly mobilize for and participate in a presidential election that is likely to produce on balance the opposite policy consequences from those that the people have voted for. Rather than worrying about imaginary threats of dictatorship, we ought to be worried today about an electoral system that may be regularly frustrating the popular will.

MYERS v. UNITED STATES

272 U.S. 52 (1926)

Opinion: Taft, joined by Van Devanter, Sutherland, Butler, Sanford, Stone
Dissent: Holmes
Dissent: McReynolds
Dissent: Brandeis

This is the first of three cases included in this chapter that concern the power of the president to remove executive officers. In this case, the Court decided that the president has full power to remove individuals exercising executive functions. This decision, however, was qualified over the course of time. The majority decision here and the dissent of U.S. Supreme Court Justice Louis Brandeis are part of a debate that has persisted from the time of the writing of the Constitution. In your opinion, what, if any, are the appropriate limits on the power of the president to remove executive officers? As you begin to read these cases, you should consider what implications the power of the president to appoint executive officers has for his removal power. Is it essential to democratic accountability that the president have the authority to hire and fire? As you consider this, you might pick up on the possible tension noted by Justice Brandeis between the efficiency of the executive function and the risk that the president will retain arbitrary power.

MR. CHIEF JUSTICE TAFT *delivered the opinion of the Court.*

This case presents the question whether, under the Constitution, the President has the exclusive power of removing executive officers of the United States whom he has appointed by and with the advice and consent of the Senate.

Myers was, on July 21, 1917, appointed by the President, by and with the advice and consent of the Senate, to be a postmaster of the first class at Portland, Oregon, for a term of four years. On January 20, 1920, Myers' resignation was demanded. He refused the demand. On February 2, 1920, he was removed from office by order of the Postmaster General, acting by direction of the President. He protested to the Department against his removal, and continued to do so until the end of his term. He pursued no other occupation, and drew compensation for no other service during the interval. On April 21, 1921, he brought this suit in the Court of Claims for his salary from the date of his removal, which, as claimed by supplemental petition filed after July 21, 1921, the end of his term, amounted to $8,838.71.

By the 6th section of the Act of Congress of July 12, 1876, under which Myers was appointed with the advice and consent of the Senate as a first-class postmaster, it is provided that

> Postmasters of the first, second and third classes shall be appointed and may be removed by the President by and with the advice and

> consent of the Senate and shall hold their offices for four years unless sooner removed or suspended according to law.

The Senate did not consent to the President's removal of Myers during his term. If this statute, in its requirement that his term should be four years unless sooner removed by the President by and with the consent of the Senate, is valid, the appellant is entitled to recover his unpaid salary for his full term. The Government maintains that the requirement is invalid for the reason that, under Article II of the Constitution the President's power of removal of executive officers appointed by him with the advice and consent of the Senate is full and complete without consent of the Senate. If this view is sound, the removal of Myers by the President without the Senate's consent was legal. We are therefore confronted by the constitutional question, and cannot avoid it.

The question where the power of removal of executive officers appointed by the President by and with the advice and consent of the Senate was vested was presented early in the first session of the First Congress. There is no express provision respecting removals in the Constitution, except as Section 4 of Article II provides for removal from office by impeachment. The subject was not discussed in the Constitutional Convention. Under the Articles of Confederation, Congress was given the power of appointing certain executive officers of the Confederation, and, during the Revolution and while the Articles were given effect, Congress exercised the power of removal.

First. Mr. Madison insisted that Article II, by vesting the executive power in the President, was intended to grant to him the power of appointment and removal of executive officers except as thereafter expressly provided in that Article. He pointed out that one of the chief purposes of the Convention was to separate the legislative from the executive functions. He said:

> If there is a principle in our Constitution, indeed in any free Constitution, more sacred than another, it is that which separates the Legislative, Executive and Judicial powers. If there is any point in which the separation of the Legislative and Executive powers ought to be maintained with great caution, it is that which relates to officers and offices.

1 Annals of Congress, 581.

Their union under the Confederation had not worked well, as the members of the convention knew. Montesquieu's view that the maintenance of independence as between the legislative, the executive, and the judicial branches was a security for the people had their full approval. Accordingly, the Constitution was so framed as to vest in the Congress all legislative powers therein granted, to vest in the President the executive power, and to vest in one Supreme Court and such inferior courts as Congress might establish the judicial power. From this division on principle, the reasonable construction of the Constitution must be that the branches should be kept separate in all cases in which they were not expressly blended, and the Constitution should be expounded to blend them no more than it affirmatively requires.

The vesting of the executive power in the President was essentially a grant of the power to execute the laws. But the President, alone and unaided, could not execute the laws. He must execute them by the assistance of subordinates. As he is charged specifically to take care that they be faithfully executed, the reasonable implication, even in the absence of express words, was that, as part of his executive power, he should select those who were to act for him under his direction in the execution of the laws. The further implication must be, in the absence of any express limitation respecting removals, that, as his selection of administrative officers is essential to the execution of the laws by him, so must be his power of removing those for whom he cannot continue to be responsible.

The executive power was given in general terms, strengthened by specific terms where emphasis was regarded as appropriate, and was limited by direct expressions where limitation was needed, and the fact that no express limit was placed on the power of removal by the Executive was convincing indication that none was intended.

The reason for the principle is that those in charge of and responsible for administering functions of government who select their executive subordinates need, in meeting their responsibility, to have the power to remove those whom they appoint.

For the reasons given, we must therefore hold that the provision of the law of 1876, by which the unrestricted power of removal of first class postmasters is denied to the President, is in violation of the Constitution, and invalid.

MR. JUSTICE BRANDEIS, *dissenting.*

The Act of July 12, 1876, c. 17, §6, 19 Stat. 78, 80, reenacting earlier legislation, provided that "postmasters of the first, second, and third classes shall be appointed and may be removed by the President by and with the advice and consent of the Senate, and shall hold their offices for four years unless sooner removed or suspended according to law." That statute has been in force unmodified for half a century. Throughout the period, it has governed a large majority of all civil offices to which appointments are made by and with the advice and consent of the Senate. May the President, having acted under the statute insofar as it creates the office and authorizes the appointment, ignore, while the Senate is in session, the provision which prescribes the condition under which a removal may take place?

It is this narrow question, and this only, which we are required to decide.

In *Marbury v. Madison*, it was assumed, as the basis of decision, that the President, acting alone, is powerless to remove an inferior civil officer appointed for a fixed term with the consent of the Senate, and that case was long regarded as so deciding. In no case has this Court determined that the President's power of removal is beyond control, limitation, or regulation by Congress. Nor has any lower federal court ever so decided. This is true of the power as it affects officers in the Army or the Navy and the high political officer like heads of departments, as well as of the power in respect to inferior statutory offices in the executive branch. Continuously for the last fifty-eight years, laws comprehensive in character, enacted from time to time with the approval of the President, have made removal from the great majority of the inferior presidential offices dependent upon the consent of the Senate. Throughout that period these laws have been continuously applied. We are requested to disregard the authority of *Marbury v. Madison* and to overturn this long established constitutional practice.

The contention that Congress is powerless to make consent of the Senate a condition of removal by the President from an executive office rests mainly upon the clause in §1 of Article II which declares that "The executive Power shall be vested in a President." The argument is that appointment and removal of officials are executive prerogatives; that the grant to the President of "the executive Power" confers upon him, as inherent in the office, the power to exercise these two functions without restriction by Congress, except insofar as the power to restrict his exercise of them is expressly conferred upon Congress by the Constitution; that, in respect to appointment, certain restrictions of the executive power are so provided for; but that, in respect to removal, there is no express grant to Congress of any power to limit the President's prerogative.

It is true that the exercise of the power of removal is said to be an executive act, and that, when the Senate grants or withholds consent to a removal by the President, it participates in an executive act. But the Constitution has confessedly granted to Congress the legislative power to create offices, and to prescribe the tenure thereof, and it has not in terms denied to Congress the power to control removals.

The separation of the powers of government did not make each branch completely autonomous. It left each in some measure dependent upon the others, as it left to each power to exercise, in some respects, functions in their nature executive, legislative and judicial. Obviously the President cannot secure full execution of the laws, if Congress denies to him adequate means of doing so. Full execution may be defeated because Congress declines to create offices indispensable for that purpose. Or because Congress, having created the office, declines to make the indispensable appropriation. Or because Congress, having both created the office and made the appropriation, prevents, by restrictions which it imposes, the appointment of officials who in quality and character are indispensable to the efficient execution of the law. If, in any such way, adequate means are denied to the President, the fault will lie with Congress. The President performs his full constitutional duty if, with the means and instruments provided by Congress and within the limitations prescribed by it, he uses his best endeavors to secure the faithful execution of the laws enacted. *Compare Kendall v. United States.* Checks and balances were established in order that this should be "a government of laws, and not of men."

The doctrine of the separation of powers was adopted by the convention of 1787 not to promote efficiency, but to preclude the exercise of arbitrary power. The purpose was not to avoid friction but, by means of the inevitable friction incident to the distribution of the governmental powers among three departments, to save the people from autocracy. In order to prevent arbitrary executive action, the Constitution provided in terms that presidential appointments be made with the consent of the Senate, unless Congress should otherwise provide, and this clause was construed by Alexander Hamilton in *The Federalist*, No. 77, as requiring like consent to removals.

Nothing in support of the claim of uncontrollable power can be inferred from the silence of the Convention of 1787 on the subject of removal. For the outstanding fact remains that every specific proposal to confer such uncontrollable power upon the President was rejected. In America, as in England, the conviction prevailed then that the people must look to representative assemblies for the protection of their liberties. And protection of the individual, even if he be an official, from the arbitrary or capricious exercise of power was then believed to be an essential of free government.

HUMPHREY'S EXECUTOR v. UNITED STATES

295 U.S. 602 (1935)

Opinion: Sutherland, joined by Hughes, Van Devanter, McReynolds, Brandeis, Butler, Stone, Roberts, Cardozo

In this case, the Supreme Court considered the constitutionality of a legislative act that limited the power of the president to remove from office individuals performing "quasi-legislative" or "quasi-judicial" functions. The Court decided that the president does not have limitless authority to remove such officers. To what extent does the reasoning in this case mark a departure from that in Myers v. United States, *in which the Court decided that the president has complete power to remove executive officers? Is it in fact possible to differentiate in a meaningful way between officers that perform quasi-legislative or quasi-judicial functions and those that perform purely executive duties? In other words, does this case provide a useful constitutional standard?*

MR. JUSTICE SUTHERLAND *delivered the opinion of the Court.*

Plaintiff brought suit in the Court of Claims against the United States to recover a sum of money alleged to be due the deceased for salary as a Federal Trade Commissioner from October 8, 1933, when the President undertook to remove him from office, to the time of his death on February 14, 1934.

William E. Humphrey, the decedent, on December 10, 1931, was nominated by President Hoover to succeed himself as a member of the Federal Trade Commission, and was confirmed by the United States Senate. He was duly commissioned for a term of seven years expiring September 25, 1938; and, after taking the required oath of office, entered upon his duties. On July 25, 1933, President Roosevelt addressed a letter to the commissioner asking for his resignation, on the ground "that the aims and purposes of the Administration with respect to the work of the Commission can be carried out most effectively with personnel of my own selection," but disclaiming any reflection upon the commissioner personally or upon his services. The commissioner replied, asking time to consult his friends.

The commissioner declined to resign, and on October 7, 1933, the President wrote him:

> Effective as of this date, you are hereby removed from the office of Commissioner of the Federal Trade Commission.

Humphrey never acquiesced in this action, but continued thereafter to insist that he was still a member of the commission, entitled to perform its duties and receive the compensation provided by law at the rate of $10,000 per annum. Upon these and other facts set forth in the certificate, which we deem it unnecessary to recite, the following questions are certified:

> 1. Do the provisions of section 1 of the Federal Trade Commission Act, stating that "any commissioner may be removed by the President for inefficiency, neglect of duty, or malfeasance in office," restrict or limit the power of the President to remove a commissioner except upon one or more of the causes named?
>
> If the foregoing question is answered in the affirmative, then—
>
> 2. If the power of the President to remove a commissioner is restricted or limited as shown by the foregoing interrogatory and the answer made thereto, is such a restriction or limitation valid under the Constitution of the United States?

The Federal Trade Commission Act creates a commission of five members to be appointed by the President by and with the advice and consent of the Senate, and §1 provides:

> Not more than three of the commissioners shall be members of the same political party. The first commissioners appointed shall continue in office for terms of three, four, five, six, and seven years, respectively, from the date of the taking effect of this Act, the term of each to be designated by the President, but their successors shall be appointed for terms of seven years, except that any person chosen to fill a vacancy shall be appointed only for the unexpired term of the commissioner whom he shall succeed. The commission shall choose a chairman from its own membership. No commissioner shall engage in any other business, vocation, or employment. Any commissioner may be removed by the President for inefficiency, neglect of duty, or malfeasance in office.

The legislative reports in both houses of Congress clearly reflect the view that a fixed term was necessary to the effective and fair administration of the law.

The debates in both houses demonstrate that the prevailing view was that the commission was not to be "subject to anybody in the government, but . . . only to the people of the United States"; free from "political domination or control" or the "probability or possibility of such a thing"; to be "separate and apart from any existing department of the government—not subject to the orders of the President."

Thus, the language of the act, the legislative reports, and the general purposes of the legislation as reflected by the debates all combine to demonstrate the Congressional intent to create a body of experts who shall gain experience by length of service—a body which shall be independent of executive authority *except in its selection*, and free to exercise its judgment without the leave or hindrance of any other official or any department of the government. To the accomplishment of these purposes it is clear that Congress was of opinion that length and certainty of tenure would vitally contribute. And to hold that, nevertheless, the members of the commission continue in office at the mere will of the President might be to thwart, in large measure, the very ends which Congress sought to realize by definitely fixing the term of office.

We conclude that the intent of the act is to limit the executive power of removal to the causes enumerated, the existence of none of which is claimed here, and we pass to the second question.

To support its contention that the removal provision of §1, as we have just construed it, is an unconstitutional interference with the executive power of the President, the government's chief reliance is *Myers v. United States.* That case has been so recently decided, and the prevailing and dissenting opinions so fully review the general subject of the power of executive removal, that further discussion would add little of value to the wealth of material there collected. These opinions examine at length the historical, legislative and judicial data bearing upon the question, beginning with what is called "the decision of 1789" in the first Congress and coming down almost to the day when the opinions were delivered. Nevertheless, the narrow point actually decided was only that the President had power to remove a postmaster of the first class without the advice and consent of the Senate as required by act of Congress.

The office of a postmaster is so essentially unlike the office now involved that the decision in the *Myers* case cannot be accepted as controlling our decision here. A postmaster is an executive officer restricted to the performance of executive functions. He is charged with no duty at all related to either the legislative or judicial power. The actual decision in the *Myers* case finds support in the theory that such an officer is merely one of the units in the executive department, and, hence, inherently subject to the exclusive and illimitable power of removal by the

Chief Executive, whose subordinate and aid he is. It goes no farther; much less does it include an officer who occupies no place in the executive department, and who exercises no part of the executive power vested by the Constitution in the President.

The Federal Trade Commission is an administrative body created by Congress to carry into effect legislative policies embodied in the statute in accordance with the legislative standard therein prescribed, and to perform other specified duties as a legislative or as a judicial aid. Such a body cannot in any proper sense be characterized as an arm or an eye of the executive. Its duties are performed without executive leave, and, in the contemplation of the statute, must be free from executive control. In administering the provisions of the statute in respect of "unfair methods of competition"—that is to say, in filling in and administering the details embodied by that general standard—the commission acts in part *quasi*-legislatively and in part *quasi*-judicially. In making investigations and reports thereon for the information of Congress under §6, in aid of the legislative power, it acts as a legislative agency. Under §7, which authorizes the commission to act as a master in chancery under rules prescribed by the court, it acts as an agency of the judiciary. To the extent that it exercises any executive function—as distinguished from executive power in the constitutional sense—it does so in the discharge and effectuation of its *quasi*-legislative or *quasi*-judicial powers, or as an agency of the legislative or judicial departments of the government.

If Congress is without authority to prescribe causes for removal of members of the trade commission and limit executive power of removal accordingly, that power at once becomes practically all-inclusive in respect of civil officers with the exception of the judiciary provided for by the Constitution. The Solicitor General, at the bar, apparently recognizing this to be true, with commendable candor, agreed that his view in respect of the removability of members of the Federal Trade Commission necessitated a like view in respect of the Interstate Commerce Commission and the Court of Claims. We are thus confronted with the serious question whether not only the members of these *quasi*-legislative and *quasi*-judicial bodies, but the judges of the legislative Court of Claims, exercising judicial power (*Williams v. United States*), continue in office only at the pleasure of the President.

We think it plain under the Constitution that illimitable power of removal is not possessed by the President in respect of officers of the character of those just named. The authority of Congress, in creating *quasi*-legislative or *quasi*-judicial agencies, to require them to act in discharge of their duties independently of executive control cannot well be doubted, and that authority includes, as an appropriate incident, power to fix the period during which they shall continue in office, and to forbid their removal except for cause in the meantime. For it is quite evident that one who holds his office only during the pleasure of another cannot be depended upon to maintain an attitude of independence against the latter's will.

The fundamental necessity of maintaining each of the three general departments of government entirely free from the control or coercive influence, direct or indirect, of either of the others has often been stressed, and is hardly open to serious question. So much is implied in the very fact of the separation of the powers of these departments by the Constitution, and in the rule which recognizes their essential coequality. The sound application of a principle that makes one master in his own house precludes him from imposing his control in the house of another who is master there.

The power of removal here claimed for the President falls within this principle, since its coercive influence threatens the independence of a commission which is not only wholly disconnected from the executive department, but which, as already fully appears, was created by Congress as a means of carrying into operation legislative and judicial powers, and as an agency of the legislative and judicial departments.

The result of what we now have said is this: whether the power of the President to remove an officer shall prevail over the authority of Congress to condition the power by fixing a definite term and precluding a removal except for cause will depend upon the character of the office; the *Myers* decision, affirming the power of the President alone to make the removal, is confined to purely executive officers, and, as to officers of the kind here under consideration, we hold that no removal can be made during the prescribed term for which the officer is appointed except for one or more of the causes named in the applicable statute. To the extent that, between the decision in the *Myers* case, which sustains the unrestrictable power of the President to remove purely executive officers, and our present decision that such power does not extend to an office such as that here involved, there shall remain a field of doubt, we leave such cases as may fall within it for future consideration and determination as they may arise.

Table 4.1. List of Administrative Agencies, Their Function, and Year Created

Agency Name	Function	Year Created
Agency for International Development	Supports economic growth, health, and democracy around the globe	1961
Bureau of Indian Affairs	Administers programs for American Indian tribes and Alaska natives, such as social services, natural resources management, and disaster relief	1824
Bureau of Labor Statistics	Measures working conditions, labor market activity, and price changes in the national economy	1884 as Bureau of Labor; transferred to Department of Labor in 1913 where it is located today
Centers for Medicare and Medicaid Services	Administers the federal insurance programs for the elderly and the poor	1977 as Health Care Financing Administration
Environmental Protection Agency	Enforces federal environmental legislation	1970
Government Accountability Office	Monitors federal government spending	1921
Immigration and Customs Enforcement	Enforces federal criminal and civil legislation related to immigration, trade, customs, and border control	2003
Securities and Exchange Commission	Regulates the securities industry	1934
Social Security Administration	Administers Social Security retirement, disability, and survivors' benefits programs	1935 as Social Security Board

YOUNGSTOWN SHEET & TUBE CO. v. SAWYER

343 U.S. 579 (1952)

Opinion: Black, joined by Frankfurter, Douglas, Jackson, Burton
Concurrence: Frankfurter
Concurrence: Douglas
Concurrence: Jackson
Concurrence: Burton
Concurrence: Clark
Dissent: Vinson, joined by Reed, Minton

Does the president's authority as Chief Executive and Commander-in-Chief enable him to take control of domestic private steel industries producing materials for the military during the Korean War? This case addresses that question in the context of a factory. During that war, steel workers were in a highly contentious negotiation with the mill owners, and the workers threatened to go on strike. But a strike in the steel mills might have cut off vital war supplies for troops fighting thousands of miles away in Korea. President Harry Truman ordered the secretary of commerce to seize most of the country's steel mills. The owners went to Court, arguing that President Truman had violated their property rights and usurped legislative power by acting beyond his constitutional authority.

In this case, the Court had to consider the limits of executive power and the relationship between the legislative and executive branches. Pay close attention not only to the majority opinion written by U.S. Supreme Court Justice Hugo Black, but also to Justice Robert H. Jackson's concurrence, in which he proposes a framework for determining the proper level of constitutional scrutiny that should be applied to executive action under different political circumstances—a framework that continues to shape constitutional rulings in this area to this day. Note particularly the difference between how the Court might treat executive action in the absence of congressional authorization and the Court's view of executive actions that are opposed by Congress. But what should happen where Congress is silent, or its views are ambiguous or unclear? What happens in Justice Jackson's "zone of twilight"? Is Justice Jackson's framework a compelling reading of the Constitution's provisions for the separation of powers?

MR. JUSTICE BLACK *delivered the opinion of the Court.*

We are asked to decide whether the President was acting within his constitutional power when he issued an order directing the Secretary of Commerce to take possession of and operate most of the Nation's steel mills. The mill owners argue that the President's order amounts to lawmaking, a legislative function which the Constitution has expressly confided to the Congress, and not to the President. The Government's position is that the order was made on findings of the President that his action was necessary to avert a national catastrophe which would inevitably result from a stoppage of steel production, and that, in meeting this grave emergency, the President was acting within the aggregate of his constitutional powers as the Nation's Chief Executive and the Commander in Chief of the Armed Forces of the United States. The issue emerges here from the following series of events:

In the latter part of 1951, a dispute arose between the steel companies and their employees over terms and conditions that should be included in new collective bargaining agreements. Long-continued conferences failed to resolve the dispute. On December 18, 1951, the employees' representative, United Steelworkers of America, CIO, gave notice of an intention to strike when the existing bargaining agreements expired on December 31. The Federal Mediation and Conciliation Service then intervened in an effort to get labor and management to agree. This failing, the President on December 22, 1951, referred the dispute to the Federal Wage Stabilization Board to investigate and make recommendations for fair and equitable terms of settlement. This Board's report resulted in no settlement. On April 4, 1952, the Union gave notice of a nation-wide strike called to begin at 12:01 A.M. April 9. The indispensability of steel as a component of substantially all weapons and other war materials led the President to believe that the proposed work stoppage would immediately jeopardize our national defense and that governmental seizure of the steel mills was necessary in order to assure the continued availability of steel. Reciting these considerations for his action, the President, a few hours before the strike was to begin, issued Executive Order 10340. . . . The order directed the Secretary of Commerce to take possession of most of the steel mills and keep them running. The Secretary immediately issued his own possessory orders, calling upon the presidents of the various seized companies to serve as operating managers for the United States. They were directed to carry on their activities in accordance with regulations and directions of the Secretary. The next morning the President sent a message to Congress reporting his action. Cong. Rec. April 9, 1952, p. 3962. Twelve days later, he sent a second message. Cong. Rec. April 21, 1952, p. 4192. Congress had taken no action.

Obeying the Secretary's orders under protest, the companies brought proceedings against him in the District Court. Their complaints charged that the seizure was not authorized by an act of Congress or by any constitutional provisions. The District Court was asked to declare the orders of the President and the Secretary invalid and to issue preliminary and permanent injunctions restraining their enforcement. Opposing the motion for preliminary injunction, the United States asserted that a strike disrupting steel production for even a brief period would so endanger the well being and safety of the Nation that the President had "inherent power" to do what he had done—power "supported by the Constitution, by historical precedent, and by court decisions."

The President's power, if any, to issue the order must stem either from an act of Congress or from the Constitution itself. There is no statute that expressly authorizes the President to take possession of property as he did here. Nor is there any act of Congress to which our attention has been directed from which such a power can fairly be implied. Indeed, we do not understand the Government to rely on statutory authorization for this seizure. There are two statutes which do authorize the President to take both personal and real property under certain conditions. However, the Government admits that these conditions were not met, and that the President's order was not rooted in either of the statutes. The Government refers to the seizure provisions of one of these statutes (§201(b) of the Defense Production Act) as "much too cumbersome, involved, and time-consuming for the crisis which was at hand."

Moreover, the use of the seizure technique to solve labor disputes in order to prevent work stoppages was not only unauthorized by any congressional enactment; prior to this controversy, Congress had refused to adopt that method of settling labor disputes. When the Taft-Hartley Act was under consideration in 1947, Congress rejected an amendment which would have authorized such governmental seizures in cases of emergency. Apparently it was thought that the technique of seizure, like that of compulsory arbitration, would interfere with the process of collective bargaining. Consequently, the plan Congress adopted in that Act did not provide for seizure under any circumstances. Instead, the plan sought to bring about settlements by use of the customary devices of mediation, conciliation, investigation by boards of inquiry, and public reports. In some instances, temporary injunctions were authorized to provide cooling-off periods. All this failing, unions were left free to strike after a secret vote by employees as to whether they wished to accept their employers' final settlement offer.

It is clear that, if the President had authority to issue the order he did, it must be found in some provision of the Constitution. And it is not claimed that express constitutional language grants this power to the President. The contention is that presidential power should be implied from the aggregate of his powers under the Constitution. Particular reliance is placed on provisions in Article II which say that "The executive Power shall be vested in a President . . . "; that "he shall take Care that the Laws be faithfully executed," and that he "shall be Commander in Chief of the Army and Navy of the United States."

The order cannot properly be sustained as an exercise of the President's military power as Commander in Chief of the Armed Forces. The Government attempts to do so by citing a number of cases upholding broad powers in military commanders engaged in day-to-day fighting in a theater of war. Such cases need not concern us here. Even though "theater of war" be an expanding concept, we cannot with faithfulness to our constitutional system hold that the Commander in Chief of the Armed Forces has the ultimate power as such to take possession of private property in order to keep labor disputes from stopping production. This is a job for the Nation's lawmakers, not for its military authorities.

Nor can the seizure order be sustained because of the several constitutional provisions that grant executive power to the President. In the framework of our Constitution, the President's power to see that the laws are faithfully executed refutes the idea that he is to be a lawmaker. The Constitution limits his functions in the lawmaking process to the recommending of laws he thinks wise and the vetoing of laws he thinks bad. And the Constitution is neither silent nor equivocal about who shall make laws which the President is to execute. The first section of the first article says that "All legislative Powers herein granted shall be vested in a Congress of the United States. . . ."

The President's order does not direct that a congressional policy be executed in a manner prescribed by Congress — it directs that a presidential policy be executed in a manner prescribed by the President. The preamble of the order itself, like that of many statutes, sets out reasons why the President believes certain policies should be adopted, proclaims these policies as rules of conduct to be followed, and again, like a statute, authorizes a government official to promulgate additional rules and regulations consistent with the policy proclaimed and needed to carry that policy into execution. The power of Congress to adopt such public policies as those proclaimed by the order is beyond question. It can authorize the taking of private property for public use. It can make laws regulating the relationships between employers and employees, prescribing rules designed to settle labor disputes, and fixing wages and working conditions in certain fields of our economy. The Constitution does not subject this lawmaking power of Congress to presidential or military supervision or control.

The Founders of this Nation entrusted the lawmaking power to the Congress alone in both good and bad times. It would do no good to recall the historical events, the fears of power, and the hopes for freedom that lay behind their choice. Such a review would but confirm our holding that this seizure order cannot stand.

MR. JUSTICE JACKSON, *concurring in the judgment and opinion of the Court.*

That comprehensive and undefined presidential powers hold both practical advantages and grave dangers for the country will impress anyone who has served as legal adviser to a President in time of transition and public anxiety. While an interval of detached reflection may temper teachings of that experience, they probably are a more realistic influence on my views than the conventional materials of judicial decision which seem unduly to accentuate doctrine and legal fiction. But, as we approach the question of presidential power, we half overcome mental hazards by recognizing them. The opinions of judges, no less than executives and publicists, often suffer the infirmity of confusing the issue of a power's validity with the cause it is invoked to promote, of confounding the permanent executive office with its temporary occupant. The tendency is strong to emphasize transient results upon policies — such as wages or stabilization — and lose sight of enduring consequences upon the balanced power structure of our Republic.

A judge, like an executive adviser, may be surprised at the poverty of really useful and unambiguous authority applicable to concrete problems of executive power as they actually present themselves. Just what our forefathers did envision, or would have envisioned had they foreseen modern conditions, must be divined from materials almost as enigmatic as the dreams Joseph was called upon to interpret for Pharaoh. A century and a half of partisan debate and scholarly speculation yields no net result, but only supplies more or less apt quotations from respected sources on each side of any question. They largely cancel each other. And court decisions are indecisive because of the judicial practice of dealing with the largest questions in the most narrow way.

The actual art of governing under our Constitution does not, and cannot, conform to judicial definitions of the power of any of its branches based on isolated clauses, or even single Articles torn from context. While the Constitution diffuses power the better to secure liberty, it also contemplates that practice will integrate the dispersed powers into a workable government. It enjoins upon its branches separateness but interdependence, autonomy but reciprocity. Presidential powers are not fixed but fluctuate depending upon their disjunction or conjunction with those of Congress. We may well begin by a somewhat over-simplified grouping of practical situations in which a President may doubt, or others may challenge, his powers, and by distinguishing roughly the legal consequences of this factor of relativity.

1. When the President acts pursuant to an express or implied authorization of Congress, his authority is at its maximum, for it includes all that he possesses in his own right plus all that Congress can delegate. In these circumstances, and in these only, may he be said (for what it may be worth) to personify the federal sovereignty. If his act is held unconstitutional under these circumstances, it usually means that the Federal Government, as an undivided whole, lacks power. A seizure

executed by the President pursuant to an Act of Congress would be supported by the strongest of presumptions and the widest latitude of judicial interpretation, and the burden of persuasion would rest heavily upon any who might attack it.

2. When the President acts in absence of either a congressional grant or denial of authority, he can only rely upon his own independent powers, but there is a zone of twilight in which he and Congress may have concurrent authority, or in which its distribution is uncertain. Therefore, congressional inertia, indifference or quiescence may sometimes, at least, as a practical matter, enable, if not invite, measures on independent presidential responsibility. In this area, any actual test of power is likely to depend on the imperatives of events and contemporary imponderables, rather than on abstract theories of law.

3. When the President takes measures incompatible with the expressed or implied will of Congress, his power is at its lowest ebb, for then he can rely only upon his own constitutional powers minus any constitutional powers of Congress over the matter. Courts can sustain exclusive presidential control in such a case only by disabling the Congress from acting upon the subject. Presidential claim to a power at once so conclusive and preclusive must be scrutinized with caution, for what is at stake is the equilibrium established by our constitutional system.

Into which of these classifications does this executive seizure of the steel industry fit? It is eliminated from the first by admission, for it is conceded that no congressional authorization exists for this seizure. That takes away also the support of the many precedents and declarations which were made in relation, and must be confined, to this category.

Can it then be defended under flexible tests available to the second category? It seems clearly eliminated from that class, because Congress has not left seizure of private property an open field, but has covered it by three statutory policies inconsistent with this seizure.

None of these were invoked. In choosing a different and inconsistent way of his own, the President cannot claim that it is necessitated or invited by failure of Congress to legislate upon the occasions, grounds and methods for seizure of industrial properties.

This leaves the current seizure to be justified only by the severe tests under the third grouping, where it can be supported only by any remainder of executive power after subtraction of such powers as Congress may have over the subject. In short, we can sustain the President only by holding that seizure of such strike-bound industries is within his domain and beyond control by Congress. Thus, this Court's first review of such seizures occurs under circumstances which leave presidential power most vulnerable to attack and in the least favorable of possible constitutional postures.

The Solicitor General seeks the power of seizure in three clauses of the Executive Article, the first reading, "The executive Power shall be vested in a President of the United States of America." Lest I be thought to exaggerate, I quote the interpretation which his brief puts upon it: "In our view, this clause constitutes a grant of all the executive powers of which the Government is capable." If that be true, it is difficult to see why the forefathers bothered to add several specific items, including some trifling ones.

The example of such unlimited executive power that must have most impressed the forefathers was the prerogative exercised by George III, and the description of its evils in the Declaration of Independence leads me to doubt that they were creating their new Executive in his image.

The clause on which the Government next relies is that "The President shall be Commander in Chief of the Army and Navy of the United States. . . ." These cryptic words have given rise to some of the most persistent controversies in our constitutional history. Of course, they imply something more than an empty title. But just what authority goes with the name has plagued presidential advisers who would not waive or narrow it by nonassertion, yet cannot say where it begins or ends. It undoubtedly puts the Nation's armed forces under presidential command. Hence, this loose appellation is sometimes advanced as support for any presidential action, internal or external, involving use of force, the idea being that it vests power to do anything, anywhere, that can be done with an army or navy.

Assuming that we are in a war *de facto*, whether it is or is not a war *de jure*, does that empower the Commander in Chief to seize industries he thinks necessary to supply our army? The Constitution expressly places in Congress power "to raise and support Armies" and "to provide and maintain a Navy." This certainly lays upon Congress primary responsibility for supplying the armed forces. Congress alone controls the raising of revenues and their appropriation, and may determine in what manner and by what means they shall be spent for military and naval procurement. I suppose no one would doubt that Congress can take over war supply as a Government enterprise. On the other hand, if Congress sees fit to rely on free private enterprise collectively bargaining with free labor for support and maintenance of our armed forces, can the Executive, because of lawful disagreements incidental to that process, seize the facility for operation upon Government-imposed terms?

There are indications that the Constitution did not contemplate that the title Commander in Chief *of the Army and Navy* will constitute him also Commander in Chief of the country, its industries and its inhabitants. He has no monopoly of "war powers," whatever they are. While Congress cannot deprive the President of the command of the army and navy, only Congress can providc him an army or navy to command.

That military powers of the Commander in Chief were not to supersede representative government of internal affairs seems obvious from the Constitution and from elementary American history.

We should not use this occasion to circumscribe, much less to contract, the lawful role of the President as Commander in Chief. I should indulge the widest latitude of interpretation to sustain his exclusive function to command the instruments of national force, at least when turned against the outside world for the security of our society. But, when it is turned inward not because of rebellion, but because of a lawful economic struggle between industry and labor, it should have no such indulgence.

The third clause in which the Solicitor General finds seizure powers is that "he shall take Care that the Laws be faithfully executed. . . ." That authority must be matched against words of the Fifth Amendment that "No person shall be . . . deprived of life, liberty or property, without due process of law. . . ." One gives a governmental authority that reaches so far as there is law, the other gives a private right that authority shall go no farther. These signify about all there is of the principle that ours is a government of laws, not of men, and that we submit ourselves to rulers only if under rules.

In the practical working of our Government, we already have evolved a technique within the framework of the Constitution by which normal executive powers may be considerably expanded to meet an emergency. Congress may and has granted extraordinary authorities which lie dormant in normal times but may be called into play by the Executive in war or upon proclamation of a national emergency.

Under this procedure, we retain Government by law—special, temporary law, perhaps, but law nonetheless. The public may know the extent and limitations of the powers that can be asserted, and persons affected may be informed from the statute of their rights and duties.

The executive action we have here originates in the individual will of the President, and represents an exercise of authority without law. No one, perhaps not even the President, knows the limits of the power he may seek to exert in this instance, and the parties affected cannot learn the limit of their rights. We do not know today what powers over labor or property would be claimed to flow from Government possession if we should legalize it, what rights to compensation would be claimed or recognized, or on what contingency it would end. With all its defects, delays and inconveniences, men have discovered no technique for long preserving free government except that the Executive be under the law, and that the law be made by parliamentary deliberations. Such institutions may be destined to pass away. But it is the duty of the Court to be last, not first, to give them up.

MR. JUSTICE DOUGLAS, *concurring.*

There can be no doubt that the emergency which caused the President to seize these steel plants was one that bore heavily on the country. But the emergency did not create power; it merely marked an occasion when power should be exercised. And the fact that it was necessary that measures be taken to keep steel in production does not mean that the President, rather than the Congress, had the constitutional authority to act. The Congress, as well as the President, is trustee of the national welfare. The President can act more quickly than the Congress. The President, with the armed services at his disposal, can move with force, as well as with speed. All executive power—from the reign of ancient kings to the rule of modern dictators—has the outward appearance of efficiency.

Legislative power, by contrast, is slower to exercise. There must be delay while the ponderous machinery of committees, hearings, and debates is put into motion. That takes time, and, while the Congress slowly moves into action, the emergency may take its toll in wages, consumer goods, war production, the standard of living of the people, and perhaps even lives. Legislative action may indeed often be cumbersome, time-consuming, and apparently inefficient. But, as Mr. Justice Brandeis stated in his dissent in *Myers v. United States*:

> The doctrine of the separation of powers was adopted by the Convention of 1787 not to promote efficiency, but to preclude the exercise of arbitrary power. The purpose was not to avoid friction, but, by means of the inevitable friction incident to the distribution of the governmental powers among three departments, to save the people from autocracy.

We therefore cannot decide this case by determining which branch of government can deal most expeditiously with the present crisis. The answer must depend on the allocation of powers under the Constitution. That, in turn, requires an analysis of the conditions giving rise to the seizure, and of the seizure itself.

The legislative nature of the action taken by the President seems to me to be clear. When the United States takes over an industrial plant to settle a labor controversy, it is condemning property. The seizure of the plant is a taking in the constitutional sense. *United States v. Pewee Coal*

Co. A permanent taking would amount to the nationalization of the industry. A temporary taking falls short of that goal. But though the seizure is only for a week or a month, the condemnation is complete, and the United States must pay compensation for the temporary possession. *United States v. General Motors Corp.*; *United States v. Pewee Coal Co., supra.*

The power of the Federal Government to condemn property is well established. *Kohl v. United States.* It can condemn for any public purpose, and I have no doubt but that condemnation of a plant, factory, or industry in order to promote industrial peace would be constitutional. But there is a duty to pay for all property taken by the Government. The command of the Fifth Amendment is that no "private property be taken for public use, without just compensation." That constitutional requirement has an important bearing on the present case.

The President has no power to raise revenues. That power is in the Congress by Article I, Section 8 of the Constitution. The President might seize, and the Congress, by subsequent action, might ratify the seizure. But, until and unless Congress acted, no condemnation would be lawful. The branch of government that has the power to pay compensation for a seizure is the only one able to authorize a seizure or make lawful one that the President has effected. That seems to me to be the necessary result of the condemnation provision in the Fifth Amendment. It squares with the theory of checks and balances expounded by Mr. Justice Black in the opinion of the Court, in which I join.

We could not sanction the seizures and condemnations of the steel plants in this case without reading Article II as giving the President not only the power to execute the laws, but to make some. Such a step would most assuredly alter the pattern of the Constitution.

MR. JUSTICE FRANKFURTER, *concurring.*

The question before the Court comes in this setting. Congress has frequently—at least 16 times since 1916—specifically provided for executive seizure of production, transportation, communications, or storage facilities. In every case, it has qualified this grant of power with limitations and safeguards. This body of enactments demonstrates that Congress deemed seizure so drastic a power as to require that it be carefully circumscribed whenever the President was vested with this extraordinary authority. The power to seize has uniformly been given only for a limited period or for a defined emergency, or has been repealed after a short period. Its exercise has been restricted to particular circumstances such as "time of war or when war is imminent," the needs of "public safety" or of "national security or defense," or "urgent and impending need." The period of governmental operation has been limited, as, for instance, to "sixty days after the restoration of productive efficiency." Seizure statutes usually make executive action dependent on detailed conditions: for example, (a) failure or refusal of the owner of a plant to meet governmental supply needs or (b) failure of voluntary negotiations with the owner for the use of a plant necessary for great public ends. Congress often has specified the particular executive agency which should seize or operate the plants or whose judgment would appropriately test the need for seizure. Congress also has not left to implication that just compensation be paid; it has usually legislated in detail regarding enforcement of this litigation-breeding general requirement.

Congress, in 1947, was again called upon to consider whether governmental seizure should be used to avoid serious industrial shutdowns. Congress decided against conferring such power generally and in advance, without special Congressional enactment to meet each particular need. Under the urgency of telephone and coal strikes in the winter of 1946, Congress addressed itself to the problems raised by "national emergency" strikes and lockouts. The termination of wartime seizure powers on December 31, 1946, brought these matters to the attention of Congress with vivid impact. A proposal that the President be given powers to seize plants to avert a shutdown where the "health or safety" of the Nation was endangered was thoroughly canvassed by Congress, and rejected. No room for doubt remains that the proponents as well as the opponents of the bill which became the Labor Management Relations Act of 1947 clearly understood that, as a result of that legislation, the only recourse for preventing a shutdown in any basic industry, after failure of mediation, was Congress. Authorization for seizure as an available remedy for potential dangers was unequivocally put aside. The Senate Labor Committee, through its Chairman, explicitly reported to the Senate that a general grant of seizure powers had been considered and rejected in favor of reliance on *ad hoc* legislation, as a particular emergency might call for it. An amendment presented in the House providing that, where necessary "to preserve and protect the public health and security," the President might seize any industry in which there is an impending curtailment of production, was voted down after debate, by a vote of more than three to one.

On a balance of considerations, Congress chose not to lodge this power in the President. It chose not to make available in advance a remedy to which both industry and labor were fiercely hostile. In deciding that authority to seize should be given to the President only after full consideration of the particular situation should show such legislation to be necessary, Congress presumably acted on experience with similar industrial conflicts in the past. It evidently assumed that industrial shutdowns in basic industries are not instances of spontaneous generation, and that danger warnings are sufficiently plain before the event to give ample opportunity to start the legislative process into action.

In any event, nothing can be plainer than that Congress made a conscious choice of policy in a field full of perplexity and peculiarly within legislative responsibility for choice. In formulating legislation for dealing with industrial conflicts, Congress could not more clearly and emphatically have withheld authority than it did in 1947. Perhaps as much so as is true of any piece of modern legislation, Congress acted with full consciousness of what it was doing, and in the light of much recent history. Previous seizure legislation had subjected the powers granted to the President to restrictions of varying degrees of stringency. Instead of giving him even limited powers, Congress, in 1947, deemed it wise to require the President, upon failure of attempts to reach a voluntary settlement, to report to Congress if he deemed the power of seizure a needed shot for his locker. The President could not ignore the specific limitations of prior seizure statutes. No more could he act in disregard of the limitation put upon seizure by the 1947 Act.

It cannot be contended that the President would have had power to issue this order had Congress explicitly negated such authority in formal legislation. Congress has expressed its will to withhold this power from the President as though it had said so in so many words. The authoritatively expressed purpose of Congress to disallow such power to the President and to require him, when in his mind the occasion arose for such a seizure, to put the matter to Congress and ask for specific authority from it, could not be more decisive if it had been written into the Labor Management Relations Act of 1947.

It is one thing to draw an intention of Congress from general language and to say that Congress would have explicitly written what is inferred, where Congress has not addressed itself to a specific situation. It is quite impossible, however, when Congress did specifically address itself to a problem, as Congress did to that of seizure, to find secreted in the interstices of legislation the very grant of power which Congress consciously withheld. To find authority so explicitly withheld is not merely to disregard in a particular instance the clear will of Congress. It is to disrespect the whole legislative process and the constitutional division of authority between President and Congress.

To be sure, the content of the three authorities of government is not to be derived from an abstract analysis. The areas are partly interacting, not wholly disjointed. The Constitution is a framework for government. Therefore, the way the framework has consistently operated fairly establishes that it has operated according to its true nature. Deeply embedded traditional ways of conducting government cannot supplant the Constitution or legislation, but they give meaning to the words of a text or supply them. It is an inadmissibly narrow conception of American constitutional law to confine it to the words of the Constitution and to disregard the gloss which life has written upon them. In short, a systematic, unbroken, executive practice, long pursued to the knowledge of the Congress and never before questioned, engaged in by Presidents who have also sworn to uphold the Constitution, making as it were such exercise of power part of the structure of our government, may be treated as a gloss on "executive Power" vested in the President by §1 of Art. II.

Down to the World War II period, the record is barren of instances comparable to the one before us.

A scheme of government like ours no doubt at times feels the lack of power to act with complete, all-embracing, swiftly moving authority. No doubt a government with distributed authority, subject to be challenged in the courts of law, at least long enough to consider and adjudicate the challenge, labors under restrictions from which other governments are free. It has not been our tradition to envy such governments. In any event, our government was designed to have such restrictions. The price was deemed not too high in view of the safeguards which these restrictions afford.

MR. CHIEF JUSTICE VINSON, *with whom* **MR. JUSTICE REED** *and* **MR. JUSTICE MINTON** *join, dissenting.*

The President of the United States directed the Secretary of Commerce to take temporary possession of the Nation's steel mills during the existing emergency because "a work stoppage would immediately jeopardize and imperil our national defense and the defense of those joined with us in resisting aggression, and would add to the continuing danger of our soldiers, sailors, and airmen engaged in combat in the field." In passing upon the question of Presidential powers in this case, we must first consider the context in which those powers were exercised.

Those who suggest that this is a case involving extraordinary powers should be mindful that these are extraordinary times. A world not yet recovered from the devastation of World War II has been forced to face the threat of another and more terrifying global conflict.

In 1950, when the United Nations called upon member nations "to render every assistance" to repel aggression in Korea, the United States furnished its vigorous support. For almost two full years, our armed forces have been fighting in Korea, suffering casualties of over 108,000 men. Hostilities have not abated. The "determination of the United Nations to continue its action in Korea to meet the aggression" has been reaffirmed. Congressional support of the action in Korea has been manifested by provisions for increased military manpower and equipment and for economic stabilization, as hereinafter described.

As an illustration of the magnitude of the over-all program, Congress has appropriated $130 billion for our own defense and for military assistance to our allies since the June, 1950, attack in Korea.

Over $5½ billion were appropriated for military assistance for fiscal year 1952, the bulk of that amount to be devoted to purchase of military equipment.

Congress, recognizing the "grim fact . . . that the United States is now engaged in a struggle for survival" and that "it is imperative that we now take those necessary steps to make our strength equal to the peril of the hour," granted authority to draft men into the armed forces. As a result, we now have over 3,500,000 men in our armed forces.

Appropriations for the Department of Defense, which had averaged less than $13 billion per year for the three years before attack in Korea, were increased by Congress to $48 billion for fiscal year 1951 and to $60 billion for fiscal year 1952.

The President has the duty to execute the foregoing legislative programs. Their successful execution depends upon continued production of steel and stabilized prices for steel. Accordingly, when the collective bargaining agreements between the Nation's steel producers and their employees, represented by the United Steel Workers, were due to expire on December 31, 1951, and a strike shutting down the entire basic steel industry was threatened, the President acted to avert a complete shutdown of steel production.

One is not here called upon even to consider the possibility of executive seizure of a farm, a corner grocery store or even a single industrial plant. Such considerations arise only when one ignores the central fact of this case — that the Nation's entire basic steel production would have shut down completely if there had been no Government seizure. Even ignoring for the moment whatever confidential information the President may possess as "the Nation's organ for foreign affairs," the uncontroverted affidavits in this record amply support the finding that "a work stoppage would immediately jeopardize and imperil our national defense."

Plaintiffs do not remotely suggest any basis for rejecting the President's finding that any stoppage of steel production would immediately place the Nation in peril.

Plaintiffs' counsel tells us that "sooner or later" the mills will operate again. That may satisfy the steel companies and, perhaps, the Union. But our soldiers and our allies will hardly be cheered with the assurance that the ammunition upon which their lives depend will be forthcoming — "sooner or later," or, in other words, "too little and too late."

Accordingly, if the President has any power under the Constitution to meet a critical situation in the absence of express statutory authorization, there is no basis whatever for criticizing the exercise of such power in this case.

A review of executive action demonstrates that our Presidents have on many occasions exhibited the leadership contemplated by the Framers when they made the President Commander in Chief, and imposed upon him the trust to "take Care that the Laws be faithfully executed." With or without explicit statutory authorization, Presidents have at such times dealt with national emergencies by acting promptly and resolutely to enforce legislative programs, at least to save those programs until Congress could act. Congress and the courts have responded to such executive initiative with consistent approval.

History bears out the genius of the Founding Fathers, who created a Government subject to law but not left subject to inertia when vigor and initiative are required.

Focusing now on the situation confronting the President on the night of April 8, 1952, we cannot but conclude that the President was performing his duty under the Constitution to "take Care that the Laws be faithfully executed"—a duty described by President Benjamin Harrison as "the central idea of the office."

The President reported to Congress the morning after the seizure that he acted because a work stoppage in steel production would immediately imperil the safety of the Nation by preventing execution of the legislative programs for procurement of military equipment. And, while a shutdown could be averted by granting the price concessions requested by plaintiffs, granting such concessions would disrupt the price stabilization program also enacted by Congress. Rather than fail to execute either legislative program, the President acted to execute both.

Much of the argument in this case has been directed at straw men. We do not now have before us the case of a President acting solely on the basis of his own notions of the public welfare. Nor is there any question of unlimited executive power in this case. The President himself closed the door to any such claim when he sent his Message to Congress stating his purpose to abide by any action of Congress, whether approving or disapproving his seizure action. Here, the President immediately made sure that Congress was fully informed of the temporary action he had taken only to preserve the legislative programs from destruction until Congress could act.

The absence of a specific statute authorizing seizure of the steel mills as a mode of executing the laws has not until today been thought to prevent the President from executing the laws. Unlike an administrative commission confined to the enforcement of the statute under which it was created, or the head of a department when administering a particular statute, the President is a constitutional officer charged with taking care that a "mass of legislation" be executed. Flexibility as to mode of execution to meet critical situations is a matter of practical necessity.

Whatever the extent of Presidential power on more tranquil occasions, and whatever the right of the President to execute legislative programs as he sees fit without reporting the mode of execution to Congress, the single Presidential purpose disclosed on this record is to faithfully execute the laws by acting in an emergency to maintain the *status quo*, thereby preventing collapse of the legislative programs until Congress could act. The President's action served the same purposes as a judicial stay entered to maintain the *status quo* in order to preserve the jurisdiction of a court. In his Message to Congress immediately following the seizure, the President explained the necessity of his action in executing the military procurement and anti-inflation legislative programs and expressed his desire to cooperate with any legislative proposals approving, regulating or rejecting the seizure of the steel mills. Consequently, there is no evidence whatever of any Presidential purpose to defy Congress or act in any way inconsistent with the legislative will.

In *United States v. Midwest Oil Co., supra,* this Court approved executive action where, as here, the President acted to preserve an important matter until Congress could act—even though his action in that case was contrary to an express statute. In this case, there is no statute prohibiting the action taken by the President in a matter not merely important, but threatening the very safety of the Nation. Executive inaction in such a situation, courting national disaster, is foreign to the concept of energy and initiative in the Executive as created by the Founding Fathers. The Constitution was itself "adopted in a period of grave emergency. . . . While emergency does not create power, emergency may furnish the occasion for the exercise of power." The Framers knew, as we should know in these times of peril, that there is real danger in Executive weakness. There is no cause to fear Executive tyranny so long as the laws of Congress are being faithfully executed. Certainly there is no basis for fear of dictatorship when the Executive acts, as he did in this case, only to save the situation until Congress could act.

Faced with the duty of executing the defense programs which Congress had enacted and the disastrous effects that any stoppage in steel production would have on those programs, the President acted to preserve those programs by seizing the steel mills. There is no question that the possession was other than temporary in character, and subject to congressional direction—either approving, disapproving, or regulating the manner in which the mills were to be administered and returned to the owners. The President immediately informed Congress of his action, and clearly stated his intention to abide by the legislative will. No basis for claims of arbitrary action, unlimited powers, or dictatorial usurpation of congressional power appears from the facts of this case. On the contrary, judicial, legislative and executive precedents throughout our history demonstrate that, in this case, the President acted in full conformity with his duties under the Constitution.

IMMIGRATION AND NATURALIZATION SERVICE v. CHADHA

462 U.S. 919 (1983)

Opinion: Burger, joined by Brennan, Marshall, Blackmun, Stevens, O'Connor
Concurrence: Powell
Dissent: White
Dissent: Rehnquist, joined by White

In this case, the Supreme Court considered the constitutionality of a congressional act allowing for one House of Congress to invalidate by way of "legislative veto" a particular decision made by the executive branch. As you know, the veto power is usually thought of as a presidential prerogative, exercised in order to stop legislation passed by the House and the Senate. A central issue in this case is whether the procedure violates the Presentment Clause of Article I, Section 7 of the Constitution, which requires that every bill passed by Congress "shall . . . be presented to the President of the United States." Notice, too, the Court's discussion of the fact that the Constitution created Congress as a bicameral body, and its requirement that all legislation must pass through both the House and Senate. Can Congress ensure that the law is carried out in accordance with the will of the people if it cannot invalidate particular executive decisions? Is the Court correct that congressional policy determinations that do not include both Houses are constitutionally problematic? How is the legislative veto different from other instances in which one House can act alone without the other, such as the Senate's entitlement to ratify treaties? Consider here the debate between U.S. Supreme Court Justice Byron White, who argues that the Court should ask if this innovative process is actually the best way to assure the functional integrity of the separation of powers, and the majority, who insist that the formal requirements of the Presentment and Bicameralism Clauses must be respected. As you read this case, consider whether you think there must be some flexibility in the structure of the U.S. government to allow it to meet modern challenges, including the growth of the government itself.

CHIEF JUSTICE BURGER *delivered the opinion of the Court.*

[The case at hand] presents a challenge to the constitutionality of the provision in §244(c)(2) of the Immigration and Nationality Act, 66 Stat. 216, as amended, 8 U.S.C. §1254(c)(2), authorizing one House of Congress, by resolution, to invalidate the decision of the Executive Branch, pursuant to authority delegated by Congress to the Attorney General of the United States, to allow a particular deportable alien to remain in the United States.

Chadha is an East Indian who was born in Kenya and holds a British passport. He was lawfully admitted to the United States in 1966 on a nonimmigrant student visa. His visa expired on June 30, 1972. On October 11, 1973, the District Director of the Immigration and Naturalization Service ordered Chadha to show cause why he should not be deported for having "remained in the United States for a longer time than permitted." Pursuant to §242(b) of the Immigration and Nationality Act (Act), a deportation hearing was held before an Immigration Judge on January 11, 1974. Chadha conceded that he was deportable for overstaying his visa, and the hearing was adjourned to enable him to file an application for suspension of deportation under §244(a)(1) of the Act.

After Chadha submitted his application for suspension of deportation, the deportation hearing was resumed on February 7, 1974. On the basis of evidence adduced at the hearing, affidavits submitted with the application, and the results of a character investigation conducted by the INS, the Immigration Judge, on June 25, 1974, ordered that Chadha's deportation be suspended. The Immigration Judge found that Chadha met the requirements of §244(a)(1): he had resided continuously in the United States for over seven years, was of good moral character, and would suffer "extreme hardship" if deported.

Pursuant to §244(c)(1) of the Act, the Immigration Judge suspended Chadha's deportation and a report of the suspension was transmitted to Congress.

Once the Attorney General's recommendation for suspension of Chadha's deportation was conveyed to Congress, Congress had the power under §244(c)(2) of the Act, to veto the Attorney General's determination that Chadha should not be deported.

On December 12, 1975, Representative Eilberg, Chairman of the Judiciary Subcommittee on Immigration, Citizenship, and International Law, introduced a resolution opposing "the granting of permanent residence in the United States to [six] aliens," including Chadha. The resolution was referred to the House Committee on the Judiciary. On December 16, 1975, the resolution was discharged from further consideration by the House Committee on the Judiciary and submitted to the House of Representatives for a vote. The resolution had not been printed and was not made available to other Members of the House prior to or at the time it was voted on. So far as the record before us shows, the House consideration of the resolution was based on Representative Eilberg's statement from the floor that

> [i]t was the feeling of the committee, after reviewing 340 cases, that the aliens contained in the resolution [Chadha and five others] did not meet these statutory requirements, particularly as it relates to hardship; and it is the opinion of the committee that their deportation should not be suspended.

Ibid. The resolution was passed without debate or recorded vote. Since the House action was pursuant to §244(c)(2), the resolution was not treated as an Art. I legislative act; it was not submitted to the Senate or presented to the President for his action.

We turn now to the question whether action of one House of Congress under §244(c)(2) violates strictures of the Constitution. We begin, of course, with the presumption that the challenged statute is valid. Its wisdom is not the concern of the courts; if a challenged action does not violate the Constitution, it must be sustained.

By the same token, the fact that a given law or procedure is efficient, convenient, and useful in facilitating functions of government, standing alone, will not save it if it is contrary to the Constitution. . . .

Justice White undertakes to make a case for the proposition that the one-House veto is a useful "political invention," and we need not challenge that assertion. We can even concede this utilitarian argument, although the long-range political wisdom of this "invention" is arguable.

But policy arguments supporting even useful "political inventions" are subject to the demands of the Constitution, which defines powers and, with respect to this subject, sets out just how those powers are to be exercised.

Explicit and unambiguous provisions of the Constitution prescribe and define the respective functions of the Congress and of the Executive in the legislative process. Since the precise terms of those familiar provisions are critical to the resolution of these cases, we set them out verbatim. Article I provides:

> All legislative Powers herein granted shall be vested in a Congress of the United States, which shall consist of a Senate ***and*** House of Representatives.

Art. I, §1. (Emphasis added.)

> Every Bill which shall have passed the House of Representatives ***and*** the Senate, ***shall***, before it becomes a law, be presented to the President of the United States. . . .

Art. I, §7, cl. 2. (Emphasis added.)

> ***Every*** Order, Resolution, or Vote to which the Concurrence of the Senate and House of Representatives may be necessary (except on a question of Adjournment) ***shall*** be presented to the President of the United States; and before the Same shall take Effect, ***shall*** be approved by him, or being disapproved by him, ***shall*** be repassed by two thirds of the Senate and House of Representatives, according to the Rules and Limitations prescribed in the Case of a Bill.

Art. I, §7, cl. 3. (Emphasis added.)

These provisions of Art. I are integral parts of the constitutional design for the separation of powers. We have recently noted that "[t]he principle of separation of powers was not simply an abstract generalization in the minds of the Framers: it was woven into the document that they drafted in Philadelphia in the summer of 1787." *Buckley v. Valeo.* Just as we relied on the textual provision of Art. II, §2, cl. 2, to vindicate the principle of separation of powers in *Buckley*, we see that the purposes underlying the Presentment Clauses, Art. I, §7, cls. 2, 3, and the bicameral requirement of Art. I, §1, and §7, cl. 2, guide our resolution of the important question presented in these cases. The very structure of the

Articles delegating and separating powers under Arts. I, II, and III exemplifies the concept of separation of powers, and we now turn to Art. I.

B. The Presentment Clauses

The records of the Constitutional Convention reveal that the requirement that all legislation be presented to the President before becoming law was uniformly accepted by the Framers. Presentment to the President and the Presidential veto were considered so imperative that the draftsmen took special pains to assure that these requirements could not be circumvented. During the final debate on Art. I, §7, cl. 2, James Madison expressed concern that it might easily be evaded by the simple expedient of calling a proposed law a "resolution" or "vote," rather than a "bill." As a consequence, Art. I, §7, cl. 3, was added.

The decision to provide the President with a limited and qualified power to nullify proposed legislation by veto was based on the profound conviction of the Framers that the powers conferred on Congress were the powers to be most carefully circumscribed. It is beyond doubt that law-making was a power to be shared by both Houses and the President.

The President's role in the lawmaking process also reflects the Framers' careful efforts to check whatever propensity a particular Congress might have to enact oppressive, improvident, or ill-considered measures. The President's veto role in the legislative process was described later during public debate on ratification:

> It establishes a salutary check upon the legislative body, calculated to guard the community against the effects of faction, precipitancy, or of any impulse unfriendly to the public good, which may happen to influence a majority of that body.
>
> . . . The primary inducement to conferring the power in question upon the Executive is to enable him to defend himself; the secondary one is to increase the chances in favor of the community against the passing of bad laws, through haste, inadvertence, or design.

The Federalist No. 73 (A. Hamilton). The Court also has observed that the Presentment Clauses serve the important purpose of assuring that a "national" perspective is grafted on the legislative process:

> The President is a representative of the people just as the members of the Senate and of the House are, and it may be, at some times, on some subjects, that the President elected by all the people is rather more representative of them all than are the members of either body of the Legislature, whose constituencies are local and not countrywide. . . .

Myers v. United States, supra, at 123.

C. Bicameralism

The bicameral requirement of Art. I, §§1, 7, was of scarcely less concern to the Framers than was the Presidential veto, and indeed the two concepts are interdependent. By providing that no law could take effect without the concurrence of the prescribed majority of the Members of both Houses, the Framers reemphasized their belief, already remarked upon in connection with the Presentment Clauses, that legislation should not be enacted unless it has been carefully and fully considered by the Nation's elected officials. In the Constitutional Convention debates on the need for a bicameral legislature, James Wilson, later to become a Justice of this Court, commented:

> Despotism comes on mankind in different shapes, sometimes in an Executive, sometimes in a military, one. Is there danger of a Legislative despotism? Theory & practice both

> proclaim it. If the Legislative authority be not restrained, there can be neither liberty nor stability; and it can only be restrained by dividing it within itself, into distinct and independent branches. In a single house there is no check but the inadequate one of the virtue & good sense of those who compose it.

However familiar, it is useful to recall that, apart from their fear that special interests could be favored at the expense of public needs, the Framers were also concerned, although not of one mind, over the apprehensions of the smaller states. Those states feared a commonality of interest among the larger states would work to their disadvantage; representatives of the larger states, on the other hand, were skeptical of a legislature that could pass laws favoring a minority of the people. It need hardly be repeated here that the Great Compromise, under which one House was viewed as representing the people and the other the states, allayed the fears of both the large and small states.

We see therefore that the Framers were acutely conscious that the bicameral requirement and the Presentment Clauses would serve essential constitutional functions. The President's participation in the legislative process was to protect the Executive Branch from Congress and to protect the whole people from improvident laws. The division of the Congress into two distinctive bodies assures that the legislative power would be exercised only after opportunity for full study and debate in separate settings. The President's unilateral veto power, in turn, was limited by the power of two-thirds of both Houses of Congress to overrule a veto, thereby precluding final arbitrary action of one person. It emerges clearly that the prescription for legislative action in Art. I, §§1, 7, represents the Framers' decision that the legislative power of the Federal Government be exercised in accord with a single, finely wrought and exhaustively considered, procedure.

Although not "hermetically" sealed from one another, *Buckley v. Valeo*, the powers delegated to the three Branches are functionally identifiable. When any Branch acts, it is presumptively exercising the power the Constitution has delegated to it. When the Executive acts, he presumptively acts in an executive or administrative capacity as defined in Art. II. And when, as here, one House of Congress purports to act, it is presumptively acting within its assigned sphere.

Beginning with this presumption, we must nevertheless establish that the challenged action under §244(c)(2) is of the kind to which the procedural requirements of Art. I, §7, apply. Not every action taken by either House is subject to the bicameralism and presentment requirements of Art. I. Whether actions taken by either House are, in law and fact, an exercise of legislative power depends not on their form, but upon "whether they contain matter which is properly to be regarded as legislative in its character and effect."

Examination of the action taken here by one House pursuant to §244(c)(2) reveals that it was essentially legislative in purpose and effect. In purporting to exercise power defined in Art. I, §8, cl. 4, to "establish an uniform Rule of Naturalization," the House took action that had the purpose and effect of altering the legal rights, duties, and relations of persons, including the Attorney General, Executive Branch officials and Chadha, all outside the Legislative Branch. Section 244(c)(2) purports to authorize one House of Congress to require the Attorney General to deport an individual alien whose deportation otherwise would be canceled under §244. The one-House veto operated in these cases to overrule the Attorney General and mandate Chadha's deportation; absent the House action, Chadha would remain in the United States. Congress has acted, and its action has altered Chadha's status.

The legislative character of the one-House veto in these cases is confirmed by the character of the congressional action it supplants. Neither the House of Representatives nor the Senate contends that, absent the veto provision in §244(c)(2), either of them, or both of them acting together, could effectively require the Attorney General to deport an alien once the Attorney General, in the exercise of legislatively delegated authority, had determined the alien should remain in the United States. Without the challenged provision in §244(c)(2), this could have been achieved, if at all, only by legislation requiring deportation. Similarly, a veto by one House of Congress under §244(c)(2) cannot be justified as an attempt at amending the standards set out in §244(a)(1), or as a repeal of §244 as applied to Chadha. Amendment and repeal of statutes, no less than enactment, must conform with Art. I.

The nature of the decision implemented by the one-House veto in these cases further manifests its legislative character. After long experience with the clumsy, time-consuming private bill procedure, Congress made a deliberate choice to delegate to the Executive Branch, and specifically to the Attorney General, the authority to allow deportable aliens to remain in this country in certain specified circumstances. It is not disputed that this choice to delegate authority is precisely the kind of decision that can be implemented only in accordance with the procedures set out in Art. I. Disagreement with the Attorney General's decision on Chadha's deportation — that is, Congress' decision to deport Chadha — no less than Congress' original choice to delegate to the Attorney General the authority to make that decision, involves determinations of policy that Congress can implement in only one way; bicameral passage followed by presentment to the President. Congress must abide by its delegation of authority until that delegation is legislatively altered or revoked.

Finally, we see that, when the Framers intended to authorize either House of Congress to act alone and outside of its prescribed bicameral legislative role, they narrowly and precisely defined the procedure for such action. There are four provisions in the Constitution, explicit and unambiguous, by which one House may act alone with the unreviewable force of law, not subject to the President's veto:

> (a) The House of Representatives alone was given the power to initiate impeachments. Art. I, §2, cl. 5;
>
> (b) The Senate alone was given the power to conduct trials following impeachment on charges initiated by the House, and to convict following trial. Art. I, §3, cl. 6;
>
> (c) The Senate alone was given final unreviewable power to approve or to disapprove Presidential appointments. Art. II, §2, cl. 2;
>
> (d) The Senate alone was given unreviewable power to ratify treaties negotiated by the President. Art. II, §2, cl. 2.

Clearly, when the Draftsmen sought to confer special powers on one House, independent of the other House, or of the President, they did so in explicit, unambiguous terms. These carefully defined exceptions from presentment and bicameralism underscore the difference between the legislative functions of Congress and other unilateral but important and binding one-House acts provided for in the Constitution. These exceptions are narrow, explicit, and separately justified; none of them authorize the action challenged here. On the contrary, they provide further support for the conclusion that congressional authority is not to be implied, and for the conclusion that the veto provided for in §244(c)(2) is not authorized by the constitutional design of the powers of the Legislative Branch. . . .

We hold that the congressional veto provision in §244(c)(2) is severable from the Act, and that it is unconstitutional.

JUSTICE POWELL, *concurring in the judgment.*

The Court's decision, based on the Presentment Clauses, Art. I, §7, cls. 2 and 3, apparently will invalidate every use of the legislative veto. The breadth of this holding gives one pause. Congress has included the veto in literally hundreds of statutes, dating back to the 1930's. Congress clearly views this procedure as essential to controlling the delegation of power to administrative agencies. One reasonably may disagree with Congress' assessment of the veto's utility, but the respect due its judgment as a coordinate branch of Government cautions that our holding should be no more extensive than necessary to decide these cases. In my view, the cases may be decided on a narrower ground. When Congress finds that a particular person does not satisfy the statutory criteria for permanent residence in this country, it has assumed a judicial function in violation of the principle of separation of powers. Accordingly, I concur only in the judgment. . . .

II

On its face, the House's action appears clearly adjudicatory. The House did not enact a general rule; rather, it made its own determination that six specific persons did not comply with certain statutory criteria. It thus undertook the type of decision that traditionally has been left to other branches. Even if the House did not make a *de novo* determination, but simply reviewed the Immigration and Naturalization Service's findings, it still assumed a function ordinarily entrusted to the federal courts. *See* 5 U.S.C. §704 (providing generally for judicial review of final agency action); *cf. Foti v. INS* (holding that courts of appeals have jurisdiction to review INS decisions denying suspension of deportation). Where, as here, Congress has exercised a power "that cannot possibly be regarded as merely in aid of the legislative function of Congress," *Buckley v. Valeo*, the decisions of this Court have held that Congress impermissibly assumed a function that the Constitution entrusted to another branch.

The impropriety of the House's assumption of this function is confirmed by the fact that its action raises the very danger the Framers sought to avoid—the exercise of unchecked power. In deciding whether Chadha deserves to be deported, Congress is not subject to any internal constraints that prevent it from arbitrarily depriving him of the right to remain in this country. Unlike the judiciary or an administrative agency, Congress is not bound by established substantive rules. Nor is it subject to the procedural safeguards, such as the right to counsel and a hearing before an impartial tribunal, that are present when a court or an agency adjudicates individual rights. The only effective constraint on Congress' power is political, but Congress is most accountable politically when it prescribes rules of general applicability. When it decides rights of specific persons, those rights are subject to "the tyranny of a shifting majority."

Chief Justice Marshall observed:

> It is the peculiar province of the legislature to prescribe general rules for the government of society; the application of those rules to individuals in society would seem to be the duty of other departments.

Fletcher v. Peck. In my view, when Congress undertook to apply its rules to Chadha, it exceeded the scope of its constitutionally prescribed authority. I would not reach the broader question whether legislative vetoes are invalid under the Presentment Clauses.

JUSTICE WHITE, *dissenting.*

Today the Court not only invalidates §244(c)(2) of the Immigration and Nationality Act, but also sounds the death knell for nearly 200 other statutory provisions in which Congress has reserved a "legislative veto." For this reason, the Court's decision is of surpassing importance. And it is for this reason that the Court would have been well advised to decide the cases, if possible, on the narrower grounds of separation of powers, leaving for full consideration the constitutionality of other congressional review statutes operating on such varied matters as war powers and agency rulemaking, some of which concern the independent regulatory agencies.

The prominence of the legislative veto mechanism in our contemporary political system and its importance to Congress can hardly be overstated. It has become a central means by which Congress secures the accountability of executive and independent agencies. Without the legislative veto, Congress is faced with a Hobson's choice: either to refrain from delegating the necessary authority, leaving itself with a hopeless task of writing laws with the requisite specificity to cover endless special circumstances across the entire policy landscape, or, in the alternative, to abdicate its lawmaking function to the Executive Branch and independent agencies. To choose the former leaves major national problems unresolved; to opt for the latter risks unaccountable policymaking by those not elected to fill that role. Accordingly, over the past five decades, the legislative veto has been placed in nearly 200 statutes. The device is known in every field of governmental concern: reorganization, budgets, foreign affairs, war powers, and regulation of trade, safety, energy, the environment, and the economy.

. . . [T]he legislative veto is more than "efficient, convenient, and useful." It is an important, if not indispensable, political invention that allows the President and Congress to resolve major constitutional and policy differences, assures the accountability of independent regulatory agencies, and preserves Congress' control over lawmaking. Perhaps there are other means of accommodation and accountability, but the increasing reliance of Congress upon the legislative veto suggests that the alternatives to which Congress must now turn are not entirely satisfactory.

II

If the legislative veto were as plainly unconstitutional as the Court strives to suggest, its broad ruling today would be more comprehensible. But the constitutionality of the legislative veto is anything but clear-cut. The issue divides scholars, courts, Attorneys General, and the two other branches of the National Government. If the veto devices so flagrantly disregarded the requirements of Art. I as the Court today suggests, I find it incomprehensible that Congress, whose Members are bound by oath to uphold the Constitution, would have placed these mechanisms in nearly 200 separate laws over a period of 50 years.

The reality of the situation is that the constitutional question posed today is one of immense difficulty over which the Executive and Legislative Branches — as well as scholars and judges — have understandably disagreed. That disagreement stems from the silence of the Constitution on the precise question: the Constitution does not directly authorize or prohibit the legislative veto. Thus, our task should be to determine whether the legislative veto is consistent with the purposes of Art. I and the principles of separation of powers which are reflected in that Article and throughout the Constitution. We should not find the lack of a specific constitutional authorization for the legislative veto surprising, and I would not infer disapproval of the mechanism from its absence. From the summer of 1787 to the present, the Government of the United States has become an endeavor far beyond the contemplation of the Framers. Only within the last half century has the complexity and size of the Federal Government's responsibilities grown so greatly that the Congress must rely on the legislative veto as the most effective, if not the only, means to insure its role as the Nation's lawmaker. But the wisdom of the Framers was to anticipate that the Nation would grow and new problems of governance would require different solutions. Accordingly, our Federal Government was intentionally chartered with the flexibility to respond to contemporary needs without losing sight of fundamental democratic principles. This was the spirit in which Justice Jackson penned his influential concurrence in the *Steel Seizure Case*:

> The actual art of governing under our Constitution does not and cannot conform to judicial definitions of the power of any of its branches based on isolated clauses or even single Articles torn from context. While the Constitution diffuses power the better to secure liberty, it also contemplates that practice will integrate the dispersed powers into a workable government.

Youngstown Sheet & Tube Co. v. Sawyer.

This is the perspective from which we should approach the novel constitutional questions presented by the legislative veto. In my view, neither Art. I of the Constitution nor the doctrine of separation of powers is violated by this mechanism by which our elected Representatives preserve their voice in the governance of the Nation.

III

B

. . . The Court's holding today that all legislative-type action must be enacted through the lawmaking process ignores that legislative authority is routinely delegated to the Executive Branch, to the independent regulatory agencies, and to private individuals and groups.

This Court's decisions sanctioning such delegations make clear that Art. I does not require all action with the effect of legislation to be passed as a law.

When agencies are authorized to prescribe law through substantive rulemaking, the administrator's regulation is not only due deference, but is accorded "legislative effect." These regulations bind courts and officers of the Federal Government, may preempt state law, and grant rights to and impose obligations on the public. In sum, they have the force of law.

If Congress may delegate lawmaking power to independent and Executive agencies, it is most difficult to understand Art. I as prohibiting Congress from also reserving a check on legislative power for itself. Absent the veto, the agencies receiving delegations of legislative or quasi-legislative power may issue regulations having the force of law without bicameral approval and without the President's signature. It is thus not apparent why the reservation of a veto over the exercise of that legislative power must be subject to a more exacting test. In both cases, it is enough that the initial statutory authorizations comply with the Art. I requirements.

Under the Court's analysis, the Executive Branch and the independent agencies may make rules with the effect of law while Congress, in whom the Framers confided the legislative power, Art. I, §1, may not exercise a veto which precludes such rules from having operative force. If the effective functioning of a complex modern government requires the delegation of vast authority which, by virtue of its breadth, is legislative or "quasi-legislative" in character, I cannot accept that Art. I—which is, after all, the source of the nondelegation doctrine — should forbid Congress to qualify that grant with a legislative veto.

C

The Court also takes no account of perhaps the most relevant consideration: however resolutions of disapproval under §244(c)(2) are formally characterized, in reality, a departure from the *status quo* occurs only upon the concurrence of opinion among the House, Senate, and President. Reservations of legislative authority to be exercised by Congress should be upheld if the exercise of such reserved authority is consistent with the distribution of and limits upon legislative power that Art. I provides.

1

The history of the Immigration and Nationality Act makes clear that §244(c)(2) did not alter the division of actual authority between Congress and the Executive. At all times, whether through private bills, or through affirmative concurrent resolutions, or through the present one-House veto, a permanent change in a deportable alien's status could be accomplished only with the agreement of the Attorney General, the House, and the Senate.

2

The central concern of the presentment and bicameralism requirements of Art. I is that, when a departure from the legal *status quo* is undertaken, it is done with the approval of the President and both Houses of Congress — or, in the event of a Presidential veto, a two-thirds majority in both Houses. This interest is fully satisfied by the operation of §244(c)(2). The President's approval is found in the Attorney General's action in recommending to Congress that the deportation order for a given alien be suspended. The House and the Senate indicate their approval of the Executive's action by not passing a resolution of disapproval within the statutory period. Thus, a change in the legal *status quo* — the deportability of the alien — is consummated only with the approval of each of the three relevant actors. The disagreement of any one of the three maintains the alien's preexisting status: the Executive may choose not to recommend suspension; the House and Senate may each veto the recommendation. The effect on the rights and obligations of the affected individuals and upon the legislative system is precisely the same as if a private bill were introduced but failed to receive the necessary approval.

Thus understood, §244(c)(2) fully effectuates the purposes of the bicameralism and presentment requirements.

Nor does §244 infringe on the judicial power, as Justice Powell would hold. Section 244 makes clear that Congress has reserved its own judgment as part of the statutory process. Congressional action does not substitute for judicial review of the Attorney General's decisions. The Act provides for judicial review of the refusal of the Attorney General to suspend a deportation and to transmit a recommendation to Congress. *INS v. Jong Ha Wang* (per curiam). But the courts have not been given the authority to review whether an alien should be given permanent status; review is limited to whether the Attorney General has properly applied the statutory standards for essentially denying the alien a recommendation that his deportable status be changed by the Congress.

V

I regret that I am in disagreement with my colleagues on the fundamental questions that these cases present. But even more I regret the destructive scope of the

Court's holding. It reflects a profoundly different conception of the Constitution than that held by the courts which sanctioned the modern administrative state. Today's decision strikes down in one fell swoop provisions in more laws enacted by Congress than the Court has cumulatively invalidated in its history. I fear it will now be more difficult to "insur[e] that the fundamental policy decisions in our society will be made not by an appointed official, but by the body immediately responsible to the people," *Arizona v. California* (Harlan, J., dissenting in part). I must dissent.

BOWSHER v. SYNAR

478 U.S. 714 (1986)

Opinion: Burger, joined by Brennan, Powell, Rehnquist, O'Connor
Concurrence: Stevens, joined by Marshall
Dissent: White
Dissent: Blackmun

In this case, the Court considers the constitutionality of an act in which Congress allocated power to the comptroller general, an executive official who is subject to removal from office by congressional action, to play a critical role in the execution of its legislation. Would this unconstitutionally allow Congress to not only create legislation, but also to execute it? If so, is this a usurpation of executive power? Just how separate must the powers of the legislative and executive branches be? Is it possible to fully separate the two? How does the ability to fire an official relate to the broader issue of separation of powers?

CHIEF JUSTICE BURGER *delivered the opinion of the Court.*

The question presented by these appeals is whether the assignment by Congress to the Comptroller General of the United States of certain functions under the Balanced Budget and Emergency Deficit Control Act of 1985 violates the doctrine of separation of powers.

On December 12, 1985, the President signed into law the Balanced Budget and Emergency Deficit Control Act of 1985, popularly known as the "Gramm-Rudman-Hollings Act." The purpose of the Act is to eliminate the federal budget deficit. To that end, the Act sets a "maximum deficit amount" for federal spending for each of fiscal years 1986 through 1991. The size of that maximum deficit amount progressively reduces to zero in fiscal year 1991. If in any fiscal year the federal budget deficit exceeds the maximum deficit amount by more than a specified sum, the Act requires across-the-board cuts in federal spending to reach the targeted deficit level, with half of the cuts made to defense programs and the other half made to nondefense programs. The Act exempts certain priority programs from these cuts.

These "automatic" reductions are accomplished through a rather complicated procedure, spelled out in §251, the so-called "reporting provisions" of the Act. Each year, the Directors of the Office of Management and Budget (OMB) and the Congressional Budget Office (CBO) independently estimate the amount of the federal budget deficit for the upcoming fiscal year. If that deficit exceeds the maximum targeted deficit amount for that fiscal year by more than a specified amount, the Directors of OMB and CBO independently calculate, on a program-by-program basis, the budget reductions necessary to ensure that the deficit does not exceed the maximum deficit amount. The Act then requires the Directors to report jointly their deficit estimates and budget reduction calculations to the Comptroller General.

The Comptroller General, after reviewing the Directors' reports, then reports his conclusions to the President. §251(b). The President, in turn, must issue a "sequestration" order mandating the spending reductions specified by the Comptroller General. §252. There follows a period during which Congress may by legislation reduce spending to obviate, in whole or in part, the need for the sequestration order. If such reductions are not enacted, the sequestration order becomes effective and the spending reductions included in that order are made.

Anticipating constitutional challenge to these procedures, the Act also contains a "fallback" deficit reduction process to take effect "[i]n the event that any of the reporting procedures described in section 251 are invalidated." §274(f). Under these provisions, the report prepared by the Directors of OMB and the CBO is submitted directly to a specially created Temporary Joint Committee on Deficit Reduction, which must report in five days to both Houses a joint resolution setting forth the content of the Directors' report. Congress then must vote on the resolution under special rules, which render amendments out of order. If the resolution is passed and signed by the President, it then serves as the basis for a Presidential sequestration order.

Within hours of the President's signing of the Act, Congressman Synar, who had voted against the Act, filed a complaint seeking declaratory relief that the Act was unconstitutional. Eleven other Members later joined Congressman Synar's suit. A virtually identical lawsuit was also filed by the National Treasury Employees Union. The Union alleged that its members had been injured as a result of the Act's automatic spending reduction provisions, which have suspended certain cost-of-living benefit increases to the Union's members.

We noted recently that "[t]he Constitution sought to divide the delegated powers of the new Federal Government into three defined categories, Legislative, Executive, and Judicial." *INS v. Chadha.* The declared purpose of separating and dividing the powers of government, of course, was to "diffus[e] power the better to secure liberty." *Youngstown Sheet & Tube Co. v. Sawyer*, (Jackson, J., concurring). Justice Jackson's words echo the famous warning of Montesquieu, quoted by James Madison in *The Federalist* No. 47, that " 'there can be no liberty where the legislative and executive powers are united in the same person, or body of magistrates'. . . ." *The Federalist* No. 47, p. 325 (J. Cooke ed. 1961).

Even a cursory examination of the Constitution reveals the influence of Montesquieu's thesis that checks and balances were the foundation of a structure of government that would protect liberty. The Framers provided a vigorous Legislative Branch and a separate and wholly independent Executive Branch, with each branch responsible ultimately to the people. The Framers also provided for a Judicial Branch equally independent, with "[t]he judicial Power . . . extend[ing] to all Cases, in Law and Equity, arising under this Constitution, and the Laws of the United States." Art. III, §2.

That this system of division and separation of powers produces conflicts, confusion, and discordance at times is inherent, but it was deliberately so structured to assure full, vigorous, and open debate on the great issues affecting the people, and to provide avenues for the operation of checks on the exercise of governmental power.

The Constitution does not contemplate an active role for Congress in the supervision of officers charged with the execution of the laws it enacts. The President appoints "Officers of the United States" with the "Advice and Consent of the Senate. . . ." Art. II, §2. Once the appointment has been made and confirmed, however, the Constitution explicitly provides for removal of Officers of the United States by Congress only upon impeachment by the House of Representatives and conviction by the Senate. An impeachment by the House and trial by the Senate can rest only on "Treason, Bribery or other high Crimes and Misdemeanors." Art. II, §4. A direct congressional role in the removal of officers charged with the execution of the laws beyond this limited one is inconsistent with separation of powers.

. . . [We] conclude that Congress cannot reserve for itself the power of removal of an officer charged with the execution of the laws except by impeachment. To permit the execution of the laws to be vested in an officer answerable only to Congress would, in practical terms, reserve in Congress control over the execution of the laws.

The structure of the Constitution does not permit Congress to execute the laws; it follows that Congress cannot grant to an officer under its control what it does not possess.

To permit an officer controlled by Congress to execute the laws would be, in essence, to permit a congressional veto. Congress could simply remove, or threaten to remove, an officer for executing the laws in any fashion found to be unsatisfactory to Congress. This kind of congressional control over the execution of the laws, *Chadha* makes clear, is constitutionally impermissible.

The dangers of congressional usurpation of Executive Branch functions have long been recognized. "[T]he debates of the Constitutional Convention, and the *Federalist Papers*, are replete with expressions of fear that the Legislative Branch of the National Government will aggrandize itself at the expense of the other two branches." *Buckley v. Valeo*. Indeed, we also have observed only recently that "[t]he hydraulic pressure inherent within each of the separate Branches to exceed the outer limits of its power, even to accomplish desirable objectives, must be resisted." *Chadha, supra*, at 951. With these principles in mind, we turn to consideration of whether the Comptroller General is controlled by Congress.

The critical factor lies in the provisions of the statute defining the Comptroller General's office relating to removability. Although the Comptroller General is nominated by the President from a list of three individuals recommended by the Speaker of the House of Representatives and the President *pro tempore* of the Senate, *see* 31 U.S.C. §703(a)(2), and confirmed by the Senate, he is removable only at the initiative of Congress. He may be removed not only by impeachment, but also by joint resolution of Congress "at any time" resting on any one of the following bases:

(i) permanent disability;
(ii) inefficiency;
(iii) neglect of duty;
(iv) malfeasance; or
(v) a felony or conduct involving moral turpitude.

31 U.S.C. §703(e)(1)B.

The statute permits removal for "inefficiency," "neglect of duty," or "malfeasance." These terms are very broad and, as interpreted by Congress, could sustain removal of a Comptroller General for any number of actual or perceived transgressions of the legislative will. The Constitutional Convention chose to permit impeachment of executive officers only for "Treason, Bribery, or other high Crimes and Misdemeanors." It rejected language that would have permitted impeachment for "maladministration," with Madison arguing that "[s]o vague a term will be equivalent to a tenure during pleasure of the Senate."

In constitutional terms, the removal powers over the Comptroller General's office dictate that he will be subservient to Congress.

It is clear that Congress has consistently viewed the Comptroller General as an officer of the Legislative Branch. The Reorganization Acts of 1945 and 1949, for example, both stated that the Comptroller General and the GAO are "a part of the legislative branch of the Government." 59 Stat. 616; 63 Stat. 205. Similarly, in the Accounting and Auditing Act of 1950, Congress required the Comptroller General to conduct audits "as an agent of the Congress." 64 Stat. 835.

Over the years, the Comptrollers General have also viewed themselves as part of the Legislative Branch. Against this background, we see no escape from the conclusion that, because Congress has retained removal authority over the Comptroller General, he may not be entrusted with executive powers. The remaining question is whether the Comptroller General has been assigned such powers in the Balanced Budget and Emergency Deficit Control Act of 1985.

Appellants suggest that the duties assigned to the Comptroller General in the Act are essentially ministerial and mechanical, so that their performance does not constitute "execution of the law" in a meaningful sense. On the contrary, we view these functions as plainly entailing execution of the law in constitutional terms. Interpreting a law enacted by Congress to implement the legislative mandate is the very essence of "execution" of the law. Under §251, the Comptroller General must exercise judgment concerning facts that affect the application of the Act. He must also interpret the provisions of the Act to determine precisely what budgetary calculations are required. Decisions of that kind are typically made by officers charged with executing a statute.

The executive nature of the Comptroller General's functions under the Act is revealed in §252(a)(3), which gives the Comptroller General the ultimate authority to determine the budget cuts to be made.

By placing the responsibility for execution of the Balanced Budget and Emergency Deficit Control Act in the hands of an officer who is subject to removal only by itself, Congress, in effect, has retained control over the execution of the Act, and has intruded into the executive function. The Constitution does not permit such intrusion.

JUSTICE WHITE, *dissenting.*

The Court, acting in the name of separation of powers, takes upon itself to strike down the Gramm-Rudman-Hollings Act, one of the most novel and far-reaching legislative responses to a national crisis since the New Deal. The basis of the Court's action is a solitary provision of another statute that was passed over 60 years ago and has lain dormant since that time. I cannot concur in the Court's action. Like the Court, I will not purport to speak to the wisdom of the policies incorporated in the legislation the Court invalidates; that is a matter for the Congress and the Executive, both of which expressed their assent to the statute barely half a year ago. I will, however, address the wisdom of the Court's willingness to interpose its distressingly formalistic view of separation of powers as a bar to the attainment of governmental objectives through the means chosen by the Congress and the President in the legislative process established by the Constitution....

II

If, as the Court seems to agree, the assignment of "executive" powers under Gramm-Rudman-Hollings to an officer not removable at will by the President would not, in itself, represent a violation of the constitutional scheme of separated powers, the question remains whether, as the Court concludes, the fact that the officer to whom Congress has delegated the authority to implement the Act is removable by a joint resolution of Congress should require invalidation of the Act. The Court's decision, as I have stated above, is based on a syllogism: the Act vests the Comptroller with "executive power"; such power may not be exercised by Congress or its agents; the Comptroller is an agent of Congress because he is removable by Congress; therefore the Act is invalid. I have no quarrel with the proposition that the powers exercised by the Comptroller under the Act may be characterized as "executive" in that they involve the interpretation and carrying out of the Act's mandate. I can also accept the general proposition that, although Congress has considerable authority in designating the officers who are to execute legislation, *see supra*, at 760-764, the constitutional scheme of separated powers does prevent Congress from reserving an executive role for itself or for its "agents." *Buckley v. Valeo* at 120-141; *id.* at 267-282 (White, J., concurring in part and dissenting in part). I cannot accept, however, that the exercise of authority by an officer removable for cause by a joint resolution of Congress is analogous to the impermissible execution of the law by Congress itself, nor would I hold that the congressional role in the removal process renders the Comptroller an "agent" of the Congress, incapable of receiving "executive" power....

The Act vesting budget-cutting authority in the Comptroller General represents Congress' judgment that the delegation of such authority to counteract ever-mounting deficits is "necessary and proper" to the exercise of the powers granted the Federal Government by the Constitution; and the President's approval of the statute signifies his unwillingness to reject the choice made by Congress. *Cf. Nixon v. Administrator of General Services.* Under such circumstances, the role of this Court should be limited to determining whether the Act so alters the balance of authority among the branches of government as to pose a genuine threat to the basic division between the lawmaking power and the power to execute the law. Because I see no such threat, I cannot join the Court in striking down the Act.

I dissent.

MORRISON v. OLSON

487 U.S. 654 (1988)

Opinion: Rehnquist, joined by Brennan, White, Marshall, Blackmun, Stevens, O'Connor
Dissent: Scalia

Calls for limits on executive power came with full force after the Watergate scandal of the Nixon administration. President Richard Nixon had been accused of hiring burglars to break into the headquarters of the Democratic National Committee at the Watergate complex in Washington, D.C. The scandal eventually resulted in his resignation. During the scandal, President Nixon tried to exercise what many considered to be inappropriate control over the investigation of the break-in. Specifically, he ordered one Attorney General, Elliot Richardson, to fire an independent prosecutor, Archibald Cox, who had been appointed to investigate the Watergate break-in. Richardson resigned rather than fire Cox, but a subsequent acting Attorney General, Robert Bork, who was later nominated but not confirmed to serve on the Supreme Court, did fire Cox. These events raised traditional worries about the excessive power of the president, in particular when it came to investigations about his or her own wrongdoing. During the Carter administration, Congress passed a series of reforms that included a provision to ensure the independence of attorneys charged with investigating the executive branch.

This case concerns the constitutionality of a law allowing for the appointment of an independent counsel who may be removed from office not by the president, but only by the attorney general, and even then only under extremely narrow and specific circumstances. It raises questions about the extent to which Congress may limit the power of the president to appoint and remove officials that perform executive functions. To what extent does the reasoning in this case build upon or depart from the reasoning in previous cases on the issue of the president's power to remove executive officers? Does this case repudiate Myers v. United States *and reaffirm* Humphrey's Executor v. United States? *To what extent should Congress be able to create executive offices that are independent from the control of the president? How specifically should the separation of powers be maintained? Also, if the president did have the power to fire any attorney charged with investigating him or her, would it be possible for that person to do his or her job effectively? Pay close attention to the arguments about democratic accountability in the dissent by U.S. Supreme Court Justice Antonin Scalia.*

CHIEF JUSTICE REHNQUIST *delivered the opinion of the Court.*

This case presents us with a challenge to the independent counsel provisions of the Ethics in Government Act of 1978, 28 U.S.C. §§49, 591 *et seq.* (1982 ed., Supp. V). We hold today that these provisions of the Act do not violate the Appointments Clause of the Constitution, Art. II, §2, cl. 2, or the limitations of Article III, nor do they impermissibly interfere with the President's authority under Article II in violation of the constitutional principle of separation of powers.

Briefly stated, Title VI of the Ethics in Government Act, 28 U.S.C. §§591-599 (1982 ed., Supp. V), allows for the appointment of an "independent counsel" to investigate and, if appropriate, prosecute certain high ranking Government officials for violations of federal criminal laws. The Act requires the Attorney General, upon receipt of information that he determines is "sufficient to constitute grounds to investigate whether any person [covered by the Act] may have violated any Federal criminal law," to conduct a preliminary investigation of the matter. When the Attorney General has completed this investigation, or 90 days has elapsed, he is required to report to a special court (the Special Division) created by the Act "for the purpose of appointing independent counsels." 28 U.S.C. §49 (1982 ed., Supp. V). If the Attorney General determines that "there are no reasonable grounds to believe that further investigation is warranted," then he must notify the Special Division of this result. In such a case, "the division of the court shall have no power to appoint an independent counsel." §592(b)(1). If, however, the Attorney

General has determined that there are "reasonable grounds to believe that further investigation or prosecution is warranted," then he "shall apply to the division of the court for the appointment of an independent counsel."

Upon receiving this application, the Special Division "shall appoint an appropriate independent counsel and shall define that independent counsel's prosecutorial jurisdiction." §593(b).

With respect to all matters within the independent counsel's jurisdiction, the Act grants the counsel "full power and independent authority to exercise all investigative and prosecutorial functions and powers of the Department of Justice, the Attorney General, and any other officer or employee of the Department of Justice." §594(a).... In addition, whenever a matter has been referred to an independent counsel under the Act, the Attorney General and the Justice Department are required to suspend all investigations and proceedings regarding the matter. §597(a).

Two statutory provisions govern the length of an independent counsel's tenure in office. The first defines the procedure for removing an independent counsel. Section 596(a)(1) provides:

> An independent counsel appointed under this chapter may be removed from office, other than by impeachment and conviction, only by the personal action of the Attorney General and only for good cause, physical disability, mental incapacity, or any other condition that substantially impairs the performance of such independent counsel's duties.

If an independent counsel is removed pursuant to this section, the Attorney General is required to submit a report to both the Special Division and the Judiciary Committees of the Senate and the House "specifying the facts found and the ultimate grounds for such removal." §596(a)(2). Under the current version of the Act, an independent counsel can obtain judicial review of the Attorney General's action by filing a civil action in the United States District Court for the District of Columbia. The reviewing court is authorized to grant reinstatement or "other appropriate relief." §596(a)(3).

The other provision governing the tenure of the independent counsel defines the procedures for "terminating" the counsel's office. Under §596(b)(1), the office of an independent counsel terminates when he or she notifies the Attorney General that he or she has completed or substantially completed any investigations or prosecutions undertaken pursuant to the Act. In addition, the Special Division, acting either on its own or on the suggestion of the Attorney General, may terminate the office of an independent counsel at any time if it finds that "the investigation of all matters within the prosecutorial jurisdiction of such independent counsel . . . have been completed or so substantially completed that it would be appropriate for the Department of Justice to complete such investigations and prosecutions." §596(b)(2).

Finally, the Act provides for congressional oversight of the activities of independent counsel. An independent counsel may from time to time send Congress statements or reports on his or her activities. §595(a)(2). The "appropriate committees of the Congress" are given oversight jurisdiction in regard to the official conduct of an independent counsel, and the counsel is required by the Act to cooperate with Congress in the exercise of this jurisdiction. §595(a)(1). The counsel is required to inform the House of Representatives of "substantial and credible information which [the counsel] receives . . . that may constitute grounds for an impeachment." §595(c). In addition, the Act gives certain congressional committee members the power to "request in writing that the Attorney General apply for the appointment of an independent counsel." §592(g)(1). The Attorney General is required to respond to this request within a specified time, but is not required to accede to the request. §592(g)(2).

The proceedings in this case provide an example of how the Act works in practice. In 1982, two Subcommittees of the House of Representatives issued subpoenas directing the Environmental Protection Agency (EPA) to produce certain documents relating to the efforts of the EPA and the Land and Natural Resources Division of the Justice Department to enforce the "Superfund Law." At that time, appellee Olson was the Assistant Attorney General for the Office of Legal Counsel (OLC), appellee Schmults was Deputy Attorney General, and appellee Dinkins was the Assistant Attorney General for the Land and Natural Resources Division. Acting on the advice of the Justice Department, the President ordered the Administrator of EPA to invoke executive privilege to withhold certain of the documents on the ground that they contained "enforcement-sensitive information." The Administrator obeyed this order and withheld the documents. In response, the House voted to hold the Administrator in contempt, after which the Administrator and the United States together filed a lawsuit against the House. The conflict abated in March, 1983, when the administration agreed to give the House Committees limited access to the documents.

The following year, the House Judiciary Committee began an investigation into the Justice Department's role in the controversy over the EPA documents. During this investigation, appellee Olson testified before a House Subcommittee on March 10, 1983. Both before and after that testimony, the Department complied with several Committee requests to produce certain documents. Other documents were at first withheld, although these documents were eventually disclosed by the Department after the Committee learned of their existence. In 1985, the majority members of the Judiciary Committee published a lengthy report on the Committee's investigation. The report not only criticized various officials in the Department of Justice for their role in the EPA executive privilege dispute, but it also suggested that appellee Olson had given false and misleading testimony to the Subcommittee on March 10, 1983, and that appellees Schmults and Dinkins had wrongfully withheld certain documents from the Committee, thus obstructing the Committee's investigation. The Chairman of the Judiciary Committee forwarded a copy of the report to the Attorney General with a request, pursuant to 28 U.S.C. §592(c), that he seek the appointment of an independent counsel to investigate the allegations against Olson, Schmults, and Dinkins.

The Attorney General directed the Public Integrity Section of the Criminal Division to conduct a preliminary investigation. The Section's report concluded that the appointment of an independent counsel was warranted to investigate the Committee's allegations with respect to all three appellees. After consulting with other Department officials, however, the Attorney General chose to apply to the Special Division for the appointment of an independent counsel solely with respect to appellee Olson.

On April 23, 1986, the Special Division appointed James C. McKay as independent counsel to investigate "whether the testimony of . . . Olson and his revision of such testimony on March 10, 1983, violated either 18 U.S.C. §1505 or §1001, or any other provision of federal law." The court also ordered that the independent counsel

> shall have jurisdiction to investigate any other allegation of evidence of violation of any

> Federal criminal law by Theodore Olson developed during investigations, by the Independent Counsel, referred to above, and connected with or arising out of that investigation, and Independent Counsel shall have jurisdiction to prosecute for any such violation.

Order, Div. No. 86-1 (CADC Special Division, April 23, 1986). McKay later resigned as independent counsel, and on May 29, 1986, the Division appointed appellant Morrison as his replacement, with the same jurisdiction.

In January, 1987, appellant asked the Attorney General pursuant to §594(e) to refer to her as "related matters" the Committee's allegations against appellees Schmults and Dinkins. The Attorney General refused to refer the matters, concluding that his decision not to request the appointment of an independent counsel in regard to those matters was final under §592(b)(1). Appellant then asked the Special Division to order that the matters be referred to her under §594(e). On April 2, 1987, the Division ruled that the Attorney General's decision not to seek appointment of an independent counsel with respect to Schmults and Dinkins was final and unreviewable under §592(b)(1), and that therefore the court had no authority to make the requested referral. The court ruled, however, that its original grant of jurisdiction to appellant was broad enough to permit inquiry into whether Olson may have conspired with others, including Schmults and Dinkins, to obstruct the Committee's investigation.

Following this ruling, in May and June, 1987, appellant caused a grand jury to issue and serve subpoenas on appellees. All three appellees moved to quash the subpoenas, claiming, among other things, that the independent counsel provisions of the Act were unconstitutional, and that appellant accordingly had no authority to proceed.

The Appointments Clause of Article II reads as follows:

> [The President] shall nominate, and by and with the Advice and Consent of the Senate, shall appoint Ambassadors, other public Ministers and Consuls, Judges of the supreme Court, and all other Officers of the United States, whose Appointments are not herein otherwise provided for, and which shall be established by Law: but the Congress may by Law vest the Appointment of such inferior Officers, as they think proper, in the President alone, in the Courts of Law, or in the Heads of Departments.

U.S. Const., Art. II, §2, cl. 2. The parties do not dispute that "[t]he Constitution for purposes of appointment . . . divides all its officers into two classes." *United States v. Germaine*. As we stated in *Buckley v. Valeo*:

> Principal officers are selected by the President with the advice and consent of the Senate. Inferior officers Congress may allow to be appointed by the President alone, by the heads of departments, or by the Judiciary.

The initial question is, accordingly, whether appellant is an "inferior" or a "principal" officer. If she is the latter, as the Court of Appeals concluded, then the Act is in violation of the Appointments Clause.

The line between "inferior" and "principal" officers is one that is far from clear, and the Framers provided little guidance into where it should be drawn. We need not attempt here to decide exactly where the line falls between the two types of officers, because, in our view, appellant clearly falls on the "inferior officer" side of that line. Several factors lead to this conclusion.

First, appellant is subject to removal by a higher Executive Branch official. . . . Second, appellant is empowered by the Act to perform only certain, limited duties. An independent counsel's role is restricted primarily to investigation and, if appropriate, prosecution for certain federal crimes....

Third, appellant's office is limited in jurisdiction. Not only is the Act itself restricted in applicability to certain federal officials suspected of certain serious federal crimes, but an independent counsel can only act within the scope of the jurisdiction that has been granted by the Special Division pursuant to a request by the Attorney General. Finally, appellant's office is limited in tenure. There is concededly no time limit on the appointment of a particular counsel. Nonetheless, the office of independent counsel is "temporary" in the sense that an independent counsel is appointed essentially to accomplish a single task, and when that task is over, the office is terminated, either by the counsel herself or by action of the Special Division....

This does not, however, end our inquiry under the Appointments Clause. Appellees argue that, even if appellant is an "inferior" officer, the Clause does not empower Congress to place the power to appoint such an officer outside the Executive Branch. They contend that the Clause does not contemplate congressional authorization of "interbranch appointments," in which an officer of one branch is appointed by officers of another branch. The relevant language of the Appointments Clause is worth repeating. It reads:

> . . . but the Congress may by Law vest the Appointment of such inferior Officers, as they think proper, in the President alone, in the courts of Law, or in the Heads of Departments.

On its face, the language of this "excepting clause" admits of no limitation on interbranch appointments. Indeed, the inclusion of "as they think proper" seems clearly to give Congress significant discretion to determine whether it is "proper" to vest the appointment of, for example, executive officials in the "courts of Law."

We do not mean to say that Congress' power to provide for interbranch appointments of "inferior officers" is unlimited. In addition to separation of powers concerns, which would arise if such provisions for appointment had the potential to impair the constitutional functions assigned to one of the branches, *Siebold* itself suggested that Congress' decision to vest the appointment power in the courts would be improper if there was some "incongruity" between the functions normally performed by the courts and the performance of their duty to appoint. 100 U.S. at 398.

In this case, however, we do not think it impermissible for Congress to vest the power to appoint independent counsel in a specially created federal court. We thus disagree with the Court of Appeals' conclusion that there is an inherent incongruity about a court having the power to appoint prosecutorial officers. We have recognized that courts may appoint private attorneys to act as prosecutor for judicial contempt judgments. *See Young v. United States ex rel. Vuitton et Fils S.A.* In *Go-Bart Importing Co. v. United States*, we approved court appointment of United States commissioners, who exercised certain limited prosecutorial powers. *Id.* at 353, n. 2. In *Siebold*, as well, we indicated that judicial appointment of federal marshals, who are "executive officer[s]," would not be inappropriate.

Congress of course was concerned when it created the office of independent counsel with the conflicts of interest that could arise in situations when the Executive Branch is called upon to investigate its own high-ranking officers. If it were to remove the appointing authority from the Executive Branch, the most logical place to put it was in the Judicial Branch. In the light of the Act's provision making the judges of the Special Division ineligible to participate in any matters relating to an independent counsel they have appointed,

28 U.S.C. §49(f) (1982 ed., Supp. V), we do not think that appointment of the independent counsel by the court runs afoul of the constitutional limitation on "incongruous" interbranch appointments.

Appellees next contend that the powers vested in the Special Division by the Act conflict with Article III of the Constitution. We have long recognized that by the express provision of Article III, the judicial power of the United States is limited to "Cases" and "Controversies." *See Muskrat v. United States.* As a general rule, we have broadly stated that "executive or administrative duties of a nonjudicial nature may not be imposed on judges holding office under Art. III of the Constitution." *Buckley*, at 123 (citing *United States v. Ferreira*; *Hayburn's Case*). The purpose of this limitation is to help ensure the independence of the Judicial Branch and to prevent the judiciary from encroaching into areas reserved for the other branches. *See United States Parole Comm'n v. Geraghty.* With this in mind, we address in turn the various duties given to the Special Division by the Act.

Most importantly, the Act vests in the Special Division the power to choose who will serve as independent counsel and the power to define his or her jurisdiction. §593(b). Clearly, once it is accepted that the Appointments Clause gives Congress the power to vest the appointment of officials such as the independent counsel in the "courts of Law," there can be no Article III objection to the Special Division's exercise of that power, as the power itself derives from the Appointments Clause, a source of authority for judicial action that is independent of Article III. Appellees contend, however, that the Division's Appointments Clause powers do not encompass the power to define the independent counsel's jurisdiction. We disagree. In our view, Congress' power under the Clause to vest the "Appointment" of inferior officers in the courts may, in certain circumstances, allow Congress to give the courts some discretion in defining the nature and scope of the appointed official's authority. Particularly when, as here, Congress creates a temporary "office" the nature and duties of which will by necessity vary with the factual circumstances giving rise to the need for an appointment in the first place, it may vest the power to define the scope of the office in the court as an incident to the appointment of the officer pursuant to the Appointments Clause. This said, we do not think that Congress may give the Division unlimited discretion to determine the independent counsel's jurisdiction. In order for the Division's definition of the counsel's jurisdiction to be truly "incidental" to its power to appoint, the jurisdiction that the court decides upon must be demonstrably related to the factual circumstances that gave rise to the Attorney General's investigation and request for the appointment of the independent counsel in the particular case.

We are more doubtful about the Special Division's power to terminate the office of the independent counsel pursuant to §596(b)(2). As appellees suggest, the power to terminate, especially when exercised by the Division on its own motion, is "administrative" to the extent that it requires the Special Division to monitor the progress of proceedings of the independent counsel and come to a decision as to whether the counsel's job is "completed." §596(b)(2). It also is not a power that could be considered typically "judicial," as it has few analogues among the court's more traditional powers. Nonetheless, we do not, as did the Court of Appeals, view this provision as a significant judicial encroachment upon executive power or upon the prosecutorial discretion of the independent counsel.

The termination provisions of the Act do not give the Special Division anything approaching the power to remove the counsel while an investigation or court proceeding is still underway—this power is vested solely in the Attorney General. As we see it, "termination" may occur only when the duties of the counsel are truly "completed" or "so substantially completed" that there remains no need for any continuing action by the independent counsel. It is basically a device for removing from the public payroll an independent counsel who has served his or her purpose, but is unwilling to acknowledge the fact. So construed, the Special Division's power to terminate does not pose a sufficient threat of judicial intrusion into matters that are more properly within the Executive's authority to require that the Act be invalidated as inconsistent with Article III.

We now turn to consider whether the Act is invalid under the constitutional principle of separation of powers. Two related issues must be addressed: the first is whether the provision of the Act restricting the Attorney General's power to remove the independent counsel to only those instances in which he can show "good cause," taken by itself, impermissibly interferes with the President's exercise of his constitutionally appointed functions. The second is whether, taken as a whole, the Act violates the separation of powers by reducing the President's ability to control the prosecutorial powers wielded by the independent counsel.

Unlike both *Bowsher* and *Myers*, this case does not involve an attempt by Congress itself to gain a role in the removal of executive officials other than its established powers of impeachment and conviction. The Act instead puts the removal power squarely in the hands of the Executive Branch; an independent counsel may be removed from office, "only by the personal action of the Attorney General, and only for good cause." §596(a)(1). There is no requirement of congressional approval of the Attorney General's removal decision, though the decision is subject to judicial review. §596(a)(3). In our view, the removal provisions of the Act make this case more analogous to *Humphrey's Executor v. United States*, and *Wiener v. United States*, than to *Myers* or *Bowsher*.

. . . Appellees contend that *Humphrey's Executor* and *Wiener* are distinguishable from this case because they did not involve officials who performed a "core executive function." They argue that our decision in *Humphrey's Executor* rests on a distinction between "purely executive" officials and officials who exercise "quasi-legislative" and "quasi-judicial" powers. In their view, when a "purely executive" official is involved, the governing precedent is *Myers*, not *Humphrey's Executor*. And, under *Myers*, the President must have absolute discretion to discharge "purely" executive officials at will.

We undoubtedly did rely on the terms "quasi-legislative" and "quasi-judicial" to distinguish the officials involved in *Humphrey's Executor* and *Wiener* from those in *Myers*, but our present considered view is that the determination of whether the Constitution allows Congress to impose a "good cause"–type restriction on the President's power to remove an official cannot be made to turn on whether or not that official is classified as "purely executive." The analysis contained in our removal cases is designed not to define rigid categories of those officials who may or may not be removed at will by the President, but to ensure that Congress does not interfere with the President's exercise of the "executive power" and his constitutionally appointed duty to "take care that the laws be faithfully executed" under Article II. . . .

Considering for the moment the "good cause" removal provision in isolation from the other parts of the Act at issue in this case, we cannot say that the imposition of a "good cause" standard for removal by itself unduly trammels on executive authority. There is no real dispute that the functions performed by the independent counsel are "executive" in the sense that they are law enforcement functions that typically have been undertaken by officials within the Executive Branch. As we noted above, however, the independent counsel is an inferior officer under the Appointments Clause, with limited jurisdiction and tenure and lacking policymaking or significant administrative authority. Although the counsel exercises no small amount of discretion and judgment in deciding how to carry out his or her duties under the Act, we simply do not see how the President's need to control the exercise of that discretion is so central to the functioning of the Executive Branch as to require as a matter of constitutional law that the counsel be terminable at will by the President.

Nor do we think that the "good cause" removal provision at issue here impermissibly burdens the President's power to control or supervise the independent counsel, as an executive official, in the execution of his or her duties under the Act. This is not a case in which the power to remove an executive official has been completely stripped from the President, thus providing no means for the President to ensure the "faithful execution" of the laws. Rather, because the independent counsel may be terminated for "good cause," the Executive, through the Attorney General, retains ample authority to assure that the counsel is competently performing his or her statutory responsibilities in a manner that comports with the provisions of the Act. Here, as with the provision of the Act conferring the appointment authority of the independent counsel on the special court, the congressional determination to limit the removal power of the Attorney General was essential, in the view of Congress, to establish the necessary independence of the office. We do not think that this limitation as it presently stands sufficiently deprives the President of control over the independent counsel to interfere impermissibly with his constitutional obligation to ensure the faithful execution of the laws.

The final question to be addressed is whether the Act, taken as a whole, violates the principle of separation of powers by unduly interfering with the role of the Executive Branch. Time and again we have reaffirmed the importance in our constitutional scheme of the separation of governmental powers into the three coordinate branches. As we stated in *Buckley v. Valeo*, the system of separated powers and checks and balances established in the Constitution was regarded by the Framers as "a self-executing safeguard against the encroachment or aggrandizement of one branch at the expense of the other." *Id.* at 122. We have not hesitated to invalidate provisions of law which violate this principle. On the other hand, we have never held that the Constitution requires that the three Branches of Government "operate with absolute independence." *United States v. Nixon*. In the often-quoted words of Justice Jackson:

> While the Constitution diffuses power the better to secure liberty, it also contemplates that practice will integrate the dispersed powers into a workable government. It enjoins upon its branches separateness but interdependence, autonomy but reciprocity.

Youngstown Sheet & Tube Co. v. Sawyer (concurring opinion).

We observe first that this case does not involve an attempt by Congress to increase its own powers at the expense of the Executive Branch. Unlike some of our previous cases, most recently *Bowsher v. Synar*, this case simply does not pose a "dange[r] of congressional usurpation of Executive Branch functions." at 727; *see also INS v. Chadha*. Indeed, with the exception of the power of impeachment—which applies to all officers of the United States—Congress retained for itself no powers of control or supervision over an independent counsel. The Act does empower certain Members of Congress to request the Attorney General to apply for the appointment of an independent counsel, but the Attorney General has no duty to comply with the request, although he must respond within a certain time limit. §592(g). Other than that, Congress' role under the Act is limited to receiving reports or other information and oversight of the independent counsel's activities, §595(a), functions that we have recognized generally as being incidental to the legislative function of Congress. *See McGrain v. Daugherty*.

Similarly, we do not think that the Act works any judicial usurpation of properly executive functions. As should be apparent from our discussion of the Appointments Clause above, the power to appoint inferior officers such as independent counsel is not, in itself, an "executive" function in the constitutional sense, at least when Congress has exercised its power to vest the appointment of an inferior office in the "courts of Law." We note nonetheless that, under the Act, the Special Division has no power to appoint an independent counsel *sua sponte*; it may only do so upon the specific request of the Attorney General, and the courts are specifically prevented from reviewing the Attorney General's decision not to seek appointment, §592(f). In addition, once the court has appointed a counsel and defined his or her jurisdiction, it has no power to supervise or control the activities of the counsel.

Finally, we do not think that the Act "impermissibly undermine[s]" the powers of the Executive Branch, *Schor supra*, at 856, or "disrupts the proper balance between the coordinate branches [by] prevent[ing] the Executive Branch from accomplishing its constitutionally assigned functions," *Nixon v. Administrator of General Services, supra*, at 443. It is undeniable that the Act reduces the amount of control or supervision that the Attorney General and, through him, the President exercises over the investigation and prosecution of a certain class of alleged criminal activity. The Attorney General is not allowed to appoint the individual of his choice; he does not determine the counsel's jurisdiction; and his power to remove a counsel is limited. Nonetheless, the Act does give the Attorney General several means of supervising or controlling the prosecutorial powers that may be wielded by an independent counsel. Most importantly, the Attorney General retains the power to remove the counsel for "good cause," a power that we have already concluded provides the Executive with substantial ability to ensure that the laws are "faithfully executed" by an independent counsel. No independent counsel may be appointed without a specific request by the Attorney General, and the Attorney General's decision not to request appointment if he finds "no reasonable grounds to believe that further investigation is warranted" is committed to his unreviewable discretion. The Act thus gives the Executive a degree of control over the power to initiate an investigation by the independent counsel. In addition, the jurisdiction of the independent counsel is defined with reference to the facts submitted by the Attorney General, and once a counsel is appointed, the Act requires that the counsel abide by Justice Department policy unless it is not "possible" to do so. Notwithstanding the fact that the counsel is to some degree "independent" and free from Executive supervision to a greater extent than other federal prosecutors, in our view, these features of the Act give the

Executive Branch sufficient control over the independent counsel to ensure that the President is able to perform his constitutionally assigned duties.

In sum, we conclude today that it does not violate the Appointments Clause for Congress to vest the appointment of independent counsel in the Special Division; that the powers exercised by the Special Division under the Act do not violate Article III; and that the Act does not violate the separation of powers principle by impermissibly interfering with the functions of the Executive Branch.

JUSTICE SCALIA, *dissenting.*

. . . The notion that every violation of law should be prosecuted, including—indeed, *especially*—every violation by those in high places, is an attractive one, and it would be risky to argue in an election campaign that that is not an absolutely overriding value. *Fiat justitia, ruat coelum.* Let justice be done, though the heavens may fall. The reality is, however, that it is not an absolutely overriding value, and it was with the hope that we would be able to acknowledge and apply such realities that the Constitution spared us, by life tenure, the necessity of election campaigns. I cannot imagine that there are not many thoughtful men and women in Congress who realize that the benefits of this legislation are far outweighed by its harmful effect upon our system of government, and even upon the nature of justice received by those men and women who agree to serve in the Executive Branch. But it is difficult to vote not to enact, and even more difficult to vote to repeal, a statute called, appropriately enough, the Ethics in Government Act. If Congress is controlled by the party other than the one to which the President belongs, it has little incentive to repeal it; if it is controlled by the same party, it dare not. By its shortsighted action today, I fear the Court has permanently encumbered the Republic with an institution that will do it great harm.

Worse than what it has done, however, is the manner in which it has done it. A government of laws means a government of rules. Today's decision on the basic issue of fragmentation of executive power is ungoverned by rule, and hence ungoverned by law. It extends into the very heart of our most significant constitutional function the "totality of the circumstances" mode of analysis that this Court has in recent years become fond of. Taking all things into account, we conclude that the power taken away from the President here is not really too much. The next time executive power is assigned to someone other than the President, we may conclude, taking all things into account, that it *is* too much. That opinion, like this one, will not be confined by any rule. We will describe, as we have today (though I hope more accurately) the effects of the provision in question, and will authoritatively announce: "The President's need to control the exercise of the [subject officer's] discretion is so central to the functioning of the Executive Branch as to require complete control." This is not analysis; it is *ad hoc* judgment. And it fails to explain why it is not true that—as the text of the Constitution seems to require, as the Founders seemed to expect, and as our past cases have uniformly assumed—all purely executive power must be under the control of the President.

The *ad hoc* approach to constitutional adjudication has real attraction, even apart from its work-saving potential. It is guaranteed to produce a result, in every case, that will make a majority of the Court happy with the law. The law is, by definition, precisely what the majority thinks, taking all things into account, it *ought* to be. I prefer to rely upon the judgment of the wise men who constructed our system, and of the people who approved it, and of two centuries of history that have shown it to be sound. Like it or not, that judgment says, quite plainly, that "[t]he executive Power shall be vested in a President of the United States."

CLINTON v. CITY OF NEW YORK

524 U.S. 417 (1998)

Opinion: Stevens, joined by Rehnquist, Kennedy, Souter, Thomas, Ginsburg
Concurrence: Kennedy
Partial Concurrence, Partial Dissent: Scalia, joined by O'Connor and by Breyer in Part III
Dissent: Breyer, joined by O'Connor, Scalia in Part III

This case concerns the constitutionality of the Line Item Veto Act of 1996, which granted to the president the power to nullify particular provisions of congressional acts. The Court decided that the "line item veto" as granted in the Act violates the Presentment Clause of the Constitution. U.S. Supreme Court Justice Stephen Breyer, however, questions this conclusion in his dissent. Could the line item veto in fact serve a legitimate and constitutional political purpose? For example, the line item veto would allow the president to eliminate the provisions unrelated to the topic of the bill that members of Congress often insert in major legislation. Even if the line item veto could be valuable in a democratic society, is it right to employ it? According to U.S. Supreme Court Justice Anthony Kennedy, "Failure of political will does not justify unconstitutional remedies." Do you agree, or do you think the ends justify the means? Does the majority's approach elevate form over substance?

JUSTICE STEVENS *delivered the opinion of the Court.*

The Line Item Veto Act (Act), 110 Stat. 1200, 2 U.S.C. §691 *et seq.* (1994 ed., Supp. II), was enacted in April 1996 and became effective on January 1, 1997. The following day, six Members of Congress who had voted against the Act brought suit in the District Court for the District of Columbia challenging its constitutionality. On April 10, 1997, the District Court entered an order holding that the Act is unconstitutional. *Byrd v. Raines.* In obedience to the statutory direction to allow a direct, expedited appeal to this Court, see §§692(b)-(c), we promptly noted probable jurisdiction and expedited review, 520 U.S. ___ (1997). We determined, however, that the Members of Congress did not have standing to sue because they had not "alleged a sufficiently concrete injury to have established Article III standing," *Raines v. Byrd*; thus, "in . . . light of [the] overriding and time-honored concern about keeping the Judiciary's power within its proper constitutional sphere," *id.*, we remanded the case to the District Court with instructions to dismiss the complaint for lack of jurisdiction.

Less than two months after our decision in that case, the President exercised his authority to cancel one provision in the Balanced Budget Act of 1997, and two provisions in the Taxpayer Relief Act of 1997. Appellees, claiming that they had been injured by two of those cancellations, filed these cases in the District Court. That Court again held the statute invalid, and we again expedited our review. We now hold that these appellees have standing to challenge the constitutionality of the Act and, reaching the merits, we agree that the cancellation procedures set forth in the Act violate the Presentment Clause, Art. I, §7, cl. 2, of the Constitution.

I

We begin by reviewing the canceled items that are at issue in these cases.

Section 4722(c) of the Balanced Budget Act

Title XIX of the Social Security Act, 79 Stat. 343, as amended, authorizes the Federal Government to transfer huge sums of money to the States to help finance medical care for the indigent. In 1991, Congress directed that those federal subsidies be reduced by the amount of certain taxes levied by the States on health care providers. In 1994, the Department of Health and Human Services (HHS) notified the State of New York that 15 of its taxes were covered by the 1991 Act, and that as of June 30, 1994, the statute therefore required New York to return $955 million to the United States. The notice advised the State that it could apply for a waiver on certain statutory grounds. New York did request a waiver for those tax programs, as well as for a number of others, but HHS has not formally acted on any of those waiver requests. New York has estimated that the amount at issue for the period from October 1992 through March 1997 is as high as $2.6 billion.

Because HHS had not taken any action on the waiver requests, New York turned to Congress for relief. On August 5, 1997, Congress enacted a law that resolved the issue in New York's favor. Section 4722(c) of the Balanced Budget Act of 1997 identifies the disputed taxes and provides that they "are deemed to be permissible health care related taxes and in compliance with the requirements" of the relevant provisions of the 1991 statute.

On August 11, 1997, the President sent identical notices to the Senate and to the House of Representatives canceling "one item of new direct spending," specifying §4722(c) as that item, and stating that he had determined that "this cancellation will reduce the Federal budget deficit." He explained that §4722(c) would have permitted New York "to continue relying upon impermissible provider taxes to finance its Medicaid program" and that "[t]his preferential treatment would have increased Medicaid costs, would have treated New York differently from all other States, and would have established a costly precedent for other States to request comparable treatment."

Section 968 of the Taxpayer Relief Act

A person who realizes a profit from the sale of securities is generally subject to a capital gains tax. Under existing law, however, an ordinary business corporation can acquire a corporation, including a food processing or refining company, in a merger or stock-for-stock transaction in which no gain is recognized to the seller; the seller's tax payment, therefore, is deferred. If, however, the purchaser is a farmers' cooperative, the parties cannot structure such a transaction because the stock of the cooperative may be held only by its members; thus, a seller dealing with a farmers' cooperative cannot obtain the benefits of tax deferral.

In §968 of the Taxpayer Relief Act of 1997, Congress amended §1042 of the Internal Revenue Code to permit owners of certain food refiners and processors to defer the recognition of gain if they sell their stock to eligible farmers' cooperatives. The purpose of the amendment, as repeatedly explained by its sponsors, was "to facilitate the transfer of refiners and processors to farmers' cooperatives." The amendment to §1042 was one of the 79 "limited tax benefits" authorized by the Taxpayer Relief Act of 1997 and specifically identified in Title XVII of that Act as "subject to [the] line item veto."

On the same date that he canceled the "item of new direct spending" involving New York's health care programs, the President also canceled this limited tax benefit. In his explanation of that action, the President endorsed the objective of encouraging "value-added farming through the purchase by farmers' cooperatives of refiners or processors of agricultural goods," but concluded that the provision lacked safeguards and also "failed to target its benefits to small-and-medium-size cooperatives."

II

Appellees filed two separate actions against the President and other federal officials challenging these two cancellations. The plaintiffs in the first case are the City of New York, two hospital associations, one hospital, and two unions representing health care employees. The plaintiffs in the second are a farmers' cooperative consisting of about 30 potato growers in Idaho and an individual farmer who is a member and officer of the cooperative. The District Court consolidated the two cases and determined that at least one of the plaintiffs in each had standing under Article III of the Constitution.

IV

The Line Item Veto Act gives the President the power to "cancel in whole" three types of provisions that have been signed into law: "(1) any dollar amount of discretionary budget authority; (2) any item of new direct spending; or (3) any limited tax benefit." It is undisputed that the New York case involves an "item of new direct spending" and that the Snake River case involves a "limited tax benefit" as those terms are defined in the Act. It is also undisputed that each of those provisions had been signed into law pursuant to Article I, §7, of the Constitution before it was canceled.

The Act requires the President to adhere to precise procedures whenever he exercises his cancellation authority. In identifying items for cancellation he must consider the legislative history, the purposes, and other relevant information about the items. He must determine, with respect to each cancellation, that it will "(i) reduce the Federal budget deficit; (ii) not impair any essential Government functions; and (iii) not harm the national interest." Moreover, he must transmit a special message to Congress notifying it of each cancellation within five calendar days (excluding Sundays) after the enactment of the canceled provision. It is undisputed that the President meticulously followed these procedures in these cases.

A cancellation takes effect upon receipt by Congress of the special message from the President. If, however, a "disapproval bill" pertaining to a special message is enacted into law, the cancellations set forth in that message become "null and void." The Act sets forth a detailed expedited procedure for the consideration of a "disapproval bill," but no such bill was passed for either of the cancellations involved in these cases. A majority vote of both Houses is sufficient to enact a disapproval bill. The Act does not grant the President the authority to cancel a disapproval bill, but he does, of course, retain his constitutional authority to veto such a bill.

The effect of a cancellation is plainly stated in §691e, which defines the principal terms used in the Act. With respect to both an item of new direct spending and a limited tax benefit, the cancellation prevents the item "from having legal force or effect." Thus, under the plain text of the statute, the two actions of the President that are challenged in these cases prevented one section of the Balanced Budget Act of 1997 and one section of the Taxpayer Relief Act of 1997 "from having legal force or effect." The remaining provisions of those statutes, with the exception of the second canceled item in the latter, continue to have the same force and effect as they had when signed into law.

In both legal and practical effect, the President has amended two Acts of Congress by repealing a portion of each. "[R]epeal of statutes, no less than enactment, must conform with Art. I." *INS v. Chadha.* There is no provision in the Constitution that authorizes the President to enact, to amend, or to repeal statutes. Both Article I and Article II assign responsibilities to the President that directly relate to the lawmaking process, but neither addresses the issue presented by these cases. The President "shall from time to time give to the Congress Information on the State of the Union, and recommend to their Consideration such Measures as he shall judge necessary and expedient. . . ." Art. II, §3. Thus, he may initiate and influence legislative proposals. Moreover, after a bill has passed both Houses of Congress, but "before it become[s] a Law," it must be presented to the President. If he approves it, "he shall sign it, but if not he shall return it, with his Objections to that House in which it shall have originated, who shall enter the Objections at large on their Journal, and proceed to reconsider it." Art. I, §7, cl. 2. His "return" of a bill, which is usually described as a "veto," is subject to being overridden by a two-thirds vote in each House.

There are important differences between the President's "return" of a bill pursuant to Article I, §7, and the exercise of the President's cancellation authority pursuant to the Line Item Veto Act. The constitutional return takes place *before* the bill becomes law; the statutory cancellation occurs *after* the bill becomes law. The constitutional return is of the entire bill; the statutory cancellation is of only a part. Although the Constitution expressly authorizes the President to play a role in the process of enacting statutes, it is silent on the subject of unilateral Presidential action that either repeals or amends parts of duly enacted statutes.

There are powerful reasons for construing constitutional silence on this profoundly important issue as equivalent to an express prohibition. The procedures governing the enactment of statutes set forth in the text of Article I were the product of the great debates and compromises that produced the Constitution itself. Familiar historical materials provide abundant support for the conclusion that the power to enact statutes may only "be exercised in accord with a single, finely wrought and exhaustively considered, procedure." *Chadha.* Our first President understood the text of the Presentment Clause as requiring that he either "approve all the parts of a Bill, or reject it in toto." What has emerged in these cases from the President's exercise of his statutory cancellation powers, however, are truncated versions of two bills that passed both Houses of Congress. They are not the product of the "finely wrought" procedure that the Framers designed.

VI

Although they are implicit in what we have already written, the profound importance of these cases makes it appropriate to emphasize three points.

First, we express no opinion about the wisdom of the procedures authorized by the Line Item Veto Act. . . .

Second, although appellees challenge the validity of the Act on alternative grounds, the only issue we address concerns the "finely wrought" procedure commanded by the Constitution. *Chadha.*

Third, our decision rests on the narrow ground that the procedures authorized by the Line Item Veto Act are not authorized by the Constitution. The Balanced Budget Act of 1997 is a 500-page document that became "Public Law 105-33" after three procedural steps were taken: (1) a bill containing its exact text was approved by a majority of the Members of the House of Representatives; (2) the Senate approved precisely the same text; and (3) that text was signed into law by the President. The Constitution explicitly requires that each of those three steps be taken before a bill may "become a law." Art. I, §7. If one paragraph of that text had been omitted at any one of those three stages, Public Law 105-33 would not have been validly enacted. If the Line Item Veto Act were valid, it would authorize the President to create a different law — one whose text was not voted on by either House of Congress or presented to the President for signature. Something that might be known as "Public Law 105-33 as modified by the President" may or may not be desirable, but it is surely not a document that may "become a law" pursuant to the procedures designed by the Framers of Article I, §7, of the Constitution.

If there is to be a new procedure in which the President will play a different role in determining the final text of what may "become a law," such change must come not by legislation but through the amendment procedures set forth in Article V of the Constitution.

JUSTICE KENNEDY, *concurring.*

A nation cannot plunder its own treasury without putting its Constitution and its survival in peril. The statute before us, then, is of first importance, for it seems undeniable the Act will tend to restrain persistent excessive spending. Nevertheless, for the reasons given by Justice Stevens in the opinion for the Court, the statute must be found invalid. Failure of political will does not justify unconstitutional remedies.

I write to respond to my colleague Justice Breyer, who observes that the statute does not threaten the liberties of individual citizens, a point on which I disagree. The argument is related to his earlier suggestion that our role is lessened here because the two political branches are adjusting their own powers between themselves. To say the political branches have a somewhat free hand to reallocate their own authority would seem to require acceptance of two premises: first, that the public good demands it, and second, that liberty is not at risk. The former premise is inadmissible. The Constitution's structure requires a stability which transcends the convenience of the moment. The latter premise, too, is flawed. Liberty is always at stake when one or more of the branches seek to transgress the separation of powers.

Separation of powers was designed to implement a fundamental insight: concentration of power in the hands of a single branch is a threat to liberty. *The Federalist* states the axiom in these explicit terms: "The accumulation of all powers, legislative, executive, and judiciary, in the same hands . . . may justly be pronounced the very definition of tyranny." *The Federalist* No. 47.

In recent years, perhaps, we have come to think of liberty as defined by that word in the Fifth and Fourteenth Amendments and as illuminated by the other provisions of the Bill of Rights. The conception of liberty embraced by the Framers was not so confined. They used the principles of separation of powers and federalism to secure liberty in the fundamental political sense of the term, quite in addition to the idea of freedom from intrusive governmental acts. The idea and the promise were that when the people delegate some degree of control to a remote central authority, one branch of government ought not possess the power to shape their destiny without a sufficient check from the other two. In this vision, liberty demands limits on the ability of any one branch to influence basic political decisions.

It follows that if a citizen who is taxed has the measure of the tax or the decision to spend determined by the Executive alone, without adequate control by the citizen's Representatives in Congress, liberty is threatened. Money is the instrument of policy and policy affects the lives of citizens. The individual loses liberty in a real sense if that instrument is not subject to traditional constitutional constraints.

The principal object of the statute, it is true, was not to enhance the President's power to reward one group and punish another, to help one set of taxpayers and hurt another, to favor one State and ignore another. Yet these are its undeniable effects. The law establishes a new mechanism which gives the President the sole ability to hurt a group that is a visible target, in order to disfavor the group or to extract further concessions from Congress. The law is the functional equivalent of a line item veto and enhances the President's powers beyond what the Framers would have endorsed.

It is no answer, of course, to say that Congress surrendered its authority by its own hand; nor does it suffice to point out that a new statute, signed by the President or enacted over his veto, could restore to Congress the power it now seeks to relinquish. That a congressional cession of power is voluntary does not make it innocuous. The Constitution is a compact enduring for more than our time, and one Congress cannot yield up its own powers, much less those of other Congresses to follow.

JUSTICE BREYER, *with whom* **JUSTICE O'CONNOR** *and* **JUSTICE SCALIA** *join as to Part III, dissenting.*

I

In my view the Line Item Veto Act does not violate any specific textual constitutional command, nor does it violate any implicit Separation of Powers principle. Consequently, I believe that the Act is constitutional.

II

I approach the constitutional question before us with three general considerations in mind. *First*, the Act represents a legislative effort to provide the President with the power to give effect to some, but not to all, of the expenditure and revenue-diminishing provisions contained in a single massive appropriations bill. And this objective is constitutionally proper.

When our Nation was founded, Congress could easily have provided the President with this kind of power. In that time period, our population was less than four million, federal employees numbered fewer than 5,000, annual federal budget outlays totaled approximately $4 million, and the entire operative text of Congress's first general appropriations law [contained only four provisions].

At that time, a Congress, wishing to give a President the power to select among appropriations, could simply have embodied each appropriation in a separate bill, each bill subject to a separate Presidential veto.

Today, however, our population is about 250 million, the Federal Government employs more than four million people, the annual federal budget is $1.5 trillion, and a typical budget appropriations bill may have a dozen titles, hundreds of sections, and spread across more than 500 pages of the Statutes at Large. Congress cannot divide such a bill into thousands, or tens of thousands, of separate appropriations bills, each one of which the President would have to sign, or to veto, separately. Thus, the question is whether the Constitution permits Congress to choose a particular novel *means* to achieve this same, constitutionally legitimate, end.

Second, the case in part requires us to focus upon the Constitution's generally phrased structural provisions, provisions that delegate all "legislative" power to Congress and vest all "executive" power in the President. The Court, when applying these provisions, has interpreted them generously in terms of the institutional arrangements that they permit.

Indeed, Chief Justice Marshall, in a well-known passage, explained,

> "To have prescribed the means by which government should, in all future time, execute its powers, would have been to change, entirely, the character of the instrument, and give it the properties of a legal code. It would have been an unwise attempt to provide, by immutable rules, for exigencies which, if foreseen at all, must have been seen dimly, and which can be best provided for as they occur."

McCulloch v. Maryland.

This passage calls attention to the genius of the Framers' pragmatic vision, which this Court has long recognized in cases that find constitutional room for necessary institutional innovation.

Third, we need not here referee a dispute among the other two branches. And, as the majority points out,

> "When this Court is asked to invalidate a statutory provision that has been approved by both Houses of the Congress and signed by the President, particularly an Act of Congress that confronts a deeply vexing national problem, it should only do so for the most compelling constitutional reasons."

These three background circumstances mean that, when one measures the *literal* words of the Act against the Constitution's *literal* commands, the fact that the Act may closely resemble a different, literally unconstitutional, arrangement is beside the point. To drive exactly 65 miles per hour on an interstate highway closely resembles an act that violates the speed limit. But it does not violate that limit, for small differences matter when the question is one of literal violation of law. No more does this Act literally violate the Constitution's words.

III

The Court believes that the Act violates the literal text of the Constitution. A simple syllogism captures its basic reasoning:

> Major Premise: The Constitution sets forth an exclusive method for enacting, repealing, or amending laws.
>
> Minor Premise: The Act authorizes the President to "repea[l] or amen[d]" laws in a different way, namely by announcing a cancellation of a portion of a previously enacted law.
>
> Conclusion: The Act is inconsistent with the Constitution.

I find this syllogism unconvincing, however, because its Minor Premise is faulty. When the President "canceled" the two appropriation measures now before us, he did not *repeal* any law nor did he *amend* any law. He simply *followed* the law, leaving the statutes, as they are literally written, intact.

To understand why one cannot say, *literally speaking*, that the President has repealed or amended any law, imagine how the provisions of law before us might have been, but were not, written. Imagine that the canceled New York health care tax provision at issue here, Pub. L. 105-33, §4722(c), 111 Stat. 515 . . . , had instead said the following:

> Section One. Taxes . . . that were collected by the State of New York from a health care provider before June 1, 1997 and for which a waiver of provisions [requiring payment] have been sought . . . are deemed to be permissible health care related taxes . . . ***provided however that the President may prevent the just-mentioned provision from having legal force or effect if he determines x, y and z.*** (Assume x, y and z to be the same determinations required by the Line Item Veto Act.)

Whatever a person might say, or think, about the constitutionality of this imaginary law, there is one thing the English language would prevent one from saying. One could not say that a President who "prevent[s]" the deeming language from "having legal force or effect" has either *repealed* or *amended* this particular hypothetical statute. Rather, the President has *followed* that law to the letter. He has exercised the power it explicitly delegates to him. He has executed the law, not repealed it.

Because one cannot say that the President's exercise of the power the Act grants is, literally speaking, a "repeal" or "amendment," the fact that the Act's procedures differ from the Constitution's exclusive procedures for enacting (or repealing) legislation is beside the point. The Act *itself* was enacted in accordance with these procedures, and its failure to require the President to satisfy those procedures does not make the Act unconstitutional.

IV

Because I disagree with the Court's holding of literal violation, I must consider whether the Act nonetheless violates Separation of Powers principles — principles that arise out of the Constitution's vesting of the "executive Power" in "a President," U.S. Const., Art. II, §1, and "[a]ll legislative Powers" in "a Congress," Art. I, §1. There are three relevant Separation of Powers questions here: (1) Has Congress given the President the wrong kind of power, *i.e.*, "non-Executive" power? (2) Has Congress given the President the power to "encroach" upon Congress' own constitutionally reserved territory? (3) Has Congress given the President too much power, violating the doctrine of "nondelegation"? These three limitations help assure "adequate control by the citizen's representatives in Congress," upon which Justice Kennedy properly insists. And with respect to *this* Act, the answer to all these questions is "no."

A

Viewed conceptually, the power the Act conveys is the right kind of power. It is "executive." As explained above, an exercise of that power "executes" the Act. Conceptually speaking, it closely resembles the kind of delegated authority — to spend or not to spend appropriations, to change or not to change tariff rates — that Congress has frequently granted the President, any differences being differences in degree, not kind.

B

The Act does not undermine what this Court has often described as the principal function of the Separation of Powers, which is to maintain the tripartite structure of the Federal Government — and thereby protect individual liberty — by providing a "safeguard against the encroachment or aggrandizement of one branch at the expense of the other." *Buckley v. Valeo (per curiam)*; *Mistretta v. United States.*

[O]ne cannot say that the Act "encroaches" upon Congress' power, when Congress retained the power to insert, by simple majority, into any future appropriations bill, into any section of any such bill, or into any phrase of any section, a provision that says the Act will not apply.

Nor can one say the Act's grant of power "aggrandizes" the Presidential office. The grant is limited to the context of the budget. It is limited to the power to spend, or not to spend, particular appropriated items, and the power to permit, or not to permit, specific limited exemptions from generally applicable tax law from taking effect. These powers resemble those the President has exercised in the past on other occasions. The delegation of those powers to the President may strengthen the Presidency, but any such change in Executive Branch authority seems minute when compared with the changes worked by delegations of other kinds of authority that the Court in the past has upheld.

C

The "nondelegation" doctrine represents an added constitutional check upon Congress' authority to delegate power to the Executive Branch. And it raises a more serious constitutional obstacle here. The Constitution permits Congress to "see[k] assistance from another branch" of Government, the "extent and character" of that assistance to be fixed "according to common sense and the inherent necessities of the governmental co-ordination." *J. W. Hampton, Jr., & Co. v. United States*, 276 U.S., at 406. But there are limits on the way in which Congress can obtain such assistance; it "cannot delegate any part of its legislative power except under the limitation of a prescribed standard." *United States v. Chicago, M., St. P. & P. R. Co.* Or, in Chief Justice Taft's more familiar words, the Constitution permits only those delegations where Congress "shall lay down by legislative act an *intelligible principle* to which the person or body authorized to [act] is directed to conform." *J.W. Hampton, supra*, at 409 (emphasis added).

The Act before us seeks to create such a principle in three ways. The first is procedural. The Act tells the President that, in "identifying dollar amounts [or] . . . items . . . for cancellation" (which I take to refer to his selection of the amounts or items he will "prevent from having legal force or effect"), he is to "consider," among other things,

> "the legislative history, construction, and purposes of the law which contains [those amounts or items, and] . . . any specific sources of information referenced in such law or . . . the best available information. . . ."

2 U.S.C. §691(b) (1994 ed., Supp. II).

The second is purposive. The clear purpose behind the Act, confirmed by its legislative history, is to promote "greater fiscal accountability" and to "eliminate wasteful federal spending and . . . special tax breaks." H.R. Conf. Rep. No. 104-491, p. 15 (1996).

The third is substantive. The President must determine that, to "prevent" the item or amount "from having legal force or effect" will "reduce the Federal budget deficit; . . . not impair any essential Government functions; and . . . not harm the national interest." 2 U.S.C. §691(a)(A) (1994 ed., Supp. II).

The resulting standards are broad. But this Court has upheld standards that are equally broad, or broader.

V

In sum, I recognize that the Act before us is novel. In a sense, it skirts a constitutional edge. But that edge has to do with means, not ends. The means chosen do not amount literally to the enactment, repeal, or amendment of a law. Nor, for that matter, do they amount literally to the "line item veto" that the Act's title announces. Those means do not violate any basic Separation of Powers principle. They do not improperly shift the constitutionally foreseen balance of power from Congress to the President. Nor, since they comply with Separation of Powers principles, do they threaten the liberties of individual citizens. They represent an experiment that may, or may not, help representative government work better. The Constitution, in my view, authorizes Congress and the President to try novel methods in this way. Consequently, with respect, I dissent.

SYNTHESIS QUESTIONS FOR FURTHER DISCUSSION: CHAPTER 7

1. Throughout this chapter, we investigate conflicts between the executive and the legislative branches. Justice Robert H. Jackson's concurrence in *Youngstown Sheet & Tube Co. v. Sawyer* lays out a three-part test for determining the extent of the president's power in a case of controversy:

> "1. When the President acts pursuant to an express or implied authorization of Congress, his authority is at its maximum, for it includes all that he possesses in his own right plus all that Congress can delegate. . . .
>
> 2. When the President acts in absence of either a congressional grant or denial of authority, he can only rely upon his own independent powers, but there is a zone of twilight in which he and Congress may have concurrent authority, or in which its distribution is uncertain. . . .
>
> 3. When the President takes measures incompatible with the expressed or implied will of Congress, his power is at its lowest ebb, for then he can rely only upon his own constitutional powers minus any constitutional powers of Congress over the matter. . . ."

This three-part framework is suggested as a way that the Court might adjudicate between executive and congressional authority. But does the Court assume in *Youngstown Sheet & Tube Co. v. Sawyer* that it rightly has the power to adjudicate these disputes? Should it have this power? The lawyers representing the president suggested that *Youngstown Sheet & Tube Co. v. Sawyer* was rightly in the first category, while the Court found it to be in the third. Should the Court have the final word in this controversy, or is this a political question best settled between the executive and legislative branches?

These questions are related to the issues of judicial authority and supremacy introduced in Chapter 1. Is it possible for the Court to be the primary or exclusive institution for discerning whether an issue concerns congressional or executive authority without usurping the legitimate power of the other branches?

2. President Harry Truman's decision to seize the steel mills, the issue at stake in *Youngstown Sheet & Tube Co. v. Sawyer*, took place during the Korean War. In defining the second category of presidential authority, Justice Jackson suggests that any "actual test of power is likely to depend on the imperatives of events and contemporary imponderables." Should the fact that the country was involved in a military conflict give the Court more reason to defer to congressional power? To executive power? Given that the president is the Commander-in-Chief, should his command over the military include the power to support the armed forces, even if doing so might infringe on domestic property rights? It is important to consider whether the context of war should automatically provide the president with greater domestic power, and if so, when, why, and how much? In the following chapter, the question will arise as to the president's power over foreign affairs at times of war. It will be important to keep in mind how his authority over foreign matters compares with that in the domestic realm, even in times of military crisis.

3. An "Old Whig" expressed the concern that the Constitution will empower the executive to such a degree that the president will become like a king. His argument focuses in part on the massive power a Commander-in-Chief is likely to wield among his or her own people. One aspect of executive power that the Founders likely did not anticipate derives from the vast network that makes up the administrative agencies in the federal government. Such agencies include the Federal Communications Commission (FCC), the Internal Revenue Service (IRS), and the Federal Election Commission (FEC). This is a different kind of power from that usually wielded by monarchs in that its power is dispersed throughout many different regulatory bodies rather than consolidated in one office. Do such agencies pose a threat to democratic self-governance and the rule of law? Defenders of congressional power might argue that the so-called legislative veto was simply a way to deflect a new threat to congressional authority posed by administrative agencies. Specifically, the ability of the INS or other executive agencies to carry out executive policy that does not reflect the legislative will could potentially undermine the power of the people to make laws. Given that these agencies are not elected and are not directly under the control of the president, what is the source of their legitimacy? Should Congress have the power to "veto" particular administrative choices that do not reflect congressional intent? If Congress lacks such power, does this jeopardize democratic self-government? Does it give the executive too much power? Consider the arguments against the "legislative veto" presented by the Court in *INS v. Chadha*.

4. While *INS v. Chadha* raises questions about whether administrative agencies might undermine the Congress's power to enact legislation according to the people's will, another modern development might present a threat to the president's power. Bills passed by Congress are often joined together into one large "omnibus" bill. In effect, they combine many different policy issues and controversies into one package. In order to combat this practice, the president asserted his power to carry out a line item veto. In other words, the president claimed to have the power to veto particular lines of legislative bills rather than having to veto the entire bill or nothing at all. Would this expand the veto power too far, or is it a way to ensure that the president, an elected official, has a sufficiently robust role in evaluating legislation passed by Congress by ensuring that the decision to veto can be based on the merits of a particular policy? Why did the Court rule against the line item veto in *Clinton v. City of New York*?

5. The excerpt from Alexander Hamilton's *The Federalist No. 70* emphasized why executive power should rest in one "unitary" government official — the president. Drawing on that thought, contemporary defenders of the unitary executive stress that there can be no "fourth" branch of government not under the total control of the executive or the legislature. Clearly, however, administrative agencies, whose officers must be confirmed by Congress, have some shared authority at the moment of appointment. But does this shared authority extend to the ability to remove an officer from one of those agencies? Defenders of the unitary executive theory suggest not. They argue that the Founders, through the Constitution, granted the authority to the executive to fire. As you read the excerpts from James Madison and Hamilton, is there any evidence for this claim? In their article, Lawrence Lessig and Cass Sunstein argue that there is not, but still go on to consider efficiency and other grounds for the claims of a unitary executive. Does the lack of an ability to fire the heads of administrative agencies constitute a threat to the executive power? Does the existence of these agencies themselves fit into one branch of government?

KEY TERMS

bicameralism: The principle that the legislative branch should be composed of two chambers.

executive privilege: Areas in which the president might be immune or exempt from certain powers of Congress, including the subpoena power.

legislative veto: A statutory mechanism formerly used by Congress to permit overriding an executive agency's action or determination.

line item veto: A proposed presidential power to veto specific sections of a bill, rather than the whole bill.

prerogative: The discretionary power of the president not subject to control by legislation.

unitary executive: The notion that the executive power must be held solely by one individual, not a committee. Its modern usage suggests that executive power should not be shared with the legislative branch or with independent agencies in matters such as the appointment and removal of officers. Also a theory associated with presidential control over federal agencies and with expanded presidential power during wartime.

CHAPTER 8

FOREIGN AFFAIRS AND THE POWER TO DECLARE WAR

Who has the power to declare war? Is it always necessary to declare war before engaging in military operations?

Whereas in the previous chapter we examined the general framework for evaluating conflicts between the president and Congress, we focus now on how these conflicts should be resolved in matters of foreign affairs. The question about the degree to which the president has exclusive power in foreign affairs has been controversial since first U.S. President George Washington's administration. The first reading in this chapter includes excerpts from the "Pacificus-Helvidius" debate between Alexander Hamilton and James Madison. In this debate, Hamilton and Madison initiate what would become a central debate over whether and how power over foreign affairs is shared. In Hamilton's view, it is an inherent and exclusive power of the president to engage in foreign relations, except where that power has been explicitly limited by the Constitution, or assigned to another branch. Hamilton's arguments deeply worried Thomas Jefferson, but since he was a member of President Washington's cabinet, he turned to James Madison (then a member of Congress) to challenge and refute Hamilton's arguments. Madison articulated a far more robust role for Congress in the making of foreign policy.

The question of the power to declare war, which the Constitution formally grants to Congress, has only been used five times in the nation's history: the War of 1812, the Mexican-American War, the Spanish-American War, World War I, and World War II. As a result, most of the conflicts to which the United States has been a party have occurred in what U.S. Supreme Court Justice Robert H. Jackson called the "zone of twilight" in his *Youngstown Sheet & Tube Co. v. Sawyer* decision. In the reading by John Hart Ely, the author criticizes Congress and the president for failing to live up to their constitutional obligations in bringing the nation to war. He calls for greater deliberation and the establishment of a national consensus before entry to war. His arguments rebut the resolutions authorizing the use of force in the cases of the Vietnam and Iraq conflicts, excerpts of which are included as well. The article by John Yoo challenges Ely and defends a strong and autonomous role of the executive in determining when to engage in armed combat. Yoo extends the idea of the unitary executive and makes appeals to inherent presidential power in defending this robust role for the president.

We begin our case selection with the *Prize Cases*, which concerned whether President Abraham Lincoln could create a naval blockade of ports in the South during the Civil War without a formal declaration of war. The case reflected a trend towards presidential authority not only in war, but also more generally in cases of foreign affairs, which would continue into the twentieth century. In *United States v. Curtiss-Wright Export Corp.*, the Court considers whether Congress can delegate broad power to the executive in foreign affairs, as well as the source and scope of the president's independent power in foreign policy—themes that are developed in *Dames & Moore v. Regan.* These cases offer examples of the Court struggling to define just what might constitute congressional authorization and how to treat congressional silence in foreign affairs. In *Goldwater v. Carter*, the Court is asked to intervene and protect congressional prerogatives even where Congress itself has not directly confronted the president. While the Court declined to make a formal ruling in this case, *Goldwater v. Carter* does generate a set of important opinions about how and when the Court should—and should not—intervene in the separation of powers in foreign affairs, with some of the justices insisting that this constitutes a "political question" that should not be resolved by the Court.

When it invokes the political question doctrine, the Court refuses to decide the substance of the case because it considers the subject matter to be outside its jurisdiction. As you read *Goldwater v. Carter*, you might consider the differences and similarities between the issues in that case and those in the other cases we examine in this chapter.

As you read this chapter, you should continue to keep in mind the framework and debate from Chapter 7. In particular, ask yourself whether Yoo correctly applies the idea of the unitary executive discussed in Chapter 7 to the president's power in foreign affairs. Specifically, you should ask whether Yoo's position is qualitatively different from those advanced in Chapter 7 by Steven Calabresi, as well as Lawrence Lessig and Cass Sunstein, or whether these views are continuous.

THE PROCLAMATION OF NEUTRALITY OF 1793 AND THE PACIFICUS-HELVIDIUS DEBATE

The following debate between Alexander Hamilton and James Madison arose over President George Washington's official proclamation of neutrality with regard to the conflict between European powers, specifically war between France and Great Britain, which the French revolutionary government declared in February 1793. As you will see in this excerpt, the proclamation, issued April 22, 1793, requires American citizens to remain neutral in these conflicts and declares that the American government will not aid citizens who fail to obey this dictate. What is constitutionally significant about this proclamation was that it was made unilaterally, without the consent of Congress. The proclamation was therefore an early example of what would come to be a fundamental debate over the president's power to make foreign policy outside of the formal grants he was given by the Constitution. In the following debate, Hamilton takes the position that Congress can impose no limit on the president's foreign policy power. But as you will see, Madison challenges this position, arguing that the powers granted to the president do not include the power to make this proclamation. After the proclamation was issued and the debate ensued, Congress passed the Neutrality Act of 1794, bolstering President Washington's stated position of neutrality with congressional authorization.

PRESIDENT GEORGE WASHINGTON'S PROCLAMATION OF NEUTRALITY, 1793

Whereas it appears that a state of war exists between Austria, Prussia, Sardinia, Great Britain, and the United Netherlands, of the one part, and France on the other; and the duty and interest of the United States require, that they should with sincerity and good faith adopt and pursue a conduct friendly and impartial toward the belligerant Powers;

I have therefore thought fit by these presents to declare the disposition of the United States to observe the conduct aforesaid towards those Powers respectfully; and to exhort and warn the citizens of the United States carefully to avoid all acts and proceedings whatsoever, which may in any manner tend to contravene such disposition.

And I do hereby also make known, that whatsoever of the citizens of the United States shall render himself liable to punishment or forfeiture under the law of nations, by committing, aiding, or abetting hostilities against any of the said Powers, or by carrying to any of them those articles which are deemed contraband by the modern usage of nations, will not receive the protection of the United States, against such punishment or forfeiture; and further, that I have given instructions to those officers, to whom it belongs, to cause prosecutions to be instituted against all persons, who shall, within the cognizance of the courts of the United States, violate the law of nations, with respect to the Powers at war, or any of them.

In testimony whereof, I have caused the seal of the United States of America to be affixed to these presents, and signed the same with my hand. Done at the city of Philadelphia, the twenty-second day of April, one thousand seven hundred and ninety-three, and of the Independence of the United States of America the seventeenth.

ALEXANDER HAMILTON AND JAMES MADISON, PACIFICUS-HELVIDIUS DEBATE OF 1793

Pacificus (Alexander Hamilton)

No. 1

***

The objections [to President Washington's Proclamation of Neutrality] fall under four heads:

1. That the proclamation was without authority.
2. That it was contrary to our treaties with France.

3. That it was contrary to the gratitude which is due from this to that country, for the succors afforded to us in our own revolution.

4. That it was out of time and unnecessary. . . .

The inquiry then is, what department of our government is the proper one to make a declaration of neutrality, when the engagements of the nation permit, and its interests require that it should be done?

A correct mind will discern at once, that it can belong neither to the legislature nor judicial department, and of course must belong to the executive.

The legislative department is not the organ of intercourse between the United States and foreign nations. It is charged neither with making nor interpreting treaties. It is therefore not naturally that member of the government, which is to pronounce the existing condition of the nation, with regard to foreign powers, or to admonish the citizens of their obligations and duties in consequence; still less is it charged with enforcing the observance of those obligations and duties.

It is equally obvious, that the act in question is foreign to the judiciary department. The province of that department is to decide litigations in particular cases. It is indeed charged with the interpretation of treaties, but it exercises this function only where contending parties bring before it a specific controversy. It has no concern with pronouncing upon the external political relations of treaties between government and government. This position is too plain to need being insisted upon.

It must then of necessity belong to the executive department to exercise the function in question, when a proper case for it occurs.

It appears to be connected with that department in various capacities — As the organ of intercourse between the nation and foreign nations; as the interpreter of the national treaties, in those cases in which the judiciary is not competent, that is, between government and government; as the power which is charged with the execution of the laws, of which treaties form a part; as that which is charged with the command and disposition of the public force. . . .

The second article of the Constitution of the United States, section first, establishes this general proposition, that "the EXECUTIVE POWER shall be vested in a President of the United States of America." . . .

The general doctrine of our Constitution . . . is that the executive power of the nation is vested in the President; subject only to the exceptions and qualifications, which are expressed in the instrument.

Two of [the exceptions are] . . . the participation of the senate in the appointment of officers, and in the making of treaties. A third remains to be mentioned; the right of the legislature "to declare war, and grant letters of marque and reprisal." . . .

If on the one hand, the legislature have a right to declare war, it is on the other, the duty of the executive to preserve peace, till the declaration is made; and in fulfilling this duty, it must necessarily possess a right of judging what is the nature of the obligations which the treaties of the country impose on the government; and when it has concluded that there is nothing in them inconsistent with neutrality, it becomes both its province and its duty to enforce the laws incident to that state of the nation. The executive is charged with the execution of all laws, the law of nations, as well as the municipal law, by which the former are recognized and adopted. It is consequently bound, by executing faithfully the laws of neutrality, when the country is in a neutral position, to avoid giving cause of war to foreign powers. . . .

The right of the executive to receive ambassadors and other public ministers, may serve to illustrate the relative duties of the executive and legislative departments. This right includes that of judging, in the case of a revolution of government in a foreign country, whether the new rulers are competent organs of the national will, and ought to be recognized, or not; which, where a treaty antecedently exists between the United States and such nation, involves the power of continuing or suspending its operation. For until the new government is acknowledged, the treaties between the nations, so far at least as regards public rights, are of course suspended.

This power of determining virtually upon the operation of national treaties, as a consequence of the power to receive public ministers, is an important instance of the right of the executive, to decide upon the obligations of the country with regard to foreign nations. To apply it to the case of France, if there had been a treaty of alliance, offensive and defensive between the United States and that country, the unqualified acknowledgment of the new government would have put the United States in a condition to become an associate in the war with France, and would have laid the legislature under an obligation, if required, and there was otherwise no valid excuse, of exercising its power of declaring war.

This serves as an example of the right of the executive, in certain cases, to determine the condition of the nation, though it may, in its consequences, affect the exercise of the power of the legislature to declare war. Nevertheless, the executive cannot thereby control the exercise of that power. The legislature is still free to perform its duties, according to its own sense of them; though the executive, in the exercise of its constitutional powers, may establish an antecedent state of things, which ought to weigh in the legislative decision.

The division of the executive power in the Constitution, creates a concurrent authority in the cases to which it relates.

Hence, in the instance stated, treaties can only be made by the president and senate jointly; but their activity may be continued or suspended by the President alone. . . .

It deserves to be remarked, that as the participation of the senate in the making of treaties, and the power of the legislature to declare war, are exceptions out of the general "executive power" vested in the President, they are to be construed strictly, and ought to be extended no further than is essential to their execution.

While, therefore, the legislature can alone declare war, can alone actually transfer the nation from a state of peace to a state of hostility, it belongs to the "executive power" to do whatever else the law of nations, cooperating with the treaties of the country, enjoin in the intercourse of the United States with foreign powers.

In this distribution of authority, the wisdom of our Constitution is manifested. It is the province and duty of the executive to preserve to the nation the blessings of peace. The legislature alone can interrupt them by placing the nation in a state of war. . . .

Helvidius (James Madison)

No. 1

***

Let us examine [the doctrine being propounded by Pacificus]:

In the general distribution of powers, we find that of declaring war expressly vested in the congress, where every other legislative power is declared to be vested; and without any other qualifications than what is common to every other legislative act. The constitutional idea of this power would seem then clearly to be, that it is of a legislative and not an executive nature.

This conclusion becomes irresistible, when it is recollected, that the constitution cannot be supposed to have placed either any power legislative in its nature, entirely among executive powers, or any power executive in its nature, entirely among legislative powers, without charging the constitution, with that kind of intermixture and consolidation of different powers, which would violate a fundamental principle in the organization of free governments. If it were not unnecessary to enlarge on this topic here, it could be shown, that the constitution was originally vindicated, and has been constantly expounded, with a disavowal of any such intermixture.

The power of treaties is vested jointly in the president and in the senate, which is a branch of the legislature. From this arrangement merely, there can be no inference that would necessarily exclude the power from the executive class: since the senate is joined with the president in another power, that of appointing to offices, which, as far as relate to executive offices at least, is considered as of an executive nature. Yet on the other hand, there are sufficient indications that the power of treaties is regarded by the constitution as materially different from mere executive power, and as having more affinity to the legislative than to the executive character.

. . . [T]hat treaties, when formed according to the constitutional mode, are confessedly to have force and operation of laws, and are to be a rule for the courts in controversies between man and man, as much as any other laws. They are even emphatically declared by the constitution to be "the supreme law of the land."

So far the argument from the constitution is precisely in opposition to the doctrine. As little will be gained in its favour from a comparison of the two powers, with those particularly vested in the president alone.

As there are but few, it will be most satisfactory to review them one by one.

"The president shall be commander in chief of the army and navy of the United States, and of the militia when called into the actual service of the United States."

There can be no relation worth examining between this power and the general power of making treaties. And instead of being analogous to the power of declaring war, it affords a striking illustration of the incompatibility of the two powers in the same hands. Those who are to conduct a war cannot in the nature of things, be proper or safe judges, whether a war ought to be commenced, continued, or concluded. They are barred from the latter functions by a great principle in free government, analogous to that which separates the sword from the purse, or the power of executing from the power of enacting laws. . . .

Thus it appears that by whatever standard we try this doctrine, it must be condemned as no less vicious in theory than it would be dangerous in practice. It is countenanced neither by the writers on law; nor by the nature of the powers themselves; nor by any general arrangements, or particular expressions, or plausible analogies, to be found in the constitution.

Whence then can the writer have borrowed it?

There is but one answer to this question.

The power of making treaties and the power of declaring war, are royal prerogatives in the British government, and are accordingly treated as executive prerogatives by British commentators. . . .

No. 2

***

Leaving however to the leisure of the reader deductions which the author, having omitted, might not choose to own, I proceed to the examination of one, with which that liberty cannot be taken.

"However true it may be (says he) that the right of the legislature to declare war includes the right of judging, whether the legislature be under obligations to make war or not, it will follow that the executive is in any case excluded from a similar right of judging in the execution of its own functions."...

A concurrent authority in two independent departments, to perform the same function with respect to the same thing, would be as awkward in practice, as it is unnatural in theory.

If the legislature and executive have both a right to judge of the obligations to make war or not, it must sometimes happen, though not at present, that they will judge differently. The executive may proceed to consider the question today; may determine that the United States are not bound to take part in a war, and, in the execution of its functions, proclaim that declaration to all the world. Tomorrow the legislature may follow in the consideration of the same subject; may determine that the obligations impose war on the United States, and, in the execution of its functions, enter into a constitutional declaration, expressly contradicting the constitutional proclamation.

In what light does this present the constitution to the people who established it? In what light would it present to the world a nation, thus speaking, through two different organs, equally constitutional and authentic, two opposite languages, on the same subject, and under the same existing circumstances?

But it is not with the legislative rights alone that this doctrine interferes. The rights of the judiciary may be equally invaded. For it is clear that if a right declared by the constitution to be legislative, leaves, notwithstanding, a similar right in the executive, whenever a case for exercising it occurs, in the course of its functions; a right declared to be judiciary and vested in that department may, on the same principle, be assumed and exercised by the executive in the course of its functions; and it is evident that occasions and pretexts for the latter interference may be as frequent as for the former. So again the judiciary department may find equal occasions in the execution of its functions, for usurping the authorities of the executive; and the legislature for stepping into the jurisdiction of both. And thus all the power of government, of which a partition is so carefully made among the several branches, would be thrown into absolute hotchpot and exposed to a general scramble....

John Hart Ely

WAR AND RESPONSIBILITY

Chapter 1: The Constitutional Framework

Princeton, NJ: Princeton University Press (1993)

This system will not hurry us into war; it is calculated to guard against it. It will not be in the power of a single man, or a single body of men, to involve us in such distress; for the important power of declaring war is vested in the legislature at large....

—James Wilson

I didn't have to get permission from some old goat in the United States Congress to kick Saddam Hussein out of Kuwait.

— George [H.W.] Bush

One of the recurrent discoveries of academic writing about constitutional law — an all but certain ticket to tenure — is that from the standpoint of twentieth-century observers, the "original understanding" of the document's framers and ratifiers can be obscure to the point of inscrutability. Often this is true. In this case, however, it isn't. The power to declare war was constitutionally vested in Congress. The debates, and early practice, establish that this meant that all wars, big or small, "declared" in so many words or not — most weren't, even then — had to be legislatively authorized. Indeed, only one delegate to either the Philadelphia convention or any of the state ratifying conventions, Pierce Butler, is recorded as suggesting that authority to start a war be vested in the president. Elbridge Gerry, backed by others, responded that he "never expected to hear in a republic a motion to empower the Executive alone to declare war," and Butler subsequently disowned his earlier view.

There were several reasons for the founders' determination to vest the decision to go to war in the legislative process. The one they mentioned most often is the most obvious, a determination not to let such decisions be taken easily. The founders assumed that peace would (and should) be the customary state of the new republic — James Madison characterized war as "among the greatest of national calamities" — and sought to arrange the Constitution so as to assure that expectation. Their assumption was not that Congress was any more expert on the subject of war than the executive — if anything they assumed the contrary — but rather that requiring its assent would reduce the number of occasions on which we would become thus involved. There were various statements by influential framers to the effect that executives tended to be more warlike than legislative bodies.

Madison's is typical: "The constitution supposes, what the History of all Governments demonstrates, that the Executive is the branch of power most interested in war, and most prone to it. It has accordingly with studied care, vested the question of war in the Legislature." Patently the point was not to exclude the executive from the decision — if the president's not on board we're not going to have much of a war — but rather to "clog" the road to combat by requiring the concurrence of a number of people of various points of view. Justice Story wrote in 1833, "[T]he power of declaring war is not only the highest sovereign prerogative; but . . . it is in its own nature and effects so critical and calamitous, that it requires the utmost deliberation, and the successive review of all the councils of the nation." To invoke a more contemporary image, it takes more than one key to launch a missile: It should take quite a number to start a war.

Two other rationales that played a role can be highlighted by examining the (debated) decision to involve the House of Representatives in the decision to go to war. The House was certainly not included because of any perceived expertise: Indeed, because of its assumed lack thereof it was excluded from such foreign policy processes as the approval of treaties. Rather, authorization by the entire Congress was foreseeably calculated, for one thing, to slow the process down, to insure that there would be a pause, a "sober second thought," before the nation was plunged into anything as momentous as war. Thus in defense of including the House, Story wrote that "[l]arge bodies necessarily move slowly; and where the co-operation of different bodies is required, the retardation of any measure must be proportionately increased." (Occasionally there won't be time for such deliberation, but we shall see that that is something the framers foresaw and accommodated.)

The House was included for another reason as well, that it was conceived as "the people's house." Given the way the burdens of war get distributed, it was felt that the people's representatives should have a say. (It was felt further that the involvement of "the people's representatives" would increase the participation of the people themselves in the debate.) The requirement of authorization by both houses of Congress was thus also calculated to increase the probability that the American people would support any war we entered into. The founders didn't need a Vietnam to teach them that wars unsupported by the people at large are unlikely to succeed. (Indeed, the difficulties of keeping the colonial troops in the field during the Revolution provided the beginnings of a similar lesson.)

This point applies a fortiori to the legislature. Unless Congress has unequivocally authorized a war at the outset, it is a good deal more likely later to undercut the effort, leaving it in a condition that satisfies neither the allies we induced to rely on us, our troops who fought and sometimes died, nor for that matter anyone else except, conceivably, the enemy. Admiral James Stockdale, who spent seven and a half years as a prisoner of war in Hanoi, put it well: "Our Constitution as written protected our fighting men from shedding blood in pointless exercises while a dissenting Congress strangled the effort. But what has evolved . . . affords them no such protection." Thus, he concludes, we cannot afford "to fight any more wars without a thoroughgoing national commitment in advance." In fact this is a position often taken, understandably, by military men. For example, General Alexander Haig testified at his confirmation hearing for the position of Secretary of State, "Heaven help us as a nation if we once again indulge in the expenditure of precious American blood without a clear demonstration of popular support for it. I think the legislature is the best manifestation of popular support."

It is true that an early draft of the Constitution vested the power "to make war" in Congress, and this language was changed during the editing process to the power "to declare war." This change was made for two reasons. The first was to make clear that once hostilities were congressionally authorized, the president, as "commander in chief," would assume tactical control (without constant congressional interference) of the way they were conducted. (Proponents of broad executive authority to involve the nation in military hostilities often rely on the constitutional designation of the president as "Commander in Chief of the Army and Navy of the United States," but the record is entirely clear that all this was meant to convey was command of the armed forces once Congress had authorized a war, that it did not carry authority to start one.) The second reason for the change in language was to reserve to the president the power, without advance congressional authorization, to "repel sudden attacks."

THE COUNTERARGUMENT FROM OBSOLESCENCE

The need for Presidents to have that power [to use force abroad without congressional approval], particularly in the modern age, should be obvious to almost everyone.

— *Robert Bork*

The clarity of the Constitution on this question leaves two strategies open to advocates of executive authority to start wars — though it can be demonstrated quite rapidly that neither will work. The first is simply to assert that the Constitution does not fit today's world — that it is, in a word, obsolete. In fact this is a line that is rarely taken in so many words, as the conventions of constitutional discourse do not recognize it as a legitimate move. For good reason: The most archaic-sounding provisions of our founding document, their purposes intelligently unpacked, generate commands of complete contemporary relevance. If there is a consensus that one of those commands has become unworkably burdensome — their point, of course, is to be at least somewhat burdensome — the appropriate response is repeal by the constitutionally prescribed method, not a unilateral declaration by the burdened official that the provision no longer applies, at least not to him.

In any event, the constitutional requirement that Congress express its formal approval before the president leads the nation into war is not remotely obsolete: The purposes that underlay it were rendered sufficiently transparent to permit their mapping onto contemporary conditions. Occasionally — though nowhere near as often as enthusiasts would have us believe — military emergencies can develop faster than Congress can convene and react. That was also true, however, in the late eighteenth century — in fact it was probably truer then than it is today, given that (a) Congress was out of session most of the time and it took weeks, not hours, to round its members up, and (b) its members and committees did not have significant staffs. The founders understood this, though, and consequently reserved to the president authority to respond on his own to "sudden attacks" until there was time for Congress to convene and confer: In such situations the president could respond militarily and seek authorization simultaneously.

It probably is the case, however, that enemy actions not actually amounting to attacks on the United States can more obviously threaten our national security now than they could when the Constitution was agreed to. This raises the question whether the reserved emergency presidential authority to "repel sudden attacks" should be (1) limited to actual attacks on United States territory or (2) "functionally" extended to other situations where a clear danger to our national security has developed so unexpectedly, and immediate military response is so imperative, that advance congressional authorization to respond militarily simply cannot be awaited (though such authorization must be requested, at the latest, simultaneously with the issuance of the order dispatching the troops, our military response discontinued if such authorization is not promptly forthcoming).

At first blush the language seems mildly helpful: "attack" might or might not mean "attack on the United States," but "sudden" does seem to suggest that time urgency is the point. This is building too much on too little, however, as the phrase appears not in the document but in Madison's notes on the debates. We therefore will make better progress by inquiring into the *purpose* of the reservation of authority to repel sudden attacks. One animating idea could have been that there would in the event of an attack on the United States inevitably be a consensus that a military response was in order, and thus a requirement of congressional approval would be a needless formality. If that was the idea, however, a limitation to actual attacks on U.S. territory seems highly questionable: The *preclusion* of such an attack by a preemptive strike seems likely to garner a similar consensus, as for that matter would an American military response to, say, a Soviet invasion of Mexico or Canada. But then how about Guatemala, Great Britain, or Japan? Thus if we construe the reservation in "likely consensus" terms we confront two choices, each unacceptable. Either we limit it to actual attacks on the United States, which seems to undershoot the posited rationale and thus constitute a questionable approach to constitutional language, or we expand it to all cases where the executive believes that "all sensible people" would agree with his response, in which case we can be quite certain it would be invoked whenever the executive himself thought a military response appropriate. (The tendency of virtually everyone to assume that all rational people, properly advised, would agree with him is one I assume I need not annotate.)

The most natural alternative construction of the reservation would focus on the word "sudden" and assume the point was to give the president authority to respond without advance authorization when there has not been time to secure it (so long as he seeks it simultaneously and subsides if it is not promptly forthcoming). This path appears more promising. In the first place, it fits a general theory of emergency power entertained by some of the founders, that under emergency conditions the executive can properly act in excess of legislative authorization, so long as he makes swift and full disclosure to the legislature and subsides if they do not approve. Second, it parallels a similar reservation of extraordinary military authority another section of Article I made in favor of the *states:* "No State shall, without the Consent of Congress . . . engage in War, unless actually invaded, *or* in such imminent Danger as will not admit of delay." Finally, unlike the "most sensible persons would agree" rationale, "there wasn't time to secure advance authorization so we had to seek it simultaneously" seems susceptible to principled limitation and thus may be given the sort of functional construction we are accustomed to according constitutional language. Thus although the point is arguable, I am inclined to construe the president's reserved authority to go ahead and respond militarily (and seek congressional authorization simultaneously) as extending to genuine and serious threats to our national security beyond actual attacks on United States territory.

Thus construed, the constitutional command is certainly not obsolete: In fact other changes have made it more urgent than ever. In the nineteenth century—indeed, up until World War II—the nation took quite seriously the founders' fear of a "standing army": Thus in order to lead the nation into combat the president needed not only a declaration of war or comparable statement of authorization, but also statutory authority to raise an army and a congressional appropriation of the funds needed to support it. Now, of course, we do effectively have a standing army, which means that today the requirement of congressional authorization is all that stands in the way of unfettered executive discretion to commit it to combat.

Another fact that might render the requirement of congressional authorization particularly important today is that at least for the present we have an all-volunteer army, thereby eliminating what might at certain periods in our history have been regarded as a further source of potential resistance to half-baked military schemes, namely draftees from all social classes (including politically influential ones) and their families and friends. I won't linger long on this one, however. This "check" was probably never terribly significant: I know I didn't emerge from basic training programmed for independent thinking. (For the moment at least it seems to be professional soldiers who provide the most reliable brake on the ill-conceived military schemes of amateurs, though obviously not so reliable that we should continue to tolerate the exclusion of Congress from the process.) Worth more attention is the fact that we have spent much of the late twentieth century in an era of "divided government" (president from one party, Congress from the other). Thank God it didn't happen, but as of, say, February 1992, the risk that the executive might start a war to demonstrate toughness and "leadership" in perilous political times (when, for example, the economy refuses to "jump-start" in time for an upcoming election) seemed anything but remote.

As far as the need to bring the American people on board is concerned, another change—actually in this case a return to the earlier traditions of the republic—seems relevant. We now have a citizenry more willing than those of prior decades to take on the administration on questions of foreign policy, particularly questions of war and peace. That this change too (at least assuming, as I do, that national unity behind authorized wars is generally a desirable goal) has increased the importance of the congressional authorization requirement was noted well in a student paper I received in the spring of 1991:

> [T]his writer must enter a personal note.... The congressional process that led to the authorization of January 12, 1991, had a significant bearing on my own attitude towards the war once it began. I was highly doubtful of the march to war, agreeing (as did congressional opponents of the war resolution) that the Iraqis ought to be ejected from Kuwait, but believing that sanctions and blockade were a wiser course, and that war was both hazardous and not necessary. Had President Bush gone to war by fiat, without authority from Congress . . . I believe I would have marched against it. But the war was in fact duly authorized, and I therefore believed it best to reserve my own doubts and not actively oppose a war which was entered into in a constitutional manner.

Another change of conditions repeatedly pressed by proponents of unencumbered presidential power is that the possible consequences of war are more serious now than they were in the eighteenth century. But this one too turns out on a moment's reflection to argue the other way—*in favor of* the original conclusion that "no one man should hold the power of bringing this oppression upon us." The fact that we can all be blown to kingdom come only reinforces the need, where there is time, for a "sober second thought" before war is entered into, and a collective judgment that it should be.

Of course, if he asked, the president probably would usually receive rather readily the support of both Congress and the American people when he decided to have a war. (Admittedly this is somewhat hard to judge, as of late congressional and popular opinion has generally not been permitted to register until the war is under way, at which point support notoriously increases.) From childhood we Americans are programmed to fall in when the bugle sounds, a fact that has caused no small percentage of my friends to ask me why, if approval is a foregone conclusion, I'm wasting my time worrying about increasing participation in such decisions. Is there any reason to suppose, given their respective performances, that Congress will prove wiser on issues of war and peace than the president? Actually I think our history does support, if slightly, the founders' judgment that Congress (if only because it is necessarily more deliberate) tends to be more responsible in this area than the executive. To answer the question on its own (comparative) terms, however, is to miss the point. The constitutional strategy was to require more than one set of keys to open the Pandora's box of war. As usual, Alexander Bickel said it well: "Singly, either the President or Congress can fall into bad errors. . . . So they can together too, but that is somewhat less likely, and in any event, together they are all we've got."

THE COUNTERARGUMENT FROM PRACTICE

The other argument that we can ignore the original demand of the Constitution here — this one is made more explicitly — is an argument from post-ratification practice, that the behavior of various presidents, and the acquiescence of various congresses, during the 200 years since the document was adopted have in essence amended it, effectively eliminating the requirement of congressional authorization. The most obvious answer here is one the Supreme Court has given many times, that past violations are only that — violations — and cannot change the meaning of the Constitution: "That an unconstitutional action has been taken before surely does not render that same action any less unconstitutional at a later date." Though that's got to be generally right, it may oversimplify somewhat, unduly assimilating constitutional provisions of relevantly different types. If, for example, the question before the Court were whether a certain action was appropriately classified as within the "legislative power" or the "executive power" — *and* there were no more precise provision suggesting an answer — one would rightly expect the judges to be interested in how various presidents and congresses, most particularly *early* presidents and congresses, had by action and acquiescence effectively classified it. Our question, however, does not present a case of one or more vague documentary vessels that must receive their meaning from subsequent experience. In language and recorded purpose the War Clause made an unmistakable point that needed no further gloss: Acts of war must be authorized by Congress. In cases like this the Court is quite right: Usurpation isn't precedent, it's usurpation.

Assume this were not so, however, and that on some oddly repotted "adverse possession" theory, post-ratification practice in violation of the Constitution could change it, still the argument could not work in this context. At the very least we would require "a systematic, unbroken, executive practice, long pursued to the knowledge of the Congress and never before questioned," a pattern that on every count is manifestly lacking here. Of course real life is never entirely neat and clean, but the original constitutional understanding was quite consistently honored from the framing until 1950. And when certain presidents did play a little fast and loose with congressional prerogatives — Polk at the start of the Mexican War; Wilson and Roosevelt, respectively, in the events leading up to the First and Second World Wars — they obscured or covered up the actual facts, pledging public fealty to the constitutional need for congressional authorization of military action. It is therefore impossible to build the occasional nonconforming presidential actions of this period into an argument that they had gradually altered the constitutional plan. Shifts of constitutional power, to the extent they are possible at all, must be accomplished in the open.

John Yoo

THE CONTINUATION OF POLITICS BY OTHER MEANS: THE ORIGINAL UNDERSTANDING OF WAR POWERS

84 Cal. L. Rev. 167 (Mar. 1996)

INTRODUCTION

Since the end of the Cold War, our nation has turned to the use of force in its foreign relations more frequently than some might have hoped. The increase in military interventions — in Lebanon, Grenada, the Persian Gulf, Panama, Kuwait, Somalia, Haiti, and now Bosnia — has been accompanied by increasing academic criticism of the way in which the federal government makes war. This criticism, which represents a diversity of political and intellectual positions, is striking both for its uniformity of opinion and its harshness of tone. Critics of the current war powers landscape accuse Presidents from Harry Truman to George Bush of waging "unconstitutional" wars, portray Congress as shirking its constitutional responsibilities, and point to the "powerful whiff of hypocrisy" found in the judiciary's hands-off attitude.

According to these scholars, the post–World War II era has witnessed nothing less than "the disappearance of the separation of powers, the system of checks and balances, as it applies to decisions to go to war." Arguing that the Framers intended Congress to have exclusive control over the decision to go to war, they interpret the Declare War Clause as a separation of powers provision that not only empowers Congress, but also limits executive abilities to make war. Under this approach, in order to wage war, the President must receive a declaration of war or its "functional equivalent" from Congress. Should the President overstep these constitutional boundaries, the federal courts must intervene to right the balance by declaring the war unconstitutional or even by enjoining the President's actions.

Historical practice, however, has contrasted starkly with these constitutional arguments. Congress has issued a declaration of war only five times in its history. The post-1945 era has borne witness to a litany of undeclared wars and an even longer list of less significant uses of the military. The President has initiated conflict, often without any formal signs of congressional approval, and certainly without a declaration of war. With few exceptions, the federal courts either have refused to hear constitutional challenges to these wars, or have upheld the propriety of the executive action.

This divergence of academic theory and political practice has led to an unusual arrangement of ideology and constitutional interpretation. "Liberals" who opposed unilateral executive authority have turned to the Framers' intent for support, arguing for a Constitution with a meaning fixed by the history of its drafting. "Conservatives" who favored enhanced presidential war powers have invoked the lessons of the recent past and the nation's post-ratification history to buttress a vision of a Constitution that has adapted to a dangerous world.

This Article argues, in a sense, that both sides are wrong. It agrees with the methodology employed by the critics of executive dominance over war powers but disagrees with their conclusions. When interpreting the text of the Constitution, we should seek to determine the meaning of its terms as understood by those who adopted its provisions. As the majority of scholars in the war powers area recognize, this is the best starting point to interpret the Constitution. As a written document, the Constitution's meaning does not change from the meaning it held for its drafters. Otherwise the Constitution's meaning would be as inconstant as, to paraphrase Horace, the times, or the mores.

Most works have focused on the short discussion of the Declare War Clause at the Constitutional Convention and a few selected comments from *The Federalist.* Others rely heavily on post-ratification evidence from the first quarter-century of the nation's youth to fill in the Constitution's perceived ambiguities. But these approaches fail to recognize that the Framers neither acted in a historical vacuum, nor wrote on a constitutional tabula rasa. Nor can we take as dispositive private comments that were not made known to the state ratifying conventions or to the people.

The historical evidence reveals a Constitution that does not prescribe one exclusive method for going to war. A war may be constitutional, even if no declaration of war has issued or if the President has acted unilaterally, so long as one branch has not usurped the textually enumerated power of another. The Constitution establishes a war-making process that can vary with the circumstances and with the relative political power of the President and Congress. It assumes that the political branches will exercise their constitutional powers sometimes cooperatively and sometimes antagonistically. Moreover, the Constitution did not inadvertently allocate all war powers to the two political branches; rather, the nature of the mutable process it created made judicial supervision unworkable and undesirable.

The Framers established a system which was designed to encourage presidential initiative in war, but which granted Congress an ultimate check on executive actions. Congress could express its opposition to executive war decisions only by exercising its powers over funding and impeachment. The Framers established this system because they were not excessively worried by the prospect of unilateral executive action. The President was seen as the protector and representative of the People. In contrast, the Framers expressed a deep concern regarding the damage that Congress, and the interest groups that could dominate it, might cause in the delicate areas of war and foreign policy.

Original understanding analysis illuminates the general framework that the Framers erected and what their expectations were. Because the Constitution fails to specify an exact relationship between the President and Congress in the area of war, examination of post-ratification practice confirms our understanding of the allocation of war powers between the branches. Ultimately, however, it is the constitutional framework that endures, while the exact processes of going to war within that framework may change over time.

I. WAR POWERS: ALLOCATION, PRACTICE, AND CRITICISM

A. The Constitutional Text

As with all constitutional questions, an analysis of war powers should begin with the constitutional text, which allocates war-making authority not to a single branch of government, but to both the executive and legislative departments. Article I gives Congress the power to "declare War, grant Letters of Marque and Reprisal, and make Rules concerning Captures on Land and Water." Congress also has the authority to "raise and support Armies," to "provide and maintain a Navy," to "make Rules for the Government and Regulation of the land and naval Forces," to "provide for calling forth the Militia to execute the Laws of the Union, suppress Insurrections and repel Invasions," and to "provide for organizing, arming, and disciplining, the Militia." Congress also possesses other powers related to foreign affairs, including the power to regulate international commerce, to establish immigration rules, to pass laws punishing piracy and felonies committed on the high seas, and to give its advice and consent to the appointment of ambassadors and the making of treaties.

Compared to this impressive list, the powers of the President at first glance appear somewhat paltry. Article II states that "the President shall be Commander in Chief of the Army and Navy of the United States, and of the Militia of the several States, when called into the actual Service of the United States." The President's other enumerated powers include the authority to receive ambassadors and, with the advice and consent of the Senate, to make treaties and appoint ambassadors. Finally, Article II vests "the executive Power" and the duty to execute the laws in the President.

The judiciary's powers are limited in the area of war powers, although the federal courts do have jurisdiction over cases that may relate to foreign affairs. Article III vests the judicial power of the United States in the federal courts, and gives them jurisdiction over cases arising under the Constitution, treaties, and other laws of the United States. No provision explicitly authorizes the federal courts to intervene directly in war powers questions.

1. Congress and President

The Constitution's division of authority establishes a framework that has evolved into the operational system of war powers we have today. The experiences of World Wars I and II might lead one to assume that because Congress declared war in those two wars, the Constitution requires a declaration to trigger the President's powers as Commander in Chief. However, formal declarations of war have constituted the exception rather than the rule in American history. . . . Although declarations of war have been rare, Congress has never been wholly absent from the war powers equation. For much of the nineteenth and early twentieth centuries, Congress assented to presidential uses of force abroad. Interventions undertaken without congressional approval were, for the most part, small-scale actions to protect American property, citizens, or honor abroad that had little risk of significant combat. Larger-scale actions required the President to seek congressional approval for expanded military forces. Given this relative inter-branch harmony, it is not surprising that the judiciary was not an active participant in war powers.

With the establishment of a large peacetime military force in the twentieth century, the prospect of unilateral presidential war-making appeared, concerns about congressional control emerged, and questions about the role of the judiciary arose. The Cold War period provoked almost continual struggles between the two branches over war powers. . . . A period of presidential weakness in the aftermath of the Vietnam War and Watergate prompted congressional efforts to assert control over the war-making process. In 1973, Congress passed the War Powers Resolution over President Nixon's veto to fulfill the intent of the framers . . . and insure that the collective judgment of both the Congress and the President will apply to the introduction of United States Armed Forces into hostilities, or into situations where imminent involvement in hostilities is clearly indicated by the circumstances, and to the continued use of such forces in hostilities or in such situations.

The Resolution further declares Congress' belief that the President can exercise his Commander-in-Chief powers "only pursuant to (1) a declaration of war, (2) specific statutory authorization, or (3) a national emergency created by attack upon the United States, its territories or possessions, or its armed forces." The Resolution attempts to prevent the President from sending the American military into combat without congressional approval, except in emergency situations.

Congress included three mechanisms in the Resolution designed to assure congressional participation in the war-making process. First, "the President in every possible instance shall consult with Congress" before introducing the armed forces into hostilities, whether imminent or actual. Second, the President must report to Congress within forty-eight hours of sending the military into (a) hostilities or imminent hostilities, (b) into the territory of another nation equipped for combat, or (c) in numbers which substantially increase the size of the American forces stationed in a foreign nation. This report must explain why the President sent the troops, describe the constitutional and legislative authority for the action, and estimate the scope and duration of the intervention.

The reporting requirement then triggers the third requirement: the controversial sixty-day clock. Once the President has reported military intervention to Congress, the Resolution requires the President to terminate the intervention within sixty days. Three events can forestall removal of American forces: (1) a declaration of war or specific congressional authorization; (2) congressional extension of the sixty-day period; or (3) congressional inability to meet due to armed attack on the United States. The President may also extend the sixty-day period once for thirty days if he certifies that the additional time is necessary to permit the safe withdrawal of American armed forces. Finally, the Resolution permits Congress to terminate an unauthorized presidential use of military force at any time by concurrent resolution.

Most commentators would agree that the Resolution has not proven to be a resounding success. No President has ever acknowledged its constitutionality, and no President has ever formally complied with its terms. The high watermark of presidential recognition of the Resolution was President Ford's messages to Congress in which he took "note" of the Resolution when he sent military forces to evacuate Americans from South Vietnam and Cambodia and to rescue American sailors in the S.S. *Mayaguez* incident . . . of military action in messages that used similar language.

Despite presidential noncompliance, Congress has never sought to enforce the Resolution's terms either by using section

5's concurrent resolution mechanism or by removing funding for the military action. Congressional inaction has led challengers of the president's use of military force to seek judicial declarations that the President has violated the Constitution.

2. The Courts and the War Powers

Although individual members of Congress have criticized presidential actions in these various wars, Congress as a body has never sought to block executive war-making in the courts. But individuals who have been adversely affected by these military interventions have challenged presidential action by seeking redress in the courts. These actions have met with little success, because the Supreme Court has deferred to the conduct of international relations by the other branches, particularly the President. By relying on doctrines including political questions, ripeness, mootness, and standing, and by refusing to grant a writ of certiorari, the Court has studiously avoided becoming embroiled in war powers disputes.

From the earliest days of the Republic, the Court has recognized that the other branches must permit the President some amount of discretion in the conduct of foreign relations. When Chief Justice John Marshall was a Congressman, he declared that the President was "the sole organ of the nation in its external relations." Later, when he wrote *Marbury v. Madison*, Marshall made clear that there were "questions in their nature political" which were entrusted to the executive branch and removed from judicial review.

In discussing whether the Jefferson administration could withhold Marbury's commission, Marshall wrote:

> By the constitution of the United States, the president is invested with certain important political powers, in the exercise of which he is to use his own discretion, and is accountable only to his country in his political character, and to his own conscience. . . . The subjects are political . . . and being entrusted to the executive, the decision of the executive is conclusive.
>
> . . . Questions in their nature political, or which are, by the constitution and laws, submitted to the executive, can never be made in this court.

Even when faced with the modern wars of the twentieth century, the Court has continued to recognize that foreign affairs questions often are beyond judicial competence. In 1918, the Court in *Oetjen v. Central Leather Co.* declared, "The conduct of the foreign relations of our Government is committed by the Constitution to the Executive and Legislative—'the political'—Departments of the Government, and the propriety of what may be done in the exercise of this political power is not subject to judicial inquiry or decision." The twentieth-century Court also has held that the political question doctrine applies to the determination of when war has ended and whether the United States has recognized a foreign government.

The foremost statement of the convergence of judicial deference and executive discretion in foreign affairs came in Justice Sutherland's opinion in *United States v. Curtiss-Wright Export Corp.*:

> Not only . . . is the federal power over external affairs in origin and essential character different from that over internal affairs, but participation in the exercise of the power is significantly limited. In this vast external realm, with its important, complicated, delicate and manifold problems, the President alone has the power to speak or listen as a representative of the nation. It is important to bear in mind that we are here dealing . . . [with] the very delicate, plenary and exclusive power of the President as the sole organ of the federal government in the field of international relations. . . .

Baker v. Carr expresses the modern version of the political question doctrine. Although not a foreign affairs case, several of *Baker*'s justiciability factors apply with vigor to war powers and foreign affairs issues. Although "it is error to suppose that every case or controversy which touches foreign relations lies beyond judicial cognizance," Justice Brennan commented:

> Not only does resolution of such issues frequently turn on standards that defy judicial application, or involve the exercise of a discretion demonstrably committed to the executive or legislature; but many such questions uniquely demand single-voiced statement of the Government's views.

Baker's broad definition of the political question doctrine has permitted enhanced presidential powers in foreign affairs, primarily because the "single-voiced statement of the Government's views" has come almost exclusively from the executive branch. Over time, Chief Justice Marshall's original doctrine of presidential discretion in certain political areas involving the "nation, not individual rights," has neatly dovetailed with the President's growing control over foreign affairs.

Given these broad doctrines, it should come as no surprise that the Supreme Court has avoided challenges to the use of the war power. In the Korean and Vietnam Wars, for example, the Court regularly refused to grant a writ of certiorari for cases brought by draftees challenging the wars' constitutionality. Several times, Justice Douglas dissented from the denial of certiorari on the ground "that the constitutional questions raised by conscription for a presidential war are both substantial and justiciable," but to no avail. Moreover, lower courts faced with Vietnam War suits regularly dismissed them as presenting political questions.

The judicial tradition of deference has continued during the post-Vietnam era, even in the context of the War Powers Resolution. When various plaintiffs challenged the Reagan administration's use of the American military in Central America in 1982 and the Persian Gulf in 1987, the D.C. Circuit dismissed the suits as presenting non-justiciable political questions. When twenty-nine Members of Congress sued President Reagan for allegedly sending illegal aid to El Salvador in violation of the War Powers Resolution, the same court held that whether the President had to comply with the Resolution's terms presented a non-justiciable political question.

Even though the modern Supreme Court has never ruled on the proper constitutional allocation of war powers among the three branches, what Professor Reisman calls an "operational code of competence" has formed among them. In other words, the President, Congress, and the federal courts have acted according to a set of norms and rules that they deem authoritative. In the war powers context, the President has taken the primary role in deciding when and how to wage war. Congress has fallen into the role of approving the interventions either through authorization before operations have begun or appropriations after the fact, while the judicial branch has abstained from inter-branch war powers disputes because they raise non-justiciable political questions. Put less charitably, we have a system which Professor Koh describes as one of "executive initiative, congressional acquiescence, and judicial tolerance." Professor Koh's views are emblematic of a growing consensus among international and constitutional law scholars that the President's war powers grasp exceeds his constitutional reach.

C. The Academic Critique: The President Against the Professors

For the most part, legal academia has sharply criticized the current state of war powers. In a series of recent books, foreign relations and international law scholars such as John Hart Ely, Louis Henkin, Michael Glennon, Thomas Franck, Louis Fisher, and Harold Koh have taken the Presidents to task for waging unconstitutional war and have chastised the courts for abdicating their duty to adjudicate war power cases. These scholars rest their arguments on three bases: first, that the Framers intended Congress to exercise exclusive control over the decision to go to war; second, that modern separation of powers doctrine requires congressional approval of war; and third, that the courts have a constitutional duty to determine the proper allocation of war-making power between the President and Congress.

In a curious reversal of roles, the war powers question displays critics of the legal theories of the Reagan and Bush administrations readily invoking the intent of the Framers. They claim that the Declare War Clause, in light of their reading of the thoughts of the Constitution's drafters, clearly indicates that the Framers intended that Congress play an equal, if not paramount, role in the decision to go to war. This original intent argument is an important part of the academic critique of presidential power that this Article intends to refute....

IV. THE NEW CONSTITUTION

A. The Constitutional Text in Context

Our analysis begins with the constitutional text. In order to understand what the Constitution requires, we must place its text in the legal context of its day. Those who ratified the Constitution would not have understood its provisions in a vacuum, but instead would have compared and contrasted the document with both their legal understanding of the words and their understanding of how these provisions operated in the world of the eighteenth century.

The Framers included the declaration of war in the Constitution as a device to facilitate the federal government's representation of the nation in international affairs, and to make clear that the declaration of war was a power of the national government, not the state governments. As we have seen, a declaration of war performed a primarily juridical function under eighteenth-century international law, and it was this understanding that the Framers drew upon in giving Congress the authority to declare war. Critics, however, have misinterpreted it as primarily a separation of powers vehicle.

... [I]n the eighteenth-century mind, a declaration of war was not the same thing as a domestic authorization of war. In fact, a declaration of war was understood as what its name suggests: a declaration. Like a declaratory judgment, a declaration of war represented the judgment of Congress, acting in a judicial capacity (as it does in impeachments), that a state of war existed between the United States and another nation. Such a declaration could take place either before or after hostilities had commenced. While the power to "declare" war adds to Congress' store of powers, it does little to alter the relative domestic authorities of the executive and legislative branches. Its primary function was to trigger the international laws of war, which would clothe in legitimacy certain actions taken against one's own and enemy citizens. This was the meaning attributed to a declaration of war by seventeenth and eighteenth-century scholars on the laws of nations.

The Framers turned to international law to define phrases such as to "declare war" because it was international law (and international politics) which gave these powers meaning. Consistent with Chief Justice John Marshall's holding in *The Schooner Charming Betsy* that international law serves as a canon for statutory construction, it is appropriate to use international law as a canon of construction in the constitutional context.

American jurists in the decades following the ratification of the Constitution continued to interpret the declaration as a notification mechanism that defined the wartime rights of citizens and neutrals. Thus, Americans of the eighteenth century would have understood that the power to declare war dealt with setting the formal, legal relationship between two nations, and not with authorizing real hostilities. Once war was declared, a citizen of the United States could seize a ship flying French colors regardless of the state of relations between the two nations. However, if Congress has not declared a state of hostilities, the citizen must return the ship and pay damages; if a declaration has issued, he may sell the ship as a prize. But in neither case is a declaration of war necessary to "authorize," ex ante, the seizure of the ship.

Of course, in legitimating hostilities, this core function of a declaration of war could be thought to "authorize" war by justifying federal wartime policies. Because the declaration of war has a primary domestic effect of notifying the citizens of their new rights and obligations, it grants the government a different standard of conduct in relation to those rights and duties. Thus, a declaration of war would permit the government to treat its citizens in a way that restricted peacetime liberties in favor of a more effective war effort. The Fifth Amendment, for example, generally guarantees the right to an indictment or presentment by grand jury for capital crimes, "except in cases arising in the land or naval forces, or in the Militia, when in actual service in time of War or public danger." In time of war, Congress may authorize seizure of property belonging to foreigners without the need for compensations as required by the Takings Clause. During the Quasi-War, Federalists clamored for a declaration of war against France, because it would allow the passage at home of broad sedition laws, higher taxes, an expanded peacetime army, and other war measures. Thus, a declaration of war had a domestic function, which permitted new government actions in light of the changed legal status of its citizens. A declaration of war did not grant permission for executive action abroad, as we would expect of an "authorization" of war, but only set the stage for the exercise of domestic wartime powers, primarily by Congress.

Interpreting "declaration" to mean a judgment of a current status of relations, not an authorization of war, provides a new understanding of Congress' role in war, one which is not purely legislative. We should conceptualize the war clause as vesting the legislature with a judicial function, which involves a capacity for judgment in the manner of a court, rather than the enactment of positive law in the style of a legislature. Formally vesting one branch of government with powers that another branch inherently ought to exercise did not trouble the Framers. They gave the President the right to veto legislation, which they thought of as a legislative power; they gave the President and the Senate the power to enter into treaties, which they also believed to be a legislative function. It is this formal mixing of powers that underlies Madison's famous argument in *The Federalist* No. 47 that the departments of government might have a "partial agency in, or . . . controul over the acts of each other."

Thinking of Congress as exercising judicial functions comes more easily when we consider that Article I already vests the legislature with the power of impeachment. Impeachment requires the Senate to act as nothing less than a court of first and last resort. As the Supreme Court implicitly recognized in *Nixon v. United States*, the Constitution vests Congress with a judicial function in impeachment, thereby precluding the federal courts from subsequent review. Although the Court in *Nixon* did not make the connection suggested here, and instead relied upon the political question doctrine, it reached the correct result because the Constitution already vests all judicial power over impeachments to Congress. In other words, the Court could not permit itself to review impeachment proceedings because to do so would vest Article III courts with appellate jurisdiction in derogation of the Senate's own judicial powers.

Analogizing to impeachment supports the legitimacy of the Article III courts' refusal to review war powers cases. Because the Constitution has vested Congress with the entire judicial power to decide whether the United States is in a state of war, no role for the courts is warranted. To be sure, the courts may still adjudicate cases that involve the ramifications of the nation's wartime or peacetime status, such as insurance cases that have wartime clauses. But the Constitution's allocation of the power "to declare war" in Congress divests the courts of any judicial power in war, just as the impeachment clause deprives the courts of any involvement in impeachments. The courts simply must accept the actions of the political branches in war matters as valid indications of whether a state of war exists.

CONCLUSIONS

This study has shown that the Framers ntended Congress to participate in war-making by controlling appropriations. Although the Constitution gives the President the initiative in war by virtue of his powers over foreign relations and the military, it also forces the President to seek money and support from Congress at every turn. In making decisions whether to raise and support the requested forces, Congress can judge the benefits of a particular war as well as influence its means and ends. Such was the practice under the British Constitution and under the early American governments, elements of which provided models for the drafters of the new federal Constitution. Such was the explanation given by the supporters of the Constitution to its opponents.

Contrary to the arguments by today's scholars, the Declare War Clause does not add to Congress' store of war powers at the expense of the President. Rather, the Clause gives Congress a judicial role in declaring that a state of war exists between the United States and another nation, which bears significant legal ramifications concerning the rights and duties of American citizens. Congress' power to declare war also has the additional effect of ousting the courts from war powers disputes, because it deprives the courts of the ability to second-guess Congress' determination of whether a formal state of war exists.

The Framers also may have believed judicial participation unwarranted because of the structure established in the war powers area. The potentially conflicting powers of the President and Congress establishes a system that demanded no constitutionally correct method of waging war, but instead permits flexible decision-making based on each branch's exercise of its powers. Aside perhaps from policing against the most extreme violations of those grants by another branch — such as if Congress attempted to "fire" the President as Commander in Chief — the courts have no constitutional standards to apply to a process the Framers left intentionally undefined. Instead, the Framers understood that the legislature and the executive would use their powers to defend the prerogatives of their departments, as well as to pursue their policy preferences against a recalcitrant coordinate branch. The Framers expected the branches to cooperate to wage a successful war, but also anticipated conflict should the two disagree.

A President sometimes must chart a risky course toward war because the Constitution places him squarely at the tiller. He is not alone; the Congress is at his side, either funding his decisions or frustrating them. This cooperative, and yet competitive, relationship has produced many different wars, and many different ways of going to war, in American history. It is perhaps ironic that as the United States today turns to its military more often in international affairs, the historical roots of war powers are so little understood by academia, or so ambiguously defined by the courts. The recent examples of presidential war-making and congressional inaction do not violate the Constitution, nor should they cause the confusion they appear to. Instead, the elasticity of the war power process has resulted directly from the Framers' conscious design. They established an arena with wide markers to permit the executive and legislative branches to work in harmony, or to struggle for primacy, over issues of war.

As shown in Panama, Kuwait, Somalia, Haiti, and Bosnia, the end of the Cold War has not produced a relaxation in the need for American military force abroad. The approach of a new millennium does not seem to bring the prospects of a millennial peace any closer, either to the world or to the President and the Congress. Indeed the continuing struggle between the branches over the powers of war is only the fulfillment of the Framers' design and in the best interests of the People.

PRIZE CASES

67 U.S. 635 (1863)

Opinion: Grier, joined by Wayne, Swayne, Miller, Davis
Dissent: Nelson, joined by Clifford, Catron, Taney

On April 27, 1861, in the midst of the Civil War, President Abraham Lincoln ordered a naval blockade of southern ports in order to cut off supplies to insurrectionists. The central question in this case is whether President Lincoln had authority to order a blockade given that war had not been formally declared. The Court decided that the southern rebellion clearly instigated a state of war, warranting President Lincoln's actions. Notice that this case puts into tension the president's role as Commander-in-Chief and the role of Congress in declaring war.

In recent times, the question of what exactly constitutes a state of war has become increasingly complicated. Could a terrorist attack on the United States be considered an act of war warranting the president to engage in military conflict without congressional approval? The Civil War was not fought against an autonomous state, and terrorist networks generally transcend state boundaries. Does this case provide a relevant precedent for these kinds of issues?

MR. JUSTICE GRIER *delivered the opinion of the Court.*

Had the President a right to institute a blockade of ports in possession of persons in armed rebellion against the Government, on the principles of international law, as known and acknowledged among civilized States?

Neutrals have a right to challenge the existence of a blockade *de facto*, and also the authority of the party exercising the right to institute it. They have a right to enter the ports of a friendly nation for the purposes of trade and commerce, but are bound to recognize the rights of a belligerent engaged in actual war, to use this mode of coercion, for the purpose of subduing the enemy.

That a blockade *de facto* actually existed, and was formally declared and notified by the President on the 27th and 30th of April, 1861, is an admitted fact in these cases. That the President, as the Executive Chief of the Government and Commander-in-chief of the Army and Navy, was the proper person to make such notification has not been, and cannot be disputed.

The right of prize and capture has its origin in the "*jus belli*," and is governed and adjudged under the law of nations. To legitimate the capture of a neutral vessel or property on the high seas, a war must exist *de facto*, and the neutral must have knowledge or notice of the intention of one of the parties belligerent to use this mode of coercion against a port, city, or territory, in possession of the other.

Let us enquire whether, at the time this blockade was instituted, a state of war existed which would justify a resort to these means of subduing the hostile force. War has been well defined to be, "That state in which a nation prosecutes its right by force." The parties belligerent in a public war are independent nations. But it is not necessary, to constitute war, that both parties should be acknowledged as independent nations or sovereign States. A war may exist where one of the belligerents claims sovereign rights as against the other.

Insurrection against a government may or may not culminate in an organized rebellion, but a civil war always begins by insurrection against the lawful authority of the Government. A civil war is never solemnly declared; it becomes such by its accidents — the number, power, and organization of the persons who originate and carry it on. . . .

By the Constitution, Congress alone has the power to declare a national or foreign war. It cannot declare war against a State, or any number of States, by virtue of any clause in the Constitution. The Constitution confers on the President the whole Executive power. He is bound to take care that the laws be faithfully executed. He is Commander-in-chief of the Army and Navy of the United States, and of the militia of the several States when called into the actual service of the United States. He has no power to initiate or declare a war either against a foreign nation or a domestic State. But, by the Acts of Congress of February 28th, 1795, and 3d of March, 1807, he is authorized to call out the militia and use the military and naval forces of the United States in case of invasion by foreign nations and to suppress insurrection against the government of a State or of the United States.

If a war be made by invasion of a foreign nation, the President is not only authorized but bound to resist force by force. He does not initiate the war, but is bound to accept the challenge without waiting for any special legislative authority. And whether the hostile party be a foreign invader or States organized in rebellion, it is nonetheless a war although the declaration of it be "unilateral."

This greatest of civil wars was not gradually developed by popular commotion, tumultuous assemblies, or local unorganized insurrections. However long may have been its previous conception, it nevertheless sprung forth suddenly from the parent brain, a Minerva in the full panoply of war. The President was bound to meet it in the shape it presented itself, without waiting for Congress to baptize it with a name; and no name given to it by him or them could change the fact. It is not the less a civil war, with belligerent parties in hostile array, because it may be called an "insurrection" by one side, and the insurgents be considered as rebels or traitors. It is not necessary that the independence of the revolted province or State be acknowledged in order to constitute it a party belligerent in a war according to the law of nations.

Whether the President, in fulfilling his duties as Commander-in-chief in suppressing an insurrection, has met with such armed hostile resistance and a civil war of such alarming proportions as will compel him to accord to them the character of belligerents is a question to be decided by him, and this Court must be governed by the decisions and acts of the political department of the Government to which this power was entrusted. "He must determine what degree of force the crisis demands." The proclamation of blockade is itself official and conclusive evidence to the Court that a state of war existed which demanded and authorized a recourse to such a measure under the circumstances peculiar to the case.

. . . [T]herefore, we are of the opinion that the President had a right, *jure belli*, to institute a blockade of ports in possession of the States in rebellion which neutrals are bound to regard.

MR. JUSTICE NELSON, *dissenting.*

... The cases of the *United States v. Palmer*, *Divina Pastora*, and 4 *ibid.* 52, and that class of cases to be found in the reports are referred to as furnishing authority for the exercise of the war power claimed for the President in the present case. These cases hold that, when the Government of the United States recognizes a state of civil war to exist between a foreign nation and her colonies, but remaining itself neutral, the Courts are bound to consider as lawful all those acts which the new Government may direct against the enemy, and we admit the President who conducts the foreign relations of the Government may fitly recognize or refuse to do so, the existence of civil war in the foreign nation under the circumstances stated.

But this is a very different question from the one before us, which is whether the President can recognize or declare a civil war, under the Constitution, with all its belligerent rights, between his own Government and a portion of its citizens in a state of insurrection. That power, as we have seen, belongs to Congress. We agree when such a war is recognized or declared to exist by the warmaking power, but not otherwise, it is the duty of the Courts to follow the decision of the political power of the Government....

Upon the whole, after the most careful consideration of this case which the pressure of other duties has admitted, I am compelled to the conclusion that no civil war existed between this Government and the States in insurrection till recognized by the Act of Congress 13th of July, 1861; that the President does not possess the power under the Constitution to declare war or recognize its existence within the meaning of the law of nations, which carries with it belligerent rights, and thus change the country and all its citizens from a state of peace to a state of war; that this power belongs exclusively to the Congress of the United States, and, consequently, that the President had no power to set on foot a blockade under the law of nations, and that the capture of the vessel and cargo in this case, and in all cases before us in which the capture occurred before the 13th of July, 1861, for breach of blockade, or as enemies' property, are illegal and void, and that the decrees of condemnation should be reversed, and the vessel and cargo restored.

MR. CHIEF JUSTICE TANEY, MR. JUSTICE CATRON *and* **MR. JUSTICE CLIFFORD,** *concurred in the dissenting opinion of* **MR. JUSTICE NELSON.**

UNITED STATES v. CURTISS-WRIGHT EXPORT CORP.

299 U.S. 304 (1936)

Opinion: Sutherland, joined by Hughes, Van Devanter, Brandeis, Butler, Roberts, Cardozo
Dissent (not filed): McReynolds

Defenders of a unitary executive in foreign policy with exclusive control over matters of foreign relations, such as John Yoo, often cite United States v. Curtiss-Wright *as supportive of their position. The case itself centers on two questions: Can the national government impose an arms embargo that will interfere with the rights of an American company to do business with foreign governments in a troubled region in South America? And if so, can the president decide whether and when to impose this embargo? Notice that U.S. Supreme Court Justice George Sutherland cites a joint resolution of Congress authorizing presidential action in this matter, which raises the question of delegation of powers. As you read this case, you should ask whether the president's power in this matter comes from his or her constitutional powers in foreign relations or from the statute in question. Does the case support the theory of a president with the discretion to act alone in matters of international relations? What is meant by the claim quoted by Justice Sutherland from former U.S. Supreme Court Chief Justice John Marshall, that the president is the "sole organ" in matters of international relations?*

Notice too that Justice Sutherland introduces a distinction between the national government's authority in internal domestic matters and external foreign policy matters. Is the president less constrained by the need to consult Congress in foreign as opposed to domestic matters?

MR. JUSTICE SUTHERLAND *delivered the opinion of the Court.*

On January 27, 1936, an indictment was returned in the court below, the first count of which charges that appellees, beginning with the 29th day of May, 1934, conspired to sell in the United States certain arms of war, namely fifteen machine guns, to Bolivia, a country then engaged in armed conflict in the Chaco, in violation of the Joint Resolution of Congress approved May 28, 1934, and the provisions of a proclamation issued on the same day by the President of the United States pursuant to authority conferred by §1 of the resolution.

It is contended that, by the Joint Resolution, the going into effect and continued operation of the resolution was conditioned (a) upon the President's judgment as to its beneficial effect upon the reestablishment of peace between the countries engaged in armed conflict in the Chaco; (b) upon the making of a proclamation, which was left to his unfettered discretion, thus constituting an attempted substitution of the President's will for that of Congress; (c) upon the making of a proclamation putting an end to the operation of the resolution, which again was left to the President's unfettered discretion, and (d) further, that the extent of its operation in particular cases was subject to limitation and exception by the President, controlled by no standard. In each of these particulars, appellees urge that Congress abdicated its essential functions and delegated them to the Executive.

Whether, if the Joint Resolution had related solely to internal affairs, it would be open to the challenge that it constituted an unlawful delegation of legislative power to the Executive we find it unnecessary to determine. The whole aim of the resolution is to affect a situation entirely external to the United States and falling within the category of foreign affairs. The determination which we are called to make, therefore, is whether the Joint Resolution, as applied to that situation, is vulnerable to attack under the rule that forbids a delegation of the lawmaking power. In other words, assuming (but not deciding) that the challenged delegation, if it were confined to internal affairs, would be invalid, may it nevertheless be sustained on the ground that its exclusive aim is to afford a remedy for a hurtful condition within foreign territory?

It will contribute to the elucidation of the question if we first consider the differences between the powers of the federal government in respect of foreign or external affairs and those in respect of domestic or internal affairs. That there are differences between them, and that these differences are fundamental, may not be doubted.

The two classes of powers are different both in respect of their origin and their nature. The broad statement that the federal government can exercise no powers except those specifically enumerated in the Constitution, and such implied powers as are necessary and proper to carry into effect the enumerated powers, is categorically true only in respect of our internal affairs. In that field, the primary purpose of the Constitution was to carve from the general mass of legislative powers then possessed by the states such portions as it was thought desirable to vest in the federal government, leaving those not included in the enumeration still in the states. *Carter v. Carter Coal Co.* That this doctrine applies only to powers which the states had is self-evident. And since the states severally never possessed international powers, such powers could not have been carved from the mass of state powers, but obviously were transmitted to the United States from some other source. During the colonial period, those powers were possessed exclusively by, and were entirely under the control of, the Crown. By the Declaration of Independence, "the Representatives of the United States of America" declared the United [not the several] Colonies to be free and independent states, and, as such, to have "full Power to levy War, conclude Peace, contract Alliances, establish Commerce, and to do all other Acts and Things which Independent States may of right do."

As a result of the separation from Great Britain by the colonies, acting as a unit, the powers of external sovereignty passed from the Crown not to the colonies severally, but to the colonies in their collective and corporate capacity as the United States of America. Even before the Declaration, the colonies were a unit in foreign affairs, acting through a common agency—namely the Continental Congress, composed of delegates from the thirteen colonies. When, therefore, the external sovereignty of Great Britain in respect of the colonies ceased, it immediately passed to the Union. *See Penhallow v. Doane.* That fact was given practical application almost at once. The treaty of peace, made on September 23, 1783, was concluded between his Brittanic Majesty and the "United States of America." 8 Stat.—European Treaties—80.

The Union existed before the Constitution, which was ordained and established, among other things, to form "a more perfect Union." Prior to that event, it is clear that the Union, declared by the Articles of Confederation to be "perpetual," was the sole possessor of external sovereignty, and in the Union it remained without change save insofar as the Constitution, in express terms, qualified its exercise.

It results that the investment of the federal government with the powers of external sovereignty did not depend upon the affirmative grants of the Constitution. The powers to declare and wage war, to conclude peace, to make treaties, to maintain diplomatic relations with other sovereignties, if they had never been mentioned in the Constitution, would have vested in the federal government as necessary concomitants of nationality. Neither the Constitution nor the laws passed in pursuance of it have any force in foreign territory unless in respect of our own citizens (*see American Banana Co. v. United Fruit Co.*), and operations of the nation in such territory must be governed by treaties, international understandings and compacts, and the principles of international law. As a member of the family of nations, the right and power of the United States in that field are equal to the right and power of the other members of the international family. Otherwise, the United States is not completely sovereign. The power to acquire territory by discovery and occupation (*Jones v. United States*), the power to expel undesirable aliens (*Fong Yue Ting v. United States*), the power to make such international agreements as do not constitute treaties in the constitutional sense (*Altman & Co. v. United States*; Crandall, *Treaties, Their Making and Enforcement,* 2d ed., p. 102 and note 1), none of which is expressly affirmed by the Constitution, nevertheless exist as inherently inseparable from the conception of nationality. This the court recognized, and, in each of the cases cited, found the warrant for its conclusions not in the provisions of the Constitution, but in the law of nations.

Not only, as we have shown, is the federal power over external affairs in origin and essential character different from that over internal affairs, but participation in the exercise of the power is significantly limited. In this vast external realm, with its important, complicated, delicate and manifold problems, the President alone has the power to speak or listen as a representative of the nation. He makes treaties with the advice and consent of the Senate; but he alone negotiates. Into the field of negotiation the Senate cannot intrude, and Congress itself is powerless to invade it. As Marshall said in his great argument of March 7, 1800, in the House of Representatives, "The President is the sole organ of the nation in its external relations, and its sole representative with foreign nations."

It is important to bear in mind that we are here dealing not alone with an authority vested in the President by an exertion of legislative power, but with such an authority plus the very delicate, plenary and exclusive power of the President as the sole organ of the federal government in the field of international relations — a power which does not require as a basis for its exercise an act of Congress but which, of course, like every other governmental power, must be exercised in subordination to the applicable provisions of the Constitution. It is quite apparent that if, in the maintenance of our international relations, embarrassment — perhaps serious embarrassment — is to be avoided and success for our aims achieved, congressional legislation which is to be made effective through negotiation and inquiry within the international field must often accord to the President a degree of discretion and freedom from statutory restriction which would not be admissible were domestic affairs alone involved. Moreover, he, not Congress, has the better opportunity of knowing the conditions which prevail in foreign countries, and especially is this true in time of war. He has his confidential sources of information. He has his agents in the form of diplomatic, consular and other officials. Secrecy in respect of information gathered by them may be highly necessary, and the premature disclosure of it productive of harmful results.

When the President is to be authorized by legislation to act in respect of a matter intended to affect a situation in foreign territory, the legislator properly bears in mind the important consideration that the form of the President's action or, indeed, whether he shall act at all — may well depend, among other things, upon the nature of the confidential information which he has or may thereafter receive, or upon the effect which his action may have upon our foreign relations. This consideration, in connection with what we have already said on the subject, discloses the unwisdom of requiring Congress in this field of governmental power to lay down narrowly definite standards by which the President is to be governed.

In the light of the foregoing observations, it is evident that this court should not be in haste to apply a general rule which will have the effect of condemning legislation like that under review as constituting an unlawful delegation of legislative power. The principles which justify such legislation find overwhelming support in the unbroken legislative practice which has prevailed almost from the inception of the national government to the present day.

We deem it unnecessary to consider *seriatim* the several clauses which are said to evidence the unconstitutionality of the Joint Resolution as involving an unlawful delegation of legislative power. It is enough to summarize by saying that, both upon principle and in accordance with precedent, we conclude there is sufficient warrant for the broad discretion vested in the President to determine whether the enforcement of the statute will have a beneficial effect upon the reestablishment of peace in the affected countries; whether he shall make proclamation to bring the resolution into operation; whether and when the resolution shall cease to operate and to make proclamation accordingly, and to prescribe limitations and exceptions to which the enforcement of the resolution shall be subject.

GOLDWATER v. CARTER

444 U.S. 996 (1979)

Concurrence: Rehnquist, joined by Burger, Stewart, Stevens
Concurrence: Powell, Marshall
Concurrence: Blackmun, White
Dissent: Brennan

This case centers on President Jimmy Carter's decision to nullify unilaterally a treaty that had been signed with Taiwan limiting U.S. relations with China. President Carter had argued that while treaty ratification requires the advice and consent of the Senate, treaty nullification does not. As you will see, U.S. Supreme Court then–Associate Justice William Rehnquist in his opinion, joined by three other justices, argues that this issue is a political question and therefore an issue that the Court should not decide. In other words, four justices argued that this decision should be left to the other branches to resolve on their own. To what extent does this case differ from others concerning the authority of the president over foreign affairs in which the Court did make a decision about what was required by the Constitution? Is the Court justified in removing itself from certain political disputes such as the one discussed here? Notice, too, the concurrence by U.S. Supreme Court Justice Lewis Powell, who provided the crucial fifth vote. Justice Powell suggests that the Court should not decide this case on the merits, but he provides a very different rationale from Justice Rehnquist for that decision.

MR. JUSTICE REHNQUIST, *with whom* **THE CHIEF JUSTICE, MR. JUSTICE STEWART,** *and* **MR. JUSTICE STEVENS** *join, concurring in the judgment.*

I am of the view that the basic question presented by the petitioners in this case is "political," and therefore nonjusticiable because it involves the authority of the President in the conduct of our country's foreign relations and the extent to which the Senate or the Congress is authorized to negate the action of the President. In *Coleman v. Miller*, a case in which members of the Kansas Legislature brought an action attacking a vote of the State Senate in favor of the ratification of the Child Labor Amendment, Mr. Chief Justice Hughes wrote in what is referred to as the "Opinion of the Court":

> "We think that . . . the question of the efficacy of ratifications by state legislatures, in the light of previous rejection or attempted withdrawal, should be regarded as a political question pertaining to the political departments, with the ultimate authority in the Congress in the exercise of its control over the promulgation of the adoption of the Amendment.
>
> "The precise question as now raised is whether, when the legislature of the State, as we have found, has actually ratified the proposed amendment, the Court should restrain the state officers from certifying the ratification to the Secretary of State, because of an earlier rejection, and thus prevent the question from coming before the political departments. We find no basis in either Constitution or statute for such judicial action. Article V, speaking solely of ratification, contains no provision as to rejection. . . ."

Id. at 307 U.S. 450.

Thus, Mr. Chief Justice Hughes' opinion concluded that "Congress, in controlling the promulgation of the adoption of a constitutional amendment, has the final determination of the question whether, by lapse of time, its proposal of the amendment had lost its vitality prior to the required ratifications." *Id.* at 307 U.S. 456.

I believe it follows *a fortiori* from *Coleman* that the controversy in the instant case is a nonjusticiable political dispute that should be left for resolution by the Executive and Legislative Branches of the Government. Here, while the Constitution is express as to the manner in which the Senate shall participate in the ratification of a treaty, it is silent as to that body's participation in the abrogation of a treaty. In this respect, the case is directly analogous to *Coleman, supra.* As stated in *Dyer v. Blair* (three-judge court):

> "A question that might be answered in different ways for different amendments must surely be controlled by political standards, rather than standards easily characterized as judicially manageable."

In light of the absence of any constitutional provision governing the termination of a treaty, and the fact that different termination procedures may be appropriate for different treaties (*see, e.g.*, 444 U.S. 1, *infra*), the instant case, in my view, also "must surely be controlled by political standards."

I think that the justifications for concluding that the question here is political in nature are even more compelling than in *Coleman,* because it involves foreign relations — specifically, a treaty commitment to use military force in the defense of a foreign government if attacked. . . .

The present case differs in several important respects from *Youngstown Sheet & Tube Co. v. Sawyer,* cited by petitioners as authority both for reaching the merits of this dispute and for reversing the Court of Appeals. In *Youngstown,* private litigants brought a suit contesting the President's authority under his war powers to seize the Nation's steel industry, an action of profound and demonstrable domestic impact. Here, by contrast, we are asked to settle a dispute between coequal branches of our Government, each of which has resources available to protect and assert its interests, resources not available to private litigants outside the judicial forum. Moreover, as in *Curtiss-Wright,* the effect of this action, as far as we can tell, is "entirely external to the United States, and [falls] within the category of foreign affairs." Finally, as already noted, the situation presented here is closely akin to that presented in *Coleman,* where the Constitution spoke only to the procedure for ratification of an amendment, not to its rejection.

Having decided that the question presented in this action is nonjusticiable, I believe that the appropriate disposition is for this Court to vacate the decision of the Court of Appeals and remand with instructions for the District Court to dismiss the complaint. . . .

MR. JUSTICE POWELL, *concurring.*

Although I agree with the result reached by the Court, I would dismiss the complaint as not ripe for judicial review.

I

This Court has recognized that an issue should not be decided if it is not ripe for judicial review. *Buckley v. Valeo* (per curiam). Prudential considerations persuade me that a dispute between Congress and the President is not ready for judicial review unless and until each branch has taken action asserting its constitutional authority. Differences between the President and the Congress are commonplace under our system. The differences should, and almost invariably do, turn on political, rather than legal, considerations. The Judicial Branch should not decide issues affecting the allocation of power between the President and Congress until the political branches reach a constitutional impasse. Otherwise, we would encourage small groups, or even individual Members, of Congress to seek judicial resolution of issues before the normal political process has the opportunity to resolve the conflict.

In the present posture of this case, we do not know whether there ever will be an actual confrontation between the Legislative and Executive Branches. . . . If the Congress chooses not to confront the President, it is not our task to do so. I therefore concur in the dismissal of this case.

II

Mr. Justice Rehnquist suggests, however, that the issue presented by this case is a nonjusticiable political question which can never be considered by this Court. I cannot agree. In my view, reliance upon the political question doctrine is inconsistent with our precedents. As set forth in the seminal case of *Baker v. Carr*, the doctrine incorporates three inquiries: (i) does the issue involve resolution of questions committed by the text of the Constitution to a coordinate branch of Government? (ii) would resolution of the question demand that a court move beyond areas of judicial expertise? (iii) do prudential considerations counsel against judicial intervention? In my opinion the answer to each of these inquiries would require us to decide this case if it were ready for review.

First, the existence of "a textually demonstrable constitutional commitment of the issue to a coordinate political department," *ibid.*, turns on an examination of the constitutional provisions governing the exercise of the power in question. *Powell v. McCormack*. No constitutional provision explicitly confers upon the President the power to terminate treaties. Further, Art. II, §2, of the Constitution authorizes the President to make treaties with the advice and consent of the Senate. Article VI provides that treaties shall be a part of the supreme law of the land. These provisions add support to the view that the text of the Constitution does not unquestionably commit the power to terminate treaties to the President alone. *Cf. Gilligan v. Morgan*; *Luther v. Borden*.

Second, there is no "lack of judicially discoverable and manageable standards for resolving" this case; nor is a decision impossible "without an initial policy determination of a kind clearly for nonjudicial discretion." *Baker v. Carr, supra,* at 369 U.S. 217. We are asked to decide whether the President may terminate a treaty under the Constitution without congressional approval. Resolution of the question may not be easy, but it only requires us to apply normal principles of interpretation to the constitutional provisions at issue. *See Powell v. McCormack, supra,* at 395 U.S. 548-549. The present case involves neither review of the President's activities as Commander in Chief nor impermissible interference in the field of foreign affairs. Such a case would arise if we were asked to decide, for example, whether a treaty required the President to order troops into a foreign country. But "it is error to suppose that every case or controversy which touches foreign relations lies beyond judicial cognizance." *Baker v. Carr, supra,* at 369 U.S. 211. This case "touches" foreign relations, but the question presented to us concerns only the constitutional division of power between Congress and the President.

A simple hypothetical demonstrates the confusion that I find inherent in Mr. Justice Rehnquist's opinion concurring in the judgment. Assume that the President signed a mutual defense treaty with a foreign country and announced that it would go into effect despite its rejection by the Senate. Under Mr. Justice Rehnquist's analysis, that situation would present a political question even though Art. II, §2, clearly would resolve the dispute. Although the answer to the hypothetical case seems self-evident because it demands textual, rather than interstitial, analysis, the nature of the legal issue presented is no different from the issue presented in the case before us. In both cases, the Court would interpret the Constitution to decide whether congressional approval is necessary to give a Presidential decision on the validity of a treaty the force of law. Such an inquiry demands no special competence or information beyond the reach of the Judiciary. *Cf. Chicago & Southern Air Lines v. Waterman S.S. Corp.*

Finally, the political question doctrine rests in part on prudential concerns calling for mutual respect among the three branches of Government. Thus, the Judicial Branch should avoid "the potentiality of embarrassment [that would result] from multifarious pronouncements by various departments on one question." Similarly, the doctrine restrains judicial action where there is an "unusual need for unquestioning adherence to a political decision already made." *Baker v. Carr, supra,* at 369 U.S. 217.

If this case were ripe for judicial review, *see* Part I *supra,* none of these prudential considerations would be present. Interpretation of the Constitution does not imply lack of respect for a coordinate branch. *Powell v. McCormack, supra,* at 395 U.S. 548. If the President and the Congress had reached irreconcilable positions, final disposition of the question presented by this case would eliminate, rather than create, multiple constitutional interpretations. The specter of the Federal Government brought to a halt because of the mutual intransigence of the President and the Congress would require this Court to provide a resolution pursuant to our duty "'*to say what the law is.*'" *United States v. Nixon,* quoting *Marbury v. Madison*. . . .

MR. JUSTICE BLACKMUN, *with whom* **MR. JUSTICE WHITE** *joins, dissenting in part.*

In my view, the time factor and its importance are illusory; if the President does not have the power to terminate the treaty (a substantial issue that we should address only after briefing and oral argument), the notice of intention to terminate surely has no legal effect. It is also indefensible, without further study, to pass on the issue of justiciability or on the issues of standing or ripeness. While I therefore join in the grant of the petition for certiorari, I would set the case for oral argument and give it the plenary consideration it so obviously deserves.

MR. JUSTICE BRENNAN, *dissenting.*

I respectfully dissent from the order directing the District Court to dismiss this case, and would affirm the judgment of the Court of Appeals insofar as it rests upon the President's well established authority to recognize, and withdraw recognition from, foreign governments. App. to Pet. for Cert. 27A-29A.

In stating that this case presents a nonjusticiable "political question," Mr. Justice Rehnquist, in my view, profoundly misapprehends the political question principle as it applies to matters of foreign relations. Properly understood, the political question doctrine restrains courts from reviewing an exercise of foreign policy judgment by the coordinate political branch to which authority to make that judgment has been "constitutional[ly] commit[ted]." 369 U.S. 211-213 (1962). But the doctrine does not pertain when a court is faced with the antecedent question whether a particular branch has been constitutionally designated as the repository of political decisionmaking power. *Cf. Powell v. McCormack.* The issue of decisionmaking authority must be resolved as a matter of constitutional law, not political discretion; accordingly, it falls within the competence of the courts.

The constitutional question raised here is prudently answered in narrow terms.

Abrogation of the defense treaty with Taiwan was a necessary incident to Executive recognition of the Peking Government, because the defense treaty was predicated upon the now-abandoned view that the Taiwan Government was the only legitimate political authority in China. Our cases firmly establish that the Constitution commits to the President alone the power to recognize, and withdraw recognition from, foreign regimes.

DAMES & MOORE v. REGAN

453 U.S. 654 (1981)

Opinion: Rehnquist, joined by Burger, Brennan, Stewart, White, Marshall, Blackmun, by Powell in all but n.6 and by Stevens in all but Part V
Concurrence: Stevens
Partial Concurrence, Partial Dissent: Powell

In negotiating for the release of American hostages captured in the Iranian hostage crisis in 1979, President Jimmy Carter ordered the transfer of Iranian assets and the settlement of legal claims brought against the state of Iran by companies in the United States to an international tribunal in Algeria. A central question in this case is whether President Carter had the authority to take such action. The Court decided that he did. But why? Here, the Dames & Moore Company argued that its right to have U.S. courts adjudicate its claims had been overridden by President Carter without congressional authorization. Then–Associate Justice William Rehnquist, in his opinion for the Court, explained that a federal statute and subsequent amendments, while not explicitly authorizing what had been done here, did in fact suggest broad congressional approval. Justice Rehnquist revisits Justice Robert H. Jackson's categories from the Steel Seizure Case *and also engages in a discussion of the distinctions that can or should be made between "internal" and "external" affairs. To what degree does this case present a challenge to the distinction between internal and external affairs relied upon in* United States v. Curtiss-Wright? *Moreover, what role does the congressional action cited by Justice Rehnquist play in this case? Is it crucial to the president's power to act, or is it merely an additional piece of evidence that he has been granted this power by the Constitution?*

JUSTICE REHNQUIST *delivered the opinion of the Court.*

The questions presented by this case touch fundamentally upon the manner in which our Republic is to be governed. Throughout the nearly two centuries of our Nation's existence under the Constitution, this subject has generated considerable debate. We have had the benefit of commentators such a John Jay, Alexander Hamilton, and James Madison writing in *The Federalist Paper* at the Nation's very inception, the benefit of astute foreign observers of our system such as Alexis de Tocqueville and James Bryce writing during the first century of the Nation's existence, and the benefit of many other treatises, as well as more than 400 volumes of reports of decisions of this Court. As these writings reveal, it is doubtless both futile and perhaps dangerous to find any epigrammatical explanation of how this country has been governed. Indeed, as Justice Jackson noted, "[a] judge . . . may be surprised at the poverty of really useful and unambiguous authority applicable to concrete problems of executive power as they actually present themselves." *Youngstown Sheet & Tube Co. v. Sawyer* (concurring opinion).

As we now turn to the factual and legal issues in this case, we freely confess that we are obviously deciding only one more episode in the never-ending tension between the President exercising the executive authority in a world that presents each day some new challenge with which he must deal, and the Constitution under which we all live and which no one disputes embodies some sort of system of checks and balances.

On November 4, 1979, the American Embassy in Tehran was seized and our diplomatic personnel were captured and held hostage. In response to that crisis, President Carter, acting pursuant to the International Emergency Economic Powers Act, 91 Stat. 1626, 50 U.S.C. §§1701-1706 (1976 ed., Supp. III) (hereinafter IEEPA), declared a national emergency on November 14, 1979, and blocked the removal or transfer of "all property and interests in property of the Government of Iran, its instrumentalities and controlled entities and the Central Bank of Iran which are or become subject to the jurisdiction of the United States. . . ." Exec. Order No. 12170, 3 CFR 457 (1980).

On December 19, 1979, petitioner Dames & Moore filed suit in the United States District Court for the Central District of California against the Government of Iran, the Atomic Energy Organization of Iran, and a number of Iranian banks. In its complaint, petitioner alleged that its wholly owned subsidiary, Dames & Moore International, S.R.L., was a party to a written contract with the Atomic Energy Organization, and that the subsidiary's entire interest in the contract had been assigned to petitioner. Under the contract, the subsidiary was to conduct site studies for a proposed nuclear power plant in Iran. As provided in the terms of the contract, the Atomic Energy Organization terminated the agreement for its own convenience on June 30, 1979. Petitioner contended, however, that it was owed $3,436,694.30 plus interest for services performed under the contract prior to the date of termination. The District Court issued orders of attachment directed against property of the defendants, and the property of certain Iranian banks was then attached to secure any judgment that might be entered against them.

On January 20, 1981, the Americans held hostage were released by Iran pursuant to an Agreement entered into the day before and embodied in two Declarations of the Democratic and Popular Republic of Algeria. The Agreement stated that "[i]t is the purpose of [the United States and Iran] . . . to terminate all litigation as between the Government of each party and the nationals of the other, and to bring about the settlement and termination of all such claims through binding arbitration." In furtherance of this goal, the Agreement called for the establishment of an Iran–United States Claims Tribunal which would arbitrate any claims not settled within six months.

On January 19, 1981, President Carter issued a series of Executive Orders implementing the terms of the agreement.

On February 24, 1981, President Reagan issued an Executive Order in which he "ratified" the January 19th Executive Orders. Exec. Order No. 12294, 46 Fed. Reg. 14111. Moreover, he "suspended" all "claims which may be presented to the . . . Tribunal," and provided that such claims "shall have no legal effect in any action now pending in any court of the United States."

On April 28, 1981, petitioner filed this action in the District Court for declaratory and injunctive relief against the United States and the Secretary of the Treasury, seeking to prevent enforcement of the

Executive Orders and Treasury Department regulations implementing the Agreement with Iran. In its complaint, petitioner alleged that the actions of the President and the Secretary of the Treasury implementing the Agreement with Iran were beyond their statutory and constitutional powers, and, in any event, were unconstitutional to the extent they adversely affect petitioner's final judgment against the Government of Iran and the Atomic Energy Organization, its execution of that judgment in the State of Washington, its prejudgment attachments, and its ability to continue to litigate against the Iranian banks.

Not infrequently in affairs between nations, outstanding claims by nationals of one country against the government of another country are "sources of friction" between the two sovereigns. *United States v. Pink*. To resolve these difficulties, nations have often entered into agreements settling the claims of their respective nationals. Consistent with that principle, the United States has repeatedly exercised its sovereign authority to settle the claims of its nationals against foreign countries. Though those settlements have sometimes been made by treaty, there has also been a longstanding practice of settling such claims by executive agreement, without the advice and consent of the Senate. Under such agreements, the President has agreed to renounce or extinguish claims of United States nationals against foreign governments in return for lump-sum payments or the establishment of arbitration procedures.

It is clear that the practice of settling claims continues today. Since 1952, the President has entered into at least 10 binding settlements with foreign nations, including an $80 million settlement with the People's Republic of China.

Crucial to our decision today is the conclusion that Congress has implicitly approved the practice of claim settlement by executive agreement. This is best demonstrated by Congress' enactment of the International Claims Settlement Act of 1949, 64 Stat. 13, as amended, 22 U.S.C. §1621 *et seq.* (1976 ed. and Supp. IV). The Act had two purposes: (1) to allocate to United States nationals funds received in the course of an executive claims settlement with Yugoslavia, and (2) to provide a procedure whereby funds resulting from future settlements could be distributed. By creating a procedure to implement future settlement agreements, Congress placed its stamp of approval on such agreements.

Over the years, Congress has frequently amended the International Claims Settlement Act to provide for particular problems arising out of settlement agreements, thus demonstrating Congress' continuing acceptance of the President's claim settlement authority. With respect to the Executive Agreement with the People's Republic of China, for example, Congress established an allocation formula for distribution of the funds received pursuant to the Agreement. As with legislation involving other executive agreements, Congress did not question the fact of the settlement or the power of the President to have concluded it.

In addition to congressional acquiescence in the President's power to settle claims, prior cases of this Court have also recognized that the President does have some measure of power to enter into executive agreements without obtaining the advice and consent of the Senate. In *United States v. Pink*, for example, the Court upheld the validity of the Litvinov Assignment, which was part of an Executive Agreement whereby the Soviet Union assigned to the United States amounts owed to it by American nationals so that outstanding claims of other American nationals could be paid.

In light of all of the foregoing — the inferences to be drawn from the character of the legislation Congress has enacted in the area, such as the IEEPA and the Hostage Act, and from the history of acquiescence in executive claims settlement — we conclude that the President was authorized to suspend pending claims pursuant to Executive Order No. 12294. As Justice Frankfurter pointed out in *Youngstown*, "a systematic, unbroken, executive practice, long pursued to the knowledge of the Congress and never before questioned . . . may be treated as a gloss on 'Executive Power' vested in the President by §1 of Art. II." Past practice does not, by itself, create power, but "long-continued practice, known to and acquiesced in by Congress, would raise a presumption that the [action] had been [taken] in pursuance of its consent. . . ." *United States v. Midwest Oil Co.* Such practice is present here, and such a presumption is also appropriate. In light of the fact that Congress may be considered to have consented to the President's action in suspending claims, we cannot say that action exceeded the President's powers.

Finally, we reemphasize the narrowness of our decision. We do not decide that the President possesses plenary power to settle claims, even as against foreign governmental entities.

But where, as here, the settlement of claims has been determined to be a necessary incident to the resolution of a major foreign policy dispute between our country and another, and where, as here, we can conclude that Congress acquiesced in the President's action, we are not prepared to say that the President lacks the power to settle such claims.

CONGRESSIONAL RESOLUTIONS RELATING TO U.S. MILTARY ACTIONS

In order to clarify when the president has the power to engage the armed forces of the United States in military conflicts, Congress passed the 1973 War Powers Resolution. This resolution sets out specific guidelines for how the president may use the armed forces and under which circumstances he must ask for and obtain congressional approval for military action. Considered highly controversial and constitutionally suspect by many, the 1973 War Powers Resolution still provides the basic framework for obtaining authorization for U.S. military engagements. Does the resolution clarify the relationship between Congress and the president when it comes to the power to engage in armed conflict? Is it a positive development in our understanding of the constitutional doctrine of separation of powers?

We have included below the text of several congressional resolutions relating to the authorization of U.S. military actions: the Gulf of Tonkin Resolution, which authorized the military engagement in Vietnam and was passed before the War Powers Resolution; the War Powers Resolution of 1973, which lays out the proper procedures for the authorization of U.S. military engagements; and the Authorization for Use of Military Force of 2001, which effectively authorized military intervention in Afghanistan and the "War on Terror."

Gulf of Tonkin Resolution (1964)

JOINT RESOLUTION of Congress H.J. Res. 1145

To promote the maintenance of international peace and security in southeast Asia.

Whereas naval units of the Communist regime in Vietnam, in violation of the principles of the Charter of the United Nations and of international law, have deliberately and repeatedly attacked United States naval vessels lawfully present in international waters, and have thereby created a serious threat to international peace; and

Whereas these attacks are part of a deliberate and systematic campaign of aggression that the Communist regime in North Vietnam has been waging against its neighbors and the nations joined with them in the collective defense of their freedom; and

Whereas the United States is assisting the peoples of southeast Asia to protect their freedom and has no territorial, military or political ambitions in the area, but desires only that these peoples should be left in peace to work out their own destinies in their own way: Now, therefore, be it

Resolved by the Senate and House of Representatives of the United States of America in Congress assembled, That the Congress approves and supports the determination of the President, as Commander in Chief, to take all necessary measures to repel any armed attack against the forces of the United States and to prevent further aggression.

Sec. 2. The United States regards as vital to its national interest and to world peace the maintenance of international peace and security in southeast Asia. Consonant with the Constitution of the United States and the Charter of the United Nations and in accordance with its obligations under the Southeast Asia Collective Defense Treaty, the United States is, therefore, prepared, as the President determines, to take all necessary steps, including the use of armed force, to assist any member or protocol state of the Southeast Asia Collective Defense Treaty requesting assistance in defense of its freedom.

Sec. 3. This resolution shall expire when the President shall determine that the peace and security of the area is reasonably assured by international conditions created by action of the United Nations or otherwise, except that it may be terminated earlier by concurrent resolution of the Congress.

War Powers Resolution (1973)

Public Law 93-148
93rd Congress
H.J. Res. 542
November 7, 1973

JOINT RESOLUTION

Concerning the war powers of Congress and the President. Resolved by the Senate and the House of Representatives of the United States of America in Congress assembled.

SEC. 1. SHORT TITLE. This joint resolution may be cited as the "War Powers Resolution."

SEC. 2. PURPOSE AND POLICY. (a) It is the purpose of this joint resolution to fulfill the intent of the framers of the Constitution of the United States and insure that the collective judgement of both the Congress and the President will apply to the introduction of United States Armed Forces into hostilities, or into situations where imminent involvement in hostilities is clearly indicated by the circumstances, and to the continued use of such forces in hostilities or in such situations.

(b) Under article I, section 8, of the Constitution, it is specifically provided that the Congress shall have the power to make all laws necessary and proper for carrying into execution, not only its own powers but also all other powers vested by the Constitution in the Government of the United States, or in any department or officer thereof.

(c) The constitutional powers of the President as Commander-in-Chief to introduce United States Armed Forces into hostilities, or into situations where imminent involvement in hostilities is clearly indicated by the circumstances, are exercised only pursuant to (1) a declaration of war, (2) specific statutory authorization, or (3) a national emergency created by attack upon the United States, its territories or possessions, or its armed forces.

SEC. 3. CONSULTATION. The President in every possible instance shall consult with Congress before introducing United States Armed Forces into hostilities or into situation where imminent involvement in hostilities is clearly indicated by the circumstances, and after every such introduction shall consult regularly with the Congress until United States Armed Forces are no longer engaged in hostilities or have been removed from such situations.

SEC. 4. REPORTING. (a) In the absence of a declaration of war, in any case in which United States Armed Forces are introduced—

(1) into hostilities or into situations where imminent involvement in hostilities is clearly indicated by the circumstances;

(2) into the territory, airspace or waters of a foreign nation, while equipped for combat, except for deployments which relate solely to supply, replacement, repair, or training of such forces; or

(3) in numbers which substantially enlarge United States Armed Forces equipped for combat already located in a foreign nation; the president shall submit within 48 hours to the Speaker of the House of Representatives and to the President pro tempore of the Senate a report, in writing, setting forth—

(A) the circumstances necessitating the introduction of United States Armed Forces;

(B) the constitutional and legislative authority under which such introduction took place; and

(C) the estimated scope and duration of the hostilities or involvement.

(b) The President shall provide such other information as the Congress may request in the fulfillment of its constitutional responsibilities with respect to committing the Nation to war and to the use of United States Armed Forces abroad.

(c) Whenever United States Armed Forces are introduced into hostilities or into any situation described in subsection (a) of this section, the President shall, so long as such armed forces continue to be engaged in such hostilities or situation, report to the Congress periodically on the status of such hostilities or situation as well as on the scope and duration of such hostilities or situation, but in no event shall he report to the Congress less often than once every six months.

SEC. 5. CONGRESSIONAL ACTION. (a) Each report submitted pursuant to section 4(a)(1) shall be transmitted to the Speaker of the House of Representatives and to the President pro tempore of the Senate on the same calendar day. Each report so transmitted shall be referred to the Committee on Foreign Affairs of the House of Representatives and to the Committee on Foreign Relations of the Senate for appropriate action. If, when the report is transmitted, the Congress has adjourned sine die or has adjourned for any period in excess of three calendar days, the Speaker of the House of Representatives and the President pro tempore of the Senate, if they deem it advisable (or if petitioned by at least 30 percent of the membership of their respective Houses) shall jointly request the President to convene Congress in order that it may consider the report and take appropriate action pursuant to this section.

(b) Within sixty calendar days after a report is submitted or is required to be submitted pursuant to section 4(a)(1), whichever is earlier, the President shall terminate any use of United States Armed Forces with respect to which such report was submitted (or required to be submitted), unless the Congress (1) has declared war or has enacted a specific authorization for such use of United States Armed Forces, (2) has extended by law such sixty-day period, or (3) is physically unable to meet as a result of an armed attack upon the United States. Such sixty-day period shall be extended for not more than an additional thirty days if the President determines and certifies to the Congress in writing that unavoidable military necessity respecting the safety of United States Armed Forces requires the continued use of such armed forces in the course of bringing about a prompt removal of such forces.

(c) Notwithstanding subsection (b), at any time that United States Armed Forces are engaged in hostilities outside the territory of the United States, its possessions and territories without a declaration of war or specific statutory authorization, such forces shall be removed by the President if the Congress so directs by concurrent resolution. . . .

SEC. 8. INTERPRETATION OF JOINT RESOLUTION. (a) Authority to introduce United States Armed Forces into hostilities or into situations wherein involvement in hostilities is clearly indicated by the circumstances shall not be inferred—

(1) from any provision of law (whether or not in effect before the date of the enactment of this joint resolution), including any provision contained in any appropriation Act, unless such provision specifically authorizes the introduction of United States Armed Forces into hostilities or into such situations and stating that it is intended to constitute specific statutory authorization within the meaning of this joint resolution; or

(2) from any treaty heretofore or hereafter ratified unless such treaty is implemented by legislation specifically authorizing the introduction of United

States Armed Forces into hostilities or into such situations and stating that it is intended to constitute specific statutory authorization within the meaning of this joint resolution.

(b) Nothing in this joint resolution shall be construed to require any further specific statutory authorization to permit members of United States Armed Forces to participate jointly with members of the armed forces of one or more foreign countries in the headquarters operations of high-level military commands which were established prior to the date of enactment of this joint resolution and pursuant to the United Nations Charter or any treaty ratified by the United States prior to such date.

(c) For purposes of this joint resolution, the term "introduction of United States Armed Forces" includes the assignment of members of such armed forces to command, coordinate, participate in the movement of, or accompany the regular or irregular military forces of any foreign country or government when such military forces are engaged, or there exists an imminent threat that such forces will become engaged, in hostilities.

(d) Nothing in this joint resolution—

(1) is intended to alter the constitutional authority of the Congress or of the President, or the provision of existing treaties; or (2) shall be construed as granting any authority to the President with respect to the introduction of United States Armed Forces into hostilities or into situations wherein involvement in hostilities is clearly indicated by the circumstances which authority he would not have had in the absence of this joint resolution. . . .

Authorization for Use of Military Force (2001)

Public Law 107-40 [S.J. RES. 23]
107th CONGRESS
September 18, 2001

JOINT RESOLUTION

To authorize the use of United States Armed Forces against those responsible for the recent attacks launched against the United States.

Whereas, on September 11, 2001, acts of treacherous violence were committed against the United States and its citizens; and

Whereas, such acts render it both necessary and appropriate that the United States exercise its rights to self-defense and to protect United States citizens both at home and abroad; and

Whereas, in light of the threat to the national security and foreign policy of the United States posed by these grave acts of violence; and

Whereas, such acts continue to pose an unusual and extraordinary threat to the national security and foreign policy of the United States; and

Whereas, the President has authority under the Constitution to take action to deter and prevent acts of international terrorism against the United States: Now, therefore, be it

Resolved by the Senate and House of Representatives of the United States of America in Congress assembled,

Section 1. Short Title. This joint resolution may be cited as the 'Authorization for Use of Military Force.'

Section 2. Authorization for Use of United States Armed Forces. (a) IN GENERAL — That the President is authorized to use all necessary and appropriate force against those nations, organizations, or persons he determines planned, authorized, committed, or aided the terrorist attacks that occurred on September 11, 2001, or harbored such organizations or persons, in order to prevent any future acts of international terrorism against the United States by such nations, organizations or persons.

(b) War Powers Resolution Requirements —

(1) SPECIFIC STATUTORY AUTHORIZATION — Consistent with section 8(a)(1) of the War Powers Resolution, the Congress declares that this section is intended to constitute specific statutory authorization within the meaning of section 5(b) of the War Powers Resolution.

(2) APPLICABILITY OF OTHER REQUIREMENTS — Nothing in this resolution supercedes any requirement of the War Powers Resolution.

SYNTHESIS QUESTIONS FOR FURTHER DISCUSSION: CHAPTER 8

1. In many ways, the eighteenth-century dialogue between Alexander Hamilton and James Madison, known as the Pacificus-Helvidius debate, set the stage for the modern discussion of presidential power in foreign affairs. The Pacificus-Helvidius debate concerned the president's power to unilaterally declare neutrality in a foreign dispute. In what ways does Hamilton's defense of the president's unilateral power to declare neutrality parallel John Yoo's defense of modern presidential power in regard to the "Declare War" Clause? In what ways does it differ? In what ways does Madison's objection to President George Washington's unilateral action prefigure John Hart Ely's insistence that Congress be involved in foreign affairs? One difference between the eighteenth-century debate between Madison and Hamilton and the twentieth-century debate between Yoo and Ely concerns topic area. While Madison and Hamilton are concerned with the power to declare neutrality, Ely and Yoo are concerned with war. Does this suggest a limit to drawing parallels between these two debates?

2. What would Hamilton and Madison have made of the controversies at issue in *United States v. Curtiss-Wright* and *Dames & Moore v. Regan*? Do these twentieth-century controversies raise issues they could not have imagined? What would Madison and Hamilton have made of the political question doctrine in *Goldwater v. Carter*?

3. The Constitution gives Congress the power to declare war. But what exactly constitutes a war? Is a declaration of war necessary to "make" or "engage" in war? Are the semantic distinctions raised by Yoo instructive in thinking about presidential power and its limits? This problem seems especially pronounced in the case of the Civil War. Can the Court assert that the controversies in the *Prize Cases* occurred during a time of war?

4. Ely's argument in *War and Responsibility* was largely motivated by and concerned with events relating to the Vietnam War. Although war in Vietnam was never officially declared, most people referred to it as a war. Was military involvement in Vietnam unconstitutional given that Congress never passed a formal declaration of war? Advocates of the view that it was a constitutional armed action appeal to the Gulf of Tonkin resolution passed by Congress in 1964. Can such resolutions serve as the equivalent of a war declaration?

KEY TERMS

justiciable: Adjective describing a controversy that can be adjudicated by the courts.

prerogative: The discretionary power of the president not subject to control by legislation.

unitary executive: The notion that the executive power must be held solely by one individual, not a committee. Its modern usage suggests that executive power should not be shared with the legislative branch or with independent agencies in matters such as the appointment and removal of officers. Also a theory associated with presidential control over federal agencies and with expanded presidential power during wartime.

CHAPTER 9

THE PRESIDENCY AND THE RULE OF LAW

Is the president ever above the law? How can the other branches provide effective checks and balances against the president? Should the president have any role in finding constitutional meaning?

We conclude this part with an examination of the relationship between the executive and the rule of law. While it is the role of the Court to interpret law and of Congress to make it, much of the executive's task is to execute the law. But some authors have suggested that the executive function goes beyond mere execution and also involves a role for the president in interpreting the Constitution itself. Others have even suggested a "prerogative power" that enables such a large degree of discretion that the president is in fact beyond the law, at least in some circumstances.

The arguments against the proposition that the president is above or beyond the law are to be found in the fundamental principles of constitutional democracy. Indeed, the notion that we are a "nation of laws, not men," is meant to contrast constitutional democracy with monarchy. In absolute monarchy, the sovereign has unlimited ability to act as he or she pleases. But in a constitutional democracy, the people, and not their leader, are sovereign, and the constraints on governmental power apply to all political actors, including the executive. As we have seen, the structure of the Constitution subjects presidential authority, such as appointment and removal power, to limits imposed by Congress and the Constitution.

But the presidency also has a great deal of implied power that stems from the president's status as the Chief Executive. In order to carry out the execution of the law, discretion is involved. Not every action will be governed by principles and laws beyond the president's judgment. To what extent does the possibility of this inherent power require immunity from scrutiny of his or her actions? Is the president's workplace so sacred that it must be immunized from public scrutiny? As you read John Locke and Harvey Mansfield, who defend not only discretion for the presidency but arguably a degree of immunity from the law, consider whether some of the structures that bind the presidency need to be loosened when it comes to subjecting the president to judicial scrutiny. Is the president ever truly above the law? What are the ramifications of the various responses to this question? In considering the question and its implications, recall the following quote from *The Federalist No. 70*, excerpted in Chapter 7: "Every man the least conversant in Roman history, knows how often that republic was obliged to take refuge in the absolute power of a single man, under the formidable title of Dictator."

The cases *United States v. Nixon, Nixon v. Fitzgerald,* and *Clinton v. Jones* ask whether sitting presidents can be subject to lawsuits. These cases generally suggest that the president can in fact be sued, though they make clear that the president is no ordinary citizen. While some of the readings in this chapter suggest that the president's extraordinary power might be reason for immunity, it is also important to consider the other side. Consider as you read these cases whether it is precisely because the president has so much power that he or she should be subject to lawsuits. Are personal lawsuits an appropriate way for citizens to check presidential power in addition to the structural checks that are inherent in our system of government?

As you read these cases, consider whether they refute the idea of "presidential prerogative," or the notion that the president is sometimes beyond the law. Do you agree with these decisions? Should the president be given more or less leeway than they allow?

John Locke

SECOND TREATISE OF GOVERNMENT

Chapter XIV: Of Prerogative

WHERE the legislative and executive power are in distinct hands, as they are in all moderated monarchies and well-framed governments, there the good of the society requires that several things should be left to the discretion of him that has the executive power. For the legislators not being able to foresee and provide by laws for all that may be useful to the community, the executor of the laws, having the power in his hands, has by the common law of Nature a right to make use of it for the good of the society, in many cases where the municipal law has given no direction, till the legislative can conveniently be assembled to provide for it; nay, many things there are which the law can by no means provide for, and those must necessarily be left to the discretion of him that has the executive power in his hands, to be ordered by him as the public good and advantage shall require; nay, it is fit that the laws themselves should in some cases give way to the executive power, or rather to this fundamental law of Nature and government—*viz.*, that as much as may be all the members of the society are to be preserved. For since many accidents may happen wherein a strict and rigid observation of the laws may do harm, as not to pull down an innocent man's house to stop the fire when the next to it is burning; and a man may come sometimes within the reach of the law, which makes no distinction of persons, by an action that may deserve reward and pardon; it is fit the ruler should have a power in many cases to mitigate the severity of the law, and pardon some offenders, since the end of government being the preservation of all as much as may be, even the guilty are to be spared where it can prove no prejudice to the innocent.

This power to act according to discretion for the public good, without the prescription of the law and sometimes even against it, is that which is called prerogative; for since in some governments the law-making power is not always in being and is usually too numerous, and so too slow for the dispatch requisite to execution, and because, also, it is impossible to foresee and so by laws to provide for all accidents and necessities that may concern the public, or make such laws as will do no harm, if they are executed with an inflexible rigor on all occasions and upon all persons that may come in their way; therefore there is a latitude left to the executive power to do many things of choice which the laws do not prescribe.

This power, whilst employed for the benefit of the community and suitably to the trust and ends of the government, is undoubted prerogative, and never is questioned. For the people are very seldom or never scrupulous or nice in the point or questioning of prerogative whilst it is in any tolerable degree employed for the use it was meant — that is, for the good of the people, and not manifestly against it. But if there comes to be a question between the executive power and the people about a thing claimed as a prerogative, the tendency of the exercise of such prerogative, to the good or hurt of the people, will easily decide that question.

It is easy to conceive that in the infancy of governments, when commonwealths differed little from families in number of people, they differed from them too but little in number of laws; and the governors, being as the fathers of them, watching over them for their good, the government was almost all prerogative. A few established laws served the turn, and the discretion and care of the ruler supplied the rest. But when mistake or flattery prevailed with weak princes, to make use of this power for private ends of their own and not for the public good, the people were fain, by express laws, to get prerogative determined in those points wherein they found disadvantage from it, and declared limitations of prerogative in those cases which they and their ancestors had left in the utmost latitude to the wisdom of those princes who made no other but a right use of it — that is, for the good of their people.

And therefore they have a very wrong notion of government who say that the people have encroached upon the prerogative when they have got any part of it to be defined by positive laws. For in so doing they have not pulled from the prince anything that of right belonged to him, but only declared that that power which they indefinitely left in his or his ancestors' hands, to be exercised for their good, was not a thing which they intended him, when he used it otherwise. For the end of government being the good of the community, whatsoever alterations are made in it tending to that end cannot be an encroachment upon anybody; since nobody in government can have a right tending to any other end; and those only are encroachments which prejudice or hinder the public good. Those who say otherwise speak as if the prince had a distinct and separate interest from the good of the community, and was not made for it; the root and source from which spring almost all those evils and disorders which happen in kingly governments. And indeed, if that be so, the people under his government are not a society of rational creatures, entered into a community for their mutual good, such as have set rulers over themselves, to guard and promote that good; but are to be looked on as a herd of inferior creatures under the dominion of a master, who keeps them and works them for his own pleasure or profit. If men were so void of reason and brutish as to enter into society upon such terms, prerogative might indeed be, what some men would have it, an arbitrary power to do things hurtful to the people.

But since a rational creature cannot be supposed, when free, to put himself into subjection to another for his own harm (though where he finds a good and wise ruler he may not, perhaps, think it either necessary or useful to set precise bounds to his power in all things), prerogative can be nothing but the people's permitting their rulers to do several things of their own free choice where the law was silent, and sometimes too against the direct letter of the law, for the public good and their acquiescing in it when so done. For as a good prince, who is mindful of the trust put into his hands and careful of the good of his people, cannot have too much prerogative — that is, power to do good, so a weak and ill prince, who would claim that power his predecessors exercised, without the direction of the law, as a prerogative belonging to him by right of his office, which he may exercise at his pleasure to make or promote an interest distinct from that of the public, gives the people an occasion to claim their right and limit that power, which, whilst it was exercised for their good, they were content should be tacitly allowed.

And therefore he that will look into the history of England will find that prerogative was always largest in the hands of our wisest and best princes, because the people observing the whole tendency of their actions to be the public good, or if any human frailty or mistake (for princes are but men, made as others) appeared in some small declinations from that end, yet it was visible the main of their conduct tended to nothing but the care of the public. The people, therefore, finding reason to be satisfied with these princes, whenever they acted without, or contrary to the letter of the law, acquiesced in what they did, and without the least complaint, let them enlarge their prerogative as they pleased, judging rightly that they did nothing herein to the prejudice of their laws, since they acted conformably to the foundation and end of all laws — the public good.

Such God-like princes, indeed, had some title to arbitrary power by that argument that would prove absolute monarchy the best government, as that which God Himself governs the universe by, because such kings partake of His wisdom and goodness. Upon this is founded that saying, "That the reigns of good princes have been always most dangerous to the liberties of their people." For when their successors, managing the government with different thoughts, would draw the actions of those good rulers into precedent and make them the standard of their prerogative — as if what had been done only for the good of the people was a right in them to do for the harm of the people, if they so pleased — it has often occasioned contest, and sometimes public disorders, before the people could recover their original right and get that to be declared not to be prerogative which truly was never so; since it is impossible that anybody in the society should ever have a right to do the people harm, though it be very possible and reasonable that the people should not go about to set any bounds to the prerogative of those kings or rulers who themselves transgressed not the bounds of the public good. For *"prerogative is nothing but the power of doing public good without a rule."*

The power of calling parliaments in England, as to precise time, place, and duration, is certainly a prerogative of the king, but still with this trust, that it shall be made use of for the good of the nation as the exigencies of the times and variety of occasion shall require. For it being impossible to foresee which should always be the fittest place for them to assemble in, and what the best season, the choice of these was left with the executive power, as might be best subservient to the public good and best suit the ends of parliament.

The old question will be asked in this matter of prerogative, "*But who shall be judge when this power is made a right use of?*" I answer: Between an executive power in being, with such a prerogative, and a legislative that depends upon his will for their convening, there can be no judge on earth. As there can be none between the legislative and the people, should either the executive or the legislative, when they have got the power in their hands, design, or go about to enslave or destroy them, the people have no other remedy in this, as in all other cases where they have no judge on earth, but to appeal to Heaven; for the rulers in such attempts, exercising a power the people never put into their hands, who can never be supposed to consent that anybody should rule over them for their harm, do that which they have not a right to do. And where the body of the people, or any single man, are deprived of their right, or are under the exercise of a power without right, having no appeal on earth they have a liberty to appeal to Heaven whenever they judge the cause of sufficient moment. And therefore, though the people cannot be judge, so as to have, by the constitution of that society, any superior power to determine and give effective sentence in the case, yet they have reserved that ultimate determination to themselves which belongs to all mankind, where there lies no appeal on earth, by a law antecedent and paramount to all positive laws of men, whether they have just cause to make their appeal to Heaven. And this judgment they cannot part with, it being out of a man's power so to submit himself to another as to give him a liberty to destroy him; God and Nature never allowing a man so to abandon himself as to neglect his own preservation. And since he cannot take away his own life, neither can he give another power to take it. Nor let any one think this lays a perpetual foundation for disorder; for this operates not till the inconvenience is so great that the majority feel it, and are weary of it, and find a necessity to have it amended. And this the executive power, or wise princes, never need come in the danger of; and it is the thing of all others they have most need to avoid, as, of all others, the most perilous.

Harvey Mansfield

THE CASE FOR THE STRONG EXECUTIVE: UNDER SOME CIRCUMSTANCES, THE RULE OF LAW MUST YIELD TO THE NEED FOR ENERGY

The Wall Street Journal, Wednesday, May 2, 2007

Complaints against the "imperial presidency" are back in vogue. With a view to President Bush, the late Arthur M. Schlesinger Jr. expanded and reissued the book of the same name he wrote against Richard Nixon, and Bush critics have taken up the phrase in a chorus. In response John Yoo and Richard Posner (and others) have defended the war powers of the president.

This is not the first time that a strong executive has been attacked and defended, and it will not be the last. Our Constitution, as long as it continues, will suffer this debate—I would say, give rise to it, preside over and encourage it. Though I want to defend the strong executive, I mainly intend to step back from that defense to show why the debate between the strong executive and its adversary, the rule of law, is necessary, good and—under the Constitution—never-ending.

In other circumstances I could see myself defending the rule of law. Americans are fortunate to have a Constitution that accommodates different circumstances. Its flexibility keeps it in its original form and spirit a "living constitution," ready for change, and open to new necessities and opportunities. The "living constitution" conceived by the Progressives actually makes it a prisoner of ongoing events and perceived trends. To explain the constitutional debate between the strong executive and the rule of law I will concentrate on its sources in political philosophy and, for greater clarity, ignore the constitutional law emerging from it.

The case for a strong executive should begin from a study, on this occasion a quick survey, of the American republic. The American republic was the first to have a strong executive that was intended to be republican as well as strong, and the success, or long life, of America's Constitution qualifies it as a possible model for other countries. Modern political science beginning from Machiavelli abandoned the best regime featured by classical political science because the best regime was utopian or imaginary. Modern political scientists wanted a practical solution, and by the time of Locke, followed by Montesquieu, they learned to substitute a model regime for the best regime; and this was the government of England. The model regime would not be applicable everywhere, no doubt, because it was not intended to be a lowest common denominator. But it would show what could be done in the best circumstances.

The American Founders had the ambition to make America the model regime, taking over from England. This is why they showed surprising respect for English government, the regime they had just rebelled against. America would not only make a republic for itself, but teach the world how to make a successful republic and thus improve republicanism and save the reputation of republics. For previous republics had suffered disastrous failure, alternating between anarchy and tyranny, seeming to force the conclusion that orderly government could come only from monarchy, the enemy of republics.

Previous republics had put their faith in the rule of law as the best way to foil one-man rule. The rule of law would keep power in the hands of many, or at least a few, which was safer than in the hands of one. As the way to ensure the rule of law, Locke and Montesquieu fixed on the separation of powers. They were too realistic to put their faith in any sort of higher law; the rule of law would be maintained by a legislative process of institutions that both cooperated and competed.

Now the rule of law has two defects, each of which suggests the need for one-man rule. The first is that law is always imperfect by being universal, thus an average solution even in the best case, that is inferior to the living intelligence of a wise man on the spot, who can judge particular circumstances. This defect is discussed by Aristotle in the well-known passage in his "Politics" where he considers "whether it is more advantageous to be ruled by the best man or the best laws."

The other defect is that the law does not know how to make itself obeyed. Law assumes obedience, and as such seems oblivious to resistance to the law by the "governed," as if it were enough to require criminals to turn themselves in. No, the law must be "enforced," as we say. There must be police, and the rulers over the police must use energy (Alexander Hamilton's term) in addition to reason. It is a delusion to believe that governments can have energy without ever resorting to the use of force.

The best source of energy turns out to be the same as the best source of reason — one man. One man, or, to use Machiavelli's expression, *uno solo*, will be the greatest source of energy if he regards it as necessary to maintaining his own rule. Such a person will have the greatest incentive to be watchful, and to be both cruel and merciful in correct contrast and proportion. We are talking about Machiavelli's prince, the man whom in apparently unguarded moments he called a tyrant.

The American Founders heeded both criticisms of the rule of law when they created the presidency. The president would be the source of energy in government, that is, in the administration of government, energy being a neutral term that might include Aristotle's discretionary virtue and Machiavelli's tyranny — in which only partisans could discern the difference. The founders of course accepted the principle of the rule of law, as being required by the republican genius of the American people. Under this principle, the wise man or prince becomes and is called an "executive," one who carries out the will and instruction of others, of the legislature that makes the law, of the people who instruct or inspire the legislature. In this weak sense, the dictionary definition of "executive," the executive forbears to rule in his own name as one man. This means that neither one-man wisdom nor tyranny is admitted into the Constitution as such; if there is need for either, the need is subordinated to, or if you will, covered over by, the republican principle of the rule of law.

Yet the executive subordinated to the rule of law is in danger of being subordinate to the legislature. This was the fault in previous republics. When the separation of powers was invented in 17th-century England, the purpose was to keep the executive subordinate; but the trouble was the weakness of a subordinate executive. He could not do his job, or he could do his job only by overthrowing or cowing the legislature, as Oliver Cromwell had done. John Locke took the task in hand, and made a strong executive in a manner that was adopted by the American Founders.

Locke was a careful writer, so careful that he did not care if he appeared to be a confused writer. In his "Second Treatise of Government" he announces the supremacy of the legislature, which was the slogan of the parliamentary side in the English Civil War, as the principle that should govern a well-made constitution. But as the argument proceeds, Locke gradually "fortifies" (to use James Madison's term) the executive. Locke adds other related powers to the subordinate power of executing the laws: the federative power dealing with foreign affairs, which he presents as conceptually distinct from the power of executing laws but naturally allied; the veto, a legislative function; the power to convoke the legislature and to correct its representation should it become corrupt; and above all, the prerogative, defined as "the power of doing public good without a rule." Without a rule! Even more: "sometimes too against the direct letter of the law." This is the very opposite of law and the rule of law—and "prerogative" was the slogan of the king's party in the same war.

Thus Locke combined the extraconstitutional with the constitutional in a contradiction; besides saying that the legislature is "the supreme power" of the commonwealth, he speaks of "the supreme executive power." Locke, one could say, was acting as a good citizen, bringing peace to his country by giving both sides in the Civil War a place in the constitution. In doing so he ensured that the war would continue, but it would be peaceful because he also ensured that, there being reason and force on both sides, neither side could win conclusively.

The American Constitution adopted this fine idea and improved it. The American Founders helped to settle Locke's deliberate confusion of supremacy by writing it into a document and ratifying it by the people rather than merely scattering it in the treatise of a philosopher. By being formalized the Constitution could become a law itself, but a law above ordinary law and thus a law above the rule of law in the ordinary sense of laws passed by the legislature. Thus some notion of prerogative—though the word "prerogative" was much too royal for American sensibilities—could be pronounced legal inasmuch as it was constitutional. This strong sense of executive power would be opposed, within the Constitution, to the rule of law in the usual, old-republican meaning, as represented by the two rule-of-law powers in the Constitution, the Congress which makes law and the judiciary which judges by the law.

The American Constitution signifies that it has fortified the executive by vesting the president with "the executive power," complete and undiluted in Article II, as opposed to the Congress in Article I, which receives only certain delegated and enumerated legislative powers. The president takes an oath "to execute the Office of President" of which only one function is to "take care that the laws be faithfully executed." In addition, he is commander-in-chief of the military, makes treaties (with the Senate), and receives ambassadors. He has the power of pardon, a power with more than a whiff of prerogative for the sake of a public good that cannot be achieved, indeed that is endangered, by executing the laws. In the *Federalist*, as already noted, the executive represents the need for energy in government, energy to complement the need for stability, satisfied mainly in the Senate and the judiciary.

Energy and stability are necessary in every form of government, but in their previous, sorry history, republics had failed to meet these necessities. Republican government cannot survive, as we would say, by ideology alone. The republican genius is dominant in America, where there has never been much support for anything like an *ancien régime,* but support for republicanism is not enough to make a viable republic. The republican spirit can actually cause trouble for republics if it makes people think that to be republican it is enough merely to oppose monarchy. Such an attitude tempts a republican people to republicanize everything so as to make government resemble a monarchy as little as possible.

Although the *Federalist* made a point of distinguishing a republic from a democracy (by which it meant a so-called pure, nonrepresentative democracy), the urge today to democratize everything has similar bad effects. To counter this reactionary republican (or democratic, in today's language) belief characteristic of short-sighted partisans, the *Federalist* made a point of holding the new, the novel, American republic to the test of good government as opposed merely to that of republican government.

The test of good government was what was necessary to all government. Necessity was put to the fore. In the first papers of the *Federalist,* necessity took the form of calling attention to the present crisis in America, caused by the incompetence of the republic established by the Articles of Confederation. The crisis was both foreign and domestic, and it was a crisis because it was urgent. The face of necessity, the manner in which it first appears and is most impressive, is urgency—in Machiavelli's words, *la necessità che non da tempo* (the necessity that allows no time). And what must be the character of a government's response to an urgent crisis? Energy. And where do we find energy in the government? In the executive. Actually, the *Federalist* introduces the need for energy in government considerably before it associates energy with the executive. To soothe republican partisans, the strong executive must be introduced by stages.

One should not believe that a strong executive is needed only for quick action in emergencies, though that is the function mentioned first. A strong executive is requisite to oppose majority faction produced by temporary delusions in the people. For the *Federalist,* a strong executive must exercise his strength especially against the people, not showing them "servile pliancy." Tocqueville shared this view. Today we think that a strong president is one who leads the people, that is, one who takes them where they want to go, like Andrew Jackson. But Tocqueville contemptuously regarded Jackson as weak for having been "the slave of the majority." Again according to the *Federalist,* the American president will likely have the virtue of responsibility, a new political virtue, now heard so often that it seems to be the only virtue, but first expounded in that work.

"Responsibility" is not mere responsiveness to the people; it means doing what the people would want done if they were apprised of the circumstances. Responsibility requires "personal firmness" in one's character, and it enables those who love fame—"the ruling passion of the noblest minds"—to undertake "extensive and arduous enterprises."

Only a strong president can be a great president. Americans are a republican people but they admire their great presidents. Those great presidents—I dare not give a complete list—are not only those who excelled in the emergency of war but those, like Washington, Lincoln and Franklin Roosevelt, who also deliberately planned and executed enterprises for shaping or reshaping the entire politics of their country.

This admiration for presidents extends beyond politics into society, in which Americans, as republicans, tolerate, and appreciate, an amazing amount of one-man rule. The CEO (chief executive officer) is found at the summit of every corporation including universities. I suspect that appreciation for private executives in democratic society was taught by the success of the Constitution's invention of a strong executive in republican politics.

The case for a strong executive begins from urgent necessity and extends to necessity in the sense of efficacy and even greatness. It is necessary not merely to respond to circumstances but also in a comprehensive way to seek to anticipate and form them. "Necessary to" the survival of a society expands to become "necessary for" the good life there, and indeed we look for signs in the way a government acts in emergencies for what it thinks to be good after the emergency has passed. A free government should show its respect for freedom even when it has to take it away. Yet despite the expansion inherent in necessity, the distinction between urgent crises and quiet times remains. Machiavelli called the latter *tempi pacifici*, and he thought that governments could not take them for granted. What works for quiet times is not appropriate in stormy times. John Locke and the American Founders showed a similar understanding to Machiavelli's when they argued for and fashioned a strong executive.

In our time, however, an opinion has sprung up in liberal circles particularly that civil liberties must always be kept intact regardless of circumstances. This opinion assumes that civil liberties have the status of natural liberties, and are inalienable. This means that the Constitution has the status of what was called in the 17th-century natural public law; it is an order as natural as the state of nature from which it emerges. In this view liberty has just one set of laws and institutions that must be kept inviolate, lest it be lost.

But Locke was a wiser liberal. His institutions were "constituted," less by creation than by modification of existing institutions in England, but not deduced as invariable consequences of disorder in the state of nature. He retained the difference, and so did the Americans, between natural liberties, inalienable but insecure, and civil liberties, more secure but changeable. Because civil liberties are subject to circumstances, a free constitution needs an institution responsive to circumstances, an executive able to be strong when necessary.

The lesson for us should be that circumstances are much more important for free government than we often believe. Civil liberties are for majorities as well as minorities, and no one should be considered to have rights against society whose exercise would bring society to ruin. The usual danger in a republic is tyranny of the majority, because the majority is the only legitimate dominant force. But in time of war the greater danger may be to the majority from a minority, and the government will be a greater friend than enemy to liberty. Vigilant citizens must be able to adjust their view of the source of danger, and change front if necessary. "Civil liberties" belong to all, not only to the less powerful or less esteemed, and the true balance of liberty and security cannot be taken as given without regard to the threat. Nor is it true that free societies should be judged solely by what they do in quiet times; they should also be judged by the efficacy, and the honorableness, of what they do in war in order to return to peace.

The American Constitution is a formal law that establishes an actual contention among its three separated powers. Its formality represents the rule of law, and the actuality arises from which branch better promotes the common good in the event, or in the opinion of the people. In quiet times the rule of law will come to the fore, and the executive can be weak. In stormy times, the rule of law may seem to require the prudence and force that law, or present law, cannot supply, and the executive must be strong. In judging the circumstances of a free society, two parties come to be formed around these two outlooks. These outlooks may not coincide with party principles because they often depend on which branch a party holds and feels obliged to defend: Democrats today would be friendlier to executive power if they held the presidency—and Republicans would discover virtue in the rule of law if they held Congress.

The terms of the disagreement over a strong executive go back to the classic debate between Hamilton (as Pacificus) and Madison (as Helvidius) in 1793–94. Hamilton argued that the executive power, representing the whole country with the energy necessary to defend it, cannot be limited or exhausted. Madison replied that the executive power does not represent the whole country but is determined by its place in the structure of government, which is executing the laws. If carrying on war goes beyond executing the laws, that is all the more reason why the war power should be construed narrowly. Today Republicans and Democrats repeat these arguments when the former declare that we are at war with terrorists and the latter respond that the danger is essentially a matter of law enforcement.

As to the contention that a strong executive prompts a policy of imperialism, I would admit the possibility, and I promise to think carefully and prayerfully about returning Texas to Mexico. In its best moments, America wants to be a model for the world, but no more. In its less good moments, America becomes disgusted with the rest of the world for its failure to imitate our example and follow our advice. I believe that America is more likely to err with isolationism than with imperialism, and that if America is an empire, it is the first empire that always wants an exit strategy. I believe too that the difficulties of the war in Iraq arise from having wished to leave too much to the Iraqis, thus from a sense of inhibition rather than imperial ambition.

UNITED STATES v. NIXON

418 U.S. 683 (1974)

Opinion: Burger, joined by Douglas, Brennan, Stewart, White, Marshall, Blackmun, Powell

On June 17, 1972, five men were arrested for breaking into the Democratic National Committee headquarters at the Watergate building in Washington, D.C. Over time, it became apparent that these men broke into the office under orders from individuals in the administration of President Richard Nixon. As part of the investigation of this crime, a subpoena was issued requiring President Nixon to produce tapes, memoranda, and other documents relating to meetings that he held with certain individuals. President Nixon released some but not all of the requested materials and filed a motion to quash the subpoena. He claimed that the meetings in question were protected by executive privilege. In the case at hand, the Court considered the president's claim.

This case raises important questions about executive power, specifically in circumstances of suspected criminal activity in the executive branch. Is the president entitled to secrecy in his official meetings, or are his activities and words always a part of the public record? Here the Court explicitly endorses the idea that a president has a legitimate claim to privilege in certain matters. But how far does that claim extend? What is the best means to ensure that the president does not overstep his bounds? Do the courts have the authority to make such determinations?

MR. CHIEF JUSTICE BURGER *delivered the opinion of the Court.*

This litigation presents for review the denial of a motion, filed in the District Court on behalf of the President of the United States, in the case of *United States v. Mitchell*, to quash a third-party subpoena *duces tecum* issued by the United States District Court for the District of Columbia, pursuant to Fed. Rule Crim. Proc. 17(c). The subpoena directed the President to produce certain tape recordings and documents relating to his conversations with aides and advisers. The court rejected the President's claims of absolute executive privilege, of lack of jurisdiction, and of failure to satisfy the requirements of Rule 17(c).

On March 1, 1974, a grand jury of the United States District Court for the District of Columbia returned an indictment charging seven named individuals with various offenses, including conspiracy to defraud the United States and to obstruct justice. Although he was not designated as such in the indictment, the grand jury named the President, among others, as an unindicted coconspirator. On April 18, 1974, upon motion of the Special Prosecutor, a subpoena *duces tecum* was issued pursuant to Rule 17(c) to the President by the United States District Court and made returnable on May 2, 1974. This subpoena required the production, in advance of the September 9 trial date, of certain tapes, memoranda, papers, transcripts, or other writings relating to certain precisely identified meetings between the President and others. The Special Prosecutor was able to fix the time, place, and persons present at these discussions because the White House daily logs and appointment records had been delivered to him. On April 30, the President publicly released edited transcripts of 43 conversations; portions of 20 conversations subject to subpoena in the present case were included. On May 1, 1974, the President's counsel filed a "special appearance" and a motion to quash the subpoena under Rule 17(c). This motion was accompanied by a formal claim of privilege. At a subsequent hearing, further motions to expunge the grand jury's action naming the President as an unindicted coconspirator and for protective orders against the disclosure of that information were filed or raised orally by counsel for the President.

II. JUSTICIABILITY

In the District Court, the President's counsel argued that the court lacked jurisdiction to issue the subpoena because the matter was an intra-branch dispute between a subordinate and superior officer of the Executive Branch, and hence not subject to judicial resolution. That argument has been renewed in this Court with emphasis on the contention that the dispute does not present a "case" or "controversy" which can be adjudicated in the federal courts. The President's counsel argues that the federal courts should not intrude into areas committed to the other branches of Government. He views the present dispute as essentially a "jurisdictional" dispute within the Executive Branch which he analogizes to a dispute between two congressional committees. Since the Executive Branch has exclusive authority and absolute discretion to decide whether to prosecute a case, it is contended that a President's decision is final in determining what evidence is to be used in a given criminal case. Although his counsel concedes that the President has delegated certain specific powers to the Special Prosecutor, he has not "waived nor delegated to the Special Prosecutor the President's duty to claim privilege as to all materials . . . which fall within the President's inherent authority to refuse to disclose to any executive officer." The Special Prosecutor's demand for the items therefore presents, in the view of the President's counsel, a political question under *Baker v. Carr*, 369 U.S. 186 (1962), since it involves a "textually demonstrable" grant of power under Art. II.

The mere assertion of a claim of an "intra-branch dispute," without more, has never operated to defeat federal jurisdiction; justiciability does not depend on such a surface inquiry. In *United States v. ICC*, the Court observed, "courts must look behind names that symbolize the parties to determine whether a justiciable case or controversy is presented."

Our starting point is the nature of the proceeding for which the evidence is sought — here, a pending criminal prosecution. It is a judicial proceeding in a federal court alleging violation of federal laws, and is brought in the name of the United States as sovereign. Under the authority of Art. II, §2, Congress has vested in the Attorney General the power to conduct the criminal litigation of the United States Government. It has also vested in him the power to appoint subordinate officers to assist him in the discharge of his duties. Acting pursuant to those statutes, the Attorney General has delegated the authority to represent the United States in these particular matters to a Special Prosecutor with unique authority and tenure. The regulation gives the Special Prosecutor explicit power to contest the invocation of executive privilege in the process of seeking evidence deemed relevant to the performance of these specially delegated duties.

So long as this regulation is extant, it has the force of law. In *United States ex rel. Accardi v. Shaughnessy*, regulations of the Attorney General delegated certain of his discretionary powers to the Board of Immigration Appeals and required that Board to exercise its own discretion on appeals in deportation cases. The Court held that, so long as the Attorney General's regulations remained operative, he denied himself the authority to exercise the discretion delegated to the Board even though the original authority was his and he could reassert it by amending the regulations.

Here, as in *Accardi*, it is theoretically possible for the Attorney General to amend or revoke the regulation defining the Special Prosecutor's authority. But he has not done so. So long as this regulation remains in force, the Executive Branch is bound by it, and indeed the United States, as the sovereign composed of the three branches, is bound to respect and to enforce it. Moreover, the delegation of authority to the Special Prosecutor in this case is not an ordinary delegation by the Attorney General to a subordinate officer: with the authorization of the President, the Acting Attorney General provided in the regulation that the Special Prosecutor was not to be removed without the "consensus" of eight designated leaders of Congress.

The demands of and the resistance to the subpoena present an obvious controversy in the ordinary sense, but that alone is not sufficient to meet constitutional standards. In the constitutional sense, controversy means more than disagreement and conflict; rather it means the kind of controversy courts traditionally resolve. Here at issue is the production or nonproduction of specified evidence deemed by the Special Prosecutor to be relevant and admissible in a pending criminal case. It is sought by one official of the Executive Branch within the scope of his express authority; it is resisted by the Chief Executive on the ground of his duty to preserve the confidentiality of the communications of the President. Whatever the correct answer on the merits, these issues are "of a type which are traditionally justiciable." *United States v. ICC.*

Moreover, since the matter is one arising in the regular course of a federal criminal prosecution, it is within the traditional scope of Art. III power. *Id.* at 198.

In light of the uniqueness of the setting in which the conflict arises, the fact that both parties are officers of the Executive Branch cannot be viewed as a barrier to justiciability. It would be inconsistent with the applicable law and regulation, and the unique facts of this case, to conclude other than that the Special Prosecutor has standing to bring this action, and that a justiciable controversy is presented for decision.

IV. THE CLAIM OF PRIVILEGE

A

... [W]e turn to the claim that the subpoena should be quashed because it demands "confidential conversations between a President and his close advisors that it would be inconsistent with the public interest to produce." The first contention is a broad claim that the separation of powers doctrine precludes judicial review of a President's claim of privilege. The second contention is that, if he does not prevail on the claim of absolute privilege, the court should hold as a matter of constitutional law that the privilege prevails over the subpoena *duces tecum.*

In the performance of assigned constitutional duties, each branch of the Government must initially interpret the Constitution, and the interpretation of its powers by any branch is due great respect from the others. The President's counsel, as we have noted, reads the Constitution as providing an absolute privilege of confidentiality for all Presidential communications. Many decisions of this Court, however, have unequivocally reaffirmed the holding of *Marbury v. Madison,* that "[i]t is emphatically the province and duty of the judicial department to say what the law is." No holding of the Court has defined the scope of judicial power specifically relating to the enforcement of a subpoena for confidential Presidential communications for use in a criminal prosecution, but other exercises of power by the Executive Branch and the Legislative Branch have been found invalid as in conflict with the Constitution. Since this Court has consistently exercised the power to construe and delineate claims arising under express powers, it must follow that the Court has authority to interpret claims with respect to powers alleged to derive from enumerated powers.

Our system of government "requires that federal courts on occasion interpret the Constitution in a manner at variance with the construction given the document by another branch." *Powell v. McCormack, supra,* at 549.

Notwithstanding the deference each branch must accord the others, the "judicial Power of the United States" vested in the federal courts by Art. III, §1, of the Constitution can no more be shared with the Executive Branch than the Chief Executive, for example, can share with the Judiciary the veto power, or the Congress share with the Judiciary the power to override a Presidential veto. Any other conclusion would be contrary to the basic concept of separation of powers and the checks and balances that flow from the scheme of a tripartite government. We therefore reaffirm that it is the province and duty of this Court "to say what the law is" with respect to the claim of privilege presented in this case.

B

In support of his claim of absolute privilege, the President's counsel urges two grounds, one of which is common to all governments and one of which is peculiar to our system of separation of powers. The first ground is the valid need for protection of communications between high Government officials and those who advise and assist them in the performance of their manifold duties; the importance of this confidentiality is too plain to require further discussion. Human experience teaches that those who expect public dissemination of their remarks may well temper candor with a concern for appearances and for their own interests to the detriment of the decisionmaking process. Whatever the nature of the privilege of confidentiality of Presidential communications in the exercise of Art. II powers, the privilege can be said to derive from the supremacy of each branch within its own assigned area of constitutional duties. Certain powers and privileges flow from the nature of enumerated powers; the protection of the confidentiality of Presidential communications has similar constitutional underpinnings.

The second ground asserted by the President's counsel in support of the claim of absolute privilege rests on the doctrine of separation of powers. Here it is argued that the independence of the Executive Branch within its own sphere insulates a President from a judicial subpoena in an ongoing criminal prosecution, and thereby protects confidential Presidential communications.

However, neither the doctrine of separation of powers nor the need for confidentiality of high-level communications, without more, can sustain an absolute, unqualified Presidential privilege of immunity from judicial process under all circumstances. The President's need for complete candor and objectivity from advisers calls for great deference from the courts. However, when the privilege depends solely on the broad, undifferentiated claim of public interest in the confidentiality of such conversations, a confrontation with other values arises. Absent a claim of need to protect military, diplomatic, or sensitive national security secrets, we find it difficult to accept the argument that even the very important interest in confidentiality of Presidential communications is significantly diminished by production of such material for *in camera* inspection with all the protection that a district court will be obliged to provide.

The impediment that an absolute, unqualified privilege would place in the way of the primary constitutional duty of the Judicial Branch to do justice in criminal prosecutions would plainly conflict with the function of the courts under Art. III. In designing the structure of our Government and dividing and allocating the sovereign power among three co-equal branches, the Framers of the Constitution sought to provide a comprehensive system, but the separate powers were not intended to operate with absolute independence.

To read the Art. II powers of the President as providing an absolute privilege as against a subpoena essential to enforcement of criminal statutes on no more than a generalized claim of the public interest in confidentiality of nonmilitary and nondiplomatic discussions would upset the constitutional balance of "a workable government" and gravely impair the role of the courts under Art. III.

C

Since we conclude that the legitimate needs of the judicial process may outweigh Presidential privilege, it is necessary to resolve those competing interests in a manner that preserves the essential functions of each branch. The right and indeed the duty to resolve that question does not free the Judiciary from according high respect to the representations made on behalf of the President.

The expectation of a President to the confidentiality of his conversations and correspondence, like the claim of confidentiality of judicial deliberations, for example, has all the values to which we accord deference for the privacy of all citizens and, added to those values, is the necessity for protection of the public interest in candid, objective, and even blunt or harsh opinions in Presidential decisionmaking. A President and those who assist him must be free to explore alternatives in the process of shaping policies and making decisions, and to do so in a way many would be unwilling to express except privately. These are the considerations justifying a presumptive privilege for Presidential communications. The privilege is fundamental to the operation of Government, and inextricably rooted in the separation of powers under the Constitution.

But this presumptive privilege must be considered in light of our historic commitment to the rule of law. This is nowhere more profoundly manifest than, in our view, that "the twofold aim [of criminal justice] is that guilt shall not escape or innocence suffer." *Berger v. United States.* We have elected to employ an adversary system of criminal justice in which the parties contest all issues before a court of law. The need to develop all relevant facts in the adversary system is both fundamental and comprehensive. The ends of criminal justice would be defeated if judgments were to be founded on a partial or speculative presentation of the facts.

In this case, the President challenges a subpoena served on him as a third party requiring the production of materials for use in a criminal prosecution; he does so on the claim that he has a privilege against disclosure of confidential communications. He does not place his claim of privilege on the ground they are military or diplomatic secrets. As to these areas of Art. II duties, the courts have traditionally shown the utmost deference to Presidential responsibilities.

No case of the Court, however, has extended this high degree of deference to a President's generalized interest in confidentiality. Nowhere in the Constitution, as we have noted earlier, is there any explicit reference to a privilege of confidentiality, yet to the extent this interest relates to the effective discharge of a President's powers, it is constitutionally based.

The right to the production of all evidence at a criminal trial similarly has constitutional dimensions. The Sixth Amendment explicitly confers upon every defendant in a criminal trial the right "to be confronted with the witnesses against him" and "to have compulsory process for obtaining witnesses in his favor." Moreover, the Fifth Amendment also guarantees that no person shall be deprived of liberty without due process of law. It is the manifest duty of the courts to vindicate those guarantees, and to accomplish that it is essential that all relevant and admissible evidence be produced.

In this case, we must weigh the importance of the general privilege of confidentiality of Presidential communications in performance of the President's responsibilities against the inroads of such a privilege on the fair administration of criminal justice. The interest in preserving confidentiality is weighty indeed, and entitled to great respect. However, we cannot conclude that advisers will be moved to temper the candor of their remarks by the infrequent occasions of disclosure because of the possibility that such conversations will be called for in the context of a criminal prosecution.

On the other hand, the allowance of the privilege to withhold evidence that is demonstrably relevant in a criminal trial would cut deeply into the guarantee of due process of law and gravely impair the basic function of the court. A President's acknowledged need for confidentiality in the communications of his office is general in nature, whereas the constitutional need for production of relevant evidence in a criminal proceeding is specific and central to the fair adjudication of a particular criminal case in the administration of justice. Without access to specific facts, a criminal prosecution may be totally frustrated. The President's broad interest in confidentiality of communications will not be vitiated by disclosure of a limited number of conversations preliminarily shown to have some bearing on the pending criminal cases.

We conclude that, when the ground for asserting privilege as to subpoenaed materials sought for use in a criminal trial is based only on the generalized interest in confidentiality, it cannot prevail over the fundamental demands of due process of law in the fair administration of criminal justice. The generalized assertion of privilege must yield to the demonstrated, specific need for evidence in a pending criminal trial.

NIXON v. FITZGERALD

457 U.S. 731 (1982)

Opinion: Powell, joined by Burger, Rehnquist, Stevens, O'Connor
Concurrence: Burger
Dissent: White, joined by Brennan, Marshall, Blackmun
Dissent: Blackmun, joined by Brennan, Marshall

This case concerns the extent to which the president is immune from civil suit for actions made by him in his official capacity. It suggests a variety of questions. Is the president personally liable for the decisions he makes? Is it possible to distinguish adequately between the president as a person and the president as an officer of government? Do public needs, as the Court seems to suggest, justify the denial of civil claims brought against the president by private individuals?

JUSTICE POWELL *delivered the opinion of the Court.*

The plaintiff in this lawsuit seeks relief in civil damages from a former President of the United States. The claim rests on actions allegedly taken in the former President's official capacity during his tenure in office. The issue before us is the scope of the immunity possessed by the President of the United States.

I

In January, 1970 the respondent A. Ernest Fitzgerald lost his job as a management analyst with the Department of the Air

Force. Fitzgerald's dismissal occurred in the context of a departmental reorganization and reduction in force, in which his job was eliminated. In announcing the reorganization, the Air Force characterized the action as taken to promote economy and efficiency in the Armed Forces.

Respondent's discharge attracted unusual attention in Congress and in the press. Fitzgerald had attained national prominence approximately one year earlier, during the waning months of the Presidency of Lyndon B. Johnson. On November 13, 1968, Fitzgerald appeared before the Subcommittee on Economy in Government of the Joint Economic Committee of the United States Congress. To the evident embarrassment of his superiors in the Department of Defense, Fitzgerald testified that cost-overruns on the CA transport plane could approximate $2 billion. He also revealed that unexpected technical difficulties had arisen during the development of the aircraft.

Concerned that Fitzgerald might have suffered retaliation for his congressional testimony, the Subcommittee on Economy in Government convened public hearings on Fitzgerald's dismissal. The press reported those hearings prominently, as it had the earlier announcement that his job was being eliminated by the Department of Defense. At a news conference on December 8, 1969, President Richard Nixon was queried about Fitzgerald's impending separation from Government service. The President responded by promising to look into the matter. Shortly after the news conference, the petitioner asked White House Chief of Staff H.R. Haldeman to arrange for Fitzgerald's assignment to another job within the administration. It also appears that the President suggested to Budget Director Robert Mayo that Fitzgerald might be offered a position in the Bureau of the Budget.

Fitzgerald's proposed reassignment encountered resistance within the administration. In an internal memorandum of January 20, 1970, White House aide Alexander Butterfield reported to Haldeman that "Fitzgerald is no doubt a top-notch cost expert, but he must be given very low marks in loyalty; and after all, loyalty is the name of the game." Butterfield therefore recommended that "[w]e should let him bleed, for a while at least." There is no evidence of White House efforts to reemploy Fitzgerald subsequent to the Butterfield memorandum.

Absent any offer of alternative federal employment, Fitzgerald complained to the Civil Service Commission. In a letter of January 20, 1970, he alleged that his separation represented unlawful retaliation for his truthful testimony before a congressional Committee. The Commission convened a closed hearing on Fitzgerald's allegations on May 4, 1971.

After hearing over 4,000 pages of testimony, the Chief Examiner for the Civil Service Commission issued his decision in the Fitzgerald case on September 18, 1973. The Examiner held that Fitzgerald's dismissal had offended applicable civil service regulations. The Examiner based this conclusion on a finding that the departmental reorganization in which Fitzgerald lost his job, though purportedly implemented as an economy measure, was in fact motivated by "reasons purely personal to" respondent. As this was an impermissible basis for a reduction in force, the Examiner recommended Fitzgerald's reappointment to his old position or to a job of comparable authority.

Following the Commission's decision, Fitzgerald filed a suit for damages in the United States District Court. In it, he raised essentially the same claims presented to the Civil Service Commission. . . .

IV

Here a former President asserts his immunity from civil damages claims of two kinds. He stands named as a defendant in a direct action under the Constitution and in two statutory actions under federal laws of general applicability. In neither case has Congress taken express legislative action to subject the President to civil liability for his official acts.

Applying the principles of our cases to claims of this kind, we hold that petitioner, as a former President of the United States, is entitled to absolute immunity from damages liability predicated on his official acts. We consider this immunity a functionally mandated incident of the President's unique office, rooted in the constitutional tradition of the separation of powers and supported by our history.

A

The President occupies a unique position in the constitutional scheme. Article II, §1, of the Constitution provides that "[t]he executive Power shall be vested in a President of the United States. . . ." This grant of authority establishes the President as the chief constitutional officer of the Executive Branch, entrusted with supervisory and policy responsibilities of utmost discretion and sensitivity.

In arguing that the President is entitled only to qualified immunity, the respondent relies on cases in which we have recognized immunity of this scope for governors and cabinet officers. We find these cases to be inapposite. The President's unique status under the Constitution distinguishes him from other executive officials.

Because of the singular importance of the President's duties, diversion of his energies by concern with private lawsuits would raise unique risks to the effective functioning of government. As is the case with prosecutors and judges — for whom absolute immunity now is established — a President must concern himself with matters likely to "arouse the most intense feelings." Yet, as our decisions have recognized, it is in precisely such cases that there exists the greatest public interest in providing an official "the maximum ability to deal fearlessly and impartially with" the duties of his office. This concern is compelling where the officeholder must make the most sensitive and far-reaching decisions entrusted to any official under our constitutional system. Nor can the sheer prominence of the President's office be ignored. In view of the visibility of his office and the effect of his actions on countless people, the President would be an easily identifiable target for suits for civil damages. Cognizance of this personal vulnerability frequently could distract a President from his public duties, to the detriment of not only the President and his office but also the Nation that the Presidency was designed to serve.

B

Courts traditionally have recognized the President's constitutional responsibilities and status as factors counseling judicial deference and restraint. For example, while courts generally have looked to the common law to determine the scope of an official's evidentiary privilege, we have recognized that the Presidential privilege is "rooted in the separation of powers under the Constitution." *United States v. Nixon.* It is settled law that the separation of powers doctrine does not bar every exercise of jurisdiction over the President of the United States. But our cases also have established that a court, before exercising jurisdiction, must balance the constitutional weight of the interest to be served against the dangers of intrusion on the authority and functions of the Executive Branch. When judicial action is needed to serve broad public interests—as when the Court acts not in derogation of the separation of powers, but to maintain their proper balance, *cf. Youngstown Sheet & Tube Co. v. Sawyer, supra,* or to vindicate the public interest in an ongoing criminal prosecution, *see United States v. Nixon, supra*—the exercise of jurisdiction has been held warranted. In the case of this merely private suit for damages based on a President's official acts, we hold it is not.

C

In defining the scope of an official's absolute privilege, this Court has recognized that the sphere of protected action must be related closely to the immunity's justifying purposes. Frequently our decisions have held that an official's absolute immunity should extend only to acts in performance of particular functions of his office. But the Court also has refused to draw functional lines finer than history and reason would support. In view of the special nature of the President's constitutional office and functions, we think it appropriate to recognize absolute Presidential immunity from damages liability for acts within the "outer perimeter" of his official responsibility.

It clearly is within the President's constitutional and statutory authority to prescribe the manner in which the Secretary will conduct the business of the Air Force. Because this mandate of office must include the authority to prescribe reorganizations and reductions in force, we conclude that petitioner's alleged wrongful acts lay well within the outer perimeter of his authority.

V

A rule of absolute immunity for the President will not leave the Nation without sufficient protection against misconduct on the part of the Chief Executive. There remains the constitutional remedy of impeachment. In addition, there are formal and informal checks on Presidential action that do not apply with equal force to other executive officials. The President is subjected to constant scrutiny by the press. Vigilant oversight by Congress also may serve to deter Presidential abuses of office, as well as to make credible the threat of impeachment. Other incentives to avoid misconduct may include a desire to earn reelection, the need to maintain prestige as an element of Presidential influence, and a President's traditional concern for his historical stature.

The existence of alternative remedies and deterrents establishes that absolute immunity will not place the President "above the law." For the President, as for judges and prosecutors, absolute immunity merely precludes a particular private remedy for alleged misconduct in order to advance compelling public ends.

JUSTICE WHITE, *with whom* **JUSTICE BRENNAN, JUSTICE MARSHALL,** *and* **JUSTICE BLACKMUN** *join, dissenting.*

. . . The Court intimates that its decision is grounded in the Constitution. If that is the case, Congress cannot provide a remedy against Presidential misconduct, and the criminal laws of the United States are wholly inapplicable to the President. I find this approach completely unacceptable. I do not agree that, if the Office of President is to operate effectively, the holder of that Office must be permitted, without fear of liability and regardless of the function he is performing, deliberately to inflict injury on others by conduct that he knows violates the law. . . .

Attaching absolute immunity to the Office of the President, rather than to particular activities that the President might perform, places the President above the law. It is a reversion to the old notion that the King can do no wrong. . . .

IV

The majority may be correct in its conclusion that "[a] rule of absolute immunity . . . will not leave the Nation without sufficient protection against misconduct on the part of the Chief Executive." . . . Such a rule will, however, leave Mr. Fitzgerald without an adequate remedy for the harms that he may have suffered. More importantly, it will leave future plaintiffs without a remedy, regardless of the substantiality of their claims. The remedies in which the Court finds comfort were never designed to afford relief for individual harms. Rather, they were designed as political safety valves. Politics and history, however, are not the domain of the courts; the courts exist to assure each individual that he, as an individual, has enforceable rights that he may pursue to achieve a peaceful redress of his legitimate grievances.

I find it ironic, as well as tragic, that the Court would so casually discard its own role of assuring "the right of every individual to claim the protection of the laws," *Marbury v. Madison*, in the name of protecting the principle of separation of powers. Accordingly, I dissent.

CLINTON v. JONES

520 U.S. 681 (1997)

Opinion: Stevens, joined by Rehnquist, O'Connor, Scalia, Kennedy, Souter, Thomas, Ginsburg
Concurrence: Breyer

This case deals with the question of whether suits may be brought against the president for offenses allegedly committed before his entrance into office. The Court decided that the president was not immune from such suits. Is there a tension between the decision in this case and the Court's decision in Nixon v. Fitzgerald? *Lawsuits against the president inevitably require a great deal of attention from the administration. Would the nation be better served if civil suits against the president were delayed until after completion of his term of office, or is it best to ensure that he be held immediately accountable for prior actions?*

JUSTICE STEVENS *delivered the opinion of the Court.*

This case raises a constitutional and a prudential question concerning the Office of the President of the United States. Respondent, a private citizen, seeks to recover damages from the current occupant of that office based on actions allegedly taken before his term began. The President submits that in all but the most exceptional cases the Constitution requires federal courts to defer such litigation until his term ends and that, in any event, respect for the office warrants such a stay. Despite the force of the arguments supporting the President's submissions, we conclude that they must be rejected.

Petitioner, William Jefferson Clinton, was elected to the Presidency in 1992, and re-elected in 1996. His term of office expires on January 20, 2001. In 1991 he was the Governor of the State of Arkansas. Respondent, Paula Corbin Jones, is a resident of California. In 1991 she lived in Arkansas, and was an employee of the Arkansas Industrial Development Commission.

On May 6, 1994, she commenced this action in the United States District Court for the Eastern District of Arkansas by filing a complaint naming petitioner and Danny Ferguson, a former Arkansas State Police officer, as defendants. As the case comes to us, we are required to assume the truth of the detailed — but as yet untested — factual allegations in the complaint.

Those allegations principally describe events that are said to have occurred on the afternoon of May 8, 1991, during an official conference held at the Excelsior Hotel in Little Rock, Arkansas. The Governor delivered a speech at the conference; respondent — working as a state employee — staffed the registration desk. She alleges that Ferguson persuaded her to leave her desk and to visit the Governor in a business suite at the hotel, where he made "abhorrent" sexual advances that she vehemently rejected. She further claims that her superiors at work subsequently dealt with her in a hostile and rude manner, and changed her duties to punish her for rejecting those advances. Finally, she alleges that after petitioner was elected President, Ferguson defamed her by making a statement to a reporter that implied she had accepted petitioner's alleged overtures, and that various persons authorized to speak for the President publicly branded her a liar by denying that the incident had occurred.

Respondent seeks actual damages of $75,000, and punitive damages of $100,000. With the exception of the last charge, which arguably may involve conduct within the outer perimeter of the President's official responsibilities, it is perfectly clear that the alleged misconduct of petitioner was unrelated to any of his official duties as President of the United States and, indeed, occurred before he was elected to that office.

In response to the complaint, petitioner promptly advised the District Court that he intended to file a motion to dismiss on grounds of Presidential immunity, and requested the court to defer all other pleadings and motions until after the immunity issue was resolved.

Petitioner's principal submission — that "in all but the most exceptional cases," the Constitution affords the President temporary immunity from civil damages litigation arising out of events that occurred before he took office — cannot be sustained on the basis of precedent.

Only three sitting Presidents have been defendants in civil litigation involving their actions prior to taking office. Complaints against Theodore Roosevelt and Harry Truman had been dismissed before they took office; the dismissals were affirmed after their respective inaugurations. Two companion cases arising out of an automobile accident were filed against John F. Kennedy in 1960 during the Presidential campaign. After taking office, he unsuccessfully argued that his status as Commander in Chief gave him a right to a stay under the Soldiers' and Sailors' Civil Relief Act of 1940. The motion for a stay was denied by the District Court, and the matter was settled out of court. Thus, none of those cases sheds any light on the constitutional issue before us.

The principal rationale for affording certain public servants immunity from suits for money damages arising out of their official acts is inapplicable to unofficial conduct. In cases involving prosecutors, legislators, and judges we have repeatedly explained that the immunity serves the public interest in enabling such officials to perform their designated functions effectively without fear that a particular decision may give rise to personal liability.

That rationale provided the principal basis for our holding that a former President of the United States was "entitled to absolute immunity from damages liability predicated on his official acts," *Fitzgerald*, (citing *Ferri v. Ackerman*). Our central concern was to avoid rendering the President "unduly cautious in the discharge of his official duties."

This reasoning provides no support for an immunity for *unofficial* conduct. As we explained in *Fitzgerald*, "the sphere of protected action must be related closely to the immunity's justifying purposes." Because of the President's broad responsibilities, we recognized in that case an immunity from damages claims arising out of official acts extending to the "outer perimeter of his authority." But we have never suggested that the President, or any other official, has an immunity that extends beyond the scope of any action taken in an official capacity.

Moreover, when defining the scope of an immunity for acts clearly taken *within* an official capacity, we have applied a functional approach. "Frequently our decisions have held that an official's absolute immunity should extend only to acts in performance of particular functions of his office." Hence, for example, a judge's absolute immunity does not extend to actions performed in a purely administrative capacity. As our opinions have made clear, immunities are grounded in "the nature of the function performed, not the identity of the actor who performed it."

Petitioner's effort to construct an immunity from suit for unofficial acts grounded purely in the identity of his office is unsupported by precedent.

Petitioner's strongest argument supporting his immunity claim is based on the text and structure of the Constitution. He does not contend that the occupant of the Office of the President is "above the law," in the sense that his conduct is entirely immune from judicial scrutiny. The President argues merely for a postponement of the judicial proceedings that will determine whether he violated any law. His argument is grounded in the character of the office that was created by Article II of the Constitution, and relies on separation of powers principles that have structured our constitutional arrangement since the founding.

As a starting premise, petitioner contends that he occupies a unique office with powers and responsibilities so vast and important that the public interest demands that he devote his undivided time and attention to his public duties. He submits that—given the nature of the office—the doctrine of separation of powers places limits on the authority of the Federal Judiciary to interfere with the Executive Branch that would be transgressed by allowing this action to proceed.

We have no dispute with the initial premise of the argument. It does not follow, however, that separation of powers principles would be violated by allowing this action to proceed. The doctrine of separation of powers is concerned with the allocation of official power among the three co-equal branches of our Government.

Of course the lines between the powers of the three branches are not always neatly defined. But in this case there is no suggestion that the Federal Judiciary is being asked to perform any function that might in some way be described as "executive." Respondent is merely asking the courts to exercise their core Article III jurisdiction to decide cases and controversies. Whatever the outcome of this case, there is no possibility that the decision will curtail the scope of the official powers of the Executive Branch. The litigation of questions that relate entirely to the unofficial conduct of the individual who happens to be the President poses no perceptible risk of misallocation of either judicial power or executive power.

Rather than arguing that the decision of the case will produce either an aggrandizement of judicial power or a narrowing of executive power, petitioner contends that—as a by-product of an otherwise traditional exercise of judicial power—burdens will be placed on the President that will hamper the performance of his official duties. We have recognized that "[e]ven when a branch does not arrogate power to itself . . . the separation of powers doctrine requires that a branch not impair another in the performance of its constitutional duties." *Loving v. United States*. As a factual matter, petitioner contends that this particular case—as well as the potential additional litigation that an affirmance of the Court of Appeals judgment might spawn—may impose an unacceptable burden on the President's time and energy, and thereby impair the effective performance of his office.

Petitioner's predictive judgment finds little support in either history or the relatively narrow compass of the issues raised in this particular case. As we have already noted, in the more than 200-year history of the Republic, only three sitting Presidents have been subjected to suits for their private actions. If the past is any indicator, it seems unlikely that a deluge of such litigation will ever engulf the Presidency. As for the case at hand, if properly managed by the District Court, it appears to us highly unlikely to occupy any substantial amount of petitioner's time.

In sum, "[i]t is settled law that the separation of powers doctrine does not bar every exercise of jurisdiction over the President of the United States." *Fitzgerald*. If the Judiciary may severely burden the Executive Branch by reviewing the legality of the President's official conduct, and if it may direct appropriate process to the President himself, it must follow that the federal courts have power to determine the legality of his unofficial conduct. The burden on the President's time and energy that is a mere by-product of such review surely cannot be considered as onerous as the direct burden imposed by judicial review and the occasional invalidation of his official actions. We therefore hold that the doctrine of separation of powers does not require federal courts to stay all private actions against the President until he leaves office.

We add a final comment on two matters that are discussed at length in the briefs: the risk that our decision will generate a large volume of politically motivated harassing and frivolous litigation, and the danger that national security concerns might prevent the President from explaining a legitimate need for a continuance.

We are not persuaded that either of these risks is serious. Most frivolous and vexatious litigation is terminated at the pleading stage or on summary judgment, with little if any personal involvement by the defendant. Moreover, the availability of sanctions provides a significant deterrent to litigation directed at the President in his unofficial capacity for purposes of political gain or harassment. History indicates that the likelihood that a significant number of such cases will be filed is remote. Although scheduling problems may arise, there is no reason to assume that the District Courts will be either unable to accommodate the President's needs or unfaithful to the tradition—especially in matters involving national security—of giving "the utmost deference to Presidential responsibilities." Several Presidents, including petitioner, have given testimony without jeopardizing the Nation's security. In short, we have confidence in the ability of our federal judges to deal with both of these concerns.

If Congress deems it appropriate to afford the President stronger protection, it may respond with appropriate legislation. As petitioner notes in his brief, Congress has enacted more than one statute providing for the deferral of civil litigation to accommodate important public interests. If the Constitution embodied the rule that the President advocates, Congress, of course, could not repeal it. But our holding today raises no barrier to a statutory response to these concerns.

The Federal District Court has jurisdiction to decide this case. Like every other citizen who properly invokes that jurisdiction, respondent has a right to an orderly disposition of her claims.

JUSTICE BREYER, *concurring in the judgment.*

I agree with the majority that the Constitution does not automatically grant the President an immunity from civil lawsuits based upon his private conduct. . . .

In my view, however, once the President sets forth and explains a conflict between judicial proceeding and public duties, the matter changes. At that point, the Constitution permits a judge to schedule a trial in an ordinary civil damages action (where postponement normally is possible without overwhelming damage to a plaintiff) only within the constraints of a constitutional principle — a principle that forbids a federal judge in such a case to interfere with the President's discharge of his public duties. I have no doubt that the Constitution contains such a principle applicable to civil suits, based upon Article II's vesting of the entire "executive Power" in a single individual, implemented through the Constitution's structural separation of powers, and revealed both by history and case precedent. . . .

This case is a private action for civil damages in which, as the District Court here found, it is possible to preserve evidence and in which later payment of interest can compensate for delay. The District Court in this case determined that the Constitution required the postponement of trial during the sitting President's term. It may well be that the trial of this case cannot take place without significantly interfering with the President's ability to carry out his official duties. Yet, I agree with the majority that there is no automatic temporary immunity and that the President should have to provide the District Court with a reasoned explanation of why the immunity is needed; and I also agree that, in the absence of that explanation, the court's postponement of the trial date was premature. For those reasons, I concur in the result.

SYNTHESIS QUESTIONS FOR FURTHER DISCUSSION: CHAPTER 9

1. "When the president does it that means it is not illegal." Former President Richard Nixon uttered these words in a famous interview with David Frost in 1977. Do John Locke and Harvey Mansfield agree with this statement? What arguments do they present for it?

2. The idea of "sovereign immunity" suggests that government officials should not be subject to lawsuits. The idea goes back to a time of monarchy when the monarch was not thought to be bound by the law in a manner similar to the rest of the population. Did the Founders mean to extend the idea of prerogative to U.S. presidents? Is there a justification for such power that does not rest on the idea of monarchy? For instance, *United States v. Nixon* and *Clinton v. Jones* suggest limits on the power of the president to assert executive privilege to be immune from lawsuits. But are there cases in which such limits might in fact impair the president's ability to govern? The president's communications with other White House officials are generally considered part of the public record. Might this hinder the president from speaking as freely as he or she might otherwise?

KEY TERMS

executive privilege: Areas in which the president might be immune or exempt from certain powers of Congress, including the subpoena power.

justiciable: Adjective describing a controversy that can be adjudicated by the courts.

prerogative: The discretionary power of the president not subject to control by legislation.

unitary executive: The notion that the executive power must be held solely by one individual, not a committee. Its modern usage suggests that executive power should not be shared with the legislative branch or with independent agencies in matters such as the appointment and removal of officers. Also a theory associated with presidential control over federal agencies and with expanded presidential power during wartime.

GLOSSARY

bicameralism The principle that the legislative branch should be composed of two chambers.

bill of attainder Legislation that declares an individual guilty of a crime without the benefit of a trial.

Democratic-Republican Party The party of Thomas Jefferson, the President of the United States when *Marbury v. Madison* was decided.

departmentalism The view that the various branches of government ought to have a say in constitutional interpretation.

dual-sovereignty The theory that suggests that both the states and the federal government are sovereign entities under the Constitution. On this theory, each retains certain exclusive powers. In particular, it holds that the Tenth Amendment and other provisions ensure a particular role for state power and limit federal power.

enumerated powers Those powers specifically granted to Congress by the Constitution, in contrast to the states' more general police powers to regulate the "welfare, health, safety, and morals" of its population.

ex post facto law A law retroactively imposed on parties, in contrast to laws that govern future action.

executive privilege Areas in which the president might be immune or exempt from certain powers of Congress, including the subpoena power.

Federalist Party The party of President John Adams, Chief Justice John Marshall, and William Marbury.

implied powers Powers not explicitly stated in the Constitution, but thought granted by general phrases such as the Necessary and Proper Clause and the General Welfare Clause, often thought central to the decision in *McCulloch v. Maryland.*

judicial review The power to strike down legislative or executive acts on grounds that they are incompatible with a provision or provisions of the Constitution.

judicial supremacy The view that the Court is the final and supreme interpreter of constitutional meaning.

justiciable Adjective describing a controversy that can be adjudicated by the courts.

legislative veto A statutory mechanism formerly used by Congress to permit overriding an executive agency's action or determination.

line item veto A proposed presidential power to veto specific sections of a bill, rather than the whole bill.

New Federalism The philosophy usually associated with the Reagan revolution, which sought to retrench the role of the federal government in the economic sphere; this also might refer to the Court's jurisprudence in pulling back congressional power under the Commerce Clause.

original jurisdiction The power of the Court to be the first court to hear a case. This is in contrast to appellate jurisdiction, where the Court reviews a lower court decision.

per curiam opinion An unsigned opinion issued on behalf of the Court.

plenary powers. Exclusive powers explicitly granted to Congress, not shared with the states.

prerogative The discretionary power of the president not subject to control by legislation.

Progressive movement A movement of the early twentieth century that sought increased roles for government in guaranteeing basic welfare for all and increased federal regulation of the economy and in stimulating economic growth.

standing doctrine The doctrine the Court uses to determine whether an individual has suffered a constitutionally cognizable harm sufficient to permit his or her claim to be heard in federal court.

unitary executive The notion that the executive power must be held solely by one individual, not a committee. Its modern usage suggests that executive power should not be shared with the legislative branch or with independent agencies in matters such as the appointment and removal of officers. Also a theory associated with presidential control over federal agencies and with expanded presidential power during wartime.

TABLE OF CASES

Principal cases are in italics.

INDEX